AMNESTY INTERNATIONAL

Amnesty International is a global movement of 2.8 million supporters, members and activists who campaign for internationally recognized human rights to be respected and protected. Its vision is for every person to enjoy all of the human rights enshrined in the Universal Declaration of Human Rights and other international human rights standards.

Amnesty International's mission is to conduct research and take action to prevent and end grave abuses of all human rights – civil, political, social, cultural and economic. From freedom of expression and association to physical and mental integrity, from protection from discrimination to the right to housing – these rights are indivisible.

Amnesty International is funded mainly by its membership and public donations. No funds are sought or accepted from governments for investigating and campaigning against human rights abuses. Amnesty International is independent of any government, political ideology, economic interest or religion.

Amnesty International is a democratic movement whose major policy decisions are taken by representatives from all national sections at International Council meetings held every two years. The members of the International Executive Committee, elected by the Council to carry out its decisions, are Bernard Sintobin (Belgium Flemish – International Treasurer), Pietro Antonioli (Italy), Guadalupe Rivas (Mexico), Tjalling J.S. Tiemstra (Netherlands – co-opted member), Vanushi Rajanayagam Walters (New Zealand), Julio Torales (Paraguay), Louis Mendy (Senegal), Euntae Go (South Korea), Christine Pamp (Sweden – Vice-Chair) and Peter Pack (UK – Chair).

First published in 2010 by
Amnesty International
Publications
International Secretariat
Peter Benenson House
1 Easton Street
London WC1X 0DW
United Kingdom

© Copyright
Amnesty International
Publications 2010
Index: POL 10/001/2010

ISBN: 978-0-86210-455-9
ISSN: 0309-068X

A catalogue record for this book
is available from the British
Library.

Original language: English

Photographs:
All photographs appear with full
credits and captions elsewhere
in the report.

Printed on 100% recycled
post-consumer waste paper by
Pureprint Group
East Sussex
United Kingdom

Pureprint is a CarbonNeutral®
company, and uses only
vegetable-oil-based inks.

www.amnesty.org

AMNESTY
INTERNATIONAL

AMNESTY INTERNATIONAL REPORT 2010
THE STATE OF THE WORLD'S HUMAN RIGHTS

10

FOREWORD
Pursuing justice: for all rights, for all people
by Claudio Cordone, interim Secretary General

PART 1
Regional overviews
Africa/1
Americas/11
Asia-Pacific/21
Europe and Central Asia/31
Middle East and North Africa/41

PART 2
Country entries
Afghanistan/55
Albania/58
Algeria/60
Angola/62
Argentina/64
Armenia/66
Australia/67
Austria/68
Azerbaijan/69
Bahamas/71
Bahrain/72
Bangladesh/73
Belarus/75
Belgium/77
Benin/78
Bolivia/79
Bosnia and Herzegovina/80
Brazil/84
Bulgaria/87
Burkina Faso/89
Burundi/90
Cambodia/92
Cameroon/94
Canada/96
Central African Republic/98
Chad/100
Chile/102
China/104
Colombia/108
Congo (Republic of)/112
Côte d'Ivoire/113
Croatia/114

Cuba/117
Cyprus/119
Czech Republic/120
Democratic Republic of the Congo/122
Denmark/125
Djibouti/126
Dominican Republic/127
Ecuador/129
Egypt/130
El Salvador/134
Equatorial Guinea/135
Eritrea/137
Estonia/139
Ethiopia/139
Fiji/142
Finland/143
France/144
Gambia/146
Georgia/148
Germany/149
Ghana/151
Greece/152
Guatemala/155
Guinea/156
Guinea-Bissau/158
Guyana/160
Haiti/161
Honduras/163
Hungary/165
India/166
Indonesia/170
Iran/172
Iraq/176
Ireland/180
Israel and the Occupied Palestinian Territories/182
Italy/185
Jamaica/188
Japan/189
Jordan/191
Kazakhstan/193
Kenya/195
Korea (Democratic People's Republic of)/198
Korea (Republic of)/200
Kuwait/201
Kyrgyzstan/202
Laos/203

CONTENTS
ANNUAL REPORT
2010

Latvia/204
Lebanon/205
Liberia/207
Libya/209
Lithuania/212
Macedonia/213
Madagascar/215
Malawi/216
Malaysia/217
Maldives/219
Mali/220
Malta/221
Mauritania/221
Mexico/223
Moldova/227
Mongolia/229
Montenegro/230
Morocco/Western Sahara/231
Mozambique/234
Myanmar/236
Namibia/239
Nepal/239
Netherlands/241
New Zealand/242
Nicaragua/243
Niger/245
Nigeria/246
Oman/249
Pakistan/250
Palestinian Authority/254
Papua New Guinea/256
Paraguay/257
Peru/259
Philippines/261
Poland/263
Portugal/264
Puerto Rico/265
Qatar/266
Romania/267
Russian Federation/269
Rwanda/273
Saudi Arabia/275
Senegal/278
Serbia/280
Sierra Leone/284
Singapore/286

Slovakia/287
Slovenia/289
Solomon Islands/290
Somalia/291
South Africa/295
Spain/298
Sri Lanka/301
Sudan/304
Suriname/307
Swaziland/308
Sweden/311
Switzerland/312
Syria/313
Taiwan/316
Tajikistan/317
Tanzania/319
Thailand/320
Timor-Leste/322
Togo/323
Trinidad and Tobago/324
Tunisia/325
Turkey/328
Turkmenistan/331
Uganda/333
Ukraine/336
United Arab Emirates/338
United Kingdom/339
United States of America/343
Uruguay/347
Uzbekistan/348
Vanuatu/351
Venezuela/351
Viet Nam/353
Yemen/355
Zimbabwe/358

PART 3
Selected international and
regional human rights treaties
International human rights treaties/368
Regional human rights treaties/382

PART 4
Contact Amnesty International/394
I want to help/398
Index/400

COUNTRY DATA

The facts at the top of each individual country entry in this report have been drawn from the following sources:

All **Life expectancy** and **Adult literacy** figures are from the UN Development Programme's Human Development Index, found at http://hdr.undp.org/en/media/HDR_2009_EN_Complete.pdf

The latest figures available were Life expectancy at birth (2007) and Adult literacy rate (percentage aged 15 and above, 1999-2007).

Data refer to national literacy estimates from censuses or surveys conducted between 1999 and 2007, unless otherwise specified. For more information, see the UNDP website or www.uis.unesco.org

Some countries that fall into the UNDP's 'high human development' bracket have been assumed by the UNDP to have a literacy rate of 99% for purposes of calculating the Human Development Index. Where this is the case, we have omitted the figure.

All **Population** figures are for 2009 and **Under-5 mortality** figures are estimates for the period 2005-2010, both drawn from the UN Fund for Population Activities' Demographic, Social and Economic Indicators, found at http://unfpa.org/swp/2009/en/pdf/EN_SOWP09.pdf

Population figures are there solely to indicate the number of people affected by the issues we describe. Amnesty International acknowledges the limitations of such figures, and takes no position on questions such as disputed territory or the inclusion or exclusion of certain population groups.

Some country entries in this report have no reference to some or all of the above categories. Such omissions are for a number of reasons, including the absence of the information in the UN lists cited above.

These are the latest available figures at the time of going to print, and are for context purposes only. Due to differences in methodology and timeliness of underlying data, comparisons across countries should be made with caution.

THE FOLLOWING ABBREVIATIONS ARE USED IN THIS REPORT:

ASEAN	Association of South East Asian Nations
AU	African Union
ECOWAS	Economic Community of West African States
European Committee for the Prevention of Torture	European Committee for the Prevention of Torture and Inhuman or Degrading Treatment or Punishment
European Convention on Human Rights	(European) Convention for the Protection of Human Rights and Fundamental Freedoms
EU	European Union
ICRC	International Committee of the Red Cross
ILO	International Labour Organization
NATO	North Atlantic Treaty Organization
NGO	non-governmental organization
OAS	Organization of American States
OSCE	Organization for Security and Co-operation in Europe
UN	United Nations
UN Children's Convention	Convention on the Rights of the Child
UN Convention against Racism	International Convention on the Elimination of All Forms of Racial Discrimination
UN Convention against Torture	Convention against Torture and Other Cruel, Inhuman or Degrading Treatment or Punishment
UNDP	UN Development Programme
UNHCR, the UN refugee agency	UN High Commissioner for Refugees
UNICEF	UN Children's Fund
UN Migrant Workers Convention	International Convention on the Protection of the Rights of All Migrant Workers and Members of Their Families
UN Refugee Convention	Convention relating to the Status of Refugees
UN Special Rapporteur on human rights defenders	Special Rapporteur on the situation of human rights defenders
UN Special Rapporteur on indigenous people	Special Rapporteur on the situation of human rights and fundamental freedoms of indigenous people
UN Special Rapporteur on racism	Special Rapporteur on contemporary forms of racism, racial discrimination, xenophobia and related intolerance
UN Special Rapporteur on torture	Special Rapporteur on torture and other cruel, inhuman or degrading treatment or punishment
UN Women's Convention	Convention on the Elimination of All Forms of Discrimination against Women
WHO	World Health Organization

Residents of Atfet Al-Moza in Al-Duwayqa, Egypt, built wooden homes on the rubble of their demolished houses. Residents were forcibly evicted from Al-Duwayqa, Establ Antar and Ezbet Khayrallah, all informal settlements in Greater Cairo. August 2009.

© Amnesty International

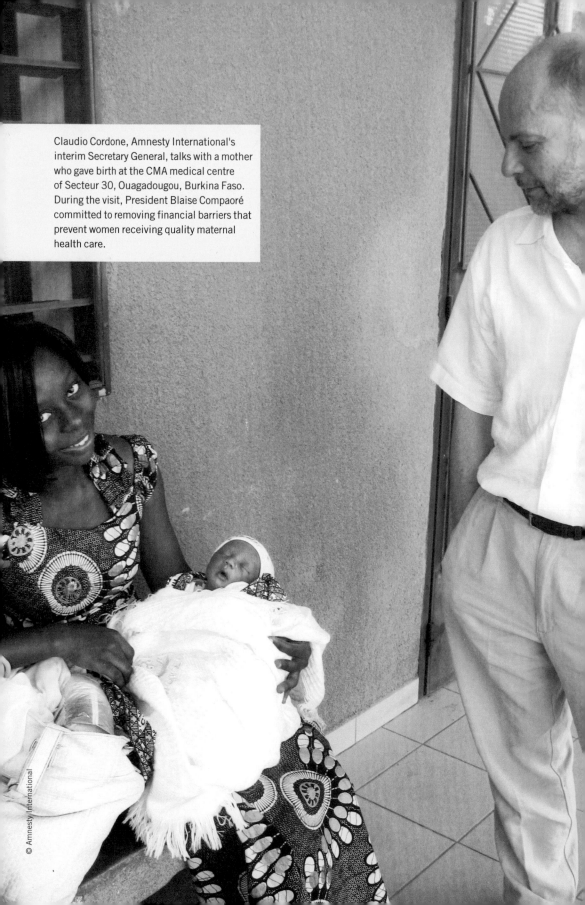

Claudio Cordone, Amnesty International's interim Secretary General, talks with a mother who gave birth at the CMA medical centre of Secteur 30, Ouagadougou, Burkina Faso. During the visit, President Blaise Compaoré committed to removing financial barriers that prevent women receiving quality maternal health care.

PURSUING JUSTICE: FOR ALL RIGHTS, FOR ALL PEOPLE

Claudio Cordone

Between January and May 2009, some 300,000 Sri Lankans were trapped on a narrow strip of land between the retreating Liberation Tigers of Tamil Eelam (LTTE) and the advancing Sri Lankan military. As reports of abuses by both sides increased, the UN Security Council failed to intervene. At least 7,000 people were killed – some have put the figure as high as 20,000. The Sri Lankan government dismissed all reports of war crimes by its forces and rejected calls for an international inquiry, while failing to hold any credible, independent investigations of its own. The UN Human Rights Council convened a special session, but power plays led to member states approving a resolution drafted by the Sri Lankan government, complimenting itself on its success against the LTTE. By the end of the year, despite further evidence of war crimes and other abuses, no one had been brought to justice.

One would be hard pressed to imagine a more complete failure to hold to account those who abuse human rights.

Thinking about it, I remembered the foreword to the *Amnesty International Report* published in 1992. Entitled "Getting away with murder", it highlighted many countries where political and military leaders responsible for ordering or condoning killings, enforced disappearances, systematic rape and other torture, faced no threat of being held to account. Sri Lanka figured prominently as an example, its then government having failed to bring to justice those responsible for tens of thousands of extrajudicial killings and enforced disappearances in the violent 1988-90 suppression of an internal insurgency.

So the obvious question is, has anything changed over the last two decades? And looking at Sri Lanka in 2009, or indeed at the situations in Colombia or Gaza, it would be easy to conclude, not really; and if not, why pursue accountability at all? But that would be to overlook the significant progress that has been made in less than 20 years – despite old and new challenges – which ensures it is now harder for perpetrators to secure impunity.

Yes, the law's reach is still far from complete. Some situations evade scrutiny altogether; in others, justice simply takes too long. But there is progress. Moreover, the demand for accountability has extended beyond the familiar territory of redress for killings or torture, to the denial of basic human rights to food, education, housing and health, which we all also need to live our lives in dignity.

Accountability – the achievements

To be accountable is to be held responsible for an action you have taken, or failed to take, that has a direct consequence on others. It is a broad concept: one can speak of political accountability, tested, for example, in elections; or moral accountability, measured perhaps by a society's values.

International human rights standards are focused primarily on establishing legal accountability. People have rights that must be set out in and protected by law; those in power have duties, also established in law, to respect, protect and fulfil individual rights.

Ensuring accountability is important because, first and foremost, those who have suffered harm have a right to truth and justice. Victims and their relatives must have the wrongs done to them acknowledged and see those responsible brought to account. If victims are to receive reparation, finding out what happened, by whom and why, is as important as bringing to justice those responsible for abuses.

Accountability also allows us to look ahead. It provides a measure of deterrence for those who might commit crimes, and it provides a basis on which to build reforms of state and international institutions. Efficient and effective mechanisms for accountability can help states make better policies and laws, and monitor their impact on people's lives.

During the past two decades, a global campaign has succeeded in establishing a role for international justice. Its achievements include the establishment in 1998 of the International Criminal Court (ICC) built on the foundations of international tribunals that dealt with genocide, crimes against humanity and war crimes in the former Yugoslavia and Rwanda.

2009 was a watershed year, when a sitting head of state, President Omar Al Bashir of Sudan, was named in an arrest warrant by the ICC on five counts of crimes against humanity (murder, extermination, forcible transfer of population, torture and rape) and two counts of war crimes (for the targeting of civilians).

By the end of 2009, the ICC Prosecutor had opened investigations in three situations referred by the states where the crimes occurred – Uganda, Democratic Republic of the Congo (DRC) and Central African Republic (CAR) and one where the Security Council referred the situation (Darfur, Sudan). He also requested authorization from the Pre-Trial Chamber to open another investigation (Kenya). The ICC has summoned a leader of an armed group in Darfur, and issued arrest warrants for a militia leader, a senior government official and the President in Sudan, and issued arrest warrants for leaders of armed groups in Uganda, the DRC and CAR. These are important steps to implement the principle that all those committing war crimes or crimes against humanity should be held equally to account, whether they belong to government or other forces.

In recent years, the ICC Prosecutor has expanded the geographical scope of his work by beginning preliminary examinations of four situations outside Africa – Afghanistan, Colombia, Georgia, and the 2008-09 conflict in Gaza and southern Israel.

The process whereby states (110 by the end of 2009) ratify the Rome Statute of the ICC has spurred national legal reform so that national courts are being given jurisdiction over crimes under international law, allowing suspects to be brought to book abroad when – and crucially only when – they enjoy impunity at home. Despite some setbacks in the development of universal jurisdiction in 2009, such as the decision in Spain only to pursue cases where there was a Spanish victim, lawyers have initiated cases and some were advancing before national courts across the Americas, Europe and Africa. In South Africa in December, two NGOs challenged in court the decision by the authorities not to open investigations under South Africa's universal jurisdiction law into alleged crimes against humanity committed in Zimbabwe by individuals known to travel to South Africa. By the end of the year more than 40 states had enacted legislation since 1998 maintaining or strengthening universal jurisdiction over crimes under international law, helping fill a small part of the global justice gap.

Such investigations and prosecutions have transformed the way governments and the general public see crimes under international law. More and more, these cases are seen for what they are: serious crimes to be investigated and prosecuted, as opposed to political issues to be resolved through diplomatic channels. Having campaigned hard with my colleagues to hold former Chilean President Augusto Pinochet to account following his arrest in London in 1998, I am particularly encouraged by this shift in perception.

Throughout Latin America, national courts and governments are re-opening investigations into crimes long shielded by amnesty laws. These developments show how even decades after the events, with numerous amnesties and other measures of impunity designed to block prosecutions, civil society will still fight to tear down barriers to truth, justice and reparation.

Among a number of landmark judgments was the conviction in April 2009 of former President Alberto Fujimori of Peru for crimes against humanity, which brought some closure for the relatives of those kidnapped, tortured and extrajudicially executed by military death squads in three cases in the early 1990s. In October, the Supreme Court of Uruguay found that the amnesty law enacted to provide impunity for gross human rights violations in the late 1980s was null and void because it was inconsistent with Uruguay's obligations under international law. And as 2009 drew to a close, Argentine prosecutors began presenting evidence in one of the most important trials since the demise of the military government (1976-1983) involving 17 members of the armed forces and police charged with torture, enforced disappearance and murder at the notorious Escuela Superior de Mecánica de la Armada (Naval Mechanics School).

The pursuit of justice extended far beyond Latin America. Sierra Leone, for example, came closer to reconciliation with its past in 2009 as all trials in the Special Court for Sierra Leone were concluded apart from that of former President of Liberia Charles Taylor, which was ongoing. And in Asia, one of Cambodia's most notorious Khmer Rouge commanders finally faced trial for war crimes and crimes against humanity committed more than 30 years ago. Kaing Guek Eav, also known as Duch, was the commander of Security Office S-21 where at least 14,000 people are believed to have been tortured and then killed between April 1975 and January 1979. It was the first trial by the "Extraordinary Chambers in the Courts of Cambodia" – such a temporary tribunal must give way to a functioning national justice system as soon as practical, but at least it allowed survivors to have their suffering acknowledged.

In 2009, even powerful states found they could not always hide from the law. While some European states were lukewarm in pursuing violations within the context of the US-led "war on terror", an Italian court convicted 22 CIA operatives, one US Air Force officer and two Italian military intelligence agents in November for their involvement in the 2003 abduction of Usama Mustafa Hassan Nasr (Abu Omar) from a street in Milan. Abu Omar had then been rendered to Egypt, where he was held in secret for 14 months, and allegedly tortured. The trial took place largely because the Milan prosecutor's office was determined to enforce the law, despite pressure from its own government to drop the case, and although none of the US agents was ever arrested, or physically present in court.

The existence of the ICC has inspired more serious attention to the issue of accountability even in states where those responsible might otherwise have felt immune because they have not formally accepted the court's jurisdiction. The UN Human Rights Council created an independent fact-finding mission led by South African judge Richard Goldstone, previously Prosecutor of the International Criminal Tribunals for Rwanda and the former Yugoslavia, to investigate alleged violations during the 22-day conflict in Gaza and southern Israel that ended in January 2009. The Goldstone report found that both Israeli forces and Hamas (and other Palestinian groups) committed war crimes and, possibly, crimes against humanity. This echoed the findings of Amnesty

International's field missions to Gaza and southern Israel during the conflict and in its immediate aftermath.

The Goldstone report stated that "[t]he prolonged situation of impunity has created a justice crisis". It recommended that if the two sides failed to carry out investigations and ensure accountability, the Security Council should exercise its authority and refer the situation to the ICC. In November 2009, the UN General Assembly gave Israel and the Palestinian side three months to show they were willing and able to undertake investigations that met international standards.

In an example of prompt response by the international community, the UN set up an International Commission of Inquiry to investigate the events of 28 September in Conakry (Guinea), where more than 150 people were killed, and women were raped in public, when security forces violently repressed a peaceful demonstration in a stadium. The Inquiry found in December that crimes against humanity had been committed and recommended a referral to the ICC, which initiated a preliminary examination.

Finally, the last two decades have seen an exponential growth in "transitional justice" mechanisms, with many countries emerging from prolonged armed conflict or political repression to confront their past with different models of accountability. During 2009, truth and reconciliation processes and their follow-up were in progress in Liberia, the Solomon Islands and Morocco/Western Sahara – the only country in the Middle East and North Africa Region to have confronted past abuses in such a way, although without including a criminal justice component. As we gathered Amnesty International's relevant records to assist that process, covering decades of research on individual cases, it was clear to all of us that accountability must accompany truth-telling if reconciliation based on justice is to be achieved. The temptation remains to 'let bygones be bygones', but experience has shown that allowing perpetrators, literally, to 'get away with murder' can make for a precarious and often short-lived peace.

Power and politicization – obstacles to justice

While legal accountability for crimes under international law is more of a possibility today than ever before, events in 2009 confirmed that two formidable obstacles stand in the way. These must be addressed if we hope to spread meaningful accountability across the full spectrum of rights. The first is the fact that powerful states continue to stand above the law, outside effective international scrutiny. The other is that powerful states manipulate the law, shielding their allies from scrutiny and pushing for accountability mainly when politically expedient. In so doing, they provide a pretext for other states or block of states to politicize justice in the same way.

Although 110 states ratified the Rome Statute to the ICC by the end of 2009, only 12 out of the G20 countries had done so. Among others, China, India, Indonesia, Russia, Turkey and the USA have stood aside from, if not deliberately undermined, international justice efforts.

Having excluded itself from the jurisdiction of the ICC, the USA faces less external pressure to address its own abuses committed in the context of its counter-terrorism strategy. When President Barack Obama took office and ordered the closure of the Guantánamo Bay detention facility within a year, as well as the end of the secret detention programme and the use of so-called "enhanced interrogation techniques", the signs were promising. However, by the end of 2009 the Guantánamo detentions were still ongoing and little progress had been made in holding anyone accountable for the violations there and in the other aspects of the US-led "war on terror".

China too shields its actions from international scrutiny. In July 2009, violent riots followed a police crackdown on an initially peaceful protest by Uighurs in Urumqi, Xinjiang Uighur Autonomous Region. The Chinese government restricted access to information, arrested non-violent protesters, and set up quick, unfair trials, sentencing many to death and executing nine within months of the violence. In December, a further 13 were sentenced to death, and 94 more arrested. The short and controlled access journalists were allowed after the violence is no substitute for proper international scrutiny – China failed to respond to a request from the UN Rapporteur on torture to visit the area. Any claim by the government that it is ensuring accountability is not credible when the supposed accountability is cloaked in secrecy and a rush to executions.

Despite an EU-commissioned independent inquiry that concluded that all sides in the 2008 Georgia-Russia conflict were responsible for violations of international humanitarian and human rights law, neither Russia nor Georgia had brought anyone to account by the end of the year, and 26,000 people were still unable to return home. It was increasingly clear that Russia would use its power to shield both its own soldiers and Georgia's breakaway regions of South Ossetia (and Abkhazia) from international scrutiny. Specifically, Russia opposed the extension of the mandates of two crucial international monitoring missions in Georgia belonging to the Organization for Security and Co-operation in Europe and the UN. This left the European Union Monitoring Mission as the sole international observer body operating in Georgia, with no access to areas controlled by Russia or the de facto South Ossetian and Abkhazian authorities in the post-conflict zone.

Indonesia, another financial heavyweight with membership of the G20, has for more than 10 years failed to ensure accountability for the victims of human rights violations committed during Timor-Leste's 1999 UN-sponsored independence referendum and the previous 24 years of Indonesian occupation. Despite various national and internationally sponsored justice initiatives over the last decade, most of those suspected of having committed crimes against humanity in 1999 are still at large. Of those who have been prosecuted in Indonesia, all have been acquitted.

The second obstacle – the politicization of international justice – makes the pursuit of accountability subservient to a political agenda of supporting allies and undermining rivals. The USA, for example, and European Union states, used their position within the

UN Security Council to continue to shield Israel from strong measures of accountability for its actions in Gaza. In a display of counter political bias, the UN Human Rights Council, initially resolved to investigate only alleged Israeli violations. To his credit, Judge Richard Goldstone, subsequently appointed to lead that investigation, insisted that the UN Fact-Finding Mission should examine alleged violations by both Israel and Hamas. Also at the UN Human Rights Council, not a single Asian or African state voted against the resolution that applauded the Sri Lankan government's conduct of the war against the LTTE.

The unwillingness of the powerful to apply the same standards to themselves and their political allies plays into the hands of others who can then justify their own double standards, sometimes placing a misguided notion of "regional solidarity" above solidarity with the victims. Nowhere can this be seen more clearly than in the initial response of African states to the ICC's arrest warrant for President Al Bashir. Despite the seriousness of the crimes alleged, in July the Assembly of the African Union (AU), chaired by Libya, reiterated a request to the UN Security Council to suspend the proceedings against the Sudanese President, decided that AU member states would not co-operate with the ICC in his arrest and surrender, and requested the African Commission to convene a preparatory meeting to discuss amendments to the Rome Statute to be submitted to the 2010 Review Conference.

After travelling freely around countries not party to the Rome Statute, President Al Bashir was then invited by Turkey, Nigeria, Uganda and Venezuela. After an outcry from civil society, however, the tide began to shift. South Africa said it would fulfil its obligations as a party to the Rome Statute, and Brazil, Senegal and Botswana made clear their readiness to arrest him if he arrived. Nevertheless, at the end of 2009, President Al Bashir was still at large, and still alleging that the effort to prosecute him was politically motivated and biased against Africa. For hundreds of thousands of displaced people in Darfur, the nightmare of further violence and abuses continues, with the prospect of the war in Southern Sudan resuming and the hardship intensifying.

Challenges ahead – accountability for all rights

The obstacles to implementing accountability for mass atrocities in conflicts or political repression are real, but the debate at least has been won: no one denies the principle that war crimes or crimes against humanity or enforced disappearances should be punished. Yet when it comes to the mass abuses of economic, social and cultural rights, there is no comparable effort to bring law and accountability to bear. Not the same thing, many will say. And true enough, massacring civilians is different from denying a population its right to education. But such denials are still flouting international law and impacting adversely on people's lives. They must, therefore, be pursued through international accountability.

The task is to convince world leaders that, no less than the conflict in Darfur, the problem is a human rights crisis.

Consider the right to health, and specifically the scourge of maternal mortality. Every year, more than half a million women die from pregnancy-related complications. Maternal mortality rates for women in Sierra Leone, Peru, Burkina Faso and Nicaragua – to name a few countries on which Amnesty International focused in 2009 – are directly affected by human rights abuses. As I witnessed personally in Sierra Leone and Burkina Faso, the governments in these countries acknowledge the problem and are taking steps to tackle it. But they – along with civil society – need to make greater efforts to address the key human rights issues that contribute to the high rates of preventable deaths, such as gender discrimination, early marriage, the denial of women's sexual and reproductive rights, and barriers to accessing essential health care. In this, they must be supported by the international community.

Human rights law recognizes that adequate resources are a crucial condition for the realization of some aspects of economic, social and cultural rights and so demands "progressive realization" of those aspects "to the maximum of available resources". But governments cannot simply use the issue of resource constraint as an excuse. The existence of preventable maternal mortality in a country is not just a simple reflection of how poor or rich a country is. Angola, for example, has a much higher maternal mortality ratio than Mozambique, despite the fact that Mozambique is much poorer. Or take Guatemala, with a GDP per capita nearly double the size of Nicaragua, but higher maternal mortality ratios.

Consider also the right to housing. In 2009 Amnesty International addressed the plight of tens of thousands left homeless in N'Djamena, Chad, after forced evictions, as well as that of the inhabitants of slums in Cairo, Egypt, who remained at risk of being killed by landslides or other hazards, due to the authorities' failure to provide adequate housing. In Nairobi, Kenya, Amnesty International marched with inhabitants from Kibera, the largest slum in Africa, and other slums to demand their right to adequate housing and services. In Gaza, one of the consequences of the 2008-09 conflict highlighted by Amnesty International has been the extensive destruction of houses coupled with a continuing blockade which prevents construction materials from entering Gaza. The blockade, which amounts to collective punishment, a crime under international law, hits hardest the most vulnerable.

What the people in the situations mentioned above have in common more than anything else is their poverty. It is the poor who are most discriminated against and where the need for protection of all the rights in the Universal Declaration of Human Rights is most evident. Discrimination is a key driver of poverty, and is often reflected in the allocation of government spending and policies. And most of the people living in poverty in the world, and the ones suffering most discrimination in law and practice, are women. Safe pregnancies, safe homes, safe routes to school or work – none of these should be the preserve of men or of the wealthy.

There are some positive steps towards ensuring legal accountability for the denial of basic economic, social and cultural rights. Increasingly, national courts are intervening to protect these rights and to demand changes to government policy so that minimum rights to health, housing, education and food do not go unfulfilled. And they are being spurred to go further by international mechanisms.

In a ground-breaking decision in November 2009, for example, the ECOWAS (Economic Community of West African States) Community Court of Justice in Abuja declared that education is a human right to which all Nigerians are entitled. The Court said that the right to education can be enforced legally and dismissed all objections brought by the government that education was "a mere directive policy of the government and not a legal entitlement of the citizens".

In another example, in Miercurea Ciuc, Romania, a Roma community which has been living in metal cabins and shacks next to a sewage treatment plant since 2004, after being forcibly evicted from a crumbling building in the centre of the town, lodged an appeal in December 2008 with the European Court of Human Rights. The community, supported by local NGOs, had exhausted national remedies for reparations when rulings in their favour by national courts amounted to nothing in practical terms.

The possibility of international accountability in this field took a leap forward in September 2009 with the opening for signature of the Optional Protocol to the International Covenant on Economic, Social and Cultural Rights. The Protocol establishes, for the first time, an international mechanism for individual complaints. It will also support efforts within countries to ensure that effective remedies are available to victims.

Increased accountability for the denial of basic economic, social and cultural rights has become ever more important in view of the combined effects of the food, energy, and financial crises which are estimated to have pushed many million more people into poverty. The respect for all human rights, including economic, social and cultural rights, must be an integral part of all national and international responses to the crises.

But governments are not the only actors contributing to such a crisis. Global business is growing in power and influence. Decisions companies make and the influence they wield can profoundly impact people's human rights. Too many companies exploit the absence of effective regulation or work hand in glove with abusive and often corrupt governments, with devastating consequences.

Over the past 15 years, we have seen the expansion of law to protect global economic interests, through a range of international investment and trade agreements backed by enforcement mechanisms. But while economic interests have been able to make the law work for them, those harmed by their operations have often seen the law recede in the face of corporate power.

December 2009 marked the 25th anniversary of the catastrophic leak of deadly chemicals from Union Carbide's pesticide plant in Bhopal, India. Thousands died and an estimated 100,000 people are still suffering the health consequences of that leak today. Despite efforts by survivors of the Bhopal disaster to pursue justice through courts in

India and the USA, a quarter of a century after the leak, rehabilitation is still far short of what is needed and no one has ever been held to account for the leak or its aftermath.

Meaningful accountability for corporations remains rare. Attempts to secure justice are thwarted by ineffective legal systems, lack of access to information, corporate interference with legal and regulatory systems, corruption and powerful state-corporate alliances. Although transnational businesses, by definition, operate across borders, the legal and jurisdictional obstacles to bringing court actions against companies abroad remain significant. Global business operates in a global economy but in the absence of a global rule of law.

Yet, despite the enormous challenges, individuals and communities affected by transnational companies are increasingly bringing civil actions in an effort to both hold companies to account and gain some form of remedy. In Nigeria, the oil industry has operated for 50 years without effective regulatory controls. The consequence has been widespread damage to the environment and human rights. Justice in Nigeria has proved elusive for most of the communities whose lives and livelihoods have been damaged. In December 2009 a Dutch court agreed to proceed in a civil case against Shell brought by four Nigerians seeking compensation for oil-spill damages to their livelihood.

In a high-profile civil action in the UK in 2009, the oil-trading company Trafigura agreed a US$45 million out of court settlement with some 30,000 people affected by the dumping of toxic waste in Abidjan in Côte d'Ivoire. The waste was brought to Abidjan in 2006 on board the ship *Probo Koala*, which had been chartered by Trafigura. The waste was then dumped in various locations around the city. More than 100,000 people sought medical attention for a range of health problems and there were 15 reported deaths.

Such out of court settlements may bring a small measure of justice for victims, but they often involve serious limitations and do not offer full reparation or accountability. In the Côte d'Ivoire case, critical aspects of the human rights impact of the toxic waste dumping remain unaddressed. Far more needs to be done to address the legal and jurisdictional gaps that currently facilitate corporate impunity. Companies which in increasing numbers profess commitment to human rights should actively promote such efforts.

The next global plan – accountability for all rights

World leaders will gather at the UN in September 2010 to review progress on their promises to improve the lives of the world's poor, set out in the Millennium Development Goals (MDGs). On the evidence available, we are falling far short of the goals set for 2015. The cost of this failure is to deprive hundreds of millions of people of their right to live in dignity – not just to enjoy their political freedoms, but also to have access to food, housing, health care, education and security, as enshrined in the Universal Declaration of Human Rights. Freedom from fear, and freedom from want – that remains the goal.

There must now be a comparable effort to harness the same energy used to set up the ICC and the international mechanisms for justice, to bring more accountability to a global economic and political order that fails to take all human rights into account. New thinking is needed. The MDG targets cannot simply be just promises. They must be based on the legal commitments governments have made to meet basic human rights, and as such there must be mechanisms to hold governments to account to meet these commitments. There must be effective remedies when states fail to do so.

Accountability would be enhanced if efforts to meet the MDGs took full account of the views of those living in poverty. Individuals have the right to participate in and to have free access to information about decisions that affect their lives. There has been little genuine participation of rights holders themselves in the MDGs. And the MDG process must also ensure proper scrutiny of those governments who pursue national policies – including those with international effect – that undermine the realization of the basic rights embedded in the Goals. All governments, but especially those of the G20, which claim a greater role in global leadership, should be held accountable for whether their policies translate into tangible improvements in the lives of the world's poor.

In this effort to secure the delivery of all human rights for all people, states and non-state actors should be constantly reminded of their legal obligations and responsibilities. More than ever before, human rights activists, community organizations, lawyers and others are joining together to do so, working with those in power when sharing common objectives, but otherwise challenging them by seeking institutional and individual measures of accountability. The human rights movement is itself becoming more global and diverse, connecting ever better across borders and disciplines in pursuit of a comprehensive human rights project.

As we enter the second decade of the millennium, Amnesty International is working alongside partners in such a global movement, seeking to reassert the value of universal human rights; to show how they cannot be divided up or parcelled off, and how they are directly relevant to people's full life experience. In so doing, we recommit ourselves to a vision of human rights whereby – beyond states, armed groups and companies – each individual is an agent of change, with rights as well as responsibilities. Each of us has rights to demand respect, protection and fulfilment from the state and society, but also responsibilities to respect the rights of others and act in solidarity with each other to fulfil the promise of the Universal Declaration.

Women and children escape the fighting in Maidan, northwest Pakistan, 27 April 2009. Conflict between the Pakistani Taleban and government security forces displaced more than 2 million people.

AMNESTY INTERNATIONAL REPORT 2010
PART ONE: REGIONAL OVERVIEWS

Pregnant women in a village in Koinadugu district, northern Sierra Leone, February 2009. Free care for pregnant women and children was among the plans announced by the President to try to combat high levels of maternal mortality.

AFRICA

*"No one ever asked the Sudanese themselves if they want the arrest
warrant against their President. [But] undoubtedly, yes: it's time."*

This Sudanese activist reflected the feelings of many in the region
when the International Criminal Court (ICC) issued its arrest warrant for
President Omar Al Bashir of Sudan in March. President Al Bashir was
accused, as indirect perpetrator, of war crimes - specifically attacking
civilians and pillaging – and crimes against humanity – specifically for
murder, extermination, forcible transfer, torture and rape. This was a
powerful and welcome signal sent to those suspected of being
responsible for gross human rights violations: that nobody is above the
law, and that the rights of victims should be upheld.

Members of civil society in Africa frequently stressed the
importance of strengthening international justice, and called on the
African Union (AU) and its member states to work with the ICC, but in
July, the AU Assembly adopted a resolution stipulating it would not
collaborate with the Court in surrendering President Al Bashir. The AU
also reiterated its request to the UN Security Council to suspend the
ICC proceedings against President Al Bashir, and expressed its intention
to seek to limit the Prosecutor's discretion to initiate investigations and
prosecutions. Although some AU states seemed to disagree with the
position taken by the AU as a whole, their voices were drowned out by
the more vocal opponents of the ICC.

The stark contrast from many leaders in Africa between their
human rights rhetoric and the absence of concrete action to respect,
protect and promote human rights, is not new. But hardly ever has it
been demonstrated so unequivocally as with their reaction to President
Al Bashir's arrest warrant. This triggered a wide – and still ongoing –
debate in Africa on the role of international justice in ensuring
accountability for gross violations of international human rights and
humanitarian law.

Sadly, there are numerous other examples from 2009 that
demonstrate the lack of political will in Africa to ensure accountability
on any scale.

Conflict

Members of armed opposition groups and government security forces in Central African Republic, Chad, Democratic Republic of the Congo (DRC), Somalia and Sudan continued to commit human rights abuses with impunity in those parts of the countries affected by armed conflict or insecurity.

In Somalia, there was no functioning justice system and no effective mechanism was put in place to monitor human rights abuses. The conflict between the various armed groups and government forces resulted in thousands of civilian casualties due to the indiscriminate and disproportionate nature of many of the military operations conducted by all parties to the conflict, especially around the capital Mogadishu. Civilians were often targeted in attacks and densely populated areas were shelled. Military assistance, including shipments of arms from the USA, to the Transitional Federal Government, without adequate safeguards in place to ensure that such assistance does not lead to gross human rights violations, risked exacerbating the situation. The conflict in Somalia also continued to have implications for stability in the rest of the Horn of Africa.

In eastern DRC, sexual violence, attacks against civilians, looting and recruitment and use of child soldiers continued unabated. Joint military operations of the national Congolese army (FARDC) and the UN peacekeeping force (MONUC) against the armed group the Democratic Liberation Forces of Rwanda (FDLR) displaced thousands more people, destroyed villages and killed and wounded thousands. The FDLR continued to target civilians. MONUC was heavily criticized for its support to the FARDC in these military operations as the national army was also responsible for numerous human rights violations.

UN and AU peacekeepers, often with a mandate to protect the civilian population, were also attacked.

The arrest in Germany in November of Ignace Murwanashyaka, President of the FDLR, and his deputy, Straton Musoni, was a positive development and demonstrated the contribution universal jurisdiction can make in addressing impunity. The government of the DRC refused to arrest former rebel commander Bosco Ntaganda and surrender him to the ICC, even though the government is legally obliged to do so as an arrest warrant has been issued. Other senior FARDC officers accused of war crimes or other serious human rights violations have not been suspended from duty or brought to justice.

In March, the AU mandated a panel under former South African President Thabo Mbeki, to explore ways of ensuring accountability as well as reconciliation in Darfur. The report of the Mbeki panel, released in October, contained a wide range of recommendations to obtain justice, establish the truth about past and ongoing human rights abuses and seek reparations for those affected by human rights abuses or their relatives. The Mbeki panel recognized the role the ICC plays in addressing impunity.

And yet, although a number of countries indicated that President Al Bashir would be at risk of arrest if he were to visit, many others, such as Egypt, Ethiopia and Eritrea were more than pleased to receive the Sudanese President. And the government of Sudan ignored international attempts at justice and continued to refuse to arrest former government minister Ahmad Harun and militia leader Ali Kushayb even though warrants from the ICC have been outstanding against both of them for war crimes and crimes against humanity since April 2007.

Conflict between various communities in South Sudan increased, specifically in Jonglei, leading to thousands of people being displaced and numerous others killed and wounded, including civilians.

Any help humanitarian organizations might have been able to offer people was hampered by the difficult working environment in the country, partly due to the general insecurity and partly because they were often targeted by parties to the conflict or bandits. This was also the case in the DRC, eastern Chad, and Somalia. UN and AU peacekeepers, often with a mandate to protect the civilian population, were also attacked in these four countries.

Accountability and reparations for past human rights violations were often not effectively addressed in post-conflict situations either. In Liberia, for example, the Truth and Reconciliation Commission, established to shed light on the human rights violations committed during the period 1979-2003, published its final report in 2009 and recommended establishing an extraordinary criminal tribunal to investigate and prosecute those suspected of having committed crimes under international law. However, concrete steps need to be taken by the authorities to implement these recommendations.

In Burundi, there was only limited progress in establishing a Truth and Reconciliation Commission and a Special Tribunal within the Burundian justice system to investigate Burundi's violent history and to prosecute, if established, crimes of genocide, war crimes and crimes against humanity.

Good news came primarily from the Special Court for Sierra Leone, which concluded all its trials in 2009, including those at the appeal stage, except that of former President of Liberia Charles Taylor, which continued throughout the year. However, the reparations programme in Sierra Leone lacked means to be of much significance for the people affected by human rights abuses during the 1991-2002 conflict. The

UN Security Council also extended in December the mandate of the International Criminal Tribunal for Rwanda until the end of 2012 to ensure it could finalize the trials.

By the end of 2009, Senegal had still not started the trial of former Chadian President Hissène Habré, as requested by the AU, allegedly due to lack of resources. However, requests from Senegal for financial assistance were deemed excessive by international donors.

Public security concerns

The lack of commitment to address impunity was also reflected in the attitude of many governments in the region towards human rights violations committed by their law enforcement and other security officers. It was not unusual in 2009 for security forces to use excessive force and to commit unlawful killings, including extrajudicial executions.

On 7 February, the Presidential Guard in Madagascar fired live ammunition at unarmed demonstrators marching on the Presidential Palace in Antananarivo, killing at least 31 people. No independent and impartial investigation was conducted into the unlawful killings despite requests from the victims' relatives and human rights organizations.

In Nigeria, hundreds of people are unlawfully killed every year by the police, and 2009 was no exception. These unlawful killings, many of which may be extrajudicial executions, and which occur in police stations, at road blocks or in the street, are hardly ever investigated. Those who live in poverty face a greater risk of being killed as they are not in a position to bribe police officers. The law in Nigeria provides more grounds for lethal force than those permitted by international human rights law and standards.

There was no indication that the government of Cameroon had initiated investigations into the unlawful killings of about 100 people in 2008 when security forces cracked down on violent demonstrations against the increased cost of living and a constitutional amendment to extend the President's term of office. The government of Kenya did not take measures to ensure accountability for human rights violations committed during the post-election violence in 2007-08 when more than 1,000 people were killed. As a result, the Prosecutor of the ICC sought authorization from the Court to investigate possible crimes against humanity during the post-election violence in Kenya.

On 28 September, more than 150 people were unlawfully killed in Guinea when security forces violently repressed a peaceful demonstration in a stadium in the capital Conakry. Women participating in the demonstration were raped in public. No credible investigations were initiated by the authorities so the UN set up an international

The work of journalists was restricted in numerous ways, and the list of governments in 2009 that repressed basic freedoms and the right of their people to information, is long.

Commission of Inquiry. It concluded that crimes against humanity had been committed and recommended referral to the ICC.

At least here there was political will among the UN, AU and the Economic Community of West African States (ECOWAS) to act swiftly to determine the facts and identify those responsible. Unfortunately, this was more an exception than a rule in the region.

The problems in 2009 were compounded by the fact that security forces continued to be poorly paid, inadequately trained and ill-equipped. In many states security forces were still primarily a tool for repression and not for maintaining law and order, or for serving the public. In this way the demand for accountability was squashed by further violations.

Repression of dissent

In many countries, journalists, political opponents, trade union activists, and human rights defenders had their rights to freedom of expression, association and peaceful assembly violated. Across the region, governments' reaction to criticism was often to discredit and attack the messenger, including through intimidation, arbitrary arrests, enforced disappearances and sometimes killings. In some countries the judiciary lacks independence and magistrates are intimidated – so the judiciary becomes yet another tool of repression.

The work of journalists was restricted in numerous ways and the list of governments in 2009 that repressed basic freedoms and the right of their people to information is long: in Angola, journalists faced lawsuits for "abusing the media" and defamation charges leading to prison sentences; in Cameroon, a journalist was sentenced to three years' imprisonment for publishing "false news" and others were charged with insulting government officials; journalists were also arrested in the DRC, Eritrea, Gambia, Nigeria and Uganda for their work; Sudan and Chad deported several foreign journalists and media laws restricting their work were introduced or remained in place in both countries as well as in Rwanda and Togo; print media in Sudan were heavily censored for most of the year; in Madagascar, Nigeria, Senegal and Uganda, various media outlets were closed down; in Côte d'Ivoire, Republic of Congo, Djibouti, Ethiopia, Guinea, Kenya, Senegal, Swaziland and Tanzania, journalists were harassed and intimidated; in Somalia, nine journalists were killed and many others fled the country, as they and human rights activists were also threatened by members of armed groups.

Human rights activists were intimidated for their work across the region, and sometimes arrested, including in Burkina Faso, Chad, the DRC, Mauritania, Swaziland and Zimbabwe. Other countries, including Ethiopia, passed legislation restricting the legitimate work of civil society. In Gambia, the President reportedly threatened to kill anyone wishing to destabilize the country and specifically threatened human rights defenders. In Kenya, two prominent human rights defenders were killed in broad daylight in Nairobi by unidentified gunmen. In Burundi, a human rights defender working on corruption, including within the police, was stabbed to death at his home.

Political opponents of the government, or people perceived to be, were arbitrarily arrested in many countries, including Cameroon, Chad, Republic of Congo, Equatorial Guinea, Ethiopia, Guinea, Guinea-Bissau, Madagascar, Niger and Zimbabwe. Those in detention were regularly tortured or otherwise ill-treated. Some political opponents remained victims of enforced disappearances, including in Chad and Gambia. Military personnel in Guinea Bissau killed a number of political and military figures.

In some countries, such as Republic of Congo, Guinea, Madagascar, Mauritania and Uganda, demonstrations were violently repressed.

People on the move

The ongoing armed conflicts and insecurity in the region meant hundreds of thousands of people remained displaced in 2009, often living in camps, in precarious conditions with limited access to water, sanitation, health, education and food. Many of the internally displaced in northern Uganda returned to their homes but had no access to basic services.

Refugees and asylum-seekers in Kenya, Tanzania and Uganda were forcibly returned, or were at risk of being so, to their countries of origin where they still faced persecution or other risks. In South Africa the police response to xenophobic attacks against migrants and refugees, and destruction of their property, was often inadequate.

In Mauritania, migrants continued to be arbitrarily arrested and detained before being expelled, a policy put in place by the authorities as a result of pressure from European states to control migration. Angola expelled an estimated 160,000 DRC nationals in a process fraught with abuses, including reports that Angolan security forces subjected those expelled to wide-ranging ill-treatment including sexual abuse. Some died during the expulsion. In retaliation, the DRC expelled thousands of Angolan citizens, including refugees.

One positive development of 2009 was the adoption by the AU of the Convention for the Protection and Assistance of Internally Displaced Persons in Africa, recognizing the specific vulnerability and needs of displaced people.

Ongoing armed conflicts and insecurity in the region meant hundreds of thousands of people remained displaced in 2009.

Housing – forced evictions

The rapid urbanization in the region also causes displacement. Every year, tens of thousands of people end up living in informal settlements, often in very precarious living conditions with no access to basic services such as water, sanitation, health and education.

People have no access to adequate housing, no security of tenure and are at risk of forced evictions. The forced evictions often lead to the loss of their livelihood and their meagre possessions, and drive people deeper into poverty. Those evicted are hardly ever consulted, are not given advance notice of the evictions and are not granted compensation or adequate alternative housing. In 2009 the trend continued, and mass forced evictions took place in Angola, Chad, Equatorial Guinea, Ghana, Kenya and Nigeria.

Economic concerns – corporate accountability

The lack of corporate accountability resulted in a range of human rights abuses. In eastern DRC, the exploitation of natural resources, specifically in the mining industry, continued to fuel the conflict. Armed groups as well as the national army were involved in the exploitation of natural resources and were trading with private economic actors. Children were working in some of the mines.

In the Niger Delta in Nigeria, the situation deteriorated as security forces committed human rights violations during their military operations against armed groups. Armed groups kidnapped numerous oil workers and their relatives and attacked oil installations. The oil industry damaged the environment and had a negative impact on the standard of living and livelihood of local people. Laws and regulations to protect the environment were poorly enforced, and impunity for past human rights abuses continued, further contributing to poverty and conflict.

Due to corruption, nearly 30,000 victims of the 2006 dumping of toxic waste in Côte d'Ivoire were at risk of missing out on the compensation granted to them by the multinational corporation Trafigura in an out of court settlement in the UK.

Discrimination

Discrimination against people based on their perceived or real sexual orientation continued in various countries. Lesbian, gay, bisexual and transgender people as well as human rights activists working with and for them were harassed and intimidated. Some faced arbitrary arrest and detention as well as ill-treatment. New legislation to further criminalize homosexuality was introduced or debated in parliaments across the region.

Burundi, for example, adopted a new penal code in April that criminalized consensual same-sex relations. In Uganda, an Anti-Homosexuality Bill was introduced for consideration by parliament, building on the existing discriminatory laws by proposing new offences such as the "promotion of homosexuality". The Bill also sought to impose the death penalty and life imprisonment for some offences. In Nigeria, discussions continued on the draft Same Gender Marriage Bill, which would criminalize not only people of the same sex who get married, but also their witnesses or officiators.

In Cameroon and Senegal, men faced harassment, arbitrary arrest and detention, torture and unfair trials because they were suspected of engaging in same-sex relationships. In Malawi, two people were arrested and charged with "indecent practices between males" at the end of December, following a "traditional engagement ceremony". They were reportedly ill-treated while in detention.

More positive was the public statement in Rwanda by the Minister of Justice that homosexuality would not be criminalized, as sexual orientation was considered a private matter.

People were also discriminated against across the region for their gender, ethnicity, religion and identity. Discrimination and violence against women and girls prevailed in many societies and in different forms. Women and girls continued to be raped, particularly in situations of armed conflict such as in Chad, the DRC and Sudan. Some countries also recorded high levels of domestic violence although in most no proper reporting or investigating system was in place. Most women and girls faced numerous obstacles to obtain access to justice. Discrimination and the low status of women in countries such as Burkina Faso and Sierra Leone affected their ability to seek health care, and contributed to high levels of maternal mortality. Traditional harmful practices continued, including female genital mutilation and early marriage.

In Sudan, women were arrested and flogged for wearing trousers – which were considered "indecent or immoral". In Somalia, al-Shabab ("youth") militias closed women's organizations. In northern districts of Sierra Leone, women were not allowed to contest chieftaincy elections. An attempt to address the inequality of women in law sparked protests in Mali, and Nigeria still has to adopt legislation to incorporate the UN Women's Convention, almost 25 years after it chose to ratify this treaty.

In Mauritania, Special Rapporteurs of the UN highlighted the ongoing marginalization of black Mauritanian people. Several religious groups remained banned in Eritrea and people were persecuted due to their religion. In Burundi and Tanzania, killings and mutilations of albino people continued, driven by cultural and religious beliefs.

Some suspected of involvement in the killings were convicted of murder in Tanzania.

Conclusion

Lack of accountability in Africa was not only reflected in the reluctance of many states to investigate and prosecute those responsible for crimes under international law, or to collaborate with the ICC on the arrest of President Al Bashir. The lack of accountability for human rights abuses – by local and central authorities, law enforcement agencies, armed groups and corporate actors – continued to be a systemic problem across the region. Unless it is addressed, there will be no lasting improvement in the realization of all human rights as enshrined in the Universal Declaration of Human Rights and regional and international human rights treaties.

The AU should lead by example, but in certain situations it has become part of the problem. The call for accountability from civil society has become stronger over the years in Africa, but commitment from the political leadership is required to make significant change.

REGIONAL
OVERVIEWS
AFRICA

In a landmark ruling on 7 April 2009 in Lima, Peru's former President Alberto Fujimori was sentenced to 25 years' imprisonment for grave human rights violations.

AMERICAS

"People ask 'why don't you forgive?'," says Tita Radilla Martínez. "Because they don't tell me what they did to my father. Is he dead or alive? They say 'don't re-open the wound'. Re-open? The wound is open – it never healed."

It has been more than 30 years since Tita Radilla Martínez last saw her father, Rosendo Radilla. He was 60 years old when he was forcibly disappeared in 1974. The social activist and former mayor was last seen in a military barracks in Guerrero State, Mexico.

His family's hopes for truth and justice were rekindled by a decision from the Inter-American Court of Human Rights, which in November condemned Mexico for failing to adequately investigate his enforced disappearance.

Hundreds of thousands of people were killed, forcibly disappeared, tortured and many more forced into exile, during the period of military rule in Latin America from the 1960s to the mid 1980s. Return to civilian, democratically elected governments has not, however, overcome the legacy of impunity for most of these crimes. Indeed, a lack of accountability for abuses during this dark period of history has helped perpetuate policies and practices that feed continuing violations. The failure to bring those responsible, at all levels of authority, to justice sends a clear signal that those in power are above the law.

In recent years, however, a growing number of Latin American countries have made important advances towards tackling impunity, recognizing that reconciliation is an empty concept unless it is built on truth, justice and reparation. Until very recently most prosecutions and convictions were directed at low-ranking security personnel directly responsible for the crime; there was little or no effort to bring to justice those with ultimate responsibility for ruthlessly eliminating dissent and opposition.

But in April, a democratically elected head of state was convicted of human rights violations for the first time. Former Peruvian President Alberto Fujimori was sentenced to 25 years' imprisonment for grave human rights violations committed in 1991, including torture, enforced disappearances and extrajudicial executions. The conviction finally shows the region that nobody is exempt from justice. The judges concluded that former President Alberto Fujimori bore individual criminal responsibility because he had effective military command over those who committed the crimes.

Alberto Fujimori was not the only former leader on trial in the year. The trial of former Surinamese President Lieutenant Colonel Désiré Bouterse (1981-1987) and 24 others – accused of killing 13 civilians and two army officers at a military base in Paramaribo in December 1982 – resumed in 2009. Gregorio Álvarez, former general and de facto President of Uruguay (1980-1985) was sentenced to 25 years in prison, for the kidnapping and killing of 37 activists in Argentina in 1978.

In Colombia, the Council of State confirmed the dismissal of an army general for human rights violations. Álvaro Velandia Hurtado and three other army officers were dismissed for the torture, enforced disappearance and extrajudicial execution of Nidia Erika Bautista in 1987. The country also saw retired army general Jaime Uscátegui sentenced to 40 years in prison in November for his involvement in a massacre of 49 civilians by right-wing paramilitaries in Mapiripán in 1997.

During Argentina's 1976-1983 military regimes, the ESMA Naval Mechanics School served as a clandestine detention centre, where thousands of people were forcibly disappeared, or tortured, or both. Seventeen former ESMA officers, among them Alfredo Astiz, finally went on trial for human rights abuses, including torture and murder, including that of two French nuns, a journalist and three founder members of the Madres de Plaza de Mayo human rights group. Alfredo Astiz was first prosecuted in relation to these crimes in 1985 but amnesty laws, since-repealed, halted the proceedings.

In May, Sabino Augusto Montanaro, Interior Minister during the regime of General Alfredo Stroessner in Paraguay, was arrested after voluntarily returning to the country from exile. He faces trial for human rights violations including crimes allegedly committed under Operación Condor – a regional security co-operation against perceived political opponents. In September, more than 165 retired ex-agents of the Chilean National Intelligence Directorate (DINA) were charged in Chile for their roles in the operation, as well as in other cases of torture and enforced disappearance in the early years of Chile's military regime.

Despite this important progress in a growing number of emblematic cases of past human rights violations, justice for most of the hundreds of thousands of victims of past human rights violations remained elusive. Amnesty laws continued to hamper efforts in El Salvador, Brazil and Uruguay to hold violators accountable, and a national referendum in Uruguay on the annulment of the 1986 Law

Many ... investigations in 2009 were obstructed or collapsed; and the hopes and expectations of families for truth, justice and reparation remained frustrated.

on the Expiration of the Punitive Claims of the State (Expiry Law) failed
to reach the required majority needed to overturn the law. In the run-up
to the referendum, however, the Uruguayan Supreme Court reached
an historic ruling on the unconstitutionality of the law in the case of
Nibia Sabalsagaray, a young activist opponent who was tortured and
killed in 1974. The ruling, along with interpretations made by the
Executive to limit the application of the law, allowed for some progress
on justice.

In a somewhat swifter process, people who suffered human rights
violations in Oaxaca, Mexico, in 2006 during violent political protests,
may find their justice a step closer – with the finalization of the Supreme
Court investigation into the political crisis four years ago. It concluded
that the state governor and other senior officials should be held
accountable, but no steps were taken to indict them.

However, many other investigations in 2009 were obstructed or
collapsed; and the hopes and expectations of families for truth, justice
and reparation remained frustrated. A Mexican federal court, for
example, closed the case of genocide against former President Luis
Echeverría, and the armed forces in Brazil continued to block progress
into past abuses. In December, President Luiz Inácio Lula da Silva
announced the creation of a truth commission to investigate torture,
killings and enforced disappearances during the military rule of 1964
to 1985, as a part of the Third National Human Rights Plan. Following
concerted pressure from the military, there were concerns that the
proposal could be watered down.

And little progress was made in bringing to justice those
responsible for human rights violations in the context of US conduct in
the "war on terror".

International justice

As well as national prosecutions' attempts to combat impunity in Latin
America, international justice continued to play an important role in
2009. In June, Chile became the final state in South America to ratify
the Rome Statute establishing the International Criminal Court, and in
November, the declaration under Article 124 of the Rome Statute, by
which Colombia had declared that for seven years it did not accept the
jurisdiction of the Court with respect to war crimes, came to an end,
paving the way for investigations into war crimes and crimes against
humanity.

In January, a Spanish National Court charged 14 Salvadoran army
officers and soldiers with crimes against humanity and state terrorism
for the killings of six Jesuit priests, their housekeeper and her 16-year-
old daughter at the Central American University in El Salvador in

November 1989. In August, a Paraguayan judge ordered the extradition of former army doctor Norberto Bianco to Argentina to face trial for his alleged role in the illegal detention of more than 30 women and subsequent appropriation of their children in 1977 and 1978 during the military regime.

The trial of former Chilean Military Prosecutor General Alfonso Podlech in connection with the enforced disappearance of four people in the 1970s, including former priest Omar Venturelli, began in Italy in November. That same month, a US court ruled that sufficient grounds existed to try former Bolivian President Sánchez de Lozada and former Defence Minister Carlos Sánchez Berzaín in the USA in a civil suit for damages in relation to charges of crimes against humanity including extrajudicial executions in 2003.

Public security concerns

The public security situation affecting many countries continued to cause great concern. Murder rates for women and men continued to rise, in particular in Mexico, Guatemala, Honduras, El Salvador and Jamaica. Millions of people in Latin America and the Caribbean's poorest communities were plagued by violent criminal gangs and repressive, discriminatory and corrupt responses by law enforcement officials. At the same time, members of the security forces, especially the police, were required to work in ways that often put their own lives at risk.

As organized criminal networks extended their activities from drug trafficking, to kidnapping and trafficking of people, including women and children, the risks to irregular migrants and other vulnerable groups intensified. Governments in the region typically did very little to collect data and analyze these new problems, and even less to prevent abuses or bring to justice those responsible.

A general trend in 2009 towards an arms build-up in the region led to concern about the potential impact on human rights for people already living in fragile or non-existent security.

Official efforts to address escalating crime were often undermined by allegations of grave human rights violations, including enforced disappearances, torture and other ill-treatment. In Brazil, Jamaica, Colombia and Mexico, the security forces were accused of committing hundreds of unlawful killings – the vast majority of which were dismissed as "killings while resisting arrest" or simply dismissed as false allegations designed to dishonour the security forces.

Despite reports of serious human rights violations by armed and security force personnel, Colombia and Mexico continued to receive significant security co-operation from the USA, and more is expected under the terms of the Merida Initiative – a heavily financed agreement between Mexico (and other certain Central American countries) and the USA to combat organized crime.

Some countries encouraged alternative public security projects – a crucial initiative for challenging illegal policing methods – but they frequently fell short of expectations, and they were criticized by the affected communities in the Dominican Republic and Jamaica, for example, as further delaying urgently needed policing reform, and failing to address the broader needs of the communities.

Conflict and crisis

A general trend in 2009 towards an arms build-up in the region led to concern about the potential impact on human rights for people already living in fragile or non-existent security.

The civilian population in Colombia continued to bear the brunt of the 40-year-old internal armed conflict. All the warring parties – the security forces, paramilitaries, and guerrilla groups – to the conflict continued to abuse human rights and violate international humanitarian law. Indigenous Peoples, social leaders and human rights defenders were among the most vulnerable. At least 3 million and possibly as many as 5 million people have been forcibly displaced as a result of the long-running, armed conflict. As many as 286,000 were forced from their homes in 2009 alone. Women continued to suffer sexual violence, communities continued to be subjected to hostage-taking, enforced disappearances, forced recruitment of children, indiscriminate attacks, and those deemed a particular risk to each party's interests faced death threats to intimidate them.

Insecurity and instability were not limited to Colombia, however. In a disturbing echo of the past, Honduras experienced the first military-backed coup d'état in Latin America since Venezuela's in 2002. Months of political turbulence and instability followed, which November elections failed to resolve. The security forces met protests against the coup with excessive use of force, intimidation and attacks against opponents. Freedom of expression was curtailed as several media outlets were closed and there were reports of violence against women and the killing of more than 10 transgender women. The Tegucigalpa-San José accord – brokered by the international community and which included a truth commission to clarify responsibilities – made no progress and the de facto government remained in power at the end of the year.

Hemispheric relations

Hopes and expectations for a new era of hemispheric relations were initially borne out by US pledges on partnership. When President Barack Obama addressed the Fifth Summit of the Americas in Trinidad and Tobago in April, he promised an era of mutual respect and a multilateral approach. However, by the end of the year, relations were strained by the

Honduras crisis, US policy on Cuba and Colombia's agreement to allow the USA to use some of its military bases. Growing tensions between several Latin American countries – Colombia with neighbours Ecuador and Venezuela, and Peru with neighbours Chile and Bolivia – also hampered efforts to move towards greater regional integration.

Economic concerns – poverty

Deep and persistent inequalities continue to exist in the Americas, especially in access to education, income levels, health and nutritional status, exposure to violence and crime, and access to basic services.

Although some Latin American and Caribbean countries were not as severely affected by the international financial crisis as initially feared, an estimated 9 million more people were tipped into poverty in the region in 2009. This reversed the recent trend of reducing income poverty, fuelled by economic growth. With varying degrees of commitment, states took measures to protect the most vulnerable sectors of the population from the crisis and avoided regressive measures in social rights. However, social expenditure in Latin America and the Caribbean is still extremely low and there is a lack of long-term policies to combat the human rights violations suffered by people living in poverty. Those most affected continued to be those already discriminated against, such as women, children and Indigenous communities.

Giving birth safely in 2009 continued to be the privilege of only the most affluent women in the region. In every country – including high-income economies the USA and Canada – already marginalized women, such as African Americans or Native American women, had the highest risk of death from complications in pregnancy or childbirth – disparities which in the USA had been unchanged for the past 25 years.

Violence against women and girls

Violence against women and girls remained endemic. The number of reported cases of domestic violence, rape and sexual abuse, and the killing and mutilation of women's bodies after having been raped, rose in Mexico, Guatemala, El Salvador, Honduras, Nicaragua and Haiti. In several countries, in particular Nicaragua, Haiti and the Dominican Republic, data suggested that more than half these victims were girls.

Discrimination against women, and the lack of rigorous investigations into complaints of violence, was highlighted by several international bodies. The Inter-American Court of Human Rights, for example, condemned Mexico for failing to act diligently to prevent or effectively investigate or remedy the abduction and murder of three women in Chihuahua in 2001. The authorities in several countries,

Despite the simple legal fact of a woman's own right to life and health, the issue [of abortion] continued to polarize opinion and emotion.

including Uruguay, Venezuela and the Dominican Republic, acknowledged they were unable to deal with the level of complaints relating to violence against women, even though specialist gender units were established in a number of criminal justice systems. Medical care for survivors was often deficient or wholly lacking.

Implementation of laws to ensure respect for women's rights and prevent violence remained slow, especially in Argentina, Mexico, Jamaica and Venezuela. A number of countries, mainly those in the Caribbean, introduced reforms but fell short of international human rights standards by not criminalizsing rape in all circumstances.

Abortion in cases of rape or when the health of the mother is at risk was accessible and available in a number of countries including Colombia, Mexico Federal District, Cuba and the USA. In many other countries where it is allowed legally, in practice there were obstacles to access. Steps were taken towards decriminalizing abortion in certain circumstances in Peru. However, constitutional reforms introduced in the Dominican Republic and 17 Mexican states to protect the right to life from the moment of conception, raised fears that a total prohibition on abortion may follow. Total prohibitions on abortion in all circumstances remained in place in Chile, El Salvador and Nicaragua.

Despite the simple legal fact of a woman's own right to life and health, the issue continued to polarize opinion and emotion, with campaigners and health care professionals involved in abortions receiving threats and a US doctor being killed.

On a more positive note, steps were taken to uphold the rights of lesbian, gay, bisexual and transgender people (LGBT). Mexico City passed a ground-breaking bill legalizing gay marriage. However, Honduras, Peru and Chile failed to protect their LGBT communities from harassment or intimidation, along with Caribbean countries such as Jamaica and Guyana.

Indigenous Peoples

Discrimination against Indigenous Peoples remained both systemic and systematic across the region. Decisive action to protect Indigenous Peoples' rights did not match rhetoric. There was a general failure to consider Indigenous rights in decisions to do with licensing oil, logging and other resource concessions. The right to free, prior and informed consent about matters that may impact Indigenous Peoples' lives is defined in the 2007 UN Declaration on the Rights of Indigenous Peoples. In Canada, Peru, Argentina, Chile and Paraguay, Amnesty International documented cases where the authorities failed to establish a robust process to ensure this right was upheld in development project proposals.

REGIONAL
OVERVIEWS
AMERICAS

Massive oil and gas developments continued to be carried out in Canada, for example, without the consent of the Lubicon Cree in northern Alberta, undermining their use of traditional lands and contributing to high levels of poor health and poverty.

Throughout the region, evictions of Indigenous Peoples from their ancestral lands were reported. Threats, intimidation and violence against Indigenous leaders and community members were common.

A new Constitution in Bolivia which took effect in February, asserted the centrality and plurality of Indigenous identities in the country and set out a framework for reform, including by elevating Indigenous jurisdiction to be equal to current judicial processes.

Indigenous Peoples across the region campaigned throughout the year for their social, civil, economic, cultural and political rights to be upheld. They were frequently met with intimidation, harassment, excessive use of force, spurious charges and detention. In Queretaro, Mexico, one Indigenous woman was released but two others remained in prison at the end of the year, pending the outcome of their retrial on the basis of fabricated criminal charges. In Peru, Indigenous leaders were charged with rebellion, sedition and conspiracy against the state, without any evidence, following the dispersal of a road blockade by hundreds of Indigenous people in which scores of protesters were injured and 33 people killed – including 23 police officers. In Colombia, the authorities often falsely accused Indigenous communities and their leaders of links to the guerrilla forces.

Despite the progress made in an important number of emblematic cases of past human rights violations, the legal, jurisdictional and political obstacles that have helped entrench impunity in the region, remained formidable in 2009.

Counter-terror and security

The new US administration seemed to promise substantive change in some of the policies that have damaged international human rights protections over the previous seven years. An end to the CIA secret detention programme, for example, and the release of some information on the legal opinions that had been issued in support of that programme, were welcome. But not all promises translated into reality. The deadline set by President Obama on his second day in office to close the detention facility at Guantánamo within a year drifted as domestic party politics trumped the human rights of the detainees. The positive move by the new administration to turn to the ordinary federal courts to try some Guantánamo detainees was tarnished by its decision to retain military commissions for others.

Meanwhile, detentions at Bagram airbase in Afghanistan continued as if under the old administration, and the USA failed to meet its legal obligation to ensure accountability and remedy for human rights violations committed in the counter-terrorism context since September 2001.

Death penalty

There were 52 executions in the USA during the year. Although this was the highest judicial death toll in the USA since 2006, it was still well down on the peaks of the late 1990s. Death sentencing continued on its downward trend – even in Texas and Virginia, which account for almost half of all executions carried out in the USA since 1977. Around 100 people were sentenced to death nationwide compared with around 300 a decade and a half earlier. In March, New Mexico became the 15th state to abolish the death penalty, but three months later, Connecticut's Governor vetoed an attempt to do likewise by the state legislature.

Although death sentences were handed down in the Bahamas, Guyana and Trinidad and Tobago, no executions were carried out.

Conclusion

Despite the progress made in an important number of emblematic cases of past human rights violations, the legal, jurisdictional and political obstacles that have helped entrench impunity in the region, remained formidable in 2009.

However, across the region, victims of human rights violations, their families and human rights defenders supporting them continued to defy intimidation, threats and harassment and campaigned vigorously to hold governments and armed groups to their obligations to respect international and domestic human rights standards.

Tita Radilla Martínez demanded the Mexican government comply with the Inter American Court, which ordered the end of military jurisdiction for all human rights cases, so the truth of her father's enforced disappearance, along with hundreds of others, would finally be established. They need justice. The time for rhetoric is over.

Vedanta's alumina refinery at Lanjigarh, seen from Kenduguda village, Orissa, India, March 2009. Marginalized communities, including landless farmers and Adivasis, in several states were threatened with forced evictions to accommodate industrial and other business projects.

ASIA-PACIFIC

"We left everything behind. We have nothing now... The Taleban were very cruel to us, and then the government began bombing so we had to flee with whatever we could gather. So who can we turn to?"

This schoolteacher spoke to Amnesty International as she was fleeing the intense fighting that forced more than 2 million people out of their homes in Pakistan's North West Frontier Province and the Federally Administered Tribal Areas (FATA), abutting the Afghan border.

Her sentiments apply equally to the millions of other people across the Asia-Pacific region who have been forced, whether through insecurity or economic necessity, to leave their homes and, in many cases, their countries.

At the beginning of the year, nearly half a million Pakistanis were already displaced. Although the communities Amnesty International spoke to had been subject to the Taleban's harsh practices – including public executions, torture, and severe restrictions on women and girls' ability to receive health care and attend school – most explained that they had fled out of fear of the Pakistani government's brutal counter-insurgency offensives. Indeed, by April, as the Taleban aggressively extended their control to areas within easy driving distance of Islamabad, the government launched another major assault, prompting 2 million more people to flee.

The government's response to the long-standing conflict in the north-western border with Afghanistan has vacillated between appeasement and extreme violence; neither strategy indicating a government committed to protecting the rights of the Pakistani people. In fact, there is a clear link between the surging conflict and decades of successive Pakistani governments ignoring the rights of the millions who live in the difficult terrain of north-western Pakistan, evading accountability for current or past abuses. Even now, the people of the Tribal Areas bordering Afghanistan do not have the same rights as the other citizens of Pakistan: under the colonial era Frontier Crimes Regulation (1901) that still governs most administrative and judicial aspects of their lives, they are outside the writ of Pakistan's national assembly as well as the judiciary. Pakistanis living in the FATA region are legally subject to collective punishment, that is, the government can punish any and all members of a tribe for crimes committed on its territory, or for "acting in a hostile or unfriendly manner" or in any way abetting or failing to provide evidence of a crime. At the same time, the residents of FATA suffer some of the highest levels of maternal mortality, infant mortality, and illiteracy (particularly for girls and women) in the entire region.

By the end of 2009, millions of people across the Asia-Pacific region were still waiting for their governments to protect their rights. Whether in their own homes or in makeshift shelters, accountability for the injustice they suffer remained an ideal celebrated more often in the breach, especially for the marginalized and powerless. But for people on the move, whether crossing international frontiers as refugees, asylum-seekers and migrant workers, or travelling within the borders of their own country due to displacement or for work; nobody assumed responsibility for them. They lacked the standing to assert their human rights, and they faced violations of all of them: civil, political, economic, social and cultural.

Conflict

The vast majority of the people displaced by armed conflict sought shelter within the borders of their own country. Most were lucky enough to receive humanitarian assistance to stave off immediate starvation or deadly disease, but the vast majority of the displaced suffered from insufficient sanitation, health care, and education.

They had no way of speaking out about their situation or getting redress for the wrongs that had led to their displacement in the first place.

Some 300,000 Sri Lankans were trapped on a narrow coastal strip of north-eastern Sri Lanka from January to mid May between the retreating Liberation Tigers of Tamil Eelam (LTTE) and the advancing Sri Lankan military. In many instances, the LTTE prevented them from fleeing, while the government rained shells upon the area. Many thousands were killed.

There was little sign that the Sri Lankan authorities would provide accountability for any of the atrocities allegedly committed by both sides during the fighting, especially in its final bloody phase, despite a promise to UN Secretary-General Ban Ki Moon.

The Sri Lankan government also promised to allow hundreds of thousands of Sri Lankan Tamils who survived the war to return home, but in fact more than 100,000 remained in military-run camps by year's end, denied their freedom of movement. Many of them had previously survived months of difficult conditions as they were forced to travel with retreating LTTE forces who forcibly recruited civilians, including children, and in some cases used them as human shields. The government of Sri Lanka, citing varying security concerns, barred

Afghan women again paid a high price in the conflict, as the Taleban targeted women human rights defenders and activists as well as schools and health clinics, particularly those for girls and women.

independent monitors from freely assessing the detained population's well-being. This lack of access stymied efforts to gather information about violations of humanitarian law during the long conflict, and consequently blocked accountability.

Tens of thousands of Afghans were displaced by a combination of escalating violence by the Taleban and the inability of the central government and its international allies to improve the country's political and economic situation. The Afghan Taleban were responsible for some two thirds of the more than 2,400 civilian casualties, with the peak of the attacks occurring as the Taleban tried to disrupt the presidential election.

Despite the Taleban's attacks, millions of Afghans turned out to exercise their right to vote on election day, only to have their selection undermined as a result of the failure of the Afghan government and its international supporters to provide an adequate human rights protection mechanism. Supporters of the main candidates, including President Hamid Karzai, intimidated and harassed political activists and journalists before, during, and after the elections. The balloting itself was immediately criticized by independent observers as fraudulent, and the process of verifying the results dragged on for months, further eroding the election's legitimacy and the Afghan people's right to participate in the conduct of their public affairs.

Afghan women again paid a high price in the conflict, as the Taleban targeted women human rights defenders and activists as well as schools and health clinics, particularly those for girls and women, while ongoing insecurity eroded the very modest gains Afghan women had made since the fall of the Taleban government.

In the conflict-afflicted Philippines island of Mindanao, more than 200,000 civilians continued to live in camps or makeshift shelters, sometimes surrounded by a heavy military presence despite the July ceasefire between the Philippine army and the insurgent Moro Islamic Liberation Front. A significant element in the fighting was the lawlessness of paramilitary groups and militias, controlled and funded by local politicians and operating without any legal accountability.

The history of impunity for these forces formed the backdrop to the shocking, execution-style killing of at least 57 people, including more than 30 journalists, on 23 November on the eve of registration for local gubernatorial elections. The egregious nature of the crime led the government to impose martial law briefly to reimpose its writ and press charges against several members of the powerful Ampatuan family, which has dominated the province's politics for a decade.

REGIONAL OVERVIEWS
ASIA-PACIFIC

Repression of dissent

In other parts of the Asia-Pacific region, it was not sharp conflict that spurred the dislocation of people and the subsequent denial of their rights, but rather ongoing repression.

Thousands of people fled North Korea and Myanmar to get away from their governments' ongoing and systematic violation of human rights. North Koreans mainly sought to escape political repression and the country's economic crisis by crossing the Chinese border illegally. If caught by the Chinese authorities and forcibly returned, they faced detention, forced labour and torture, with some deaths occurring while in custody.

China considered all undocumented North Koreans as economic migrants, rather than refugees, and continued to prevent the UN refugee agency, UNHCR, from having access to them. In 2009, the UN Special Rapporteur on the situation of human rights in the Democratic People's Republic of Korea stated that most North Korean border crossers into China were entitled to international protection because of the threat of persecution or punishment upon return.

North Korean authorities also continued to bar their own citizens from freely moving around inside the country. People had to obtain official permission to travel. Although the authorities have reportedly relaxed enforcement of such rules, as thousands have left their homes in search of food or economic opportunities, people remained vulnerable under the current law and were often subjected to extortion by officials.

Thousands of people were displaced in Myanmar as government security forces routinely violated the laws of war in campaigns against armed opposition groups from several of the country's ethnic minorities. The government continued to repress political dissent, with 2,100 political prisoners in detention. The most prominent detainee, Aung San Suu Kyi, who has been in detention for 13 of the past 20 years, mostly under house arrest, was sentenced to 18 more months under house arrest on 11 August after an unfair trial by a court in Yangon's Insein prison. The charges stemmed from the uninvited visit of a US man who swam to her house and spent two nights there in early May.

The year witnessed another painful reminder of the desperation of Myanmar's Rohingyas, a persecuted Muslim minority from western Myanmar, when thousands of them fled on boats sailing for Thailand and Malaysia. The Thai security forces, intent on preventing an influx of refugees, expelled hundreds of them, setting them adrift in unseaworthy boats with little or no food and water.

> The discrimination that migrant workers faced throughout the region, even in their own countries, formed the backdrop to one of the worst recent outbreaks of unrest in China's Xinjiang Uighur Autonomous Region.

As the year was ending, Thai authorities also forcibly returned around 4,500 Lao Hmong, including 158 recognized refugees and many others fleeing persecution, to Laos. The Lao government refused requests from the UN and others to be allowed access to monitor the conditions of those who were returned.

In December, the Chinese government successfully pressed Cambodian authorities to return 20 Uighur asylum-seekers who were fleeing the crackdown after the July unrest in the Xinjiang Uighur Autonomous Region (XUAR). The move was part of China's increasingly assertive strategy of pushing other governments to avoid any support for dissenting voices within China. The Chinese government stepped up its pressure on all internal challenges, detaining and harassing dozens of lawyers and human rights defenders. In particular, Chinese authorities targeted the signatories of Charter '08, a document calling for greater respect for human rights and popular participation.

China maintained its position as the world's leading executioner, although the exact extent of the problem remained shrouded in China's state secrecy laws.

Economic concerns

The vast majority of people who left their homes in the Asia-Pacific region were driven by economic need. Millions of people in China who had moved to the country's economic hubs were forced back to their homes in rural areas, more aware of the growing inequities between China's newly wealthy and the millions still living with inadequate health care and education.

In 2009, as in all recent years, millions left their homes in countries such as the Philippines, Nepal, Indonesia and Bangladesh, to pursue livelihoods in others, namely South Korea, Japan and Malaysia, or even further abroad. Despite some improvements in the national and bilateral legal frameworks governing the hiring, transportation and treatment of migrant labourers, most of those participating in this massive global flow of migrant labour were not able to enjoy their rights fully. In many cases, this was due to government practices, but they also often found themselves as easy targets of heightened racism and xenophobia in economically difficult times.

The discrimination that migrant workers faced throughout the region, even in their own countries, formed the backdrop to one of the worst recent outbreaks of unrest in China's Xinjiang Uighur Autonomous Region. The protests began with non-violent demonstrations against government inaction after a violent riot at a factory in Shaoguan, Guangdong province, resulted in two deaths.

On 26 June, hundreds of Uighur workers clashed with thousands of Han Chinese workers at a factory where Uighurs had been recruited from the XUAR. By early July, the protests in the XUAR had turned into full scale riots, with reports that more than 190 people were killed. Perhaps unsurprisingly, given the decades of official marginalization and discrimination of the Uighur community, the authorities blamed Uighur activists for the violence, without allowing for independent monitoring or proper trials. China executed at least nine of those they blamed within months, and the authorities pledged to respond to further unrest with a heavy hand.

One of the starkest examples of the abuse of migrant workers came to light in Malaysia, where foreign workers made up a fifth of the total workforce. Official records divulged this year showed that Malaysian authorities caned almost 35,000 migrants between 2002 and 2008, many for immigration offences – cruel and degrading punishment on a monumental scale. In addition to undocumented workers, documented workers whose passports have been withheld by their employers, asylum-seekers and refugees were also at risk of being caned. Thousands of migrant workers languished in detention centres falling short of international standards, often with little due process or legal protection.

Even where migrant workers received greater legal protection, their marginalized status still made them vulnerable to abuse. In South Korea – one of the first Asian countries to legally recognize the rights of migrant workers – the state failed to protect migrant workers from being abused by their employers, trafficked for sexual exploitation, and denied their wages for long periods.

Housing – forced evictions

In many other cases, economic motives prompted authorities to forcibly evict people from their homes. Cambodian authorities, for example, forcibly evicted low-income families from a redevelopment site in central Phnom Penh after three years of harassing and intimidating them. In another example, Cambodian authorities evicted 31 families living with HIV and AIDS in Phnom Penh, and took the majority of them to a grossly inadequate resettlement site with limited access to crucial health care.

In India, the development of aluminium mining and processing facilities in the eastern state of Orissa threatened to dislocate thousands of Indigenous people who hold the site to be sacred. In the two years that Vedanta's aluminium refinery at Lanjigarh has been running, local communities have had to contend with contaminated water, polluted air and constant dust and noise. Further plans to open a mine in the

> **In many other cases, economic motives prompted authorities to forcibly evict people from their homes.**

Niyamgiri Hills threatened to undermine the lives and livelihoods of the Dongria Kondh, an Adivasi Indigenous community.

In April 2009, the Indian authorities gave Sterlite Industries India Ltd and the state-owned Orissa Mining Corporation permission to mine bauxite in Dongria Kondh traditional lands for the next 25 years.

In Papua New Guinea, police forcibly evicted the residents of around 100 houses near the Porgera mine operated by a subsidiary of Canadian transnational corporation Barrick Gold.

In Viet Nam, a mob, apparently with official backing, evicted nearly 200 Buddhist monks and nuns from a monastery in central Viet Nam. The group had been sheltering there since they were evicted from another monastery in September, by a similar mob. The authorities denied any involvement, but consistently failed to provide any protection for the monks and nuns, or ensure they were offered suitable alternative accommodation.

In each case, the destruction of their home significantly undermined the ability of the people concerned to enjoy their rights, and to get redress for the violations of them.

Environmental displacement

In a year when the Copenhagen Climate Change summit sought, and failed, to achieve a global consensus to address environmental change, it was easy to see the impact of large-scale shifts in the human environment. The government of the Maldives held a cabinet meeting underwater just before the Copenhagen meeting – a stunt that graphically captured the very real possibility that the small island state would disappear under the Indian Ocean sooner rather than later. Several Pacific states also announced that they feared being submerged.

In Tibet and Nepal where the headwaters of some of the world's most important rivers are located, and in Bangladesh, the possibility of catastrophic droughts or floods prompted dislocation and attendant political instability. Thus environmental concerns led to human rights challenges – and as is often the case, it was the poorest and most marginalized communities who were most susceptible to the realities of the physical environment, and less likely to receive assistance from their own governments.

Conclusion

By and large, the countries in the Asia-Pacific region have not responded adequately to the challenges of protecting the rights of those who have left their homes behind. Most countries in the region have not even ratified the 1951 Refugee Convention or its 1967

Protocol, which sets out the rights of people who have fled their country due to persecution or clear danger.

Frameworks to protect the rights of internally displaced people remained even more poorly developed, compared with the international legal framework for the treatment of refugees and asylum-seekers. But the greatest challenge for the protection of dislocated people in the region remained the poor record of accountability for many of the region's governments.

Nowhere was this more apparent than in the case of Sri Lanka. The UN Human Rights Council on 27 May passed a deeply flawed resolution on Sri Lanka that not only ignored calls for an international investigation into alleged atrocities during the conflict, but actually commended the Sri Lankan government. Global politics and expediency trumped concern for the wellbeing of hundreds of thousands of Sri Lankans. The international community also continued to ignore the large-scale human rights violations that forced thousands of the country's citizens to flee from their homes.

China and India, apparently vying for access to Myanmar's resources, did not use their political and economic influence to curb the Myanmar government's practice of excluding internal critics like Aung San Suu Kyi, or of ending the repression of various ethnic minorities. Even the widely reported spectacle of the Rohingyas adrift on the sea did not prompt appropriate action from Myanmar's neighbours in the Association of South East Asian Nations (ASEAN).

All ASEAN members finally ratified the ASEAN Charter, containing several provisions addressing human rights, including one that called for the establishment of a human rights body. Nevertheless, most countries in the region had still not signed up to many of the major global human rights treaties. In particular, Amnesty International believes that the region shirked its responsibility to establish a clear regional response to the ongoing problems created by flows of people across borders, or the underlying human rights problems that prompt such movements.

There are strong indications that the rate of movement of people across the globe, within and across borders, is going to increase, whether as a result of conflict, economic need, or environmental disruptions.

There are strong indications that the rate of movement of people across the globe, within and across borders, is going to increase, whether as a result of conflict, economic need, or environmental disruptions. Yet there are no signs that the international community is amending and adapting the current legal framework to address this development. What is required is an acknowledgement that people leave their homes for a variety of reasons, and that, whatever the reason, every human is still entitled to enjoy the full range of their human rights.

Individual nation states cannot always address the migration of their own people – whether because the scale of internal movement is too great, or because it crosses regional and global borders. This understanding has grown in recent decades but must accelerate further to accommodate the reality of a global population on the move.

The people of the Asia-Pacific region constitute a major portion of the global population of migrant workers, refugees, asylum-seekers, and internally displaced people. They are waiting for the region's governments and regional groups to follow and facilitate these trends.

REGIONAL OVERVIEWS
ASIA-PACIFIC

A man mourns Natalia Estemirova at a memorial for the human rights defender and journalist murdered in July 2009 in Chechnya. Human rights activists working across the Russian Federation continued to face harassment and death.

EUROPE AND CENTRAL ASIA

"I dream of living somewhere in peace with my daughter, becoming a grandmother and being kind to my grandchildren, but I still have a task to fulfil here... This is a declaration of war, we have to fight for justice, we cannot give up."

Natalia Estemirova, talking to Amnesty International in 2009, after the murder of her friend and fellow human rights defender Stanislav Markelov.

At 8.30 on a July morning in the Chechen capital of Grozny, leading human rights defender Natalia Estemirova was dragged off the street into a waiting car, shouting to witnesses that she was being abducted. Later that day her body was found with gunshot wounds, dumped in the neighbouring Russian republic of Ingushetia.

This was a tragedy on a number of levels: for her 15-year-old daughter who she had brought up alone; for the people of Chechnya who lost a tireless, courageous voice seeking to document the abuses they suffer and their lack of justice; and for civil society, in Russia and abroad, for whom she was an invaluable partner in the fight for respect of human rights.

It would also be a tragedy doomed to repetition, should the Russian legal system again prove utterly ineffective in ensuring accountability for the life of another activist who braved death threats and intimidation to demand justice for others.

This was not, sadly, an isolated story. Across Europe and Central Asia, governments failed to live up to their responsibilities to protect human rights defenders, and made continued efforts to suppress those who sought to publicize abuses, articulate alternative views or hold different beliefs. Many governments used repressive measures, or exploited the seeming indifference of the international community, to shield themselves from accountability. They continued to erode human rights, evade their obligations, and suffer a failure of political will in addressing key abuses.

Counter-terror and security

One of the most striking cases in point is that of renditions. The involvement of European states in the global programme of rendition and secret detention operated by the CIA in the years after 2001 has long been known. But despite repeated denials and obfuscation by individual governments, we now have clear evidence of the involvement.

Most governments, however, still failed to seek effective and transparent accountability for these human rights abuses, either at the national level or through European institutions. Some initiatives that had been taken remained unsatisfactory. A German parliamentary inquiry into German involvement in renditions concluded in July 2009, but exonerated all German state actors, despite compelling evidence to the contrary. A German court had previously issued warrants for the arrest of 13 CIA agents for their involvement in the rendition of Khalid al-Masri but the government refused to transmit these warrants. The methods, evidence and findings of an investigation into the existence of an alleged secret prison in Poland, finally begun in 2008, still remained secret. Other European states reportedly implicated in such abuses, including Romania, did even less to ensure accountability for them. Several European states ignored the rulings of the European Court of Human Rights against the return of suspects of terrorism to countries where they were at risk of torture. In February, the Court ruled that Italy's expulsion of Sami Ben Khemais Essid to Tunisia violated the prohibition of *refoulement*. In August, Italy returned Ali ben Sassi Toumi to Tunisia, where he was held incommunicado for eight days.

There were some other signs of progress towards accountability, however. In November, an Italian court convicted 22 CIA agents, one US military officer and two Italian agents for their involvement in the abduction and rendition of Abu Omar – a man kidnapped in broad daylight from an Italian street and then illegally transferred via Germany to Egypt where he said he was tortured. The prosecution of those involved had faced serious obstacles due to restrictions on the evidence available to prosecutors on grounds of national security. And in December a European government admitted for the first time that a secret "black site" had existed on its territory after a Lithuanian parliamentary committee concluded that a CIA secret detention facility had been constructed there. The committee found that officials from the Lithuanian State Security Department had assisted in the construction of the site, and knew of CIA flights landing without border checks, but failed to notify the President or Prime Minister – an echo of concerns raised elsewhere about the lack of oversight of intelligence and security agencies.

The signature response of European states to the challenges of large and mixed flows of irregular migration was to repress them.

In other areas too, security trumped human rights in government agendas, to the detriment of both. In waves of arbitrary detentions, the security forces in Uzbekistan swept up a range of individuals and their relatives on suspicion of involvement with banned Islamist parties and armed groups accused of attacks throughout the country. Among those detained were men and women who attended unregistered mosques, studied under independent imams, had travelled or studied abroad, or had relatives who lived abroad or were suspected of affiliation to banned Islamist groups. Many were believed to have been detained without charge or trial for lengthy periods, amid reports of torture. In Kazakhstan, the security forces continued to use counter-terrorism operations to target minority groups perceived as a threat to national and regional security. Groups particularly affected were asylum-seekers and refugees from Uzbekistan, and members or suspected members of Islamic groups or Islamist parties, either unregistered or banned in Kazakhstan. A total failure of political will to uphold the rule of law and address impunity in Chechnya continued to lead to destabilization across Russia's North Caucasus region.

Armed opposition groups continued to cause death and destruction in parts of the region, including in the North Caucasus, Spain, Greece and Turkey.

People on the move

Real or perceived risks for security also continued to drive the debate in other areas, providing fertile ground for populist rhetoric particularly in relation to migration, and exclusion of the 'other'.

The signature response of European states to the challenges of large and mixed flows of irregular migration was to repress them, resulting in a consistent pattern of human rights violations linked to the interception, detention and expulsion by states of foreign nationals, including those seeking international protection. In May, for example, the lives and safety of hundreds of migrants and asylum-seekers on three vessels in the Mediterranean were placed at risk first by a squabble between the Italian and Maltese authorities over their obligations to respond to maritime distress calls, and then by the Italian government's unprecedented decision to send those in the boats to Libya – a country with no functioning asylum procedure – without assessing their protection needs.

Some others, including Turkey and Ukraine, also forcibly returned refugees and asylum-seekers to countries where they risked serious human rights violations. Other asylum-seekers facing obstacles in accessing help included those in Greece and Turkey who could be unlawfully detained and expelled due to the absence of a fair asylum procedure, or denied necessary guidance and legal support to pursue their claims.

Many countries such as Greece and Malta also routinely detained migrants and asylum-seekers, and in inappropriate conditions.

Across the region, hundreds of thousands of people remained displaced by the conflicts that accompanied the collapse of the former Yugoslavia and the Soviet Union, often unable to return owing to their legal status – or lack of it – and discriminated against in accessing rights including property tenure. They were joined by some 26,000 people still unable to return home after the 2008 conflict between Russia and Georgia.

Discrimination

A climate of racism and intolerance in many countries fuelled ill-treatment of migrants, and helped to keep them and other marginalized groups excluded from society, blocking their rights to access services, participate in government and be protected by the law. The marginalization was heightened in 2009 by fears of the economic downturn, and accompanied in many countries by a sharp rise in racism and hate speech in public discourse. The endorsement by Swiss voters in November of a constitutional ban on the construction of minarets was an example of the dangers of popular initiatives transforming rights into privileges.

Many asylum-seekers and migrants were subject to discrimination and exclusion from services and employment, and experienced extreme poverty. In Italy, new legislation as part of a security package established the criminal offence of "irregular migration". Many feared the new law would deter irregular migrants from accessing education and medical care – and indeed protection by law enforcement officials – for fear of being reported to the police. This was especially the case given existing provisions in the criminal code obliging civil servants (such as teachers or local authority employees, including those in charge of issuing identity cards) to report all criminal acts to the police or judicial authorities. In the UK, hundreds of thousands of rejected asylum-seekers – whose inability to leave the country was often outside their control – lived in destitution and faced significant limits on their access to free health care, with the majority relying on the charity of others. In Germany, irregular migrants and their children had limited access to health care, education, and judicial remedies in cases of labour rights violations.

One of the most profound illustrations of systemic discrimination was against the Roma, who remained largely excluded from public life. Roma families were frequently unable to enjoy full access to housing,

Authorities in a number of countries continued to foster a climate of intolerance against the lesbian, gay, bisexual and transgender communities.

education, employment and health services. In some cases, such as in Kosovo, one factor was a lack of personal documents enabling them to register their residency and status. One of the routes out of the vicious cycle of poverty and marginalization – education – was denied to many Romani children who continued to be placed in substandard, segregated classes or schools, including in the Czech Republic and Slovakia. Negative stereotyping as well as physical and cultural isolation also blighted future prospects. Unlawful forced evictions of Roma in places such as Italy, Serbia and Macedonia drove them further into poverty. In many places Roma faced increasingly overt public hostility. The Hungarian police strengthened a special task force to 120 officers to investigate a series of attacks against the Romani community, including murders, after widespread concern that initial investigations were ineffective.

Authorities in a number of countries continued to foster a climate of intolerance against the lesbian, gay, bisexual and transgender (LGBT) communities, making it harder for their voices to be heard and their rights to be protected. In August, the Lithuanian parliament adopted a controversial law that institutionalized homophobia. It could be used to prohibit any legitimate discussion of homosexuality, impede the work of human rights defenders and further stigmatize LGBT people. In Turkey, discrimination in law and practice against people based on their sexual orientation and gender identity continued. Five transgender women were murdered, and in only one case was a conviction secured. The Belarusian authorities denied an application by a group of 20 people to hold a small public awareness action about LGBT issues. Their excuse was that the request did not include copies of contracts with the local police department, the health clinic, and the waste disposal services to cover the expenses of ensuring public order, safety and for cleaning up after the action.

Member states of the EU continued to block a new regional directive on non-discrimination, which would simply close a legal protection gap for those experiencing discrimination outside of employment on the grounds of disability, belief, religion, sexual orientation and age.

Repression of dissent

In many areas across the region the space for independent voices and civil society shrunk, as freedoms of expression, association and religion remained under attack.

It remained very dangerous for individuals who did speak out. In Russia, human rights defenders, journalists and opposition activists were killed, beaten or received death threats. In both Serbia and

REGIONAL OVERVIEWS
EUROPE AND CENTRAL ASIA

Croatia, the authorities failed to protect people working to highlight issues such as war crimes, transitional justice, corruption and organized crime – women human rights defenders in the former, journalists in the latter, were subject to continued intimidation and attacks. Human rights defenders in Turkey continued to be prosecuted for their legitimate work documenting and reporting on alleged human rights violations. And dissenting views in the country were still met with criminal prosecutions and intimidation.

Independent journalists were harassed or imprisoned in places such as Azerbaijan, or physically attacked by unidentified individuals in places such as Armenia or Kyrgyzstan, where the assaults were sometimes fatal. Independent newspapers and journalists in Tajikistan continued to face criminal and civil lawsuits for criticizing the government, resulting in self-censorship of the media. In Turkmenistan, all printed and electronic media remained under state control, and the authorities continued to block websites run by dissidents and exiled members of the opposition. Journalists, as well as human rights defenders, faced increased harassment in Kazakhstan and Uzbekistan.

Public events were banned in Belarus and peaceful demonstrators were detained. Civil society organizations faced many obstacles in trying to register while any activity on behalf of a non-registered organization remained a criminal offence. In Moldova, despite a progressive Law on Assemblies which was passed in 2008, police and local authorities continued to unduly restrict the right to freedom of peaceful assembly by banning demonstrations, imposing limitations and detaining peaceful protesters.

In many places the space for freedom of religion and belief contracted further. In Uzbekistan, for example, religious communities continued to be under strict government control and to have their right to freedom of religion compromised. Those most affected were members of unregistered groups such as Christian Evangelical congregations and Muslims worshipping in mosques outside state control. The authorities in Tajikistan continued to close, confiscate and destroy Muslim and Christian places of worship, without explanation. Some 70 Jehovah's Witnesses were serving prison terms in Armenia for refusing to perform compulsory military service on grounds of conscience.

Impunity in post-conflict situations

Although some progress was made in tackling impunity for crimes committed on the territory of the former Yugoslavia during the wars of the 1990s, insufficient efforts by domestic courts meant that many perpetrators of war crimes and crimes against humanity continued to

> **Victims of torture and other ill-treatment, often fuelled by racism and discrimination, and frequently used to extract confessions, were likewise too often failed by justice systems which did not hold to account those responsible.**

evade justice. Witness support and protection measures in all courts in Bosnia and Herzegovina, for example, were inadequate. This meant that in some cases victims, including survivors of war crimes of sexual violence, were not able to access justice.

Although a report by an international fact-finding mission commissioned by the EU confirmed that violations of international human rights and humanitarian law had been committed by Georgian, Russian and South Ossetian forces during the 2008 war, and called on all sides of the conflict to address the consequences of the war, no side conducted comprehensive investigations into these violations.

For too many others, however, accountability was still a long way off, including for those waiting for justice from the international community. The relatives of two men killed by Romanian forces serving with the UN in Kosovo in 2007 were still among them, although an internal UN investigation had held the troops responsible for the deaths through the improper use of rubber bullets. The Romanian authorities failed to respond to these findings and in March the UN Special Representative in Kosovo, citing security reasons, refused to allow a public hearing into the failure of the UN troop mission to bring to justice members of the Romanian Formed Police Unit.

Torture and other ill-treatment

Victims of torture and other ill-treatment, often fuelled by racism and discrimination, and frequently used to extract confessions, were likewise too often failed by justice systems which did not hold to account those responsible. Obstacles to accountability included lack of prompt access to a lawyer, failure by prosecutors to vigorously pursue investigations, victims' fear of reprisals, low penalties imposed on convicted police officers, and the absence of properly resourced and independent systems for monitoring complaints and investigating serious police misconduct. Such failures continued in countries such as Greece, France, Moldova, Russia, Spain, Turkey and Uzbekistan.

For some, however, there was limited redress although it was long in coming. In a unanimous judgment in June, the European Court of Human Rights ruled that Sergei Gurgurov had been a victim of torture in Moldova in 2005. The following month the Office of Moldova's Prosecutor General opened a criminal case, almost four years after Sergei Gurgurov first said he had been tortured by police officers. The Prosecutor General's Office had previously responded to all requests for a criminal investigation to be opened by saying that the injuries he claimed were the result of torture at the hands of police officers had been self-inflicted.

Violence against women and girls

Violence against women and girls in the home remained pervasive across the region for all ages and social groups. Only a small proportion of women, however, officially reported this abuse. They were deterred by fear of reprisals from abusive partners, the idea of bringing 'shame' on their family, for reasons of financial insecurity. Mostly, the widespread impunity enjoyed by perpetrators meant they knew there was little point.

Entrenched societal attitudes, and a backlash of traditional discourses in many places across the region in 2009, led to woefully inadequate provision of services to protect victims of domestic violence. In Tajikistan, such services including shelters and adequate alternative housing were virtually non-existent. Women and girls there were even more vulnerable to domestic violence because of early and unregistered marriages and an increased early drop-out rate from school. The number of shelters available in Turkey remained far below the one per settlement of 50,000 people required by domestic law. Moscow, a city of more than 10 million people, had only one shelter. It held 10 women.

Women also frequently lost confidence that the relevant authorities would regard this abuse as a crime, rather than a private matter, and deal with it as such, therefore official reporting rates were exceptionally low. Failure to bridge that confidence gap not only hampered justice in individual cases, but also impeded efforts to tackle such abuses across society by hiding the full extent and nature of the problem.

Certain groups remained particularly vulnerable across the spectrum of violence against women. Migrant women, for example in Spain, continued to face additional difficulties in obtaining justice and specialist services. In Bosnia and Herzegovina, the survivors of war crimes of sexual violence continued to be denied access to economic and social rights, and to adequate reparation to rebuild their lives. Many were also unable to find a job as they still suffered from the physical and psychological consequences of their experiences during the war.

Death penalty

In a continuing positive trend, the Russian Constitutional Court decided in November to extend a 10-year moratorium on executions and recommended abolishing the death penalty completely, saying that the path towards full abolition was irreversible. A parliamentary working group was established in Belarus to examine the introduction of a moratorium. Judges, however, continued to hand down death sentences in a process which remained shrouded in secrecy – prisoners and their relatives were not informed about the date of the

It is sadly still the case, that the reality of protection from human rights abuses for many of those within [Europe's] borders falls short of the rhetoric.

execution, the body was not given to the relatives and they were not told where the burial place was. The use of the death penalty in Belarus was also compounded by a flawed criminal justice system, with credible evidence that torture and other ill-treatment were used to extract "confessions" and that condemned prisoners did not have access to effective appeal mechanisms.

Conclusion

Europe has a regional human rights architecture which is unrivalled elsewhere in the world. It also guards a proud reputation as a beacon of human rights. It is sadly still the case, however, that the reality of protection from human rights abuses for many of those within its borders falls short of the rhetoric.

One of the clear opportunities that arose in 2009 to uphold Europe's obligations, was the entry into force of the EU Lisbon Treaty. This opened up new possibilities to strengthen human rights and fundamental freedoms: the EU Charter of Fundamental Rights is now binding on the EU institutions as well as on member states (with the exception of three), and the EU is enabled to accede to the European Convention on Human Rights.

While this was another welcome component of the human rights framework, the gap is still implementation at a national level. Each individual state across the region has a primary obligation to ensure all within its borders enjoy the full range of human rights guaranteed by the international community of which they are a part. The experience of the past year shows that many states fail in this duty, but also that there is no lack of courageous people who dare to stand up, whatever the personal cost, and work to hold them accountable.

REGIONAL OVERVIEWS
EUROPE AND CENTRAL ASIA

Hundreds of thousands of people turn out to protest against the disputed result of the presidential election at a mass rally in Azadi (Freedom) square in Tehran, Iran, 15 June 2009.

MIDDLE EAST AND NORTH AFRICA

"They showed me a photocopied piece of paper that read: 'Since the election, some people want to create chaos and unrest. It is asked that quick action is taken... to identify the organizers and the collaborators.' It was pretty strange for me. I asked, 'How is this related to me?' They explained it was a general warrant. Then they brought me to the car."

Shiva Nazar Ahari, an Iranian human rights defender arrested on 14 June, describing her arrest by Intelligence Ministry officials.

The year opened with Israeli military jets pounding Gaza, as part of a 22-day conflict that killed hundreds of Palestinian civilians, and closed with mounting repression in Iran, as thousands of demonstrators again took to the streets to protest over the disputed outcome of the presidential election and the ruthless clampdown on dissent that followed.

Both cases, in their different ways, illustrated the need for accountability if long-standing cycles of human rights abuse are to be brought to an end. Both also illustrate the obstacles to achieving such accountability. Following the Gaza conflict, an authoritative UN investigation found that the parties to the conflict, Israel and Hamas, had committed war crimes and possible crimes against humanity and called for them to hold credible investigations and bring the perpetrators to account, yet neither had taken effective steps to do this by the end of the year.

The Iranian authorities, meanwhile, seemed more intent on covering up than investigating allegations of rape and other torture of detainees. They also sought to transfer the blame for killings committed by their forces onto those who spoke out against them, rather than comply with their obligations under international law to properly investigate human rights violations and hold those responsible to account. As the architects of the abuse, they had much to hide.

The events in Gaza and Iran were also both illustrations – in the starkest form – of the continuing insecurity faced by millions throughout the Middle East and North Africa region. As in previous years, 2009 witnessed deep-seated political, religious and ethnic divisions spawning patterns of intolerance, injustice and violent conflict, in which those who speak up for human rights or call for reform all too often do so at their peril. These divisions and tensions were also exacerbated in 2009 by foreign involvement in the region – particularly the presence of foreign military forces – and by the impact of the global financial crisis.

Conflict and insecurity

The short, sharp conflict in Gaza and southern Israel at the beginning of the year was marked on both sides by a callous disregard for the lives of civilians who consequently comprised the vast majority of those killed and injured.

Likewise, it was civilians, people trying to go about their daily lives amid the turmoil around them, who bore the brunt of the internal conflict that continued to grip much of Iraq. Overall, the number of those killed there fell in 2009 compared to previous years; even so, numerous civilians were killed. Many died in bomb explosions in Baghdad and other cities, perpetrated by shadowy armed groups who often seemed to select their targets with the aim of killing and maiming as many civilians as possible, and provoking sectarian feuds. Others were abducted and murdered by armed militias connected to parties represented in the Iraqi parliament.

In Yemen too, many thousands of civilians were displaced from their homes – they numbered close to 200,000 by the end of 2009 – and an unknown number were killed amid renewed, more intense fighting between government forces and armed adherents of a Shi'a minority cleric killed in 2004. The conflict, in the northerly Sa'da Governorate, spilled over into neighbouring Saudi Arabia, whose troops also clashed with the Shi'a rebels.

Meanwhile, the Yemen government increasingly resorted to repressive methods to try and contain growing unrest and protests in the south against alleged discrimination amid the country's burgeoning economic woes.

Attacks by armed groups, including groups apparently aligned to al-Qa'ida, killed civilians in states such as Algeria and Egypt. Such attacks, and the waves of arrests of suspects that usually followed, added to the general climate of insecurity in the region. They also pointed to a propensity by governments to resort to repression and abuse of human rights in response to opposition, including peaceful opposition, rather than address underlying political, economic or social grievances.

In all too many states, those who had the courage or temerity to question government policies or criticize their human rights records were still liable to find themselves branded as enemies of the state.

Repression of dissent

If these were the most extreme manifestations, the political insecurity that pervades the region was evidenced also by a pattern of governmental intolerance of even peaceful criticism and dissent. In states such as Libya, Saudi Arabia and Syria, authoritarian governments allowed virtually no space for free speech or independent political activity. In Libya, there was some slight opening up and Amnesty International was permitted to visit for the first time in five years, but rights to freedom of expression, association and assembly all continued to be severely curtailed.

In Egypt, leaders of the Muslim Brotherhood – all civilians – sentenced to imprisonment after an unfair trial before a military court in 2008 had their sentences confirmed and members and supporters of the organization, officially banned but commanding wide support, continued to be harassed and detained. In the West Bank, the Fatah-led Palestinian Authority cracked down on supporters of Hamas; in Gaza, the de facto Hamas administration targeted supporters of Fatah – in both areas, detainees were tortured or otherwise ill-treated and bystanders were killed and injured in gunfights between opposing factions.

The Moroccan authorities, meanwhile, were increasingly intolerant of those advocating independence for Western Sahara, administered by Morocco since 1975, and of Sahrawi human rights defenders. In November, they summarily expelled Aminatou Haidar to the Canary Islands, claiming that she had renounced her nationality, only relenting and allowing her to return home to Laayoune in the face of mounting international pressure after she had been on hunger strike for a month and had put her life at risk in defence of her human rights.

In all too many states, those who had the courage or temerity to question government policies or criticize their human rights records were still liable to find themselves branded as enemies of the state and detained or sentenced to prison terms.

In Syria, human rights lawyer Muhannad al-Hassani was arrested in July and faced a possible 15-year prison term for exposing the deficiencies of a notorious special court used to try political suspects. He was banned from practising as a lawyer by the official Bar Association. Veteran political activist and lawyer Haytham al-Maleh, despite being 78 years old, likewise faced a possible 15-year sentence for comments he made in a TV interview.

Some even paid with their lives: in Libya, Fathi el-Jahmi, a long-standing government critic, was flown to Jordan for belated medical treatment after over five years of detention when it became clear that his death was imminent; he died some two weeks later.

REGIONAL
OVERVIEWS
MIDDLE EAST AND
NORTH AFRICA

Freedom of expression and the media

In most countries of the region, the media was closely controlled. Editors and journalists had to operate within both written and unwritten rules, and to steer clear of subjects considered taboo – including criticism of the ruler, his family and circle, official corruption or other abuse of power by those in authority. The alternative was to be subjected to harassment, arrest or prosecution on criminal defamation charges. It was not only the mainstream media that suffered in this way. In Egypt and Syria, for example, the authorities detained and sentenced bloggers on account of their writings, and all across the region state authorities blocked access to internet sites that carried comment or information they considered averse to their interests. In Iran, this was taken to extremes in the months following the June presidential election; the authorities cut phone and email communications to try and prevent the truth emerging, particularly pictures taken on mobile phones of violent attacks on demonstrators by the thuggish paramilitary Basij and other government strong-arm men.

In Tunisia, the authorities used trumped-up charges to prosecute some of their critics while at the same time manipulating the media to smear and defame others. The law acted as no protection for those targeted. After the main journalists' union in the country called for greater media freedom, its leadership was ousted and replaced by a new board that then came out openly advocating the President's re-election for an unprecedented fifth term. Human rights defenders too remained subject to continuing harassment, oppressive surveillance and other breaches of their rights by the Tunisian authorities despite the human rights-friendly image that the government sought to cultivate internationally.

Public 'security'

In Egypt and Syria, the authorities maintained decades-long states of emergency which equipped their security police with exceptional powers to arrest and detain suspects, to hold them incommunicado and under conditions which facilitated torture and other ill-treatment and abuse. Israel continued to operate a system of military law over the Palestinians in the West Bank, while Palestinians in Gaza were subjected to Israeli laws that afforded them even fewer rights.

Throughout the region, governments allowed their security forces exceptional licence in the name of upholding state security and defending against threats to the public, although often such forces were used to pursue partisan political interests and to maintain monopolies on power in the face of calls for greater openness, free elections and political change.

> **Torture and other ill-treatment remained endemic and, for the most part, were committed with impunity.**

Consequently, torture and other ill-treatment remained endemic and, for the most part, were committed with impunity. It was common practice throughout the region for political suspects to be detained incommunicado, often for weeks or months at a time, in secret or undisclosed prisons where they were tortured and abused to make them "confess", to name and so put at risk others with whom they were associated, to make them become informers or simply to terrorize them. Many such detainees were then brought to trial, often before special courts whose procedures ran counter to those prescribed under international fair trial standards, routinely ignoring their complaints of torture and convicting them on the basis of their forced 'confessions'.

In Iran, the authorities mounted a series of "show trials" reminiscent of those associated with some of the most totalitarian regimes of the 20th century to punish those accused of leading the outburst of popular protest that greeted the official result of the presidential election. In Saudi Arabia, the government announced that more than 300 people had been sentenced on terrorism-related charges but disclosed no details of the trials, which were held in secret, closed to outside observers and, it appeared, even to defence lawyers. One death sentence was said to have been imposed; other defendants received prison terms of up to 30 years.

Several governments in the region continued to use the death penalty extensively, justifying the practice on the grounds both that it was required by Shari'a law and that it deterred crime and guaranteed public security; in a number of other states, the authorities did not carry out executions. The main offenders were Iran, Iraq and Saudi Arabia, in all of which large numbers of executions were carried out, often after legal proceedings that failed to comply with international standards of fair trial. In Iran, moreover, the victims included juvenile offenders sentenced for crimes committed when they were younger than 18. By contrast, the authorities in states such as Algeria, Lebanon, Morocco and Tunisia, while they continued to impose death sentences, maintained de facto moratoriums under which no executions have been carried out in recent years, reflecting the growing international trend towards ending executions.

Economic concerns – housing and livelihoods
Despite efforts by the new US administration to build momentum for a revived Middle East peace process, the divide between Israelis and Palestinians was further deepened in 2009 – not only by the deaths and destruction caused during Operation "Cast Lead" but also by the impact of Israel's unremitting blockade of the Gaza Strip. Begun in June

2007, the blockade continued to cut off almost 1.5 million Palestinians from the rest of the world, isolating them in Gaza's cramped confines, and greatly limiting the import of essential goods and supplies. This gratuitous exacerbation of the privations already suffered by the inhabitants of Gaza seriously hampered their access to health care and education and destroyed industries and livelihoods. Imposed ostensibly to deter rocket-firing into Israel by Palestinian armed groups, the blockade was nothing less than an outrage – the imposition of collective punishment on the entire population of Gaza. All too predictably, it hit hardest on the most vulnerable – children, the elderly, the homeless and the sick, including those in need of medical treatment outside Gaza – not the armed militants responsible for rocket firing.

The Gaza blockade and Israeli policies in the West Bank – including house demolitions, roadblocks and restrictions on movement – all contributed to the impoverishment of Palestinians as if by design. Elsewhere in the region, millions of people lived in informal settlements – slums – in various degrees of poverty. In Greater Cairo, for example, many resided in areas that the Egyptian authorities designated as "unsafe" due to the constant threat of sudden rock falls or the presence of high-voltage cables. The residents were liable to be forcibly evicted without any or adequate consultation. Others, re-housed after a lethal rockslide in 2008 which left more than 100 dead, complained that they had no security of tenure in their new abodes.

Discrimination

Across the region, women and girls continued to face legal and other discrimination and to be denied the opportunity to access their rights such as to education, health and political participation. In most countries, family and personal status laws rendered women legally inferior to men in relation to inheritance, divorce and custody over their children, and caused them to be inadequately protected against violence within the family or on account of their gender. States such as Iraq, Jordan and Syria retained laws which allow men who commit violence against women to escape punishment if their crimes are deemed to be committed "in a fit of rage" and to uphold family "honour" or to receive only minimal punishment; in Syria, it represented an advance when the President decreed in July that men who killed or injured women relatives on such grounds should receive a penalty of at least two years in prison.

So-called honour killings of women were reported in Jordan, the Palestinian Authority and Syria. In Iraq, women were attacked and threatened for not adhering to strict moral codes and women detainees told a parliamentary committee that they had been raped in detention.

Women and girls continued to face legal and other discrimination and to be denied the opportunity to access their rights.

In Iran, the authorities continued to target women human rights defenders and activists leading the popular campaign for an end to discrimination against women in law.

Some advances were made in 2009, however. In Kuwait, four women were directly elected to parliament for the first time, after women were given the right to vote and run for office in 2005. In Saudi Arabia, the first woman government minister was appointed – for women's education. In Yemen, the law was changed to allow Yemeni women with foreign husbands to pass on their nationality to their children, but a proposal to raise the marriage age for girls was left pending, although early and forced marriages of girls reportedly remain common and may contribute to Yemen's notably high rate of maternal mortality. Qatar acceded to the UN Women's Convention in June but with reservations, while the governments of Algeria and Jordan lifted some of their previous reservations to the treaty but maintained others and therefore continue to undermine the essence of the Convention as a means of ending gender discrimination.

In the oil- and gas-rich states of the Gulf, it was migrant workers – mostly from Asia – whose labour underpinned the national economies and helped build the world's tallest skyscraper, opened amid great fanfare in December in Dubai. They did the heavy lifting but when it came to human rights, they were near the bottom of the heap: abused, exploited and often required to live in squalid conditions out of sight of the opulence. At the very bottom, both in the Gulf and in countries such as Lebanon, were the migrant domestic workers, almost all of them women. They were generally excluded even from the weak labour law protections that existed for migrants working in construction and other industry. They were among the most vulnerable to exploitation and abuse, triply discriminated against as foreigners, as unprotected workers and as women.

Throughout the region, the situation of foreign migrants gave serious cause for concern. Thousands of suspected irregular migrants from sub-Saharan Africa seeking to obtain work or travel on to Europe were detained in Algeria, Libya and other states or summarily expelled; some were reported to have been beaten or otherwise abused. Egyptian security forces shot dead at least 19 migrants trying to cross into Israel and forcibly returned 64 to Eritrea despite the risks to their human rights that they faced there. The Algerian government made "illicit" exit from the country, by its own nationals as well as foreigners, a crime. A draft law before the Israeli parliament prescribed a range of prison sentences to be imposed on foreigners who entered Israel illegally, with the heaviest sentences reserved for particular nationalities.

Refugees and asylum-seekers also rarely received the protection that is their right. In Lebanon, the large and long-resident Palestinian refugee community continued to be denied access to adequate housing, work and the realization of other economic and social rights; thousands who fled from Nahr al-Bared camp to escape fighting in 2007 had still not been able to return to their former homes more than two years after the fighting had ceased. Moreover, a process aimed to remedy the position of the estimated several thousand refugees without official papers – "non-IDs" – was halted by the Lebanese security authorities.

Women, migrants, refugees: these were not alone in suffering discrimination and violence in 2009. In Iran, Iraq and other states, members of ethnic and religious minorities were subject to discrimination and violent attacks. In Syria, thousands of Kurds were effectively stateless and Kurdish minority activists were detained and imprisoned. In Qatar, members of a tribe blamed for a failed coup attempt in 1996 continued to be denied nationality, and so denied employment and other rights. Other minorities facing discrimination included the lesbian, gay, bisexual and transgender community. In Egypt, for example, suspected gay men were targeted for prosecution under a debauchery law and subjected to degrading treatment; and in Iraq, gay men were abducted, tortured, murdered and mutilated by Islamist militias, with those responsible not held to account.

All across the region, state authorities have shown themselves either reluctant or downright unwilling to honour their international treaty obligations to protect and promote human rights.

Accounting for the past

2009 saw little progress towards addressing past human rights violations despite the continuing, valiant efforts of many survivors and victims' families to learn the truth of what occurred and to seek justice. The Algerian government appeared ever more determined to blot out the enforced disappearances and killings of the 1990s from public memory, and the Syrian government showed no interest in clarifying the fate of those who disappeared under the rule of the current President's father. In Lebanon, human rights groups won a court order for the findings of an earlier official investigation into enforced disappearances to be disclosed but there was little sign that the government, a balancing act of different factions, was willing to pursue the truth with vigour. The Special Tribunal for Lebanon was established in the Netherlands with a mandate to prosecute the perpetrators of one set of political crimes – the assassination of former Lebanese Prime Minister Rafic Hariri and related attacks – but was not complemented by measures to investigate many others. In Morocco/Western Sahara, legal and institutional reforms recommended years earlier by the groundbreaking Equity and Reconciliation Commission had yet to be implemented and still no steps had been taken to bring justice to those whose rights were violated under the rule of King Hassan II, when state violence against dissidents and opponents was particularly extreme. In Iraq, those accused of committing crimes under Saddam Hussain continued to be brought to trial but before a seriously flawed court which handed out further death sentences. In Libya, relatives of prisoners killed at Abu Salim prison in 1996 still awaited the outcome of a belated – and apparently secret – official inquiry.

Conclusion

Ten years on from the start of a new millennium, much – so much – remains to be done to give reality to the human rights set out more than 60 years earlier in the Universal Declaration of Human Rights. In particular, all across the region, state authorities have shown themselves either reluctant or downright unwilling to honour their international treaty obligations to protect and promote human rights. This trend has been exacerbated in face of the threat posed by terrorism, while that threat is also used as a convenient justification for clamping down further on legitimate criticism and dissent. Even so, all across the region, courageous individuals remain undeterred and continue to speak out for what is their right and their due, and in support of the rights of others. They are our inspiration.

REGIONAL OVERVIEWS
MIDDLE EAST AND NORTH AFRICA

Two girls from the Romani community in Miercurea Ciuc, Romania, hold drawings of the houses they would like to live in. May 2009.

AMNESTY INTERNATIONAL REPORT 2010
PART TWO: COUNTRY ENTRIES

10

Bodies of people killed in Conakry, Guinea, on 28 September 2009. More than 150 people were killed when security forces violently repressed a peaceful demonstration against the participation of President Camara in presidential elections.

AFGHANISTAN

ISLAMIC REPUBLIC OF AFGHANISTAN

Head of state and government:	Hamid Karzai
Death penalty:	retentionist
Population:	28.2 million
Life expectancy:	43.6 years
Under-5 mortality (m/f):	233/238 per 1,000
Adult literacy:	28 per cent

Afghan people continued to suffer widespread human rights violations and violations of international humanitarian law more than seven years after the USA and its allies ousted the Taleban. Access to health care, education and humanitarian aid deteriorated, particularly in the south and south-east of the country, due to escalating armed conflict between Afghan and international forces and the Taleban and other armed groups. Conflict-related violations increased in northern and western Afghanistan, areas previously considered relatively safe.

Background

The Taleban and other anti-government groups stepped up attacks against civilians, including attacks on schools and health clinics, across the country. Allegations of electoral fraud during the 2009 presidential elections reflected wider concerns about poor governance and endemic corruption within the government. Afghans faced lawlessness associated with a burgeoning illegal narcotics trade, a weak and inept justice system and a systematic lack of respect for the rule of law. Impunity persisted, with the government failing to investigate and prosecute top government officials widely believed to be involved in human rights violations as well as illegal activities.

The UN ranked Afghanistan the second poorest out of 182 countries in its index of human development. The country had the second highest maternal mortality rate in the world. Only 22 per cent of Afghans had access to clean drinking water.

Impunity – national elections

The failure to implement the 2005 Action Plan on Peace, Justice and Reconciliation and disband illegal armed groups allowed individuals suspected of serious human rights violations to stand for and hold public office.

The Afghan government and its international supporters failed to institute proper human rights protection mechanisms ahead of the August elections. The elections were marred by violence and allegations of widespread electoral fraud, including ballot box stuffing, premature closure of polling stations, opening unauthorized polling stations and multiple voting.

Despite a public outcry, President Karzai's post re-election cabinet included several figures facing credible and public allegations of war crimes and serious human rights violations committed during Afghanistan's civil war, as well as after the fall of the Taleban.

Armed conflict
Abuses by armed groups

Civilian casualties caused by the Taleban and other insurgent groups increased. Between January and September, armed groups carried out more than 7,400 attacks across the country, according to the Afghanistan NGO Safety Office. The UN registered more than 2,400 civilian casualties, some two-thirds of whom were killed by the Taleban.

Violence peaked in August during the election period, with many of the attacks indiscriminate or targeted at civilians. Used as polling stations, schools and clinics were vulnerable to attack. According to the UN, at least 16 schools and one clinic were attacked by the Taleban and insurgent groups on election day.

■ On 11 February, the Taleban launched suicide bomb and gun attacks on three Afghan government buildings in Kabul, killing at least 26 people, 20 of them civilians, and injuring more than 60 others, mostly civilians.

■ On 17 September, a suicide car bomb on an International Security Assistance Force convoy in Kabul killed at least 18 people, including 10 civilians, and injured more than 30 civilians. The Taleban claimed responsibility for the attack.

■ At least 30 civilians were killed and 31 wounded in attacks by the Taleban on election day.

■ On 8 October, a Taleban suicide car bomb exploded outside the Indian Embassy in Kabul, killing 13 civilians and two police officers and injuring another 60 civilians and 13 police officers.

■ On 28 October, Taleban fighters stormed a UN guesthouse in Kabul, killing five foreign UN employees, one Afghan civilian and two Afghan security personnel.

A

The attack was the deadliest in years for the UN in Afghanistan, leading it to relocate more than 600 foreign staff outside the country.

The Taleban and other armed groups continued to attack school buildings and target teachers and pupils. A total of 458 schools, the majority in the south, were closed across the country due to insecurity, affecting 111,180 students. The Taleban particularly targeted girls' schools.

■ In May, a gas attack on a girls' school in Kapisa province resulted in more than 84 students being taken to hospital.

Violations by Afghan and international forces

International forces revised their rules of engagement to minimize civilian casualties, but civilian deaths as a result of operations by international and Afghan security forces increased in the first half of the year. NATO and US forces lacked a coherent and consistent mechanism for investigating civilian casualties and providing accountability and compensation to victims.

■ On 4 September, NATO airstrikes near the village of Amarkhel in Kunduz province killed up to 142 people, of whom reportedly 83 were civilians. Although it was in a position to do so, NATO failed to effectively warn civilians that they were going to launch an imminent attack in the area (see Germany entry).

■ On 27 August, NATO forces supporting Afghan army units attacked a clinic in Paktika province, where a Taleban leader was reportedly being treated. The attack violated international humanitarian law which protects combatants no longer fighting due to injury from attack.

■ On 4 May, US airstrikes in Bala Baluk district in the western province of Farah led to the deaths of more than 100 civilians. NATO and US military officials reported that Taleban militants were hiding among civilian populations to instigate attacks on civilians.

Freedom of expression – journalists

The Taleban and other armed groups stepped up attacks against Afghan journalists and blocked nearly all reporting in areas under their control. Journalists were also intimidated and attacked by the government.

The Taleban attempted to disrupt media coverage of the elections. Media workers faced intimidation and interference from supporters of President Karzai and other candidates, in particular rival presidential candidate, Abdullah Abdullah. Two journalists and two media workers were killed by government forces and armed groups, and many more were physically attacked.

As in previous years, the government failed to thoroughly investigate killings of and attacks on journalists.

■ In July, five journalists were beaten by police officers in Herat for reporting on a public demonstration and police corruption.

■ On 11 March, Jawed Ahmad, an Afghan journalist working for an international news organization, was killed by insurgents in Kandahar province.

■ In September, Sayed Parwiz Kambakhsh was pardoned by President Karzai and given political asylum in a third country. He had been serving a 20-year prison term for "blasphemy" for allegedly distributing an article questioning the role of women in Islam.

Violence against women and girls

Women and girls continued to face widespread discrimination, domestic violence, and abduction and rape by armed individuals. They continued to be trafficked, traded in settlement of disputes and debts, and forced into marriages, including under-age marriages. In some instances women and girls were specifically targeted for attack by the Taleban and other armed groups.

Women human rights defenders continued to suffer from violence, harassment, discrimination and intimidation by government figures as well as the Taleban and other armed groups.

■ In April 2009, the Taleban assassinated Sitara Achekzai, a secretary of the Kandahar Provincial Council and prominent women's rights activist.

Legal developments

The government introduced two laws concerning women.

■ In March, the Shi'a Personal Status Law, which contained several discriminatory provisions against Shi'a women, was passed. The law was amended in July following criticism by Afghan women's groups and the international community. Some discriminatory provisions remained.

■ In August, the Elimination of Violence Against Women law was passed by the Afghan President and Cabinet. The law criminalized violence against women, including domestic violence. Parliamentary approval of the law remained pending.

A

Lack of humanitarian access

Insurgent activity, particularly in the southern and eastern provinces, prevented many humanitarian and aid agencies from operating there. Attacks against aid workers by the Taleban and other armed groups increased considerably, including in the north. There were 172 attacks against NGOs and aid workers, resulting in 19 people dead, 18 injured and 59 abducted. The conflict impaired humanitarian access to some of the worst affected areas in the south and east, affecting the delivery of essential aid and medical care to millions. In March alone, 13 aid convoys were attacked and looted by armed groups.

Right to health

The conflict continued to have an adverse impact on health facilities. Some health clinics and facilities, particularly in the south, suffered as a result of operations by both sides of the conflict, which had a devastating effect on civilians' access to health care.
■ Two Basic Health Centres in the Nawa and Garamseer districts of Helmand province were occupied by international and national military forces in August and used as a military base. In September, the clinic in Nawa district reopened and the clinic in Garamseer district was moved to a new location.
■ On 6 September, International Security Assistance Force (ISAF) troops raided and searched a hospital run by the Swedish Committee for Afghanistan in Wardak province.

Internally displaced people

UNHCR, the UN refugee agency, estimated that 297,000 Afghans were displaced from their homes, with more than 60,000 in 2009 alone. The majority of the displaced had fled the ongoing fighting in the south, east and south-eastern areas. Thousands were also displaced by drought conditions, flash floods and food shortages in central and northern areas.

Thousands of displaced people were living in makeshift camps in Kabul and Herat with inadequate shelter and very little access to food, drinking water, health care services and education.

A total of 368,786 refugees returned to Afghanistan from Iran and Pakistan during the year, according to UNHCR. Some returnees were displaced from their places of origin because of scarce economic opportunities and limited access to land, housing, drinking and irrigation water, health care and education. In several instances, the returnees' land and property were occupied by local militias allied with the government.

Thousands of displaced Pakistanis, who fled military operations in the north-western parts of Pakistan – the Federally Administered Tribal Areas and Swat valley – were sheltering in Kunar, Khost and Paktika provinces in eastern Afghanistan (see Pakistan entry).

Arbitrary arrests and detentions

Hundreds of Afghans continued to be arbitrarily detained, without clear legal authority and due process. Some 700 Afghans remained in detention at the US base at Bagram airport without charge or trial in "security internment" of indefinite length. On 15 November, the USA inaugurated a new "improved" detention facility adjacent to the Bagram facility but continued to withhold detainees' rights to due process (see USA entry).

NATO and US forces continued to hand over detainees to the National Directorate of Security (NDS), Afghanistan's intelligence service, where they were at risk of torture and other ill-treatment, arbitrary detention and unfair trials.

Law enforcement officials illegally detained – and in some cases even tried – people on charges not provided for in the Penal Code, such as breaches of contractual obligations, family disputes, as well as so-called "moral crimes". The NDS arrested and detained people, including journalists, for acts considered a "risk to public or state security and safety", which have been vaguely defined in Afghan law.

Justice system

In its national report to the UN Human Rights Council in February, the government acknowledged weaknesses in the justice system, including lack of access to justice for women, corruption and lack of presumption of innocence.

Trial proceedings fell below international standards of fairness, including by not providing adequate time for the accused to prepare their defence, lack of legal representation, reliance on insufficient evidence or evidence gathered through torture and other ill-treatment, and the denial of the defendants' right to call and examine witnesses.

A

Death penalty

The lower courts sentenced 133 people to death, of whom 24 had their sentences upheld by the Supreme Court of Afghanistan. At least 375 people remained on death row.

Amnesty International visits/reports

🚗 Amnesty International delegates visited Afghanistan in April, May, October and December.

▤ Getting away with murder? The impunity of international forces in Afghanistan (ASA 11/001/2009)

▤ Afghanistan: Three concrete steps to improve conditions for Afghans (ASA 11/004/2009)

▤ Afghanistan: 10-point human rights agenda for President Karzai (ASA 11/017/2009)

ALBANIA

REPUBLIC OF ALBANIA

Head of state:	Bamir Topi
Head of government:	Sali Berisha
Death penalty:	abolitionist for all crimes
Population:	3.2 million
Life expectancy:	76.5 years
Under-5 mortality (m/f):	18/17 per 1,000
Adult literacy:	99 per cent

Women increasingly reported domestic violence and sought legal protection, although many later withdrew complaints. There were arrests and convictions for the trafficking of women for forced prostitution. Some detainees in police stations and prisons alleged torture or other ill-treatment. Detention conditions in police stations and many prisons were often very poor, despite some improvements in the treatment of prisoners. Adult orphans were denied their legal right to adequate housing.

Background

In April Albania became a member of NATO and applied for membership of the EU. In November the European Council agreed that Albania should be considered for EU candidate status. National elections were narrowly won in June by the governing Democratic Party and its allies. The main opposition party, the Socialist Party, boycotted parliament in protest against voting irregularities. Unemployment, particularly among young people, was high. Corruption in the judiciary and government remained a serious problem.

Violence against women and children

Women, particularly in urban centres, increasingly reported domestic violence. Nonetheless, many incidents went unreported and women frequently withdrew complaints under family pressure and for lack of economic independence. According to official figures, in the first nine months of the year, 990 occurrences of domestic violence, mostly against women, were reported. Courts dealt with 640 petitions from victims for protection orders. Domestic violence was not a specific offence in the criminal code, and was generally only prosecuted when it resulted in death, severe injury or was accompanied by threats to life.

■ In October Lirie Neziri and her four children sought refuge from her repeatedly violent husband at a hospital in Pukë, where they spent a week sleeping on the floor. Following media coverage, police arrested her husband, and she and the children were given temporary shelter at a social centre in Shkodër.

Trafficking in human beings

According to the US State Department Trafficking in Persons Report 2009, issued in June, Albania remained a source country for men, women and children trafficked for the purposes of sexual exploitation and forced labour, including forced begging. The report stated that the government "does not fully comply with the minimum standards for the elimination of trafficking; however, it is making significant efforts to do so." Prosecutions remained scarce because victims feared reprisals by their traffickers, or were pressured by their families to withdraw complaints. During 2009 the Serious Crimes Court convicted five people of trafficking women for prostitution and four of trafficking children.

■ Agron Alijaj was arrested in Fier in January. In 2008 he had allegedly seduced a 14-year-old girl and taken her to Kosovo, where he forced her to work as a prostitute.

■ In January Astrit Pata and his son Nelgert were fined and sentenced to 15 and 16 years' imprisonment respectively for trafficking two women and forcing them to work as prostitutes.

Enforced disappearances

■ The trial of former officers of the National Intelligence Service, Ilir Kumbaro, Arben Sefgjini and Avni Koldashi, which began in 2008, continued. They were charged with the abduction and "torture with serious consequences" of three men in 1995. Proceedings against a fourth defendant were separated because of his ill-health. The fate of one of the victims, Remzi Hoxha, an ethnic Albanian from Macedonia, remained unknown. Despite the serious charges against him, Arben Sefgjini was in May appointed head of the newly established Probation Service within the Ministry of Justice. Ilir Kumbaro was tried in his absence. He had been arrested in 2008 while living in the UK under a false name; in December he was released after his appeal against extradition to Albania was upheld in a UK court, on the grounds that his arrest warrant was no longer valid.

Torture and other ill-treatment

Police and prison guards allegedly tortured or otherwise ill-treated detainees. In January the European Committee for the Prevention of Torture's report on its visit to Albania in June 2008 stated that "ill-treatment by the police... often appears to be related to an overemphasis on confessions during criminal investigations". The Committee had received allegations of serious ill-treatment in police stations in Korça, Pogradec and Elbasan, and at Korça remand centre. The authorities subsequently said that disciplinary measures had been taken against several officials at Korça remand centre.

■ In April Edison Lleshi, aged 15, threw himself out of a window of the police station in Peshkopi, breaking a leg and sustaining other injuries. The Ombudsperson concluded that he did this after being beaten and threatened by police officers who had questioned him about a theft. Disciplinary measures were taken against seven police officers, and a criminal investigation was started against one of them.

Detention conditions

A new prison was opened in Durrës and a reformatory for juvenile offenders in Kavajë. Classes were started in several prisons for inmates who were illiterate or had not completed compulsory education. Following the establishment of a Probation Service in April, a number of prisoners were released on probation, which helped to reduce overcrowding.

Conditions in many prisons and remand centres remained harsh owing to old, poorly maintained and insanitary buildings. The National Mechanism for the Prevention of Torture, under the Ombudsperson, inspected 12 prisons and some 30 police stations. It concluded that conditions in many were below national and international human rights standards for the detention of prisoners, despite an EC-funded programme for penitentiary reform. Medical facilities were often inadequate, and there was little specialist treatment available for prisoners with mental illnesses. In almost all cases, the Ombudsperson called for major reconstruction or repairs to detention areas at police stations. He also criticized the frequent lack of separate areas for women and minors in police stations. Minors were sometimes held with adults, and women in the offices of the judicial police or in corridors.

■ In February the Ombudsperson concluded that the physical conditions at Burrel prison were irredeemably bad, and recommended its closure.

■ In May Prison 302 and the women's remand section of Tirana Prison 313 were found to be infested with vermin.

Right to adequate housing

Under Albanian law, registered orphans up to the age of 30 are among the vulnerable groups to be prioritized when social housing is allocated. However, the law was not implemented. Over 200 adults who were orphaned as children, including those who completed their secondary education in June, continued to share rooms in often dilapidated and insanitary sections of school dormitories. Very few earned enough to rent private accommodation. In the face of a huge demand for social housing, such programmes were limited, and the income criteria for eligibility were set too high for this group. In November President Topi called for a review of legislation to provide better care for orphans under 18 years and to secure them housing and employment as adults. However, by the end of the year their situation had not improved.

Amnesty International visit/report

🚍 Amnesty International delegates visited Albania in June.
📄 Albania: Promises to orphans should be a serious commitment (EUR 11/002/2009)

ALGERIA

PEOPLE'S DEMOCRATIC REPUBLIC OF ALGERIA

Head of state:	Abdelaziz Bouteflika
Head of government:	Ahmed Ouyahia
Death penalty:	abolitionist in practice
Population:	34.9 million
Life expectancy:	72.2 years
Under-5 mortality (m/f):	35/31 per 1,000
Adult literacy:	75.4 per cent

People suspected of terrorism-related activities were arrested and detained incommunicado; some faced unfair trials. The authorities harassed human rights defenders, lawyers and journalists, and prosecuted some for criticizing government officials. New legislation was introduced to criminalize irregular migration. The authorities again took no action to investigate thousands of cases of enforced disappearance and other grave abuses committed in the past and to bring the perpetrators to justice.

Background

On 9 April, Abdelaziz Bouteflika was re-elected President after constitutional changes adopted in 2008 allowed him to stand for a third term. On 19 April, he expressed his continuing commitment to the process of "national reconciliation" initiated when he first came to power in 1999. Under the process, the government has enacted amnesty and other measures that institutionalize impunity for the massive human rights abuses committed during the internal conflict of the 1990s and effectively deny victims their rights to truth, justice and adequate reparation. During his election campaign, he proposed the introduction of an amnesty for armed groups.

Armed groups continued to mount attacks, but there were fewer indiscriminate attacks on civilians than in preceding years. Some 30 civilians were reported to have been killed in such attacks, mostly bomb explosions in public places, and some 90 members of the security forces. Dozens of alleged members of armed groups were reported to have been killed in clashes with the security forces or search operations; in most cases, the precise circumstances were unclear, prompting fears that some people may have been extrajudicially executed. Al-Qa'ida Organization in the Islamic Maghreb was believed to be the main active armed Islamist group in Algeria.

The year was also punctuated with a series of strikes, protests and riots in different areas by people protesting against unemployment, low wages, housing shortages and other problems.

In August, the government promulgated Law 09-04 and issued a presidential decree to make the Algerian National Advisory Commission for the Promotion and Protection of Human Rights (CNCPPDH) more transparent and independent. In March, the Sub-Committee on Accreditation of the International Coordinating Committee of National Institutions had recommended not to fully accredit the CNCPPDH for failing to comply with the Paris Principles on national human rights institutions.

Counter-terror and security

The Department of Information and Security (DRS), military intelligence, continued to arrest terrorism suspects and detain them incommunicado for weeks or months, during which they were at risk of torture or other ill-treatment.

The right to fair trial of individuals suspected of terrorism was not respected. Some faced proceedings in military courts. Some were denied access to legal counsel, particularly while held in pre-trial detention. The authorities failed to investigate allegations of torture and other ill-treatment of detainees and the courts continued to accept "confessions" allegedly obtained under torture or other duress, without investigation, as a basis for convicting defendants.

■ Moussa Rahli was taken away by plain-clothed security officials from his home in Ouled Aïssa, Boumerdes province, on 17 March. He was detained incommunicado for about 50 days before his family learned that he was being detained at the military barracks in Blida. Although a civilian, he was expected to be tried before a military court on terrorism-related charges. His trial had not taken place by the end of 2009.

■ Mohamed Rahmouni, also a civilian, continued to be detained at Blida military barracks awaiting trial before a military court on terrorism-related charges. Arrested in July 2007, he was held incommunicado for the first six months of his detention. The authorities did not permit him to have access to or be represented by the lawyer of his choice; he was assigned a lawyer, whom he did not accept, by the military court.

On 17 January, Bachir Ghalaab became the eighth Algerian national to be returned from the US prison at Guantánamo Bay. All eight were at liberty. Two awaited trial on charges of belonging to a terrorist group active abroad. Bachir Ghalaab and two others remained under judicial control for investigation. In November a court in Algiers cleared Feghoul Abdelli and Mohammed Abd Al Al Qadir of charges of belonging to a terrorist group abroad and document forgery. The eighth man was cleared of all charges without being referred for trial.

Freedom of expression

Journalists, human rights defenders and others were prosecuted on defamation and other criminal charges apparently because of their criticism of the authorities' human rights record or of public officials and institutions.

■ Hafnaoui Ghoul, a journalist and human rights activist with the Djelfa branch of the Algerian League for the Defence of Human Rights (LADDH), was convicted by the Court of First Instance of Djelfa on charges of defamation and contempt of a public institution in two separate trials on 27 October. He was sentenced to a total of four months' imprisonment, two of them suspended, fined and told to pay damages. He appealed in both cases and remained at liberty pending the outcome. Judicial proceedings were taken against him after officials in Djelfa complained about articles he had written in *Wasat* newspaper alleging mismanagement and corruption. In January, he was the victim of a knife attack in the street by a person unknown.

■ Kamal Eddine Fekhar, a LADDH member and political activist within the Front of Socialist Forces (FFS), faced prosecution in several cases. In October, the Court of First Instance of Ghardaia sentenced him to a suspended six-month prison term and a fine for "insult", which he denied. He was also awaiting trial on charges of inciting the burning of a police car in February, for which he was arrested in June, placed under judicial control and had his passport confiscated. His arrest followed a call by the FFS for a strike in Ghardaia on 1 June to protest against an alleged miscarriage of justice.

■ The appeal of human rights lawyer Amine Sidhoum remained pending before Algeria's highest court. Amine Sidhoum was convicted in 2008 of bringing the judiciary into disrepute, in relation to comments

attributed to him in a 2004 newspaper article. He was sentenced to a suspended six-month prison term and a fine.

Enforced disappearances

The authorities took no steps to investigate the thousands of enforced disappearances that took place during the internal conflict of the 1990s.

■ No progress was made towards uncovering the truth about the fate of Fayçal Benlatreche who disappeared in 1995, and in bringing those responsible to justice. His father, who had continued to campaign for truth and justice over many years and who founded the Association of the Families of the Disappeared in Constantine, died in September.

In August, a government minister was reported to have said that almost 7,000 families of the disappeared had accepted financial compensation from the state, totalling 11 billion dinars (about US$14 million). Farouk Ksentini, head of the CNCPPDH, was reported to have called for an official public apology to be made to the families of the disappeared but to have described some of their demands for truth and justice as impossible to realize.

Associations of families of the disappeared faced harassment and constraints to their work, but nevertheless continued to hold protests.

■ Law enforcement officials prevented participants from gaining access to a private venue in Bachedjarah, Algiers, on 16 June to attend a conference organized by associations of families of the disappeared and victims of "terrorism".

■ The local authorities in Jijel did not respond to the application for registration deposited in May by the newly formed Association of Mich'al of Children of the Disappeared in Jijel, despite being obliged by law to do so within 60 days. Other associations of families of the disappeared active for years have not been able to legally register.

Migrants' rights

On 25 February, the President approved amendments to the Penal Code which, among other things, criminalized "illicit" exit from Algeria by using forged documents or travelling via locations other than official border exit ports, restricting freedom of movement and criminalizing migration. Such "illicit" exit was made punishable by prison terms of between two and six months and/or fines. Nonetheless, thousands of Algerians and other nationals sought to migrate irregularly to Europe from Algeria; hundreds, possibly many more, were intercepted at sea or while preparing to depart by boat, and the media reported that many people were tried and sentenced under the new "illicit" exit provisions.

No official statistics were available concerning the number of foreign nationals expelled from Algeria, but in its initial report to the UN Committee on Migrant Workers in June 2008, the government said that an average of 7,000 foreign nationals were turned back at the borders or expelled from Algeria annually. Many such expulsions are believed to be carried out without due process and without adequate safeguards.

Discrimination against women

On 15 July, Algeria lifted reservations to Article 9.2 of the Convention on the Elimination of All Forms of Discrimination against Women (CEDAW), pertaining to equal rights of women in respect to the nationality of their children. Amendments to the Nationality Code in 2005 had already permitted Algerian women married to non-nationals to confer nationality on their children. A number of discriminatory provisions remain in the Family Code, particularly regarding marriage, divorce, child custody and inheritance – as reflected in Algeria's continued reservation to several other articles of CEDAW.

Death penalty

More than 100 people were sentenced to death, but the authorities maintained the de facto moratorium on executions in force since 1993. The majority of sentences were imposed in terrorism-related trials, mostly in the absence of the accused, but some were imposed on defendants convicted of premeditated murder.

In June, the government's rejection of a bill to abolish the death penalty proposed by an opposition parliamentarian was made public.

Amnesty International report

A legacy of impunity: A threat to Algeria's future (MDE 28/001/2009)

ANGOLA

REPUBLIC OF ANGOLA
Head of state:	José Eduardo dos Santos
Head of government:	António Paulo Kassoma
Death penalty:	abolitionist for all crimes
Population:	18.5 million
Life expectancy:	46.5 years
Under-5 mortality (m/f):	220/189 per 1,000
Adult literacy:	67.4 per cent

The government continued to make commitments towards the provision of social housing. However, forced evictions persisted, including one of the largest carried out in recent years. Extrajudicial executions, excessive use of force, arbitrary arrests and detentions, and torture and other ill-treatment by police were reported. Human rights organizations faced less intimidation, although journalists were harassed and prosecuted for their work.

Background

In September, President José Eduardo dos Santos marked 30 years as head of state. Presidential elections expected in 2009 were further postponed pending approval of a new Constitution. Three types of constitutional models were proposed and drafts of these were circulated for public debate. One version would allow for the President to be elected directly by parliament. No decisions on the models had been made by the end of the year. In December, President dos Santos announced that elections would probably not be held for another three years.

Heavy rains at the beginning of the year caused floods in many parts of the country. Tens of thousands of people lost their homes, including an estimated 25,000 people in the southern province of Cunene in March.

In September, Angola agreed a deal with the International Monetary Fund (IMF) for loans of up to US$890 million.

Right to adequate housing – forced evictions

In July, the government announced that it would exempt some imported building materials from taxes in a bid to make housing more affordable for the poor. The same month it was announced that the USA would lend Angola US$400 million to help it build 1 million homes for the poor in the next five years.

Despite these initiatives, forced evictions continued. In July, over 3,000 families (an estimated 15,000 people) were forcibly evicted from the neighbourhoods of Bagdad and Iraque in Luanda. These evictions were on a larger scale than those seen in recent years. Government officials justified their actions by stating that those forcibly evicted had illegally occupied and built homes on land earmarked by the government for development. However, some of those evicted said that they had legal title to the land. There were also forced evictions in Benguela province and tens of thousands of families remained at risk of forced eviction throughout the country.

Police

The police continued to carry out human rights violations, including excessive use of force and extrajudicial executions. Few officers were brought to justice and little information was made available about action taken against police for past human rights violations.

■ At the end of January, a police officer in Namibe province chased and then shot dead Roberto Yava Chivondu as he travelled home on a motorbike. The police officer indicated for him to stop but he did not. The wife and niece of Roberto Yava Chivondu, who were also on the motorbike, were injured when they fell off after the shooting. The officer, who had allegedly killed someone else in a previous incident, was convicted of Roberto Yava's killing in June by Namibe Provincial Court and sentenced to 20 years' imprisonment.

■ In August, a police officer in Lobito city, Benguela province, shot Jorge Euclia in the abdomen during a police operation to arrest a group of young suspects. The officer fired three shots at Jorge Euclia as he tried to stop the police officer from beating his brother. Jorge Euclia needed intensive care treatment for his injuries but survived. The Benguela Provincial Police Commander stated that Jorge Euclia had been shot not by police but by one of the suspects. No investigation was carried out and no one was held responsible for the shooting.

■ In September, the trial began before Luanda Provincial Court of seven police officers charged with killing eight youths in the Largo da Frescura area of Luanda in July 2008. The trial had not concluded by the end of the year.

Arbitrary arrests, torture and other ill-treatment

Arbitrary arrests and detentions by the police were reported. Most of the arrests were accompanied by excessive use of force. Police were also reported to have tortured and otherwise ill-treated detainees in Lunda Norte province.

■ On 1 April, four members of the Commission of the Legal Sociological Manifesto of the Protectorate of Lunda Tchokwe in Lunda Norte province took a manifesto to the police command in Cuango, Lunda Norte province. There, the four men – Calixto Kulunga, Modesto Timóteo, Bento Majimo and Zeferino Rui Muatxingo – were reportedly arrested and beaten by police to obtain the names and addresses of other Commission members. This was followed by the arrest and detention of about 270 people who had been identified by the four men. The majority of those arrested were released. However, the four men and some 30 other members of the Commission remained in detention in the Conduege Prison in Lunda Norte, where they were allegedly tortured. They were to be tried in November for crimes against the state, but the trial was postponed.

Human rights defenders

In March, the Constitutional Court decided it was not competent to hear a case against the Association for Justice, Peace and Democracy. The case called for the closure of the association on the grounds that its founding documents breached Angolan law. The Constitutional Court sent the case to the Supreme Court for adjudication.

Freedom of expression – journalists

Journalists continued to face harassment in the form of lawsuits and other restrictions. At least three journalists were accused of abusing the media, while another received a suspended prison sentence for defamation. The editor of *Folha 8* newspaper had his passport seized in May as he attempted to leave the country for Namibia. He was told that he was on a list of people forbidden from leaving the country.

■ In July, the Director of *A Capital* newspaper was reportedly called in for questioning by the Criminal Police on suspicion of "attacking the honour and dignity of the head of state", a criminal offence. The accusation was based on a complaint by the Public Prosecutor's Office regarding an article that appeared in the paper criticizing the President. No decision had been made on the case by the end of the year.

■ Also in July, Luanda Provincial Court sentenced journalist Eugénio Mateus to a three-month suspended prison term for defamation of the armed forces. The charges were brought as a result of a complaint by the army's chief of staff for an article Eugénio Mateus had written in 2007 criticizing the army for, among other things, excessive drinking of alcohol.

Cabinda province
Sporadic fighting continued in Cabinda province between the Armed Forces of Angola and the military wing of the Front for the Liberation of the Cabinda State (FLEC).

■ The trial of five individuals arrested and charged with crimes against the state in Cabinda province in 2008 started in March. In May, four were acquitted and one was sentenced to 18 months in prison for possession of firearms. All five were released, including the one sentenced because of the time he had already spent in pre-trial detention.

■ In August, prisoner of conscience José Fernando Lelo was released after he was acquitted on appeal by the Supreme Military Court, which ruled there was insufficient evidence to maintain the conviction. In September 2008, the Cabinda Military Court had sentenced him to 12 years in prison for crimes against the security of the state and instigating a rebellion. Also in August, the Supreme Military Court increased on appeal the sentences from 13 years to between 22 and 24 years of five soldiers sentenced with José Fernando Lelo in September 2008. The five had been convicted of attempted armed rebellion and other military crimes and sentenced to 13 years' imprisonment.

Migrants' rights
The authorities continued to expel undocumented migrants, mainly nationals from the Democratic Republic of the Congo (DRC). However, many of those expelled claimed to have rights to remain in Angola. Towards the end of September, the DRC authorities began expelling Angolans in retaliation (see DRC entry).

The mass expulsions were carried out under deplorable conditions and accompanied by human rights violations, including physical and at times sexual violence by the armed forces. Large numbers of people were transported to borders in overcrowded vehicles and there were reports that some died of asphyxiation. Many family members, including children, were separated during the expulsions and those deported were left in remote areas without food and shelter. Refugees from both countries were affected by these expulsions.

In October, both countries agreed to stop the expulsions. The Angolan government worked with a UN inter-agency commission to deal with the resultant humanitarian situation in Uíge and Zaire provinces. No action was known to have been taken against anyone for the human rights violations that accompanied the expulsions.

Amnesty International visits/reports
🚌 Applications for visas made by Amnesty International in October 2008 were not granted. In October 2009 Amnesty International lodged new applications but these too had not been granted by the end of the year.

▢ Unjust, unlawful, unacceptable: Forced evictions in Angola (AFR 12/002/2009)

▢ Angola: Submission to the UN Universal Periodical Review (AFR 12/005/2009)

ARGENTINA

ARGENTINE REPUBLIC
Head of state and government:	Cristina Fernández
Death penalty:	abolitionist for all crimes
Population:	40.3 million
Life expectancy:	75.2 years
Under-5 mortality (m/f):	17/14 per 1,000
Adult literacy:	97.6 per cent

Indigenous communities faced eviction from their traditional lands, despite legal guarantees. Criminal proceedings to bring to justice those responsible for past human rights violations continued. Conditions of detention remained a serious concern.

Background
Protests and demonstrations against unemployment, high levels of urban crime, poor housing and other social concerns were widespread. A monthly allowance for each child, payable to unemployed or low-income parents or those working in the informal

sector, was established by government decree in October in an attempt to tackle social exclusion.

Indigenous Peoples' rights

Indigenous communities continued to face eviction orders in breach of international standards and of a 2006 national emergency law temporarily suspending the execution of eviction orders or the removal of Indigenous communities from traditional lands. Lack of progress regarding the nationwide land survey led Congress to extend the applicability of the 2006 law until November 2013.

Indigenous communities were denied their right to free, prior and informed consent in projects involving exploitation of natural resources on Indigenous lands.

Around 150 Mapuches faced criminal charges in connection with protests over land rights and against judicial eviction orders in Neuquén Province.

■ In October, 68-year-old Javier Chocobar, a member of the Indigenous Diaguita community of Los Chuschagasta, Tucumán Province, was killed by a landowner attempting to drive the community off their ancestral land. The landowner and two other men were under investigation at the end of the year.

■ A lawsuit lodged in 2001 by members of the Indigenous Pilagá community in El Descanso, Formosa Province, remained pending at the end of 2009. The case involved irrigation works carried out in 1997, which the community believe affect their traditional territories. The right to free, prior and informed consent over a major infrastructure development in the province was not upheld.

Impunity – justice for past violations

There was progress in bringing to justice key perpetrators of past human rights violations. However, insufficient resources led to protracted delays. According to the Prosecution Co-ordination Unit, more than 600 people were facing criminal proceedings for human rights violations, including enforced disappearances, at the end of the year. Trials resulted in more than 30 convictions during the year.

■ In December, two men broke into the premises of the Buenos Aires Province Human Rights Office. Files concerning cases involving alleged illegal police activities were stolen, as were some other documents related to cases of past human rights violations about to come to trial.

■ In August, Santiago Omar Riveros, commander of the notorious Campo de Mayo detention centre during Argentina's military regime (1976 to 1983), was sentenced to life imprisonment. He was convicted of torturing and beating to death 15-year-old Floreal Avellaneda and of abducting his mother, Iris Pereyra, one month after the 1976 military coup.

■ In March, two former military officials and three former police officials were sentenced to life imprisonment in San Luis Province. They were found guilty of the killing of Graciela Fiochetti, the enforced disappearance and killing of Pedro Valentín Ledezma and Sandro Santana Alcaraz and of the torture of Víctor Carlos Fernández. All four victims had been detained in September 1976.

■ In October, former general Jorge Olivera Róvere was sentenced to life imprisonment after being found guilty of four cases of homicide and a number of cases of illegal deprivation of liberty. Another former general was also sentenced to life imprisonment in the same case. Three other former members of the military were acquitted.

■ In December, 17 former navy officers, including captain Alfredo Astiz, went on trial charged with crimes against humanity committed at Argentina's biggest secret detention centre, the Navy School of Mechanics, under the military government. Alfredo Astiz was charged with the killings of two French nuns and the enforced disappearance of an Argentine journalist, among other crimes.

■ In a trial that finished in December in Córdoba Province, former military general Luciano Benjamín Menéndez was sentenced to life imprisonment for the third time.

Threats against witnesses

There were further reports that witnesses in trials relating to past human rights violations were threatened, particularly those living in isolated rural areas, despite protection programmes.

■ In May, Orlando Argentino González, a survivor of a secret detention centre in Tucumán Province, failed to appear in court to testify after receiving several threats.

■ The whereabouts of Jorge Julio López, the main witness and complainant in the case against former Director of Investigations of the Buenos Aires Provincial Police Miguel Etchecolatz, remained unknown. Investigations into his disappearance in September 2006 made no progress during the year.

A

Prison conditions

Poor conditions, violence, overcrowding, lack of adequate health services, torture and other ill-treatment were reported in prisons and detention centres in Santiago del Estero and Mendoza provinces. The national authorities failed to set up a mechanism for the prevention of torture as required by the Optional Protocol to the UN Convention against Torture.

Violence against women and girls

Gender-based violence remained a serious concern. Legislation to prevent and punish violence against women was enacted in April. This provides for free legal assistance for women who experience violence and sets out protocols for the collection and systematic recording of official data on gender-based violence. However, at the end of the year, the law had yet to be implemented.

ARMENIA

REPUBLIC OF ARMENIA

Head of state:	Serzh Sargsyan
Head of government:	Tigran Sargsyan
Death penalty:	abolitionist for all crimes
Population:	3.1 million
Life expectancy:	73.6 years
Under-5 mortality (m/f):	29/25 per 1,000
Adult literacy:	99.5 per cent

Impunity for perpetrators of human rights violations persisted. Freedom of expression was restricted and journalists were attacked. The ban on holding demonstrations in the centre of the capital, Yerevan, which had been introduced in March 2008 during the state of emergency, remained in place. Protection of women and girls against violence fell short of international standards. The government failed to provide a genuine alternative to military service.

Background

On 19 June, the National Assembly granted an amnesty for opposition activists imprisoned in relation to the events in Yerevan, in March 2008. The amnesty covered those who had not been charged with violent crimes and had been sentenced to prison terms of less than five years. Those who did not fall under the amnesty had their sentences halved. On 1 and 2 March 2008, violent demonstrations had taken place in Yerevan to protest against the presidential election results of 19 February, in which opposition candidate Levon Ter-Petrossian lost to incumbent President Serzh Sargsyan.

Some progress was made in Azerbaijan-Armenian talks over the disputed territory of Nagorno-Karabakh, a predominantly ethnic Armenian enclave within Azerbaijan that broke away following the 1990 war. On 2 November, following talks in Moscow, Armenia and Azerbaijan signed a joint agreement aimed at resolving the dispute on the basis of international law.

Violence against women and girls

In its concluding observations published in February, the Committee on the Elimination of Discrimination against Women expressed concern about the lack of legislation referring to domestic violence and the absence of a responsible state institution. The Committee called on the authorities "to enact, without delay, legislation specifically addressing domestic violence against women", and to provide sufficient shelters.

A draft law on domestic violence was under discussion by the authorities, but had not been presented to parliament by the end of the year. During 2009, only one shelter for victims of domestic violence, run by the Women's Rights Centre, was operational.

Impunity

In October, four police officers were charged with using force against members of the public during the demonstrations on 1 March 2008. By the end of the year, no independent inquiry had been conducted into allegations of use of force by police during the March 2008 events. In June 2008, an ad hoc parliamentary commission had been established to investigate the events, but did not function because the opposition refused to participate. A separate fact-finding group made up of representatives from diverse political factions and the Ombudsperson was disbanded by presidential decree in June 2009, before it became operational.

The prosecution in the case of the shooting of Mikael Danielian, a human rights activist, was discontinued in May on the grounds that the perpetrator had allegedly acted in self-defence. In May 2008, Mikael Danielian was shot at point-blank range with a pneumatic gun by a former leader of the pro-government Armenian Progressive Party. Human rights groups voiced concern that key witness statements had not been considered by the prosecution. Mikael Danielian lodged an appeal against this decision, but no decision was made on his appeal by the end of the year.

Freedom of expression

On 30 April, Argishti Kiviryan, a lawyer and journalist, was severely beaten by a group of unidentified men outside his home in Yerevan. The attackers reportedly beat him with sticks and attempted to shoot him. The OSCE Representative for Media Freedom called on the authorities to investigate the attack and expressed concern about the lack of investigations into violent attacks against journalists, contributing to a climate of impunity. In July, two suspects were detained. The investigation was ongoing at the end of the year.

Discrimination – Jehovah's Witnesses

Alternative civilian service to conscription continued to be under the control of the military. Conscientious objectors had to wear military uniform, were disciplined by the Military Prosecutor's office and were forbidden to hold prayer meetings. As of 1 November, 71 Jehovah's Witnesses were serving prison sentences of 24 to 36 months for refusing to perform military service on grounds of conscience.

In October, the European Court of Human Rights ruled that there had not been a violation of the right to freedom of conscience and religion when Vahan Bayatyan was sentenced to two and a half years' imprisonment for his refusal to perform military service on religious grounds. The Court held that "the right of conscientious objection was not guaranteed by any article of the Convention". In a dissenting opinion, one of the Court judges stated that the judgement failed to reflect the almost universal acceptance that the right to conscientious objection is fundamental to the rights to freedom of thought, conscience and religion. Vahan Bayatyan is currently appealing to the Grand Chamber against this ruling.

AUSTRALIA

AUSTRALIA
Head of state: Queen Elizabeth II, represented by Quentin Bryce
Head of government: Kevin Rudd
Death penalty: abolitionist for all crimes
Population: 21.3 million
Life expectancy: 81.4 years
Under-5 mortality (m/f): 6/5 per 1,000

Indigenous people continued to be discriminated against throughout the Northern Territory. A change to immigration regulations meant that asylum-seekers could work while their applications are processed. The largest public consultation on human rights was completed in September. Recommendations included the establishment of a national Human Rights Act.

Background

In 2007, the Australian government launched the Northern Territory Intervention in response to a report on sexual abuse in the Northern Territory. As part of the intervention, the Government suspended the Racial Discrimination Act and Northern Territory anti-discrimination legislation. This resulted in more than 45,000 Aboriginal people being subjected to racially discriminatory measures, including compulsory income management.

Indigenous Peoples' rights

In April, the government announced support for the UN Declaration on the Rights of Indigenous Peoples, reversing Australia's previous opposition to the Declaration.

In March, the UN Committee on the Elimination of Racial Discrimination requested that the Australian government ensure it complies with the UN Convention against Racism in applying the Northern Territory Intervention.

In August, the UN Special Rapporteur on indigenous people visited Australia and concluded that measures under the Intervention overtly discriminate against Aboriginal peoples, infringe their right to self-determination and further stigmatize communities.

A

Violence against women and girls

In April, the Federal Government accepted the report of the National Council to Reduce Violence Against Women and their Children and committed to develop a national plan of action by 2010.

Refugees and asylum-seekers

In July, immigration regulations were changed to allow more asylum-seekers to work while their applications are processed. In September, the government stopped charging asylum-seekers for the cost of their detention.

In November, a Bill was passed in the Senate to implement protection for asylum-seekers. The Bill gave asylum-seekers who fall outside the scope of the UN Refugee Convention protection from forcible return.

Four thousand Australian islands remained outside Australia's migration zone. Those who arrived by boat were processed on Christmas Island and granted fewer rights and less access to services than those who arrived by plane.

Legal, constitutional or institutional developments

In May, Australia signed the UN Optional Protocol to the Convention against Torture and acceded to the Optional Protocol to the Convention on the Rights of Persons with Disabilities in September.

An extensive National Human Rights Consultation, completed in September, recommended a Human Rights Act for Australia. No government commitment was made to support an Act.

Counter-terror and security

Australian law allowing pre-charge detention for terrorism suspects remained in force.

Police and security forces

■ In June, a Queensland man died after police shocked him with a stun weapon which had been discharged 28 times. A Commission of Inquiry ordered an overhaul of police training and operational policy, and stated that stun guns should be used only when there is a "risk of serious injury".

Deaths in custody

Following a report on the death in custody of an Aboriginal man in 2008, the West Australian government changed custody procedures and training for law enforcement officers but failed to legislate for the humane treatment of prisoners.

Amnesty International visit

🚌 In November, Amnesty International's Secretary General visited Australia.

AUSTRIA

REPUBLIC OF AUSTRIA

Head of state:	Heinz Fischer
Head of government:	Werner Faymann
Death penalty:	abolitionist for all crimes
Population:	8.4 million
Life expectancy:	79.9 years
Under-5 mortality (m/f):	6/5 per 1,000

Allegations of ill-treatment and racism by law-enforcement officials continued. The rights of asylum-seekers and migrants were violated and undermined by the authorities.

Racism

Non-white Austrians were more likely to be suspected of crime and ill-treated by police. Complaints of police ill-treatment from members of ethnic minorities were often followed by an inadequate response by both the police force and the judicial system; complaints were not properly investigated, and police officers were seldom prosecuted and lightly sanctioned.

■ Between April and mid-2009 the Viennese police conducted a large-scale operation based on ethnic profiling. In April, in response to a rise in burglaries, law enforcement officials were instructed to carry out searches in the houses of all known people of Georgian and Moldovan origin, without concrete grounds of suspicion, in order to question the residents and to establish whether they possessed stolen goods or burglary tools.

Torture and other ill-treatment

The authorities failed to implement safeguards against torture and other ill-treatment.

■ Torture victim Bakary J., a Gambian citizen, had still not received compensation or any form of rehabilitation. He had been tortured by three police officers in Vienna in 2006 and was still at risk of deportation for residing illegally in the country. On 20 November, the Disciplinary Appeal Commission decided to dismiss from office two police officers involved in the case. A third officer, now retired, lost all pension benefits relating to his public employment.

Police and security forces

Reports of human rights violations and excessive use of force by law enforcement officers continued to be made. The authorities failed to investigate and adequately sentence such cases in line with international standards, leading to a high degree of impunity.

- 14-year-old Florian P. died and a 17-year-old was seriously wounded after a burglary in Krems in August, allegedly from shots fired by two police officers. A prompt and impartial investigation failed to take place. The police officers involved were interrogated only days later by colleagues, not by the Public Prosecutor's office, as provided by law. In September, an expert appointed by the Public Prosecutor found that the account of the incident given by one police officer was grossly incorrect, which led to delays in the investigation. Despite his injuries, the 17-year-old suspect was immediately interrogated in hospital and was denied his right for a "trusted third party" to be present. At the end of the year the investigation was still ongoing.
- On 13 January 2009, 27-year-old Chechen refugee Umar Israilov was killed, reportedly by Chechen assailants in Vienna. Umar Israilov had stated publicly that he had been tortured by President Kadyrov and his security forces in Chechnya and had filed a complaint with the European Court of Human Rights in 2006 on the grounds of torture. Umar Israilov's lawyer explained the case in detail to the police, and repeatedly asked them to protect him, but the authorities failed to implement an adequate response.

Migrants' and asylum-seekers' rights

On 21 October, the parliament adopted new legislation amending the 2005 law on aliens. The new provisions, due to come into force on 1 January 2010, considerably increased the number of cases where asylum-seekers had to be detained, in contravention of international human rights standards. The Interior Ministry terminated the contracts of almost all independent NGOs providing legal advice to asylum-seekers, thus limiting their ability to obtain asylum or international protection and to challenge the reasons for their detention and deportation.

Amnesty International visit/report

- An Amnesty International delegate visited Austria in April
- Victim or suspect: A question of colour – racial discrimination in the Austrian justice system (EUR 13/002/2009)

AZERBAIJAN

REPUBLIC OF AZERBAIJAN

Head of state:	Ilham Aliyev
Head of government:	Artur Rasizade
Death penalty:	abolitionist for all crimes
Population:	8.8 million
Life expectancy:	70 years
Under-5 mortality (m/f):	54/52 per 1,000
Adult literacy:	99.5 per cent

Restrictions on freedom of expression were tightened. Legislation and practice on the prohibition of torture and other ill-treatment fell short of international standards, including in the failure to investigate torture allegations. Independent journalists and civil society activists continued to face harassment and imprisonment on charges of hooliganism and libel. The authorities failed to conduct a thorough investigation into the death in custody of a human rights defender who was convicted after an unfair trial and denied necessary medical care.

Background

Some progress was made in talks between Azerbaijan and Armenia over the disputed territory of Nagorno-Karabakh, a predominantly ethnic Armenian enclave within Azerbaijan that broke away following the 1990 war. On 2 November, following talks in Moscow, Armenia and Azerbaijan signed a joint agreement aimed at resolving their dispute over Nagorno-Karabakh on the basis of international law. Some 600,000 people internally displaced by the conflict continued to have restricted access to their economic and social rights.

Torture and other ill-treatment

In November the UN Committee against Torture expressed concern at Azerbaijan's failure to implement the Convention against Torture in legislation and practice, including by prosecuting those responsible for torture. The Committee was also concerned at the extradition of Chechens to the Russian Federation and of Kurds to Turkey, where they risked torture.

■ In January the Supreme Court overturned the decision on the convictions of Dmitri Pavlov, Maksim Genashilkin and Ruslan Bessonov made by the Baku Appeal Court in July 2008. The convictions of the three juveniles in June 2007, on charges of murdering another teenager, had been based on confessions allegedly extracted under torture. The Supreme Court found that the Appeal Court had failed to summon witnesses, cross-examine them about contradicting testimonies, or investigate allegations of forced confessions. In June the Appeal Court reviewed the case for the third time but reportedly failed to rectify the errors identified by the Supreme Court.

Freedom of expression

Street protests were effectively banned. Youth opposition activists who attempted to hold demonstrations in Baku in January were reportedly arrested by police.

In March, Parliament passed several amendments to the laws regulating the mass media. These allowed the closure of media outlets for the "abuse of freedom of speech and a journalist's rights", vaguely defined as distributing information that threatened the "integrity of the state" or violated public order.

The constitutional referendum in March resulted in further restrictive measures in the Constitution and legislation. These prohibited the photographing, filming or recording of people without their consent, even in the public domain, effectively preventing the reporting of events of public interest. Opposition supporters and groups attempting to campaign against the referendum were reportedly intimidated and harassed by the police.

Independent journalists and civil society activists continued to be charged and imprisoned with the criminal offences of defamation and hooliganism. The UN Human Rights Council, concluding a Universal Periodic Review of human rights in June, called on Azerbaijan to decriminalize defamation and reverse its ban on foreign radio broadcasters. The UN Human

Rights Committee in August urged the government to end direct and indirect restrictions on freedom of expression.

■ In November a court in Baku sentenced two well-known youth activists, Emin Abdullayev (blogger name Emin Milli) and Adnan Hajizade, to 30 and 24 months' imprisonment respectively. They had been convicted of hooliganism and inflicting minor bodily harm. The charges were reportedly fabricated to punish their non-violent dissenting views as part of a continued clampdown on government critics.

In the autonomous republic of Naxçivan, an Azerbaijani exclave bordered by Iran and Armenia, the authorities continued to harass and obstruct the work of journalists.

■ In January Hakimeldosu Mehdiyev, Elman Abbasov and Mehman Mehdiyev, correspondents of the NGO Institute for Reporters' Freedom and Safety, and Malahat Nasibova, a correspondent for Radio Free Europe/Radio Liberty, were reportedly attacked and prevented from filming by local authorities while investigating reports of police abuse in Heydarabad village. Hakimeldosu Mehdiyev said he was beaten by local police, then forced into his car and expelled from the village.

Human rights defenders

Human rights defenders remained under pressure. New regulations for NGOs came into effect in September introducing unspecified financial reporting obligations and a requirement for foreign NGOs to obtain authorization from the Ministry of Justice in order to operate in Azerbaijan.

■ In March a defamation suit against human rights activist Leila Yunus was withdrawn by the Ministry of Internal Affairs. She had been charged with criminal libel in December 2008 after reporting allegations of human rights abuses made in the course of a public criminal trial she was monitoring.

The authorities failed to conduct a prompt, thorough or impartial investigation into the death in prison, apparently following medical neglect, of a seriously ill human rights defender.

■ In August, Novruzali Mammadov, a 67-year-old Talysh minority activist, died in a prison hospital. He had been serving a 10-year prison sentence for treason after a trial in June 2008 that was reportedly unfair and politically motivated because of his activities in promoting the Talysh language and culture. A thorough

A

investigation into his death, including into whether he had been denied necessary medical treatment, was not carried out.

Amnesty International report

📄 Azerbaijan: Independent journalists under siege (EUR 55/004/2009)

BAHAMAS

COMMONWEALTH OF THE BAHAMAS

Head of state:	Queen Elizabeth II, represented by Arthur Hanna
Head of government:	Hubert Ingraham
Death penalty:	retentionist
Population:	0.3 million
Life expectancy:	73.2 years
Under-5 mortality (m/f):	14/12 per 1,000
Adult literacy:	95.8 per cent

At least two people were sentenced to death; no executions were carried out. There were reports of excessive use of force by members of the security forces and of ill-treatment and discrimination against migrants.

Police and security forces

There were continuing reports of excessive use of force by members of the Royal Bahamas Police Force.
■ On 9 July, police pursuing two suspected robbers shot and killed 18-year-old Brenton Smith as he was walking with a friend in the capital, Nassau. Initial police reports alleging that Brenton Smith had been involved in the robbery were subsequently withdrawn. A coroner's inquiry began in November, but was adjourned until mid-January 2010.

Asylum-seekers' and migrants' rights

There were reports of ill-treatment at the Carmichael Road Detention Centre which holds migrants, including children with their families. In February, a national newspaper published several allegations of recent ill-treatment of detainees. One man, for example, alleged that he was beaten so severely that he lost several fingernails and toenails. The findings of a Department of Immigration commission set up to investigate the allegations had not been made public by the end of the year.

There were reports of ill-treatment by immigration officials and members of the security forces during the deportation of migrants, the vast majority of whom were Haitians.

Violence against women

In March, at the UN Human Rights Council, the government rejected recommendations to criminalize rape within marriage. However, in July, a bill was introduced to Parliament to amend provisions of the 1991 Sexual Offences and Domestic Violence Act which exclude rape within marriage from the definition of rape. Discussions were continuing at the end of the year.

Death penalty

At least two people were sentenced to death.

In August the authorities announced that four death row prisoners had had their death sentences confirmed. Their sentences had been reviewed following a 2006 ruling by the UK-based Judicial Committee of the Privy Council that the mandatory death penalty is unconstitutional in the Bahamas. In October, the authorities began proceedings to move to execute one of the four men, but they were halted after his lawyers lodged an appeal before the Privy Council. Fourteen other men were awaiting re-sentencing at the end of the year.

At the adoption of the UN Universal Periodic Review outcome in March, the Bahamas rejected a wide range of recommendations regarding the death penalty.

Amnesty International reports

📄 Bahamas: Fear for safety/ill-treatment – Detainees at the Carmichael Road Detention Centre (AMR 14/001/2009)
📄 Human Rights Council adopts Universal Periodic Review outcome on Bahamas: Amnesty International regrets rejection of recommendations to abolish the death penalty (AMR 14/002/2009)

B

BAHRAIN

KINGDOM OF BAHRAIN

Head of state:	King Hamad bin 'Issa Al Khalifa
Head of government:	Shaikh Khalifa bin Salman Al Khalifa
Death penalty:	retentionist
Population:	0.8 million
Life expectancy:	75.6 years
Under-5 mortality (m/f):	13/13 per 1,000
Adult literacy:	88.8 per cent

The government took steps to promote human rights and to improve conditions for some migrant workers. However, it continued to penalize criticism of the royal family and failed to investigate allegations of torture in 2008. One person remained at risk of execution.

Background

In November, a royal decree established a national human rights institution. Its mandate includes promoting awareness of human rights in Bahrain and proposing legal reforms. The government said it was considering withdrawing some reservations entered by Bahrain when ratifying key international human rights treaties. It also said it would introduce various legal reforms and provide human rights training to judicial and other officials.

In March, the security forces shot and injured demonstrators in Sitra and al-Duraz who were protesting against alleged land seizures and for the release of prisoners sentenced after violent protests in 2007 and 2008. The authorities denied the use of excessive force and said the security forces had intervened when the protests became violent.

Justice system – trials and prisoner releases

Three Shi'a activists – Hassan Meshaima', 'Abd al-Jalil al-Singace and Mohammad Habib al-Muqdad – appeared before the High Criminal Court in March. They and 32 other defendants, some of whom were being tried in their absence, were accused of financing and planning acts of violence with the aim of overthrowing the government. Thirteen of the accused, who had been arrested on 15 December 2008 and later shown on television "confessing", alleged that they had been detained incommunicado and tortured. They said they had been subjected to electric shocks, beaten while suspended by their arms, and held for prolonged periods with their hands and feet bound. Before the trial concluded, all the defendants were released in April under a royal pardon. A total of 178 prisoners, including political prisoners, were released under the pardon.

The authorities failed to investigate alleged torture of detainees in late 2008.

Freedom of expression

The government remained especially sensitive to criticism of the monarchy. Amendments to the 2002 Press and Publications Law, proposed in 2008, remained pending before the House of Representatives. If implemented, the amendments would remove imprisonment as a penalty for those convicted of criticizing the King or "inciting hatred of the regime".

In January, the Ministry of Information and Culture blocked a number of websites, blogs and discussion forums, including some deemed to "incite hatred and sectarian violence". Hundreds of websites were said to remain blocked at the end of the year.

■ 'Abdul Hadi al-Khawaja, a human rights defender, was charged under Articles 92, 160, 165 and 168 of the Penal Code in January after he criticized the royal family. He was accused of calling for the use of force to change the political system, inciting hatred against the country's rulers and inciting unrest by deliberately spreading rumours. He was also banned from travelling abroad. He denied the accusations. The charges were dropped in accordance with the royal pardon in April.

■ In February, Lamees Dhaif was charged under the Penal Code after she published several articles on alleged judicial corruption in *al-Waqt* daily newspaper. She faced possible imprisonment or a fine if convicted of insulting a public authority. At the end of the year, the case was still being investigated.

Migrants' rights

In May, the government announced a revision of the sponsorship system – known as *kafala* – through which foreign migrant workers obtain employment. The new system, which came into force on 1 August, permits foreign workers to change their employment without obtaining their current employer's consent. The *kafala* had previously prevented workers from changing their employers or leaving the country, facilitating exploitation and abuse of workers' rights by employers, including non-payment of wages. The reform does not apply to migrant domestic workers, mostly women, who remain particularly vulnerable to abuse by employers.

Death penalty

In November, the Court of Cassation upheld the death sentence against Jassim Abdulmanan, a Bangladeshi national. He was sentenced to death in 2007 for premeditated murder. The execution was pending ratification by the King.

Amnesty International visits

🚍 In March, Amnesty International observed the trial of the 35 people accused of terrorism-related offences. The same month, an Amnesty International delegate participated in an international conference on human trafficking.

BANGLADESH

PEOPLE'S REPUBLIC OF BANGLADESH

Head of state:	Zillur Rahman (replaced Iajuddin Ahmed in February)
Head of government:	Sheikh Hasina (replaced Fakhruddin Ahmed in January)
Death penalty:	retentionist
Population:	162.2 million
Life expectancy:	65.7 years
Under-5 mortality (m/f):	58/56 per 1,000
Adult literacy:	53.5 per cent

At least 74 people including civilians and army officers were killed during a Bangladesh Rifles (BDR) mutiny in February. After the mutiny, over 3,000 BDR personnel were detained, at least 48 of whom died in custody. Police and security forces were implicated in the alleged extrajudicial executions of up to 70 criminal suspects. At least 64 people were sentenced to death and at least three were executed. Women continued to be victims of acid attacks, rape, beatings and other attacks, with little preventive action from the authorities.

Background

The Awami League government took office in January, ending two years of an army-backed state of emergency under a civilian caretaker government. The new government endorsed some institutional reforms which the caretaker government had initiated under temporary legislation. These included the Human Rights Commission Act which Parliament enacted in July. The government also set up the Information Commission in July after Parliament passed the Right to Information Act in March.

Repression of dissent

Police continued to use unnecessary and excessive force against protesters.

■ In September, dozens of police attacked peaceful protesters with batons in Dhaka at a rally organized by the National Committee to Protect Oil, Gas, Mineral Resources, Power and Ports. At least 20 protesters, including one of their leaders, Professor Anu Mohammed, were injured. Some 1,000 protesters were calling for greater transparency in the government's decision to award contracts to international oil companies. There was no independent investigation of the attack.

BDR rebellion – torture and fear of unfair trials

Members of the BDR launched a large-scale mutiny in February at the BDR headquarters in Dhaka. Mutineers killed at least 74 people, including six civilians, 57 army officers, one army soldier, nine *jawans* (lowest BDR rank), and one as yet unidentified person. Thousands of BDR personnel were subsequently confined to barracks and denied all outside contact. Reports soon emerged that scores – possibly hundreds – of BDR personnel suffered human rights violations, including torture, for possible involvement in the mutiny. At least 20 BDR personnel died in custody between March and May alone. BDR officials claimed that four men committed suicide, and 16 died from natural causes. By 10 October, the total number of BDR personnel who died in custody was 48. There were allegations that torture may have been the cause or a contributing factor in some of these deaths. An official committee set up in May to investigate the deaths had not submitted its report by year's end.

An official investigation into the circumstances of

the mutiny failed to establish its causes. Another investigation by the Criminal Investigation Department of the police to identify charges against more than 3,000 BDR personnel awaiting trial had not submitted its report by year's end. The government confirmed in September that trials for killings, hostage-taking and looting would take place in civilian courts. It was not clear what resources, particularly in terms of additional training for judges, were available to courts to provide fair trials to such an unprecedented number of defendants.

Indigenous Peoples' rights

The government began in August to disband major army camps in the Chittagong Hill Tracts (CHT) to meet one of several unimplemented agreements of the 1997 CHT peace accord. The accord, signed by the government and CHT representatives, recognized the rights of Indigenous Peoples living in the area and ended more than two decades of insurgency. The government took no action to resolve other unimplemented agreements, including a dispute over land ownership which Indigenous Peoples allege the army confiscated from them during the insurgency and gave to non-Indigenous Bangladeshis whom the government encouraged to settle there.

Extrajudicial executions

Prime Minister Sheikh Hasina pledged in February and October that the government would end extrajudicial executions. However, up to 70 people reportedly died in "crossfire" in the first nine months of the year. Police authorities usually characterized suspected extrajudicial executions as deaths from "crossfire" or after a "shoot-out".

■ Family members of Mohsin Sheikh, aged 23, and Mohammad Ali Jinnah, aged 22, two Awami League student leaders, alleged that Rapid Action Battalion (RAB) personnel shot the two men dead in Dhaka in May. The RAB claimed that the men disregarded a warning to stop at a checkpoint. It said that in the "gunfight" that followed, the men were shot dead. An autopsy of the bodies showed that none of the bullets fired by RAB officers had gone astray, which suggested that this was a planned killing and not a "gunfight". Police subsequently opened criminal investigations against 10 RAB personnel, but no one was brought to justice.

Violence against women

Newspapers reported at least 21 cases where a husband had killed his wife because her family could not afford to give him dowry money. Police sources said they had received at least 3,413 complaints of beating and other abuse of women over dowry disputes between January and October. In many of the known cases, prosecution led to conviction, but the authorities failed to develop, fund and implement an action programme to actively prevent violence against women. Women's rights groups said many cases of violence against women, such as the alleged rape of sex workers in police custody, were not reported for fear of reprisal and lack of protection.

■ In October, Smrity Begum died after she was allegedly forced by her husband to swallow poison. He had demanded a motorbike from Smrity Begum's family as her dowry, which they could not afford. Police charged the husband with murder.

Legal, constitutional or institutional developments

The Minister of Law, Justice and Parliamentary Affairs announced in August that a tribunal would be set up to hear cases of people accused of human rights abuses during the 1971 independence war, but no such tribunals were set up.

Death penalty

Five men found guilty of killing then President Sheikh Mujibur Rahman in 1975 had their death sentences upheld by the Supreme Court in November. At least 64 people were sentenced to death and at least three were executed.

Amnesty International visits/reports

🚌 Amnesty International delegates visited Bangladesh in April and May.

📋 Looking for justice: Mutineers on trial in Bangladesh (ASA 13/006/2009)

📋 Bangladesh: Appeals for commutation of death sentences (ASA 13/007/2009)

BELARUS

REPUBLIC OF BELARUS

Head of state:	Alyaksandr Lukashenka
Head of government:	Syarhey Sidorski
Death penalty:	retentionist
Population:	9.6 million
Life expectancy:	69 years
Under-5 mortality (m/f):	14/9 per 1,000
Adult literacy:	99.7 per cent

The government continued to hand down death sentences. Public events were banned and peaceful demonstrators were detained or ill-treated in police custody. The rights to freedom of association and expression were restricted. Inadequate measures were taken to counter violence against women. State control over the media continued.

Background

European institutions continued their engagement with Belarus. In June, the Parliamentary Assembly of the Council of Europe voted to restore Special Guest Status to the Belarusian parliament on several conditions. Besides a moratorium on the death penalty and registration of the human rights organization *Nasha Viasna* (Our Spring), terms included the immediate and unconditional lifting of sentences of restricted freedom imposed on several young people for their participation in a peaceful demonstration in January 2008. However, these terms were not met by the end of the year. In November, the EU Council reviewed the decision made in October 2008 and decided not to end the travel restrictions on senior Belarus officials, but to extend the suspension until October 2010. The majority of printed and electronic media remained under state control, and the state press distribution system maintained its monopoly. Two independent newspapers – *Narodnaya Volya* (People's Will) and *Nasha Niva* (Our Field) – were allowed once again to use the state press distribution system.

Death penalty

On 29 June, the House of Representatives set up a working group to draft proposals on imposing a moratorium on the death penalty. However, Belarus continued to hand down death sentences despite international pressure. Two men were sentenced to death for murder in the course of the year. On 29 June, Brest regional court sentenced 30-year-old Vasily Yuzepchuk to death; and on 22 July, Minsk regional court sentenced 25-year-old Andrei Zhuk to death. Both death sentences were upheld on appeal.

■ In January, Vasily Yuzepchuk and another unnamed man were detained and charged with first-degree murder, following the murder of six elderly women between November 2007 and January 2008. On 29 June, both men were found guilty by Brest regional court. The second man, convicted as his accomplice, was sentenced to life imprisonment. Vasily Yuzepchuk was sentenced to death. On 2 October, the Supreme Court turned down his appeal and he subsequently applied for clemency. Vasily Yuzepchuk, originally from Ukraine, belongs to the marginalized Roma ethnic group, and may have an intellectual disability. His lawyer stated that the investigation and trial were fundamentally flawed and that Vasily Yuzepchuk had been beaten to force him to confess. On 12 October, the UN Human Rights Committee called on the Belarusian government not to execute Vasily Yuzepchuk until it had considered the case.

Freedom of assembly

The authorities continued to violate the right to freedom of assembly by not permitting demonstrations and public actions in accordance with the very restrictive Law on Public Events. There were allegations that excessive force was used to disperse non-violent demonstrations, and peaceful demonstrators were detained.

■ On 12 February, an application by a group of 20 people to hold a small public awareness action about lesbian, gay, bisexual and transgender issues was refused by the Gomel city administration. They said that the application did not include copies of contracts with the local police department, the health clinic and the waste disposal services to cover the expenses of ensuring public order, safety and for cleaning up after the action. Gomel District Court held that the application had been refused in accordance with the Law on Public Events and turned down the appeal.

■ Peaceful legal demonstrations to mark the anniversary of the disappearance of leading opposition figures Viktor Hanchar and Anatoly Krasouski, held on the 16th day of every month, were regularly dispersed using force. Viktor Hanchar and

B

Yury Zakharenko, as well as businessman Anatoly Krasouski and journalist Dmitry Zavadsky, were subjected to enforced disappearances in 1999 and 2000. On 16 September, police officers in Minsk allegedly used excessive force to disperse demonstrators and detained 31 people for over three hours before releasing them without charge. The demonstrators reported that they had been standing silently holding portraits of the disappeared when approximately 40 men in plain clothes approached and started to beat them, closely followed by riot police who detained them and took them by bus to Tsentralny District police department. According to one demonstrator, police officers did not explain the reason for their arrest and some of the detainees were beaten in the bus. At the police station they were reportedly made to stand facing the wall for three hours and subjected to verbal abuse, threats and beating. On 17 September, the Presidency of the European Union expressed concern about the crackdown on peaceful demonstrations in Minsk the previous day and urged the Belarusian authorities to refrain from excessive use of force in dealing with peaceful demonstrations.

Prisoners of conscience

Several people continued to be held under "restricted freedom" following participation in a peaceful protest in January 2008. The conditions of "restricted freedom" are so severe that they amount to house arrest. Furthermore, although the sentence of "restricted freedom" is imposed by a judge, the details of the restrictions can be changed arbitrarily by the police officer in charge of the case without any possibility to appeal. This makes it very difficult for those convicted to comply with the conditions of their sentence.

■ On 7 July, Artsyom Dubski was sentenced to one year in prison by the Asipovichi district court in the Mahilyow region, and on 15 June Maxim Dashuk was sentenced to one year and three months of further "restricted freedom" by the Maskouski district court in Minsk. Both were convicted for violating the terms of earlier sentences imposed for their participation in the January 2008 protest and Amnesty International considers them to be prisoners of conscience. These young men had been among 11 people who were given sentences of up to two years of "restricted freedom" for "taking part in or organizing actions that gravely disturb

public order". As of November 2009, five out of the original 11 had received amnesties, one had had his restrictions reduced, and three remained abroad.

Human rights defenders

Civil society organizations faced many obstacles in registering with the authorities before being permitted to operate.

■ On 26 January, the human rights organization *Nasha Viasna* (previously known as *Viasna*), applied for registration and was refused for a third time. The Ministry of Justice rejected the application on several grounds: previous convictions of the group's members on administrative charges; inaccuracies in the list of founders; the failure to describe the mechanism for electing the Chair and the Secretary; the absence of the organization's name on one document; and that the headquarters were too cramped. On 22 March, the Supreme Court upheld the decision of the Ministry of Justice after an appeal by the founders on 19 March. On 25 April, the founders applied again and on 28 May, registration was again refused by the Ministry of Justice. In addition to the reasons cited in previous refusals the Ministry of Justice claimed that the second part of the organization's name was not in line with its statute. On 16 June 2009, the founders of Nasha Viasna appealed against this decision, but refusal of registration was again upheld by the Supreme Court on 12 August.

Violence against women

On 21 January, a new Law on Crime Prevention came into effect which for the first time specifically referred to domestic violence and called on state bodies including the Ministry of Internal Affairs to investigate all cases of domestic violence and to prosecute the perpetrators. However, adequate structures and resources to respond to violence against women were lacking. At the end of the year only two shelters for victims of domestic violence were financed from a combination of state and non-governmental funding.

Amnesty International visits/report

🚌 An Amnesty International delegate visited Belarus in March and November.

📄 Ending executions in Europe: Towards abolition of the death penalty in Belarus (EUR 49/001/2009)

BELGIUM

KINGDOM OF BELGIUM

Head of state:	King Albert II
Head of government:	Yves Leterme (replaced Herman Van Rompuy in November)
Death penalty:	abolitionist for all crimes
Population:	10.6 million
Life expectancy:	79.5 years
Under-5 mortality (m/f):	6/5 per 1,000

Following numerous public protests, measures were introduced to allow some irregular migrants to regularize their status. The Federal Ombudsperson criticized conditions inside closed centres for migrants and asylum-seekers and called for reform. Many asylum-seekers were living in inadequate housing or were homeless. Belgium granted residency to one former Guantánamo Bay detainee. Allegations of ill-treatment and excessive use of force by law enforcement officials continued.

Refugees and asylum-seekers

The federal government agency responsible for the reception of asylum-seekers (Fedasil) was repeatedly condemned by the administrative courts for failing to provide housing to asylum-seekers. Figures from a national NGO estimated that more than 200 asylum-seekers, including families with children, were sleeping in the street in October. According to official figures published in September, on any given day at least 1,100 asylum-seekers were housed in hotels and homeless shelters due to insufficient places in official housing.

The Secretary of State for Integration announced in October that pre-fabricated modules or "containers" would be installed in the grounds of existing Fedasil housing centres by July 2010 to house 700 asylum-seekers. It was also announced that an additional 16 million euros would be budgeted in 2010 for housing asylum-seekers.

For the first time in more than a decade Belgium introduced a refugee resettlement programme. Forty-seven Iraqi refugees living in Jordan and Syria, comprising single women with or without children, arrived in Belgium in September.

Arbitrary arrests and detentions

■ According to information received by Amnesty International, at least one person refused asylum may have been arbitrarily detained after he finished serving his prison sentence. Saber Mohammed, an Iraqi asylum-seeker, was convicted of terrorism-related offences by the Brussels Court of Appeal in 2005. On 27 October 2007, after completing his prison sentence, he was immediately put into administrative detention pending expulsion to Iraq. He had made an asylum claim in November 2000, but this was rejected in 2005. A second asylum claim was made in November 2007. In February 2009, the Commissioner-General for Refugees and Stateless Persons rejected Saber Mohammed's claim for asylum. Saber Mohammed lodged an appeal with the Council for Alien Disputes against the initial negative decision. The Council rejected his claim for refugee status, but noted in its decision that Saber Mohammed would be at risk of torture and other serious human rights violations if returned to Iraq. Saber Mohammed was released from administrative detention on 5 March 2009, the day after his appeal. He was immediately placed under a compulsory residence order by the Ministry for Migration and Asylum obliging him to reside within the Sint-Niklaas commune area and register with the police twice daily. At the end of the year Saber Mohammed's asylum claim remained under appeal to the Council of State. He had submitted a claim to the European Court of Human Rights regarding arbitrary detention and inhuman treatment.

Migrants' rights

In July the federal government issued an instruction on regularization proceedings for irregular migrants who can demonstrate local integration in Belgium and have been awaiting regularization for an extended period of time. Numerous public protests, occupations and hunger strikes by irregular migrants preceded the introduction of this measure.

In July the Office of the Federal Ombudsperson published the findings of its investigation into closed centres for irregular migrants and rejected asylum-seekers in Belgium. The Ombudsperson reaffirmed that detention for the purpose of migration control should be used only as a last resort and noted that this principle was not always respected in Belgium. The Ombudsperson also expressed concerns about the living conditions inside closed centres, noted

B

serious deficiencies in the system for dealing with individual complaints, and called for the introduction of legal advice services inside the closed centres. This recommendation was also made by the Council of Europe Commissioner for Human Rights in his report on his 2008 visit to Belgium published in June. He additionally called on the Belgian authorities to stop automatically detaining asylum-seekers who make claims at the border and to improve conditions in the closed centres.

Counter-terror and security
On 8 October, a detainee from the US detention facility at Guantánamo Bay was transferred to Belgium. The Belgian authorities confirmed that the released detainee would have residency status entitling him to a work permit.

Excessive use of force – police and security forces
There were continued reports of ill-treatment and excessive use of force by law enforcement officials.
■ In March the family of Ebenizer Sontsa, a rejected asylum-seeker from Cameroon who committed suicide after an attempted deportation from Brussels airport in April 2008, submitted a complaint of torture and assault against the police officers suspected of ill-treating him during the failed expulsion.

BENIN

REPUBLIC OF BENIN

Head of state and government:	Thomas Boni Yayi
Death penalty:	abolitionist in practice
Population:	8.9 million
Life expectancy:	61 years
Under-5 mortality (m/f):	123/118 per 1,000
Adult literacy:	40.5 per cent

Several demonstrations were banned. At least one person died in detention reportedly as a result of ill-treatment. Prison conditions remained poor due to overcrowding. At least five people were sentenced to death.

Freedom of assembly
In May, the authorities banned public gatherings in two departments in the north of the country for alleged security reasons. In July, the authorities banned several demonstrations organized in Cotonou by trade unions protesting against corruption and the rising cost of essential goods.

Torture and other ill-treatment – death in custody
■ In February, Adam Yessoufa, who was arrested by the gendarmerie of Karimama in the north of the country, died in custody reportedly after being beaten by security forces. The case was brought before the local prosecutor but the results of any inquiry were not made public and no one was charged.

Prison conditions
Prisons remained overcrowded. The prison of Abomey in the centre of the country reportedly had six times more people in detention than its capacity, resulting in harsh conditions for prisoners.

Death penalty
In November and December, at least five people were sentenced to death in their absence by the Parakou Court of Appeal. The last execution known to have been carried out was in 1987.

B

BOLIVIA

PLURINATIONAL STATE OF BOLIVIA

Head of state and government:	Evo Morales Ayma
Death penalty:	abolitionist for ordinary crimes
Population:	9.9 million
Life expectancy:	65.4 years
Under-5 mortality (m/f):	65/56 per 1,000
Adult literacy:	90.7 per cent

A number of initiatives in the area of economic, social and cultural rights resulted in improvements in education and health services and in the recognition of the land rights of Indigenous Peoples and *campesinos* (peasant farmers). Further weakening of the judicial system undermined fair trial guarantees.

Background

In December, President Evo Morales won a second term in office, gaining a two-thirds majority for his party in the legislature. A new Constitution was approved by voters in January and promulgated in February following more than two years of political negotiation. The Constitution asserts the centrality of Bolivia's "plurinational" Indigenous majority and contains provisions to advance economic, social and cultural rights.

Political violence diminished, but political polarization continued to affect public life. In April, an elite police unit killed three men suspected of organizing an armed plot against the central government in the city of Santa Cruz, an opposition stronghold. Concerns were subsequently raised about the way in which the investigations were conducted.

Investigations into some 140 cases of reported rapes in Manitoba Mennonite communities were initiated. Young girls were alleged to be among the victims.

Justice system

There were continuing concerns about the independence of the judiciary. Political tensions undermined the ability of key institutions to discuss proposals for reform of the judiciary in a co-ordinated manner.

The last remaining Constitutional Court judge resigned in June, leaving a backlog of over 4,000 cases and no mechanism for oversight of constitutional guarantees

There were concerns that the continuing instability and politicization in the justice system could weaken the application of international fair trial standards. In 2009, many judges and law officers, including several Supreme Court judges, were disqualified and charged with procedural irregularities. Among them was Supreme Court President Eddy Fernández who was suspended in May on the grounds that he had allegedly intentionally delayed the "Black October" case (see below) with intent.

Legal challenges hindered progress in several high-profile cases, leading to allegations of political interference. For example, challenges over jurisdiction slowed progress in the case relating to the outbreak of violence in September 2008 in Pando department which left 19 people, mostly campesinos, dead. Allegations that judges assigned to some cases failed to act with impartiality resulted in further procedural challenges.

Two special commissions established by the Chamber of Deputies in 2008 presented their findings on both the racist violence that occurred in Sucre in May 2008 and the Pando massacre. At the end of the year, a number of local officials and leaders were on trial charged with torture and public order offences in Sucre. The Deputies recommended that over 70 people, including former Pando Prefect Leopoldo Fernández, be charged for their role in the Pando massacre. A trial was expected to start in early 2010.

Impunity

In May, the trial began of 17 senior officials, including former President Gonzalo Sánchez de Lozada, in connection with the "Black October" events of October 2003 in which at least 67 people were killed and more than 400 injured in clashes between the security forces and demonstrators protesting against government proposals to sell off national gas resources. At the end of the year, Gonzalo Sánchez de Lozada remained in the USA awaiting the outcome of an extradition request. Several former ministers charged in the case left Bolivia during 2009, thus evading prosecution.

In November, a US court ruled that sufficient grounds existed to try Gonzalo Sánchez de Lozada and former Defence Minister Carlos Sánchez Berzaín in the USA in a civil suit for damages in relation to charges of crimes against humanity and carrying out extrajudicial executions.

Former Interior Minister Luis Arce Gómez was extradited from the USA to Bolivia. On arrival he was given a 30-year prison sentence. He had been convicted in 1993 of enforced disappearance, torture, genocide and murder committed in 1980 and 1981.

Forensic work to locate the remains of members of an armed opposition movement who were forcibly disappeared in 1970 began in July in Teoponte, a rural area 300km from La Paz. By the end of the year, nine bodies had been found. The search for the remains of around 50 others believed to have died in the area was continuing at the end of the year.

The Ministry of Defence approved a procedure allowing documentation relating to past human rights violations to be requested from the armed forces. President Morales initially insisted that no files existed relating to people who were forcibly disappeared under previous governments.

Indigenous Peoples' rights

In May, the UN Permanent Forum on Indigenous Issues published a report which acknowledged the steps taken by the Bolivian authorities to identify servitude, forced labour, bonded labour and enslavement of captive families. The report criticized entrenched interests prevalent in lowland prefectures and civic committees that allowed such abuses to continue.

■ In July, the Vice-Minister for Land announced a new programme to settle approximately 2,000 families from Cochabamba and La Paz departments to 200,000 hectares of lands identified as federal land in Pando department. In August, the first families were moved to these lands. However, there were concerns about the lack of infrastructure and services available to them and the programme was cancelled.

Women's rights

A government initiative to reduce maternal mortality began in May, granting mothers a cash incentive to attend free pre- and post-natal check-ups. Take-up was high, but there were reports that women who did not have birth certificates encountered obstacles in accessing this health care. Health professionals reported an increase in the number of clandestine abortions and teenage pregnancies during the year, but there were no comprehensive reliable figures to confirm this.

Amnesty International visit

🚍 Amnesty International delegates visited Bolivia in August.

BOSNIA AND HERZEGOVINA

BOSNIA AND HERZEGOVINA

Head of state:	rotating presidency - Željko Komšić, Nebojša Radmanović, Haris Silajdžić
Head of government:	Nikola Špirić
Death penalty:	abolitionist for all crimes
Population:	3.8 million
Life expectancy:	75.1 years
Under-5 mortality (m/f):	17/12 per 1,000
Adult literacy:	96.7 per cent

The country continued to be increasingly divided along ethnic lines. Progress in prosecution of war crimes cases committed during the 1992-1995 war remained slow. The authorities continued to fail to address the situation of women who were raped during the war by not providing them with adequate access to justice and reparations.

Background

Relations between members of the three main ethnic groups – Serbs, Croats and Bosnian Muslims (Bosniaks) – worsened dramatically. Some senior politicians used increasingly nationalistic rhetoric. In some instances this took the form of public, verbal attacks on state institutions, including on the independence of the justice system. Some politicians made statements denying certain war crimes had ever taken place, even though the courts had passed verdicts on them, and convicted those responsible.

On several occasions Serb representatives boycotted state institutions, paralyzing their work.

Talks facilitated by the international community to strengthen the state institutions and amend the constitution ended in failure in October.

In response to the economic crisis the authorities announced a reduction in the social welfare budget. This disproportionally affected the most vulnerable groups and was met with public outcry.

The international community continued to maintain its presence in Bosnia and Herzegovina (BiH). In March Austrian diplomat Valentin Inzko replaced Miroslav Lajčák as the High Representative – head of a civilian peace implementation agency created by the 1995 Dayton Peace Agreement. The High Representative also acted as the EU Special Representative.

The EU continued to maintain its peacekeeping force with approximately 2,000 troops as well as a police mission with approximately 150 international staff.

In October, BiH was elected as a non-permanent member of the UN Security Council for the 2010-2011 term.

International justice

At the end of 2009, seven war crimes cases concerning BiH were pending before the UN International Criminal Tribunal for the former Yugoslavia (Tribunal). In addition, three cases were on appeal.

■ The Tribunal started the trial of Radovan Karadžić in October. He was charged with two counts of genocide. The first was related to crimes committed between 31 March and 31 December 1992 in a number of municipalities in BiH, which included killings, torture and forcible transfer or deportation which aimed at the destruction of Bosnian Croats and Bosnian Muslims as ethnic or religious groups. The second covered the killing of more than 7,000 men and boys in July 1995 in Srebrenica. There were five counts of crimes against humanity, including persecution, extermination, murder and deportation of non-Serbs. The indictment also contained four charges of violations of the laws or customs of war such as hostage-taking and spreading terror among the civilian population.

Radovan Karadžić boycotted the proceedings from the beginning by repeatedly refusing to appear in the courtroom. In November, the presiding judge appointed a lawyer to represent him in his absence. The trial was adjourned until March 2010 to enable the court-appointed lawyer to prepare for the case.

■ In July, the Trial Chamber of the Tribunal convicted Milan and Sredoje Lukić of war crimes and crimes against humanity, including the burning to death of at least 119 Bosnian Muslims in Višegrad in 1992. The charges had included murder, persecution, extermination and torture of the civilian population in

the Višegrad area during the 1992-1995 war, and Milan and Sredoje Lukić were sentenced to life and 30 years' imprisonment respectively. However, despite extensive evidence already collected by the Tribunal, the charges related to war crimes of sexual violence had not been included in the indictment. Since its creation in 1993, the Tribunal has prosecuted only 18 cases including charges of war crimes of sexual violence related to the war in BiH.

Justice system

Witness support and protection measures in all courts in BiH were inadequate. This meant that in some cases victims, including survivors of war crimes of sexual violence, were not able to access justice.

War crimes prosecutions continued before the War Crimes Chamber (WCC) of the State Court of BiH. By the end of the year, the WCC had delivered 39 final verdicts since its creation in 2005. There were 57 cases pending at trial and appeals panel stage.

Some war crimes trials of low-level perpetrators were also held in the local courts in both of the semi-autonomous entities of the country – the Federation of BiH (FBiH) and Republika Srpska (RS) – as well as in Brčko District. However, the capacity of the courts and prosecutors of FBiH and RS to prosecute war crimes cases remained inadequate.

In December 2008, the authorities had adopted a State Strategy for the Work on War Crimes in an attempt to address all outstanding war crimes cases. In the absence of a centralized case file database, there had been varying estimates of between 6,000 and 16,000 war crimes case files open at different stages of prosecution registered in all jurisdictions. However, implementation of the strategy in 2009 was extremely slow and obstructed by a lack of political will. Verbal attacks on the justice system and denial of war crimes by some senior politicians in the country further undermined the country's efforts to prosecute war crimes cases.

In October, the State Parliament of BiH rejected the extension of the mandate of international judges and prosecutors working in the WCC. Following the move, several human rights organizations, including Amnesty International, expressed serious concerns about whether the justice system of BiH was ready to prosecute war crimes cases in accordance with the highest international fair trial standards, without the support of these international judges and prosecutors.

On 14 December 2009, the High Representative used his special powers to overrule the State Parliament's decision and extended their mandate.

Discrimination
Survivors of war crimes of sexual violence
The survivors of war crimes of sexual violence continued to be denied access to economic and social rights. The authorities failed to respond to the needs of those survivors and did not provide adequate reparation, which would have enabled them to rebuild their lives.

Many women who were raped during the war continued to live in poverty, and were unable to find a job as they still suffered from the physical and psychological consequences of their war-time experience.

Provision of psychological support for survivors was inadequate and many of the women could not access the healthcare system. They were also discriminated against in access to social benefits compared with other groups of victims of war.

Minority rights
On 22 December 2009 the Grand Chamber of the European Court of Human Rights in Strasbourg ruled that the power-sharing provisions in the Constitution of BiH violated the right to free elections and prohibition of discrimination by not allowing members of minorities to stand for election to the State Presidency and the House of Peoples of the State Parliament.

In 2006, Dervo Sejdić (Roma) and Jakob Finci (Jewish) filed a complaint to the European Court of Human Rights claiming that their right to be elected to the political bodies of BiH and the principle of prohibition of discrimination were violated by the Constitution of BiH. They were both well-known public figures and intended to run for election to the State Presidency and the House of Peoples but were prevented from doing so as the Constitution of BiH restricted the right to be elected to those bodies only to the members of the three "constitutive nations" of BiH (Bosnian Muslim, Croats and Serbs).

Enforced disappearances
Progress in identifying the whereabouts of victims of enforced disappearance during the 1992-1995 war remained slow and was obstructed by the lack of co-operation between the authorities of FBiH and the RS.

According to different estimates, the whereabouts of between 10,000 and 12,000 people remained unknown. In addition, some 3,000 bodies which had been located and exhumed were still unidentified. Exhumations conducted by the Missing Persons Institute continued at different locations.

■ In August, the body of Colonel Avdo Palić of the Army of Bosnia and Herzegovina was identified. He had been subjected to enforced disappearance in July 1995, allegedly by members of the Bosnian Serb Army. According to media reports the body was exhumed from a mass grave in Rogatica in 2001 in RS, but it took almost eight years to identify it.

The state authorities failed to create a database of missing persons and to open the Fund for Support to the Families of Missing Persons, both of which were envisaged by the Law on Missing Persons adopted in 2004.

In the absence of adequate measures by the authorities to address the issue, some relatives of victims sought justice before international human rights institutions.

■ In 2009, the Advocacy Centre - TRIAL (ACT), an NGO based in Geneva, lodged five individual communications to the UN Human Rights Committee on behalf of the relatives of victims of enforced disappearance in BiH. The NGO alleged multiple violations of human rights due to the lack of investigation, criminal prosecution, reparations and effective remedy following the disappearance of their relatives.

ACT submitted an additional 16 complaints to the European Court of Human Rights on behalf of the relatives of the disappeared.

■ In October, the Union of Associations of Families of Missing and Captured Persons of RS filed 78 cases with the European Court of Human Rights on behalf of the families of disappeared Serbs. The Union alleged that the authorities had failed to respond to their continuous enquiries about the whereabouts of their relatives despite previous rulings of the Human Rights Chamber of BiH which had obliged the authorities to do so.

Refugees and internally displaced people
Fewer people returned to their pre-war places of residence in 2009 than in 2008. According to UNHCR, the UN refugee agency, as of September 2009, only 758 refugees and 216 internally displaced people had gone back to their pre-war homes.

The majority of the returns occurred to places where the returnees were in the ethnic minority. Many people, including survivors of war crimes of sexual violence, remained unable to go back to their pre-war places of residence. Many of them feared for their safety as the individuals who had perpetrated war crimes against them or members of their family continued to live in their pre-war communities and often occupied positions of power.

Discrimination in access to economic and social rights such as employment, health services and education continued to prevent many returnees from going back.

Counter-terror and security

The authorities of BiH continued to violate the rights of some individuals who had settled in BiH during or after the war and who had subsequently been granted BiH citizenship. As a result of decisions by the State Commission for the Revision of Decisions on Naturalization of Foreign Citizens, some of them lost their citizenship and deportation procedures were initiated against them.

Seven people were placed in the immigration deportation centre in Lukavica awaiting deportation to their countries of origin. If deported, they would be at risk of torture or the death penalty. The authorities continued to imprison these individuals on grounds of unspecified national security.

■ Imad al Husein remained imprisoned in the immigration deportation centre in Lukavica where he had been held since October 2008, despite the fact that no criminal charges which could justify the detention were brought against him. An appeal on the revocation of his citizenship was ongoing before the BiH judiciary and before the European Court of Human Rights.

Conditions for detainees in the immigration deportation centre in Lukavica were inadequate. During the process of revocation of citizenship, people spent several months on average in detention. The facility at Lukavica was envisaged to provide temporary custody for a few weeks only, and lacked the capacity to respond to the rights and needs of persons detained for a longer period of time, such as dietary requirements during Ramadan or a room set aside for conjugal visits.

Torture and other ill-treatment

In the majority of cases the authorities failed to take measures to tackle ill-treatment by the police and in prisons. The existing complaint mechanism was ineffective and the number of investigations by prosecutors into allegations of ill-treatment remained very low.

The State Ombudsmen issued a report in September which stated that the conditions of detention across BiH were below international standards. They cited inadequate hygiene and material conditions as well as lack of access to health services for detainees. The authorities failed to address the situation in the Zenica Prison Forensic Psychiatric Annex, where patients with mental health problems lacked adequate medical assistance.

Individuals convicted in the State Court continued to serve their sentences in prisons in FBiH and RS, as there was no BiH state prison. This caused discrepancies in their rights and material conditions while in detention.

Amnesty International visits/reports

🚗 Amnesty International delegates visited Bosnia and Herzegovina in March, September and October.

📄 "Nobody listens to us and nobody cares": Women still waiting for justice in Bosnia and Herzegovina (EUR 63/005/2009)

📄 Bosnia and Herzegovina: "Whose justice?" The women of Bosnia and Herzegovina are still waiting (EUR 63/006/2009)

📄 Bosnia and Herzegovina: Submission to the UN Universal Periodic Review (EUR 63/007/2009)

📄 Bosnia and Herzegovina: No justice for rape victims, 21 July 2009

BRAZIL

FEDERATIVE REPUBLIC OF BRAZIL

Head of state and government:	Luiz Inácio Lula da Silva
Death penalty:	abolitionist for ordinary crimes
Population:	193.7 million
Life expectancy:	72.2 years
Under-5 mortality (m/f):	33/25 per 1,000
Adult literacy:	90 per cent

Reforms in public security, though limited, signalled the authorities' recognition of the long-term neglect of this area. However, law enforcement officers continued to use excessive force and to carry out extrajudicial executions and torture with impunity. The detention system was characterized by cruel, inhuman and degrading conditions in which torture was rife. Numerous law enforcement officials were charged with involvement in organized crime and death squads. Indigenous Peoples, landless workers and small rural communities continued to be threatened and attacked for defending their land rights. Human rights defenders and social activists were the targets of threats, politically motivated charges and attacks, despite the government's national programme for the protection of human rights defenders.

Background

Nearing the end of his term in office, President Lula's government had helped enhance Brazil's role on the world stage. Brazil's policy of building a "southern" alliance to challenge long-standing "northern" power structures contributed to changes in global politics. However, at times this was achieved at the cost of supporting a broader human rights agenda, not least at the UN Human Rights Council.

At home, it was widely acknowledged that social investment by President Lula's government had helped reduce socio-economic inequalities.

In August, Brazil held its first ever national conference on public security in which civil society and law enforcement officers participated in developing government policy. In December, the government launched its third national human rights plan, which was largely welcomed by civil society. However, the plan faced staunch criticism from the military, the Catholic Church and the land lobby

regarding, respectively, measures to tackle past human rights violations, sexual and reproductive rights and land rights. These posed serious threats to the protection of human rights in the country.

Impunity for past violations

One of the proposals of the national human rights plan was a promise to set up a truth and reconciliation commission to investigate abuses under the country's military government (1964-1985). Some NGOs and relatives of victims criticized the initial proposals as the commission's remit did not appear to include the prosecution of past violators. However, even this limited proposal was strongly criticized by the Brazilian military, with the Minister of Defence attempting to further weaken it.

Nevertheless, increasing challenges were made to the long-standing impunity for crimes committed during the military era. In August, the Supreme Court ruled that Uruguayan national Colonel Manuel Cordero Piacentini could be extradited to Argentina to face charges in connection with the enforced disappearance of Uruguayan and Argentine citizens and torture in the context of Operation Condor, a joint plan by Southern Cone military governments in the 1970s and 1980s to eliminate opponents.

A submission, by the Brazilian Bar Association and a leading judicial expert, to the Supreme Court challenging the interpretation of the country's Amnesty Law was pending at the end of the year.

Police and security forces

Across the country, there were persistent reports of excessive use of force, extrajudicial executions and torture by police officers. Residents of *favelas* (shanty towns) or poor communities, often under the control of armed criminal gangs, were subjected to military-style police incursions. Police in the front line were also placed at risk and many were killed in the line of duty.

Some states launched their own stand-alone public security projects, with mixed results. The Police Pacification Units in Rio de Janeiro and the Pact for Life in Pernambuco state both claimed to have reduced crime and brought greater security to socially excluded areas. The initiatives were welcomed by some sectors of society as offering an alternative to previous repressive and abusive policing methods, although some residents in areas where the projects were implemented complained of discrimination.

B

Outside the scope of the projects, police forces continued to commit extensive violations.

The authorities continued to describe killings by police as "acts of resistance", contrary to the recommendations of the UN Special Rapporteur on extrajudicial, summary or arbitrary executions and to the third national human rights plan. Hundreds of killings were not properly investigated and little, if any, judicial action was taken. A study by the Public Security Institute attached to Rio de Janeiro's state Secretariat of Public Security found that between January 1998 and September 2009, 10,216 people were killed in the state in incidents registered as "acts of resistance". In Rio de Janeiro, police killed 1,048 people in reported "acts of resistance" during the year. In São Paulo the comparable figure was 543, an increase of 36 per cent over 2008, with killings by military police increasing by 41 per cent.

In São Paulo, the state government continued to adopt "saturation operations" in *favelas*. These operations involved military-style occupations of communities for a period of 90 days followed by police withdrawal. Members of the community of Paraisópolis, São Paulo, reported cases of torture, excessive use of force, intimidation, arbitrary and abusive searches, extortion and theft by police officers during a "saturation operation" in February.

In October, three police officers were killed in Rio de Janeiro when a police helicopter was shot down during a conflict between rival drug factions. Gang members began burning buses and driving residents from their homes in an attempt to distract police from their attack on a rival community, during which the helicopter had been downed. Police mounted a series of operations, described by a senior officer as "retaliation" during which more than 40 people were killed. These included a 24-year-old woman hit by a stray bullet as she held her 11-month-old baby, and a 15-year-old boy reportedly shot by police while putting out the rubbish.

Residents of the Acari and Maré *favelas* in Rio reported that violent police operations regularly coincided with children's return from school, putting pupils at risk and forcing schools to close. Cases of torture, intimidation, illegal and arbitrary searches, extortion and theft were also reported. It was also alleged that in Maré police rented an armoured vehicle, known as a *caveirão* (big skull), to drug traffickers involved in a turf war.

Militias

The spread of militias – armed paramilitary-style groups made up largely by off-duty law-enforcement officials – was such that one academic study claimed they controlled more of Rio de Janeiro's *favelas* than the drug factions. Using their power over communities for illicit economic and political gain, militias threatened the lives of thousands of residents and the very institutions of the state. Judges, prosecutors, police officers and a state deputy received repeated death threats from the militias. State authorities mounted a series of operations to combat the activities of the militias, leading to a number of arrests. However, the president of a parliamentary inquiry into the militias continued to criticize the failure of municipal and federal authorities to implement the inquiry's recommendations for combating the rise of the militias.

Torture and prison conditions

Detainees continued to be held in cruel, inhuman or degrading conditions. Torture was regularly used as a method of interrogation, punishment, control, humiliation and extortion. Overcrowding remained a serious problem. Gang control of detention centres resulted in high levels of violence between prisoners. Lack of independent oversight and high levels of corruption contributed to perpetuating entrenched problems of violence in the prison system, as well as in the juvenile detention system. Mechanisms for the implementation of the Optional Protocol to the UN Convention against Torture had still not been put in place by the end of the year.

Some of the harshest conditions of detention continued to be reported from Espírito Santo state. There were reports of torture, as well as of extreme overcrowding and the use of shipping containers (known as "microwaves") as cells. There were reports of prisoners dismembering other prisoners. Following extensive pressure from local human rights groups and official state and national monitoring bodies, some building projects were initiated. In March, an illegal ban on monitoring visits to the prison system was finally lifted.

In December, after evidence of torture and attempted homicide in the Urso Branco prison in the state of Rondônia, the Inter-American Court of Human Rights issued a new resolution – its seventh since 2002 – calling on the Brazilian government to ensure the safety of the prisoners held there.

B

A decision on the Attorney-General's call for federal intervention in October 2008 was still pending before the Supreme Court at the end of 2009.

Land disputes

Conflict over land continued to generate human rights abuses committed by both gunmen hired by farm owners and police officers. According to the Church-based Pastoral Land Commission, between January and mid-November 2009, 20 people were murdered in land-related conflicts in Brazil.

■ In Rio Grande do Sul state, landless worker Elton Brum da Silva was shot dead by military police in August during an eviction from the Southall ranch in São Gabriel municipality. In the aftermath of the eviction, local NGOs accused police of torture – including beating with batons, kicks, punches and the use of Tasers.

■ In August, 50 military police evicted a group of landless workers from the Pôr do Sol farm in Maranhão state, beating up several landless leaders and threatening others verbally. They set fire to houses and destroyed personal belongings, including documents.

■ In October, 20 armed, hooded men reportedly led by a local farmer attacked a settlement of 20 families in the municipality of São Mateus, in Maranhão state. Threats from gunmen to kill any families settled in the area continued following the attack.

Workers' rights

Workers' rights, especially in the agricultural sector, continued to be violated. Despite extensive efforts to combat the practice, thousands of workers were found to be held in conditions deemed analogous to slavery under national law.

In November, in a landmark ruling, a federal judge in Pará state sentenced 27 people to prison sentences ranging from three years and four months to 10 years and six months for using slave labour. The prosecutions followed reports issued between 1999 and 2008 by labour prosecutors, responsible for monitoring the implementation of labour law.

In June, the government presented the National Accord for the Improvement of Working Conditions in the Sugar Sector – a voluntary agreement between the government, industry and unions for minimum standards. The Accord followed persistent criticisms of workers' rights violations in the sugar cane industry.

Right to adequate housing

Urban homeless groups suffered threats, attacks and excessive use of force at the hands of the police. In São Paulo a series of forced evictions suggested that a policy of slum clearance to make way for development projects was being pursued without regard for the rights of those made homeless as a consequence.

■ On 18 June, riot police in São Paulo charged at a group of 200 families living by the side of the road who had been evicted on 16 June from abandoned government offices. Police used pepper spray, tear gas and batons against the residents who set up burning roadblocks. According to the Homeless Movement of Central São Paulo (Movimento dos Sem Teto do Centro, MSTC), five homeless people were injured, including a child.

■ In August, riot police used rubber bullets, tear gas and helicopters during evictions at the Olga Benário community in Capão Redondo in the south of São Paulo. Some 500 families were left homeless in extremely precarious conditions. In December, after national and international protest, the São Paulo state authorities agreed to repossess the land for social housing.

Plan for Accelerated Growth

The government and some economic analysts credited the Plan for Accelerated Growth (Programa de Aceleração do Crescimento, PAC) with ensuring the country's economic stability. However, there were reports that some of the projects threatened the human rights of local communities and Indigenous Peoples. The projects, which included the building of dams, roads and ports, were sometimes accompanied by forced evictions, loss of livelihoods and threats and attacks against protesters and human rights defenders.

■ In August, community leaders Father Orlando Gonçalves Barbosa, Isaque Dantas de Souza and Pedro Hamilton Prado received a series of death threats. The three were put under surveillance by unidentified men and armed men forced their way into Father Barbosa's house. This followed their campaign to stop the building of a port at Encontro das Águas, Manaus, Amazon state, an environmentally sensitive area and home to fishing communities. The development of the port was being funded under the PAC. On 2 September, Father Barbosa was forced to leave Manaus for his own safety.

Indigenous Peoples' rights

In March, the Supreme Court rejected a challenge to the legality of the Raposa Serra do Sol reservation in Roraima state. The ruling was seen as a victory for the Indigenous movement, but also contained a number of conditions that weakened future claims.

Mato Grosso do Sul continued to be the focus of grave human rights abuses against Indigenous Peoples in Brazil. The state government and the powerful farm lobby used the courts to block the identification of Indigenous lands. Guarani-Kaiowá communities were attacked by security guards and gunmen hired by local farmers. Local NGOs called for federal intervention to ensure the security of the Indigenous Peoples and the demarcation of their lands.

■ In October, members of the Apyka'y Guarani-Kaiowá community, who had been evicted from traditional lands in April and were living in extremely precarious conditions by the side of a highway near Dourados, Mato Grosso do Sul, were attacked in the middle of the night by armed security guards employed by local landowers. Their homes were burned and one man was shot in the leg.

■ In November, two Indigenous teachers, Genivaldo Vera and Rolindo Vera, went missing after the forced eviction of the Pirajuí Guarani-Kaiowá community from traditional lands on 30 October by a group of armed men. The body of Genivaldo Vera was subsequently found in a stream, bearing injuries consistent with torture. Rolindo Vera remained missing, feared dead at the end of the year.

In December, President Lula decreed the "homologation" (the final step in the demarcation process) of nine Indigenous lands in Roraima, Amazonas, Pará and Mato Grosso do Sul states. One week after the announcement, the Supreme Court upheld an appeal lodged by local farmers, suspending the presidential decree in relation to the Guarani-Kaiowá Arroio-Korá reservation in Mato Grosso do Sul. The Supreme Court's decision was based in part on commentaries attached to the Raposa Serra do Sol ruling which requires land claims to be based on land occupancy in 1988, when the Constitution was promulgated.

Human rights defenders

The human rights defenders programme was introduced in two further states and was operational in a total of five states by the end of 2009. However, in many cases effective protection was not provided and defenders remained at grave risk because of the lack of political will to confront systemic human rights violations.

■ In January, Manoel Mattos, Vice-President of the Workers' Party in Pernambuco state and member of the local bar association's human rights commission, was killed by two hooded men who broke into his home and shot him at point-blank range. He had long campaigned against the spread of death squads and police violence. Despite repeated death threats, federal police had withdrawn the protection he was receiving at the end of 2007.

Amnesty International visits

🚌 Amnesty International delegates visited Brazil in May and December.

BULGARIA

REPUBLIC OF BULGARIA

Head of state:	Georgi Parvanov
Head of government:	Boyko Borissov (replaced Sergey Stanishev in July)
Death penalty:	abolitionist for all crimes
Population:	7.5 million
Life expectancy:	73.1 years
Under-5 mortality (m/f):	17/13 per 1,000
Adult literacy:	98.3 per cent

The Romani community continued to face multiple and widespread discrimination, as well as the threat of forced eviction from their homes. The prolonged detention of asylum-seekers contravened EU legislation. The European Court of Human Rights found that Bulgaria had violated the prohibition of torture and degrading treatment in the European Convention on Human Rights.

Background

Following parliamentary elections, a new minority government was appointed under Prime Minister Boyko Borissov in July. The ruling Citizens for European Development party was supported by three smaller parties including the far-right Attack party, which had a history of anti-Roma and anti-Turkish speech.

Discrimination – Roma

The Romani community continued to suffer discrimination in education, housing and health care. In January, in shadow reports to the UN Committee on the Elimination of Racial Discrimination (CERD), several domestic and international NGOs highlighted frequent forced evictions of Roma. Roma in informal settlements often lacked security of tenure, exposing them to the threat of forced evictions and destitution. The European Commission against Racism and Intolerance reported in June that discrimination against Roma was widespread and included restrictions in access to public places.

Right to adequate housing

■ In September almost 50 Romani homes were demolished and the families forcibly evicted in the town of Burgas. The local council's decision to demolish houses illegally built on municipal or private land left almost 200 people, who had lived in the area for several years, without accommodation. The NGO the Bulgarian Helsinki Committee reported that police used disproportionate force during the demolitions. Despite claims by the Mayor of Burgas that the families would be provided with alternative low rent council accommodation, no alternative housing was provided; the evicted Roma were only advised to apply for municipal housing. In September members of the community, represented by the NGOs Equal Opportunities Initiative and the Centre on Housing Rights and Evictions, submitted an individual complaint against the forced eviction to the UN Human Rights Committee.

Right to health – access to social assistance

In April, the European Committee of Social Rights found Bulgaria in violation of the European Social Charter. In response to a complaint filed by the European Roma Rights Centre and the Bulgarian Helsinki Committee, the Committee ruled that the government had failed to ensure sufficient access to social assistance for people without adequate resources. The NGOs criticized an amendment to the Social Assistance Act which reduced the period in which unemployed people could obtain social assistance. They stressed that the amendment would have a disparate and unjustified effect on Roma who had been over-represented among beneficiaries. The Committee established that "adequate benefits" had to be payable to any person who was without adequate resources and in need, and that access

could not be made subject to time limits, as that might leave an applicant without basic means of subsistence.

Detention without trial

Bulgaria was again found in violation of the right to a public hearing within a reasonable time under the European Convention on Human Rights.

■ Criminal proceedings against Valentin Ivanov took more than eight years, commencing in May 1992 and ending in November 2000. The **European Court of Human Rights** ruled that this exceeded the "reasonable time" requirement, and noted that it had frequently found violations of the same right in cases against Bulgaria in the past.

Torture and other ill-treatment

Bulgaria was found to be in violation of the prohibition of torture or degrading treatment under the European Convention on Human Rights.

■ In January the **European Court of Human Rights** found that there had been a violation of the prohibition of torture and a lack of effective investigation into injuries, demonstrating that Georgi Dimitrov had been ill-treated in police custody. Arrested in 2001 on charges of fraud, he alleged after his release from prison in 2004 that he had been beaten by police officers.

In March the CERD expressed concern about ill-treatment and excessive use of force by the police against minority groups, particularly Roma. The Bulgarian Helsinki Committee and the European Roma Rights Centre submitted a shadow report to CERD in which they cited cases of police ill-treatment of individuals or use of disproportionate force by the police against Romani communities.

■ In August the Military Court of Appeals upheld the 16 to 18-year sentences imposed on five "anti-mafia" police officers convicted in 2008 of beating to death 38-year-old Angel Dimitrov in the city of Blagoevgrad. The police officers appealed against their sentences to the Supreme Court of Cassation.

Mental health institutions

NGOs continued to be critical of the admission procedures and living conditions in social care institutions for people with mental illnesses.

■ The **European Court of Human Rights** in November heard two cases regarding placements and living conditions in care homes in the towns of Pastra and

Pravda respectively. In both cases, it was claimed that individuals had been deprived of legal capacity and forcibly placed under guardianship. The European Committee for the Prevention of Torture had recommended closure of the Pastra institution in 2003 because deficiencies in its living conditions and care amounted to inhuman and degrading treatment, and the government had indicated its agreement with the recommendation in 2004.

Refugees and asylum-seekers

Asylum-seekers continued to be detained for periods of several months, or even years.

■ The European Court of Justice in November ordered the immediate release of Said Kadzoev, an asylum-seeker of Russian nationality and Chechen origin who would be at risk of torture and other ill-treatment if forcibly returned to the Russian Federation. In a landmark ruling, the Court found that the exception to the 18-month limit on the detention of asylum-seekers, proposed by the Sofia City Administrative Court, would contravene the EU directive on standards and procedures for returning illegally staying third-country nationals. Said Kadzoev was detained in 2006, and had remained in custody in spite of his lawyers' applications for less severe measures. The Court said that asylum-seekers should not be detained as a punishment for not possessing valid documents or for aggressive behaviour.

Rights of lesbian, gay, bisexual and transgender people

The second lesbian, gay, bisexual and transgender Pride march was held in Sofia in June. In the run-up to the march, the leader of the far-right party, the Bulgarian National Union, announced a "week of intolerance" as a response to the event. The march was protected by the police and no incidents were reported.

BURKINA FASO

BURKINA FASO

Head of state:	Blaise Compaoré
Head of government:	Tertius Zongo
Death penalty:	abolitionist in practice
Population:	15.8 million
Life expectancy:	52.7 years
Under-5 mortality (m/f):	160/154 per 1,000
Adult literacy:	28.7 per cent

Human rights defenders were harassed while promoting the fight against impunity. At least six people were sentenced to death. Despite continued efforts by the government, maternal mortality remained high.

Human right defenders

In January, three members of the Collective against Impunity, including Chrysogone Zougmoré, President of the Burkinabè Movement for Human and Peoples' Rights (Mouvement burkinabè des droits de l'homme et des peuples), were summoned by the gendarmerie and questioned about the organization of a demonstration to mark the 10th anniversary of the killing of prominent investigative journalist, Norbert Zongo. No serious investigation was ever conducted into the killing.

Death penalty

At least six people were sentenced to death. Among them were two people convicted of murder during the November assize court session held in Dédougou in the west of the country. The last execution known to have been carried out was in 1988.

Right to health

Despite government efforts during the previous few years to improve access to maternal health services, including a reduction of fees, maternal mortality remained high. In October, the government passed two decrees to improve access to contraceptive services, but the use of contraception remained very low.

Amnesty International visits

🚍 Amnesty International delegates visited Burkina Faso in February, June and November.

BURUNDI

REPUBLIC OF BURUNDI

Head of state and government:	Pierre Nkurunziza
Death penalty:	abolitionist for all crimes
Population:	8.3 million
Life expectancy:	50.1 years
Under-5 mortality (m/f):	177/155 per 1,000
Adult literacy:	59.3 per cent

The government suppressed the rights to freedom of expression and association by harassing or limiting the activities of some human rights defenders, journalists and opposition political parties. High levels of rape and other sexual violence against women and girls persisted. A new penal code abolished the death penalty and introduced other positive reforms. However, it also criminalized same-sex sexual relationships. Disputes continued over land ownership in the context of the mass repatriation of refugees from Tanzania.

Background

The political situation remained tense in the build-up to elections due in 2010. The government, led by the National Council for the Defence of Democracy-Forces for the Defence of Democracy (CNDD-FDD), restricted the activities of opposition parties and civil society groups.

A peace agreement was reached in April between the government and the National Liberation Forces (FNL). However, political violence increased, with opposition parties alleging that the CNDD-FDD had created a new armed youth group, provided weapons to former fighters and carried out unlawful killings. Other political parties, including the FNL, were also reported to have used violence.

The CNDD-FDD and FNL were reportedly responsible for unlawful killings and assaults of political opponents or critical members of their own parties. The CNDD-FDD mobilized their youth wing, the Imbonerakure, who were said to be often armed with sticks or clubs, and seen with state officials making arrests and carrying out community patrols.

The FNL, previously known as the Palipehutu-FNL, removed the ethnic reference from the party's official title in January, enabling its registration as a political party on 21 April. Senior members of the party were nominated to government positions on 5 June. Former fighters were entered into the demobilization programme – 5,000 of them were integrated into government and army positions under the supervision of the AU. There were complaints by former FNL fighters about demobilization pay, heightening security fears.

On 11 September, the National Assembly agreed on a long-disputed draft electoral law. The CNDD-FDD and opposition parties also agreed that commune-level elections would be held before the presidential elections.

Insecurity, often linked to criminality, remained a problem and light arms were prevalent. People had little confidence in the justice system and resorted to mob justice on numerous occasions. Violent disputes over land, sometimes involving fatalities, worsened the security situation, especially in the south.

Freedom of association

Opposition parties, including the Union for Peace and Development (UPD-Zigamibanga), the Movement for Solidarity and Democracy (MSD) and the FNL were regularly banned from holding meetings. On 18 March, the Interior Minister warned political parties against "illegal" meetings ahead of the 2010 elections. Numerous members of political opposition parties were arbitrarily detained, mostly for short periods.

■ In May, the authorities banned at extremely short notice a march organized by civil society groups to push for justice following the killing of human rights defender Ernest Manirumva (see below). The Mayor of Bujumbura cited security concerns as the reason for the ban, a reason rejected by the organizers.

Freedom of expression

Relations between the government and civil society, in particular journalists and human rights defenders, were tense.

■ Juvénal Rududura, vice-president of the trade union of non-magistrate staff at the Department of Justice, was detained at the start of the year on charges of making false statements. He had alleged corruption at the Ministry of Justice. He was provisionally released on 8 July to await trial.

■ Two prisoners of conscience – journalist Jean-Claude Kavumbagu and MSD president Alexis Sinduhije – were released in March. Jean-Claude

Kavumbagu had been arrested on 11 September 2008 and charged with defamation. He alleged in an article that the cost of President Nkurunziza's trip to see the opening ceremony of the Beijing Olympics caused some civil servants' salaries to be paid late. Alexis Sinduhije had been detained on 3 November 2008 after holding a party meeting and charged with "contempt of the head of state".

Human rights defenders

The non-governmental anti-corruption organization OLUCOME reported regular phone threats.

■ Ernest Manirumva, vice-president of OLUCOME, was stabbed to death by unidentified men at his home in Bujumbura on 8 April. Immediately prior to his death, he had been investigating police corruption, in particular that police officials were claiming salaries for posts that allegedly did not exist, as well as corruption in private companies. He had previously received several death threats. Investigations into his killing were slow, and the findings of three successive commissions of inquiry were not made public. Hilaire Ndayizamba, a prominent businessman, and two police officers were arrested on 15 October in connection with the murder.

■ On 23 November, the Interior Minister revoked the registration of the Forum for the Strengthening of Civil Society (FORSC), an umbrella organization for Burundian civil society associations. The Minister later suspended the ordinance revoking the registration, but FORSC's legal status remained unclear at the end of the year. The clampdown followed increasing intimidation and harassment of, and threats against, civil society activists working on accountability, including calls for justice for the killing of Ernest Manirumva.

Justice system – judicial interference

The government and UN took steps to reform and strengthen the judicial system, including building and renovating magistrates' courts, training magistrates, addressing overcrowding in detention facilities and reducing the backlog of criminal cases. However, significant problems remained.

Judges were sometimes put under pressure by the executive. The Ministry of Justice appointed magistrates without sufficient consultation with the Superior Council of the Magistracy. Corruption among and poor training of judges were also reported.

■ A judge who presided over the trial of Alexis Sinduhije (see above) was kidnapped on 6 May. Four

men in police uniform put a gun to his head and forced him into a car. They drove him to an undisclosed location where they beat him and accused him of receiving money from the MSD to influence the outcome of the trial. Before releasing him the same night they told him that he had three days to make a formal written statement admitting he had received money.

■ The Burundian magistrates' union SYMABU led a two-day strike in September to express their concerns over interference with the judiciary by the executive. This followed the suspension of three magistrates in Bujumbura in September for professional misconduct after they acquitted Gédéon Ntunzwenindavya, president of PA Amasekanya, a political party, on charges of threatening state security.

Legal developments

Law No.1/05 revising the Criminal Code came into force on 22 April. It abolished the death penalty and established the crimes of torture, genocide, war crimes and crimes against humanity. It also reinforced penalties for physical and sexual violence against women and raised the age of criminal responsibility to 15. However, Article 567 criminalizes same-sex relations and could lead to the persecution of Burundi's lesbian, gay, bisexual and transgender community. In response to pressure from some quarters, the government organized a large demonstration in Bujumbura on 6 March to protest against the Senate's initial decision to exclude Article 567.

Violence against women and girls

Levels of rape and other sexual violence against women and girls remained high. Most rapes were committed against minors.

Transitional justice

There was slow progress in establishing a Truth and Reconciliation Commission and a Special Tribunal within the Burundian justice system to investigate Burundi's violent history and to prosecute, if established, crimes of genocide, war crimes and crimes against humanity. However, national consultations started in July and finished in December. A network of international and national civil society organizations was closely monitoring the process. Participation was reportedly high in certain provinces.

B

Independent National Human Rights Commission

Progress towards the creation of an Independent National Human Rights Commission remained slow, with a new draft law emerging in late 2009.

Refugees and asylum-seekers

Between January and September, 29,052 Burundian refugees returned, principally from Tanzania, of whom 20,758 were refugees who had fled in 1972.

In October, the authorities began deporting up to 400 Rwandan asylum-seekers from the northern province of Kirundo, before reversing their position to make individual assessments of these cases. The refugees stated that they were fleeing unfair trials before the Rwandan *gacaca* courts and violence in the south of Rwanda.

Land disputes

Land disputes were commonplace and sometimes resulted in violent confrontations between people, including killings. Disputes were most widespread in the south, especially in the provinces of Bururi and Makamba.

Many land disputes were between returning refugees, who sought to reclaim their property, and current residents. This was particularly complicated for refugees who left Burundi in 1972, as Burundian law allows for a new occupant to become the legal owner of land after 30 years.

The work of the National Commission on land and other properties, established by the government in 2006, was hampered by its lack of legal jurisdiction over disputes and the number of complaints.

Killings of Albino children

Albino children were killed by Burundian individuals who sold the dismembered body parts to witch doctors in Tanzania.

■ An albino boy was killed on 23 February by armed individuals who forced their way into the boy's home. They tied up the parents and cut off the boy's limbs. The attackers left the house and threw a grenade into the house as they left. Arrests were made in March.

Amnesty International visit/reports

🚌 An Amnesty International delegation visited Burundi in August to conduct research.

📄 Human Rights Council adopts Universal Periodic Review outcome on Burundi (AFR 16/02/2009)

📄 Burundi abolishes the death penalty but bans homosexuality, 27 April 2009

📄 Burundi: Reverse ban on civil society group, 25 November 2009

CAMBODIA

KINGDOM OF CAMBODIA

Head of state:	King Norodom Sihamoni
Head of government:	Hun Sen
Death penalty:	abolitionist for all crimes
Population:	14.8 million
Life expectancy:	60.6 years
Under-5 mortality (m/f):	92/85 per 1,000
Adult literacy:	76.3 per cent

Forced evictions continued to affect thousands of families across the country, predominantly people living in poverty. Activists from communities affected by forced evictions and other land confiscations mobilized to join forces in protests and appeals to the authorities. A wave of legal actions against housing rights defenders, journalists and other critical voices stifled freedom of expression. The first trial to address past Khmer Rouge atrocities took place. The defendant, Duch, pleaded guilty, but later asked to be acquitted.

Background

At least 45,000 garment factory workers lost their jobs as a result of the global economic crisis and a number of companies reduced salaries. Surveys indicated growing mass youth unemployment as some 300,000 young people faced joblessness after completing their high school and bachelor degrees. For the first time, the UN Committee on Economic, Social and Cultural Rights considered Cambodia's state report, which the authorities had delayed submitting for 14 years. The Committee identified serious shortcomings in the implementation of a number of treaty obligations, including those relating to the judicial system, housing and gender inequalities. Cambodia's human rights record was reviewed under the UN Universal Periodic Review in December.

Forced evictions

Forced evictions continued to affect the lives of thousands of Cambodians. At least 26 forced evictions displaced around 27,000 people, the vast majority from communities living in poverty. In July, a number of international donors called for an end to forced evictions "until a fair and transparent mechanism for resolving land disputes is in place and a comprehensive resettlement policy" is established.
■ On 16/17 July, security forces forcibly evicted Group 78, a community group in Phnom Penh after a deeply flawed legal process. The last 60 families had no choice but to dismantle their houses and accept compensation that prevented them from living near their former homes and workplaces. Most of the families were relocated outside the city with few work prospects.

After civil society criticism, the World Bank attempted to strengthen safeguards in a multi-donor supported Land Management and Administration Project to protect security of tenure for people in urban slums and other vulnerable areas. In early September, the government responded by terminating its contract with the Bank.

Human rights defenders

The rich and powerful continued to abuse the criminal justice system to silence people protesting against evictions and land grabs. Police arrested at least 149 activists, for their peaceful defence of the right to housing.
■ On 22 March, security forces shot at unarmed villagers in Siem Reap province, injuring at least four people. The villagers, from Chikreng district, were protesting against the loss of farmland that had come under dispute. By the end of the year, no authority had investigated the shooting, but police had arrested at least 12 of the villagers, two of whom were subsequently convicted of robbery for attempting to harvest their rice on the disputed land. Seven were acquitted but remained in arbitrary detention pending a prosecutorial appeal.

Informal representatives from communities in most provinces increasingly formed grassroots networks, jointly voicing concerns over forced evictions and intimidation.

International justice

In March, the historic first hearing of the Extraordinary Chambers in the Courts of Cambodia (ECCC, Khmer Rouge Tribunal) took place with the trial of Kaing Guek Eav (known as Duch). Duch was commander of notorious security prison S-21. During the 72-day hearing, survivors and victims of Khmer Rouge atrocities heard for the first time evidence against "those most responsible". Duch admitted responsibility for crimes committed at S-21, including killing about 15,000 people.

The trial of four senior Khmer Rouge leaders was in preparation, and the International Co-Prosecutor submitted requests to open investigations into an additional five suspects. The Cambodian government spoke out against additional investigations saying they could lead to unrest, apparently in an attempt to exert influence over the tribunal.

In July, co-investigating judges decided to allow "confessions" obtained by torture as evidence in the case of Ieng Thirith. This breached the "exclusionary rule" in Article 15 of the UN Convention against Torture which binds the ECCC.

Freedom of expression

A series of prosecutions of people who criticized government policies had a stifling effect on freedom of expression.
■ Courts sentenced newspaper editor Hang Chakra, and the director of an NGO, both affiliated to the opposition Sam Rainsy Party (SRP), to prison terms for peacefully expressing views.
■ The Phnom Penh Court convicted Mu Sochua, Secretary-General of the SRP, of defamation for filing a complaint – also for defamation – against the Prime Minister. She had no legal counsel because her lawyer had withdrawn from the case after receiving threats of legal action for speaking about the case at a press conference. Mu Sochua received a non-custodial sentence.

On 10 July, one of the few remaining opposition-affiliated daily newspapers, *Moneaksekar Khmer* (Khmer Conscience), stopped publishing. The editor, Dam Sith, issued a public apology for articles, over which the government had requested a criminal investigation for "incitement".
■ By the end of the year, police had made no progress on the investigation into the murder of *Moneaksekar Khmer* reporter Khim Sambor. He had

C

been killed by unknown assailants during the July 2008 elections.

Legal, constitutional or institutional developments

On 12 October, the National Assembly passed the new Penal Code. This retained defamation as a criminal offence.

Opposition parliamentarians and civil society groups criticized a new Law on non-violent demonstrations, passed by the National Assembly in October. Authorities routinely denied permission for demonstrations and the law, if adopted, risked codifying such restrictions.

Violence against women and girls

Prosecution of rapists remained rare, due to poor law enforcement, corruption in the courts and widespread use of out-of-court financial settlements. Settlements were typically arranged by law enforcement officials and stipulated that the victim withdraw any criminal complaint. Reports indicated that rapes of women and girls, including sex workers, continued to increase, with the age of victims falling.

Amnesty International visits/reports

🚌 Amnesty International delegates visited Cambodia in March/May, September and October/December.

📄 Cambodia: Urban development or relocating slums? (ASA 23/002/2009)

📄 Cambodia: After 30 years Khmer Rouge crimes on trial (ASA 23/003/2009)

📄 Cambodia: Briefing for the UN Committee on Economic, Social and Cultural Rights: 42nd session, May 2009 (ASA 23/004/2009)

📄 Cambodia: Borei Keila – Lives at risk (ASA 23/008/2009)

CAMEROON

REPUBLIC OF CAMEROON

Head of state:	Paul Biya
Head of government:	Philémon Yang (replaced Ephraim Inoni in June)
Death penalty:	abolitionist in practice
Population:	19.5 million
Life expectancy:	50.9 years
Under-5 mortality (m/f):	151/136 per 1,000
Adult literacy:	67.9 per cent

Government opponents, journalists and human rights defenders were arrested, detained and tried for offences relating to criticism of the government or its officials. At least one man was detained for alleged same-sex sexual activities. Detention conditions remained harsh and often life-threatening. Members of the security forces implicated in human rights violations in February 2008 continued to enjoy impunity. An unknown number of prisoners were on death row.

Background

In June, President Paul Biya replaced Prime Minister Ephraim Inoni with Philémon Yang in a government reshuffle.

President Biya appointed a new electoral commission to prepare for general elections in 2011. Opposition political parties and civil society organizations called for a reform of the electoral commission known as Election Cameroon (ELECAM). Critics of the government said that the commission was dominated by supporters of the ruling Democratic Rally of the Cameroonian People (Rassemblement démocratique du peuple camérounais, RDPC).

Arrests, detentions and trials continued of former government officials and heads of government-owned companies accused of corruption. In August, the National Anti-Corruption Commission published a report accusing 47 Ministry of Agriculture officials of embezzling funds for maize production. In September, a local NGO, the Citizen Association for the Defence of Collective Interests, lodged a complaint before the High Court against the 47 officials.

Political prisoners

■ The trial of John Fru Ndi, leader of the Social Democratic Front political party, and at least 20 others charged with involvement in the murder of Grégoire Diboulé in 2006, was repeatedly adjourned and did not take place.

■ In June, the Court of Appeal in Douala confirmed the conviction and sentence against musician and political activist Pierre Lambo Sandjo by the High Court in 2008. He was convicted of taking part in the February 2008 riots and sentenced to three years in prison.

Freedom of association

Members of the Anglophone Southern Cameroons National Council (SCNC), a non-violent secessionist group, continued to face arrest and imprisonment.

■ In February, the police in Tiko, Southwest Province, arrested and briefly detained 25 SCNC members who had gone to a court to support fellow members on trial for holding an illegal meeting in October 2008.

■ In March, seven SCNC members were arrested and detained on suspicion of holding an illegal meeting. They were provisionally released on 2 April.

■ In May, the High Court in Mamfe, Southwest Province, found three SCNC leaders – including its national chairman, Nfor Ngala Nfor – guilty of belonging to a foreign organization not recognized in Cameroon and sentenced them to five months' imprisonment. The three had been awaiting trial since September 2002 when they were arrested on their return from Nigeria, where they had gone to gather support for their organization's political objectives. The court agreed with the prosecution that the SCNC was not recognized in Cameroon and was therefore an unregistered foreign organization and its members liable to prosecution under the Penal Code.

Freedom of expression – journalists and human rights defenders

The government continued to muzzle critics of its policies, including journalists and human rights defenders.

■ Lewis Medjo, director of *La Détente Libre* newspaper, was sentenced to three years' imprisonment in January. He was found guilty of "publishing false news" on account of an article alleging that President Biya was planning to force the resignation of the President of the Supreme Court.

■ In June, journalists Jacques Blaise Mvié and Charles René Nwé of *La Nouvelle* newspaper were sentenced in their absence to five years' imprisonment after the military court in Yaoundé found them guilty of insulting a government official and divulging defence secrets. The trial related to an article in the newspaper alleging that the Minister of Defence had been involved in a plot to overthrow the government.

■ In December, Jean-Bosco Talla of *Germinal* newspaper was arrested and charged with insulting President Biya. *Germinal* had published an extract from a banned book that alleges that President Biya and his predecessor, Ahmadou Ahidjo, had entered into a political pact sealed by a homosexual act. On 28 December, the High Court found Jean-Bosco Talla guilty and sentenced him to a suspended one-year prison term and a fine, and ordered him to pay costs amounting to 3,154,600 CFA francs (about US$7,000). He remained in custody at the end of the year because he failed to pay the fine. Earlier, in July, Jean-Bosco Talla had received anonymous telephone death threats after *Germinal* published a report alleging that President Biya had corruptly acquired properties in France.

Rights of lesbian, gay, bisexual and transgender people

The Penal Code criminalizes same-sex sexual relations.

In July, leaders of the Roman Catholic Church organized a demonstration in Douala to protest against Cameroon's adoption in May of the Protocol to the African Charter on Human and Peoples' Rights on the Rights of Women in Africa, known as the Maputo Protocol, which guarantees comprehensive rights to women. The church leaders accused the government of legalizing abortion and homosexuality by adopting the Protocol.

■ Yves Noe Ewane was arrested in May and charged with engaging in homosexual acts. He initially denied the charge but was reported to have been forced to admit to the offence after he was kept naked for several days and denied visits by his relatives. He was released in September.

Prison conditions

Conditions in prisons around the country continued to be harsh and life-threatening. In a report published in August, the government's National Commission for Human Rights and Freedoms stated that as many as

C

five prisoners died each year due to lack of medical attention and poor hygiene. The Commission also expressed concern at the long-term detention without trial of up to 62 per cent of the prison population, with some having been held for nine years.

Detention centres continued to be insecure and unsafe.

■ In Bamenda prison in January, many detainees were injured during a mutiny by inmates. In March, 10 inmates, including two on death row and eight convicted of rape or armed robbery, escaped.

■ In June, up to 50 inmates escaped from Yagona prison in Extreme-North province. Most were recaptured but nearly 20 were still at large at the end of the year. A further 18 inmates escaped from Meri prison in the same province.

Impunity

The government appeared not to have taken any administrative or judicial measures to investigate the unlawful killings and other human rights violations perpetrated by the security forces against civilians during violent protests in February 2008. Those who ordered or carried out the violations remained unaccountable and victims did not receive any form of redress.

Death penalty

An unknown number of prisoners were on death row. They included Jérôme Youta, who was convicted in 1999 of killing his father in a trial that he and his legal counsel said was unfair. It was unclear how many people were sentenced to death during 2009. The last known execution was in 1997.

Amnesty International visits/report

🚌 Responding to an Amnesty International report issued in January, the government denied that it had previously impeded visits by Amnesty International delegates and undertook to facilitate a visit by the organization in early 2010.

📄 Cameroon: Impunity underpins persistent abuse (AFR 17/001/2009)

CANADA

CANADA

Head of state:	Queen Elizabeth II, represented by Governor General Michaëlle Jean
Head of government:	Stephen Harper
Death penalty:	abolitionist for all crimes
Population:	33.6 million
Life expectancy:	80.6 years
Under-5 mortality (m/f):	6/6 per 1,000

Canadian officials failed to protect the rights of Indigenous peoples adequately. Concerns persisted about human rights violations associated with national security laws and practices as well as Canadian overseas mining operations.

Background

In February, Canada's human rights record was assessed under the UN Universal Periodic Review. The recommendation that Canada develop a national poverty elimination strategy was rejected by the federal government which asserted that this was a provincial or territorial responsibility.

Indigenous Peoples' rights

The authorities failed to ensure respect for Indigenous rights when issuing licences for mining, logging and petroleum and other resource extraction. The government continued to make baseless claims that the UN Declaration on the Rights of Indigenous Peoples does not apply in Canada. In September, a hearing opened before the Canadian Human Rights Tribunal into underfunding of First Nation child and family services, compared with other communities.

■ Massive oil and gas developments continued to be carried out without the consent of the Lubicon Cree in northern Alberta, undermining their use of traditional lands and contributing to high levels of poor health and poverty.

Women's rights

The high level of violence experienced by Indigenous women and girls persisted. The Native Women's Association of Canada continued to call for a comprehensive national action plan to address the violence and the underlying discrimination that contributes to it. Despite a stated commitment to stopping the violence, the Canadian government took no steps towards establishing such a plan.

Counter-terror and security
Individuals subject to immigration security certificates continued to be denied access to much of the evidence against them. The Federal Court overturned certificates against two men in October and December.

In May, the Supreme Court of Canada refused to hear an appeal concerning the Canadian military's policy of handing battlefield detainees in Afghanistan over to Afghan authorities. In November, testimony by a Canadian diplomat before a Parliamentary Committee gave rise to serious concerns about failures by senior officials to take account of the risk of torture faced by transferred prisoners.
■ In August, the Federal Court of Appeal upheld an earlier court ruling that the Canadian government must seek the repatriation of Omar Khadr, a Canadian citizen who was apprehended by US forces in Afghanistan when he was 15 years old and had been detained at Guantánamo Bay since 2002. An appeal was lodged with the Supreme Court of Canada against the ruling.

Refugees and asylum-seekers
In February, the Supreme Court of Canada refused to hear an appeal regarding the Safe Third Country refugee agreement between Canada and the USA which denies asylum-seekers who pass through the USA access to the Canadian refugee determination system.

Police and security forces
At least one person died after being stunned by police Tasers during the year, bringing the number of such deaths since 2003 to at least 26.

In February, the Royal Canadian Mounted Police (RCMP) revised its policy on Taser deployment, limiting Taser use to situations where there is a "threat to public or officer safety".

A public inquiry into the death in 2007 of Robert Dziekanski after he was stunned by a Taser continued in British Columbia. The provincial government accepted all the recommendations in the inquiry's July interim report, including raising the threshold for police use of Tasers from the standard of "active resistance" to "causing bodily harm".

In October, the RCMP and other police forces across Canada adopted directives that officers should not aim Tasers at the chests of individuals.

Death penalty
In March, the government was ordered by the Federal Court to reverse its decision not to seek clemency for Ronald Smith, a Canadian citizen who was sentenced to death in 1983 in the USA.

International justice
In May, Désiré Munyaneza, a Rwandan national, was sentenced to life imprisonment for genocide, war crimes and crimes against humanity by a court in Quebec. In November, the government charged a second Rwandan national, Jacques Mungwarere, with genocide.

Corporate accountability
A new corporate social responsibility strategy announced by the government in March failed to include binding human rights requirements. Legislation to develop a human rights framework for the overseas operations of Canadian companies active in the oil, gas and mining sector was pending at the end of the year.

Amnesty International reports
"A place to regain who we are" – Grassy Narrows First Nation, Canada (AMR 20/001/2009)

"Pushed to the edge" – The land rights of Indigenous Peoples in Canada (AMR 20/002/2009)

"Fighting for the future of our children" – Indigenous rights in the Sacred Headwaters region, British Columbia, Canada (AMR 20/003/2009)

Connecting our past to our future – The Long Point First Nation of Canada (AMR 20/010/2009)

No more stolen sisters – The need for a comprehensive response to discrimination and violence against Indigenous women in Canada (AMR 20/012/2009)

C

CENTRAL AFRICAN REPUBLIC

CENTRAL AFRICAN REPUBLIC
Head of state:	François Bozizé
Head of government:	Faustin Archange Touadéra
Death penalty:	abolitionist in practice
Population:	4.4 million
Life expectancy:	46.7 years
Under-5 mortality (m/f):	196/163 per 1,000
Adult literacy:	48.6 per cent

Tens of thousands of people remained displaced inside the country while more than 130,000 lived as refugees in neighbouring countries as a result of armed conflict. Scores of civilians were unlawfully killed or injured by fighters. Members of the security forces enjoyed impunity for human rights violations. The International Criminal Court (ICC) made progress towards the trial of Jean-Pierre Bemba. People accused of witchcraft were tortured.

Background

Despite the December 2008 Inclusive Political Dialogue (Dialogue politique inclusif, DPI) to end armed conflict, fighting continued in the north and east of the country. In a new development, some of the armed clashes, which resulted in scores of civilian deaths and the displacement of thousands of people, involved members of rival ethnic groups. Much of the intercommunal violence took place in the north-west.

Units of the Uganda People's Defence Forces (UPDF), supported by members of the Central African Armed Forces, carried out operations in eastern Central African Republic (CAR) against members of the Ugandan Lord's Resistance Army (LRA). The UPDF reported that it captured or killed several senior LRA commanders, and freed civilians abducted by the armed group.

In July, the government signed a new peace accord in Sirte, Libya, with the leader of the Democratic Front for Central African People, although this failed to end hostilities between the two parties.

Major armed groups refused to implement a recommendation of the DPI to disarm, demobilize and reintegrate (DDR) their combatants. Several of them, including the Rally of the Union of Democratic

Forces and the Popular Alliance for the Restoration of Democracy (Armée populaire pour la restauration de la démocratie, APRD) predicated their co-operation with the DDR programme on the disarmament of ethnic militia and Chadian armed groups in northern CAR.

UNICEF, the UN Children's Fund, announced in July that that it had helped demobilize about 180 child members of the APRD aged between 10 and 17 in Ouham-Pende province. In the same month, the UN refugee agency, UNHCR, held a human rights workshop for members of the APRD, government forces and a regional peacekeeping force.

Several steps were taken to prepare for general elections in 2010. In June, the National Assembly adopted an electoral code. In August, President François Bozizé issued a decree establishing an independent electoral commission charged with preparing, organizing and supervising municipal, regional, legislative and presidential elections.

Peacekeeping operations

In March, the EU-led military force (EUFOR) deployed in Chad and northern CAR was replaced by a military component of the UN Mission in the Central African Republic and Chad (MINURCAT). The UN Security Council had authorized the MINURCAT military component in January. Some 2,000 members of EUFOR stayed on under MINURCAT to provide peacekeeping cover while African and other countries took their place. However, the authorized MINURCAT strength of 5,225 had not been attained by the end of the year, while European countries continued to withdraw their troops.

The Mission for the Consolidation of Peace in Central Africa (MICOPAX), supported by the Economic Community of Central African States, remained in the CAR. The presence of MINURCAT and MICOPAX failed to protect most of the civilians at risk in northern and eastern CAR. Dozens of civilians were killed by government soldiers and armed group fighters. Nearly 20,000 people fled to neighbouring Chad and Cameroon, while more than 100,000 were displaced inside the country.

International justice – Jean-Pierre Bemba

Jean-Pierre Bemba, former Vice-President of the Democratic Republic of the Congo and leader of an armed group, continued to be detained by the ICC

C

awaiting trial in connection with crimes allegedly committed in the CAR by his armed group in 2002 and 2003. The Pre-Trial Chamber of the ICC authorized his release to await trial provided there was a country willing to host him. This drew protests from the ICC Prosecutor's office and lawyers representing victims. However, no country offered to accept him. Subsequently, the Appeals Chamber ordered Jean-Pierre Bemba to remain in custody pending trial, due to start in April 2010.

Abuses by government forces and armed groups

Government forces and armed groups killed and injured civilians in parts of the CAR affected by the armed conflict. Most of the killings by CAR armed groups were reported in Ouham, Ouham-Pende, Vakaga, Nana-Gribizi and Bamingui-Bangoran provinces. Widespread insecurity in the region made it very difficult for human rights and humanitarian organizations to establish the number of people killed or injured. Some of the victims were targeted on suspicion of supporting rival groups. Others were targeted for criticizing parties to the conflict.

■ Soule Garga, President of the National Federation of Central African Cattlekeepers, was killed in April by members of the APRD in Paoua, according to reports.

■ A local worker of the ICRC was killed in Birao in June, allegedly by members of an unspecified armed group.

LRA combatants killed a number of civilians and abducted many others in eastern CAR. The LRA repeatedly attacked areas in and around Obo during the year.

■ In April, the LRA killed two local employees of an Italian humanitarian organization known as Cooperazione Internazionale (COOPI). Two other COOPI employees were shot and wounded during the same incident.

Impunity

Government forces, particularly those belonging to the presidential guard, continued to commit serious human rights violations with impunity. A senior officer of the presidential guard who was reported in previous years to have killed and tortured with impunity carried out further human rights violations. For example, in March the officer reportedly ordered and participated in a severe beating of Daniel Sama, a police commissioner, in the capital, Bangui. The victim, who died a few hours later from his injuries, was reported to have been beaten for possessing a pistol although it had been lawfully issued to him. Although the incident was widely reported and a government minister stated that there would be an inquiry, no action was known to have been taken.

Abuses of people suspected of witchcraft

The belief that individuals can be responsible for afflicting misfortune on others, including death, remained prevalent. Those accused of witchcraft were frequently subjected to torture and other forms of cruel, inhuman or degrading treatment, or even killed. Government and security officials condoned the accusations and the ill-treatment, and took no action to protect the victims or bring those responsible for abuses to justice.

■ In July, a prison official in Mobaye, Basse-Kotto province, who accused a 15-year-old girl of using witchcraft to cause the death of his wife, ordered detainees to pour kerosene on her arms and set it alight. She suffered severe burns. The girl had been arrested in December 2008 after she was accused of causing the drowning of a 12-year-old boy. At the time of her arrest, a group of people beat her to force her to reveal her alleged accomplices, who were accused of transforming themselves into the snakes that they said drowned the boy. Under torture, the girl reportedly denounced two of her alleged accomplices, who were also arrested.

■ In September, the High Court in Bangui found four people, including two children aged 10 and 13, guilty of witchcraft and charlatanism. One of the adults on trial had denied allegations by his daughter that he had been involved in witchcraft.

CHAD

REPUBLIC OF CHAD

Head of state:	Idriss Déby Itno
Head of government:	Youssouf Saleh Abbas
Death penalty:	retentionist
Population:	11.2 million
Life expectancy:	48.6 years
Under-5 mortality (m/f):	220/201 per 1,000
Adult literacy:	31.8 per cent

Human rights abuses and instability continued to mark eastern Chad despite the deployment of a UN peace-keeping mission. Civilians and humanitarian workers were killed and abducted; women and girls were victims of rape and other violence; and children were used as soldiers. The authorities failed to take adequate action to protect civilians from attacks by bandits and armed groups. Suspected political opponents were unlawfully arrested, arbitrarily detained and tortured or otherwise ill-treated. Harassment and intimidation of journalists and human rights defenders continued. Demolition of houses and other structures continued throughout 2009, leaving thousands of people homeless.

Background

Discussions continued about the postponed legislative and presidential elections, scheduled for 2010 and 2011 respectively, and about implementation of the political agreement signed by 17 Chadian parties on 13 August 2007 in N'Djamena. The census for the election was completed on 30 June. New legislation on political parties was passed by the National Assembly on 16 July and the 30 members and the head of the electoral commission were appointed by presidential decree in July despite protests from the opposition. On 25 July, the government signed a peace agreement with the Mouvement National, a coalition of three Chadian armed opposition groups.

Several previous peace agreements signed between Chad and Sudan were not implemented. On 3 May, the two countries signed another agreement in Doha, brokered by the Qatari government. Discussion on the implementation of all the signed peace agreements continued throughout the year.

In addition to the refugees in eastern Chad (see below), at least 56,000 refugees from the Central African Republic were living in camps in the south.

Eastern Chad

The security situation remained volatile and there were widespread abuses, despite the full deployment of 806 personnel of the Détachement Intégré de Sécurité (DIS), a UN-supported Chadian security force responsible for securing towns and sites for internally displaced people (IDPs) in the east, and the presence of the UN Mission in the Central African Republic and Chad (MINURCAT). On 14 January, the UN Security Council extended MINURCAT's mandate until March 2010 and authorized the deployment of a military component to take over the European Union military operation, EUFOR. A Memorandum of Understanding between MINURCAT and the Chadian government, and a technical arrangement with EUFOR relating to the transfer of EUFOR assets to MINURCAT, were signed in February. As of 15 September, MINURCAT had deployed 2,665 troops, just over half the number pledged.

In January, eight armed opposition groups formed the Union des forces de la résistance (UFR, Union of the Forces of Resistance), a coalition led by Timane Erdimi, a former advisor and nephew of President Idriss Déby Itno. In early May, fighting erupted between the UFR and the army around the village of Am Dam on the border with Sudan. The government said that 225 opposition fighters were killed and 212 taken prisoner, and that 22 soldiers were also killed. The Chadian air force subsequently bombed Sudanese territory and in retaliation Sudanese forces bombed areas around the Chadian town of Bahai in late May. Sudan complained to the UN about Chadian attacks on its territory.

Abuses by armed groups and bandits

Chadian and Sudanese armed groups as well as bandits operating in eastern Chad killed and raped civilians and kidnapped people for ransom, including humanitarian workers. According to the UN, there were 192 attacks on humanitarian workers in eastern Chad between January and mid-October. On 13 November, six non-governmental aid agencies suspended operations in eastern Chad after a surge in attacks on humanitarian workers and relief agencies.

■ On 26 October, Michel Mitna, head of the Guereda office of the Commission nationale d'accueil et de réinsertion des réfugiés (CNAR), Chad's national refugee body, was shot dead by bandits. He was travelling in a vehicle clearly marked as belonging to UNHCR, the UN refugee agency, between Guereda and Abeché, eastern Chad. His driver was injured. The attackers escaped.

■ On 9 November, Laurent Maurice, a French agronomist employed by the International Committee of the Red Cross (ICRC), was abducted by armed men in the village of Kawa, around 20km from the Darfur border. The ICRC then suspended its operations.

Violence against women and girls
Women and girls continued to be subjected to rape and other forms of sexual violence in eastern Chad. The perpetrators of such crimes enjoyed virtual impunity.

Child soldiers
The army and armed opposition groups, as well as Sudanese armed groups, continued to recruit and use child soldiers in eastern Chad.

■ During the May fighting with the UFR, the army identified 84 child soldiers among the UFR fighters and handed them over to UNICEF, the UN Children's Fund. The children were later transferred to a transit centre.

Refugees and internally displaced people
Eastern Chad continued to host more than 260,000 refugees from Darfur in 12 refugee camps and at least 180,000 IDPs in 38 sites. Both refugees and IDPs lived in precarious conditions and lacked protection, especially when they ventured outside refugee camps or IDP sites. They were frequently attacked by Chadian and Sudanese armed groups, members of Chad's security forces, and bandits.

Enforced disappearances
The whereabouts of dozens of men who disappeared between 2006 and 2008 after arrest by government forces remained unknown. Among them was opposition leader Ibni Oumar Mahamat Saleh, arrested on 3 February 2008 and feared dead.

Arbitrary arrests and detentions
The authorities frequently arrested and arbitrarily detained people without charge. Some were held in security services' facilities where visits are not allowed.

■ On 20 July, Haroun Mahamat Abdoulaye, Sultan of the Department of Dar Tama, eastern Chad, was arrested at his home by police and then held without

charge at the security services' facility in N'Djamena. He had previously been arrested in November 2007 on suspicion of involvement with the United Front for Democratic Change, a former armed opposition group.

Violence against women and girls
Various forms of violence against women and girls continued, including female genital mutilation and forced marriage. Forced marriages were imposed on girls as young as 13, including in refugee camps and IDP sites.

■ In August, the UN Human Rights Committee called on Chad to protect a girl from sexual abuse in prison. Forced to marry when only 13 and imprisoned since 2004 on suspicion of poisoning her 70-year-old husband, she has been repeatedly raped in prison and gave birth as a result.

Freedom of expression – journalists
Journalists continued to be intimidated and harassed. Decree No.5, which was issued by the President during the state of emergency in February-March 2008, remained in force. The Decree restricted press freedom and increased penalties that could be imposed on journalists. It provided for up to five years in prison for publication of "false news" and for a new offence of "insulting the president, the head of government, ministers or foreign diplomats".

■ On 14 October, Innocent Ebode, Cameroonian chief editor of the newspaper La Voix du Tchad, was summarily deported from Chad. The authorities accused La Voix du Tchad of not respecting administrative regulations covering the publication of newspapers in Chad and its chief editor of staying illegally in Chad since his arrival in June 2009. The deportation followed an article criticizing the Environment Minister's suggestion that the Nobel Peace Prize should have been awarded to President Idriss Déby Itno for his environmental work.

■ On 28 November, Eloi Miandadji, a reporter with La Voix du Tchad, was detained for several hours and the memory card of his camera was confiscated by security personnel after he introduced himself to and requested an interview with the Minister of the Interior and Public Security. The incident happened after the Minister verbally abused Eloi Miandadji when he asked a question about the use of police vehicles. Eloi Miandadji was later made to sign a document stating that he was not going to write about his arrest or the question related to the police vehicles. The Minister told him that *La Voix du Tchad* would soon be closed. On 3 December, a N'Djamena court ordered the closure of the newspaper and the seizure of all copies of it.

Human rights defenders

Human rights defenders continued to face threats, attacks and intimidation.

■ On 13 October, Michel Barka, chairperson of the Union Syndicale du Tchad (UST), a large trade union, was followed while driving and then forced to stop. He reversed and escaped. Later the same day he was again followed, this time by a motorcyclist who pointed a gun at him.

■ Also on 13 October, Masalbaye Tenebaye, President of the Chadian Human Rights League (Ligue Tchadienne des droits de l'homme, LTDH), was followed on his way home after meeting an international partner organization. The same people followed him the next day. State officials met Masalbaye Tenebaye on 20 October and assured him that they would take measures to protect him and would investigate the incidents.

Forced evictions

People continued to be forcibly evicted in 2009 and their homes destroyed in several N'Djamena neighbourhoods, including Moursal, Chagoua and Goudji, leaving thousands homeless.

Using commercial satellite imagery, Amnesty International established that more than 3,700 structures were destroyed in the year up to January 2009. Some inhabitants were given adequate warning that their houses were going to be demolished, but most were given no notice. The houses of some were demolished despite court orders protecting them. Very few of the people forcibly evicted were given alternative housing or compensation.

■ Apollinaire Nodjohoudou Djeria, whose house was demolished in late 2008 in defiance of a court order, was told he would receive compensation in 2009 by the Mayor of N'Djamena. However, by the end of the year he had received nothing.

Amnesty International visits/reports

🚍 Amnesty International delegates visited Eastern Chad and N'Djamena in April and May.

▦ Chad: Open letter to the Security Council (AFR 20/003/2009)

▦ Chad: Broken homes, broken lives (AFR 20/007/2009)

▦ "No place for us here" – Violence against refugee women in eastern Chad (AFR 20/008/2009)

▦ Human Rights Council adopts Universal Periodic Review outcome on Chad (AFR 20/011/2009)

CHILE

REPUBLIC OF CHILE

Head of state and government:	Michelle Bachelet
Death penalty:	abolitionist for ordinary crimes
Population:	17 million
Life expectancy:	78.5 years
Under-5 mortality (m/f):	10/8 per 1,000
Adult literacy:	96.5 per cent

Further progress was made in bringing perpetrators of past human rights violations to justice. Indigenous Peoples continued to voice their land claims and demand respect for other rights amid rising tensions in the south. Obstacles to the enjoyment of sexual and reproductive rights continued to exist.

Background

In November, the Senate approved a bill to create a National Human Rights Institution that would adhere to international standards and would be empowered to initiate legal proceedings in cases of certain human rights violations.

Chile's human rights record was assessed under the UN Universal Periodic Review in May. Chile accepted all the recommendations made except those that would have brought the country's abortion laws into line with international human rights standards.

Indigenous Peoples' rights

The government announced plans to return 33,000 hectares of land to Indigenous communities in the southern IX Region. However, a decree passed in September (Decree 124) regarding procedures for consultation with and participation by Indigenous Peoples in decisions on matters directly affecting them fell far short of international standards. Efforts to incorporate recognition of Indigenous Peoples' rights into the Constitution and to introduce new legislation on land and water resources that would have a considerable impact on them were carried out without due consultation.

Large-scale development projects continued to put the livelihoods of Indigenous Peoples at risk.

■ In May, construction began on the Pascua-Lama mining project in northern Chile on the border with Argentina, despite objections from local Indigenous Diaguita Huascoaltino communities that their consent had not been given.

Mapuche Indigenous communities continued to campaign in support of their land claims and other rights. Some Mapuche groups and their supporters organized occupations and there were a number of violent clashes with the security forces. The Arauco-Malleco Co-ordinating Committee, whose aim is the creation of an autonomous Mapuche nation, claimed responsibility for a number of protest actions. In response, anti-terrorist and national security legislation dating from the military government of Augusto Pinochet (1973-1990) was applied in several cases, in breach of previous government undertakings not to do so and contrary to the recommendations of international human rights bodies.

■ On 12 August, Jaime Facundo Mendoza Collío, a 24-year-old Mapuche, died after being shot by police. He was among approximately 80 people who had occupied a farm in the community of Ercilla, Araucania region, as part of their campaign for the return of land they claim. During the police operation to evict the protesters at least eight people were injured. Forensic reports stated that Jaime Facundo Mendoza Collío was shot from behind.

■ In October, the government denied allegations that several children were injured by pellets allegedly fired by security forces outside a community meeting in a school in Temucuicui on 16 October.

Sexual and reproductive rights

Abortion remained criminalized. Obstacles to accessing emergency contraception continued. In March the Comptroller General published a decision prohibiting municipal health clinics from distributing free emergency contraception, thereby disadvantaging women who could not afford to obtain it privately.

Impunity

Chile ratified the Rome Statute of the International Criminal Court in June and the International Convention for the Protection of All Persons from Enforced Disappearance in December. In September, the government announced its intention to reopen both the National Commission on Political Imprisonment and Torture and the National Commission for Truth and Reconciliation (the Valech and Rettig Commissions) in order to allow previously unregistered cases of torture and enforced disappearance to be presented.

The Supreme Court announced that it would speed up the processing of cases of human rights violations committed during the military government of Augusto Pinochet, amid concerns that reforms to the Code of Criminal Procedure in 2010 might stall pending cases. According to official figures, between January and October, 69 former security force agents were charged, sentenced or tried in connection with human rights violations. However, by the end of October, final sentences had been handed down in only 179 out of a total of 3,186 cases.

In September, more than 165 former agents of the National Intelligence Directorate (Dirección de Inteligencia Nacional, DINA) were charged in connection with their involvement in the torture and enforced disappearance of political activists.

■ In September, the Supreme Court ruled that torture committed at the Chilean Airforce Training Unit between September 1973 and January 1975 constituted a crime against humanity. Only two people, retired colonels Edgar Cevallos Jones and Ramón Cáceres Jorquera, were sentenced in connection with these crimes.

■ The trial of former Prosecutor General Alfonso Podlech in connection with the enforced disappearance of four people in the 1970s began in Italy in November and was continuing at the end of the year.

■ In December, a judge ordered the arrest of six people after fresh investigations into the death in 1982 of former President Eduardo Frei Montalva revealed the cause of death was poisoning, rather than an infection as initially believed. The Supreme Court subsequently rejected legal challenges (*amparo*) by those charged. Lawyers for the Frei family argued that he was murdered because of his opposition to the government of Augusto Pinochet.

CHINA

PEOPLE'S REPUBLIC OF CHINA

Head of state:	Hu Jintao
Head of government:	Wen Jiabao
Death penalty:	retentionist
Population:	1,345.8 million
Life expectancy:	72.9 years
Under-5 mortality (m/f):	25/35 per 1,000
Adult literacy:	93.3 per cent

The authorities continued to tighten restrictions on freedom of expression, assembly and association due partly to sensitivities surrounding a series of landmark anniversaries, including the 60th anniversary of the People's Republic on 1 October. Human rights defenders were detained, prosecuted, held under house arrest and subjected to enforced disappearance. Pervasive internet and media controls remained. "Strike hard" campaigns resulted in sweeping arrests in the Xinjiang Uighur Autonomous Region (XUAR), particularly following violence and unrest in July. Independent human rights monitoring was prevented in Tibetan-populated regions. The authorities continued to strictly control the parameters of religious practice, with Catholic and Protestant groups practising outside official bounds being harassed, detained and sometimes imprisoned. The severe and systematic 10-year campaign against the Falun Gong continued.

Background

China was increasingly seen as a critical player in global affairs, including on such issues as Myanmar, North Korea, Iran, climate change and the global economic recovery. This contrasted with the government's increased insecurity at home stemming from a drop in the economic growth rate, rising unemployment and increased social tension associated with pervasive corruption, lack of access to adequate health care, housing and social security, and repression of civil society groups. As China's economy continued to grow, the gap between rich and poor widened.

Freedom of expression – journalists/internet

As the internet was increasingly used to disseminate news and conduct debates, the authorities tried to control its use by restricting news reporting and shutting down publications and internet sites, including ones that "slandered the country's political system", "distorted the history of the Party", "publicized Falun Gong and other evil cults", and "incited ethnic splittism". The government blocked access to content and recorded individuals' activities through new filtering software such as Blue Shield.

Following the publication of Charter 08 in December 2008, a document calling for political reform and greater protection of human rights, police questioned signatories and put them under surveillance for many months.

■ Liu Xiaobo, a prominent intellectual and signatory originally detained in December 2008, was sentenced to 11 years' imprisonment on 25 December for "inciting subversion of state power". His lawyers were given only 20 minutes to present their case, in a trial that lasted less than three hours.

Human rights defenders

Human rights defenders (HRDs), including lawyers, journalists, environmental activists, and proponents of democratic reform, were arbitrarily detained, harassed, subjected to house arrest, held in incommunicado detention, and imprisoned. Authorities tortured and ill-treated many of those in detention. Family members of HRDs, including children, continued to be targeted and were subjected to long-term house arrest and other restraints and harassment.

Police and security forces detained, harassed and abused lawyers representing politically sensitive HRDs, Falun Gong practitioners, farmers with claims against local officials regarding land rights or corruption, and those who had been involved in advocating reform of lawyers' associations. Lawyers were at particular risk of losing their licence to practise.

■ On 4 February, 10 public security bureau officers and other unidentified men abducted prominent human rights lawyer Gao Zhisheng from his home in Shanxi province. His whereabouts remained unknown at the end of the year. Gao Zhisheng's wife, Geng He, and their children arrived in the USA in March, escaping from the Chinese authorities' ongoing harassment, which included preventing their daughter from attending school.

The authorities continued to use vague laws governing the use of "state secrets" and "subversion of state power" to arrest, charge and imprison HRDs.

■ In August, HRD Tan Zuoren was charged with "inciting subversion of state power". He had organized an independent investigation into the collapse of school buildings during the May 2008 Sichuan earthquake. He had planned to publish the report prior to his detention. At the end of the year, the verdict had not been announced.

■ On 23 November, HRD Huang Qi was sentenced to three years' imprisonment for "illegally possessing state secrets". He had posted the demands of parents whose children had died in the Sichuan earthquake on his website.

Justice system

Unfair trials remained endemic. Judicial decisions remained susceptible to political interference; defendants were often unable to hire a lawyer of their own choice and were denied access to their lawyer and family; families were often not given adequate notice of trial dates and were frequently refused entry to trials. Confessions extracted through torture continued to be admitted as evidence in court.

Millions of citizens tried to present their grievances directly to government authorities through the "letters and visits" system, otherwise known as the "petitioning system". Despite being legal, police often harassed petitioners, forcibly returned them to their home provinces and detained them in illegal "black jails" or psychiatric hospitals where they were at risk of ill-treatment.

Officials continued to intimidate the parents of children who died in collapsed school buildings during the Sichuan earthquake in May 2008 and prevented them from speaking to the media or pursuing independent investigations.

Detention without trial

The authorities frequently used administrative punishments, including Re-education through Labour (RTL), to detain people without trial. According to the government, 190,000 people were held in RTL facilities, down from half a million several years ago, although the real figures were likely to be much higher. Former RTL prisoners reported that Falun Gong constituted one of the largest groups of prisoners, and political activists, petitioners and others practising their religion outside permitted bounds were common targets. The authorities used a variety of illegal forms of detention, including "black jails", "legal education classes", "study classes" and mental health institutions to detain thousands of people.

Torture and other ill-treatment and deaths in custody

Torture continued to be commonplace in places of detention, sometimes leading to death. Torture methods used on detainees included beatings, often with an electric prod, hanging by the limbs, force feeding, injecting unknown drugs and sleep deprivation.

In March, the death of a 24-year-old in a detention centre in Yunnan province triggered a heated online debate about police and "jail bullies" torturing and otherwise ill-treating inmates. The online debate led to revelations of other cases of deaths in detention and prompted an investigation by the Supreme People's Procuratorate (SPP). In July, the SPP published a report investigating 12 of the 15 deaths that occurred in detention during the first four months of the year. Of these, seven were found to have been beaten to death, three to have committed suicide, and two had died of accidental causes.

Death penalty

China continued to make extensive use of the death penalty, including for non-violent crimes. The death sentence continued to be imposed after unfair trials. Statistics on death sentences and executions remained classified as state secrets and, while executions numbered in the thousands, the government did not release actual figures.

Freedom of religion

People who practised their religion outside officially sanctioned boundaries continued to experience harassment, arbitrary detention, imprisonment and other serious restrictions on their freedom of religion. Catholic priests and bishops who refused to join the officially recognized Chinese Patriotic Catholic Association continued to be detained and held incommunicado for long periods or subjected to enforced disappearance.

■ The whereabouts of 75-year-old Monsignor James

C

Su Zhimin, an ordinary bishop from Baoding city, Hebei province, has remained unknown since his detention by police in 1996.

Police beat and detained members of Christian house-churches, who practise outside officially recognized institutions, often demolishing their churches and sending them for RTL or to prison. The government campaign against the Falun Gong intensified, with sweeping detentions, unfair trials leading to long sentences, enforced disappearances and deaths in detention following torture and ill-treatment.

■ Chen Zhenping, a Falun Gong practitioner, was sentenced to eight years in prison during a secret trial in August 2008. She was charged with "using a heretical organization to subvert the law". Before, during and after her trial, Chen Zhenping was denied access to her lawyer. In September, prison guards told her family that she had been transferred to another location, but refused to say where. Chen Zhenping's lawyers have been unable to obtain any additional information concerning her whereabouts.

Xinjiang Uighur Autonomous Region

The authorities intensified already tight restrictions on freedom of expression, association and assembly in the Xinjiang Uighur Autonomous Region (XUAR) in the north-west of China following the eruption of unprecedented violence in Urumqi on 5 July. The government reported that 197 people were killed, the majority of whom were Han killed by Uighurs, and more than 1,600 were injured. Uighurs had posted online calls for a protest in reaction to government inaction over the beatings and deaths of Uighur migrant workers by Han workers in a toy factory in Guangdong province in June.

Eyewitness accounts of events on 5 July suggest that police and security forces cracked down on peaceful Uighur demonstrators to prevent thousands from marching through the city. According to these reports, police beat peaceful protesters with batons, used tear gas to disperse the crowds, and shot directly into crowds of peaceful demonstrators with live ammunition, most likely resulting in many more deaths.

Following the unrest, the authorities detained hundreds on suspicion of participation in the protests, including boys and elderly men, in door-to-door raids. Family and friends of several detainees denied that

the detained individuals had any role in the violence or the protests. Dozens of detainees remained unaccounted for at the end of the year.

In August, the authorities announced that they were holding 718 people in connection with the unrest, and that 83 of these faced criminal charges including for murder, arson and robbery. On 9 November, the authorities announced the execution of nine individuals, after unfair trials. Based on their names, eight were Uighurs and one was Han Chinese. In December, an additional 13 individuals were sentenced to death and the authorities announced the arrest of an additional 94 people on suspicion of involvement in the July unrest.

In November, the authorities formally announced a "strike hard and punish" campaign in the region to last until the end of the year to "root out… criminals".

The authorities blamed the unrest on overseas Uighur "separatists", particularly Rebiya Kadeer, the President of the World Uyghur Congress, and failed to acknowledge the role of government policies in fuelling discontent among Uighurs. These policies included restrictions on freedom of expression, association and assembly; restrictions on religious and other cultural practices; and economic policies that discriminate against Uighurs and encourage Han migration to the region. New regulations further tightened already strict controls on the internet in the region, criminalizing its use with the vaguely defined crime of "ethnic separatism". Restrictions on internet access, international telephone calls, and text messaging, blocked in the immediate aftermath of the 5 July unrest, remained in place at the end of the year.

On 19 December, the Cambodian government forcibly returned 20 Uighur asylum-seekers to China, against UNHCR, the UN refugee agency, objections. Chinese authorities allege they had participated in the July unrest, and days later denied that the deportations were connected to a new US$1.2 billion aid package to Cambodia.

Tibet Autonomous Region

Protests which erupted in March 2008 continued on a smaller scale during the year, accompanied by persistent detentions and arrests. Two Tibetans were executed for crimes alleged to have been committed during the March 2008 unrest.

International human rights organizations reported

a rise in the number of Tibetan political prisoners prior to sensitive anniversaries, including the 50th anniversary of the failed Tibetan uprising which led to the Dalai Lama's exile. The authorities blocked communication flows to and from the region and prevented independent human rights monitoring. Tibetans' rights to freedom of expression, religion, assembly and association continued to be severely restricted. The Chinese authorities became more assertive in their international policy regarding the Tibet issue, with public statements by Chinese officials that suggested their willingness to punish countries economically and diplomatically for perceived support of the Dalai Lama and Tibetan issues.

■ In October, two Tibetan men, Losang Gyaltse and Loyar, were executed. They were convicted of arson and sentenced to death on 8 April 2009 by the Lhasa Municipal Intermediate People's Court. They had been arrested during unrest in the Tibet Autonomous Region and Tibetan-populated areas in neighbouring provinces in March 2008.

■ On 28 December, Dhondup Wangchen, an independent Tibetan film maker, was sentenced to six years imprisonment for the crime of "subverting state power" after a secret trial by the provincial court in Xining, Qinghai province. The lawyer originally hired by his family was barred from representing him, and it is unclear if he subsequently had any legal representation or was able to defend himself during the trial.

Hong Kong Special Administrative Region

On 4 June, according to organizers, over 150,000 people commemorated the 20th anniversary of the Tiananmen military crackdown, but the authorities denied entry to some Chinese and foreign activists who wished to participate. In July, tens of thousands marched for causes including an improvement in people's livelihood, democracy and freedom of speech.

Racial discrimination

The Race Discrimination Ordinance (RDO) entered into force in July. In August, the UN Committee on the Elimination of Racial Discrimination (CERD) noted that the RDO's definition of racial discrimination was not completely consistent with Article 1 of the UN Convention against Racism. CERD recommended that indirect discrimination with regard to language, immigration status and nationality be added to the definition. CERD also recommended that all government functions and powers be brought within the scope of the RDO.

Refugees and asylum-seekers

While noting planned reform in torture claims procedure, CERD recommended that the government guarantee the rights of asylum-seekers to information, interpretation, legal assistance and judicial remedies and encouraged the adoption of a refugee law with a comprehensive screening procedure for individual asylum claims. It also repeated its recommendation that the authorities ratify the 1951 Convention relating to the Status of Refugees and its 1967 Protocol.

Rights of lesbian, gay, bisexual and transgender people

On 31 December, the Hong Kong Special Administrative Region (HKSAR) government announced that amendments to the Domestic Violence Ordinance would extend protection to same-sex cohabitants and take effect on 1 January 2010. HKSAR law did not prohibit discrimination on the grounds of sexual orientation.

Macao Special Administrative Region

In June, sole candidate Fernando Chui Sai-on was elected by a 300-member election committee to become the city's Chief Executive until 2014. In September, 12 candidates were directly elected to the 29-seat legislature. The remaining legislators are appointed or chosen by functional constituencies.

In February, the Legislative Assembly passed the National Security Law covering acts of "sedition", "secession", "subversion", "treason" and "theft of state secrets". Vague definitions of the crimes could be used to abuse the rights to freedom of expression and association. Tens of Hong Kong citizens, including legislative councillors, activists, journalists and a law professor, who were attempting to participate in activities concerning the proposed new law, were denied entry to Macao. In December, three Hong Kong activists, who planned to call for the release of Liu Xiaobo during a visit by President Hu Jintao, were also denied entry.

C

COLOMBIA

REPUBLIC OF COLOMBIA

Head of state and government:	Álvaro Uribe Vélez
Death penalty:	abolitionist for all crimes
Population:	45.7 million
Life expectancy:	72.7 years
Under-5 mortality (m/f):	30/22 per 1,000
Adult literacy:	92.7 per cent

The internal armed conflict continued to have devastating consequences on the civilian population, with Indigenous communities particularly hard hit. All the warring parties – including the security forces, guerrilla groups and paramilitary groups – were responsible for serious human rights abuses and violations of international humanitarian law. Although fewer civilians were extrajudicially executed by the security forces and forcible displacement increased at a slower rate than in previous years, other human rights abuses intensified. There was a rise in killings of members of marginalized social groups and Indigenous Peoples, and in threats against human rights defenders and other activists. Witnesses to killings and victims of human rights violations and their families were threatened and harassed.

In September, the government announced it would disband the civilian intelligence service (Departamento Administrativo de Seguridad, DAS) after evidence emerged that it had illegally intercepted the communications of human rights defenders, journalists, opposition politicians and judges for at least seven years, and colluded with paramilitary groups.

The Supreme Court of Justice investigation into the "parapolitical" scandal continued to make progress. Some 80 Members of Congress – most belonging to parties from the ruling coalition – were under investigation for their alleged links to paramilitary groups.

Tensions increased with several countries in the region, especially Venezuela, following the government's decision to allow the US military to use seven military bases in Colombia.

The internal armed conflict

The warring parties failed to distinguish between civilians and combatants, resulting in forced displacement, killings of civilians, sexual violence against women, hostage-taking, enforced disappearances, forced recruitment of minors and indiscriminate attacks against the civilian population. There was a sharp increase in violence in some of the country's larger cities. This increase was attributed to the armed conflict, drug trafficking-related crimes, and acts of "social cleansing".

Some 20,000 enforced disappearances reportedly continued to be investigated by the Office of the Attorney General.

The number of internally displaced people continued to rise, although at a slower rate than in recent years. In 2009, more than 286,000 people were newly displaced, according to the NGO Consultancy for Human Rights and Displacement (Consultoría para los Derechos Humanos y el Desplazamiento, CODHES). Indigenous Peoples and Afro-descendant and campesino (peasant farmer) communities were most affected.

The government refused to support a bill, the Victims' Law, which would have granted reparation to victims of the conflict on the basis of non-discrimination, regardless of whether the perpetrator was an agent of the state or not. The bill was rejected by Congress in June.

Indigenous Peoples' rights

During his visit to Colombia in July, the UN Special Rapporteur on indigenous people described the human rights situation facing Indigenous Peoples in Colombia as "grave, critical and profoundly worrying". More than 114 Indigenous men, women and children were killed in 2009, an increase compared with 2008. More than half of those killed were members of Awá communities.

■ On 26 August, 12 Awá, including six children and an eight-month-old baby, were killed by gunmen on the *resguardo* (Indigenous reservation) of Gran Rosario in Nariño Department. One of the victims, Tulia García, had been a witness to the killing of her husband, Gonzalo Rodríguez, by the army on 23 May.
■ On 4 February, the Revolutionary Armed Forces of Colombia (Fuerzas Armadas Revolucionarias de Colombia, FARC) killed 15 Awá, including two pregnant women, in Barbacoas Municipality, Nariño Department.

Indigenous leaders and their families were also threatened.

■ On 11 May, the 12-year-old daughter of Indigenous leader Aída Quilcué was threatened at gunpoint outside her house. Aída Quilcué had been receiving protection ordered by the Inter-American Commission on Human Rights since her husband was killed by soldiers in December 2008.

In January, the Constitutional Court issued Order 004/09, which concluded that the survival of some Indigenous Peoples was at risk because of the armed conflict.

In April, the government endorsed the UN Declaration on the Rights of Indigenous Peoples. In 2007, Colombia had abstained when the Declaration was adopted by the UN General Assembly.

The civilian intelligence service

In April, the media revealed that the DAS, which operated under the direct authority of the president, had been involved in massive, long-standing, illegal espionage against human rights defenders, opposition politicians, judges and journalists to restrict or neutralize their work. The operation was reportedly carried out in close co-operation with paramilitary groups. Members of the diplomatic community in Colombia and international human rights defenders were also targeted.

In May, the Attorney General charged one former DAS director, Jorge Noguera, with homicide and membership of paramilitary groups. Some of the activists intercepted by the DAS had been subjected to death threats and spurious criminal charges. In September, President Uribe said the DAS would be abolished and a new intelligence service created.

In March, Congress approved an Intelligence Law, which outlawed intelligence gathering on individuals on the grounds of their political affiliation or membership of a trade union or social or human rights organization. In September, a decree implementing the Intelligence Law ordered a review of intelligence files compiled on those grounds by all the security services, including the military. Such files had often been used to mount unfounded criminal proceedings against activists. By the end of the year, no information was made available on the results of the review.

The 'parapolitical' scandal

Some 80 Members of Congress were under criminal investigation in 2009 for their alleged links to paramilitary groups.

In September, the Supreme Court ruled it was competent to investigate Members who had resigned their posts in an effort to ensure that their cases were investigated by the Attorney General's Office, where they hoped to be treated more leniently.

Several of the magistrates involved in investigating the scandal who had been threatened and harassed continued to receive protection measures ordered by the Inter-American Commission on Human Rights.

Extrajudicial executions by the security forces

Revelations in 2008 that the security forces had extrajudicially executed more than a dozen young men from Soacha, near the capital, Bogotá, forced the government to adopt measures to combat the problem. The number of cases of extrajudicial execution fell sharply in 2009 compared with 2008. Some 2,000 extrajudicial executions carried out by army personnel over a number of years were under investigation by the Attorney General's Office in 2009, but progress was slow. There was renewed resistance from within the military justice system to civilian jurisdiction in cases where military personnel were accused of human rights violations.

Witnesses to extrajudicial executions as well as relatives of those killed were threatened and attacked.

Following his visit to Colombia in June, the UN Special Rapporteur on extrajudicial, summary or arbitrary killings said that extrajudicial executions "were carried out in a more or less systematic fashion by significant elements within the military".

Paramilitary groups

Paramilitary groups continued to operate in many parts of the country, sometimes in collusion with sectors of the security forces. Their continued activities belied government claims that all paramilitaries had laid down their arms following a government-sponsored demobilization programme that began in 2003.

The government claimed that violence attributed to these groups was solely drug-related and criminal in nature. However, the tactics employed by these groups to terrorize the civilian population, including death threats and massacres, reflected those used by paramilitary groups prior to demobilization. Human rights defenders, community leaders and other social activists continued to be targeted by such groups.

C

There was evidence that paramilitary groups were again becoming more organized. In a report published in October, the Organization of American States' Mission to Support the Peace Process in Colombia referred to "these illegal structures' capacity for renewal, especially among their leaders, which is a challenge for the authorities to prevent their restructuring".

There was an increase in killings of people from marginalized social groups in urban areas, mostly carried out by paramilitaries. Victims included young people; the homeless; petty criminals; sex workers; lesbians, gay men, bisexual and transgender people; and drug addicts. According to the NGO Research and Popular Education Centre (Centro de Investigación y Educación Popular, CINEP), there were 184 such killings in 2009, compared with 82 in 2008.

There was an increase in efforts by paramilitary groups to exert social control over communities living in poverty through the mass distribution of threatening leaflets. In 2009, CINEP recorded 83 such threats distributed in many parts of the country, compared with 58 in 2008.

The Justice and Peace process

Only around 3,700 of the 31,000 paramilitaries who had allegedly demobilized since 2003 had participated in the Justice and Peace process by the end of 2009. However, the whereabouts of many of these were unknown. The Justice and Peace process allows former paramilitaries to benefit from reduced sentences in return for confessions about human rights violations. Some paramilitaries confessed to human rights abuses and implicated others, including people in politics, business and the military. However, the process still fell short of international standards on the rights of victims to truth, justice and reparation.

Some 90 per cent of those who were demobilized continued to escape effective investigation as a result of Decree 128 and Law 782, which grant de facto amnesties to those not under investigation for human rights violations. In June, Congress approved a law to regularize the legal status of 19,000 supposedly demobilized paramilitaries after the Supreme Court ruled in 2008 that they could not benefit from amnesties. The law authorized the Attorney General to suspend, interrupt or abandon investigations against them, thus enabling them to evade justice.

In July the Supreme Court annulled on procedural grounds the sentence handed down in March by the Justice and Peace Tribunal on the paramilitary Wilson Salazar Carrascal, alias "El Loro". By the end of the year, no paramilitary had been sentenced under the Justice and Peace process.

Most of the 18 paramilitary leaders extradited to the USA on drug-trafficking charges refused to co-operate with the Colombian justice system in its investigations into human rights violations. Colombian judicial officials experienced difficulties in gaining access to the few who did agree to co-operate.

Some paramilitaries returned a small portion of the 4-6 million hectares of land stolen by them, but there were concerns that some of these lands could again fall under the control of such groups or their backers. Some of the few original owners whose land was returned were threatened or killed.

Victims or their families participating in the Justice and Peace process, those accompanying them, and judicial officials investigating human rights violations were threatened and killed. This dissuaded many victims from participating in the process.

Guerrilla groups

The FARC and the National Liberation Army (Ejército de Liberación Nacional, ELN) continued to commit human rights abuses and serious and repeated violations of international humanitarian law, including the killing of civilians, the recruitment of children and hostage-taking.

Widespread use of anti-personnel mines by the FARC continued. In 2009, more than 111 civilians and members of the security forces were killed and 521 injured by landmines.

The FARC launched indiscriminate attacks in which civilians were the main victims.

■ On 13 January, the FARC launched an attack using explosive devices in the urban centre of Roberto Payán Municipality in Nariño Department. Six people died, including three children.

According to government figures, the overall number of kidnappings fell to 213 in 2009, from 437 in 2008. Most kidnappings were attributed to criminal gangs, but guerrilla groups were responsible for the majority of conflict-related kidnappings.

On 21 December, the FARC kidnapped and killed the Governor of Caquetá Department, Luis Francisco Cuéllar.

In February, the FARC released several high-profile hostages. Among them were Sigifredo López, a Deputy in the Valle del Cauca Assembly, who had been held captive since 2002; and former Governor of Meta Department Alán Jara, held since 2001. That same month, the FARC also released three police officers and a soldier.

Impunity

There was some progress in key human rights investigations, but impunity for human rights violations remained a serious concern.
■ In November, retired army General Jaime Uscateguí was sentenced to 40 years in prison for his part in the 1997 Mapiripán massacre in Meta Department.
■ In September, the Council of State upheld a 1995 ruling by the Office of the Procurator General dismissing General Álvaro Velandia Hurtado and three other officers from the army for their involvement in the enforced disappearance, torture and killing of Nydia Erika Bautista, a member of the M-19 guerrilla group, in 1987.

Human rights defenders

Human rights defenders, especially those working in more remote areas, were threatened and killed. Community leaders were at particular risk of attack. At least eight defenders and 39 trade unionists were killed in 2009.

Death threats targeting human rights and social activists and organizations increased; most were attributed to paramilitary groups.

Human rights defenders and social activists accused of having links with guerrilla groups continued to face criminal proceedings, often based solely on information from military intelligence files and paid informants. However, long-standing proceedings against some defenders were finally dismissed by the courts. The offices of a number of human rights organizations were broken into and sensitive information stolen.

During a visit to Colombia by the UN Special Rapporteur on human rights defenders in September, President Uribe said that human rights work was legitimate. However, high-ranking officials, including the President, continued to make statements linking such work with support for guerrilla groups.

US military aid

In 2009, the USA allocated some US$662 million in military and non-military assistance for Colombia. This included US$543.5 million from the State and Foreign Operations funding bill, of which US$305 million was earmarked for the security forces; 30 per cent of this was conditional on the Colombian authorities meeting certain human rights requirements. In August, US$55 million in security assistance withheld in 2008 was released following "positive steps" by the Colombian government on human rights. By November 2009, US$19 million in security assistance funds from 2008 and US$31 million in security assistance funds from 2009 was being withheld by the US Congress because of ongoing human rights concerns.

International scrutiny

The report on Colombia of the Office of the UN High Commissioner for Human Rights, published in March, stated that, although the government had made efforts to combat extrajudicial executions, serious violations of human rights continued to take place. It expressed concerns about continued statements by government officials linking human rights defenders and social activists with guerrilla groups; human rights abuses by guerrilla groups; and the serious risks to the civilian population posed by "illegal armed groups that have emerged since the paramilitary demobilization". The report also stressed that few victims of human rights violations had been accorded their rights to truth, justice and reparation.

In March, the UN Human Rights Council formally adopted the outcome of the December 2008 review of Colombia's human rights record under the UN Universal Periodic Review (UPR). The government made a commitment to comply with most of the recommendations, including urgent implementation of the full recommendations of the Office of the UN High Commissioner for Human Rights.

UN Special Rapporteurs on the independence of judges and lawyers; on human rights defenders; on indigenous people; and on extrajudicial, summary or arbitrary executions visited Colombia during 2009.

On 1 November, the declaration made by Colombia under Article 124 of the Rome Statute of the International Criminal Court, by which Colombia had declared that for seven years it did not accept the jurisdiction of the Court with respect to war crimes, came to an end.

C

Amnesty International visits/reports

🚍 Amnesty International delegates visited Colombia in February, July, September and October.

📄 The Curvaradó and Jiguamiandó Humanitarian Zones – Communities in resistance in Colombia (AMR 23/001/2009)

📄 The Peace Community of San José de Apartadó – Communities in resistance in Colombia (AMR 23/002/2009)

📄 Everything left behind: Internal displacement in Colombia (AMR 23/015/2009)

CONGO (REPUBLIC OF)

C

REPUBLIC OF CONGO
Head of state and government: **Denis Sassou-Nguesso**
   (replaced Isidore Mvouba as head of
   government in September)
Death penalty: **abolitionist in practice**
Population: **3.7 million**
Life expectancy: **53.5 years**
Under-5 mortality (m/f):   **135/122 per 1,000**
Adult literacy: **81.1 per cent**

The rights to freedom of expression, assembly and movement of opposition leaders and supporters were restricted, especially in the aftermath of the July presidential elections. Several opposition supporters were detained and released without charge. Three asylum-seekers arrested in 2004 remained in military custody without charge or trial.

Background

President Denis Sassou-Nguesso won presidential elections in July and was sworn in for a seven-year term in August. The Constitutional Court declared that he had won with nearly 80 per cent of the votes cast. Opposition political parties and civil society organizations described the elections as fraudulent and unfair. Several opposition presidential candidates were barred by the electoral commission from standing on the grounds that they did not fulfil all the requisite conditions. After he was sworn in, President Sassou-Nguesso appointed a new government and abolished the post of prime minister, so becoming both head of state and government.

Sporadic incidents of banditry attributed to former members of the National Resistance Council (Conseil national de résistance, CNR) took place in the Pool region. Former CNR leader Frédéric Bintsamou denied that former CNR fighters were responsible for banditry. He also said that he fully adhered to a peace agreement signed by the CNR and the government in 2003.

In March, the government said that it had destroyed nearly 3,000 weapons it had purchased from former CNR fighters as part of a programme to demobilize them. Frédéric Bintsamou said that the government had failed to demobilize his fighters and reintegrate some of them into the national security forces, as stipulated in the 2003 peace agreement. In December, Frédéric Bintsamou formally accepted the post of Delegate General in charge of promoting the values of peace and repairing the ravages of war, to which he had been appointed by President Sassou-Nguesso in 2007.

Freedom of assembly, expression and movement

As in previous years, government security forces used excessive force to suppress peaceful demonstrations. Members of opposition political parties were denied the enjoyment of their rights to freedom of assembly, expression and movement.

Three days after the July presidential elections, a number of opposition political parties held a demonstration in the capital, Brazzaville, to protest against what they called fraudulent elections. Government forces used tear gas and live ammunition to disperse the demonstrators, injuring some.

Reacting to the July demonstrations, the government banned all opposition demonstrations. They also barred opposition leaders from travelling out of the capital or the country, including former Prime Minister Ange Edouard Poungui and former president of the Congolese Bar Association Ambroise Hervé Malonga. Government and security officials said that the opposition leaders were wanted in connection with investigations into acts of violence allegedly committed during the July demonstrations. The government lifted the travel restrictions in early November after protests by the leaders affected and local human rights organizations. None of the opposition leaders subjected to restrictions was charged.

■ Four foreign journalists who covered the elections and demonstrations were harassed by the security forces. Arnaud Zajtman and Marlène Rabaud of France 24 television, and Thomas Fessy of the BBC, had their equipment confiscated. Catherine Ninin of Radio France International was reportedly threatened with violence. A government spokesman accused the journalists of publishing false information before and after the elections, and of bias towards government opponents.

Repression of dissent – arrests

Several people linked to opposition political parties were detained in the aftermath of the July elections. Former army lieutenant Céléstin Ngalouo and two others in charge of opposition presidential candidate Mathias Dzon's security were arrested soon after the July demonstrations in Brazzaville. Government officials said that those arrested were wanted in connection with shootings during the demonstrations. The opposition denied that any of their supporters had opened fire and blamed the shootings on government forces. Those arrested were released without charge several weeks later.

■ Former army colonel Ferdinand Mbahou was arrested in July after he returned from France, where he had lived for more than 10 years. He had returned to help heal rifts within the leadership of the Pan-African Union for Social Democracy (Union panafricaine pour la démocratie sociale) party. The authorities said that he was arrested in connection with inflammatory speeches he had made in France. He was still held without charge at the end of the year.

Asylum-seekers

■ Three asylum-seekers from the Democratic Republic of the Congo spent a fifth year in military detention without charge or trial. Germain Ndabamenya Etikilome, Médard Mabwaka Egbonde and Bosch Ndala Umba were arrested in 2004 in Brazzaville. Germain Ndabamenya Etikilome was seriously ill early in the year and for several weeks did not receive treatment. His health improved after he received medication. Despite many requests, the authorities failed to give any reason for the men's continued detention.

CÔTE D'IVOIRE

REPUBLIC OF CÔTE D'IVOIRE

Head of state:	Laurent Gbagbo
Head of government:	Guillaume Soro
Death penalty:	abolitionist for all crimes
Population:	21.1 million
Life expectancy:	56.8 years
Under-5 mortality (m/f):	129/117 per 1,000
Adult literacy:	48.7 per cent

Presidential elections scheduled originally for 2005 were again postponed. Government security forces and the Forces Nouvelles (New Forces), a coalition of armed groups in control of the north since 2002, continued to commit human rights abuses; harassment and physical assault remained rampant, notably at roadblocks.

Background

Despite some progress in the voter identification process and strong pressure from the international community, presidential elections, scheduled for November, were again postponed due to delays in voter registration. Disarmament of pro-government militias and armed elements of the Forces Nouvelles provided for by the 2007 Ouagadougou peace agreement continued to be impeded by mutual distrust and disagreement as to whether disarmament should be carried out before or after the elections.

In October, following a report by a UN panel of experts identifying seven instances of violations of the arms embargo by both sides, the UN Security Council renewed for a further year the embargo on arms transfers and diamond exports as well as sanctions against individuals. The Security Council stressed that these measures could be reviewed once free, fair and transparent presidential elections were held, but warned that more sanctions would be considered if the electoral process was threatened. The Security Council also decided that international peacekeeping forces would remain in the country until after the presidential elections.

Unlawful killings

The security forces were responsible for unlawful killings and widespread abuses committed to extort

C

money at checkpoints and during inspections of identity documents.

■ In January, following a quarrel between two farmers, one of them, Yao Kra, was shot dead by a gendarme reportedly at point-blank range in a village near San Pedro, some 400 kilometres west of Abidjan. His relatives lodged a complaint before the court but no progress in the case was reported and the gendarme allegedly responsible was not arrested or brought to justice.

Abuses by armed groups

Fighters and supporters of the New Forces were responsible for human rights abuses, including torture and other ill-treatment, arbitrary detention and widespread extortion. A climate of impunity prevailed due to the absence of a functioning judicial system in the north of the country.

■ In June, armed elements of the New Forces attacked the village of Pétionnara, in the centre-north of the country, a region where the exploitation of gold mines has created tensions between the population and elements of the New Forces. The armed elements raided and looted homes, fired in the air and beat people trying to resist. Some days later, officials from the New Forces came to the village and apologized for the attack but no action was apparently taken against those responsible.

Freedom of expression – media

Several journalists and newspapers were harassed by the authorities.

■ In September, Touré Moussa, director of the newspaper Nord Sud Quotidien, was briefly arrested and interrogated by gendarmes in Abidjan following publication of an article questioning promotions in the army. Some days later, he was again summoned by the gendarmerie for giving a radio interview on the reasons for his arrest.

Corporate accountability

In September, the UN Special Rapporteur on the adverse effects of the movement and dumping of toxic and dangerous products and wastes on the enjoyment of human rights presented his report on the impact of the 2006 toxic waste dumping in Abidjan. The dumping reportedly resulted in the death of 15 people and caused more than 100,000 people to seek medical assistance. The Rapporteur

identified an urgent need to address decontamination, health care and compensation issues.

Also in September, nearly 30,000 victims who had brought a claim for compensation against the multinational company Trafigura before the High Court in the UK reached an out-of-court settlement in which the company agreed to pay the claimants approximately US$45 million. However, in October an individual falsely claiming to represent all of the victims in the settlement successfully applied to an Ivorian court to freeze the money, thereby preventing its distribution, and have it transferred to his organization. In November, another Ivorian court refused his application to transfer the money but kept the freezing order in place. By the end of the year the claimants in the UK settlement were still awaiting their compensation.

Amnesty International visit/report

🚌 An Amnesty International delegation visited Côte d'Ivoire in February.

📄 Côte d'Ivoire: Authorities must ensure toxic waste compensation reaches victims, 5 November 2009

CROATIA

REPUBLIC OF CROATIA

Head of state:	Stjepan Mesić
Head of government:	Jadranka Kosor (replaced Ivo Sanader in July)
Death penalty:	abolitionist for all crimes
Population:	4.4 million
Life expectancy:	76 years
Under-5 mortality (m/f):	8/7 per 1,000
Adult literacy:	98.7 per cent

Very limited progress was made in the prosecution of cases of war crimes allegedly committed by members of the Croatian Army and police forces against Croatian Serbs and members of other minorities during the 1991-1995 war. There was a continued lack of co-operation with the International Criminal Tribunal for the former Yugoslavia (Tribunal) over military documents relating to Operation Storm in 1995. Some cases of attacks on journalists

remained unresolved. **Discrimination against Roma and Croatian Serbs, in access to economic and social rights among other things, continued.**

Background

Accession negotiations with the EU reopened in September. These had been suspended in December 2008 due to a border dispute with Slovenia as well as the lack of co-operation with the Tribunal. As a result of the negative report by the Tribunal's Chief Prosecutor, some EU member states continued to oppose opening negotiations on the judiciary and human rights chapter.

International justice – war crimes

Both the UN Human Rights Committee (HRC) and the Tribunal's Chief Prosecutor reported that Croatia continued to fail to submit to the Tribunal all outstanding military documents related to Operation Storm, conducted in 1995, for which three Croatian Army generals (Ante Gotovina, Ivan Čermak and Mladen Markač) were on trial in The Hague.

Despite statements by government representatives on the readiness and willingness of the authorities to co-operate with the Tribunal, the search for the military documents remained inconclusive.

The trial of Momčilo Perišić, which included, among other things, charges relating to the shelling of Zagreb in May 1995, continued before the Trial Chamber of the Tribunal.

The trial of Jovica Stanišić and Franko Simatović resumed in June, following its suspension in 2008. They had been charged with, among other things, racial and religious persecution, murder, deportation and inhumane acts against the non-Serb population in the Serb-controlled areas of Croatia during the 1991-1995 war.

Justice system – war crimes

The authorities continued to fail to investigate war crimes committed during the 1991-1995 war by members of the Croatian Army and police forces against Croatian Serbs and members of other minorities. A lack of political will to deal with those cases remained one of the main obstacles. The disproportionate number of cases against Croatian Serbs was demonstrated in a report in the newspaper *Jutarnji List,* where the Minister of Justice said in September that 2 per cent of the cases which had

been prosecuted by the Croatian judiciary were against ethnic Croats whereas the remaining 98 per cent included cases against Croatian Serbs and other minorities. The Minister's own view was that this was understandable, as he claimed that Croatian Serbs had committed more war crimes than ethnic Croats.

Measures designed by the government to address impunity for war crimes remained unimplemented. Only one case was under prosecution in 2009 in one of the special war crimes chambers established at four county courts in Zagreb, Osijek, Rijeka and Split. These had been established in 2003 in order to try war crimes cases outside the community where the crimes were committed, a move which was supposed to lessen potential pressure on witnesses and reduce bias.

■ In May, Branimir Glavaš and five others were convicted by the Zagreb County Court. Branimir Glavaš, who was convicted for having failed to prevent his subordinates from detaining, ill-treating and killing civilians and of having directly participated in some of the crimes in his capacity as local military leader in 1991, was sentenced to 10 years' imprisonment. The other five were found guilty of the unlawful arrest, torture and killing of Croatian Serb civilians in Osijek in 1991 and sentenced to between five and eight years' imprisonment.

Shortly after the judgement, Branimir Glavaš, who held a Bosnian passport, fled to Bosnia and Herzegovina and remained there. The Croatian authorities failed to secure his extradition as the two countries did not have an extradition agreement between them.

■ An appeal trial started in November before the Supreme Court against the verdict in the case against two Croatian Army generals, Mirko Norac and Rahim Ademi. In 2008, the Zagreb County Court acquitted Rahim Ademi of all charges, although Mirko Norac was found guilty of some of the charges and sentenced to seven years' imprisonment. The accused were both indicted for war crimes, including murders, inhumane treatment, plunder and wanton destruction of property, against Croatian Serb civilians and prisoners of war during military operations in 1993.

The action plan on prosecution of war crimes cases failed to address ethnic bias in the judiciary. The action plan envisaged that priority cases would be selected by local prosecutors. Following this plan, in the Sisak area, where approximately 100 Croatian

C

Serbs were killed or disappeared at the beginning of the war, none of the cases selected for prioritization involved Croatian Serbs as victims; in all seven priority cases, the victims were ethnic Croats. This only increased ethnic bias and widened the impunity for crimes committed by members of the Croatian Army and police forces.

In March, the UN Committee on the Elimination of Racial Discrimination (CERD) expressed its concerns at reports of ethnic discrimination in the prosecution of war crimes cases and recommended that Croatia effectively investigate and prosecute all war crimes irrespective of the ethnicity of the victims and the perpetrators.

In October, the HRC expressed concerns over impunity for war crimes, including the fact that many potential cases of war crimes remain unresolved and that the selection of cases was disproportionately directed against Croatian Serbs. The Croatian authorities were given a deadline of one year to implement these, and other, recommendations.

In October, the European Commission in its progress report on Croatia also observed that impunity for war crimes remained a problem, especially where victims were ethnic Serbs or perpetrators were members of the Croatian Army. The report stated that many crimes still had not been prosecuted due to a combination of factors, including intimidation of witnesses and reluctance of the police and prosecutors to prosecute such cases.

Freedom of expression – journalists

The authorities continued to fail to protect journalists reporting on war crimes cases and organized crime from intimidation and attacks. The slow progress in the prosecution of some of these cases created an atmosphere of impunity for the attackers.

■ There was no progress in an investigation of a physical attack on Dušan Miljuš, a journalist for the newspaper *Jutarnji List*, who was severely beaten in June 2008 by unidentified individuals in front of his house in Zagreb. The journalist continued to receive death threats.

■ In January a criminal case was opened against journalist Željko Peratović for "disseminating information likely to upset the population". The prosecution was initiated at the behest of the Minister of Interior, whom the journalist alleged was obstructing an investigation into the killing in 2000 of Milan Levar, a potential witness of the Tribunal.

■ In March, *Jutarnji List* journalist Drago Hedl and a photographer were forcibly removed from a public press conference organized by Branimir Glavaš, a member of parliament (before his conviction in May for war crimes in his capacity as local military leader in 1991 in Osijek). In previous years Drago Hedl had faced intimidation, including death threats, as a result of his investigation of war crimes committed in Osijek during the war.

In October the HRC expressed concerns about intimidation and attacks on journalists. It observed that those alleged crimes were rarely investigated and those responsible seldom brought to justice, which diminished the freedom of the press. The HRC urged Croatia to take measures to prevent the intimidation of journalists and to bring those responsible for such attacks to justice.

Discrimination
Roma

Roma continued to face discrimination in access to economic and social rights, including education, employment and housing. Measures undertaken by the authorities remained insufficient.

In April, the Grand Chamber of the European Court of Human Rights in Strasbourg held a hearing in the case of *Oršuš and others*. The case involves allegations of ethnic segregation of pupils in Roma-only classes in the Međimurje region of Croatia.

Both the CERD and the HRC expressed their concerns at the segregation of Romani pupils in the education system.

Croatian Serbs

The Croatian authorities continued to fail to guarantee the rights of Croatian Serbs, many of whom were displaced during the 1991-1995 war.

In October, the NGO Human Rights Watch reported that Croatian Serb returnees continued to face difficulties in repossessing their homes which were occupied by other tenants, often despite court judgements in their favour. Many returnees were not able to benefit from reconstruction programmes and they also faced problems in accessing employment.

In March the CERD expressed its concerns at a substantial number of unresolved cases relating to restitution of property and tenancy rights, and urged the authorities to implement fair and transparent measures to enable the sustainable return of Croatian Serbs.

In October, the HRC urged the authorities to verify the number of people not willing or not able to return, and to explore their reasons for not returning.

Right to health – mental health

In October, the HRC expressed its concerns at the ongoing use of "cage beds" as a measure to restrain mental health patients, including children in social care institutions in Croatia. It called on the country to immediately abolish the use of cage beds and to establish an inspection system in mental institutions.

Amnesty International report

📄 Briefing to the UN Human Rights Committee on the Republic of Croatia (EUR 64/001/2009)

CUBA

REPUBLIC OF CUBA

Head of state and government:	Raúl Castro Ruz
Death penalty:	retentionist
Population:	11.2 million
Life expectancy:	78.5 years
Under-5 mortality (m/f):	9/6 per 1,000
Adult literacy:	99.8 per cent

Civil and political rights continued to be severely restricted by the authorities. Government critics continued to be imprisoned; many reported that they were beaten during arrest. Restrictions on freedom of expression were commonplace. The government continued to curtail freedom of association and assembly. The US embargo against Cuba remained operational, despite increasing opposition to it within and outside the USA.

Background

Relations between Cuba and the USA improved during the year. Both governments initiated dialogues relating to migration issues and the re-establishment of a direct postal service between the two countries. Representatives of the US Congress visited Cuba in April and met the Cuban President.

The Council of Ministers underwent a major reshuffle in March and key ministers during Fidel Castro's last years in power were replaced.

In June, Cuba's 47-year suspension from the Organization of American States (OAS) was lifted. However, Cuba's participation in the OAS is conditional on its adherence to OAS principles.

In February, Cuba's human rights record was assessed under the UN Universal Periodic Review. Cuba adopted some broad undertakings but rejected most of the recommendations relating to the protection and promotion of civil and political rights. Cuba was re-elected to the Human Rights Council for another three-year term in May. The visit of the UN Special Rapporteur on torture, planned for October, was postponed by the Cuban authorities until 2010.

Prisoners of conscience

At the end of the year, 55 prisoners of conscience continued to be detained solely for the peaceful exercise of their right to freedom of expression. Prisoner of conscience Nelson Aguiar Ramírez, was released during 2009 on health grounds and Reinaldo Miguel Labrada Peña completed his sentence.

■ Human rights defenders Darsi Ferrer and his wife, Yusnaimy Jorge, were arrested on 9 July at their home in Havana City and charged with possessing or receiving illegally obtained merchandise (*receptación*). They were due to lead the "Stroll of Your Dreams" march along the Malecón, Havana's sea front, later that day. Darsi Ferrer, a physician and President of the Juan Bruno Zayas Independent Health and Human Rights Centre, which supports marginalized members of Cuban society in Havana City, was beaten by seven police officers at the Aguilera Police Station in Lawton. The couple were conditionally released shortly after midnight the same day. On 21 July, Darsi Ferrer was re-arrested and charged with "contempt of the authorities". He was refused bail and taken to Valle Grande Prison in Havana Province, a maximum security prison for convicted criminals. He remained detained awaiting trial at the end of the year.

Freedom of expression, assembly and association

Freedom of expression continued to be severely restricted. All mass media and the internet remained under state control. The authorities continued to block access to the websites of bloggers and journalists critical of the government. Criminal charges such as "dangerousness" continued to be used to restrict dissidents from exercising freedom of expression, association and assembly. Independent journalists and bloggers faced harassment. Some were threatened with criminal prosecution and a number were detained.

■ In September, Yosvani Anzardo Hernández, editor of the digital magazine *Candonga* and a correspondent for a Miami-based news website, was arrested by police officers at his home in Holguín Province. At the time of his arrest, the computer server hosting his digital magazine was confiscated. He was held at Pedernales Prison in Holguín Province during which time he was threatened with criminal prosecution under Law No. 88 on the Protection of National Independence and the Economy of Cuba. He was released without charge after two weeks.

Freedom of movement

Restrictions on freedom of movement prevented journalists and human rights and political activists from carrying out legitimate and peaceful activities.

■ In September, Yoani Sánchez, author of the popular blog *Generación Y,* was denied an exit visa by the Cuban authorities. She had been due to travel to the USA to receive the Maria Moors Cabot prize for journalism at Columbia University. She was also denied an exit visa to travel to Brazil following an invitation from the Brazilian Senate to present her book at a conference and address the legislature. In November, Yoani Sánchez and blogger Orlando Luis Pardo were forced into a car by state security agents and beaten and threatened before being released. The attackers told Yoani Sánchez "this is the end of it".

The US embargo against Cuba

The US embargo against Cuba continued to have a detrimental impact on the economic and social rights of Cubans. US legislation restricting exports of US-manufactured or patented supplies and equipment to Cuba continued to hinder access to medicine and medical technologies. UN agencies operating in Cuba were also affected by the embargo.

In April, US President Barack Obama eased travel restrictions, allowing individuals to visit relatives in Cuba and send them remittances. However, in September, he extended for another year his authority to apply financial sanctions against Cuba under the

Trading with the Enemy Act of 1917. For the 18th consecutive year, a resolution calling on the USA to end its embargo against Cuba was adopted by an overwhelming majority at the UN General Assembly. A bipartisan group of US senators introduced a bill that would allow all US citizens to travel freely to Cuba for the first time since 1962. Other bills were introduced to Congress aimed at easing or totally lifting the embargo. At the end of the year, these bills remained pending.

Death penalty

There were no executions. Three people remained on death row at the end of 2009; most death sentences had been commuted by President Raúl Castro in 2008.

■ Otto René Rodríguez Llerena and Raúl Ernesto Cruz León, both Salvadoran nationals, remained under sentence of death. They had been convicted of terrorism charges in 1999. Their appeals against the sentences were pending before the People's Supreme Court at the end of the year.

Amnesty International visits/reports

🚗 Amnesty International has not been allowed to visit Cuba since 1990.

▧ Cuba: Fear for safety – Jorge Luis García Pérez; Iris Tamara Pérez Aguilera; Carlos Michael Morales Rodriguez; Diosiris Santana Pérez; Ernesto Mederos Arrozarena (AMR 25/003/2009)

▧ Cuba: Harassment – Edgard López Moreno (AMR 25/005/2009)

▧ The US embargo against Cuba – Its impact on economic and social rights (AMR 25/007/2009)

CYPRUS

REPUBLIC OF CYPRUS

Head of state and government:	**Demetris Christofias**
Death penalty:	**abolitionist for all crimes**
Population:	**0.9 million**
Life expectancy:	**79.6 years**
Under-5 mortality (m/f):	**7/6 per 1,000**
Adult literacy:	**97.7 per cent**

Despite new legislation, trafficking in women for the purposes of sexual exploitation continued. Ten police officers accused of beating two students in 2005 were acquitted. The Law on Refugees was amended in November.

Background

Negotiations between the Greek Cypriot and Turkish Cypriot leadership continued. Among the areas under discussion were property and migration, including restitution and refugee protection. Minority and women's rights were not addressed within the negotiations.

Missing persons

The UN Committee on Missing Persons in Cyprus continued its work. Between January and September the remains of 104 individuals were exhumed from different burial sites located across the island.

Refugees' and migrants' rights

In November 2009, the (Amending) Law on Refugees transposed into domestic legislation the EU Asylum Procedures Directive. Under the new legislation and in combination with Article 146 of the Constitution, asylum applicants are entitled to submit an appeal against a negative decision at first instance to the Review Authority for Refugees or the Supreme Court. Asylum applicants can appeal against a negative decision issued by the Review Authority to the Supreme Court. Concerns were expressed that the amendments do not guarantee the right to an effective remedy before a court or tribunal as provided for in Article 39 of the Asylum Procedures Directive, since the Supreme Court's jurisdiction is limited to a review of the lawfulness and not the merits of a case. The new Law provides a free interpreter for asylum applicants when they appear

before the Review Authority and before the Supreme Court under certain conditions. It also provides for the Commissioner for the Rights of the Child to represent unaccompanied minors during asylum proceedings.

In May the UN Committee on Economic, Social and Cultural Rights expressed concern that rejected asylum-seekers and irregular migrants were held for long periods in detention and in inadequate conditions.

In September the police conducted a sweep of migrants living in the old part of Nicosia. Serious concerns were expressed by the Ombudsperson over the way the operation was conducted, such as house raids and the setting up of roadblocks in city streets.

In November the authorities rescued 110 Romanian workers brought to Cyprus by a trafficking ring. The 110 Romanians were living in squalid conditions in a shed in the Nicosia suburb of Tseri.

Violence against women and girls

In May the UN Committee on Economic, Social and Cultural Rights expressed continuing concerns at the extent of trafficking in women for the purposes of sexual exploitation. This was despite the abolition of the system of artists' visas in 2008, which had contributed to trafficking.

Police and security forces

In March the Nicosia Criminal Court acquitted 10 police officers on trial for offences including cruel, inhuman and degrading treatment. They were accused of excessive use of force on two handcuffed students, Marcos Papageorghiou and Yiannos Nicolaou, in December 2005. The acquittal was controversial because of the existence of videotaped footage of the ill-treatment. In November the public prosecutor filed an appeal against the acquittal.

C

CZECH REPUBLIC

CZECH REPUBLIC
Head of state:	Václav Klaus
Head of government:	Jan Fischer (replaced Mirek Topolánek in May)
Death penalty:	abolitionist for all crimes
Population:	10.4 million
Life expectancy:	76.4 years
Under-5 mortality (m/f):	5/4 per 1,000

Parliament passed anti-discrimination legislation blocked for several years by presidential opposition. Anti-Roma hate speech and marches by far-right parties and groups increased. Roma continued to be segregated in education and housing. Although the government apologized for the forced sterilization of Romani women in the past, individual complainants were refused compensation by the courts.

Background

In March the government of Prime Minister Mirek Topolánek lost a vote of no confidence and was replaced in May by an interim government led by Jan Fischer.

Parliament adopted anti-discrimination legislation in June, overturning a veto by President Klaus and fulfilling obligations under the EU Race and Employment Equality Directives after several years' delay. The new law guaranteed the right to equal treatment and banned discrimination in areas including education, employment and housing.

Discrimination – Roma

Roma faced increasingly overt public hostility, as well as segregation in schools and housing and discrimination in employment.

Attacks on Roma

In March the Supreme Administrative Court, citing insufficient evidence, rejected a government proposal to dissolve the far-right Workers' Party, which organized vigilante patrols targeting Roma.

The European Commission against Racism and Intolerance (ECRI) expressed concern in a report in September at mounting anti-Roma hate speech in public discourse and at repeated demonstrations by extreme right-wing groups. It recommended vigorous implementation of laws prohibiting racist violence and incitement to hatred.

■ On 4 April far-right groups organized a march through the Romani district in the town of Přerov. The Workers' Party, which initially announced the march, later distanced itself from the event. About 500 demonstrators, chanting anti-Roma slogans and joined by local inhabitants, marched through the town and the Romani neighbourhood. Around 700 police officers prevented direct attacks on Roma, but violence later broke out as demonstrators attacked riot and mounted police.

■ On 18 April in the village of Vítkov, Molotov cocktails were thrown into the home of a Romani family, where Pavel Kudrik lived with his partner, four daughters and two other family members. The fire completely destroyed their home and seriously injured the parents. Their two-year-old daughter, Natálka, had burns over 80 per cent of her body, was in an induced coma for three months and in hospital for over seven months. In August the police arrested 12 suspects: four were charged in connection with the attack; eight were released without charge. The police said the suspects were supporters of far-right groups. According to Czech Television, they were supporters of the Autonomous Nationalists, an organization allegedly linked to the Workers' Party.

■ In October the police arrested eight suspects accused of attacks on Roma in Havířov in November 2008. The case was before the Regional Court in Ostrava at the end of 2009.

Education

Two years after the European Court of Human Rights ruled that the Czech Republic had discriminated against Romani children by placing them in special schools, Romani children continued to be segregated. They were still over-represented in elementary schools and classes for pupils with "mild mental disabilities" or in segregated mainstream schools and classes. This was despite the Schools Act in force since 2005, which abolished the category of "special schools" for pupils with mild mental disabilities. Such classes and schools often provided inferior education.

The Czech NGO People in Need reported in February that the education system tended to exclude pupils with special educational needs. An analysis of the segregation of children from disadvantaged backgrounds, commissioned by the Ministry of Education and published in April, found that almost half of Romani pupils in elementary schools either failed their grade or were transferred to special schools.

■ In April the Prague City Court rejected a complaint by Jaroslav Suchý against the Ministry of Education that he had suffered discrimination and been denied the right to education. Jaroslav Suchý said that he had been placed in a special school because of his membership of the Romani community. The Court ruled that he had not proved his case and that the placement had been justified by a psychological assessment.

■ In May Valašské Meziříčí Town Council announced a plan to create special classes for Roma and non-Roma in the first grade of the local mainstream school. The proposal was presented as an attempt to address the special education needs of Romani pupils. After criticism from the Minister for Human Rights and the Ministry of Education, the Council eventually withdrew the plan.

Housing

Roma continued to experience segregation in housing. In its September report, ECRI recorded no positive developments in tackling this issue and highlighted the government's failure to hold to account local authorities that do not fulfil housing rights.

■ Z§vůle Práva, a Czech NGO that provides legal advice to Roma, brought cases against local authorities: in July alleging ethnic segregation of Roma in housing in Kladno, and in August alleging discrimination against Roma in accessing permanent residence status in the city of Ostrava.

Enforced sterilization of Romani women

There was some movement towards acknowledging responsibility for enforced sterilizations carried out in the past. In November the Prime Minister expressed regret over the illegal sterilizations, and asked the Minister of Health to report on the implementation of existing regulations that prohibited them. According to the Group of Women Harmed by Forced Sterilization, a Czech NGO, at least 100 women may have been sterilized against their will. Although most forced sterilizations were carried out in the 1970s and 1980s, the most recent reportedly occurred in 2007.

■ In October the Constitutional Court dismissed a claim for financial compensation from a Romani woman who had been illegally sterilized, on the grounds that her legal action was beyond the time limit for such claims. She had received an apology from a hospital in Vitkovice after the Regional Court in Ostrava decided in 2005 that the doctors acted illegally when they carried out the sterilization without her informed consent. The Minister for Human Rights subsequently announced that the state was nevertheless obliged to take a position that reflected the non-reversible impact of sterilization on women's lives.

Torture and other ill-treatment

In March the National Defender of Rights (Ombudsperson) reported that some psychiatric institutions continued to use restraint beds even where there was no risk to the patients or their environment. Restraint beds were in some cases included in the inventory of institutions. In September, the Ministry of Health issued a methodological guide to regulate the use of restraint techniques, including net-beds. In 2004 the European Committee for the Prevention of Torture had recommended the immediate withdrawal from service of cage-beds and the removal as soon as possible of net-beds as means for managing patients or residents in a state of agitation.

Amnesty International visits/report

🚌 Amnesty International delegates visited the Czech Republic in February and April.

📕 Injustice renamed: Discrimination in education of Roma persists in Czech Republic (EUR 73/003/2009)

C

DEMOCRATIC REPUBLIC OF THE CONGO

DEMOCRATIC REPUBLIC OF THE CONGO

Head of state:	Joseph Kabila
Head of government:	Adolphe Muzito
Death penalty:	retentionist
Population:	66 million
Life expectancy:	47.6 years
Under-5 mortality (m/f):	209/187 per 1,000
Adult literacy:	67.2 per cent

Serious violations of international humanitarian and human rights law were committed in eastern Democratic Republic of the Congo (DRC) by armed groups and the national army, notably in the context of government military operations against the Democratic Liberation Forces of Rwanda (FDLR) armed group. Government military, intelligence and police services were responsible for serious and sometimes politically motivated human rights violations across the country, including frequent arbitrary arrests, acts of torture and other ill-treatment, and sexual violence. Scores of people were sentenced to death; no executions were reported. There were growing official restrictions on the freedom of the press and a number of threats or attacks against human rights defenders. Relations between the DRC and Angola deteriorated, culminating in a reciprocal arbitrary mass expulsion of migrants and refugees in September.

Armed conflict

In January, Congolese and Rwandan government forces launched a joint military offensive against the FDLR in North-Kivu province. Rwandan forces withdrew in February. A second offensive against the FDLR, known as Kimia II, was launched by the national army (FARDC) in March, with the support of the UN peacekeeping mission to the DRC, MONUC. Kimia II was extended to South-Kivu province in July and continued in both provinces at the end of the year. In October, the UN Special Rapporteur on extrajudicial, summary or arbitrary executions described military operations against the FDLR as "catastrophic" from a human rights perspective.

The military operations followed a rapprochement between the governments of the DRC and Rwanda and a peace deal in early 2009 to end the rebellion by the Rwanda-backed National Congress for the Defence of the People (CNDP) armed group in North-Kivu. As part of the peace deal, large numbers of CNDP and other armed group fighters were hurriedly integrated into the FARDC and took a leading role in anti-FDLR operations. The government failed to vet, train or properly pay these newly integrated forces. Former armed group chains of command were left intact. Lack of effective government control over these forces contributed to poor respect for human rights by the FARDC.

MONUC's support of Kimia II, although authorized by UN Security Council resolution, was criticized because of war crimes and other serious human rights violations committed by the FARDC and, in retaliation, by the FDLR. MONUC's strength at the end of the year stood at around 20,000 personnel, concentrated in eastern DRC.

FARDC military operations, supported by Ugandan government forces and MONUC, continued against the Lord's Resistance Army (LRA) in north-eastern DRC. The LRA was responsible for violations of international humanitarian law, including the killing and abduction of civilians.

In June, a government and UN Stabilization and Reconstruction (STAREC) Plan for eastern DRC was announced. The plan aims to consolidate security and state authority, assist war-affected populations and relaunch economic activity. A key part of the plan involves progressively deploying police as well as administrative and judicial authorities to replace the FARDC in the east. The plan faced considerable challenges, not least the continuing insecurity in the east and the absence of essential government reform of its armed forces.

Intercommunal violence flared around Dongo, Equateur province in the north-west in November, leaving at least 100 people dead and an estimated 92,000 displaced.

Unlawful killings

Armed groups and government forces were responsible for hundreds of unlawful killings and attacks on humanitarian personnel, committed particularly in the context of Kimia II.

■ In the course of anti-FDLR operations, FARDC soldiers unlawfully killed at least 100 civilians, mostly women and children, in a refugee camp at Shalio, Walikale territory, North-Kivu province, between 27 and 30 April.
■ In apparent retaliation, on 10 May the FDLR unlawfully killed at least 96 civilians in Busurungi, Walikale territory. Some of the victims were burned alive in their homes.

Violence against women and girls
Military operations in eastern DRC were attended by an upsurge in rapes. High levels of rape were also reported in other areas of the country unaffected by conflict, including the cities of Lubumbashi and Kinshasa.
■ In June, an NGO medical centre reported receiving around 60 new cases a month of women and girls who had been raped in southern Lubero territory, North-Kivu, by FARDC, FDLR and other militia forces.

Children's rights
A new Child Protection Code was adopted in January. The law sets out a range of administrative, judicial, educational and health care measures to protect children. It criminalizes, among other things, acts of torture, abduction, trafficking of and sexual violence against children, and the enrolment or use of children in armed forces or groups and the police. Implementation remained weak, however.

In January, the UN Committee on the Rights of the Child concluded that the government and armed groups were responsible for wholesale violations of the Convention on the Rights of the Child, including recruitment and use of children in armed conflict, abductions, trafficking, torture and other ill-treatment, arbitrary arrest and unlawful detention of children, as well as high levels of sexual violence and economic exploitation. It expressed concern at high rates of infant mortality and low rates of school enrolment, particularly of girls. In November, the UN Children's Fund UNICEF reported that more than 43,000 children were working in mines in the DRC.
■ In April, Amnesty International delegates witnessed children working at a gold mine at Goné, Mwenga territory, South-Kivu province. Other miners were using mercury, without protection, to soak up particles of gold from mud in the riverbed.

Child soldiers
An estimated 3,000 to 4,000 children were serving with armed groups in eastern DRC, including new recruits. The LRA abducted several hundred people, mainly children, from Orientale province, north-eastern DRC, to hold in domestic or sexual slavery and to use as fighters. Many children also still served with the army, although the FARDC formally ended child recruitment in 2004. They included children associated with armed groups who were integrated into the FARDC in early 2009. The army also used children as porters during operations. UN and NGO child protection and community reintegration programmes for former child soldiers remained under-resourced.

Internally displaced people and refugees
By the end of the year, around 2 million people were internally displaced, including hundreds of thousands displaced by the Kimia II offensive. Around half of the displaced were children. Tens of thousands of displaced people in less secure areas remained outside the reach of humanitarian assistance. Many were in extremely poor health following days or weeks of flight.

An estimated 160,000 DRC nationals were expelled from Angola to the DRC between January and October, peaking in September (see Angola entry). These arbitrary mass expulsions were carried out under deplorable humanitarian conditions and accompanied by other human rights violations, including sexual violence, torture and other ill-treatment by Angolan security forces. A large number of those expelled reportedly drowned during river-crossings or were asphyxiated in overcrowded vehicles. In September, in retaliation, the DRC authorities expelled thousands of Angolan nationals, including an undetermined number of people recognized as refugees. In October, both countries agreed to stop the expulsions.

Arms trade and exploitation of natural resources
In November, the UN Group of Experts concluded that the FARDC, as well as the FDLR and other armed groups, continued to benefit from systematic exploitation of DRC's mineral and other natural resources. The Group's report highlighted instances of gold smuggling by the FDLR to Uganda, Burundi and the United Arab Emirates; of collaboration between

D

FARDC officers and the FDLR; and of suspected arms trafficking to the FDLR from Tanzania and Burundi. The report alleged that the CNDP had retained control of much of its weaponry, despite integration of its forces into the FARDC. It presented evidence of states' failure to comply with the UN arms embargo and sanctions, claiming that such instances "seriously undermined the credibility of the sanctions regime".

■ In April, an army sergeant told Amnesty International that systematic military exploitation took place at a large cassiterite mine in Walungu territory, South-Kivu province. He said that the profits were split between two FARDC army brigades and the regional army headquarters in Bukavu.

Torture and other ill-treatment

Torture and other ill-treatment remained common in military, police and intelligence service custody. Armed groups were also responsible for such abuses. Conditions in all detention centres and prisons constituted cruel, inhuman or degrading treatment. Scores of prisoners and pre-trial detainees died from starvation and treatable illnesses. Rape and other sexual abuse of female prisoners were widespread. There were frequent mass escapes from prisons and detention centres, including by army personnel accused or convicted of human rights violations.

■ Twenty women detainees were raped at Goma's Muzenze prison during an attempted mass escape in June. The women were attacked in their cells by a group of military prisoners armed with weapons smuggled into the prison.

Death penalty

Military courts sentenced scores of people to death during the year, including civilians. No executions were reported.

Human rights defenders and freedom of expression

A number of human rights activists were arbitrarily arrested and ill-treated in custody. There was an increase in death threats against human rights defenders and journalists, usually received by mobile phone text message. Two human rights defenders were prosecuted after their organizations published reports critical of the authorities. Trade unionists and journalists were arrested after they alleged corruption by government ministers and other officials. The

government threatened that local and international journalists would be tried before military courts if they published articles considered insulting to the army.

■ In September, Golden Misabiko, President of the NGO African Association for the Defence of Human Rights in Katanga province (ASADHO/Katanga), was sentenced in his absence to 12 months' imprisonment, with eight months' suspended, for "spreading false information likely to alarm or incite the population" after ASADHO/Katanga published a report alleging complicity by state officials in illegal mining at Shinkolobwe uranium mine.

■ Robert Ilunga, President of the Friends of Nelson Mandela (ANMDH) human rights NGO, was arrested by the intelligence services in Kinshasa in August. He was accused of "spreading false information" and "defamation" in relation to an ANMDH report that alleged mistreatment of workers at a factory in Kasangulu, Bas-Congo province. The report alleged that a "leading lady" was involved in the company, which the authorities believed referred to Olive Lembe, the wife of President Joseph Kabila. After nine days' incommunicado detention, Robert Ilunga was transferred to Kinshasa's central prison. He was granted provisional release by a Kinshasa court in October. No trial date was set.

Impunity

In July, the government announced a policy of "zero tolerance" for human rights violations committed by its forces. A number of soldiers and mainly junior officers were prosecuted by military field court in the Kivu provinces for human rights violations, including rape. The government, however, refused to surrender Bosco Ntaganda to the International Criminal Court (ICC), where he was wanted on war crimes charges. It also refused to suspend from duty, pending investigation and trial, other senior army officers suspected of serious human rights violations. Bosco Ntaganda and many of these officers had FARDC command roles in Kimia II. In March, a military court sentenced former militia leader Kyungu Mutanga, alias Gédéon, to death for war crimes, crimes against humanity, insurrection and "terrorism" committed in Katanga province between 2004 and 2006.

International justice

German authorities arrested Ignace Murwanashyaka, president of the FDLR, and his deputy, Straton

Musoni, in November. The arrests, on charges of crimes against humanity and war crimes committed by the FDLR in eastern DRC, reportedly followed a year-long investigation and were the first arrests of senior political or military leaders for crimes committed in the Kivu provinces. Other leaders accused of war crimes and other serious human rights abuses in the DRC remained abroad, free from prosecution. They included Laurent Nkunda, ousted military head of the CNDP, held in Rwanda since January.

The trial before the ICC of Thomas Lubanga, charged with the war crimes of recruiting and using children under the age of 15 in hostilities, began in January. The trial had not concluded by the end of the year. The ICC trial of Germain Katanga and Mathieu Ngudjolo Chui began in November. They had been jointly charged with war crimes and crimes against humanity, including the recruitment and use of children aged under 15, murder, rape and sexual slavery. Charges of war crimes and crimes against humanity against former DRC Vice-President Jean-Pierre Bemba Gombo, in ICC custody since July 2008, were confirmed in June 2009. His trial was expected to start in 2010.

Amnesty International visits/reports

🚗 Amnesty International delegates visited the country in March, July and October.

📄 Democratic Republic of Congo: Submission to the UN Universal Periodic Review (AFR 62/009/2009)

📄 Democratic Republic of Congo: Open Letter to President Kabila regarding Bosco Ntaganda (AFR 62/011/2009)

📄 Democratic Republic of Congo: More prosecutions should follow for war crimes in the Kivus (AFR 62/019/2009)

📄 Democratic Republic of Congo: Governments launching offensives against armed groups must take precautions to avoid civilian casualties, 20 January 2009

DENMARK

KINGDOM OF DENMARK

Head of state:	Queen Margrethe II
Head of government:	Lars Løkke Rasmussen (replaced Anders Fogh Rasmussen in April)
Death penalty:	abolitionist for all crimes
Population:	5.5 million
Life expectancy:	78.2 years
Under-5 mortality (m/f):	6/6 per 1,000

New provisions were introduced allowing the use of secret information in deportation and expulsion cases. The authorities planned to use "diplomatic assurances" (unenforceable promises from the countries where individuals were to be returned) to return people suspected of terrorism to countries known to practise torture. There were forcible returns to Iraq. Measures to combat violence against women were inadequate.

Counter-terror and security

In July, amendments to the Aliens Act entered into force and were applied retrospectively. The new provisions allowed for the appointment of a lawyer from an approved list, when the authorities wished to expel or deport foreign nationals on "national security grounds" based on secret information. These security-cleared lawyers would have access during closed hearings to the secret material used to justify the expulsion or deportation, but they would be barred from disclosing it to the individual concerned or his or her lawyer of choice. The measures contravened fair trial standards.

In February, the UN Special Rapporteur on torture expressed concern about plans to rely on "diplomatic assurances" when returning people suspected of terrorism to countries known to practise torture.

■ At the end of the year, the civil proceedings issued in 2007 by Ghousouallah Tarin, were ongoing. He was one of reportedly 31 Afghan nationals detained by the Danish contingent of the International Security Assistance Force in Afghanistan in 2002. He complained that after his transfer from Danish to US custody he was tortured or otherwise ill-treated. Some witnesses, who were current and former high-level employees of the Danish Ministry of Defence, had not yet testified by the end of the year.

Torture and other ill-treatment

Although amendments to the Civil and Military Criminal Codes had introduced torture as an aggravating circumstance for various criminal offences in 2008, and the Danish Criminal Code contains provisions punishing acts that amount to torture, Danish criminal law continued to omit torture as a specific crime in its own right.

The UN Special Rapporteur on torture expressed concern at, among other things, the extensive use of solitary confinement, particularly of pre-trial detainees.

Minors held on remand were regularly detained in the same facilities as adult inmates.

Police and security forces

In December, the government tabled legislation to establish a new police complaints system.

The policing of demonstrations held in December during the UN Climate Change Conference in Copenhagen gave rise to concern. There were reports of use of excessive force, such as the use of pepper spray against demonstrators who were already under police control. Of the 968 demonstrators detained under the new provisions of administrative, preventive arrest, almost all were later released without charge.

Refugees and asylum-seekers

In August, in the middle of the night, police raided a church in Copenhagen, and detained a number of Iraqi asylum-seekers who had sheltered there for months. There were complaints that the police used excessive force to remove people who were demonstrating in solidarity with the asylum-seekers.

During the year, 38 Iraqi asylum-seekers were forcibly returned to Iraq, including at least 25 to central and southern Iraq contrary to the advice of UNHCR, the UN refugee agency.

Newly arrived refugees and other aliens were still only entitled to between 45 and 65 per cent of regular welfare benefits, giving rise to concern that this would lead to their being destitute.

Violence against women and girls

In February, the UN Special Rapporteur on torture expressed concern at the high incidence of assault and sexual offences against women in Greenland. In August, the UN Committee on the Elimination of Discrimination against Women (CEDAW Committee) expressed concern at the increase in the total number of women subjected to physical violence between 2000 and 2005, and that immigrant women were most affected. The CEDAW Committee noted that foreign married women, whose immigration status depended on that of their spouses, were particularly vulnerable as victims of domestic violence. The strict seven-year residence requirement for permanent residency gave rise to concern that it may prevent women from leaving abusive relationships and seeking assistance.

The CEDAW Committee concurred with the UN Special Rapporteur on torture, that the government's emphasis on the repatriation of trafficking victims to their country of origin, rather than on their recovery and rehabilitation, was a matter of concern.

The authorities failed to address the lack of legal protection and redress for rape survivors. However, in November the government commissioned an expert committee to examine existing rape legislation and make recommendations.

DJIBOUTI

REPUBLIC OF DJIBOUTI

Head of state:	President Ismael Omar Guelleh
Head of government:	Prime Minister Dileita Mohamed Dileita
Death penalty:	abolitionist for all crimes
Population:	900,000
Life expectancy:	55.1 years
Under-5 mortality (m/f):	134/116 per 1,000
Adult literacy:	70.3 per cent

Freedom of expression was restricted. The government prevented trade unions from operating freely. Human rights defenders were harassed and intimidated by the authorities.

Background

Unemployment remained high. The global rise in food prices contributed to an increase in malnutrition among the poor. Eritrea maintained a troop presence in the disputed Ras Doumeira area and Doumeira Island.

Freedom of expression

Freedom of expression was limited. Journalists exercised self-censorship to avoid harassment by the authorities. The government imposed restrictions on the independent press. Human rights defenders' work was scrutinized by government authorities to harass and intimidate them from carrying out lawful activities.

■ On 2 July, poet Ahmed Darar Robleh was arrested for writing poetry critical of the President. He was sentenced to six months' imprisonment on 19 July.

Freedom of association

The government reportedly disrupted trade union activity.

■ On 13 October, police prevented the Union of Djibouti Workers (Union Djiboutienne du Travail, UDT) from holding a seminar at the People's Palace in Djibouti following instructions from the Office of the Prime Minister.

Security forces

■ Soldiers reportedly extorted money from Houmad Mohamed Ibrahim, a local leader in Tadjourah district. The soldiers beat him and members of his family. They transported male family members to the military barracks at Tadjourah where they were arbitrarily detained and beaten.

DOMINICAN REPUBLIC

DOMINICAN REPUBLIC

Head of state and government:	Leonel Fernández Reyna
Death penalty:	abolitionist for all crimes
Population:	10.1 million
Life expectancy:	72.4 years
Under-5 mortality (m/f):	37/29 per 1,000
Adult literacy:	89.1 per cent

At least 226 unlawful killings by the security forces were reported between January and August. Haitians and Dominico-Haitians faced widespread discrimination. Constitutional reform increased the likelihood of a total ban on abortion.

Background

The process of constitutional reform concluded in December. Positive developments included provisions for the appointment of a human rights Ombudsperson and the creation of a constitutional court. However, several civil society organizations expressed concern that many of the amendments undermined constitutional human rights guarantees.

Police and security forces

According to the General Prosecutor's Office, 226 people were killed by police between January and August 2009, a decrease of 72 over the same period in 2008. Eyewitness testimonies and other evidence indicated that many of these killings were unlawful and a number may have amounted to extrajudicial executions.

■ On 28 March 2009, Nicolas Disla was stopped in the street in Santo Domingo by three police officers in a patrol car. Eyewitnesses report that, although Nicolas Disla was unarmed and obeyed police orders, one of the officers shot him twice in the legs. The officers then handcuffed him as he lay injured and drove him away. Members of his family learned later that day that Nicolas Disla had been pronounced dead on arrival at the local hospital, with gunshot wounds to the stomach and legs. Two days later, at the funeral, one of the officers allegedly responsible for the killing tried to shoot Nicolas Disla's brother, Juan Carlos Disla. A judicial investigation into the killing was continuing at the end of the year.

D

Police used excessive force to disperse demonstrators protesting at the lack of access to clean water, poor infrastructure and frequent cuts in the electricity supply.

■ On 16 July, 13-year-old Miguel Angel Encarnacion was shot dead during a demonstration in the Santo Domingo neighbourhood of Capotillo. According to the police, the gunshots were fired by unidentified individuals. However, a commission of inquiry later confirmed reports by eyewitnesses that a police officer had fired the shots. The police officer was under investigation at the end of the year.

Discrimination – Haitian migrants and Dominico-Haitians

Access to nationality
Thousands of Dominicans continued to have their identity documents revoked on the basis of a directive issued in March 2007 by the Dominican Electoral Board. The vast majority of those whose documents were revoked were of Haitian descent. The refusal to issue identity documents resulted in people being denied access to education and health services, the right to vote and employment. Those without papers were also at risk of arbitrary detention and mass expulsion, without access to judicial review.

Expulsions
Many deportations of Haitian migrants breached international human rights standards.

■ On 4 October, 25 Haitian agricultural workers attending a training session on labour rights for migrant workers in Montecristi were arrested by soldiers and returned to Haiti the following morning. They were given no opportunity to challenge the legality of their detention, appeal against the decision, or collect their belongings or wages owed.

Lynchings
There were continued reports of mob attacks against Haitian migrants in apparent reprisal for killings of Dominican citizens or for other crimes rumoured to have been committed by Haitians. The authorities failed to take measures to combat racism and xenophobia.

■ On 2 May, Carlos Nerilus, a Haitian national, was decapitated by a group of residents who claimed he had murdered a Dominican man in Santo Domingo the previous day.

Violence against women and girls
According to the General Prosecutor's Office, the number of women killed by partners or former partners fell by 31 per cent between January and August 2009, compared with the same period in 2008. However, women's organizations stated that the true extent of such crimes may have been masked by inadequate data collection.

Sexual violence remained widespread, with girls at particular risk. For example, in July the Office of the Public Prosecutor of Santo Domingo revealed that, on average, 90 per cent of the complaints of sexual violence received involved girls under the age of 18.

Sexual and reproductive rights
Amendments to the Constitution introduced the principle of the inviolability of life from "conception to death". Women's organizations, the medical profession and other sectors of civil society expressed grave concerns that this could deny women and girls the right to life by severely limiting access to safe abortion in cases of life-threatening complications. There were also fears that it would reduce the scope for decriminalizing abortion in cases where the pregnancy is the result of rape or incest.

Amnesty International visits/report
🚌 Amnesty International delegates visited the Dominican Republic in March and September/October 2009.

📑 Dominican Republic: Submission to the UN Universal Periodic Review (AMR 27/002/2009)

ECUADOR

REPUBLIC OF ECUADOR

Head of state and government: **Rafael Vicente Correa Delgado**
Death penalty: **abolitionist for all crimes**
Population: **13.6 million**
Life expectancy: **75 years**
Under-5 mortality (m/f): **29/22 per 1,000**
Adult literacy: **91 per cent**

Scores of demonstrators were arbitrarily detained and ill-treated during mass protests against new legislation on the use of natural resources. Intimidation and threats against human rights defenders, including Indigenous and community leaders, were reported.

Background

On 26 April, President Rafael Correa was re-elected for a further four-year term. He pledged to reduce inequality and poverty and improve conditions for Indigenous Peoples.

Mass demonstrations and blockades took place throughout the year in opposition to new legislation on the use of natural resources, in particular water, and a mining law passed in January which imposed new restrictions on the constitutional right of Indigenous Peoples to be consulted over matters affecting their rights.

In October, Ecuador ratified the International Convention for the Protection of All Persons from Enforced Disappearance.

Human rights defenders

Human rights defenders, particularly Indigenous and community leaders, were intimidated and harassed. Community leaders and human rights defenders were among the scores of protesters arbitrarily detained and ill-treated in the context of mass demonstrations against the new mining law.

■ In January, human rights defender Joel Vicente Zhunio Samaniego was shot and seriously injured while being forced into a police car. He was detained without a warrant, accused of sabotaging public services during mass demonstrations against the mining law. He was held incommunicado for 18 days during which time he was beaten and threatened with death. He was later released and all charges were dropped.

■ In January, three human rights defenders, Etelvina de Jesús Misacango Chuñir, Virginia Chuñir, and Yolanda Gutama, were detained and beaten by police officers in Molleturo, Azuay province. They were accused of blockading roads during protests against the mining law earlier that month. The three women were conditionally released the following day. On 22 April, Etelvina de Jesús Misacango Chuñir was attacked by four men outside her home in the town of Molleturo. The attack was believed to have been carried out in reprisal for her opposition to mining in the area.

■ An NGO, Acción Ecológica, which had worked on environmental issues for over 20 years, had its legal status withdrawn between March and August. The move appeared to be an attempt to silence public criticism of the mining law.

Corporate accountability

In April, a Canadian law firm filed a claim against a Canadian mining company and the Toronto Stock Exchange on behalf of three people from the Intag area in Canton Cotacachi, Imbabura province. The woman and two men alleged that they had been assaulted in 2006 by private security guards acting for the company. One of the men also said that he had been subjected to threats and intimidation in several incidents in 2005, 2006 and 2007 by people allegedly linked to the company. They alleged that they were targeted because of their campaign against the opening of a copper mine in the area. The Toronto Stock Exchange was alleged to have facilitated the funding of the company despite being made aware of the potential harm to individuals. The case was pending before the Ontario Superior Court of Justice at the end of the year.

The ruling by the Provincial Court of Lago Agrio in a case brought by local communities in 1993 was deferred until 2010. The communities alleged that the oil company Chevron (formerly Texaco) was responsible for environmental damage during more than two decades of oil extraction.

Impunity

The mandate of the Truth Commission, set up in May 2007 to investigate human rights violations committed since 1984, was extended. By the end of 2009, the Commission had heard 700 testimonies relating to cases of torture, enforced disappearance, extrajudicial execution and death in custody.

E

Cases of torture and extrajudicial executions remained unresolved. Victims and relatives seeking justice and redress were threatened and intimidated.

■ Police officer Leidy Johanna Vélez Moreira and her family continued to be subjected to a campaign of intimidation by the police which began after she lodged a complaint about a police raid on her home in October 2007. The most recent incidents took place on 23 and 24 January 2009 when she and her partner were followed by police officers. The Vélez family has filed several complaints against the police, including one for the torture and killing of Leidy Johanna Vélez Moreira's brothers, Yandry Javier Vélez Moreira and Juan Miguel Vélez Cedeño, in Montecristi, Manabí province, in December 2008.

EGYPT

ARAB REPUBLIC OF EGYPT

Head of state:	**Muhammad Hosni Mubarak**
Head of government:	**Ahmed Nazif**
Death penalty:	**retentionist**
Population:	**83 million**
Life expectancy:	**69.9 years**
Under-5 mortality (m/f):	**42/39 per 1,000**
Adult literacy:	**66.4 per cent**

The government continued to use state of emergency powers to detain peaceful critics and opponents as well as people suspected of security offences or involvement in terrorism. Some were held under administrative detention orders; others were sentenced to prison terms after unfair trials before military courts. Torture and other ill-treatment remained widespread in police cells, security police detention centres and prisons, and in most cases were committed with impunity. The rights to freedom of expression, association and assembly were curtailed; journalists and bloggers were among those detained or prosecuted. Hundreds of families residing in Cairo's "unsafe areas" were forcibly evicted; some were left homeless, others were relocated but without security of tenure. Men perceived to be gay continued to be prosecuted under a "debauchery" law. At least 19 people

seeking to cross into Israel were shot dead by border guards, apparently while posing no threat. At least 269 people were sentenced to death, and at least five were executed.

Background

Egypt remained under a national state of emergency in force continuously since 1981 and most recently renewed in May 2008. In April, the government said it had completed drafting all but one section of a new, long-awaited anti-terrorism law, which was expected to pave the way for the lifting of the state of emergency. However, it was feared that the law might effectively retain emergency provisions that have facilitated human rights violations. The draft was not available by the end of 2009.

In January, there were demonstrations against the Israeli military offensive in Gaza and the Egyptian government's response to it. The authorities kept the border with the Gaza Strip closed for much of the year, including during the offensive thereby preventing Palestinians from seeking refuge in Egypt. The authorities allowed passage to the sick and wounded, and goods through the border. In December, the authorities announced that they were constructing a steel wall along the borders with Gaza in order to prevent smuggling. They refused permission to over 1,000 people from 43 countries who converged in Cairo to march to Gaza with humanitarian aid to mark the first anniversary of the Israeli military offensive; many of them were assaulted by the police.

In February, a bomb attack in Cairo killed one woman and injured 25 other people, mostly foreign tourists. In May, the authorities attributed the attack to a group associated with al-Qa'ida and the Palestinian Islamic Army, an armed group.

Former presidential candidate Ayman Nour was released from prison in February on health grounds. In November, the authorities prevented him from travelling to the USA.

There were sporadic clashes between Coptic Christians and Muslims in which several people were killed and others injured. In March, the homes of Baha'is were burned in al-Shuraniyya, a village in Sohag Governorate, reportedly after some media incited hatred and violence against Baha'is.

In April, the parliament passed the Law for the Care of Mental Patients to provide safeguards for the rights of people with mental illness.

In June, the number of seats in the parliament's lower house was increased from 454 to 518, 64 of which were reserved for women to promote greater participation by women in public life.

Draft laws were proposed that would further restrict NGOs and punish defamation of monotheistic religions or their prophets with imprisonment and fines. In November, NGOs called for a 2007 draft law, which would allow survivors of rape to obtain an abortion, to be brought before parliament for debate.

Rising food prices and poverty fuelled a wave of strikes by private and public sector workers.

Counter-terror and security

Scores of people were arrested following the February bomb attack in Cairo. In May, the authorities said they were holding seven suspects, including a French woman of Albanian origin, who they accused of recruiting foreign students and others to commit terrorist acts in Egypt and abroad. Subsequently, they detained and then deported to their home countries at least 41 foreigners, including nationals of Russia and France, who were residing in Egypt and reported to be studying Arabic and Islam. Some were reported to have been tortured or otherwise ill-treated while detained and they were given no opportunity to contest their deportation before the courts. Some were believed to be at risk of human rights violations in the countries to which they were forcibly returned.

The UN Special Rapporteur on the promotion and protection of human rights while countering terrorism visited Egypt for six days in April. His report, issued in October, criticized the government's counter-terrorism policy and practices for unduly restricting human rights. He urged the government to lift the state of emergency which, he said, had become the "norm" rather than an exceptional measure.

■ Romuald Durand, a French national, was subjected to enforced disappearance for two months after he was arrested at Cairo's international airport in April. He was handed over to the State Security Investigations (SSI) service who initially held him at Nasr City, Cairo. There, he was reported to have been kept blindfolded and handcuffed for the first 10 days, stripped naked and tortured with electric shocks while his arms and legs were tied and stretched, and threatened with rape. He was released in June without charge and deported to France.

■ In August, 22 defendants, plus four people charged in their absence, went on trial before a Cairo (Emergency) Supreme State Security Court. Among them were five Palestinians, two Lebanese nationals and a Sudanese national. The 26 faced a variety of charges, including planning to attack tourist sites, possessing explosives and passing information to Hizbullah in Lebanon. Some of them were accused of helping to dig tunnels under the border to smuggle people and goods into the Gaza Strip from Egypt and assist fighters to cross the border. They all denied the terrorism-related charges. Some told the court that they had been tortured, including with electric shocks, while held incommunicado by the SSI after their arrest in late 2008 and early 2009. In October, their defence lawyers withdrew from the court accusing it of bias against the defendants. The trial continued at the end of the year.

Administrative detention

The authorities continued to use emergency powers to detain not only people suspected of terrorism and offences against national security but also peaceful critics of the government. Some continued to be detained without charge or trial despite court orders for their release. In such cases, the Interior Ministry issued new detention orders to replace those ruled invalid by the courts, undermining the value of judicial scrutiny and oversight.

■ Hani Nazeer, a Coptic Christian and blogger from Qina, was held throughout 2009 under a succession of administrative detention orders issued by the Interior Minister. He was arrested in October 2008 when he surrendered to the police in Nagaa Hammadi, who had detained his brothers and threatened to detain his sisters to force him to surrender. This was after residents of Qina denounced him for commenting in his blog on a book they deemed insulting to Muslims. He was held at Borg al-Arab Prison near Alexandria, despite four court orders for his release. He was reported to have been pressured by security officers in prison to convert to Islam.

Unfair trials

Grossly unfair trials of civilians continued before military courts, in breach of international fair trial standards. At least three civilians were convicted in these trials, and sentenced to prison terms of up to two years.

■ In February, Ahmed Doma, a leading member of the Popular Movement to Free Egypt, a youth organization,

E

and Ahmed Kamal Abdel Aal were sentenced to one-year prison terms and fined, the former for crossing Egypt's border with the Gaza Strip during the Israeli military offensive and the latter for planning to cross. Magdy Hussein, General Secretary of the Labour Party, was sentenced to two years in prison and fined on similar grounds. In August, the Supreme Court of Military Appeals upheld his sentence.

■ The Supreme Court of Military Appeals rejected the appeals filed by 18 members of the Muslim Brotherhood organization after they were sentenced to up to seven years' imprisonment in April 2008 following an unfair trial before the Supreme Military Court of Haikstip, northern Cairo. In July, an administrative court ordered that 13 of them who had served three-quarters of their sentences should be released, but they all remained in prison at the end of the year.

Torture and other ill-treatment

Torture and other ill-treatment of detainees were systematic in police stations, prisons and SSI detention centres and, for the most part, committed with impunity. In some cases, police were reported to have threatened victims against lodging complaints. In rare cases, however, alleged torturers were prosecuted.

■ In November, an Alexandria court sentenced a police officer to five years in prison for torturing Rajai Sultan in July 2008 by beating him until he suffered a brain haemorrhage, for which he required surgery.

■ Mona Said Thabet and her husband, Yasser Naguib Mahran, were harassed and intimidated by police after she submitted a complaint to the Interior Ministry that her husband had been tortured by police at Shobra al-Khayma before his release in September 2008 because he had refused to become an informer. She reported that police slapped and beat her, stubbed out a cigarette on her face, forcibly shaved her head and threatened to rape her unless she withdraw the complaint. Instead, she filed a further complaint with the Public Prosecutor in Shobra al-Khayma, who ordered an investigation. This led local police to make new threats against her, her husband and their children. She complained to the Public Prosecutor in February, but no action was known to have been taken. In May, families from Shobra al-Khayma demonstrated in Cairo against abuses allegedly committed by the head of the SSI in Shobra al-Khayma police station and to seek the intervention of the Interior Ministry.

Deaths in custody

At least four people died in custody, apparently as a result of torture or other ill-treatment, according to reports.

■ Youssef Abu Zouhri, the brother of a spokesperson for the Palestinian organization Hamas, died in October. He was alleged to have been tortured and otherwise ill-treated at Borg al-Arab Prison, near Alexandria, following his arrest in April after he crossed from Gaza into Egypt. The authorities said his death was due to natural causes, but gave no details.

Freedom of expression – the media

The authorities maintained curbs on freedom of expression and the media. Journalists and bloggers who criticized the government were harassed, including with arrest and by being prosecuted on defamation charges. Books and foreign newspapers were censored if they commented on issues that the government considered taboo or a threat to national security.

■ Karim Amer, a blogger detained since November 2006, remained in prison even though the UN Working Group on Arbitrary Detention (WGAD) ruled in November 2008 that his detention was arbitrary and called for his release. The WGAD also criticized the imprisonment of journalists and bloggers on charges of defamation or insulting state authorities as disproportionate and a serious restraint on freedom of expression.

Freedom of assembly and association

The authorities maintained legal restrictions and other controls that limited the activities of political parties, NGOs, professional associations and trade unions. Members of the Muslim Brotherhood, which remained banned, and other opposition groups were harassed and arrested.

■ At least 34 people were arrested in April and accused of incitement and distributing leaflets calling for a national strike. They included students as well as members of political opposition groups, including the 6 April Group, the Kefaya Movement, al-Ghad and the Muslim Brotherhood. All were released uncharged.

Discrimination – suspected gay men

The authorities continued to criminalize consensual sexual acts between men.

■ Ten men arrested in January in Cairo and accused of "habitual practice of debauchery", the charge used to prosecute consensual sexual acts between men, were reported to have been beaten, slapped, kicked and insulted while detained by the Morality Police. They were tested for HIV/AIDS without their consent and forcibly subjected to anal examinations to "prove" that they had engaged in same-sex sexual conduct. Such examinations conducted without consent constitute torture. They were detained for five months for investigation and released on bail at the end of May pending their trial, which began on 31 December.

Discrimination – religious minorities

Following a Supreme Administrative Court decision in March that Baha'is could obtain identification documents without having to identify themselves as Muslims or Christians, the Interior Minister issued a decree recognizing the right of adherents of other religions to obtain official identification documents without revealing their religious faith or having to present themselves as Muslims, Christians or Jews.

Administrative courts ordered on several occasions the repeal of decisions by university and ministerial officials banning women and girls from wearing the *niqab* (face veil) in their institutions.

Right to adequate housing – forced evictions

Residents of 26 areas in Greater Cairo deemed "unsafe" in 2008 in a government master plan to develop the city by 2050 continued to face a double threat: lack of safety from possible rock falls, high-voltage power cables or other dangers; and possible forced eviction. There was little or no consultation with affected communities in the "unsafe areas".

Forced evictions were carried out in Al-Duwayqa, Establ Antar and Ezbet Khayrallah, all "unsafe areas" in which residents occupy state-owned land and are at risk from rock falls, on the basis of administrative orders issued by local authorities. The evictions were carried out without notice or prior consultation with the affected communities or any notification in writing, so hindering the possibility of legal challenge. In June, some 28 families from Atfet Al-Moza in Al-Duwayqa were left homeless when they were forcibly evicted so that the authorities could "secure" the rocky slope where they lived. In Establ Antar, some residents were told to demolish their homes or else face eviction.

From September 2008, when a rockslide killed at least 119 residents of Al-Duwayqa, to the end of 2009, the authorities rehoused some 4,000 families in an upgraded area of Al-Duwayqa. Some 1,400 other families from Establ Antar and Ezbet Khayrallah were rehoused in 6 October City, south-west of Giza, far from their source of livelihood. However, rehoused families were not given documentation providing them with legal security of tenure, and women divorced or separated from their husbands were not provided with alternative housing.

In December 2009, the Public Prosecutor indicted eight officials from the Cairo Governorate and Manshiyet Nasser Neighbourhood Authority on a charge of involuntary homicide in connection with the fatal 2008 Al-Duwayqa rockslide.

Migrants, refugees and asylum-seekers

At least 19 people were shot dead by Egyptian security forces while trying to cross the border into Israel. All were believed to be foreign nationals and migrants, refugees or asylum-seekers in Egypt. In September, the authorities defended the use of lethal force, saying it was meant to protect Egypt's borders and that it targeted "infiltrators", including smugglers of drugs and weapons.

■ In January, at least 64 Eritreans trying to cross into Israel were forcibly returned to Eritrea despite fears that they would be at risk of serious human rights violations there (see Eritrea entry).

Death penalty

At least 269 death sentences were imposed by the courts, and at least five prisoners were executed.

Amnesty International visits/reports

🚍 Amnesty International delegates visited Egypt several times in 2009 to conduct research and to attend conferences and workshops.

▤ Buried alive: Trapped by poverty and neglect in Cairo's informal settlements (MDE 12/009/2009)

▤ Egypt: Government should immediately release Musaad Abu Fagr and Karim Amer (MDE 12/029/2009)

▤ Egypt: Government must urgently rein in border guards (MDE 12/032/2009)

▤ Egyptian court overturns journalists' prison sentences, 2 February 2009

▤ Egypt: Military Court of Appeals fails to rectify injustice, 19 November 2009

EL SALVADOR

REPUBLIC OF EL SALVADOR
Head of state and government: **Carlos Mauricio Funes**
    Cartagena (replaced Elías Antonio Saca in June)
Death penalty: **abolitionist for ordinary crimes**
Population: **6.2 million**
Life expectancy: **71.3 years**
Under-5 mortality (m/f):   **29/23 per 1,000**
Adult literacy: **82 per cent**

Impunity for past human rights violations continued, although there were some positive developments. A total ban on abortion remained in place. There was a marked increase in the number of women killed.

Background

In June, President Funes took office following the election victory of the Farabundo Martí National Liberation Front (Frente Farabundo Martí para la Liberación Nacional, FMLN) earlier in the year. In November, President Funes declared a state of emergency following Hurricane Ida which left 140 dead and 140,000 displaced. El Salvador did not accede to the Rome Statute of the International Criminal Court.

Impunity

The 1993 Amnesty Law remained in place, obstructing efforts to bring to justice those responsible for past human rights violations. The new government pledged to reform the Inter-Institutional Commission for the Search for Disappeared Children established to clarify the whereabouts of some of the 700 children who disappeared during the internal armed conflict (1980-1992). The Commission had been criticized for only finding the whereabouts of some 30 of the children by the end of its mandate.

■ In October, the US Supreme Court denied a petition from the former Salvadoran Vice-Minister of Defence, Colonel Nicolás Carranza, for a review of his conviction in 2005. He was found guilty of crimes against humanity committed by units of the security forces under his control between 1979 and 1981.

■ In January, a Spanish National Court formally charged 14 army officers and soldiers with crimes against humanity and state terrorism for the killings of six Jesuit priests, their housekeeper and her 16-year-old daughter at the Central American University in November 1989.

■ In November, at a session of the Inter-American Commission on Human Rights, El Salvador accepted responsibility for the killing of Archbishop Oscar Arnulfo Romero as he said mass in a hospice in San Salvador in March 1980. The government declared its intention to fulfil the requirements of the Commission's 2000 report which included a thorough and independent investigation into the murder, reparations and repeal of the 1993 Amnesty Law.

Sexual and reproductive rights

A total ban on abortion remained in effect. Women campaigned before the Legislative Assembly for the issue to be tabled for discussion and reform.

Violence against women and girls

According to statistics provided by the Institute for Legal Medicine, some 411 women were reported to have been killed between January and September, a significant rise over 2008. In many of these cases, the women were abducted and raped and their bodies mutilated. No data was available regarding investigations into a large number of these killings.

In November, the UN Committee against Torture expressed concern about the various forms of violence against women and girls – including sexual abuse, domestic violence and killings – and the lack of rigorous investigations into complaints.

Indigenous Peoples' rights

Indigenous groups called on the new government to fulfil its pre-election commitment to sign ILO Convention No.169 and strengthen protection for Indigenous rights. In the absence of such protection, Indigenous communities continued to face discrimination and to be denied their rights regarding land and water.

EQUATORIAL GUINEA

REPUBLIC OF EQUATORIAL GUINEA

Head of state:	Teodoro Obiang Nguema Mbasogo
Head of government:	Ignacio Milán Tang
Death penalty:	retentionist
Population:	0.7 million
Life expectancy:	49.9 years
Under-5 mortality (m/f):	177/160 per 1,000
Adult literacy:	87 per cent

An alleged attack in February on the presidential palace in the capital, Malabo, led to arbitrary arrests of political opponents and others, all of whom appeared to be prisoners of conscience. Detainees were tortured with impunity. Soldiers allegedly killed at least two people unlawfully. Prisoners continued to be held incommunicado, some in isolation cells, with limited or no access to fresh air and direct sunlight. Scores of families were forcibly evicted from their homes in several cities and hundreds more remained at risk.

Background

In February, the authorities said that members of the Nigerian Movement for the Emancipation of the Niger Delta (MEND) had attacked the presidential palace in Malabo with assistance from inside Equatorial Guinea. The alleged attack led to the arrest of political opponents and a crackdown on irregular migrants. Some 500 foreign nationals, mostly Nigerians and Cameroonians, were expelled between February and May. Following the alleged attack, the Ministers of Defence and National Security were dismissed and new ones appointed. MEND denied involvement in the alleged attack.

In March, the new National Security Minister condemned the level of illegal detentions in Malabo police station, the poorly kept records of detainees, and illegal payments received by immigration officers. He warned officers against such practices, adding that their duty was to protect citizens and their property and not to violate their rights.

Law 5/09 on the Judiciary was passed in May. It provides for the creation of family courts, with competence to deal with cases of violence against women.

In November, President Obiang pardoned four South African nationals serving prison sentences of between 17 and 34 years for attempting to overthrow the Equatorial Guinean government in March 2004. A British national convicted in July 2008 of the same offence and serving a 32-year prison sentence was also pardoned.

Also in November, President Obiang won presidential elections with 95.4 per cent of the vote.

In December, the UN Human Rights Council, under its Universal Periodic Review, examined the situation of human rights in Equatorial Guinea. The government accepted in principle the recommendations of the working group. The final report was due to be adopted by the UN Human Rights Council in March 2010.

Right to adequate housing – forced evictions

Scores of families were forcibly evicted from their homes in several parts of the country and hundreds more remained at risk. In Bata, on the mainland, there were further forced evictions in the Comandachina neighbourhood where dozens of families lost their homes to make way for a luxury hotel complex and shopping centre. In Bisa, another Bata neighbourhood, over 50 families were forcibly evicted from their homes in January to make room for a promenade along the beach.

Half of Kogo's town centre was demolished in February to build a marina and promenade. Over 60 families were left homeless. Most of them were elderly people who owned their houses in which they had lived for decades. There was no consultation with the residents or adequate notification of the evictions. Just before the forced evictions, the families were offered a small plot of barren land outside town, without services or facilities, to build new homes. However, they were not given monetary compensation or other assistance, and most remained homeless.

Arbitrary arrests and detention

One prisoner of conscience, Bonifacio Nguema Ndong, was released in March having completed a one-year sentence. Five other prisoners of conscience – Cruz Obiang Ebele, Emiliano Esono Miché, Gumersindo Ramírez Faustino, Juan Ecomo Ndong and Gerardo Angüe Mangue – remained in detention.

E

Political opponents and foreign nationals were arrested following the alleged attack in February on the presidential palace. The authorities said they had captured 15 Nigerians during the attack, but did not provide further details. Between six and eight Nigerians remained in Black Beach prison without charge or trial at the end of the year. According to reports, they were traders who regularly travelled to Malabo by boat and were caught in Equatorial Guinean territorial waters. Six Equatorial Guinean fishermen in Malabo port at the time of the alleged attack were also arrested. They were released without charge about two weeks later.

In February and March in Malabo and Bata, the police arrested without warrant 10 members of the People's Union (Unión Popular) political party, including Beatriz Andeme Ondó, the wife of the party's president, Faustino Ondó Ebang. The authorities accused them of maintaining telephone contact with Faustino Ondó Ebang, a former prisoner of conscience living in Spain. All 10 were prisoners of conscience, detained solely because of their non-violent political activities. Those arrested in Bata were transferred from Bata police station to Malabo. All 10 were held in Malabo police station for two months, where they were tortured (see below) before being transferred to Black Beach prison. Eight were conditionally released in September pending charges and trial, and required to report to the police station twice a week. Marcelino Nguema and Santiago Asumo Nguema remained in prison. The 10 were charged with "acts of terrorism" in late November. They had not been tried by the end of the year.

Torture and other ill-treatment

Torture continued to be used in police stations. No investigations were carried out and perpetrators were not brought to justice.

Most of the 10 members of the People's Union arrested in February and March were tortured in Bata and Malabo police stations. Santiago Asumo told the investigating magistrate that on one occasion he was placed on the floor on his stomach, his feet tightly bound with cables, and offered money to "confess". On another occasion, the police put paper in his mouth, put him in a sack which was then tied, and suspended and beat him. Although he named those who tortured him, there was no investigation and no one was brought to justice.

■ Epifanio Pascual Nguema was arrested without a warrant on 26 February and taken to Bata police station. At about midnight on 2 March, police officers took him from his cell to the cellar and tortured him for four hours. They beat him around the kidneys, belly and genitals. For several days he passed blood in his urine and was unable to walk or stand up straight. He needed hospital treatment. He had been arrested apparently for procuring travel documents for his wife and for criticizing President Obiang. He was released uncharged in late May.

Unlawful killings

There were reports that soldiers unlawfully killed two people in the Malabo neighbourhood of Lampert in the aftermath of the alleged attack on the palace. A Nigerian man died four days after being shot by soldiers who tried to stop him in the street. Instead of stopping, the man ran and the soldiers fired at him, hitting him in the back. In the second incident, an Equatorial Guinean man was stopped by soldiers as he was returning home. They beat him severely and he died a few days later as a result of his injuries. Nobody was brought to justice for the killings.

Prison conditions

The ban on prison visits was lifted in late November. Some prisoners were held in isolation cells, in shackles, and only allowed in the yard for about 30 minutes every two to four weeks.

In police stations in Malabo and Bata, conditions were life-threatening because of overcrowding and poor hygiene and sanitation.

■ According to reports, a woman believed to be a Nigerian national died in Malabo police station on 3 March as a result of overcrowding and poor hygienic conditions. She had been arrested about two weeks earlier, following the alleged attack on the presidential palace. There was no investigation into her death.

Children's rights

At least 20 minors aged between 10 and 17 were arrested in February for receiving money from one of President Obiang's grandchildren who apparently had stolen the money. Although the age of criminal responsibility is 16 in Equatorial Guinea, all 20 were detained for nearly two months and were held in Black Beach prison, which has no facilities for juveniles.

Amnesty International reports

📄 Equatorial Guinea: Submission of the UN Universal Periodic Review (AFR 24/002/2009)

📄 Equatorial Guinea: Arrest and torture of political opponents following February attack on presidential palace (AFR 24/004/2009)

ERITREA

STATE OF ERITREA

Head of state and government:	**Isaias Afewerki**
Death penalty:	**abolitionist in practice**
Population:	**5.1 million**
Life expectancy:	**59.2 years**
Under-5 mortality (m/f):	**78/71 per 1,000**
Adult literacy:	**64.2 per cent**

Freedom of expression was severely restricted and legitimate criticism of the government suppressed. Independent journalism, political opposition, unregistered religious groups and civil society were highly restricted. Perceived critics of the government remained in detention. Deserters from the armed forces, those evading mandatory military conscription, and their families, were harassed, imprisoned and subjected to ill-treatment. Family members of detainees reported that international communication was monitored by the government and could lead to reprisals.

Background

Despite government claims of self-sufficiency, the local population remained heavily dependent on international food aid. Donor countries and inter-governmental institutions contributed millions of dollars in aid, including the European Union which gave 122 million euros in 2009. Food shortages were exacerbated by drought and desertification in certain areas. The government became increasingly reliant on a 2 per cent tax levied on most members of the Eritrean diaspora.

Large numbers of mainly young Eritreans fled to Ethiopia, Kenya, Uganda and Sudan to avoid conscription into national service.

UN Security Council (UNSC) members, the African Union and the USA accused Eritrea of supporting Somali armed opposition groups. In December, the UNSC passed Resolution 1907 imposing sanctions on Eritrea, including an arms embargo, and an assets freeze and travel ban on individuals and organizations to be determined. Eritrea maintained a troop presence in the disputed Ras Doumeira area and Doumeira Island of Djibouti, despite a UNSC resolution calling for Eritrean withdrawal.

The Eritrea-Ethiopia Boundary Commission ruling of October 2008 was not enforced. However, Eritrea stated that it would respect a decision by the Eritrea-Ethiopia Claims Commission which required the government to pay Ethiopia US$12.6 million in damages over the border war of 1998 to 2000.

Freedom of religion

Members of banned religious groups remained at risk of harassment, arrest and incommunicado detention. Only four religious institutions are officially recognized in Eritrea since 2002, namely the Eritrean Orthodox Church, Catholic Church, Lutheran Church and Islam.

■ Some 3,000 Christians from non-state sanctioned religions remained in detention.

■ The home of Pastor Tewelde Hailom, an elder of the Full Gospel Church, was raided by Eritrean security personnel on 15 October. Pastor Hailom was not placed in detention because of ill health but three others who were with him were detained. Two days later, another seven members of his congregation were also detained.

At least 22 Jehovah's Witnesses were reportedly arrested, bringing the number of those detained due to conscientious objection and religious activities to at least 61.

Prisoners of conscience and other political prisoners

The government reacted with hostility to any form of criticism and placed severe restrictions on freedom of expression, assembly and association.

Political prisoners imprisoned since the government clampdown of 2001 remained in incommunicado detention. In most cases, their whereabouts and health status remained unknown.

Prisoners of conscience included draft evaders and military deserters. Some prisoners of conscience were also failed asylum-seekers forcibly returned to Eritrea.

In early 2009 there were unconfirmed reports that nine out of 11 former government officials known as

E

the G-15 had died in detention since 2002. The group had called for government reform in 2001.

Freedom of expression – journalists

The government tightly controlled all media and reacted with hostility to any perceived criticism in state media. All independent journalism has been effectively banned since 2001.

■ Ten journalists who protested against the closure of the media in 2001 remained in incommunicado detention. Four may have died in detention since 2002.

■ On 22 February, at least 50 employees of Radio Bana were arrested by Eritrean security forces. Although some were released, an unknown number remained in detention. They were not charged with any offence.

■ In January, prisoner of conscience Dawit Isaak was reportedly transferred to an Air Force hospital in Asmara. He was believed to be seriously ill, although the extent and cause of his illness remained unclear. A journalist with the newspaper *Setit*, he was imprisoned in 2001 following the government clampdown. He was released from custody on 19 November 2005, then re-arrested two days later on his way to hospital.

Refugees and asylum-seekers

Hundreds of people reportedly fled the country each month to Sudan and Ethiopia, including those avoiding military conscription.

The UNHCR, the UN refugee agency, issued new guidelines in April, calling for the "full assessment" of all Eritrean asylum claims, owing to the deteriorating human rights situation in the country. It recommended that states refrain from all forced returns of rejected asylum-seekers to Eritrea based on an assessment of the human rights situation and treatment of past returnees. Despite this, both Egypt and Sweden forcibly returned Eritrean refugees and asylum-seekers.

■ In January, Egypt forcibly returned at least 64 Eritreans trying to cross into Israel.

At least eight people were forcibly returned to Eritrea from Sweden, contrary to UNHCR guidelines (see Sweden entry).

According to accounts by escaped detainees, Eritrean security officials were particularly interested in what failed asylum-seekers had said about Eritrea during their asylum application process. All statements about persecution in Eritrea were

perceived as acts of treason against the state.

Military conscription

National service was mandatory for men and women at least 18 years of age. Initially 18 months long, it included six months' military service and frequent forced labour, could be extended indefinitely, and was often followed by reserve duties. Much of the adult population was engaged in mandatory service. There was no exemption from military service for conscientious objectors. Penalties for evading or deserting national service were harsh, and included torture and detention without trial. Some family members of evaders and deserters were also subject to harassment, imprisonment and torture.

Jehovah's Witnesses were particularly at risk due to their conscientious objection to military service.

Torture and other ill-treatment

The authorities interrogated, tortured and otherwise ill-treated critics of the government in an attempt to deter dissenting opinion. Prisoners were often whipped, kicked or tied with ropes in painful positions for prolonged periods.

Prison conditions were dire. Many prisoners were held in underground cells or shipping containers and denied access to daylight. Conditions were overcrowded, damp and unhygienic.

Prisoners were frequently exposed to the sun for extended periods of time, or locked in metal shipping containers, which magnified extremes of heat and cold.

Religious prisoners reportedly died in custody as a result of harsh conditions and ill-treatment, or from lack of medical care for treatable diseases.

■ Two Christians, Mogos Hagos Kiflom and Mehari Gebreneguse Asegedom, reportedly died in detention in January.

■ Yemane Kahasay Andom, aged 43, of the Kale-Hiwot Church, reportedly died on 29 July due to torture. He had been held in an underground cell in isolation and was believed to have refused to sign a document renouncing his religion.

Amnesty International report

Eritrea: Submission to the UN Universal Periodic Review (AFR 64/001/2009)

E

ESTONIA

REPUBLIC OF ESTONIA
Head of state:	Toomas Hendrik Ilves
Head of government:	Andrus Ansip
Death penalty:	abolitionist for all crimes
Population:	1.3 million
Life expectancy:	72.9 years
Under-5 mortality (m/f):	11/8 per 1,000
Adult literacy:	99.8 per cent

Linguistic minorities faced continued discrimination, including in employment. A human rights organization continued to be harassed by the government. Parliament adopted provisions which could limit freedom of expression and assembly.

Discrimination – linguistic minorities

Members of the Russian-speaking minority faced discrimination. Non-Estonian speakers, mainly from the Russian-speaking minority, were denied employment due to official language requirements for various professions in the private sector and almost all professions in the public sector. Most did not have access to affordable language training that would enable them to qualify for employment.

In January, the Equal Treatment Act entered into force, prohibiting discrimination on grounds of ethnic origin, race and colour in areas such as employment, education, and social and health care. However, the measure has limited effect with regard to public sector employment, because amendments to the Public Service Act established that unequal treatment of state and municipal officials based on official language requirements should not be considered as discrimination.

Human rights defenders

In its report published in April, the Security Police Board continued to attempt to discredit the Legal Information Centre for Human Rights (LICHR), an NGO promoting and defending the rights of linguistic minorities. The report stated that Aleksei Semjonov, the LICHR director, would be a pro-Russia candidate at the 2009 European Parliamentary elections, that he was a member of the pro-minority Constitutional Party, and that he carried out activities financed and directed by the Russian authorities.

However, Aleksei Semjonov had stated publicly on 20 March that he would not take part in the European Parliamentary elections. Official information available on the internet showed that he was not a Constitutional Party member and that he did not register as an independent or party candidate for the European elections.

Freedom of expression and assembly

On 15 October, Parliament approved the so-called "Bronze Night" package (Bill N.416UE), a set of amendments to the Penal Code, the Public Service Act and the Aliens' Act. The amendments expand the definition of "an offence committed during mass disorder", which might now include acts of non-violent disobedience during peaceful demonstrations. They also provide for non-nationals, including long-term residents and those born in Estonia, to have their residence permit revoked for these offences and for other "intentional crimes against the state". This could include non-violent acts such as the symbolic destruction of national flags or those of foreign states or international organizations.

E

ETHIOPIA

FEDERAL DEMOCRATIC REPUBLIC OF ETHIOPIA
Head of state:	Girma Wolde-Giorgis
Head of government:	Meles Zenawi
Death penalty:	retentionist
Population:	82.8 million
Life expectancy:	54.7 years
Under-5 mortality (m/f):	138/124 per 1,000
Adult literacy:	35.9 per cent

Freedom of association and expression, and the work of human rights groups, were limited by new laws introduced in the first half of the year. Human rights defenders were harassed, with some fleeing the country to avoid arrest and detention. Opposition party leader Birtukan Mideksa, who was re-arrested in December 2008, continued to serve a life sentence in prison. Some 26 people were convicted in November in the trial of more than 30 former military officers and Ginbot 7 party officials accused

of plotting an armed attack on the government. Ethiopian security forces continued to carry out periodic arrests of Oromo political leaders, businessmen and their family members, who were often detained, sometimes without charge, for prolonged periods. Sporadic fighting continued between Ethiopian National Defense Forces (ENDF) and armed opposition Ogaden National Liberation Front (ONLF) in the Somali Region (known as the Ogaden). Up to 6.2 million Ethiopians, many in the Somali Region, required emergency assistance because of severe drought. International donor support for humanitarian operations was insufficient.

Background

Legislation was passed restricting civil society groups and broadening the reach of counter-terror operations. Human rights defenders chose to limit their own activities and journalists to self-censor in a climate of heightened anxiety over repression.

By the end of January, nearly all remaining Ethiopian troops based in Somalia had been withdrawn, although there were reports of sporadic cross-border incursions, particularly in the area of Beletweyne, throughout much of the year. Ethiopian government officials were also reported to have played a role in mediating negotiations between the President of Somaliland and opposition party leaders in September in Hargeisa, Somaliland. At that time, a crisis over repeated delays in national elections brought the self-declared independent country to the brink of violence (see Somalia entry).

While the government of Ethiopia hosted thousands of Eritrean, Somali and other refugees from the Horn of Africa, an increasing number of prominent opposition figures fled Ethiopia. These included human rights defenders and journalists who were harassed and intimidated by the authorities, leading them to believe that their arrest and detention could be imminent.

In September, more than 9,500 prisoners were released by the central government and by governments in the Amhara and Oromia regions, in a mass amnesty celebrating the Ethiopian New Year.

Prisoners of conscience and other political prisoners

The government continued to hold several prisoners of conscience and a large number of political prisoners in detention.

■ Former judge and Unity for Democracy and Justice Party leader Birtukan Mideksa remained in detention, serving a life sentence, since she was re-arrested in December 2008. Following international calls to improve her prison conditions, government officials moved her out of solitary confinement and she was later detained with other women prisoners. She received regular family visits but her lawyer reportedly had only intermittent access to her.

■ Twenty-six former military officers and others affiliated with the Ginbot 7 political party, led by Berhanu Negga, were convicted on several charges related to planning an attack on the government early in the year. Those detained for many months in this case included Ginbot 7 party leader Andargachew Tsige's father, 80-year-old Tsige Habtemariam, believed to be in very poor health. Eighteen of the defendants were reported to have been tortured and otherwise ill-treated upon their arrest by Ethiopian security forces in May.

■ Prisoner of conscience Sultan Fowsi Mohamed Ali, an independent mediator, remained in prison. He was arrested in Jijiga in September 2007, reportedly to prevent him from giving evidence to a UN fact-finding mission in the Somali Region.

■ Bashir Makhtal, a Canadian citizen, was sentenced to life imprisonment on 3 August. He had been convicted on 27 July on four terror-related charges, including being a member of the ONLF. The government denied allegations that his trial was unfair. Bashir Makhtal consistently denied all charges. On 4 December, the Supreme Court heard his appeal, but upheld the conviction and sentence. His brother, Hassan Makhtal, was released from prison in October and died in November, reportedly from complications due to ill-treatment in detention.

Freedom of expression

The authorities introduced various laws which negatively affected freedom of expression. Media workers were harassed by the authorities.

Charities and Societies Proclamation

In January, Parliament passed the Charities and Societies Proclamation, imposing strict controls and restrictions on civil society organizations whose work included human rights. If this law is enforced, international organizations would also be restricted from working on a range of human rights and democracy issues in Ethiopia without special permission. Similarly, local groups would be barred from human rights activities if they receive more than 10 per cent of their income from foreign sources, despite the fact that most depend heavily on support from outside Ethiopia. Even minor breaches of the law's provisions could invite severe criminal penalties, including fines and imprisonment. The Proclamation established a Charities and Societies Agency with broad discretionary power, including surveillance and interference in the management and operations of local organizations. The new law, expected to be implemented in early January 2010, puts at serious risk the ability of local and international organizations to monitor, report and advocate against human rights violations in Ethiopia. Some human rights groups scaled back their operations in the interim. Re-registration of local organizations under the new law began in October.

Anti-Terrorism Proclamation

In July, parliament passed the Anti-Terrorism Proclamation which restricted freedom of expression, and may restrict peaceful assembly and the right to a fair trial – with serious implications in the run-up to Ethiopia's 2010 parliamentary elections. According to the Proclamation, "acts of terrorism" include damage to property and disruption of public services, for which an individual could be sentenced to 15 years in prison or even the death penalty. The Proclamation's definition of "acts of terrorism" is vague and could encompass legitimate expressions of dissent.

■ In November and December, Addis Neger, a major publishing company, was threatened with closure and several of its reporters threatened with arrest, reportedly under the new Anti-Terrorism Proclamation. By the end of the year a number of journalists from the company had fled the country.

Media suppression

■ Ibrahim Mohamed Ali, editor of the *Salafiyya* newspaper, and Asrat Wedajo, editor of the former *Seife Nebelbal* newspaper, were each sentenced to one year in prison on charges linked to stories reporting human rights violations dating back to 2005. They were reportedly tried under an outdated press law which had since been superseded by a new media law passed in 2008.

■ The owners of several of the largest newspapers, which were closed during the government's 2005 media crackdown, were threatened in November with a summons to appear before the Ethiopian Supreme Court. They were asked to pay fines, imposed on them as part of their 2005 convictions, which reportedly had previously been waived.

Repression of dissent

The government of Ethiopia continued to suppress dissent in the Oromia Region of Ethiopia, and detained hundreds of people suspected of supporting the Oromo Liberation Front (OLF). Many were believed to have been held in incommunicado detention and many were detained without trial. Court proceedings were frequently and repeatedly delayed. Detainees were often held in poor conditions; some were reportedly ill-treated. Group arrests and detentions of Oromo leaders, activists and businesspeople continued sporadically throughout the year. Many of these arrests and detentions were reported to have been politically motivated.

■ Opposition political parties accused the government of arresting their members ahead of the scheduled 2010 elections; the majority of those named in lists of detainees were Oromo.

■ There were also reports of arrests, cases of rape and extrajudicial executions by government forces of suspected supporters of the ONLF in the Somali Region of Ethiopia. Although international fact-finding missions led to some alleviation of the humanitarian crisis in the region, Ethiopian authorities continued to place restrictions on humanitarian aid in some areas.

Death penalty

Death sentences were imposed but no executions were reported.

■ On 2 September, the Ethiopian Federal High Court sentenced six people to death and 97 others to prison terms on charges of genocide in relation to violence between residents of the Benishangul Gumuz and Oromia regions over a border dispute.

■ On 25 December, five men were sentenced to death, four in absentia, and 32 men and one woman to life imprisonment on charges related to an aborted coup attempt in April and May.

Amnesty International visit/reports

✈ Amnesty International delegates visited Ethiopia in September.

▥ Ethiopia: Arbitrary detention/torture or other ill-treatment: Birtukan Mideksa (AFR 25/003/2009)

▥ Ethiopia: Submission to the UN Universal Periodic Review (AFR 25/004/2009)

E

Ethiopia: Canadian citizen sentenced to life: Bashir Makhtal
(AFR 25/006/2009)

Ethiopia: Government passes repressive new legislation,
6 January 2009

Ethiopia: Government must reveal fate of political prisoners,
5 May 2009

Ethiopia: New Anti-Terrorism Proclamation jeopardizes freedom of
expression, 7 July 2009

FIJI

REPUBLIC OF THE FIJI ISLANDS

Head of state:	Ratu Epeli Nailatikau (replaced Ratu Josefa Iloilo Uluivuda in August)
Head of government:	Josaia Voreqe Bainimarama
Death penalty:	abolitionist for ordinary crimes
Population:	0.8 million
Life expectancy:	68.7 years
Under-5 mortality (m/f):	25/24 per 1,000
Adult literacy:	94.4 per cent

The suspension of the Constitution, dismissal of the judiciary and imposition of emergency regulations further undermined the protection of human rights and the rule of law. The military-led government continued to violate the right to freedom of expression and intimidate journalists and members of the public. The Fiji Human Rights Commission lacked independence and was made ineffective through a government decree. Violence against women was prevalent, with perpetrators enjoying impunity as a matter of policy.

Background

On 10 April, President Ratu Iloilo abrogated the Constitution, sacked the judiciary and declared a state of emergency using the Public Emergency Regulations (PER). These moves came a day after the Court of Appeal ruled that the military coup d'état of December 2006, and the subsequent actions of coup leader Commodore Bainimarama and President Ratu Iloilo, were illegal. Since April, media freedom was severely curtailed; the executive interfered with the independence of the judiciary and lawyers; and scores of human rights defenders, critics of the government and journalists were arrested and briefly detained, threatened or otherwise intimidated.

Legal, constitutional or institutional developments

The Revocation of Judicial Appointments Decree, introduced in April, dissolved all judicial appointments made under the Fiji Constitution. High Court judges were appointed to the judiciary six weeks later. Some judges who were dismissed in April accepted their re-appointments while others did not.

Two decrees in April and May barred the courts and the Human Rights Commission respectively from addressing issues concerning the abrogation of the Constitution and other acts of the government. The May decree also limited the Commission's powers to human rights education. In May, the Legal Practitioners' Decree removed the power to issue practising certificates to lawyers from the Fiji Law Society (FLS) and granted it to the government-appointed High Court Registrar. The Decree also excised the FLS from the Judicial Services Commission which is empowered to appoint high court judges.

■ In May, the High Court Registrar headed a raid on the office of the FLS, and removed files from the premises without a warrant.
■ Chief Magistrate Ajmal Khan and Magistrate Maika Nakora, both appointed in May, were sacked in July and August respectively without any official explanation.

Freedom of expression

The PER gave the Permanent Secretary for Information powers to revoke the licence of any media outlet that prints, publishes or broadcasts anything that portrays the government in a negative light. This led to extensive media censorship. Since April, the government used the PER to intimidate critics and human rights defenders, and arrest or detain without charge at least 20 journalists.

■ In April, several journalists were detained by the police under the PER, including one who was questioned for providing TV footage to an Australian journalist. Journalists were warned to practise "journalism of hope", meaning they should refrain from any negative reporting about the government, or face tough penalties from the authorities.
■ In May, two journalists were detained and questioned for publishing a report about the release of

several soldiers and a police officer, all of whom had been convicted of manslaughter for the death of a young man in June 2007. The government later admitted that the story was true.

■ In November, the military detained Fiji-born Australian academic Brij Lal over an interview he gave with the overseas media. The military threatened to kill him if he did not leave the country immediately. He left the next day.

Freedom of religion

In July, the government banned the Methodist Church from holding its annual church conference. Senior members of the church and a high chief were briefly detained and questioned by police, then questioned further by army officers. They were charged with offences under the PER for making arrangements for the conference to go ahead. Other churches and religious organizations were allowed to hold their annual conferences.

Police commissioner Esala Teleni introduced a "Christian crusade", a Christian outreach programme for police officers designed to curb crime. It involved police officers imparting the ethos of Christianity to members of the public through church services in town centres. This "crusade" was mandatory for all police officers regardless of their religion. Police officers who did not attend because they were of a different religious affiliation were sacked.

Violence against women and girls

Violence against women remained high with police failing to address the issue effectively. Police refrained from arresting or filing charges against suspects. Instead they forced survivors to reconcile with their violent partners as part of the police's "Christian crusade". From June to October, there were many reported cases of young girls and women being raped.

■ In July, a woman was raped and thrown into the sea. That same month, a man was charged with raping his daughters and daughter-in-law on several occasions. Fiji Women's Crisis Centre statistics showed a steady rise in the number of domestic violence cases dealt with during the year.

Amnesty International visit/report

🚗 An Amnesty International delegate visited in April.

📰 Fiji: Paradise Lost, a tale of ongoing human rights violations, April – July 2009 (ASA 18/002/2009)

FINLAND

REPUBLIC OF FINLAND

Head of state:	Tarja Halonen
Head of government:	Matti Vanhanen
Death penalty:	abolitionist for all crimes
Population:	5.3 million
Life expectancy:	79.5 years
Under-5 mortality (m/f):	5/4 per 1,000

Protection and redress for survivors of sexual violence were inadequate. Increasing numbers of asylum-seekers were transferred to other EU member states despite profound concern about reception conditions and access to fair asylum-determination procedures. Some children seeking asylum were detained. Conscientious objectors to military service were imprisoned.

International justice

The trial of François Bazaramba, a Rwandan national residing in Finland, began in September at Porvoo District Court. He faced charges of genocide, conspiracy to commit genocide and incitement to commit genocide in Rwanda in 1994 (see Rwanda entry). In September, civil society groups, including Amnesty International, called for adequate protection measures to be implemented for witnesses at the trial.

Violence against women and girls

Protection and redress for survivors of rape and other forms of sexual violence continued to be inadequate in law and in practice. Rape continued to be categorized differently in the Penal Code depending on the degree of physical violence used or threatened by the perpetrator. The conviction rate for rape remained very low and certain categories of rape and other forms of sexual abuse were investigated and prosecuted only if the victim so requested.

Refugees and asylum-seekers

Accelerated asylum-determination procedures failed to guarantee adequate protection for asylum-seekers, including by not providing a suspensive in-country right of appeal. This led to some asylum-seekers being expelled while their appeals were pending.

Increasing numbers of asylum-seekers were returned to other EU member states for determination

F

of their asylum claim under the Dublin II Regulation. Over the year, transfers under Dublin II amounted to 35 per cent of all the decisions taken by the authorities arising from asylum applications. The majority of these returns were to other EU member states where asylum-determination procedures and reception conditions, including detention, gave rise to serious concern.

Legislation continued to allow the detention of unaccompanied children seeking asylum. At least 29 children, 15 of whom were unaccompanied, were held in closed detention centres.

Prisoners of conscience – conscientious objectors to military service

The length of the civilian alternative to military service remained punitive and discriminatory; conscientious objectors were obliged to perform 362 days of alternative civilian service, more than twice the length of the most common military service – 180 days.
■ Seven conscientious objectors to military service were jailed for refusing to perform either military service or the alternative civilian service and most were serving sentences of 181 days' imprisonment.

Legal developments

In December, legislation providing a broad definition of torture as a criminal offence was adopted. However, the law contained a statute of limitations on torture.

In September, Finland signed the Optional Protocol to the Covenant on Economic, Social and Cultural Rights.

Discrimination

In March, the UN Committee on the Elimination of Racial Discrimination expressed concern at, among other things, the de facto segregation in housing experienced by migrants and Roma and the limited enjoyment by Roma of their rights to education, employment and housing.

FRANCE

FRENCH REPUBLIC

Head of state:	Nicolas Sarkozy
Head of government:	François Fillon
Death penalty:	abolitionist for all crimes
Population:	62.3 million
Life expectancy:	81 years
Under-5 mortality (m/f):	5/4 per 1,000

Allegations of police ill-treatment and excessive use of force continued. Disciplinary procedures and criminal investigations into such incidents continued to fall short of international standards. Hundreds of migrants and asylum-seekers, including unaccompanied minors, were forcibly evicted from makeshift housing in Calais. Three Afghan nationals were forcibly returned to Afghanistan. Two released Guantánamo Bay detainees were granted residency in France. There were concerns that two new police databases could undermine the presumption of innocence. Legislative reforms threatened to weaken the independent oversight of law enforcement agencies.

Police and security forces

Ill-treatment and excessive use of force by police were alleged, including in at least one fatal incident. Investigations conducted by law enforcement bodies and judicial authorities into such allegations often appeared to lack independence and impartiality and were slow to progress.
■ Ali Ziri, a 69-year-old Algerian man, died following his arrest in Argenteuil on 9 June. He was travelling in a friend's car when the two men were stopped by police. Ali Ziri's friend, Arezki Kerfali, said that they were beaten by the police officers, both at the scene and on the way to the police station. The two men were subsequently taken to hospital, where Ali Ziri died. One month later the Public Prosecutor closed the inquiry into his death stating that, on the basis of investigations conducted by the Argenteuil police, there was no evidence of ill-treatment. Arezki Kerfali was hospitalized for two days as a result of his injuries and subsequently charged with insulting a police officer. Following demands from Ali Ziri's family, an investigating judge was appointed to the case. The judge ordered a second autopsy to be conducted by

F

the Paris Medico-Legal Institute (Institut médico-légal de Paris, IML). It recorded multiple bruising on Ali Ziri's body and stated that his probable cause of death was positional asphyxia. In October, the Public Prosecutor requested further investigation into charges of involuntary homicide. The police officers concerned remained on active duty at the end of the year.

■ In July, experts from the IML concluded their examination of the hospital records of Abou Bakari Tandia, who died after sustaining fatal injuries while in police custody in January 2005. Their report stated that he had died after being shaken violently and that police testimony alleging that he had thrown himself against a wall was contradicted by the medical evidence. The hospital records, along with other important evidence, had been "lost" for several years and were only submitted to the investigating judge in January. Although the prosecutor asked for further investigation to be carried out regarding Abou Bakari Tandia's death, no action had been taken by the investigating judge at the end of the year.

■ In October, the Court of Appeal in Aix-en-Provence ordered judges investigating the death of Abdelhakim Ajimi to question two police officers on suspicion of involuntary homicide, and failing to assist a person in danger in the case of one of them. In March, five other police officers had been questioned on suspicion of failing to assist Abdelhakim Ajimi. An autopsy report stated that Abdelhakim Ajimi had suffocated as a result of the restraint techniques used on him by police officers in May 2008. The investigation was ongoing at the end of the year.

On 15 June, the then Minister of Interior announced that the annual reports of the police force internal inspectorate would be made public. However, at the end of the year no such information was available on the national police website and only a summary of statistics was available on request.

In September, the Council of State suspended the use of electro-shock weapons by local police forces, ruling that they had been introduced without adequate training and safeguards. The weapons were introduced by government decree in September 2008. National police and gendarmes continued to use such weapons.

Migrants' rights, refugees and asylum-seekers

In May, the Minister of Immigration, Integration,

National Identity and Mutually Supportive Development pursued a reform which could restrict the role of the six NGOs nominated to work in migration detention centres. The NGO Cimade launched legal challenges against the measure due to concerns that it would limit their role to providing information only and prevent them from giving legal assistance to detained migrants. In November, the Council of State upheld the reform.

In September, the Minister of Immigration stated that 20 million euros had been secured to build a new migration detention centre in the French overseas territory of Mayotte. However, no timeline was given for its construction. Photographs had been published anonymously in December 2008 showing the severe overcrowding and poor hygiene inside the existing centre.

On 22 September, approximately 300 migrants and asylum-seekers living in encampments around Calais, believed to be mostly Afghans trying to reach the UK, were detained by police. Their makeshift homes were demolished by bulldozers. According to police statements, 140 adults were taken into police custody and transferred to migration detention centres; 132 minors were taken to special accommodation centres. At the end of the year it was reported that all of the adults had been released; many were believed to have returned to the destroyed camps in Calais. Most of those released were left without shelter as a result of the destruction. Some were later granted asylum and others had asylum claims pending at the end of the year. The rest remained in France without regular status, at constant risk of being forcibly returned to their countries of origin. Further police operations against smaller encampments around Calais took place between October and December.

Three Afghan nationals, one of them detained at Calais, were forcibly returned to Afghanistan in October.

Counter-terror and security

On 3 December, the European Court of Human Rights ruled in *Daoudi v. France* that deporting a man convicted of terrorism offences to Algeria would put him at risk of torture or other ill-treatment, and would be in violation of the European Convention on Human Rights.

Guantánamo Bay detainees

France granted residency to two Algerian nationals, Lakhdar Boumediene and Saber Lahmar, who had been detained at the US detention centre in Guantánamo Bay. Both men were cleared of all charges against them by a US judge in November 2008 but could not return to Algeria due to the risk of serious human rights violations. In May, Lakhdar Boumediene arrived in France and was joined by his wife and children. Saber Lahmar arrived in France in December.

Legal, constitutional or institutional developments

On 18 October, two new police databases to collect data on individuals believed to pose a threat to public order were authorized by the government. They replaced the controversial "EDVIGE" database introduced in July 2008, which included information on individual health and sexual orientation, and on minors. However, concerns remained about the extent of the personal information collected on individuals not accused of any crime, including on children as young as 13, and the vagueness of the criteria for inclusion, such as "may pose a threat to public security".

In September, the Minister of Justice presented to the Council of Ministers draft laws proposing to merge the National Ombudsperson, the Children's Ombudsperson, and the National Commission on Security Ethics (Commission Nationale de Déontologie de la Sécurité, CNDS), which is responsible for the independent oversight of law enforcement agencies, into the new Defender of Rights institution. There was concern that this could undermine the work of the CNDS and other bodies.

Amnesty International visits/reports

🚌 Amnesty International delegates visited France in January, April and October.

📑 France: An effective mandate for the Defender of Rights (EUR 21/002/2009)

📑 Public outrage: Police officers above the law in France (EUR 21/003/2009)

GAMBIA

REPUBLIC OF THE GAMBIA

Head of state and government:	Yahya Jammeh
Death penalty:	abolitionist in practice
Population:	1.7 million
Life expectancy:	55.7 years
Under-5 mortality (m/f):	123/109 per 1,000
Adult literacy:	42.5 per cent

The government continued to stifle political and social dissent. Members of the National Intelligence Agency (NIA), army and police arbitrarily arrested and detained government opponents, human rights defenders, journalists and former security personnel. Reportedly, President Yahya Jammeh publicly threatened human rights defenders and those who co-operated with them. The authorities threatened to resume executions after more than 20 years.

Arbitrary arrests and detentions

The police, NIA and army arrested and detained people in breach of safeguards in national law. Detainees were held in official places of detention such as the Mile 2 Central Prison, the NIA headquarters and police detention centres, as well as in secret detention centres, including military barracks, secret quarters in police stations, police stations in remote areas and warehouses.

■ In March, more than 1,000 villagers from Foni Kansala district were taken to secret detention centres by "witch hunters" from Guinea and Burkina Faso dressed in red hooded outfits. The "witch hunters" were allegedly brought in by the President and accompanied by Gambian police, soldiers, NIA agents and the President's personal guards. The villagers were reportedly forced to drink hallucinogenic liquids and confess to "witchcraft". The drinks appeared to cause kidney problems and reportedly led to at least six deaths. Opposition leader Halifa Sallah, who wrote about the "witchcraft campaign" in the opposition newspaper *Foroyaa,* was detained, charged with treason and held in Mile 2 Central Prison until his case was-dropped in late March. The "witchcraft campaign" ceased after it was publicly exposed, but none of those involved in the abuses was brought to justice.

Several people were held in long-term detention without trial. Among them were at least 19 people, including Senegalese and Nigerian nationals, who were held without charge in Mile 2 Central Prison maximum security cell, one for at least 13 years.

■ At least two people arrested in connection with a March 2006 coup plot remained in detention. Alieu Lowe was held without charge or trial and Hamadi Sowe, charged with concealment of treason, was held without trial.

Freedom of expression – journalists

Freedom of expression continued to be severely limited. Journalists faced threats and harassment if they were suspected of writing stories unfavourable to the authorities or of providing information to media outlets.

■ On 15 June, seven journalists were arrested after criticizing the President for comments he made about the unsolved 2004 murder of Deyda Hydara, former editor of *The Point* newspaper. The seven were charged with defamation and sedition. One was later released on bail and charges subsequently dropped. On 6 August, the remaining six were convicted and sentenced to two years' imprisonment and a fine. Emil Touray, Secretary General of the Gambian Press Union (GPU); Sarata Jabbi Dibba, Vice President of the GPU; Pa Modou Faal, Treasurer of the GPU; Pap Saine and Ebrima Sawaneh, respectively publisher and editor of *The Point* newspaper; and Sam Sarr, editor of *Foroyaa* newspaper, were prisoners of conscience. They were released under a presidential pardon on 3 September.

Enforced disappearances

The fate and whereabouts of at least eight people arrested in previous years, including opposition supporters and journalists, remained unknown.

■ *Daily Observer* journalist Chief Ebrima Manneh, who was arrested in 2006, remained disappeared despite a 2008 ruling by the ECOWAS Community Court of Justice demanding his release and damages for his family. In October, the government denied any knowledge of his whereabouts.

■ The government continued to deny knowledge of the whereabouts of Kanyiba Kanyie, an opposition supporter arrested in September 2006.

Unlawful killings

In April, a team established by ECOWAS and the UN reported on the killing in July 2005 of more than 50 foreign nationals, most from Ghana, who were intercepted by Gambian security forces in the sea off Gambia. The report established that Gambian security forces were involved but not under government directive. The government contributed towards the funeral expenses of six Ghanaians whose bodies were found, but took no steps to bring those responsible for the killings to justice.

Death penalty

In September, the President announced that executions would resume to counter rising crime; the last known execution was in the 1980s. In October, the Director of Public Prosecutions was reported as saying that all prisoners sentenced to death would be executed by hanging as soon as possible.

One person was sentenced to death and at least 12 people were believed to be on death row at the end of the year. No executions were reported.

■ In August, Kalilou Conteh was sentenced to death by Banjul magistrate's court for murder.

Human rights defenders

On 21 September, the President reportedly threatened to kill anyone wishing to destabilize the country and specifically threatened human rights defenders and those working with them. As a result, international organizations and members of Gambia's civil society boycotted the session of the African Commission on Human and Peoples' Rights held in the Gambia in November. Two UN Special Rapporteurs and one Rapporteur serving with the African Commission condemned the President's remarks as unacceptable and in breach of all human rights instruments ratified by Gambia.

Amnesty International visit/reports

🚗 Amnesty International delegates visited Gambia in November to conduct research.

📄 Gambia: Amnesty International demands freedom for Gambians (AFR 27/005/2009)

📄 Gambia: Submission to the UN Universal Periodic Review (AFR 27/006/2009)

📄 Gambia: Amnesty International expresses solidarity with civil society in Gambia (AFR 27/008/2009)

📄 Gambia: Hundreds accused of "witchcraft" and poisoned in government campaign, 18 March 2009

📄 Gambia: Six journalists condemned to two years in Mile 2 prison, 7 August 2009

G

GEORGIA

GEORGIA
Head of state: **Mikheil Saakashvili**
Head of government: **Nikoloz Gilauri (replaced Grigol Mgaloblishvili in February)**
Death penalty: **abolitionist for all crimes**
Population: **4.3 million**
Life expectancy: **71.6 years**
Under-5 mortality (m/f):   **39/33 per 1,000**

Violations of international human rights and humanitarian law committed by Georgian and South Ossetian forces during the conflict in 2008 were not investigated further by the relevant authorities. In its aftermath, civilians in the post-conflict zone suffered from the overarching insecurity, incidents of harassment and detention. Nearly 26,000 people, mostly ethnic Georgians, were unable to return to their homes. Opposition activists and journalists reportedly suffered from harassment and alleged use of excessive force by the police.

Background

The year was marked by insecurity in and around Abkhazia and South Ossetia, regions of Georgia which had declared themselves independent in 2008, and the political crisis between April and July, when large-scale demonstrations called for the resignation of President Mikheil Saakashvili.

Armed conflict

A report by the Independent International Fact-Finding Mission on the Conflict in Georgia, commissioned by the EU and published in September, confirmed that violations of international human rights and humanitarian law were committed by Georgian, Russian and South Ossetian forces in 2008 and called on all sides of the conflict to address the consequences of the war. By the end of the year, no full investigations had been conducted by any side into the violations of human rights and international humanitarian law that took place during the 2008 war and in its immediate aftermath. A general lack of accountability persisted and there had been no comprehensive efforts undertaken to bring any of those responsible to justice.

The security situation in and around the post-conflict zones remained tense. International scrutiny and monitoring capacity were reduced significantly in June, when both the OSCE mission to Georgia and the UN Observer Mission in Georgia ended. The EU Monitoring Mission, the only remaining internationally mandated monitoring group, was denied access to areas controlled by the de facto authorities in South Ossetia and Abkhazia. There were reports of civilians being harassed and detained for alleged illegal crossing of the administrative border line between Georgia and South Ossetia.

Internally displaced people

Following what appeared to be a deliberate policy of forced displacement as part of the 2008 war, an estimated 26,000 people, mostly of Georgian ethnic origin, remained unable to return home to their villages. Most of the displaced people in Georgia had been provided with some kind of accommodation or compensation. However, concerns remained regarding their access to social and economic rights due to loss of livelihoods and lack of employment.

Violence against women

In April, the government approved the new action plan on domestic violence for 2009-10. In July, a national referral mechanism was adopted, providing guidance to identify survivors of domestic violence and to refer them to available services and assistance. The government allocated premises and prepared to set up shelters. However, by the end of the year these state shelters for victims of domestic violence were still not operational.

Freedom of assembly

Supporters of the opposition were allegedly harassed, intimidated and beaten by unidentified masked men during demonstrations between April and July. Reports stated that police officers stood by without intervening while some of these incidents took place, raising concerns about the authorities' failure to protect demonstrators and to ensure the right to freedom of assembly. While investigations were initiated into some of the reported incidents, the authorities failed to carry out full and impartial investigations and to bring those responsible to justice.

Changes to the law regulating the right to assembly and to hold demonstrations, enacted in June, set

G

stringent penalties that human rights activists feared could be used to restrict the right to freedom of assembly.

Excessive use of force

On 6 May, police officers reportedly fired impact projectiles at opposition demonstrators in a reckless manner during a violent confrontation outside the police headquarters in Tbilisi, which resulted in several people sustaining head injuries. In another incident on 15 June, police officers reportedly dispersed peaceful opposition protesters outside the Tbilisi police headquarters with excessive force, attacking the protesters using batons without any warning or prior warnings to disperse. Seventeen protesters sought medical assistance in hospital to have their wounds treated; two were hospitalized due to severe injuries. Among those injured was a representative of the Ombudsman's office who was allegedly detained and beaten by police officers. Investigations into both incidents were ongoing but had not progressed by the end of the year.

Freedom of expression

Journalists covering the demonstrations between April and June reportedly faced harassment and violence from both the authorities and opposition supporters. According to witnesses, on 15 June, police officers assaulted a number of journalists during the dispersal of an opposition protest and confiscated their audiovisual equipment. In some instances, tapes containing footage of the incident were not returned; in other cases parts of the tapes were missing.

Before and during these demonstrations, a large number of opposition activists were arrested on charges of possession of drugs and arms. The Ombudsman as well as human rights NGOs voiced concern that some might have been arrested because of their political activities and that their trials failed to meet international fair trial standards.

Amnesty International visits/reports

🚌 Amnesty International delegates visited Georgia in June and November.

📃 Civilians in the aftermath of war: The Georgia-Russia conflict one year on (EUR 04/001/2009)

📃 South Caucasus: Promptly adopt and enforce legislation on domestic violence (EUR 04/002/2009)

📃 Georgia: Police reportedly use excessive force against the demonstrators (EUR 56/001/2009)

GERMANY

FEDERAL REPUBLIC OF GERMANY

Head of state:	Horst Köhler
Head of government:	Angela Merkel
Death penalty:	abolitionist for all crimes
Population:	82.2 million
Life expectancy:	79.8 years
Under-5 mortality (m/f):	5/5 per 1,000

The absolute prohibition on torture continued to be undermined by government adherence to a policy of deportation with assurances, placing individuals at risk of serious human rights violations. Parliament concluded its inquiry into renditions (unlawful transfer of suspects between countries) and other counter-terrorism related abuses. Irregular migrants were denied their economic, social and cultural rights.

Counter-terror and security

Two criminal cases involving terrorism suspects raised concerns about the use of evidence allegedly obtained through torture.

In a case tried before the Higher Regional Court in Koblenz between December 2008 and July 2009, the prosecution's indictment relied partly on statements made by the accused while in custody in Pakistan, where he claimed he was beaten and deprived of sleep.

In April, it became known that, in June and September 2008, German investigators had interrogated a detained witness in the presence of the Uzbekistani National Security Service in Tashkent, Uzbekistan, where torture is systematic. The interrogation formed part of the criminal investigations in a case tried before the Higher Regional Court in Düsseldorf.

Regulatory rules governing the Aliens Act entered into force in October. They provide for the use of "diplomatic assurances" to justify returning terrorism suspects to places where they are at risk of torture or other cruel, inhuman or degrading treatment, in contravention of international obligations. Such assurances are unreliable and do not provide an effective safeguard against torture.

The authorities continued to accept "diplomatic assurances" from the Tunisian government as sufficient to eliminate the risk of torture in cases of planned forcible returns of Tunisian nationals

G

suspected of terrorism-related activities.

■ In March, the Administrative Court in Düsseldorf ruled in the case of a Tunisian national that "diplomatic assurances" undermine the absolute ban on torture and prohibited the forcible return of the plaintiff. The authorities challenged this ruling and the case was pending at the end of the year.

Parliament debated the report of its inquiry into renditions and secret detention in July. The report concluded that the government and intelligence services had no direct or indirect involvement in renditions and secret detention. However, Amnesty International found that both the inquiry and report provided enough evidence to conclude that Germany was complicit in human rights violations, and criticized parliament for failing to propose any measures to prevent such abuses in future. On 17 June, the Federal Constitutional Court ruled that the government had violated Constitutional Law by not providing the parliamentary committee of inquiry with relevant documents, which the government said should remain classified in order to protect the welfare of the state. The committee of inquiry did not resume its investigation.

Refugees and asylum-seekers

The number of rejected asylum-seekers forcibly returned to Syria increased considerably after a German-Syrian re-admission agreement came into force in January. Following reports of returned Syrian asylum-seekers being detained, the government ordered a risk assessment re-evaluation and recommended a de facto moratorium on deportations to Syria in mid-December.

■ Khaled Kenjo, a deported Syrian Kurd, was detained 12 days after his arrival in Syria by the State Security, a Syrian secret service agency, on 13 September. After three weeks of incommunicado detention, during which he said he was tortured, Khaled Kenjo was charged with broadcasting "false" news abroad that could damage the reputation of the state. This charge by the Military Court in Qamishli was allegedly related to his political activities in Germany.

The government negotiated a re-admission agreement with Kosovo. Several federal states forcibly returned Roma to Kosovo despite the risks faced by Roma in cases of enforced return. In November, the Council of Europe Commissioner of Human Rights expressed concern at this practice.

Migrants' rights

Irregular migrants and their children had limited access to health care, education, and judicial remedies in cases of labour rights violations. Hesse Federal State was due to change its administrative practice on 1 January 2010 so that head teachers would no longer be required to report the identity of a child to the Aliens' Authority, where foreign nationals are required to register. The new regulatory rules governing the Aliens Act state that public hospitals are exempt from reporting the identity of irregular migrants in cases of emergency treatment.

Police and security forces

In December, the Federal Court of Justice held a public hearing on Oury Jalloh, who died in police custody in 2005 from heat shock caused by a fire in his cell. At the hearing, the Court criticized the investigations. The relatives of Oury Jalloh and the Public Prosecution Office lodged an appeal against the judgement of the Dessau Regional Court which had acquitted two police officers.

In May, the Federal Agency for the Prevention of Torture started its work, under Article 3 of the Optional Protocol to the UN Convention against Torture. Concerns were raised that it lacked sufficient financial and human resources.

National scrutiny – Kunduz

The government and military came under pressure from the media and opposition parties following the general election for withholding information about a NATO airstrike near Kunduz, Afghanistan, on 4 September. Up to 142 people, including civilians, were killed (see Afghanistan entry). Consequently, three senior government and military officials were forced to resign in November. On 16 December, a parliamentary inquiry began its examination of the government's handling of the attack and its aftermath.

Economic relations and human rights

In July, the government withdrew the export credit guarantee that it had granted to a German company for its activity in the Ilısu dam project in Turkey. The decision to withdraw was jointly taken with the Swiss and Austrian governments after independent experts concluded that the project would not meet agreed standards. The construction of the dam was expected to displace at least 55,000 people, and the

G

resettlement policy did not meet international human rights standards.

Legal developments
Despite the government's announcement in 2008 that it would sign and ratify the Optional Protocol to the International Covenant on Economic, Social and Cultural Rights, it had not done so by the end of the year.

The Council of Europe Convention on Action against Trafficking in Human Beings had not been ratified by the end of the year and Germany continued to be a destination and transit country for women trafficked for sexual exploitation.

GHANA

REPUBLIC OF GHANA

Head of state and government:	**John Evans Atta Mills**
	(replaced John Agyekum Kufuor in January)
Death penalty:	**abolitionist in practice**
Population:	**23.8 million**
Life expectancy:	**56.5 years**
Under-5 mortality (m/f):	**119/115 per 1,000**
Adult literacy:	**65 per cent**

Prison conditions remained poor. Seven people were sentenced to death, but 14 death sentences were commuted to life imprisonment and there were no executions. Hundreds of people were forcibly evicted from their homes. Violence against women remained pervasive.

Background
John Evans Atta Mills was inaugurated President on 7 January.

A curfew remained in force in the northern region of Bawku, where inter-communal violence continued. Twenty-one people were reported to have been killed.

The Freedom of Information Bill, introduced in 2002, was still not passed into law.

Prison conditions
Prisons were overcrowded and under-resourced, with poor medical and sanitary facilities and insufficient bedding. Many inmates were forced to sleep in turns and on bare floors. Prisons with a capacity for about 8,000 prisoners were holding approximately 13,000, almost 30 per cent of whom were awaiting trial. In September, according to media reports, 1,021 prisoners were pardoned by the President to mark an anniversary of Dr Kwame Nkrumah, Ghana's first President.

Death penalty
Seven people were sentenced to death, according to the prison authorities, bringing to 99 the number of prisoners on death row. Among those under sentence of death were two women. Fourteen death sentences were commuted to life imprisonment and there were no executions.

Right to adequate housing – forced evictions
Threats of and actual forced evictions, particularly of marginalized people, continued. In October, the Accra Metropolitan Assembly demolished structures along the railway near Graphic Road and structures within the slum known as Abuja, affecting hundreds of people. These forced evictions deprived families of their homes and, usually, their livelihoods. Residents who had been living and working in the structures said they were not consulted about the evictions, nor offered any compensation or adequate alternative housing.

Thousands of people living in Agbogbloshie and Old Fadama settlements in Accra repeatedly came under threat of forced eviction. The Accra Metropolitan Assembly announced that the settlements would be demolished and residents would not be relocated or compensated. In November, the government indicated that people facing eviction in Old Fadama would be relocated, but no further details were given. Some residents have lived in the communities for 30 years.

Violence against women and girls
Violence against women and girls continued to be widespread, with violence in the family thought to affect one in three women. According to the police's Domestic Violence and Victim Support Unit, reported cases of violence against women and girls increased in 2009.

G

Justice system

The police often failed to bring suspects before a court within a reasonable time. The Justice for All Programme, initiated in 2007 by the Ministry of Justice and the judiciary to speed up the trials of people remanded in prison, had no significant impact.

Amnesty International report

📄 Ghana: A seven-point human rights agenda for the new government (AFR 28/001/2009)

GREECE

HELLENIC REPUBLIC

Head of state:	Karolos Papoulias
Head of government:	George A. Papandreou
	(replaced Kostas Karamanlis in October)
Death penalty:	abolitionist for all crimes
Population:	11.2 million
Life expectancy:	79.1 years
Under-5 mortality (m/f):	5/4 per 1,000
Adult literacy:	97.1 per cent

Reports continued throughout the year of incidents of ill-treatment by law enforcement officials. A new Presidential Decree left asylum-seekers without an effective right of appeal. There were reports of arbitrary expulsions of irregular migrants and possible asylum-seekers from Evros. Up to 100 people were reportedly left homeless, without access to services, following the forced eviction of a large number of irregular migrants and asylum-seekers from a campsite in Patras. Detention conditions in various immigration detention centres and prisons remained a cause of concern. Attacks by armed opposition groups resulted in injuries.

Background

Armed opposition groups launched a number of armed attacks, including on a police station. They also carried out bomb attacks: some on banks, one on the home of a member of parliament and another on the home of a Member of the European Parliament. One police officer was killed and seven others were injured, three seriously.

Refugees, asylum-seekers and migrants

There was concern about the frequent failure by police authorities at the country's points of entry to register individual asylum claims, thereby denying people access to the asylum procedure. In June, a new Presidential Decree (81/2009) introduced detrimental changes to the asylum determination procedure. Among other changes, the new decree abolished the Appeals Board and thus deprives asylum-seekers from an effective right of appeal against decisions at first instance. What remained was judicial review of cases by the Council of State, which is limited to examination of the lawfulness of the decision. In July, UNHCR, the UN refugee agency, announced its decision not to participate in asylum procedures unless substantial changes were made. At the end of the year the new government announced plans to reform the asylum determination procedure, establish a new independent Asylum Service and create screening centres for irregular migrants at the country's points of entry. Committees of Experts were set up to prepare proposals on these issues.

Several individuals were forcibly returned to countries where they risked serious human rights abuses.

■ In July, 18 Kurdish asylum-seekers of Turkish nationality, including four unaccompanied minors, were forcibly returned to Turkey. Police responsible for their detention in Chania, Crete, had refused to file asylum applications for the four minors or to forward the 14 adults' applications to the competent authorities.

Between June and August, the authorities transferred many irregular migrants and possible asylum-seekers from immigration detention centres on the Greek islands to the border region of Evros. There were reports by local and international NGOs of arbitrary expulsions of individuals from these groups.

In June, Law 3772/2009 allowed for the administrative expulsion of "aliens", even where the individual has been charged with offences punishable by a minimum of three months' imprisonment. Asylum-seekers and refugees were not excluded from the scope of the provision. The same law increased the period of administrative detention from three to six months with a possible extension of a further 12 months under certain circumstances, making a possible maximum of 18 months.

Problems such as overcrowding and poor hygiene, as well as lack of adequate food, outside exercise, access to the outside world and to health services, continued to be reported in immigration detention centres. In June, the European Committee for the Prevention of Torture concluded that "the detention conditions of the vast majority of irregular migrants deprived of their liberty in Greece remain unacceptable".

In some facilities, unaccompanied minors were detained for as long as two and half months due to a shortage of places in minors' reception centres.
■ In August, approximately 150 unaccompanied minors went on hunger strike in the Pagani immigration detention centre in Lesvos, protesting against their detention conditions. The centre was temporarily closed in November.
■ In July, a large number of irregular migrants and asylum-seekers, including unaccompanied minors, were forcibly evicted from a campsite in Patras. Between 80 and 100 people were reportedly left homeless, without access to water, sanitation or medical assistance. During the same month, approximately 100 irregular migrants were also forcibly evicted from a disused courthouse in Athens.

Racially motivated attacks against migrants and asylum-seekers increased.

In December, a draft law which provides for the granting of citizenship to second generation migrants was announced.

Torture and other ill-treatment

Protesters, lawyers and journalists were reportedly ill-treated by police following a demonstration in January.
■ The special guard responsible for the shooting of Alexis Gregoropoulos in December 2008 was charged with manslaughter with intent. The second guard was charged with complicity. Their trial was pending at the end of the year.

Incidents of excessive use of force by police during demonstrations were reported during the year. There were reports of a large number of arbitrary transfers of protesters to police stations, ill-treatment by police against some peaceful demonstrators and of police motorbikes injuring some demonstrators during the protests in December.

Reports continued throughout the year of ill-treatment by law enforcement officials, especially against members of vulnerable groups such as asylum-seekers, migrants and Roma.

■ On 3 April, Arivan Osman Aziz, a Kurdish Iraqi migrant, was reportedly severely beaten by a coastguard officer in the port of Igoumenitsa. He died as a result of his injuries four months later. An investigation had not been concluded by the end of the year.
■ In May, a police officer allegedly destroyed the Koran of a Syrian migrant during an identity check. The sworn administrative inquiry into the incident had not been concluded by the end of the year. The Muslim migrant community staged several demonstrations to protest about the incident.
■ In October, Mohamed Kamran Atif, a Pakistani migrant, died 14 days after he was reportedly subjected to torture during his arrest and detention in a police station in Piraeus. A criminal investigation was opened.
■ In October, several asylum-seekers and migrants were reportedly beaten by police guards. The incident followed their request to be let out of a smoke-filled dormitory after a protest about detention conditions and length of detention in Pagani immigration detention centre in Lesvos. Among them was a 17-year-old Palestinian who reportedly was severely beaten. An investigation was opened and some witnesses reported being intimidated.
■ The trial of a police officer charged with torturing two detainees with electric shocks in August 2002 commenced in December.

In December, the government presented a Draft Presidential Decree establishing a Bureau to deal with incidents of arbitrary behaviour by law enforcement officials. Concerns existed over the institutional independence and limited mandate of the proposed body.

Workers' rights

In June, the judge in charge of investigating the attack against trade unionist Konstantina Kuneva concluded the investigation, having failed to identify the perpetrators. Concerns were expressed by her lawyers over the quality and thoroughness of the pre-trial investigation. In November, the Council of Misdemeanours in Athens ordered the continuation of the investigation into the case.

Prison conditions

Reports were received of inhuman and degrading conditions of detention in prisons, including

G

overcrowding, inadequate facilities and lack of access to adequate medical care. Women prisoners reported that they continued to be subjected to the practice of internal examinations. In December, legislative amendments were adopted to deal with prison overcrowding and the improvement of prison conditions.

Conscientious objectors to military service

The current law on conscientious objection was still not in line with European and international standards. Conscientious objectors continued to face discrimination and even prosecution.

■ On 31 March, conscientious objector Lazaros Petromelidis was given a suspended sentence of 18 months' imprisonment on two charges of insubordination by the Athens Military Court of Appeal. In 2008, the Court of First Instance had sentenced him to three years' imprisonment on the same charges.

Freedom of expression

A report in February by the Council of Europe Commissioner for Human Rights expressed concerns about the over-restrictive practices of Greek courts in failing to register certain minority associations, and ordering the dissolution of the Xanthi Turkish Union. Similar concerns were expressed by the UN Independent Expert on Minority Issues. Despite these, and the judgments of the European Court of Human Rights in 2008, the Supreme Court of Greece upheld the refusal of the Court of Appeal to register the association "House of Macedonian Civilization" in June.

Rights of lesbian, gay, bisexual and transgender people

In March, several people were injured in a homophobic attack on a bar in Athens. It was reported that police and ambulances did not respond to the incident, despite many calls.

Trafficking in human beings

Amid concerns that the government had taken insufficient action to identify victims of trafficking, draft guidelines proposed by a coalition of NGOs, including Amnesty International, were still not adopted. Lack of state funding led to the closure of some shelters for victims of trafficking.

Violations against the Romani community

While acknowledging the special measures already adopted for the social integration of Roma, the Committee for the Elimination of Racial Discrimination (CERD) expressed its concerns in August about the obstacles faced by Roma regarding their access to work, housing, health care and education.

■ In August, at least 11 Romani families faced forced eviction from their homes on a landfill site on the island of Lefkada, and were subjected to other violations of their rights to adequate housing and health. By the end of the year, the Romani families continued to remain in the settlement. The construction work on the landfill site was completed and minor improvements had been made to the settlement. However, by the end of the year the local authorities had not taken steps to transfer the Romani community to appropriate alternative accommodation.

Amnesty International visit/reports

🚌 Amnesty International delegates visited Greece in June.

📄 Greece: Alleged abuses in the policing of demonstrations (EUR 25/001/2009)

📄 Greece: Proposed changes to asylum procedures flagrantly violate international law (EUR 25/005/2009)

📄 Greece: Amnesty International reiterates its serious concerns about detention conditions for asylum-seekers following ruling of the European Court of Human Rights (EUR 25/006/2009)

📄 Greece: Amnesty International condemns forced evictions in Patras (EUR 25/007/2009)

📄 Greece: Further forced evictions leave large numbers homeless (EUR 25/008/2009)

📄 Greece: 11 Roma families face forced eviction (EUR 25/009/2009)

📄 Greece: Amnesty International calls on the Government to create a genuinely independent and effective police complaints mechanism (EUR 25/011/2009)

GUATEMALA

REPUBLIC OF GUATEMALA

Head of state and government:	Álvaro Colom Caballeros
Death penalty:	retentionist
Population:	14 million
Life expectancy:	70.1 years
Under-5 mortality (m/f):	45/34 per 1,000
Adult literacy:	73.2 per cent

The vast majority of those responsible for grave human rights violations committed during the internal armed conflict (1960-1996) were not held to account. Violence against women and lack of access to justice for women remained a serious concern. A number of human rights defenders were attacked and threatened.

Background

In May, the lawyer Rodrigo Rosenberg was murdered. He had recorded a video accusing President Álvaro Colom and other members of his government of responsibility in the event of his death; the video was publicly circulated after he was killed. The killing and the recording provoked nationwide protests against the government and pro-government counter-protests. The UN-sponsored International Commission against Impunity in Guatemala (Comisión Internacional Contra la Impunidad en Guatemala, CICIG) investigated the case and in September facilitated the arrest of nine people, including serving and former police officers, alleged to have carried out the killing. In December two more people were arrested.

In October the UN General Assembly passed a resolution supporting the CICIG and calling on the UN and the Guatemalan government to continue assisting the CICIG in its efforts to improve criminal investigations, prosecution procedures and the implementation of public security-related legislation.

Impunity

Ten years after the publication of the *Memory of Silence* report by the UN-sponsored Historical Clarification Commission, which investigated grave and widespread human rights violations committed during the internal armed conflict, few of those responsible for these violations had been brought to justice.

In February, the Constitutional Court ordered the Ministry of Defence to hand over files relating to an ongoing legal case against several former high-ranking military officers accused of genocide against Indigenous Peoples, crimes against humanity and war crimes during the internal armed conflict. Among the crimes of which they were accused was the 1982 massacre of some 250 women, children and men in Plan de Sánchez, Baja Verapaz department. The Ministry of Defence refused to hand over all the documents, alleging that some of them had been lost. The Ministry had not raised the problem of missing documents previously, despite more than two years of legal proceedings over disclosure of the documents. By the end of the year, the documents had not been released and legal challenges to the Court's decision continued.

In August, a former member of the Civil Defence Patrols, civilian auxiliaries to the military during the armed conflict, was convicted of the enforced disappearance of six people between 1982 and 1984 in Choatalúm municipality, Chimaltenango department. The accused was sentenced to 125 years' imprisonment. In December, three former members of the Civil Defence Patrols and a retired colonel were sentenced to 50 years each for the enforced disappearance of eight people in 1981 in the village of El Jute, Chimaltenango department.

Police and security forces

The report of the UN Special Rapporteur on extrajudicial, summary or arbitrary executions issued in May noted the persistence of executions of gang members or criminal suspects. The Special Rapporteur noted that local organizations had found evidence of the continued involvement, both direct and indirect, of members of the police force in these killings. He also drew attention to the continued trend of lynchings, mostly of people suspected of robbery, and the failure of the authorities to take steps to stop these killings.

Violence against women and girls

In February, the UN Committee on the Elimination of Discrimination against Women urged the government to increase efforts to stop violence against women, reverse the persistence of high levels of poverty and social exclusion, and address the disadvantages faced by women in the labour market.

G

In March, Congress passed a law to combat sexual violence, exploitation and people trafficking. According to government figures, 717 women were killed during 2009, an increase over the previous year. Many of those killed had been raped and their bodies mutilated.

Human rights defenders

Local human rights organizations reported a number of attacks and threats against human rights defenders. Most of those responsible were not held to account.

■ In September Adolfo Ich Chamán, a local teacher and community leader, was killed in El Estor, Izabal department, in the context of an ongoing land dispute with a nickel mining company. Witnesses stated that company guards attacked and killed Adolfo Ich Chamán during a protest over an alleged attempt to forcibly evict the community. The company denied that a forced eviction had been threatened or carried out and that security guards had been involved in the killing.

■ In April, Edgar Neftaly Aldana Valencia was threatened and shots were fired at his house in San Benito, Petén department. The threats specified that he had been targeted because of his trade union activities at a nearby hospital where he had helped expose corruption and medical negligence.

No investigation had been initiated into these incidents by the end of the year.

Death penalty

No new death sentences were passed during 2009 and no one was executed. At the end of the year, 15 people remained on death row.

Amnesty International report

Police involvement in killings in Guatemala (AMR 34/010/2009)

GUINEA

REPUBLIC OF GUINEA

Head of state:	Sékouba Konaté (replaced Moussa Dadis Camara in December)
Head of government:	Kabiné Komara
Death penalty:	retentionist
Population:	10.1 million
Life expectancy:	57.3 years
Under-5 mortality (m/f):	157/138 per 1,000
Adult literacy:	29.5 per cent

Security forces extrajudicially executed more than 150 peaceful demonstrators and injured more than 1,500 others in a stadium during a protest; dozens of women were raped in public. Torture and other ill-treatment were widespread. Dozens of people were arbitrarily detained, including at secret locations. The security forces continued to enjoy impunity for human rights violations. Human rights defenders and journalists faced threats and intimidation.

Background

In January, ECOWAS endorsed the decision taken by the AU and suspended Guinea until the country re-establishes constitutional order. President Moussa Dadis Camara, head of a military junta that seized power in late 2008, promised to hold elections in 2009 and pledged that neither he nor any member of the National Council for Democracy and Development (Conseil national pour la démocratie et le développement, CNDD) would run for the presidency. The CNDD's popularity dwindled when it became clear in February that President Camara was reluctant to keep his promise.

After the 28 September stadium massacre (see below), ECOWAS and the EU imposed an arms embargo on Guinea. Targeted sanctions against members of the junta were also imposed by the AU and EU.

In December, President Camara was wounded in an assassination attempt; General Sékouba Konaté replaced him on an interim basis.

Excessive use of force and extrajudicial executions

Security forces routinely used excessive and unnecessary lethal force against peaceful demonstrators. No sanctions were taken against those responsible for unlawful killings. On several occasions, CNDD members encouraged people to lynch suspected thieves.

■ In August, one person was killed and two were seriously wounded in Kamsar when the security forces broke up demonstrations against water and electricity shortages.

■ On 28 September, more than 150 people were extrajudicially killed and over 1,500 injured when the security forces violently repressed a peaceful demonstration in Conakry. Thousands of demonstrators assembled in a stadium in response to a call by a coalition of political parties, trade unions and civil society organizations to protest against the participation of President Camara in the presidential elections planned for January 2010. The junta had banned the demonstration.

■ On 30 September, a soldier dragged a man along the main road in Bomboli before stabbing him to death. His body was left on the road.

■ Also on 30 September, in the district of La Cimenterie, Conakry, soldiers wearing red berets, who were looking for an alleged opposition supporter, stabbed to death his 75-year-old mother.

Impunity

The security forces continued to enjoy impunity. A national commission of inquiry, set up in 2007 to investigate grave human rights violations in 2006 and 2007, did not conduct any investigations.

In October, the UN Secretary-General established an International Commission of Inquiry (ICI), endorsed by the AU and ECOWAS, to investigate the grave human rights violations, including rape, committed by Guinean security forces in September. In December, the ICI submitted its report to the UN Secretary-General. The report was not officially made public. The ICI found that it was reasonable to conclude that the crimes committed on 28 September and in the immediate aftermath may constitute crimes against humanity. It also concluded that there were sufficient grounds to attribute criminal responsibility to some individuals, including President Camara; Commander Moussa Tiégboro Camara, Minister of the Special Services responsible for combating drug trafficking and organized crime; and Lieutenant Aboubacar Chérif Diakité, the President's aide-de-camp and commander of his personal bodyguards.

In October, the Prosecutor of the International Criminal Court (ICC) launched a preliminary examination to determine whether the violations of 28 September fell within the court's jurisdiction. The same month the junta set up a national commission of inquiry, which was boycotted by local civil society organizations.

Torture and other ill-treatment

Torture and other ill-treatment, including rape, sustained beatings and stabbings, were routinely committed by the security forces. Detainees were also held incommunicado at secret locations.

■ Soldiers arrested in January (see below) were beaten upon their arrival in the military barracks on Kassa Island. They were undressed and were forced to lie down with their hands tied behind their back, and then trampled and beaten.

■ People arrested after the September stadium massacre were tortured in secret detention. People searching for the bodies of their relatives or friends were arrested and beaten in military camps.

Violence against women

Sexual violence, including rape, was prevalent, especially after 28 September.

■ Dozens of women told Amnesty International that they had been raped in public on 28 September in the stadium by soldiers, including the Presidential Guard. Medical records from Conakry's Donka hospital indicated that at least 32 women protesters were raped. Several women who were arrested and transferred to a health centre after they had been raped were subsequently re-arrested. They were then held for five days, drugged and again raped by security forces.

■ The body of a woman arrested on 28 September was returned to her family a few days later showing signs of sexual violence as well as burn marks from an iron.

■ At least two women who testified before the ICI received death threats after the departure of the UN delegation in early December.

Human rights defenders

Well-established civil society groups, including the Guinean Human Rights Organization (Organisation Guinéenne des droits de l'homme, OGDH) and the National Council of Civil Society Organizations, continued to work for human rights, despite the risks, threats and intimidation.

G

Following the 28 September events, the OGDH was regularly attacked on the national radio and television.
■ Mouctar Diallo, Vice-President of the Observatoire national des droits de l'homme (ONDH), Guinea's national human rights commission, was arrested on 26 November. He was held at the Alpha Yaya military barracks in Conakry before being transferred to the detention centre PM III (Poste militaire III). He was not charged or allowed a visit by a lawyer. The authorities informed Amnesty International that Mouctar Diallo was accused of a state security offence.

Arbitrary arrests and detentions

Dozens of people were arbitrarily arrested and detained. The number of people arrested on 28 September remained unknown.
■ In January, at least 12 soldiers, including military officers, were arrested and held without charge at the Alpha Yaya military barracks. Most had worked for former President Lansana Conté. They were allowed some family visits but no access to a lawyer. In August, 11 were transferred to a detention centre on Kassa Island. The men were only wearing underwear and were tied with ropes. On Kassa, they were tortured and ill-treated (see above) and denied family visits. On 5 December, they were transferred to Conakry central prison and on 27 December to premises run by the security forces' Rapid Intervention Brigade. They had not been charged by the end of the year.
■ Four soldiers, including military officers, were arrested in April and held on Kassa Island without charge until their release in December.
■ In the run-up to the 28 September demonstration, members of the Autonomous Battalion of Airborne Troops were deployed in several districts of Conakry, including Bomboli, Hamdalaye, Mapoto and Enco 5. On 29 September, they raided Bomboli and arrested people in their homes and on the streets. They beat some of those they arrested and put them in the boots of vehicles.

Freedom of expression

Freedom of expression, particularly for journalists reporting on anti-government demonstrations or considered hostile by the CNDD, continued to be routinely restricted. Journalists working for private radio stations were intimidated and threatened; some adopted self-censorship by playing music to avoid raids.

■ In August, Diarougba Baldé, a journalist with the Kibarou website, was arrested while covering a demonstration against the CNDD. He was released a few hours later.
■ On 28 September, Moctar Bah and Amadou Diallo, respectively correspondents of the France-based RFI and the UK-based BBC radio stations, were threatened and assaulted by the security forces while covering a rally against the CNDD. Soldiers forced them to their knees in front of dead bodies. Their personal belongings were confiscated and their equipment was smashed.

Amnesty International visit/reports

🚍 An Amnesty International delegation visited Guinea in November to carry out research and hold talks with the authorities.
▤ Guinea: What has happened to the civilians and soldiers of whom there is no news? (AFR 29/006/2009)
▤ Guinea: Submission to the UN Universal Periodic Review (AFR 29/007/2009)
▤ Guinea: Details of violence emerge – Amnesty calls for international commission of inquiry, 30 September 2009
▤ Guinea: Call for suspension of military and police weapons transfers, 8 October 2009
▤ Guinea: Evidence of new arrests, harassment and illegal detentions by security forces, 3 December 2009

GUINEA-BISSAU

REPUBLIC OF GUINEA-BISSAU

Head of state:	Malam Bacai Sanhá (replaced Raimundo Pereira in September, who replaced João Bernardo "Nino" Vieira in March)
Head of government:	Carlos Gomes Júnior
Death penalty:	abolitionist for all crimes
Population:	1.6 million
Life expectancy:	47.5 years
Under-5 mortality (m/f):	207/186 per 1,000
Adult literacy:	64.6 per cent

The killing of political and military figures, including President João Bernardo "Nino" Vieira in March, exacerbated the already fragile political situation. Elections in June restored some level of stability. The armed forces interfered with the governance of the country and the judiciary. They

also committed serious human rights violations, including unlawful killings, torture and other ill-treatment, arbitrary arrests and detentions, with impunity. Human rights defenders and others received death threats.

Background

The delay in appointing a new government following elections in November 2008 increased political tension. Drug trafficking was reportedly at the root of political instability and killings, and the tension between civilian and military authorities. A new government was finally appointed in January.

In January, presidential guards known as "Aguentas", a force created by the late President João Bernardo "Nino" Vieira during the 1998-99 civil war, allegedly tried to kill the Chief of Staff of the Armed Forces, General Tagme na Waie, apparently because he had ordered their disbandment. In March, General Tagme na Waie was killed by a bomb. Soldiers accused President Vieira of ordering the killing and hours later killed him. The President of the National Assembly took over as Interim President pending a presidential election. Neither killing was properly investigated.

Prior to the presidential election in June, soldiers killed politicians close to the late President Vieira, including an election candidate. They also arbitrarily arrested and beat some parliamentarians and former ministers. Several other politicians fled the country or went into hiding.

The June election was held in an atmosphere of fear and censorship. Malam Bacai Sanhá, candidate for the ruling African Party for the Independence of Guinea and Cape Verde (PAIGC), won the election after a second round in July. He took office in September.

In August, Guinea-Bissau acceded to the Optional Protocol to the Convention on the Elimination of All Forms of Discrimination against Women and in September signed the Optional Protocol to the International Covenant on Economic, Social and Cultural Rights.

Unlawful killings

In March and June, soldiers unlawfully killed political and military figures with impunity. Despite promises by the new President, no investigations were carried out into any of the killings.

■ On 4 June, Hélder Proença, a former Minister of Defence, was killed together with his driver and bodyguard in an ambush by soldiers, some 40km from the capital, Bissau. The armed forces accused him of masterminding a plot to overthrow the government and kill the Prime Minister and the acting Chief of Staff of the Armed Forces. Two hours later, Baciro Dabó, a former Minister of the Territorial Administration and a presidential candidate, was shot dead at home by a group of about 13 soldiers.

Arbitrary arrests and detentions

Soldiers arbitrarily arrested and detained civilians and fellow soldiers whom they accused of plotting against the government. The arrests were carried out without a warrant. The detainees were held in military facilities without charge or trial for weeks or months, exceeding the 48-hour limit prescribed by law. Five soldiers accused of killing the Chief of Staff in March were arrested soon after the killing but were not brought before a magistrate to legalize their detention for several months. They had not been tried by the end of the year.

The politicians arrested in June were released without charge or trial about two months later. They included Faustino Fadut Imbali, a former Prime Minister, arrested at home by soldiers without a warrant on 5 June. He was beaten at the time of arrest and taken to the Armed Forces Headquarters where he was again beaten.

Torture and other ill-treatment

Most of those arrested in March and June were tortured in military custody, including the five soldiers detained in connection with the killing of General Tagme na Waie, according to the Guinea-Bissau Human Rights League (LGDH). In addition, people who criticized the armed forces were tortured or otherwise ill-treated in custody. No investigations were carried out into these incidents and those responsible were not brought to justice.

■ Pedro Infanda, a lawyer, was arbitrarily arrested by soldiers on 23 March, hours after holding a press conference during which he stated that one of his clients believed that the acting Chief of Staff of the Armed Forces was not competent for the job. Pedro Infanda was taken to the Amura military barracks in Bissau and tortured for the first four days of his detention. He was beaten with a wooden stick and other objects, and sustained serious injuries to his back

G

for which he required intensive care treatment in hospital.

■ At 1am on 1 April, four soldiers went to the home of Francisco José Fadul, President of the Audit Court, and beat him with the butts of their guns, causing cuts to his head and one arm. He required intensive care treatment in hospital. His wife was also beaten, but was not seriously injured. Two days before the attack, Francisco José Fadul had publicly criticized the behaviour of the armed forces and called on the government to hold the military accountable for corruption and for the killings of President Vieira and General Tagme na Waie.

Threats against physical integrity

Members of the LGDH were threatened for criticizing the military. Nobody was prosecuted for making the threats.

■ In August, the then Attorney General said that he was receiving death threats, forcing him to sleep away from his home.

Amnesty International reports

📄 Guinea-Bissau: Human rights violations in the run up to presidential elections (AFR 30/003/2009)

📄 Guinea-Bissau: Briefing for international election observers (AFR 30/005/2009)

📄 Guinea-Bissau: Submission to the UN Universal Periodic Review (AFR 30/007/2009)

GUYANA

REPUBLIC OF GUYANA

Head of state and government:	Bharrat Jagdeo
Death penalty:	retentionist
Population:	0.8 million
Life expectancy:	66.5 years
Under-5 mortality (m/f):	66/47 per 1,000
Adult literacy:	99 per cent

There were reports of human rights violations by the security forces, including unlawful killings and torture and other ill-treatment. Three people were sentenced to death; no executions were carried out.

Background

In October, Guyanese national Roger Khan was sentenced to 30 years' imprisonment in the USA on charges including drug smuggling. Following his conviction, the Guyanese government announced a police investigation into Roger Khan's involvement in a "death squad", whose members included serving and former police officers and which was reportedly responsible for the torture, enforced disappearance or killing of more than 200 people between 2002 and 2006.

In November, a coalition of opposition parties published a dossier of unsolved killings committed since 1993, including cases of unlawful killings by the security forces and former death squads, and called for an international inquiry.

Torture and other ill-treatment

There were reports of torture and ill-treatment by the security forces.

■ Three people detained in connection with a murder were tortured and ill-treated at Leonora police station in October. On 27 October, a 15-year-old boy was badly beaten and his genital area set alight when he refused to sign a confession. He was released without charge four days later and admitted to hospital. The day before, 26 October, Deonaradine Rafik had also been badly beaten and forced to sign a confession. He was charged with murder on 30 October and held in pre-trial detention until charges were withdrawn and he was released on 3 December. Nouravie Wilfred was held incommunicado for seven days and ill-treated before being released without charge on 3 December. Three police officers were awaiting trial on charges of "unlawful wounding" at the end of the year.

Violence against women and girls

A Sexual Offences Bill, which proposed amending existing gender-discriminatory legislation, was tabled in July and remained before the National Assembly at the end of the year.

Rights of lesbian, gay, bisexual and transgender people

Archaic colonial laws continued to be used to discriminate against people on grounds of their sexuality.

In February, seven people were convicted and fined under an article of the Summary Jurisdiction

(Offences) Act, which criminalizes cross-dressing for both men and women.

Right to health
In April, a National HIV/AIDS Workplace Policy was introduced. Stigma and discrimination towards people living with HIV/AIDS, however, remained a barrier to the successful implementation of treatment, particularly for lesbian, gay, bisexual and transgender people. Violations of the rights to privacy and confidentiality also continued to discourage people from seeking an HIV test or treatment.

Death penalty
Three people were sentenced to death. There were no executions. Forty-one people were on death row at the end of the year.

Amnesty International report
📄 Guyana: Tortured Guyanese man may face unfair trial (AMR 35/003/2009)

HAITI

REPUBLIC OF HAITI

Head of state:	René García Préval
Head of government:	Jean-Max Bellerive (replaced Michèle D. Pierre-Louis in November)
Death penalty:	abolitionist for all crimes
Population:	10 million
Life expectancy:	61 years
Under-5 mortality (m/f):	90/80 per 1,000
Adult literacy:	62.1 per cent

Poverty remained endemic, widespread and profound, denying millions of Haitians access to a range of human rights. Women and girls continued to experience high levels of violence. Outbreaks of mob justice and lynchings were frequent and those responsible rarely brought to justice. There were reports of ill-treatment and arbitrary arrests and killings by officials. According to the UN, prison conditions often amounted to cruel and degrading treatment or punishment. Scores of people died at sea trying to leave Haiti on boat journeys organized

by traffickers. Thousands of children used as domestic workers were at grave risk of abuse.

Background
In July, the World Bank and International Monetary Fund cancelled debts of US$1.2 billion, nearly two thirds of Haiti's national debt, and the Paris Club of creditors cancelled a further US$63 million.

Elections were held in April to renew one third of the Senate. Run-off elections took place in June in relative calm. The National Assembly agreed to initiate a series of constitutional reforms. In October, the National Assembly passed a no-confidence vote on Prime Minister Michèle D. Pierre-Louis. Jean-Max Bellerive was confirmed by Parliament as the new Prime Minister a week later.

The failure of the President to nominate a President of the Supreme Court and of the Supreme Council of the Judiciary meant that urgent reforms of the justice system were stalled. Police reform failed to progress because of delays in completing the vetting and certification of police officers.

The mandate of the UN Stabilization Mission in Haiti was extended for another year.

The right to health
Poverty was widespread and recovery from the devastating hurricane season of 2008 was slow. More than 56 per cent of Haitians lived on less than US$1 a day, according to the UNDP. Although the availability of food improved compared with 2008, in September the National Coordination for Food Security estimated that 1.9 million people were affected by food insecurity. Lack of access to clean water continued to affect millions of people, with severe consequences for health. Contaminated water was the leading cause of infant mortality and illness in children.

Children's rights
The number of juvenile courts remained inadequate. Only two were in operation in 2009: one in the capital, Port-au-Prince, and one in Cap-Haitian. Children continued to be detained in adult prisons and tried in ordinary courts which did not always respect the privacy of minors on trial. The trafficking of children within Haiti and into the Dominican Republic continued unabated, according to human rights organizations. UNICEF estimated that 175,000

H

children were employed in domestic service, which was described as a "modern form of slavery" by the UN Special Rapporteur on contemporary forms of slavery following her visit to Haiti in June.

Policing and the justice system

There were numerous reports of police ill-treatment of suspects. There were frequent reports of lynchings of suspected criminals by mobs, particularly in areas where there was no state or police presence. Those responsible were rarely brought to justice. According to the UN mission, local administrative authorities illegally carried out policing and judicial functions with the assistance of vigilante groups, leading to arbitrary arrests and killings.

According to a local human rights organization, Haiti's prison population was 5.5 times greater than its capacity. In some prisons, such as the National Penitentiary, extreme overcrowding amounted to cruel, inhuman and degrading treatment. Prolonged pre-trial detention remained the norm for criminal suspects and scores were imprisoned for actions that were not recognizable offences in law. Less than 20 per cent of the 8,833 prisoners held at the end of October 2009 had been tried and sentenced.

■ Ronald Dauphin, an activist with the Lavalas political party, completed his fourth year in detention without trial for his alleged involvement in a series of killings in February 2004 in the town of Saint-Marc. The authorities failed to accept four writs of habeas corpus filed by his lawyer. In 2007 the Appeals Court ordered a new investigation on the grounds that the previous investigation was marred by "grave procedural errors", but by the end of the year no significant progress had been made.

Violence against women and girls

Rape and other forms of sexual violence against women and girls remained widespread. During the first six months of the year, more than half of the 136 rapes reported to a Haitian women's organization involved children. Adequate structures and resources to combat violence against women were lacking and access to prophylactic medicines, including anti-retrovirals, was not available outside the main urban areas.

In January, the UN Committee on the Elimination of Discrimination against Women reviewed Haiti's first national report since the country ratified the UN Women's Convention in 1981. In February, the

Committee called on Haiti to adopt specific legislation on violence against women. By the end of the year, legislation on domestic violence had yet to be adopted by parliament.

■ In March, a 16-year-old girl was raped by five men on La Gonâve Island. The perpetrators were detained by the local police but were later released after they reportedly paid local judicial officials.

Migrants' rights

Scores of migrants died attempting to leave Haiti and escape grinding poverty. Traffickers in human beings operated with total impunity, putting the life of thousands of people at risk. Special legislation criminalizing the trafficking of human beings had not been adopted by the end of the year.

■ In July, a wooden sailboat carrying up to 200 Haitians capsized off the Turks and Caicos Islands. Seventeen Haitians died and 67 were missing feared dead. Survivors told human rights organizations that the boat had been intercepted by the Haitian Police off Cap-Haitian (northern Haiti) but the boat's captain was given permission to proceed with the trip after allegedly paying US$800 to police officers.

Impunity for past abuses

Those responsible for human rights abuses in previous years continued to evade justice.

In October, the judicial authorities designated a new magistrate to complete the investigation into the April 2000 killings of journalist Jean-Léopold Dominique and his security guard Jean-Claude Louissaint. Previous investigations by five magistrates, some of whom had been threatened because of their involvement in the case, had failed to identify the perpetrators.

Amnesty International reports

Detention without trial in Haiti: Appeal case – Release Ronald Dauphin (AMR 36/003/2009)

Overcoming poverty and abuse: Protecting girls in domestic service in Haiti (AMR 36/004/2009)

Haiti: Submission to the UN Universal Periodic Review (AMR 36/005/2009)

HONDURAS

REPUBLIC OF HONDURAS

Head of state and government:	José Manuel Zelaya Rosales, deposed in June by Roberto Micheletti
Death penalty:	abolitionist for all crimes
Population:	7.5 million
Life expectancy:	72 years
Under-5 mortality (m/f):	44/35 per 1,000
Adult literacy:	83.6 per cent

Human rights protection and the rule of law were undermined following an army-backed coup d'état in June. In the ensuing political crisis, the security forces frequently used excessive force against people who took to the streets to demonstrate. Intimidation and attacks against members of the opposition movement were widespread. There were few, if any, investigations into reports of human rights violations committed during the disturbances.

Background

President José Manuel Zelaya Rosales was forced from power on 28 June and forcibly expelled from the country by a group of opposition politicians backed by the military and led by Roberto Micheletti, former President of the National Congress and member of the Liberal Party of Honduras. A de facto government headed by Roberto Micheletti remained in power until the end of the year. In September, President Zelaya returned to the country and took up residence in the Brazilian Embassy.

The coup was condemned by much of the international community. Political negotiations mediated by the OAS to restore the elected government failed. In November, the de facto government went ahead with elections in which Porfirio ("Pepe") Lobo of the National Party won the majority of the vote, although there was reportedly a high level of abstention. He was due to take office in January 2010.

Arbitrary detention and ill-treatment

Hundreds of protesters, most of them supporters of the Zelaya government, and bystanders were arbitrarily detained, beaten and ill-treated by both police and military officials. Many detainees reported being held in unauthorized detention facilities, such as a sports stadium and military barracks.

■ A 16-year-old girl was arbitrarily detained by police in Tegucigalpa after enquiring where they were taking her father. She was detained for several hours in a cell with nine other women. One police officer took some toilet paper, soaked it in a chemical and set fire to it, releasing toxic smoke into the cell. The girl and women detained reported breathing difficulties and burning eyes and throats, in some cases lasting for several days.

■ In August, Alex Matamoros, a human rights defender working for the Centre for the Investigation and Promotion of Human Rights, was arbitrarily detained in Tegucigalpa when he intervened to stop three boys being beaten by police officers after a demonstration. Alex Matamoros was detained at Manchén Police Headquarters for nearly 12 hours before being released without charge.

Excessive use of force and unlawful killings

The use of live ammunition, rubber bullets and tear gas by the police and military led to the death of at least 10 people. The arbitrary and indiscriminate use of tear gas, with insufficient warning or precautions, caused physical harm to scores of protesters, including children. Hospitals were not given information about the chemical substances used, hindering them from providing treatment.

■ Nineteen-year-old Isis Obed Murillo died from a gunshot wound to the head on 5 July after members of the military fired live ammunition during a demonstration at Toncontín airport in Tegucigalpa. The military reportedly refused to co-operate with the investigation into his death.

■ In August, 38-year-old teacher Roger Abraham Vallejo died in hospital as a result of injuries sustained from a bullet wound to the head, reportedly fired by police during the break-up of a protest in Tegucigalpa in July.

■ In September, 16-year-old Gerson Ariel Cruz was seriously wounded by police following the break-up of a protest in Tegucigalpa. According to an eyewitness, the police chased protesters into a residential neighbourhood where they opened fire, shooting Gerson Ariel Cruz, who had taken no part in the protest. An investigation by the Special Prosecutor for Human Rights was under way at the end of the year.

H

Human rights defenders

Representatives of human rights organizations were threatened and harassed.

■ In September, around 15 police officers fired tear gas canisters into the offices of the Committee of Relatives of the Disappeared in Honduras where scores of pro-Zelaya protesters had taken refuge. Around 100 people, including children, were inside the office at the time.

■ In December, lesbian, gay, bisexual and transgender human rights activist Walter Tróchez was murdered in Tegucigalpa. Nine days earlier, he had escaped after being abducted by several masked men demanding the names and addresses of members of the opposition movement. His captors reportedly told him they had orders to kill him.

Freedom of expression and association

Several journalists were physically attacked. The de facto authorities closed Radio Globo and the television station Canal 36 intermittently from 28 June, though both media outlets were open again by the end of 2009. At times their offices were occupied by military personnel.

The de facto President issued a decree on 26 September permitting, amongst other things, the closure of newspapers and media outlets suspected of "insult[ing] public officials." Despite the fact that Congress had not passed the decree into law, police and military officials used it to authorize searches and closures of media outlets. The decree also stipulated that all public meetings or gatherings of any kind had to be authorized by the military or police in advance. The decree was revoked on 19 October.

■ In September, on his way to cover events at Radio Globo and Canal 36, Delmer Membreño, a photographer for the newspaper *El Libertador*, was forced into a truck by four men in balaclavas. The men put a hood over his head and drove off. After 90 minutes, they stopped, dragged him out and put a gun to his head. One of the men told him that he was only being allowed to live so he could deliver a death threat to the director of *El Libertador*. The men then beat Delmer Membreño and burned his face and torso with cigarettes before releasing him. An investigation into the case was continuing at the end of the year.

Violence against women

Women demonstrators and women in custody reported sexual abuse and harassment by police officers. Many women reported being beaten on the buttocks and backs of the legs by police during demonstrations. No investigations were conducted into gender-based violence during the disturbances.

■ N. was separated from her family during a demonstration in Choloma on 14 August. She was arbitrarily detained by police officers who, after dropping other detainees off at a police station, took N. to a remote location where four police officers raped her consecutively.

■ A 34-year-old woman told Amnesty International that she and her 59-year-old mother were repeatedly beaten across the back of the thighs and buttocks by police using batons during one protest.

■ "Eva", a 26-year-old woman, stated that a military officer tried to detain her and threatened her with a baton shouting, "Bitch, I am going to teach you how to be a woman."

Rights of lesbian, gay, bisexual and transgender people

Evidence emerged of a sharp rise in the number of killings of transgender women following the June coup. Between 2004 and March 2009, human rights organizations had registered 17 cases of killings of transgender women. Between the end of June and December 2009, 12 such cases were reported by local human rights organizations. No data was available about investigations into these killings.

HUNGARY

HUNGARY

Head of state:	László Sólyom
Head of government:	Gordon Bajnai (replaced Ferenc Gyurcsány in March)
Death penalty:	abolitionist for all crimes
Population:	10 million
Life expectancy:	73.3 years
Under-5 mortality (m/f):	9/8 per 1,000
Adult literacy:	98.9 per cent

A radical right-wing organization Magyar Gárda (Hungarian Guard) organized a series of marches in towns with a Romani population in eastern Hungary. Violent attacks against Roma continued.

Background

The year was marked by political and economic upheaval that led to the resignation of Prime Minister Ferenc Gyurcsány, whose cabinet was replaced by the interim government of Gordon Bajnai. Jobbik Magyarországért Mozgalom (Movement for a Better Hungary), known as Jobbik, an extreme right-wing political party with a strong anti-Roma and an increasingly anti-Semitic agenda, gained three seats at European Parliament elections in June.

In May, Hungary was elected a member of the UN Human Rights Council, and assumed its membership in June. The 20 billion euro emergency loan from international financial institutions and the EU imposed conditions on the government: it had to cut public sector wages, pensions, social benefits, and other government spending.

In July, the Budapest Court of Appeal issued a legally binding ruling banning Magyar Gárda, an organization linked to the political party Jobbik. The court ruled that Magyar Gárda's activities overstepped its rights as an association and curtailed liberties of the Roma. Later in July, Jobbik announced the re-launch of Magyar Gárda, and one of its newly elected members of the European Parliament wore a Magyar Gárda uniform to the first parliamentary session in Brussels. In December, the Supreme Court upheld the Budapest Court of Appeal ruling banning Magyar Gárda.

Counter-terror and security

In September, the Prime Minister announced that Hungary would accept one detainee from the US naval base in Guantánamo Bay, who would participate in an 18-month integration programme. A Palestinian detainee from Guantánamo Bay was transferred to Hungary on 1 December.

Racism

In February, the European Commission against Racism and Intolerance expressed concerns about a sharp rise in racism in public discourse. It also reiterated from previous reports that Roma in Hungary continued to face discrimination in access to employment, education and housing. In October, the Council of Europe's Commissioner for Human Rights expressed concerns about the rise of extremism, and appealed to all political party leaders to ensure that no xenophobic or anti-Roma statements be made in the 2010 parliamentary election campaign.

Violent attacks against Roma continued. The Hungarian National Bureau of Investigation, a police agency investigating serious crimes, strengthened a special task force to 120 officers to investigate a series of attacks against the Romani community.

■ Róbert Csorba and his son, aged five, were killed in Tatárszentgyörgy in February. After an initial examination, the local police announced that they had been found dead after a fire caused by an electrical fault in their house. Later that same day, however, the police acknowledged that evidence of gunshot wounds had been found on the bodies, but only opened a murder investigation 10 hours later. In August, the Minister of Justice stated that a disciplinary procedure against local police officers had been launched. In November, the Independent Police Complaints Commission examining the police investigation of the killings in Tatárszentgyörgy concluded that the local police had seriously violated the fundamental rights of the victims of the attack to an effective investigation.

■ Jenő Kóka, a 54-year-old Romani man, was killed in Tiszalök's Roma neighbourhood in April. He was reportedly shot dead as he left his home to start the night shift in the local chemical factory where he worked. The police stated there were similarities between Jenő Kóka's case and the earlier attacks against the Romani community.

■ Mária Balogh, a 45-year-old Romani woman, was shot dead and her 13-year-old daughter seriously

H

injured in the village of Kisléta in August. Later that month, police detained four men suspected of this killing and at least five other deadly attacks on Romani people, including the killing of Róbert Csorba and his son, and Jenő Kóka. All four suspects denied involvement in the attacks and were being held in pre-trial detention at the end of the year. The Chief of National Police said in August that they had evidence linking the suspects to acts of deadly violence against the Romani community between November 2008 and August 2009, and that racism appeared to have been the main motive. The NGO European Roma Rights Centre, however, documented the killings of nine Roma in the same period.

In September, about 400 Romani women initiated legal proceedings against Oszkár Molnár, a Member of Parliament of the opposition Fidesz party and Mayor of Edelény, over his alleged defamatory remarks on Romani women. He was also widely criticized by NGOs, other politicians and the media for his anti-Semitic comments during a local TV interview in October.

Discrimination – Roma
Forced sterilizations
■ In February, after eight years of national and international legal proceedings, the State Secretary of the Ministry of Social Affairs and Labour announced that the Ministry would provide A.S. with financial compensation for sterilizing her without her consent on 2 January 2001.

Violence against women and girls
■ The highly publicized case of Zsanett E. continued. In January the Budapest Prosecutor started an investigation into allegations that Zsanett E. had falsely accused five police officers of rape. However, as a substitutive criminal proceeding filed by Zsanett E. in 2008 was still pending, the investigation against her should not have been opened. The prosecutor's investigation against Zsanett E. was therefore suspended.

Rights of lesbian, gay, bisexual and transgender people
On 5 September, the lesbian, gay, bisexual and transgender pride march took place in Budapest with adequate police protection and no incidents reported during the march. However, a young woman was allegedly attacked by two or three anti-gay protesters after the march; she suffered injuries on her head and arms. The Budapest Police Department started an investigation into the incident, having classified it as "violence against a member of a social group" despite the amendments made in February to the criminal code introducing new crimes of homophobic and other hate-related attacks. Following calls by the Hungarian Civil Liberties Union, the police reported that investigations would proceed treating the attack under the new provisions of the criminal code.

Amnesty International visit/report
🚌 An Amnesty International delegate visited Hungary in September.
📰 Romani woman shot dead in Hungary (EUR 27/001/2009)

INDIA

REPUBLIC OF INDIA

Head of state:	Pratibha Patil
Head of government:	Manmohan Singh
Death penalty:	retentionist
Population:	1,198 million
Life expectancy:	63.4 years
Under-5 mortality (m/f):	77/86 per 1,000
Adult literacy:	66 per cent

Tighter anti-terror and security legislation in the wake of the 2008 Mumbai attacks was linked to reports of arbitrary detention and torture. Maoist violence in central India spread to West Bengal, with local communities being targeted and at least 300 civilians killed. Extrajudicial executions took place in a number of states and human rights defenders were threatened and detained arbitrarily. Judicial processes continued to fail to ensure justice for many victims of past human rights violations, violence against religious minorities and corporate abuses. Adivasis (Indigenous communities), small farmers and city dwellers living in poverty across India whose livelihoods were threatened by fast-tracked development and mining projects continued to resist moves to acquire their lands and natural resources. At least 50 people were sentenced to death but, for the fifth successive year, there were no executions.

Background

India-Pakistan peace initiatives languished, with the Indian authorities reiterating that the 2008 attacks in Mumbai had been carried out by people or groups based in Pakistan. The attacks lasted three days and killed 174 people. India-Pakistan initiatives on the Kashmir issue also failed to make progress, despite the Indian authorities resuming talks with Kashmiri leaders. Indian security forces launched co-ordinated paramilitary and police action against the spreading Maoist insurgency; there were protests over human rights abuses by both sides. About 200 people were killed in the political violence surrounding the April/May general elections and in various bomb attacks throughout the country.

Economic growth remained confined largely to key urban sectors and was tempered by global recessionary trends, security concerns and ongoing human rights abuses by state and armed groups. Government estimates from 2005 indicate that around a quarter of India's population were living below the national poverty line.

Counter-terror and security

Investigations into the 2008 terror attacks in Mumbai and elsewhere led to the detention under various security laws of more than 30 suspects without charge in several states, for periods ranging from one week to two months. Reports of unlawful killings, torture and other ill-treatment of suspects, and failure to hold independent inquiries into such incidents led to protests.

■ In October, the Supreme Court rejected a plea to hold an independent inquiry into the September 2008 killings of two young men and a police officer in a shoot-out at Batla House, Delhi. The two men were allegedly involved in the serial bomb attacks in Delhi in September 2008.

Violence between security forces, militia and Maoists

The conflict in Chhattisgarh, central India, between Maoist armed groups which are banned by the authorities and the police and paramilitary forces, spread to other states after months of political violence. Both sides abducted, tortured and killed people with impunity, often targeting civilians. The paramilitary forces include the Salwa Judum militia, widely believed to be sponsored by the state. Around

40,000 Adivasis remained internally displaced by the ongoing conflict, with 20,000 living in camps and the rest scattered in the neighbouring state of Andhra Pradesh. Human rights defenders who exposed abuses by state forces continued to be harassed by the authorities.

■ In May, Binayak Sen, a medical doctor working for the economic, social and cultural rights of Adivasis and contract labourers, and a critic of the Salwa Judum in Chhattisgarh, was released on bail after spending two years in prison. He continued to face charges of aiding Maoists.

■ On 17 September, police officers shot dead six villagers and burnt their houses in Gachanpalli, Dantewada district, Chhattisgarh.

■ On 1 October, nine villagers, including four members of one family, were killed by police officers in Gompad in Dantewada district.

■ In December, Kopa Kunjam, a member of Vanvasi Chetna Ashram, a non-governmental development organization working for the resettlement of Adivasi communities displaced by the conflict in Chhattisgarh, was arrested on politically motivated murder charges. The authorities had demolished the ashram premises in May.

The conflict spread to Lalgarh in West Bengal. Around 8,000 Adivasis remained internally displaced there, some of them in makeshift camps.

■ In September, the West Bengal authorities arrested 23 Adivasi women at Lalgarh and charged them with being Maoists, but later released 14 of them in exchange for a police official taken hostage by Maoist militants.

■ In October, Maoist militants kidnapped and killed an intelligence official and dumped his mutilated body on a highway in the neighbouring state of Jharkhand.

Unlawful killings

Unlawful killings continued to be reported from several north-eastern states, especially Manipur and Assam, where security forces and armed separatist organizations have waged low-intensity conflicts for decades. Despite ongoing protests in the north-east and Kashmir, the authorities refused to repeal the Armed Forces Special Powers Act, 1958. The UN Special Rapporteur on extrajudicial, summary or arbitrary executions stated that the Act facilitated extrajudicial executions by allowing security forces to shoot to kill in circumstances where they were not necessarily at imminent risk.

■ In March, Anil Mazumdar, editor of *Aji* daily newspaper, was shot dead by gunmen at Guwahati in Assam after he advocated peace talks between the banned United Liberation Front of Assam and the state authorities.

■ In May, Satish Loitongbam and Pebam Gunendro Singh, both from Imphal, were detained by suspected Assam Rifles personnel stationed in Manipur. Gunendro Singh was released after three days. Satish Loitongbam was taken to an unknown location and shot dead.

■ In July, Manipur police commandos shot dead Sanjit Chungkham and a pregnant woman, Rabina Devi, at Khwairamband Bazaar in Imphal. Video recordings of the event showed that Sanjit Chungkham was shot after he had been arrested.

Arbitrary arrests and detentions

In August/September, Manipur authorities responded to protests by arresting more than 10 human rights defenders after raiding their offices. Among them was Jiten Yumnam, who remained in jail under preventive detention at year's end. About 90 other people were reported to be held in preventive detention in Manipur state.

Corporate accountability

Marginalized communities across the country bore the brunt of government failures to protect them from corporate abuses.

Bhopal

Twenty-five years after the Bhopal gas leak tragedy of 1984 – one of the world's worst industrial disasters – local communities continued to suffer its effects and maintained their campaign for justice. State action continued to be inadequate and compensation insufficient, the plant site remained contaminated and the authorities repeatedly failed to deliver on promises to the survivors and their families.

Forced evictions

Marginalized communities, including landless farmers and Adivasis in several states, were threatened with forced evictions to accommodate industrial and other business projects. In some cases, Adivasis were threatened with eviction from lands defined as exclusively theirs by the Indian Constitution. Mandatory public hearings did not provide sufficient information on business or development projects, and government and business officials often excluded affected communities from decision-making processes.

■ Dongria Kondh and other Adivasi communities at Niyamgiri in Orissa resumed protests after the authorities granted environmental clearance for a bauxite mine to be operated by a subsidiary of UK-based Vedanta Resources and the Orissa Mining Corporation.

Excessive use of force

In several states, police used unnecessary or excessive force against protesters from marginalized communities. Human rights defenders campaigning for the land and environmental rights of rural communities were often detained, intimidated or harassed by the police.

■ In November, police shot dead Adivasi leaders Singanna and Andrew Nachika of the Chasi Mulia Adivasi Sangh, an organization working for Adivasi land rights at Narayanpatna in Korapur district, Orissa. The two men took part in a demonstration highlighting alleged police brutality against Adivasi communities. The police described the demonstration as an attack.

■ In October, Madhya Pradesh police used unnecessary force on peaceful protesters from the Save Narmada Movement, arresting 20 of its leaders. The protesters were demanding consultation and the implementation of judicial orders for the rehabilitation of Adivasi and other communities displaced by irrigation projects.

■ In August, Orissa authorities released Abhay Sahoo of the Communist Party of India. He had been jailed for 10 months on 20 different charges after leading a protest against the threat of forced evictions spurred by the establishment of the South Korean POSCO steel plant.

Impunity

The Indian government failed to ensure accountability for many past human rights abuses.

1984 massacre

Twenty people have so far been convicted of the targeted massacre of about 3,000 Sikhs in northern India (including Delhi) after the assassination of the then Prime Minister Indira Gandhi in 1984.

■ Public pressure forced the Central Bureau of Investigation to prosecute Jagdish Tytler and Sajjan Kumar, two Congress Party leaders accused of inciting their supporters to commit the Delhi massacres, after initially stating that there was no evidence against them. Protesters forced the ruling Congress Party to drop the two men from its list of candidates for general elections.

Human rights violations

Perpetrators of human rights violations in Punjab between 1984 and 1994, and Assam between 1998 and 2001 – including enforced disappearances and extrajudicial executions – continued to evade justice. Impunity persisted for past offences, including enforced disappearances of thousands of people during the armed conflict in Kashmir since 1989. The International People's Tribunal on Human Rights and Justice in Indian-administered Kashmir published a report documenting unmarked graves of more than 2,900 people who allegedly disappeared during the Kashmir conflict.

Communal violence

Most of those responsible for the attacks on Muslim minorities in 2002 in Gujarat and other human rights violations, including extrajudicial executions in that state, were not brought to justice. Existing cases made little progress during the year.

■ A magisterial inquiry found the killing of Ishrat Jahan and three others by Gujarat police on 16 June 2004 to be "cold-blooded murders". However, this report was challenged by the Gujarat Government in the High Court which established a Special Investigation Team to look into the case. Acting on a petition filed by the family of Ishrat Jahan, the Supreme Court stayed the proceedings before the High Court while hearing the case.

Some 15,000 people, mostly Christians, were displaced in 2008 in Orissa following violence by hundreds of supporters of Hindu nationalist organizations. By year's end, most had yet to return home. Judicial inquiries into the violence remained incomplete and the authorities failed to press charges against the majority of attackers.

An official commission indicted 68 leaders of the opposition Bharatiya Janata Party and other allied Hindu nationalist organizations for the 1992 destruction of the Babri mosque in Ayodhya. To date, no one has faced charges. Impunity continued for those who took part in the attendant violence and the ensuing massacres in some states.

In Kashmir, police and paramilitary forces killed one man and injured 150 people during a protest in June. Demonstrators were demanding an independent investigation into allegations of paramilitary forces' involvement in the sexual assault and murder of two women at Shopian, amidst reports of attempts to suppress evidence of sexual assault. An inquiry by the Central Bureau of Investigation concluded that no sexual assault took place and that the women had drowned, prompting calls for an independent investigation.

Discrimination

Dalits

Members of Dalit communities in several states continued to face attacks, social boycotts and discrimination in accessing health, education and legal services. Special laws enacted to prosecute the perpetrators of such violence and discrimination remained ineffective.

■ In August, four Dalits died of starvation in Nalanda and Jehanabad districts after members of the dominant landholding castes denied them access to food and other essential commodities.

■ During the April/May general elections, Dalit communities in several states, especially Bihar, Gujarat and Andhra Pradesh, faced intimidation and violence. On 23 April, 74 houses belonging to Dalit communities in Madhubani district, Bihar, were torched, leaving 300 people homeless.

Minority groups

In Karnataka, Hindu nationalist groups attacked several places of worship belonging to minority communities and targeted urban women and inter-religious couples.

■ On 25 January, activists from the Hindu nationalist group Sri Rama Sene attacked 10 people at a pub in Mangalore.

Workers' rights

Legislation guaranteeing rural people living in poverty a right to work for at least 100 days per year made headway in some states, but its implementation continued to rely on vigilant local communities. Human rights defenders involved in monitoring implementation faced violence and harassment.

■ On 10 February, Madhya Pradesh police arrested Shamim Modi on false charges after her organization, the Adivasi Labour Union, led a peaceful protest demanding the enforcement of laws guaranteeing labour and land rights. She spent 21 days in prison before being released. In July, the state police and forest department raided her office and arbitrarily detained 11 Adivasis. Shamim Modi, who had received threats to her life, sustained injuries during an attack in Mumbai by alleged mercenaries hired by forest contractors.

Rights of lesbian, gay, bisexual and transgender people

In a historic decision in July, the Delhi High Court rejected section 377 of the Indian Penal Code in cases of consensual sexual acts. Section 377, which criminalizes homosexuality and was introduced under British colonial rule, was deemed discriminatory and "against constitutional morality". A formal repeal of the law remained pending.

Death penalty

No executions were known to have taken place during the year, but courts sentenced at least 50 people to death.

Amnesty International visits/reports

🚌 Amnesty International delegates visited India in February/March and August/September.

📄 India: Dodging responsibility – Corporations, governments and the Bhopal disaster (ASA 20/002/2009)

📄 India: Open Letter to authorities to withdraw the clearance granted to Vedanta-Orissa Mining Corporation for bauxite mining project which could threaten Dongria Kondh indigenous communities at Niyamgiri (ASA 20/004/2009)

📄 India: Authorities should avoid excessive use of force in West Bengal (ASA 20/006/2009)

📄 India: Revoke preventive detention of human rights defender in Manipur (ASA 20/019/2009)

INDONESIA

REPUBLIC OF INDONESIA

Head of state and government:	Susilo Bambang Yudhoyono
Death penalty:	retentionist
Population:	230 million
Life expectancy:	70.5 years
Under 5-mortality (m/f):	37/27 per 1,000
Adult literacy:	92 per cent

There were violent clashes throughout the year in Papua and its population continued to face severe restrictions of their rights to freedom of expression and assembly. Members of the police reportedly used torture and other ill-treatment, and unnecessary or excessive force sometimes leading to unlawful killings throughout the archipelago. The criminal justice system remained unable to address ongoing impunity for current and past human rights violations. No one was executed during the year; however, a new by-law in Aceh provided for stoning to death. Attacks on human rights defenders continued and there were at least 114 prisoners of conscience. A new Health Law contained provisions hampering equal access to maternal health.

Background

Parliamentary elections were conducted in April. Presidential elections took place in July. President Susilo Bambang Yudhoyono was elected for a second five-year term after the first election round. The elections were conducted without any major violent incidents, except in Papua.

In July, at least nine people were killed in Jakarta in two bomb attacks.

Freedom of expression

At least 114 people were detained for peacefully expressing their views. The overwhelming majority were peaceful political activists who were sentenced to terms of imprisonment for raising prohibited pro-independence flags in Maluku or Papua.

■ In March, Buce Nahumury was sentenced to four years' imprisonment for having participated in a peaceful Cakalele dance in Ambon Maluku province in June 2007. During the dance, the "Benang Raja" flag, a symbol of the South Maluku independence movement, was unfurled in front of the President. All

22 other Cakalele dancers were serving jail sentences of between seven and 20 years.

Human rights defenders (HRDs) continued to be intimidated and harassed. At least seven HRDs faced criminal defamation charges, which carried a maximum sentence of just over five years' imprisonment under the Criminal Code. Most past human rights violations against HRDs, including torture, murder and enforced disappearances, remained unsolved and those responsible had not been brought to justice.

Although two people have been convicted of involvement in the murder of prominent HRD Munir Said Thalib (known as Munir), credible allegations were made that those responsible for his murder at the highest levels of command were still at large. Munir Said Thalib was poisoned on 7 September 2004.

Freedom of religion

Minority religious groups remained vulnerable to violent attacks by non-state actors, and were subjected to discrimination.

Students from the Christian STT Setia College continued to study and live in substandard temporary sites. They were evacuated from their school premises in Pulo, Pinang Ranti village, Makassar sub-district in East Jakarta following a violent attack by sections of the Islamic Defenders Front in July 2008. In October, at least 17 students went on hunger strike because they were at risk of forced eviction to premises which they believed were even more inadequate for people to live and study. By the end of the year, the STT Setia students continued to live and study in temporary sites in Jakarta.

Papua

Violence increased sharply around the time of parliamentary and presidential elections, creating a climate of fear and intimidation. There were reports that security forces used unnecessary or excessive force during demonstrations and tortured and ill-treated people during arrest, questioning and detention. Security forces also reportedly committed unlawful killings. Severe restrictions were imposed on the right to peaceful assembly and expression.

■ On 6 April, police opened fire on a protest in the city of Nabire, Papua province, injuring at least seven people including a 10-year-old pupil who was shot as he returned from school. A police officer was also injured by an arrow. Police beat and otherwise ill-treated Monika Zonggonau, Abet Nego Keiya and fifteen other political activists during and after arrest. On 9 April, the body of Abet Nego Keiya was found at Waharia village, Nabire district.

■ Prisoners of conscience Filep Karma and Yusak Pakage, sentenced to 15 and 10 years' imprisonment respectively, remained in jail. The two men were convicted in 2005 for raising the "Morning Star" flag.

Police

Torture remained widespread during arrest, interrogation and detention. Criminal suspects from poor and marginalized communities and peaceful political activists were particularly vulnerable to violations by police, including unnecessary or excessive use of force, sometimes resulting in death; torture and other ill-treatment; and failure to protect demonstrators and religious minorities.

■ In January, at least 75 villagers from Suluk Bongkal village in Riau province were charged with illegally claiming land. Police had arrested them in December 2008 after forcibly evicting them. In August, they were sentenced to 10 months' imprisonment and a fine of 1 million Indonesian rupiah. By the end of the year, the villagers had not received compensation, reparations or alternative adequate housing.

In January, the police issued a new regulation on the use of force in police action (No.1/2009), largely in line with the UN Basic Principles on the Use of Force and Firearms. In June, the police issued a regulation on the implementation of human rights principles (No.8/2009). However, internal and external accountability mechanisms to deal with police abuse remained weak.

Impunity

Impunity for past gross human rights violations in Aceh, Papua, Timor-Leste and elsewhere continued. The government continued to promote reconciliation with Timor-Leste at the expense of justice for crimes under the Indonesian occupation of East Timor (1975-1999).

■ In August, the government interfered with the judicial process in Timor-Leste by pressuring the Timor-Leste government to release Martenus Bere, an indicted militia leader charged with the extermination of civilians in the town of Suai and other crimes against humanity in 1999. In October, Martenus Bere was allowed to return to West Timor (Indonesia) before his case had been prosecuted by an independent court in a fair trial.

Over 300 individuals who were indicted by the UN Special Panels for Serious Crimes for crimes against humanity and other crimes remained at large and were outside the territorial jurisdiction of Timor-Leste. Most of them were believed to live in Indonesia. The government refused to facilitate the extradition of those indicted on the basis that it did not recognize the UN mandate to try Indonesian citizens in Timor-Leste.

In September, the Special Committee on Disappearances 1997-1998 of the House of People's Representatives urged the government to create an ad hoc human rights court to try those responsible for enforced disappearances. They also urged the government to ratify the International Convention for the Protection of All Persons from Enforced Disappearance. However, the government had not acted on the recommendations by the end of the year.

Death penalty

No executions were reported. However, at least 117 people remained under sentence of death.

In September, the Aceh Regional Parliament passed the local Islamic Criminal Code, which contains provisions for stoning to death for adultery and caning with up to 100 lashes for homosexuality. Although the Aceh governor refused to sign the new by-law, it came into force automatically in October.

Right to health

Maternal mortality rates remained high, particularly in poor and marginalized communities.

In September, a new Health Law was passed. Unlike the Criminal Code, the law permitted abortion in certain circumstances. Abortions were permitted provided the pregnancy could harm the mother and/or infant or, if it resulted from a rape which caused psychological trauma to the victim. Local NGOs criticized the new law as it discriminated against those who were unmarried, particularly regarding access to information on sexuality and reproduction.

Amnesty International visits/reports

🚗 Amnesty International delegates visited Indonesia in April, June and July.

📄 Indonesia: Jailed for waving a flag – Prisoners of conscience in Maluku (ASA 21/008/2009)

📄 Unfinished business: Police accountability in Indonesia (ASA 21/013/2009)

IRAN

ISLAMIC REPUBLIC OF IRAN

Head of state:	Leader of the Islamic Republic of Iran: Ayatollah Sayed 'Ali Khamenei
Head of government:	President: Dr Mahmoud Ahmadinejad
Death penalty:	retentionist
Population:	74.2 million
Life expectancy:	71.2 years
Under-5 mortality (m/f):	33/35 per 1,000
Adult literacy:	82.3 per cent

An intensified clampdown on political protest preceded and, particularly, followed the presidential election in June, whose outcome was widely disputed, deepening the long-standing patterns of repression. The security forces, notably the paramilitary Basij, used excessive force against demonstrators; dozens of people were killed or fatally injured. The authorities suppressed freedom of expression to an unprecedented level, blocking mobile and terrestrial phone networks and internet communications. Well over 5,000 people had been detained by the end of the year. Many were tortured, including some who were alleged to have been raped in detention, or otherwise ill-treated. Some died from their injuries. Dozens were then prosecuted in grossly unfair mass "show trials". Most were sentenced to prison terms but at least six were sentenced to death.

The election-related violations occurred against a background of severe repression, which persisted throughout 2009 and whose victims included members of ethnic and religious minorities, students, human rights defenders and advocates of political reform. Women continued to face severe discrimination under the law and in practice, and women's rights campaigners were harassed, arrested and imprisoned. **Torture and other ill-treatment of detainees remained rife and at least 12 people died in custody. Detainees were systematically denied access to lawyers, medical care and their families, and many faced unfair trials. Iran remained one of the states with the highest rates of execution and one of very few still to execute juvenile offenders: at least 388 people were executed, including one by stoning and at least five juveniles.**

Background

International tension persisted over Iran's nuclear enrichment programme. In March the UN Security Council voted to extend economic and political sanctions. In September, the government revealed the existence of a hitherto unknown enrichment facility.

Iran continued to host almost 1 million refugees, mostly from Afghanistan. They had limited access to social services and education.

Presidential election – widespread abuses

The authorities intensified their crackdown on critics and opponents of the government in the months preceding the 12 June presidential election, in which the incumbent, President Mahmoud Ahmadinejad, was officially declared the winner. Only three of the 474 other applicants were permitted to stand. Mass protests broke out in response to the official result, declared on 13 June, with hundreds of thousands of people taking to the streets. Security forces, notably the paramilitary Basij, were deployed to suppress the protests by force, particularly after the Supreme Leader ordered an end to demonstrations on 19 June. However, protests continued to the end of the year on significant days such as the religious festival of Ashoura on 27 December. The authorities disrupted mobile phone and internet communications, including social networking sites, to prevent information circulating. They prevented foreign journalists from covering demonstrations, expelling some, and security officials controlled the content of newspapers. Security forces raided university campuses, injuring students. The authorities accused the US and UK governments of organizing the unrest, which those governments denied.

All three defeated candidates alleged election fraud and complained to the body responsible for administering the election. It carried out a partial re-count but largely rejected the candidates' complaints. Mahmoud Ahmadinejad was sworn in for a second term on 5 August.

Unlawful killings

The Basij and other security forces used excessive force against demonstrators, beating them with batons and riding motorcycles into them to cause injury. The authorities said 43 died in the protests but opposition sources said the true total was likely to be over 100. Hundreds were injured.

■ Neda Agha Soltan, aged 27, was shot dead in a Tehran street on 20 June during a demonstration. Her dying moments were filmed. The perpetrator was identified as a member of the Basij but the authorities claimed that British and US news media had caused her death. Neda Agha Soltan's family and other mourners were harassed and intimidated by security officials when commemorating her life.

Arrests and detentions

Well over 5,000 people were detained after the election by the end of the year, including opposition politicians, journalists, academics, students, lawyers, human rights activists and army officers. Those with dual nationality or links to the USA or UK were also targeted. Some were arrested at demonstrations; others at their home or workplace; and some, who were injured, from hospital. Most, if not all, were denied access to legal representation. Many were denied access to their families and to medical care.

Hundreds of those arrested were freed within days or weeks, but scores were charged with vaguely worded offences, such as fomenting a "velvet revolution" or committing "acts against national security", and prosecuted in "show trials".

■ Mohammad Ali Abtahi, Mohsen Aminzadeh, Said Hajjarian and at least four other political leaders were detained days after the election. All were prisoners of conscience. Said Hajjarian was released on bail in October and Mohammad Ali Abtahi in November. Mohsen Aminzadeh remained in custody at the end of the year.

Rape and other torture

Some detainees were taken to the Kahrizak detention centre, south of Tehran, where they were tortured and otherwise ill-treated. Kahrizak quickly became so notorious for abuse that the Supreme Leader ordered its closure in July. By the end of the year, 12 officials were facing trial before a military court for abuses, including three for murder.

I

Compelling evidence emerged that a number of detainees, both women and men, had been raped and otherwise tortured in detention, but instead of investigating allegations thoroughly, the authorities were quick to deny them and then harassed the victims and closed the offices of a committee collecting victims' testimonies.

■ Ebrahim Sharifi, a student aged 24, testified that security officials raped him, beat him severely and subjected him to mock execution in the week following his arrest on 22 June. He tried to file a judicial complaint but went into hiding after he and his family were threatened by security officials. On 13 September a judicial panel dismissed his allegation of rape and accused him of fabricating it for political reasons and he fled Iran.

■ Mohsen Ruholamini, the son of an aide to presidential candidate Mohsen Rezaei, died on 23 July after about two weeks in Kahrizak. A coroner's report found he had suffered a heart attack and internal bleeding and had been hit repeatedly with a hard object.

Unfair trials

Mass "show trials" involving scores of detainees were staged in successive sessions beginning in August. The trials were grossly unfair. Most, if not all, defendants were denied access to lawyers. Most had been detained incommunicado for several weeks and many were reported to have been tortured or otherwise ill-treated before being brought to court. The trials were closed but excerpts broadcast on state television showed defendants making what appeared to be coerced "confessions". More than 80 were convicted and sentenced to prison terms of up to 15 years; at least six others were sentenced to death.

Human rights defenders

Human rights defenders, including minority and women's rights activists, lawyers and trade unionists, continued to face arbitrary arrest, harassment, prosecution and unfair trials throughout the year. Some were banned from travelling abroad.

■ In April, five leaders of the Haft Tapeh Sugar Cane Company Trade Union were sentenced to up to six months' imprisonment for "propaganda against the system" for criticizing conditions at their workplace when they were interviewed by foreign journalists in 2008. They began serving their sentences in November after they were upheld on appeal.

■ Five members of the Committee of Human Rights Reporters were arrested in December and others were sought by intelligence officials.

Discrimination against women

Women continued to face discrimination in law, despite some minor improvements. Women's rights campaigners, including those active in the "One Million Signatures" campaign to end legal discrimination, were harassed, detained, prosecuted and banned from travelling for collecting signatures in support of their petition.

■ On 1 February, Alieh Eghdam-Doust, a member of the Campaign for Equality, began a three-year prison sentence imposed for participating in a peaceful demonstration. She was among many women arrested during a protest in June 2006 against discriminatory laws, and the first to begin serving a prison sentence.

Freedom of expression and association

The authorities blocked websites voicing criticism, notably those of Iranian bloggers, and periodically blocked those of foreign news media reporting on Iran. In April, they warned SMS users that messages were "controlled" by a new "internet crimes" law introduced in January. They also shut down or maintained bans on tens of journals, magazines and other print media, targeted critical journalists and infiltrated and undermined independent civil society groups, such as the Society of Esfahan Human Rights Supporters. Hundreds of students faced education bans for campus activism.

■ Four students at Tehran's Amir Kabir University were arrested at their homes on 24 February for participating in a peaceful demonstration the previous day against the government's decision to bury soldiers' remains on the campus, and so facilitate unrestricted access to the campus by the Basij and other security forces. Other students were also arrested; all had been released uncharged by July.

■ Roxana Saberi, a journalist with joint US-Iranian nationality, was convicted of "collaborating with a hostile state" in a closed trial before Tehran's Revolutionary Court on 18 April following her arrest on 31 January. She was sentenced to eight years in prison, but this was reduced to a suspended two-year term following local and international criticism. She was released on 12 May and allowed to leave the country.

■ Two brothers, Arash and Kamiar Alaei, both medical doctors active in the field of HIV/AIDS treatment and prevention, were sentenced in January to six and three years' imprisonment respectively for "co-operating with an enemy government". They had been tried before a closed court on 31 December 2008. They were neither told the charges or evidence against them nor permitted by the court to call or examine witnesses. Both men were prisoners of conscience, imprisoned on account of their medical work with US and other international medical institutions.

Discrimination
Ethnic minorities
Members of Iran's ethnic minorities continued to face discrimination along with harassment and imprisonment for advocating greater respect for social and cultural rights, including the right to mother tongue education. In June, the government announced that it would allow some higher education in regional languages.

Members of the Ahwazi Arab and Azerbaijani minorities were subject to continuing repression. Members of the small Sunni Azerbaijani minority were arrested in February when they protested against cuts in water supplies. Members of the Kurdish minority suspected of belonging to banned armed opposition groups were arrested and imprisoned. Some were sentenced to death and at least one was executed, possibly in reprisal for a spate of attacks on officials in Kordestan province in September. In Sistan-Baluchistan province, home to the mostly Sunni Muslim Baluch minority, violence intensified amid increasing clashes between the security forces and members of the People's Resistance Movement of Iran (PRMI), an armed political group also known as Jondallah. On 18 October, at least 42 people, including senior Revolutionary Guards officers and civilians, were killed in an attack claimed by the PRMI.

■ On 30 May, two days after a PRMI bomb attack on a mosque in Zahedan killed at least 25 people, three men were publicly executed near the mosque for allegedly smuggling the explosives into Iran; all three had been in prison accused of other bombings when the attack happened.

Religious minorities
Members of religious minorities, including some not recognized by the government, continued to suffer discrimination, harassment, arbitrary arrest and damage to community property. Among those targeted were Sunni Muslim clerics; Shi'a clerics advocating the separation of the state from religion; members of the Dervish and Ahl-e Haqq communities; members of a philosophical association called Al-e Yasin; Christians; and members of the Baha'i community, who remained unable to access higher education. Converts from Islam were at risk of attack as well as prosecution for "apostasy", which is punishable by death.

■ Maryam Rostampour and Marzieh Amirizadeh Esmaeilabad, both Christian converts, were arrested on 5 March in Tehran for handing out Bibles and participating in religious gatherings. Both were prisoners of conscience. Released in November after acquittal in October of "acting against state security" by a Revolutionary Court, they continued to face charges of "apostasy" and "proselytizing" in a General Court.

■ Seven Baha'is, two women and five men, who were arrested in March and May 2008, remained held without trial in Evin Prison in Tehran. All faced charges of spying for Israel and "insulting religious sanctities and propaganda against the system". In May their families were told that they had also been charged with "corruption on earth", which can be punished by death.

Torture and other ill-treatment
Torture and other ill-treatment in pre-trial detention remained common, facilitated by the routine denial of access to lawyers by detainees and impunity for officials who perpetrate violations. Methods reported included severe beatings; confinement in tiny spaces; deprivation of light, food and water; and systematic denial of medical treatment. At least 12 people were believed to have died in custody in 2009 apparently as a result of ill-treatment or lack of adequate medical care. No investigations into any torture allegations were reported, except at Kahrizak.

Cruel, inhuman and degrading punishments
Sentences of flogging and judicial amputation were imposed and carried out. In February, the Supreme Court upheld a sentence in which acid would be dropped into the eyes of a man who had blinded a woman with the same liquid.

Death penalty

Iran maintained one of the highest rates of execution globally. At least 388 people were executed, including one man who was stoned to death and at least five juvenile offenders sentenced for crimes committed when they were aged under 18. At least 14 were executed in public. The actual totals were believed to be higher.

The rate of reported executions rose sharply during the unrest between the presidential election on 12 June and the inauguration on 5 August – 112 executions were recorded, an average of more than two a day.

The authorities carried out mass executions in January, March, July and August, during which a total of 77 people were executed.

At least 11 people sentenced to die by stoning and at least 136 juvenile offenders remained on death row at the end of the year.

■ Delara Darabi, a 22-year-old woman convicted of a crime she allegedly committed when aged 17, was executed on 1 May despite a two-month stay ordered by the Head of the Judiciary.

Amnesty International visits/reports

🚓 The authorities continued to deny access to Amnesty International. The organization has not been permitted to visit the country to research human rights since shortly after the Iranian Revolution in 1979.

📄 Iran: Submission to the UN Universal Periodic Review (MDE 13/009/2009)

📄 Human rights in the spotlight on the 30th anniversary of the Islamic revolution (MDE 13/010/2009)

📄 Iran: Election amid repression of dissent and unrest (MDE 13/053/2009)

📄 Iran: Election contested, repression compounded (MDE 13/123/2009)

IRAQ

REPUBLIC OF IRAQ

Head of state:	Jalal Talabani
Head of government:	Nuri al-Maliki
Death penalty:	retentionist
Population:	30.7 million
Life expectancy:	67.8 years
Under-5 mortality (m/f):	43/38 per 1,000
Adult literacy:	74.1 per cent

Government forces and armed political groups continued to commit gross human rights abuses, although the overall level of violence was lower than in previous years. Thousands of civilians were killed or seriously injured in suicide and other bomb attacks by armed political groups. The government and the US-led Multinational Force (MNF) continued to hold thousands of uncharged detainees on security grounds, some after several years, but released thousands of others. Torture and other ill-treatment of detainees by Iraqi forces, including prison guards, remained rife and were carried out with impunity. At least 1,100 prisoners were reported to be under sentence of death, many following unfair trials. The government disclosed no information about executions, but at least 120 were reported and it appeared that some were carried out in secret. At least 1.5 million people were still internally displaced within Iraq and hundreds of thousands of Iraqis were refugees abroad. New human rights violations were reported in the semi-autonomous Kurdistan region where conditions generally were much better than in the rest of Iraq.

Background

The Status of Forces Agreement (SOFA) between the governments of Iraq and the USA took effect in January, leading US troops to withdraw from Iraqi towns by 30 June and start releasing or handing over detainees to Iraqi custody. The USA also transferred control of Baghdad's Green Zone to the Iraqi government.

Prime Minister Nuri al-Maliki's State of Law Coalition won control of 10 out of 14 governorates, including Baghdad, in provincial elections held in late January in all areas except Kirkuk and the three Kurdish provinces.

The Council of Representatives (parliament) was beset by divisions, agreeing a new election law only in November. Parliamentary elections were scheduled for March 2010.

Despite the country's oil wealth, millions of Iraqis faced deepening poverty amid high unemployment and widespread government corruption. A senior government official told the UN in October that 5.6 million Iraqis were living below the poverty line, said to be a 35 per cent increase compared with the period before the US-led invasion of Iraq in 2003.

Abuses by armed groups

Armed political groups committed gross human rights abuses, including kidnapping, torture and murder. Suicide bombings and other attacks targeted public places, apparently aiming to inflict civilian casualties. Many attacks were mounted by al-Qa'ida in Iraq and by Sunni armed groups. Shi'a militia also committed abuses, including kidnapping, torture and murder. The victims included members of ethnic and religious minorities, journalists, women, gay men and other civilians.

■ At least 25 boys and men were killed in the first quarter of the year in Baghdad, apparently because they were or were perceived to be gay, after religious leaders in Baghdad's predominantly Shi'a district of al-Sadr City urged their followers to eradicate homosexuality. The perpetrators were believed to be armed Shi'a militia or members of the victims' own families or tribes. Many of the victims were kidnapped and tortured before they were murdered. Some had their bodies mutilated.

■ On 12 July, five Christian churches in Baghdad were bombed, killing four civilians and injuring at least 21 others.

■ On 13 August, at least 20 people were killed in a double suicide bombing in the town of Sinjar, a stronghold of followers of the Yazidi religion.

■ On 25 October, two suicide bombings killed at least 155 people in central Baghdad and injured more than 700. A truck bomb was detonated near the Ministries of Justice and Municipalities; minutes later a car bomb exploded outside the Baghdad Governorate building.

Detentions

On 1 January, the MNF was holding over 15,000 mostly uncharged detainees at Camp Cropper and other prisons. This total was reduced to 6,466 by

early December in accordance with the SOFA, which required that the MNF either release detainees or transfer them to Iraqi custody. Some 7,499 detainees were released after a committee comprising representatives of several Iraqi ministries reviewed their cases and they had been interrogated by security officials. At least 1,441 others, including some foreign nationals, were issued with arrest warrants or detention orders by Iraqi judicial authorities and transferred to Iraqi detention.

In September, the large MNF-run Camp Bucca prison near Um Qasr in southern Iraq was closed. Its inmates were released, transferred to Iraqi custody or moved to the two remaining MNF prisons – Camp Cropper, where most of the detained former high-ranking Ba'ath party members remained held; and Camp Taji, north of Baghdad.

■ On 8 April, a court in Baghdad's al-Karkh district ruled that there was insufficient evidence against Kadhum Ridha al-Sarraj and ordered his release. However, he was not freed by the MNF until 7 October. He had been arrested on 15 September 2008 at Erbil international airport, handed to the MNF and detained without charge at Camp Cropper, apparently because his medical research led him to be suspected of bomb-making.

Death penalty

At least 391 people were sentenced to death, bringing the total under sentence of death to at least 1,100, including at least 900 people who had exhausted all legal remedies. At least 120 executions were carried out but the true figure may have been higher as the authorities disclosed little information on executions and some were reported to have been carried out secretly.

Most death sentences were imposed after unfair trials for involvement in armed attacks, murder and other violent acts. Defendants commonly complained that "confessions" accepted as evidence against them had been obtained under torture when they were interrogated while held incommunicado in pre-trial detention, and that they could not choose their own defence lawyers. In some cases, these "confessions" were broadcast on television.

■ On 10 June, 18 men and one woman were hanged at al-Kadhimiya prison, Baghdad. The executions were not officially announced.

Trials of former officials

The Supreme Iraqi Criminal Tribunal (SICT) continued its prosecution of former senior officials and associates of former President Saddam Hussain, executed on 30 December 2006 for war crimes, crimes against humanity and other offences. The court, whose independence and impartiality have been tainted by political interference, imposed several death sentences. In late October, more than 50 members of parliament called for the SICT to be detached from the Council of Ministers headed by the Prime Minister and placed under the sole authority of the Supreme Judicial Council. They also called for the SICT's jurisdiction to be extended to cover crimes committed by civilian and military officials after 1 May 2003.

■ Watban Ibrahim al-Hassan and Sab'awi Ibrahim al-Hassan, both half-brothers of former President Saddam Hussain and respectively once Interior Minister and Head of Intelligence, were sentenced to death on 11 March for crimes against humanity. Former Deputy Prime Minister Tariq 'Aziz was sentenced to 15 years in prison, as was 'Ali Hassan al-Majid, who had already been sentenced to death in three other cases. The four were among eight people tried in connection with the killing in 1992 of 42 Baghdad merchants who had been accused of racketeering when the country was subject to UN-imposed economic sanctions. Three other accused received prison sentences ranging from six years to life; one man was acquitted.

Human rights violations by Iraqi security forces

Iraqi security forces committed gross human rights violations, including extrajudicial executions, torture and other ill-treatment, and arbitrary detentions, and did so largely with impunity. Detainees were held in heavily overcrowded prisons and detention centres, where they were abused by interrogators and prison guards. Torture methods reported included beatings with cables and hosepipes, suspension by the limbs for long periods, the application of electric shocks to the genitals and other sensitive areas, breaking of limbs, removal of toenails with pliers, and piercing the body with drills. Some detainees were alleged to have been raped.

■ In June, a human rights body affiliated to al-Diwaniya Governorate in southern Iraq accused the security forces of torturing detainees to extract "confessions". Interior Ministry investigators subsequently reported that 10 out of the 170 prisoners at al-Diwaniya prison had bruising that could have been caused by torture or other ill-treatment. Video film apparently taken by a prison guard showed a prisoner lying with his hands tied behind his back, being whipped by guards and subjected to electric shocks until he lost consciousness. One guard is heard to say, "He is done."

Human rights violations by US forces

US forces committed serious human rights violations, including unlawful killings of civilians. US military tribunals examined several court cases involving soldiers accused of crimes committed in Iraq in previous years.

■ On 1 January, US troops shot and critically wounded Hadil 'Emad, an editor for the TV station Biladi, when she was near a checkpoint in Karrada, Baghdad. The US military said that US troops shot a woman who "acted suspiciously and failed to respond to warnings."

■ On 16 September, US troops patrolling central Falluja shot dead Ahmed Latif, said to be mentally ill, apparently after he insulted and threw a shoe at them. The US authorities said he was shot because US troops suspected a grenade attack.

■ On 21 May, Steven Dale Green, a former US soldier, was sentenced to life imprisonment by a court in the USA for the rape and killing in Iraq of Abeer al-Janabi, a 14-year-old girl, and the murders of her mother, father and six-year-old sister in March 2006. Three other former soldiers were sentenced to life imprisonment in the same case.

Violence against women

Women continued to face high levels of discrimination and violence. Some were attacked in the street by armed men or received death threats from men who accused them of not adhering to strict Islamic moral codes. In May, inmates of the women's prison in al-Kadhimiya told members of the parliament's human rights committee that they had been raped in the prison or while detained elsewhere. The government provided little protection against societal and family violence.

■ Safa 'Abd al-Amir al-Khafaji, the head teacher of a girls' school in Baghdad's al-Ghadir district, was shot and seriously wounded by unidentified gunmen on 12

November 2009, soon after she announced that she would contest the elections as a candidate for the Iraqi Communist Party.

Refugees and internally displaced people

Hundreds of thousands of Iraqis were refugees in Syria, Jordan, Lebanon, Turkey and other countries, and up to 1.5 million others were internally displaced inside Iraq, although around 200,000 were reported to have returned to their homes in 2009, many because they perceived that the security situation had improved. However, they faced great challenges: many found that their homes had been destroyed or taken over by other people and had difficulty obtaining adequate food, water and energy supplies.

Camp Ashraf

Following months of rising tension, Iraqi security forces forcibly entered and took control of Camp Ashraf in Diyala Governorate on 28 and 29 July. The camp, which houses some 3,400 members or supporters of the People's Mojahedeen Organization of Iran, an Iranian opposition group, had been under US military control since 2003 prior to the SOFA. Video footage showed Iraqi security forces deliberately driving military vehicles into crowds of protesting camp residents. The security forces also used live ammunition, apparently killing at least nine camp residents, and detained 36 others who they tortured. The 36 were taken to al-Khalis police station in Diyala, where they mounted a hunger strike, and were then moved to Baghdad despite repeated judicial orders for their release. They were freed and allowed to return to Camp Ashraf in October after an international campaign. However, the government was reported to be insisting that the camp residents move to another location in southern Iraq, despite fears that they would be less safe there, and to have set 15 December as the date by which they should move or be relocated by force. By the end of the year, camp residents had still not moved.

Kurdistan region

Presidential and parliamentary elections for the semi-autonomous Kurdistan Regional Government (KRG) were held on 25 July. Masoud Barzani was re-elected as KRG President. The Kurdistan List, which includes the Kurdistan Democratic Party (KDP) and the Patriotic Union of Kurdistan (PUK), retained an overall majority in the Kurdistan parliament. The main opposition Change List won 25 of the 111 seats.

In April, KRG Prime Minister Nechirvan Barzani told visiting Amnesty International delegates that he had personally instructed the *Asayish*, the security police, and other law enforcement bodies to comply with human rights safeguards recommended by the organization and was taking steps to make the *Asayish* fully accountable. He detailed measures being taken to combat so-called honour crimes and other violence against women. Despite this and the continuing improvement in human rights in the KRG, cases of arbitrary arrest and detention were reported, as were allegations of torture and other ill-treatment, notably by the Parastin and Zanyari, respectively the security arms of the KDP and the PUK. Activists in the Change List Movement and independent journalists were subject to threats, intimidation and, in some cases, violence for criticizing the KRG or senior officials.

Arbitrary detention

At least nine detainees arrested previously continued to be held without charge or trial.

■ Walid Yunis Ahmed, a member of the Turkoman minority arrested in February 2000, spent his ninth year in detention without trial. He is reported to have been tortured after arrest, and in 2009 was held in solitary confinement in prison in Erbil.

Media freedom

Despite the introduction of a more liberal press law in 2008, journalists working for the independent media were harassed with what appeared to be politically motivated criminal lawsuits. Some were physically assaulted by men in plain clothes believed to be connected to the Parastin and Zanyari.

■ In late October, Nabaz Goran, editor of the independent *Jihan* magazine, was attacked by three unidentified men outside the newspaper office in Erbil.

Violence against women

High levels of violence against women continued to be reported, including cases of women being killed by their relatives.

■ In October, the body of Jian Ali Abdel Qader was discovered next to her family house in the village of Qadafari, Sulaimaniya. She had previously reported being subjected to family violence and sought refuge in a shelter in Sulaimaniya in July. However, she had returned to the family home after assurances for her safety had been given. Relatives, including her father, were detained in connection with her murder.

I

Amnesty International visit/reports

Amnesty International delegates visited the Kurdistan region of Iraq in April/May.

Trapped by violence: Women in Iraq (MDE 14/005/2009)

Hope and fear: Human rights in the Kurdistan region of Iraq (MDE 14/006/2009)

A thousand people face the death penalty in Iraq (MDE 14/020/2009)

Iraq: Submission to the UN Universal Periodic Review (MDE 14/022/2009)

IRELAND

REPUBLIC OF IRELAND

Head of state:	Mary McAleese
Head of government:	Brian Cowen
Death penalty:	abolitionist for all crimes
Population:	4.5 million
Life expectancy:	79.7 years
Under-5 mortality (m/f):	6/6 per 1,000

New criminal law provisions further curtailed the right to silence by allowing adverse inferences to be drawn from a person's silence during police questioning. Asylum procedures continued to be prolonged, and failed sufficiently to take children's needs into consideration. Two reports were published on the abuse of thousands of children over decades by members of the Catholic clergy. The abuse was covered up by church and state authorities. There was a shortfall in mental health services. The treatment of rape survivors by the criminal justice system gave rise to concern. The human rights of trafficking victims were not adequately protected.

Legal, constitutional or institutional developments

The Criminal Justice (Amendment) Act 2009, enacted in July, extended the remit of the jury-less Special Criminal Court to certain "organized crime" offences. Provisions of the new law also allowed adverse inferences to be drawn from a person's silence during police questioning, thereby undermining the right not to be compelled to testify against oneself. The Irish Human Rights Commission (IHRC) complained that parliament (Oireachtas) and the public had been allowed insufficient time to consider the new law.

In July, the IHRC said that the 32 per cent cut in its 2009 funding seriously hampered its statutory functions. It recommended that it should be made answerable to parliament, not to a government department.

The Civil Partnership Bill 2009, published in June, proposed to permit same-sex couples, opposite-sex couples and cohabiting companions to register civil partnerships. The Bill recognized a number of other rights and obligations previously afforded only married couples. Lesbian, gay, bisexual and transgender groups criticized it for not giving same-sex couples a right to civil marriage or addressing the unsatisfactory legal situation of children of same-sex couples.

Police and security forces

In April the IHRC, while welcoming positive initiatives underway within the police (An Garda Síochána) to make the service more human rights compliant, expressed concern at the slow pace of reform in key areas. It set out a range of recommendations on further reforms needed for the service to become more transparent and accountable. It also called for the Garda Síochána Ombudsman Commission, which deals with complaints against the police, to be sufficiently resourced to carry out its functions effectively.

Prison conditions

In October, the IHRC informed the UN Human Rights Committee that physical conditions in many prisons were unacceptable, sometimes amounting to inhuman and degrading treatment, and that in the previous 12 months overcrowding had reportedly reached severe levels, increasing the potential for violence among prisoners.

Counter-terror and security

The government cabinet committee established in 2008 to review and strengthen legislation dealing with the search and inspection of suspected rendition flights did not publish legislative proposals.

Guantánamo Bay detainees

In September, the government announced that it had accepted two former detainees from the US naval base in Guantánamo Bay, Cuba, for residence in Ireland.

Refugees and asylum-seekers

There remained concern at the length of asylum proceedings, which in some cases took three to five years. Legislation proposed in 2008 to introduce a single procedure for determining refugee status as well as other forms of protection was not enacted.

In November, the Ombudsman for Children found that unaccompanied asylum-seeking children received a lower standard of care than children in the mainstream care system, and that many resided in uninspected private hostels. She expressed concern that 419 unaccompanied children had gone missing from care between the end of 2000 and June 2009 and was critical of the response to such incidents. She also concluded that the asylum process did not take sufficient account of children's age or vulnerability.

Children's rights

In May, the report of the Commission to Inquire into Child Abuse (Ryan report) outlined the physical, emotional and sexual abuse of over 30,000 children between 1936 and 2000 placed by the state in institutions operated by Catholic religious orders. It found that the Department of Education, health boards and religious orders failed to protect children or to investigate complaints. In July, the government gave commitments to implement the Commission's recommendations, including by providing reparation to abuse survivors and addressing serious gaps in current child protection and care systems.

A report by the Dublin Archdiocese Commission of Investigation (Murphy report) into the handling of clerical child sexual abuse in the Archdiocese of Dublin between 1975 and 2004 was published in November. It found that hundreds of abuse cases were covered up by the church and state authorities, including the police.

A referendum on the incorporation of children's rights in the Constitution was further delayed.

Right to health – mental health

There was a shortfall in mental health services, especially for vulnerable groups such as children and people with intellectual disabilities. In May, the Inspector of Mental Health Services described the 247 admissions of children to adult units in 2008 as "inexcusable, counter-therapeutic and almost purely custodial".

In April, the Mental Health Commission reported on care and treatment practices in two mental health in-patient facilities in Clonmel. It found a poor and unsafe physical environment, high levels of injuries to patients in uncertain circumstances, inappropriate medication and use of seclusion, an absence of basic levels of privacy, and restrictions on movement.

Women's rights

In December, a review by the Rape Crisis Network of the criminal justice system's response in rape cases found that just 30 per cent of cases reported to the police led to prosecutions. It observed that both the police and the prosecution service assessed the credibility of a rape report against a narrow stereotype, a factor in deterring survivors from reporting their ordeal. It also found that the most common reason given by victims for considering withdrawing complaints was poor treatment by the police.

Also in December the Grand Chamber of the European Court of Human Rights held a hearing in a case concerning three women who complained that restrictions on obtaining an abortion in Ireland violated their human rights.

Trafficking in human beings

A report by the Immigrant Council of Ireland in April found that at least 102 and probably many more women and girls were trafficked into or through Ireland for sexual exploitation over a two-year period.

In June the government published a three-year national action plan to prevent and combat trafficking. Its proposal to continue housing survivors of trafficking in accommodation dedicated to asylum-seekers gave rise to concern that they would be inadequately protected from the risk of further harm. Very few victims were granted a "reflection and recovery" period.

Arms trade

The government failed to publish its first report on arms exports and brokering for the year 2008, required under the Control of Exports Act 2008.

ISRAEL AND THE OCCUPIED PALESTINIAN TERRITORIES

STATE OF ISRAEL

Head of state:	Shimon Peres
Head of government:	Binyamin Netanyahu (replaced Ehud Olmert in March)
Death penalty:	abolitionist for ordinary crimes
Population:	7.2 million (Israel); 4.3 million (OPT)
Life expectancy:	80.7 years (Israel); 73.3 years (OPT)
Under-5 mortality (m/f):	6/5 per 1,000 (Israel); 23/18 per 1,000 (OPT)
Adult literacy:	97.1 per cent (Israel); 93.8 per cent (OPT)

Israeli forces committed war crimes and other serious breaches of international law in the Gaza Strip during a 22-day military offensive code-named Operation "Cast Lead" that ended on 18 January. Among other things, they carried out indiscriminate and disproportionate attacks against civilians, targeted and killed medical staff, used Palestinian civilians as "human shields", and indiscriminately fired white phosphorus over densely populated residential areas. More than 1,380 Palestinians, including over 330 children and hundreds of other civilians, were killed. Much of Gaza was razed to the ground, leaving vital infrastructure destroyed, the economy in ruins and thousands of Palestinians homeless.

Israeli forces continued to impose severe restrictions on the movement of Palestinians in the Occupied Palestinian Territories (OPT) throughout 2009, hampering access to essential services and land. The restrictions included a military blockade of the Gaza Strip, which effectively imprisoned the 1.5 million residents and resulted in a humanitarian crisis. Despite this, Israel often stopped international aid and humanitarian assistance from entering Gaza. Permission to leave Gaza to receive medical treatment was denied or delayed for hundreds of seriously ill Palestinians and at least 28 individuals died while waiting for permission to travel. Israeli forces continued to forcibly evict Palestinians, demolish their homes and expropriate their land in the occupied West Bank, including East Jerusalem, while allowing Israeli settlements to expand on illegally confiscated Palestinian land.

Throughout the year, Israeli forces used excessive and, at times, lethal force against Palestinian civilians. Allegations of ill-treatment against Palestinian detainees continued and were rarely investigated. Hundreds were administratively detained without charge; others were serving sentences imposed after unfair military trials. Israeli soldiers and settlers who committed serious human rights abuses against Palestinians enjoyed virtual impunity.

Background

Israeli parliamentary elections in February saw a growth in support for right-wing parties and the formation of a coalition government that included the Labour party, the right-wing Likud party and the ultra-right Yisrael Beitenu.

The US government increased calls for Israel to stop settlement building as an initial step in reviving the peace process, but its calls were not heeded.

Operation 'Cast Lead'

The 22-day Israeli military offensive on Gaza, launched without warning, had the stated aim of ending rocket attacks into Israel by armed factions affiliated to Hamas and other Palestinian groups. The offensive killed more than 1,380 Palestinians and injured around 5,000, many of them seriously. More than 1,800 of the injured were children. Thousands of civilian homes, businesses and public buildings were destroyed. Entire neighbourhoods were flattened. The electricity, water and sewage systems were severely damaged, as was other vital infrastructure. Large swathes of agricultural land and many industrial and commercial properties were destroyed. Much of the destruction was wanton and deliberate, and could not be justified on grounds of military necessity. Thirteen Israelis were killed during the fighting, including three civilians killed by rockets and mortars fired by Palestinian armed groups into southern Israel (see Palestinian Authority entry).

Before and during Operation "Cast Lead" the Israeli army refused to allow into Gaza independent observers, journalists, human rights monitors and humanitarian workers, effectively cutting off Gaza from the outside world. The authorities also refused to co-operate with an investigation by the UN Human Rights Council (HRC).

The HRC report, issued in September and known as the Goldstone report, accused Israel and Hamas of war crimes and possible crimes against humanity in Gaza and southern Israel. It recommended that those responsible for war crimes be brought to justice.

The Israeli authorities did not establish any independent or impartial investigation into the conduct of its forces during Operation "Cast Lead", although there were a number of internal investigations.

Unlawful killings

Hundreds of civilians were killed by Israeli attacks using long-range high-precision munitions fired from combat aircraft, helicopters and drones, or from tanks stationed several kilometres from their target. Victims were not caught in the crossfire or when shielding militants, but killed in their homes while sleeping, carrying out daily tasks or playing. Some civilians, including children, were shot at close range when posing no threat to the lives of Israeli soldiers. Paramedics and ambulances were repeatedly attacked while rescuing the wounded, leading to several deaths.

Scores of civilians were killed and injured by less precise weapons, such as artillery shells and mortars, and flechette tank shells.

White phosphorus was repeatedly fired indiscriminately over densely populated residential areas, killing and wounding civilians and destroying civilian property.

Many of these attacks violated international law as they were disproportionate and indiscriminate; directly targeted civilians and civilian objects, including medical personnel and vehicles; failed to take all feasible precautions to minimize the risks to civilians; and failed to allow timely access to and passage of medical and relief personnel and vehicles.

■ On 4 January, Sa'adallah Matar Abu Halima and four of his children were killed in a white phosphorus attack on their home in the Sayafa area in north-west Gaza. His wife Sabah was seriously burned and told Amnesty International that she had watched her baby girl Shahed melt in her arms. Soon after the attack Israeli soldiers shot dead at close range cousins Matar and Muhammad Abu Halima as they tried to take their burned relatives to hospital.

■ During the night of 6 January, 22 members of the al-Daya family, most of them women and children, were killed when an Israeli F-16 aircraft bombed their home in the al-Zaytoun district of Gaza City.

Attacks on civilian objects

Israeli forces attacked hospitals, medical staff and ambulances as well as humanitarian facilities, including UN Relief and Works Agency for Palestine Refugees in the Near East (UNRWA) buildings. At least 15 of the 27 hospitals in Gaza were damaged, some extensively; around 30 ambulances were hit and 16 health workers were killed. Amnesty International found no evidence that Hamas or armed militants used hospitals as hiding places or to carry out attacks, and the Israeli authorities did not provide evidence to substantiate such allegations.

■ Three paramedics – Anas Fadhel Na'im, Yaser Kamal Shbeir and Raf'at Abd al-'Al – were killed on 4 January in Gaza City by an Israeli missile as they walked towards two wounded men. A 12-year-old boy, Omar Ahmad al-Barade'e, who was showing them the way, was also killed.

■ At about 6am on 17 January a white phosphorus artillery shell exploded in the UNRWA primary school in Beit Lahia, where more than 1,500 people were sheltering. Two children – Muhammad al-Ashqar and his brother Bilal – aged five and seven respectively, were killed. More than a dozen other civilians sheltering in the school were injured.

Use of civilians as 'human shields'

On several occasions Israeli soldiers used Palestinian civilians, including children, as "human shields" during military operations, or forced them to carry out dangerous tasks. Israeli soldiers also launched attacks from near inhabited houses.

■ For two days from 5 January, Israeli forces held Yousef Abu 'Ida, his wife Leila and their nine children as "human shields" in their home in Hay al-Salam, east of Jabalia, while they used the house as a military position. They then forced the family out and destroyed the house.

Humanitarian assistance blocked

Israeli forces deliberately blocked and otherwise impeded emergency relief and humanitarian assistance. They also attacked aid convoys and distribution centres, and medical personnel, prompting UNRWA and the ICRC to cut back on their operations in Gaza during the offensive.

■ Several members of the al-Sammouni family bled to death in the days following an attack on 5 January on

I

their home in the al-Zaytoun neighbourhood of Gaza City because the Israeli army did not allow ambulances or anyone else to rescue them. Children lay for three days without food or water next to the bodies of their dead relatives. In all, 29 members of the al-Sammouni family perished.

Gaza blockade – humanitarian crisis

The continuing Israeli military blockade of Gaza, in force since June 2007, deepened the ongoing humanitarian crisis. Mass unemployment, extreme poverty, food insecurity and food price rises caused by shortages left four in five Gazans dependent on humanitarian aid. The scope of the blockade and statements made by Israeli officials about its purpose showed that it was being imposed as a form of collective punishment of Gazans, a flagrant violation of international law.

Operation "Cast Lead" pushed the crisis to catastrophic levels. After it concluded, the blockade hampered or prevented reconstruction efforts. As a result, there was a further deterioration of water and sanitation services; more power cuts, causing severe problems in the summer heat and for public and health institutions; greater overcrowding in schools; more challenges for an already overstretched health system struggling with damaged facilities and higher demand; and little or no chance of economic recovery. Israel continued to deny farmers access to their land within 500m of the Gaza-Israel border, and to ban fishing further than three nautical miles from the shore.

Among those trapped in Gaza were people with serious illnesses who needed medical care outside Gaza, and students and workers needing to travel to take up university places or jobs in the West Bank or abroad.

■ Samir al-Nadim died on 1 November after his exit from Gaza for a heart operation was delayed by 22 days. By the time the Israeli authorities allowed him to leave on 29 October, he was unconscious and on a respirator. He died of heart failure in a hospital in Nablus in the West Bank.

Restrictions in the West Bank

Israel's 700km fence/wall in the West Bank, which separates many Palestinians from their land, jobs and relatives, combined with long curfews, around 600 Israeli checkpoints, roadblocks and other closure obstacles, continued to disrupt the ability of Palestinians to access basic services, including educational and health facilities.

Right to water

Israel continued to deny Palestinians in the OPT fair access to adequate, safe water supplies, hindering social and economic development and posing threats to health, in violation of its responsibilities as the occupying power. Palestinian water consumption barely reached 70 litres a day per person – well below the WHO's recommended daily minimum of 100 litres. Israeli daily per capita consumption was four times higher. The Israeli army repeatedly destroyed rainwater harvesting cisterns used by Palestinians in the West Bank on the grounds that they had been built without permission.

Forced evictions

Israeli forces forcibly evicted Palestinians and demolished their homes, particularly in East Jerusalem, on the grounds that the buildings lacked permits. Such permits are systematically denied to Palestinians. Simultaneously, Israeli settlements were allowed to expand on illegally confiscated Palestinian land. The Bedouin population of the Negev was also targeted for forced evictions.

Excessive use of force

Israeli forces used excessive force against Palestinian civilians, causing many injuries and some deaths. The security forces used tear gas, rubber-coated metal bullets and live ammunition, often when there was no serious threat to themselves or to others.

■ On 17 April, Bassem Abu Rahmeh was hit by a high-velocity Israeli tear gas canister, causing internal bleeding that quickly killed him. He was taking part in the weekly protest in Bil'in village against the security fence/wall that cuts off Bil'in from much of its agricultural land. Video footage showed that Bassem Abu Rahmeh was unarmed and posing no threat. The Israeli military said it was investigating his death.

Military justice system
Detentions without trial

The number of Palestinians held in Israeli prisons without charge or trial decreased from 564 in January to 278 in December.

■ Hamdi al-Ta'mari, a Palestinian student arrested on

18 December 2008 when he was 16 years old, continued to be administratively detained without charge in Ofer Prison near Ramallah in the West Bank until his release on 14 December. He was arrested by Israeli soldiers at gunpoint at his home in Bethlehem and, according to his family, was kicked, beaten and otherwise abused during arrest.

Unfair trials

Palestinians from the OPT, including juveniles, continued to be interrogated without a lawyer present and to be tried in military rather than civil courts, where they suffered other violations to their right to fair trial.

Prison conditions – denial of family visits

Around 900 Palestinian prisoners continued to be denied family visits, some for a third year, because Gazans have not been allowed to travel into Israel since the blockade was imposed.

Torture and other ill-treatment

Torture and other ill-treatment of Palestinians by the General Security Service (GSS) continued to be reported. Methods allegedly used included beatings, sleep deprivation and prolonged periods in stress positions. Israeli domestic law retains "necessity" as a possible justification for torture.

Impunity

Impunity remained the norm for Israeli soldiers, police and other security forces, as well as Israeli settlers, who committed serious human rights abuses against Palestinians, including unlawful killings. Violence by settlers against Palestinians included beatings, stone throwing and damaging their crops and homes. In rare cases where Israeli security personnel were convicted, the punishments were extremely lenient.

■ In June, the State Attorney's Office withdrew an indictment against Ze'ev Braude, a resident of Kiryat Arba settlement in Hebron, even though he had been filmed shooting and seriously wounding two Palestinians, Hosni Matriya and his 67-year-old father Abed al-Hai, on 4 December 2008.

Prisoners of conscience – Israeli conscientious objectors

At least six Israeli conscientious objectors were imprisoned during 2009 for refusing to serve in the Israeli army because they opposed the military occupation of the Palestinian Territories or the actions of the army in Gaza. There was increasing harassment of Israeli NGOs supporting conscientious objectors.

■ On 29 October, Or Ben David was given her first prison sentence of 20 days after she refused to serve in the army. She was back in prison at the end of the year after receiving two further sentences.

Amnesty International visits/reports

🚗 Amnesty International delegates visited Israel and the OPT in January, February, June, July, October and November.

▨ Israel/OPT: The conflict in Gaza: A briefing on applicable law, investigations and accountability (MDE 15/007/2009)

▨ Israel/OPT: Fuelling conflict – foreign arms supplies to Israel/Gaza (MDE 15/012/2009)

▨ Israel/Gaza: Operation "Cast Lead": 22 days of death and destruction (MDE 15/015/2009)

▨ Israel/Occupied Palestinian Territories: Urgent steps needed to address UN Committee against Torture's concerns (MDE 15/019/2009)

▨ Troubled waters: Palestinians denied fair access to water (MDE 15/027/2009)

ITALY

ITALIAN REPUBLIC

Head of state:	Giorgio Napolitano
Head of government:	Silvio Berlusconi
Death penalty:	abolitionist for all crimes
Population:	59.9 million
Life expectancy:	81.1 years
Under-5 mortality (m/f):	5/4 per 1,000
Adult literacy:	98.9 per cent

Unlawful forced evictions of Roma communities continued throughout the year. Efforts by the authorities to control migration jeopardized the rights of migrants and asylum-seekers. Italy continued to deport people to places where they were at risk of human rights abuses. US and Italian agents were convicted for their part in the US-led programme of renditions (unlawful transfers of terrorist suspects between countries). Deaths in custody were reported and allegations of torture and other ill-treatment by law enforcement officials continued to be made.

Discrimination

Roma continued to be denied equal access to education, housing, health care and employment. The authorities introduced new legislation which could result in discriminatory activities.

Roma – forced evictions

Unlawful forced evictions of Roma drove them further into poverty. Both Roma with Italian citizenship and those of EU or another nationality suffered the adverse effects.

■ On 31 March, Milan authorities forcibly evicted a community of about 150 Roma living under the Bacula overpass in the north of the city. Only four families, approximately 30 people, were provided with adequate alternative accommodation. The majority of Roma living in Bacula camp had been previously forcibly evicted from other camps in Milan in 2008.

■ On 11 November, city authorities forcibly evicted a community of about 350 Romani people from Via Centocelle camp, in Rome. All the community's shelters were destroyed and the municipality offered short-term shelter to approximately 70 people. Members of the community were not notified of the eviction, contrary to domestic law, which states that authorities should notify each individual, or publish an order or notice. As the order was not formalized in this way, the community could not challenge it through the courts, and stop or postpone the eviction.

Legal developments

In August, new legislation (Law 94/2009), part of the so-called "security package", enabled local authorities to authorize associations of unarmed civilians not belonging to state or local police forces to patrol the territory of a municipality. In recent years there have been documented attacks by self-organized groups against Roma and migrants. The implementation of such provision may result in discrimination and vigilantism.

Migrants' and asylum-seekers' rights

In January, Italy was criticized by the UN Working Group on Arbitrary Detention for the way migrants and asylum-seekers, including minors, were routinely detained without any individual consideration of whether their detention was necessary, and frequently without any basis in domestic law. Asylum-seekers were prohibited from leaving the reception centres where they were detained until they received a formal confirmation of the submission of their asylum claim;

completing registration formalities could take up to a month. Forced expulsions, without consideration of individual protection needs and circumstances, persisted.

Legal developments

New legislation adopted as part of the so-called "security package" (see above) established the criminal offence of "irregular migration". Criminal proceedings against asylum-seekers for entering the country illegally would only be suspended once a claim for international protection was lodged, and dismissed if international protection was granted.

There were concerns that the new law might deter irregular migrants from accessing education, medical care and protection by law enforcement officials against crimes, for fear of being reported to the police, especially given existing provisions in the criminal code obliging civil servants (such as teachers or local authority employees, including those in charge of issuing identity cards) to report all criminal acts to the police or judicial authorities.

International obligations to refugees and migrants

The Italian and Maltese governments disagreed over their obligations to carry out rescue operations at sea, leaving migrants stranded for days without water and food and posing a serious risk to their lives.

The Italian authorities took the unprecedented decision to transfer migrants and asylum-seekers rescued at sea to Tripoli, Libya, without assessing their need for refuge and international protection. Libya is not a signatory to the 1951 Geneva Refugee Convention and does not have a functioning asylum procedure in place, which limits the possibility of receiving international protection in the country. According to Italian government figures, between May and September 834 people intercepted or rescued at sea were taken to Libya, violating the principle of *non-refoulement* (prohibition on returning an individual to a country where they would risk serious human rights abuses).

■ On 6 May, three vessels with an estimated 227 people on board sent out a distress call while passing about 50 miles south of Lampedusa. The rescue operation was delayed by a dispute between Malta and Italy over who had responsibility for the boats. Eventually, the people were rescued by two Italian coastguard vessels. The coastguard took them to Tripoli, Libya, without stopping in an Italian port to assess their need for refuge and international protection.

Counter-terror and security

The authorities failed to fully co-operate with investigations into human rights abuses committed in the context of renditions and, in the name of security, continued a policy of forcibly returning third-country nationals to places where they were at risk of torture. The government accepted the return of two Guantánamo Bay detainees.

Renditions

■ On 4 November, a Criminal Court in Milan convicted 22 US agents and officials of the Central Intelligence Agency (CIA) and one US military officer in their absence. The prosecutors had issued arrest warrants for the US defendants in 2005 and in 2006, but successive Italian Justice Ministers refused to transmit them to the US government.

The accused were convicted for their involvement in the February 2003 abduction of Usama Mostafa Hassan Nasr (better known as Abu Omar). Abu Omar was kidnapped in Milan and flown via Germany to Egypt, where he was secretly detained for 14 months and allegedly tortured. Three other US nationals, including the then-CIA station chief in Rome, were granted diplomatic immunity and the cases against them were dismissed. Two Italian military agents were also convicted, and sentenced to three years' imprisonment. The cases against the former head of the Italian Military Security Service Agency and his deputy were dismissed under the "state secrets" privilege, as were the cases of three other Italians.

The Milan Court provisionally awarded Abu Omar 1 million euros and his wife, Nabila Ghali, 500,000 euros as compensation for the abuse and injustice they suffered.

Forcible returns

Despite international rulings against them, since the adoption in 2005 of legislation which provides for expedited expulsion procedures for terrorist suspects (Law 155/05, the so-called "Pisanu Law"), the authorities continued to expel several people to Tunisia, a country with a long and well-documented record of torturing and abusing prisoners.

■ On 24 February, the European Court of Human Rights ruled against Italy on its 2008 decision to expel Sami Ben Khemais Essid to Tunisia (see Tunisia entry). The Court condemned Italy for violating the principle of *non-refoulement*.

■ On 2 August, the Italian authorities returned Ali Ben Sassi Toumi to Tunisia, despite three separate rulings of the European Court of Human Rights urging them to stay his forcible return. In Tunisia, he was held incommunicado and his relatives were not informed of his whereabouts until 10 August, when he was released on bail. He continued to await his trial for terrorism-related charges at the end of the year.

Guantánamo Bay

On 30 November, Adel Ben Mabrouk and Riadh Nasseri, two Tunisian nationals formerly detained without charge by the USA at Guantánamo Bay, were transferred to Italy. Both men were detained upon arrival and faced prosecution in Italy, reportedly on charges for terrorism-related offences. At the end of the year, they remained in prison in Milan under a special security regime.

Deaths in custody, torture and other ill-treatment

There were widespread allegations of torture and other ill-treatment by law enforcement officials as well as reports of deaths in custody in disputed circumstances. Italy failed to introduce an independent police complaints body and to introduce the crime of torture in its ordinary criminal legislation.

■ The investigation in the case of Emmanuel Bonsu continued. In September 2008, Emmanuel Bonsu was arrested by municipal police officers in Parma. He was reportedly beaten and physically assaulted, resulting in long-term psychological damage. In June, 10 officers were indicted for injury, assault, abduction, slander and false testimony, and other lesser charges. The trial was still pending at the end of the year.

■ On 6 July, four police officers were sentenced to prison terms of three years and six months each for the manslaughter of Federico Aldrovandi, who died in September 2005 after being stopped by police officers in Ferrara. The police officers had not been suspended from duty during the investigation or trial, and were appealing against the sentence at the end of the year.

■ On 22 October, Stefano Cucchi died in Sandro Pertini hospital's prison wing seven days after his arrest. His family believed injuries seen on his body after his death were indicative of ill-treatment. The Public Prosecutor investigating the death of Stefano Cucchi charged three prison guards and three doctors with his manslaughter.

G8 trials

Law enforcement officials and the Public Prosecutor continued different appeals against the 2008 verdicts and sentences of abuse of protesters at Armando Diaz School and Bolzaneto prison during the G8 summit in 2001.

Amnesty International visits/reports

🚌 Amnesty International delegates visited Italy in March, July and October.

📄 Italy: Forcible return/fear of torture or other ill-treatment (EUR 30/001/2009)

📄 Italy: Obligation to safeguard lives and safety of migrants and asylum-seekers (EUR 30/007/2009)

📄 Homophobic attacks on the rise in Italy (EUR 30/010/2009)

📄 Italy: The Abu Omar case (EUR 30/012/2009)

📄 Italy: Roma community forcibly evicted (EUR 30/013/2009)

JAMAICA

JAMAICA

Head of state:	Queen Elizabeth II, represented by Kenneth Hall
Head of government:	Bruce Golding
Death penalty:	retentionist
Population:	2.7 million
Life expectancy:	71.7 years
Under-5 mortality (m/f):	28/28 per 1,000
Adult literacy:	86 per cent

Hundreds of people in inner-city communities were the victims of gang murders or police killings. Sexual violence against women and girls was widespread. There were reports of discrimination against lesbian and gay people. Two people were sentenced to death; there were no executions.

Background

The public security situation remained critical. Gang violence in marginalized inner-city communities reportedly resulted in 1,198 deaths between January and September. The Minister of National Security and the Commissioner of Police resigned in April and November respectively following criticism from the Prime Minister over the failure to reduce the murder rate.

A new Charter of Fundamental Rights and Freedoms came before Parliament in April and was still under consideration at the end of the year. The Charter, which is intended to replace Chapter III of the Constitution, was criticized by national human rights organizations on the grounds that it was too limited in scope and that there had been a lack of public consultation.

Unlawful killings

The number of reported police killings rose to 253, compared with 224 in 2008. The high number of killings, combined with eyewitness testimonies and other evidence, indicated that many of the killings were unlawful.

■ Anthony Nelson was shot dead by the police on 7 January 2009 on a construction site at Central Village, St Catherine. His companion, Ricardo Suckoo, was seriously injured. Police officers reported that the two men fired at them after being questioned for acting suspiciously. However, according to witnesses, the men were unarmed and the police shot at them after asking what they were doing on the site. At the end of the year, a ruling from the Director of Public Prosecutions on whether to pursue criminal proceedings against the police officers was still pending.

■ Dane Daley was fatally shot by the police on 27 May in Portmore, St Catherine, as he was on his way to the shops with two cousins, Tyrell and Jordan Thompson. According to Tyrell Thompson, they were stopped and ordered not to move by four armed men, whom they could not identify because it was dark. They started to run away before realizing that the men were police officers. Tyrell Thompson was shot and injured. Dane Daley was shot in the head and abdomen and died. Residents in the area said that the police were patrolling the area following previous incidents of gang shootings. An investigation into the shootings was continuing at the end of the year.

The Jamaica Constabulary Force (JCF) began implementation of the recommendations of a strategic review of the force. According to national human rights organizations, although the number of police officers trained in crime scene investigation increased, the resources made available to JCF ballistic, forensic and pathology departments remained inadequate. The independence of these departments, which remained under the direction of the police force, was also questioned.

Parliament debated draft legislation to create an independent commission to investigate abuses by the security forces but had not passed the bill by the end of the year.

Justice system

According to the Minister of Justice, by early November the implementation had begun of over 70 of the 200 recommendations to reform the justice system made by the Justice System Reform Task Force. A bill creating a special coroner's office to expedite investigations into new cases of fatal police shootings was passed by Parliament but the office had not been established by the end of the year.

More than a year and a half after it was tabled in Parliament, a bill establishing a special prosecutor to investigate corruption by state officials had still not been adopted.

Violence against women and girls

A study on the relationship between adolescent pregnancy and sexual violence carried out by health care researchers showed that 49 per cent of the 750 girls aged between 15 and 17 surveyed had experienced sexual coercion or violence. The study highlighted the need to address gender-based violence at community level.

In July, the Sexual Offences Act, which reforms and incorporates various laws relating to rape, incest and other sexual offences, was passed by Parliament. Although women's organizations welcomed the Act, they also expressed concerns about the restrictive definition of rape. The Act criminalizes rape within marriage, but only in certain circumstances.

Rights of lesbian, gay, bisexual and transgender people

During a parliamentary debate, a member of Parliament questioned the right of gay men and lesbians to form organizations and demanded life imprisonment for homosexual acts. The Prime Minister, while distancing himself from these comments, made it clear that his government would not repeal the crime of buggery, which is currently punishable by up to 10 years' imprisonment.

Death penalty

Two death sentences were handed down in 2009; no executions were carried out. There were four people on death row at the end of the year. In July the Prime Minister declared that the government would honour Parliament's decision in 2008 to retain the death penalty by resuming executions as soon as the appeal avenues available to death row prisoners were exhausted.

Amnesty International visit/report

🚗 Amnesty International delegates visited Jamaica in February.

📄 Public security reforms and human rights in Jamaica (AMR 38/001/2009)

JAPAN

JAPAN	
Head of government:	Hatoyama Yukio (replaced Aso Taro in September)
Death penalty:	retentionist
Population:	127.2 million
Life expectancy:	82.7 years
Under 5-mortality (m/f):	5/4 per 1,000

Executions continued until August when a new government took power. The newly appointed Minister of Justice called for a public debate on the death penalty and instituted a group to study "transparency" during interrogations. However, the pre-trial *daiyo kangoku* (detention) system continued. Prisoners faced prolonged periods of solitary confinement and inadequate medical access. In July, the UN Special Rapporteur on trafficking in persons expressed great concern at trafficking for labour exploitation and recommended stronger laws and labour inspections to protect migrant workers' rights.

Background

In August, Prime Minister Aso Taro called for general elections following the Liberal Democratic Party's (LDP) defeat in Tokyo local elections. The opposition Democratic Party of Japan (DPJ) was voted into power, ending more than 50 years of rule by the LDP. Hatoyama Yukio was elected Prime Minister of a coalition government with the Social Democratic Party and the People's New Party.

Justice system

In October, Minister of Justice Chiba Keiko established a committee to study transparency in the pre-trial *daiyo kangoku* system. However, she did not specify a timeline for proposals. The *daiyo kangoku* system, which allows detention of suspects for 23 days, is associated with intimidation and abusive interrogation methods aimed at obtaining confessions.

■ In June, the Tokyo High Court granted a retrial for Sugaya Toshikazu. He had been sentenced to life imprisonment in 1993 after being convicted of murdering a four-year-old girl. Sugaya Toshikazu's conviction was based on inaccurate DNA evidence and a confession obtained under the *daiyo kangoku* system. He had retracted his confession twice during the course of his trials.

Under a new lay-judge (*saiban-in*) system, citizens joined professional judges in deciding verdicts and sentencing. All serious crimes, including those carrying the death penalty, were eligible to be tried under this system.

■ In August, in the first case under the new system at Tokyo District Court, a 72-year-old man was found guilty of murder and sentenced to 15 years in prison.

Death penalty

Seven men were executed in 2009. Approximately 106 prisoners, including several mentally ill prisoners, were at risk of execution and lived in particularly harsh prison conditions.

Refugees and asylum-seekers

The government forcibly repatriated asylum-seekers to countries where they were at risk of torture and other ill-treatment. As of September, 1,123 individuals had filed asylum claims. The refugee recognition process was very time-consuming and only 15 individuals were granted refugee states, including three after appeal. Over 90 per cent of asylum-seekers were not permitted to work, did not receive health insurance and were ineligible for public assistance.

■ In April, the government deported Filipino nationals Arlan and Sarah Calderon because of their irregular status, separating them from their 13-year-old daughter, Noriko Calderon. The Ministry of Justice gave Noriko Calderon, who was born in Japan and speaks only Japanese, a choice of returning to the Philippines with her parents or remaining in Japan alone.

In July, bills revising the Immigration Control and Refugee Recognition Act and the Basic Resident Registration Law were enacted to create a new residence control and resident certificate system for foreign nationals in the next three years. Civil organizations raised concerns that undocumented foreign residents, including asylum-seekers, faced exclusion from basic public services, such as education and health care.

Violence against women and girls

In July, after considering Japan's sixth periodic report, the UN Committee on the Elimination of Discrimination against Women (CEDAW) expressed its concern at the obstacles faced by women victims of domestic and sexual violence when bringing complaints and seeking protection. It was particularly concerned at the precarious situation of immigrant women, minority women and women of vulnerable groups.

CEDAW reiterated its recommendation that Japan should urgently find a lasting solution for the situation of the "comfort women" – survivors of Japan's military sexual slavery system. This should include compensation for the victims, the prosecution of perpetrators and educating the Japanese public about these crimes. Twelve local councils adopted resolutions calling for an apology and compensation for survivors of the "comfort women" system.

Amnesty International visits/report

🚌 Amnesty International delegates visited Japan in February and April.

🗐 Hanging by a thread: mental health and the death penalty in Japan (ASA 22/005/2009)

JORDAN

HASHEMITE KINGDOM OF JORDAN

Head of state:	King Abdullah II bin al-Hussein
Head of government:	Samir Rifai (replaced Nader al-Dahabi in December)
Death penalty:	retentionist
Population:	6.3 million
Life expectancy:	72.4 years
Under-5 mortality (m/f):	24/19 per 1,000
Adult literacy:	91.1 per cent

Torture and other ill-treatment were reported and at least two men were alleged to have died as a result of police beatings. Thousands of people were held without charge or prospect of trial. Trials before the State Security Court (SSC) continued to breach international standards of fair trial. A new Societies Law opened the way for greater state interference in the work of civil society organizations. Women faced legal and other discrimination and remained inadequately protected against domestic violence; at least 24 were reported to have been victims of so-called honour killings. New regulations improved conditions for migrant domestic workers but still left them vulnerable to exploitation and abuse. At least 12 people were sentenced to death; there were no executions.

Background

In November, the King dissolved the Lower House of Parliament which had been elected in November 2007. New elections were to take place towards the end of 2010. A new cabinet was sworn in during December.

Detention without trial, torture and other ill-treatment

There were new reports of torture and other ill-treatment despite amendments to the Criminal Procedures Law that halved the maximum permissible period of detention without charge to one month in misdemeanour cases and three months in criminal cases. The amendments also require that applications to hold detainees for such periods must be judicially sanctioned.

In April, the National Centre for Human Rights (NCHR), an official body, disclosed in its report for 2008 that when carrying out unannounced inspection visits to prisons it had received complaints from inmates that they had been beaten and otherwise ill-treated by guards. The report noted that some perpetrators could escape accountability because physical evidence of abuse tended to be temporary and often there were no independent witnesses.

Thousands of people were reported to be held under the 1954 Law on Crime Prevention, which gives provincial governors power to detain people suspected of committing crimes or deemed to be "a danger to society" and to hold them indefinitely without charge or trial. In its report for 2008 the NCHR cited more than 13,000 cases of such detentions. Although outside the law's remit, governors continued to use it to detain women considered to be at risk of family violence for their "own protection".

■ Sadem Abdul Mutelib al-Saoud died in hospital on 8 November apparently as a result of injuries sustained when he was arrested and beaten by police while held at Amman's al-Hussein Security Centre in October. He fell into a coma and died three weeks later. At least four police officers were referred to a police court on 11 November in connection with the killing.

Counter-terror and security

Tens of people accused of terrorism-related or state security offences were tried before the SSC, whose procedures breach international standards for fair trial. In particular, the court continued to accept as evidence for conviction "confessions" that defendants alleged had been obtained under torture in pre-trial detention, apparently without taking adequate steps to investigate the allegations.

In September, however, the Court of Cassation set aside the life sentences imposed on eight men alleged to have been planning a terrorist attack in 2004 after concluding that their "confessions" had been coerced and were therefore invalid.

Freedom of expression, association and assembly

A new Societies Law came into force in September after it was ratified by the King. It increases government control over the legal registration, operation and activities of NGOs, provides for executive interference in their affairs and requires that they obtain official approval before they can receive funds from abroad.

J

Journalists and others remained liable to prosecution for "insulting" the King, the judiciary and religion.

■ Islam Samhan, a poet and journalist, was sentenced to one year's imprisonment and fined by the Amman Court of First Instance in June after he was convicted of insulting Islam and religious sentiment. He had been arrested in October 2008 and held for three or four days after he published a collection of his poems in which he was said to have used verses from the Qur'an. He was at liberty awaiting the outcome of an appeal.

Excessive use of force

The gendarmerie were accused of using excessive force to disperse a largely peaceful demonstration in al-Rabiah, Amman, on 9 January. Some 3,000 people had gathered to protest against Israeli attacks on the Gaza Strip when they were forcibly dispersed, apparently without warning, by gendarmerie officers using batons, water cannon and tear gas. The Public Security Directorate said it would investigate, but no findings had been disclosed publicly by the end of the year.

Police were also accused of using excessive force when carrying out some arrests.

■ Fakhri Anani Kreishan died on 14 November after he was allegedly assaulted by a police officer two days earlier outside his home in Ma'an. He was reported to have fallen into a coma after a police officer hit him on the head with a baton before dragging him down some steps. An autopsy said the main cause of death was an injury to the head caused by a hard object. A police officer was charged with his murder on 17 November and referred to a police court.

Migrants' rights – domestic workers

Tens of thousands of migrant women domestic workers continued to face economic, physical and psychological abuse by employers and representatives of recruitment agencies. They were disproportionately more likely to commit or attempt suicide than others in Jordan. In March, *al-Ghad* newspaper reported an unsourced "official statistic" that 25 domestic workers had died in the first three months of 2009, 18 from suicide and seven as a result of illness. In October, the Labour Ministry announced that 14 Sri Lankan domestic workers had attempted suicide in 2009 and said this appeared to be linked to their work conditions.

In August, the authorities introduced new regulations under the Labour Law to regulate the working conditions of all domestic workers, including migrants. They prescribe maximum working hours, rights to holiday and sick leave, and domestic workers' entitlement to regular contact with their own families. Despite addressing important issues, however, the regulations are loosely worded and open to interpretation in certain respects and they fail to specify mechanisms for determining wages and so resolve long-standing problems related to non-payment of wages or low wages. They also fail to provide effective safeguards against physical violence and sexual abuse by employers of domestic workers, the great majority of whom are women, and appear to place women at risk by requiring domestic workers to obtain their employer's permission before leaving their house.

■ An Indonesian domestic worker died on 7 March after her employers beat her apparently to "discipline" her. An autopsy found that she had been badly beaten on the head and had sustained broken ribs and severe bruising to her body. The couple who had employed her were charged with manslaughter.

Refugees

Jordan continued to host some 450,000 refugees from Iraq most of whom arrived after the US-led invasion of Iraq in 2003. Many maintained a precarious existence, without legal status and access to work or state support.

Violence and discrimination against women

Twenty-four women were reported to have been victims of "honour killings" by family members. Perpetrators of such killings continued to benefit from inappropriately lenient sentences under Article 98 of the Penal Code, which allows courts discretion to impose sentences of a minimum of three months' imprisonment on defendants considered to have killed while in a "fit of rage caused by an unlawful or dangerous act on the part of the victim". In August, the authorities established a special tribunal to try defendants accused of "honour crimes". In September, the Justice Minister said that the government planned to amend the Penal Code, including Article 98, but the proposed amendments were still awaited at the end of the year.

In May, the government told the UN Secretary-General that it would withdraw its reservation to Article 15(4) of the Convention on the Elimination of All Forms of Discrimination against Women, which guarantees women freedom of mobility and to choose their place of residence, but would maintain its reservation to other elements of Article 15, including that guaranteeing women equality under the law with men.

Death penalty

At least 12 people were sentenced to death. The Justice Minister stated that the death sentences of four people became final, with no further right to appeal, and that 40 people were under sentence of death at the end of the year. In April, the Ministry of Justice announced that the Penal Code would be amended to abolish the death penalty for a number of crimes, although it seemed that pre-meditated murder would continue to be punishable by death. The proposed amendments had not received parliamentary approval by the end of the year.

Amnesty International report

Jordan must fully investigate suspected police killings, 18 November 2009

KAZAKHSTAN

REPUBLIC OF KAZAKHSTAN

Head of state:	Nursultan Nazarbaev
Head of government:	Karim Massimov
Death penalty:	abolitionist for ordinary crimes
Population:	15.6 million
Life expectancy:	64.9 years
Under-5 mortality (m/f):	34/26 per 1,000
Adult literacy:	99.6 per cent

Confessions extracted under torture continued to be admitted as evidence in trials. Criminal proceedings failed to comply with international standards of fair trial. Torture and other ill-treatment by members of the security forces remained widespread, in particular by officers of the National Security Service in the context of operations in the name of national security, and the fight against terrorism and corruption. Freedom of expression and freedom of religion continued to be restricted.

Background

In May, President Nazarbaev approved a National Human Rights Action Plan for 2009 to 2012. This was to allay concerns of domestic and international human rights organizations that Kazakhstan was failing to comply with its human rights obligations on the eve of assuming the chairmanship of the OSCE in January 2010.

In July, the President signed amendments to a law on the internet which classified all online resources as mass media and made them subject to the same stringent rules that governed other mass media, such as criminal sanctions for criticizing the President and government officials.

Torture and other ill-treatment

In November the European Court of Human Rights ruled in the case of *Kaboulov v. Ukraine* that the extradition to Kazakhstan of any criminal suspect, including Amir Damirovich Kaboulov, would be in violation of Article 3 of the European Convention on Human Rights, as they would run a serious risk of being subjected to torture or inhuman or degrading treatment.

Despite amendments to the criminal and criminal procedural codes to clamp down on abusive practices, torture and other ill-treatment remained widespread. Confessions reportedly extracted under torture continued to be admitted as evidence in criminal trials, and individuals continued to be held in unregistered detention for longer than the three hours allowed for in national law. The lack of a clear definition of detention remained unaddressed despite recommendations of the UN Committee against Torture in November 2008.

Following his visit to Kazakhstan in May 2009, the UN Special Rapporteur on torture concluded that he "received many credible allegations of beatings with hands and fists, plastic bottles filled with sand and police truncheons and of kicking, asphyxiation through plastic bags and gas masks used to obtain confessions from suspects. In several cases, these allegations were supported by forensic medical evidence."

■ In June, Dmitri Tian and Oleg Evloev were sentenced to 25 years' and life imprisonment respectively by a

K

court in the capital Astana for the premeditated murders of a woman and her three children. Both men claimed that they had not committed the murders, but that they had been tortured in detention in order to force them to confess. According to observers of the trial, the judge instructed the jury not to consider the allegations of torture. Reportedly, a video tape recorded by the police following Oleg Evloev's arrest, showed him covered in bruises, but it was lost by the prosecution. In November, the Supreme Court turned down the appeals by both defendants. No investigations into the allegations of torture were conducted.

Prison conditions

■ Inessa Karkhu, an accountant serving an eight-year prison sentence for fraud handed down in 2007, continued to be denied essential medical treatment for glaucoma, a disease that progressively damages vision. Her condition continued to deteriorate throughout the year and it was feared that she could end up losing her sight if she was not treated as a matter of urgency. She had to rely on medication delivered by her family which became difficult when she was transferred to a prison in Almaty, some 1,000km from the capital Astana. Following international pressure, Inessa Karkhu was examined by an independent ophthalmologist in November, who found that the disease had significantly progressed and that both her eyes were affected. Nevertheless, Inessa Karkhu had not received the recommended medical treatment by December.

Counter-terror and security

The National Security Service (NSS), which carries out special operations relating to national security and corruption, continued to use counter-terrorism operations to target minority groups perceived as a threat to national and regional security. Groups particularly affected were asylum-seekers and refugees from Uzbekistan, and members or suspected members of Islamic groups or Islamist parties, either unregistered or banned in Kazakhstan. Some high-profile political actors targeted in anti-corruption operations continued to be held in arbitrary and incommunicado detention.

In May, the UN Special Rapporteur on torture stated that "some groups run larger risks of cruel, inhuman and degrading treatment than others", noting that the likeliness for foreigners to be subjected to such treatment seemed to be "higher than average".

NSS officers were accused of routinely using torture and other ill-treatment in pre-charge and pre-trial detention centres under their jurisdiction. Public Monitoring Commissions, tasked with inspecting detention facilities, were denied access to NSS detention centres.

■ In September, armed and masked NSS officers conducted a night-time raid on the homes of three refugees and two asylum-seekers from Uzbekistan in Almaty. The officers, who did not identify themselves, detained the men and took them to an unidentified location for interrogation, later identified as the NSS building in Almaty. Allegedly, the men were handcuffed and beaten which resulted in one of them having a broken nose, and plastic bags were put over their heads. They reported that the officers threatened them with extradition to Uzbekistan, allegedly for the murder of a policeman. Several hours later they were released without charge. During arrest, they were refused permission to contact their families, a legal representative or UNHCR, the UN refugee agency. A spokesperson of the NSS later denied any use of excessive force and described the raids and detentions as a mere document check.

Unfair trials

Criminal proceedings continued to fall short of international fair trial standards, undermining the rule of law.

■ In September, Evgeni Zhovtis, a prominent human rights defender and director of the Kazakhstan International Bureau for Human Rights and the Rule of Law, was sentenced to four years' imprisonment following his conviction for causing the death of a pedestrian in a traffic accident at the end of July. Evgeni Zhovtis had admitted to having hit and fatally injured the pedestrian with his car, but pleaded not guilty by default. An appeal court in October upheld the conviction. The trial reportedly fell short of meeting national and international fair trial standards. The failure to inform Evgeni Zhovtis that he was being interrogated as a suspect rather than as a witness deprived him of a number of rights during investigation, such as the right to remain silent and the right to have access to reports of forensic experts. In October, he was transferred to an open prison in Ust-Kamenogorsk. His lawyers lodged a complaint against the appeal court's decision.

Freedom of religion

The right to freedom of religion remained restricted and religious minorities continued to report harassment by police and local authorities. Muslims worshipping outside state-registered mosques, such as the Ahmadi community and followers of the Salafi movement, reported being increasingly targeted by police and the NSS.

■ In March, NSS and local police conducted several raids on an Ahmadi Muslim community in Semipalatinsk as members of the community were gathering for Friday prayers. Reportedly, those present were forced to give personal details. During one of the raids, members of the community were detained and questioned at the local police station for several hours.

In February, following a request from the President, the Constitutional Council assessed a controversial draft law on freedom of conscience which would severely restrict the rights of religious minorities. The Council held that the draft law was incompatible with the Constitution and international human rights obligations. A revision of the draft law remained pending at the end of December.

Amnesty International visit/report

🚗 Amnesty International delegates visited Kazakhstan in June.

📄 Kazakhstan: Submission to the UN Universal Periodic Review (EUR 57/001/2009)

KENYA

REPUBLIC OF KENYA

Head of state and government:	Mwai Kibaki
Death penalty:	abolitionist in practice
Population:	39.8 million
Life expectancy:	53.6 years
Under 5-mortality (m/f):	112/95 per 1,000
Adult literacy:	73.6 per cent

The authorities showed little political will to ensure that those responsible for human rights abuses committed during the post-election violence of 2007/8 were brought to justice and that victims received adequate reparations. Impunity for state security officials who carried out unlawful killings and torture was not addressed. Human rights defenders faced considerable risks and threats. Violence against women and girls remained widespread. Thousands of people were forcibly evicted from their homes. The President commuted to life imprisonment the sentences of more than 4,000 prisoners who had been on death row for prolonged periods. Courts continued to impose death sentences but there were no executions.

Background

The government introduced several measures recommended in agreements reached during the political mediation – the Kenya National Dialogue and Reconciliation – following the post-election violence of 2007/8. In February, a committee of experts was appointed to lead the process of redrafting and adopting a new Constitution. In November, the committee issued a draft Constitution for public comments. In April, the Interim Independent Electoral Review Commission was formed to oversee elections for two years until a permanent electoral body is established. In September, the government appointed members of the National Cohesion and Integration Commission mandated by a 2008 law to promote national integration. Overall, however, there was little progress in implementing fundamental reforms proposed under the agreements.

There were regular disagreements within government and between the two main political parties that formed the coalition government – the Party of National Unity and the Orange Democratic Movement. As a result, much-needed legal, constitutional, land, electoral and other reforms were delayed.

Dozens of people were killed in violence, particularly in central Kenya, involving armed community vigilante groups and members of the Mungiki vigilante group. The police failed to effectively enforce law and order.

Impunity – post-election human rights violations

No measures were implemented to ensure accountability for human rights violations, including possible crimes against humanity, committed during the post-election violence in 2007/8, when more than 1,000 people were killed.

In February Parliament rejected a Bill to establish a special tribunal to investigate and prosecute

K

suspected perpetrators of these crimes. In July the cabinet rejected the tabling of a redrafted government version of the Bill. A private members' Bill seeking to establish a special tribunal was published in August and was pending in Parliament at the end of the year.

In July the government announced plans to use the truth, justice and reconciliation process and carry out "accelerated reforms of the judiciary, the police and the investigative arms of government" to deal with human rights abuses during the post-election violence, but no timeline was given.

In July, the Office of the Prosecutor of the International Criminal Court (ICC) reiterated to the government that primary responsibility for investigations and prosecutions into crimes that may fall within the jurisdiction of the ICC lies with Kenyan authorities. At the end of the year, an application by the ICC Prosecutor filed in November to the Pre-Trial Chamber to authorize an investigation into possible crimes against humanity during the post-election violence was pending.

Police and security forces

No individual police officers or security personnel were brought to justice for unlawful killings and other violations committed in the recent past.

In February, the UN Special Rapporteur on extrajudicial, summary or arbitrary executions conducted a fact-finding mission to Kenya. His report issued in May confirmed systematic and widespread human rights violations by the police and other security personnel. It documented unlawful killings, torture and other human rights violations by the police during the post-election violence in 2007/8, in security operations against alleged members of the outlawed Mungiki vigilante group, and during a 2007 security operation in Mount Elgon in western Kenya.

In November, a government-formed task force recommended comprehensive police reform measures, including the establishment of an independent police oversight body mandated to investigate and act on complaints against the police. However, it was unclear by when and how the recommendations would be implemented.

Human rights defenders

In early March, Oscar Kingara and Paul Oulu were killed by unknown armed assailants in Nairobi. Both men worked for the Oscar Foundation, a legal aid and human rights advocacy organization, and had

provided the visiting UN Rapporteur with information about alleged police killings. No progress with investigations into the two killings was reported.

Several human rights activists, including officials of NGOs working in Nairobi and local activists based in Mount Elgon area of western Kenya, fled the country after being threatened and harassed by police and other security personnel.

Internally displaced people

Most camps hosting the majority of thousands of families displaced during the post-election violence closed down. An estimated 200,000 internally displaced people (IDPs) returned to their homes. In September, the government ordered the resettlement of all IDPs who were in camps within two weeks and announced the provision of resettlement allowances. However, as of October thousands of IDPs remained displaced in transit camps and other areas. The UN estimated that 7,249 households were being hosted in 43 transit camps in the Rift Valley province. Many IDPs complained that they did not receive government assistance in their attempt to return home or resettle. Others said that government assistance was often inadequate. Hundreds of IDP families complained that they were being forced to leave camps to return home despite fears about their security.

Violence against women and girls

Women and girls continued to face widespread gender-based violence and limited access to justice. In March, a study by the International Federation of Women Lawyers in Kenya documented that women and girls with disabilities were three times more likely to be subjected to gender-based violence than those without disabilities, and that the violence was unlikely to be reported.

Truth, Justice and Reconciliation Commission

In July, the government appointed commissioners to the Truth, Justice and Reconciliation Commission (TJRC), established following the post-election violence, and the President approved amendments to the 2008 TJRC Act through the Statute Law (Miscellaneous Amendment) Act, 2009. The 2009 law amended section 34 of the TJRC Act to stipulate that no amnesty may be recommended by the TJRC in respect of genocide, crimes against humanity and gross human rights violations. However, concerns remained about the failure of the TJRC law to provide for effective protection for victims and witnesses and for adequate reparations for victims.

Refugees and asylum-seekers

Increasingly, the authorities forcibly returned asylum-seekers to Somalia. The government did not formally reverse its January 2007 decision to close the Kenya/Somalia border, although more than 50,000 Somali refugees and asylum-seekers managed to cross into Kenya during 2009.

The humanitarian conditions in the Dadaab refugee camp hosting most Somali refugees continued to deteriorate; the camp's population was three times more than its intended capacity.

Freedom of expression

Despite concerns that the Kenya Information and Communications (Amendment) Bill would lead to unjustified restrictions on freedom of expression, the Bill became law in January. In July another new media-related law repealed provisions in the January law that granted the government power to control media broadcast content. It also provided for an independent statutory body with the power to regulate the media.

Several journalists were intimidated and threatened by state officials over stories critical of government practice.

■ In January, Francis Kainda Nyaruri, a freelance journalist based in south-western Kenya, was killed by unidentified assailants. The local press reported that his killing was thought to be linked to articles he had written about alleged corruption and other malpractices by the local police. Two suspects were reportedly arrested but no prosecution followed. Witnesses to the killing were threatened, reportedly by police.

Right to adequate housing

In September, Parliament adopted the report of the Task Force on the Mau Forest Complex, appointed by the government in 2008. The report recommends, among other things, the eviction of thousands of families who live in the forest complex. Subsequently, the government formed a unit to co-ordinate the rehabilitation of the forest, but had not issued a comprehensive plan on the recommended evictions that would avoid forced evictions as witnessed in the removal of thousands of people from parts of the forest between 2004 and 2006. The first phase of planned forest evictions in the Mau forest scheduled by the government for the coming years was carried out in November. It involved the eviction of 2,850 households comprising some 20,345 people, according to the authorities. Most evictees said they were denied adequate notice and had no alternative housing. Most ended up in temporary and makeshift displacement camps without proper access to emergency shelter and other services.

In July, almost 3,000 people were forcibly evicted from their homes in Githogoro Village, Nairobi. Police told residents that they had 72 hours to dismantle their homes before government bulldozers would move in. The evictions were ostensibly carried out as part of government plans to build a new road, the Northern Bypass.

At the end of the year, hundreds of families living in informal settlements close to the Nairobi River were still living under the immediate threat of forced eviction following a 2008 government announcement calling on residents to leave. There were no plans to ensure that any evictions would respect appropriate legal protections and other safeguards.

The government failed to fulfil its 2006 pledge to release national guidelines on evictions. It also failed to stop forced evictions until the guidelines were in place.

Some 2 million people – half of Nairobi's population – continued to live in slums and informal settlements, crammed into 5 per cent of the city's residential area. Residents suffered not only squalid conditions and lack of basic services, but also discrimination, insecurity and marginalization. Despite a national housing policy adopted in 2005 that promised the progressive realization of the right to housing, the government continued to fail to provide accessible, affordable housing. An ongoing slum upgrading process remained slow and under-resourced. Slum residents complained of being inadequately consulted about the programme's implementation.

Death penalty

In August, the President commuted to life imprisonment the death sentences of more than 4,000 prisoners. He stated that an "extended stay on death row causes undue mental anguish and suffering, psychological trauma, anxiety, while it may as well constitute inhuman treatment". He ordered a government study on whether the death penalty had any impact on the fight against crime. It was unclear whether this study was undertaken and no findings were published.

Courts continued to impose the death penalty; no executions were reported.

Amnesty International visits/reports

🚍 Amnesty International delegates visited Kenya in February, March, June, September and November. In June, Amnesty International's Secretary General led an Amnesty International high-level mission to Kenya.

📄 Kenyan authorities cannot wait for the International Criminal Court to end impunity for crimes (AFR 32/001/2009)

📄 Kenya: The unseen majority – Nairobi's two million slum-dwellers (AFR 32/005/2009)

📄 How the other half lives: Nairobi's slum-dwellers (AFR 32/006/2009)

📄 Kenya: Statement on the conclusion of the mission led by Amnesty International's Secretary General (AFR 32/007/2009)

📄 Kenya: Amnesty International calls for immediate investigation into execution-style killings of human rights activists, 6 March 2009

KOREA
(DEMOCRATIC PEOPLE'S REPUBLIC OF)

DEMOCRATIC PEOPLE'S REPUBLIC OF KOREA
Head of state:	KIM Jong-il
Head of government:	KIM Yong-il
Death penalty:	retentionist
Population:	23.9 million
Life expectancy:	67.1 years
Under 5-mortality (m/f):	63/63 per 1,000

The government continued to systematically violate the civil, political, economic, social and cultural rights of millions of North Koreans. Food shortages gripped much of the country and there were fears of increased food insecurity due to poor economic management and reduced international aid. Thousands crossed the border into China, mostly in a desperate search for food. The Chinese authorities arrested and forcibly repatriated thousands of North Koreans who faced detention, interrogation and torture. Some were subjected to enforced disappearance, which the government failed to acknowledge. Politically motivated and arbitrary detentions continued. Severe restrictions on freedom of expression and freedom of movement persisted. At least seven people were executed. Independent human rights monitors continued to be denied access.

Background

In April, North Korea expelled international nuclear inspectors. In May, North Korea announced that it had conducted a second nuclear test, after increasing tensions with the international community. In June, the UN Security Council unanimously voted to tighten sanctions targeting North Korea's nuclear and missile development programmes, and encouraged UN members to inspect cargo vessels and airplanes suspected of carrying weapons and other military material.

The second half of the year was characterized by reconciliatory measures towards the international community. In August, the authorities released two US journalists, Laura Ling and Euna Lee, following a visit by former US President Bill Clinton. The two journalists had been sentenced to 12 years' hard labour in June for illegally entering North Korean territory.

In August, a North Korean delegation attended the funeral of former South Korean President Kim Dae-jung. The authorities released four South Korean fishermen who had been detained for illegally entering its waters. In September, North Korea resumed meetings to reunite families separated during the Korean War – the first to take place for nearly two years. In October, North Korea indicated that it was willing to resume bilateral and multilateral talks on its nuclear programmes.

On 30 November, the government implemented a currency reform, exchanging old for new at a rate of 100:1. The maximum amount of money that could be converted was 300,000 won per person (approximately 150 euros). The authorities were reportedly forced to increase the exchange rate slightly following protests in North Korea's capital, Pyongyang.

Food crisis

Nearly 9 million people, more than one third of the population, suffered severe food shortages. However, international aid fell drastically following the May nuclear test and donor fatigue. Consequently, the World Food Program scaled back its emergency operation to reach only 2.4 million out of an originally planned 6 million people. The UN Secretary-General Ban Ki-moon stated that North Korea's humanitarian problems – including food shortages, a crumbling health system and lack of access to safe drinking water – seriously hampered fulfilment of the population's human rights.

Arbitrary detention, torture and other ill-treatment

Thousands of North Koreans who crossed into China mostly in search of food were apprehended by Chinese authorities and forcibly returned to North Korea. Upon return, North Korean security officials held them in detention facilities near the border for several days during which they were subjected to torture and other ill-treatment. Most were sentenced to periods not exceeding three years in labour training camps where they were subjected to forced labour for ten to twelve hours a day with no rest days. There were reports of several deaths in these detention facilities as a consequence of hard labour, inadequate food and insufficient access to medicines and medical treatment.

■ In August, following the visit of Hyundai Group chairperson Hyun Jeong-eun to North Korea, the authorities released South Korean national and Hyundai Asan employee, Yu Seong-jin. Yu had been arrested in March at the Kaesong Industrial Complex, where he was working. The North Korean government detained Yu for criticizing the government and for trying to persuade a woman to leave and go to South Korea.

Enforced disappearances

The authorities failed to acknowledge the use of enforced disappearances. Since the 1950s, the authorities have subjected North Koreans and nationals of other countries such as South Korea and Japan to enforced disappearances. North Korean family members of suspected dissidents disappeared under the principle of "guilt by association", a form of collective punishment for those associated with someone deemed hostile to the regime. Thousands of North Koreans forcibly returned from China during the year were unaccounted for.

Death penalty

The government continued to execute people by hanging or firing squad. Public executions appeared to be carried out for crimes such as murder, human trafficking, smuggling, circulating "harmful" information, disseminating religious material and espionage. According to foreign media reports, at least seven people were executed.

■ In June, Ri Hyun-ok, 33 years old, was publicly executed in the north-western city of Ryongchon (near the border with China) on charges of distributing Bibles and espionage. Ri Hyun-ok's parents, husband and three children were sent to a political prison camp in the north-eastern city of Hoeryong.

Freedom of expression and association

The government continued to impose severe restrictions on the media and to punish any form of association and expression that it deemed hostile, including religious practice. There were no known independent opposition political parties or NGOs. Local authorities continued to arrest individuals who owned unauthorized Chinese mobile phones, or sold South Korean videos.

Constitutional developments

An amended Constitution came into effect in April, making the chairman of the National Defence Commission, Kim Jong-il, North Korea's "supreme leader". Article 8 of the amended Constitution stipulated that the state should "respect and protect human rights".

International scrutiny

North Korea's human rights record was assessed under the UN Universal Periodic Review in December. The government continued to deny access to independent human rights monitors including the UN Special Rapporteur on the Human Rights Situation in the Democratic People's Republic of Korea.

K

KOREA
(REPUBLIC OF)

REPUBLIC OF KOREA
Head of state: Lee Myung-bak
Head of government: Chung Un-chan (replaced Han Seung-
                                           soo in September)
Death penalty: abolitionist in practice
Population: 48.3 million
Life expectancy: 79.2 years
Under 5-mortality (m/f):   6/6 per 1,000

Discrimination against migrant workers was widespread and many suffered extremely poor working conditions. Police arrested journalists and protesters who were exercising their right to freedom of expression. Impunity for law enforcement officials using unnecessary or excessive force during protests, evictions and immigration raids continued.

Migrants' rights

The government-run Employment Permit System (EPS) provided employers with excessive powers over migrants, which increased their vulnerability to unfair dismissal, sexual harassment and forced overtime. Industrial accidents, including fatalities, were disproportionately higher among migrant workers than national workers. Immigration officers were often not in uniform when arresting irregular migrants and failed to present a detention order or to inform detainees of their rights. Several women recruited as singers under the E-6 entertainment scheme (visas for artistic performers) were trafficked for sexual exploitation in US military camp towns. Applicants for EPS, entertainment and foreign language instruction schemes, were required to disclose their HIV status. Foreigners who tested positive were subjected to deportation.

In November, the UN Committee on Economic, Social and Cultural Rights (CESCR) recommended strengthening the monitoring of E-6 visas; mandatory training of law enforcement officials, prosecutors and judges on anti-trafficking legislation; and ensuring an effective complaint mechanism for migrant workers regardless of their immigration status. The CESCR also stated that in the current economic climate it was unreasonable for the EPS to stipulate that migrant workers must find employment within three months of leaving a job or lose their legal status. It further recommended that the state uphold the Seoul High Court's decision to grant legal status to the Migrants' Trade Union.

■ In April, a video clip captured two immigration officers in Daejeon hauling a Chinese woman to a van by the back of her jeans and shirt. One of the officers punched her in the neck without any apparent provocation.

Racism

In November, in the first conviction involving racist remarks, Incheon District Court fined Park one million won (US$865) for slander against an Indian research professor, Bonojit Hussain. Park was convicted of "personal insult" because no racial discrimination law exists.

Police and security forces

■ In January, approximately 40 evicted tenants with incendiary material barricaded themselves on a rooftop in Seoul's Yongsan district to protest against the lack of compensation following their eviction. After 25 hours without negotiations, two squads of anti-terrorist commandos supported by 1,600 riot police raided the building, which ended in the deaths of five protesters and one police officer.

The authorities prosecuted 1,258 civilians for illegal protest during demonstrations in 2008 against US beef imports. No police were prosecuted for using unnecessary or excessive force during the protests despite evidence that some officials had done so.

In September, the Constitutional Court ruled that article 10 of the Assembly and Demonstration Law, prohibiting demonstrations after sunset and before sunrise, violated the spirit of the Constitution which guaranteed freedom of assembly and association.

Freedom of expression
Internet
■ In January, blogger Park Dae-sung or "Minerva" was arrested for violating the Framework Act on Telecommunications after he posted gloomy economic forecasts. He was accused of spreading malicious rumours to destabilize the economy. In April, Park Dae-sung was acquitted, but the prosecutor's office appealed.

K

Journalists

- In March 2009, four journalists and union activists from Yonhap Television Network (YTN), a 24-hour news channel, were arrested for "interfering with business". The journalists had been calling for guarantees of editorial independence after the appointment of Ku Bon-hong, formerly an aide to President Lee Myung-bak, as YTN president.
- In June, four producers and one writer at the Munhwa Broadcasting Corporation were indicted on charges of defaming the former Agriculture Minister and negotiator on US beef imports. Prosecutors accused them of distorting facts, deliberately mistranslating and exaggerating the dangers of US beef in their television programme, *PD Notebook*, aired in April 2008. The government blamed the programme for sparking the 2008 candlelight protests against US beef imports.

Conscientious objectors

At least 696 conscientious objectors, mostly Jehovah's Witnesses, were in prison for refusing to serve in the military. The average sentence was one and a half years.

Arbitrary arrests and detentions

Eighteen individuals were arrested for offences under vague provisions of the National Security Law (NSL).

Thirty-four people charged under the NSL were prosecuted, resulting in 14 convictions. The trials of the remaining 20 were pending at the end of the year.

Death penalty

In June, the Constitutional Court heard the case of Oh, a death row inmate, who claimed that the death penalty violated human dignity and values under the Constitution. No executions took place. Fifty-seven people remained on death row.

Institutional developments

The CESCR expressed deep concern about the independence of the National Human Rights Commission of Korea (NHRCK) and its 21 per cent downsize. It recommended allocating adequate human and financial resources, and allowing individuals to file complaints of violations of economic, social and cultural rights directly to the NHRCK.

Refugees and asylum-seekers

Three hundred and twenty-four individuals applied for asylum and 321 applications were pending with the Justice Ministry. A total of 994 applications were rejected, and only 74 individuals were granted refugee status. The CESCR remained concerned that state recognition of asylum-seekers was extremely low. In June, certain asylum-seekers were given the right to work, but delays in implementation left many with no source of livelihood.

KUWAIT

STATE OF KUWAIT

Head of state:	al-Shaikh Sabah al-Ahmad al-Jaber al-Sabah
Head of government:	al-Shaikh Nasser Mohammad al-Ahmad al-Sabah
Death penalty:	retentionist
Population:	3 million
Life expectancy:	77.5 years
Under-5 mortality (m/f):	11/9 per 1,000
Adult literacy:	94.5 per cent

Migrant workers faced exploitation and abuse despite legal reforms. Critics of the government and ruling family were harassed. Thousands of Bidun remained stateless and so were unable to access their full range of rights. At least three people were sentenced to death; no executions were reported.

Background

National elections were held in May after the government resigned in March. Sixteen women stood as candidates for the 50-seat National Assembly (*Majlis al-Umma*), four of whom became the first women ever to win seats. Formal political parties remained banned.

Freedom of expression

Critics of the government and the ruling family were harassed.

- Muhamad Abdulqader al-Jasem, a journalist and well-known critic of the Prime Minister, was arrested in November and detained by the Interior Ministry's Criminal Investigation Department for 12 days and then released on bail for remarks he made at a private meeting.

Counter-terror and security

In August, the authorities said they had arrested six men suspected of belonging to an al-Qa'ida cell that was planning to attack a US base in Kuwait and a government building linked to the security services. In December, following acknowledgement by the court that the accused had been ill-treated, charges against the men were deemed unsafe and prosecutors ordered an investigation into the allegations of ill-treatment. A further hearing was scheduled for January 2010.

In October and December respectively, Khaled al-Mutairi and Fouad al-Rabia were released from US detention at Guantánamo Bay and returned to Kuwait. Neither was reported to have been detained on return, although the government established a "rehabilitation" centre, apparently to be used for Guantánamo detainees and others, near the Central Prison in Sulaybiya. Two other Kuwaitis, Fawzi al-Odah and Faiz al-Kandari, continued to be held at Guantánamo.

Women's rights

In October, the Constitutional Court ruled that the 1962 law requiring a husband's permission for a woman to obtain a passport contravened constitutional provisions guaranteeing personal freedom and gender equality.

Migrants' rights

In December, parliament agreed to amend a 1964 labour law in order to introduce a minimum wage for some jobs, increase annual leave, prohibit arbitrary dismissal, and prescribe penalties for people who trade visas or recruit workers but fail to provide employment. The new law, if approved by the Amir, would also establish an official not-for-profit body to oversee employment arrangements and conditions for migrant workers. However, it appeared that the new law would not apply to domestic workers, mostly women, who are particularly vulnerable to exploitation and abuse.

■ In March, a Filipina domestic worker was reported to have been hospitalized after she was raped and repeatedly assaulted; the police rejected her employers' allegation that she had attempted suicide.

Death penalty

At least three people were sentenced to death for murder; no executions were reported.

■ May Membriri Vecina, a Filipina domestic worker, returned to the Philippines in June following a pardon by the Amir. She had been sentenced to death in July 2007 after being convicted of murdering her employer's youngest child. At her trial, she alleged that her employer had physically and mentally abused her, causing her to become mentally ill. Her sentence had been commuted to life imprisonment in June 2008.

KYRGYZSTAN

KYRGYZ REPUBLIC

Head of state:	Kurmanbek Bakiev
Head of government:	Daniar Usenov (replaced Igor Chudinov in October)
Death penalty:	abolitionist for all crimes
Population:	5.5 million
Life expectancy:	67.6 years
Under-5 mortality (m/f):	49/42 per 1,000
Adult literacy:	99.3 per cent

There were further restrictions on freedom of expression. Three human rights defenders were deported. Security forces used torture and other ill-treatment in the fight against terrorism.

Counter-terror and security

In September, the Head of the National Security Service (NSS) openly advocated public executions, compulsory re-education and separate prison facilities for members of banned Islamic groups and Islamist parties, such as Hizb-ut-Tahrir. June and October saw clashes between security forces and armed groups allegedly affiliated to the banned Islamic Movement of Uzbekistan and trying to infiltrate the south of the country.

■ In May, the Supreme Court turned down the appeals of all 32 individuals sentenced in November 2008 to prison terms of between nine and 20 years for calling for the overthrow of the constitutional order. The sentences of a 17-year-old boy and two women were reduced. The group had been accused of membership of Hizb-ut-Tahrir and of participating in violent protests in the town of Nookat after the authorities cancelled celebrations at the end of Ramadan in October 2008. The Supreme Court did not order an investigation into allegations that the defendants had been tortured. According to reports, the women had their heads shaved and were forced to stand in freezing water, and the men had their beards set on fire, were stripped naked, tied to metal beds and beaten on the soles of their feet. Families reported that they were threatened by security officers to stop them lodging complaints about the torture allegations.

Human rights defenders

■ In February, Vitaly Ponomarev, director of the Central Asia department of the Russian NGO Memorial, was deported to Russia shortly after his arrival in Kyrgyzstan to present a report on unfair trial and torture allegations linked to the Nookat protests (see above). He was banned from re-entering the country for five years.

■ In November, Bakhrom Khamroev, a Russian human rights defender of Uzbek origin, was arbitrarily detained by NSS officers while he was conducting research for Memorial on developments relating to the Nookat protests. He was detained incommunicado for over 18 hours and interrogated about his research and his alleged links to banned Islamist groups. Following international pressure he was released and deported to Russia.

■ In December, Nigina Bakhrieva, a Tajikistani human rights defender, was banned from entering Kyrgyzstan for 10 years, reportedly for highlighting violations in relation to the Nookat protests during an international human rights training seminar in Bishkek in September.

Freedom of expression

There was an increase in violent and sometimes fatal attacks, some by masked men, on independent journalists, including stabbings, beatings and shootings.

The authorities condemned these attacks and ordered investigations, but denied any link to articles or investigations by the journalists into corruption and organized crime, among other issues.

■ In August, a former police officer confessed to the October 2007 murder of ethnic Uzbek journalist and editor Alisher Saipov, but reportedly later withdrew his confession in court, claiming that he had been tortured. The Court of First Instance decided to send the case for investigation but in December the Supreme Court overruled this decision.

LAOS

LAO PEOPLE'S DEMOCRATIC REPUBLIC
Head of state:	Choummaly Sayasone
Head of government:	Bouasone Bouphavanh
Death penalty:	abolitionist in practice
Population:	6.3 million
Life expectancy:	64.6 years
Under 5-mortality (m/f):	68/61 per 1,000
Adult literacy:	72.7 per cent

Around 4,500 Hmong asylum-seekers were returned against their will from Thailand to Laos. Lao authorities continued to severely restrict freedom of expression, assembly and association, with no independent media permitted. Lack of access by independent human rights monitors hampered assessments of the human rights situation. Natural resource management and land redevelopment led to evictions and a government official said land disputes had emerged as the country's most pressing problem.

Background

On 25 September Laos ratified the International Covenant on Civil and Political Rights; the UN Convention on the Rights of Persons with Disabilities; and the UN Convention against Corruption. A government decree on registering domestic associations took effect in November, allowing the formation of a civil society for the first time.

Chronic malnutrition remained high, with half of rural children under five years chronically malnourished, and an even higher number in isolated areas and among non-Lao-Thai ethnic groups.

L

Refugees and asylum-seekers

In December, Thai and Lao authorities co-ordinated the forcible return of around 4,500 Lao Hmong people from Thailand. An unknown number had gone to Thailand to seek asylum, but were not given the opportunity to register their claims with UNHCR, the UN refugee agency, and were forcibly returned. A few hundred returnees were resettled at designated sites, including Phalak village in Kasi district, but the whereabouts and wellbeing of the majority were not known. No independent observers were allowed unfettered access to the returnees, and resources to cope with the large influx were inadequate.

Freedom of expression

The government strictly controlled public debate, including in the media and on the internet.

■ After 10 years in prison, three surviving pro-democracy activists from the so-called October Protests continued to be held in Samkhe prison despite being due for release on 25 October. Authorities said the men had received a 20-year sentence.

■ On 2 November, security forces rounded up over 300 farmers and others who had planned to protest over loss of land and lack of economic and social support. All but nine of those arrested were released. The fate and whereabouts of the nine were unknown.

Death penalty

A de facto moratorium on executions remained in place and no executions were reported. However, secrecy remained tight around its application.

■ A British woman arrested in 2008 for suspected drug trafficking had faced a mandatory death sentence. Following an unfair trial, a court in Vientiane sentenced her to life imprisonment after it was revealed that she was pregnant, as stipulated in domestic law. She was subsequently transferred to the UK to serve the sentence.

Prison conditions

Despite widespread secrecy, reports emerged about continued harsh conditions in Lao prisons and police detention centres. There was a shortage of food and clean water. Guards beat prisoners as punishment, and wooden shackles were used on some prisoners.

Freedom of religion

According to reports from Savannakheth and Saravan provinces, local officials tried to force Christians to recant their faith. Interrogation, death threats and harassment were among the methods reported, and it appeared that recent converts to Christianity were particularly targeted.

Amnesty International reports

📄 Laos: Submission to the UN Universal Periodic Review (ASA 26/003/2009)

📄 Laos: Peaceful protesters must be released immediately (ASA 26/004/2009)

LATVIA

REPUBLIC OF LATVIA

Head of state:	Valdis Zatlers
Head of government:	Valdis Dombrovskis (replaced Ivars Godmanis in March)
Death penalty:	abolitionist for ordinary crimes
Population:	2.2 million
Life expectancy:	72.3 years
Under-5 mortality (m/f):	12/10 per 1,000
Adult literacy:	99.8 per cent

Lesbian, gay, bisexual and transgender people were exposed to harassment by state officials. There were reports of ill-treatment in prisons.

Background

The global financial crisis had a particularly marked impact on Latvia. Severe cuts in public expenditure reduced funding to the police force, to maintaining the national minimum wage and to exempting minimum incomes from tax. Public sector wages were cut by more than 20 per cent.

Rights of lesbian, gay, bisexual and transgender people

On 8 May the Commission on Meetings, Marches and Demonstrations of the Riga City Council authorized a Baltic Lesbian, Gay, Bisexual and Transgender Pride march organized by NGOs from Latvia, Estonia and Lithuania. On 13 May, however, 34 of the 60 city councillors called for the decision to be revoked, saying the march was offensive to public decency and posed a threat to public security. On 14 May the

Council withdrew permission for the march, but the following day the Riga Municipal Court overturned the ban. The march went ahead on 16 May, with protection provided by the police. Counter-demonstrators hurled homophobic verbal abuse.

Torture and other ill-treatment

In December, the European Committee for the Prevention of Torture, reporting on a visit in December 2007, expressed concern at allegations of physical ill-treatment by prison officers at Jēkabpils, Daugavpils and Jelgava prisons, and at Cēsis Correctional Centre. The Committee criticized the authorities for not fully investigating such allegations in an impartial and independent process. The Committee further reported high levels of violence between prisoners, which the authorities failed to prevent or limit. This resulted in self-harmings by inmates seeking transfer to safer prison units.

LEBANON

LEBANESE REPUBLIC

Head of state:	Michel Suleiman
Head of government:	Saad Hariri (replaced Fouad Siniora in November)
Death penalty:	retentionist
Population:	4.2 million
Life expectancy:	71.9 years
Under-5 mortality (m/f):	31/21 per 1,000
Adult literacy:	89.6 per cent

The Special Tribunal for Lebanon, established to try those responsible for killing former Prime Minister Rafic Hariri in 2005 and related attacks, opened in March, and ordered the release of four generals arbitrarily detained in connection with its investigations. Palestinian refugees continued to face discrimination, which impeded their access to work, health, education and adequate housing. Other refugees were liable to arrest and deportation. Small advances were made in establishing what happened to some of the thousands of people who were victims of enforced disappearance during the 1975-1990 civil war. Some progress was also made to improve the conditions of migrant domestic workers, although they continued to suffer widespread exploitation and abuse. At least 41 people were under sentence of death at the end of the year.

Background

Political tension remained high following June elections until the formation in November of a national unity government. Headed by Saad Hariri, son of assassinated former Prime Minister Rafic Hariri, the new government was formed after five months of negotiations between Saad Hariri's March 14 alliance and the March 8 coalition comprising Hizbullah and other parties.

Several civilians were reported to have been killed and others injured in localized outbreaks of political violence, mostly clashes between the Alawite and Sunni Muslim communities in Tripoli, and in Aisha Bakkar and Ain al-Rummaneh in Beirut.

Relations between Lebanon and Syria continued to improve, with both countries appointing ambassadors.

There was continuing tension with Israel. Several rockets were fired from southern Lebanon into Israel in January, September and October, and Israeli forces returned fire. The Israeli air force continued to violate Lebanese airspace.

Three civilians were killed and 25 injured, including children, by cluster bomb remnants and land mines left behind by Israeli forces in previous years, according to the official Lebanon Mine Action Center. In May, the Israeli authorities handed to the UN Interim Force in Lebanon data and maps showing where their forces had used cluster munitions during the 2006 war.

■ In March, Mohammed Abd al-'Aal, aged 10, lost his left leg and right hand when a cluster bomb exploded as he played near his home at Hilta in south Lebanon.

Palestinian and other refugees

Most Palestinian refugees continued living in overcrowded and often squalid conditions in 12 official refugee camps. Nearly 422,000 registered Palestinian refugees faced discriminatory laws and regulations, denying them the right to inherit property, work in around 20 professions and other basic rights.

At least 3,000 Palestinian refugees had no official ID cards – which are required for proving their residence in Lebanon, for registering births, marriages

L

and deaths, and for other essential purposes –
because they arrived in Lebanon after the Palestine
Liberation Organization was expelled from Jordan in
1971. In 2008, the authorities had issued official
temporary ID cards valid for one year to some 800
Palestinians as a step towards legalizing their status
and to enable them to move freely about the country.
In 2009, however, the General Directorate of the
General Security prevented further ID cards from
being issued, leaving Palestinian refugees facing
severe obstacles to accessing their basic rights.

Around 21,650 Palestinian refugees who were
forced to flee from Nahr al-Bared refugee camp near
Tripoli in 2007 during a 15-week battle between the
Lebanese Army and fighters belonging to Fatah al-
Islam, an armed group, remained displaced because
of the devastation and delays in reconstruction. Some
4,450 who had lived in the area adjacent to the
official camp were able to return.

Lebanon also hosted refugees from Iraq, Somalia,
Sudan and other countries who were constantly at
risk of arrest, detention and deportation irrespective of
whether they had been formally registered as
refugees by UNHCR, the UN refugee agency. In
2008, the General Directorate of the General Security
had agreed informally to allow refugees a grace period
of three months, renewable once, to find an employer
to sponsor them and provide them with a residence
permit and so regularize their status. This policy was
not maintained in 2009.

Violence and discrimination against women

Women migrant domestic workers continued to face
exploitation and physical, sexual and psychological
abuse in their workplace.

In January, the Labour Ministry introduced a
standard employment contract for migrant domestic
workers, the vast majority of whom are women. The
contract includes a job description and sets out the
rights and responsibilities of the employer and
employee, and the maximum number of working
hours. However, no monitoring process was
established to ensure employer compliance and the
change appeared insufficient to afford migrant
domestic workers effective protection.

The nationality law does not allow Lebanese women
to pass on their nationality to their spouses or
children, even if they were born in Lebanon.

■ The public prosecution and a legal commission at
the Ministry of Justice contested, in July and
September respectively, a June decision by three
judges allowing Samira Soueidan to pass on her
nationality to three of her children. No hearings on the
case had been held by the end of the year. The
children's father, an Egyptian national, had died 15
years earlier.

Special Tribunal for Lebanon

The Special Tribunal for Lebanon opened on 1 March
near the Hague in the Netherlands. One of its first
acts was to ask the Lebanese authorities to hand over
the cases of four generals who had been detained
without charge in Lebanon since August 2005 in
connection with Rafic Hariri's assassination. The
Lebanese authorities complied, and the four generals
– Jamil al-Sayyed, Mustapha Hamdan, Ali al-Hajj and
Raymond Azar – were released without charge by
order of the Special Tribunal by 29 April. In 2008, the
UN Working Group on Arbitrary Detention had found
the generals' detention to be arbitrary and unjust.

Earlier, in February, the Lebanese authorities
released on bail three other detainees – Ahmad 'Abd
al-'Aal, Mahmoud 'Abd al-'Aal and Ibrahim Jarjoura –
who had been held for three years, apparently
because they were suspected of making false
statements to the UN body investigating Rafic Hariri's
assassination and related attacks.

Arbitrary detentions

■ Yusef Cha'ban, a Palestinian refugee imprisoned for
15 years for murdering a Jordanian diplomat, was
released on 13 July after President Michel Suleiman
granted him a special pardon in recognition of the gross
miscarriage of justice in his case. He had remained in
prison even after a Jordanian court concluded in 2002
that others were responsible for the murder. Yusef
Cha'ban had been sentenced in Lebanon by the
Justice Council, a court whose judgments cannot be
appealed or revoked. In 2006, the UN Working Group
on Arbitrary Detention found that Yusef Cha'ban was
arbitrarily detained.

Enforced disappearances and abductions

Thousands of cases of enforced disappearance and
abduction carried out during the civil war remained
unresolved. In October and November, however, a
court issued preliminary decisions ordering the

L

authorities to provide it with confidential findings of investigations conducted by the Official Commission of Investigation into the Fate of the Abducted and Disappeared Persons in 2000 and relating to two mass graves in Beirut. By the end of the year, the authorities had provided only a short medical report about one mass grave.

■ In November, DNA tests concluded that human remains found in the eastern town of Aita al-Foukhar included those of Alec Collett, a British journalist who was abducted, apparently by a Palestinian armed group, in 1985 and subsequently killed.

Alleged collaborators

Dozens of men and women suspected of spying for Israel were arrested by the authorities or handed over to them after being taken captive and interrogated by Hizbullah. At least two other men arrested in 2006 were tried for collaborating with Israel.

■ In August, Mahmoud Rafeh, a retired Internal Security Forces official, went on trial before a military tribunal in Beirut. He alleged that he was tortured in pre-trial detention and forced to "confess" by Military Intelligence officials. His trial was continuing at the end of the year.

■ Joseph Sader, an employee of Middle East Airlines, was abducted in February and remained held incommunicado by a non-state group who suspected him of providing information to Israel.

Death penalty

At least 40 men and one woman were under sentence of death at the end of the year. The last executions were carried out in 2004.

A draft law to abolish the death penalty proposed by Justice Minister Ibrahim Najjar and submitted to the Council of Ministers in 2008 had not been approved by the end of 2009. The Minister pressed for the repeal of Penal Code articles that allow courts to impose death sentences.

Amnesty International reports

The Special Tribunal for Lebanon: Selective justice? (MDE 18/001/2009)

Lebanon: A human rights agenda for the elections (MDE 18/003/2009)

LIBERIA

REPUBLIC OF LIBERIA

Head of state and government:	Ellen Johnson-Sirleaf
Death penalty:	abolitionist in practice
Population:	4 million
Life expectancy:	57.9 years
Under-5 mortality (m/f):	144/136 per 1,000
Adult literacy:	55.5 per cent

The final report of the Truth and Reconciliation Commission (TRC) was released in December. Some progress was made in establishing the Independent National Human Rights Commission. Although the government made some institutional progress to address rape and other forms of sexual violence against women and girls, many cases went unreported. Serious concerns remained regarding the administration of justice, with significant judicial delays leading to overcrowding in prisons.

Background

President Ellen Johnson-Sirleaf made significant cabinet changes in April, June and July to address poor performance in key sectors, particularly the justice and security sectors.

The acquittal in April of five senior government officials – Charles Gyude Bryant, former Chairman of the National Transitional Government of Liberia (NTGL); Edwin Snowe, former Speaker of the House; and three other NTGL members – was considered a major setback in the fight against corruption. The Liberian Anti-Corruption Commission, established early in the year, started investigations on two major cases. Several government ministers were dismissed for alleged corruption.

President Johnson-Sirleaf officially closed the disarmament, demobilization, rehabilitation and reintegration programme in July, which had disarmed and demobilized 101,000 former combatants and provided reintegration for 90,000 former combatants since 2003.

There were three separate incidents of violence that involved the Armed Forces of Liberia (AFL) soldiers and Liberia National Police officers in Monrovia in February, April and May.

Mob justice prevailed on several occasions because of the public's lack of confidence in the

L

administration of justice. In June, for example, in the south-eastern city of Harper, an allegation of a ritual killing sparked a riot involving more than 2,000 people who ransacked the police station, damaged the prison and tried to kill police officers by dousing them with petrol.

A joint field mission drawn from UN peacekeeping operations in Liberia and Côte d'Ivoire visited western Côte d'Ivoire in April. It found that many of the estimated 1,500 to 2,000 Liberian combatants associated with Ivorian militias were involved in illegal exploitation of natural resources.

In September, the mandate of the UN Mission in Liberia (UNMIL) was extended for a further year, with a reduction in military and civilian personnel to approximately 8,500.

In December, the UN Security Council lifted the arms embargo on Liberia that had been in place since 1999. It also extended the travel ban and asset freeze imposed on people considered a threat to the peace process. The mandate of the Panel of Experts that monitors UN sanctions on Liberia was extended to December 2010.

No steps were taken to abolish the death penalty after its reintroduction in 2008 in violation of the Second Optional Protocol of the International Covenant on Civil and Political Rights, to which Liberia acceded in 2005.

Impunity

Little progress was made in bringing to justice people responsible for gross human rights violations during the conflict in Liberia between 1989-1996 and 1999-2003.

In January, Benjamin Yeaten, a former general of the National Patriotic Front of Liberia (NPFL) and a close associate of former President Charles Taylor, was indicted for the murders of two Deputy Ministers and a former Minister and members of his family in November 1997 and June 2003. Benjamin Yeaten was alleged to be living in Togo.

In June, the TRC concluded its work and submitted an unedited version of its report to the legislature and the President. The final report was made public in December. The TRC recommended the establishment of an extraordinary criminal tribunal to prosecute people identified as having committed crimes under international law as well as economic crimes. A total of 98 individuals were identified as the "most notorious perpetrators", including Charles Taylor and seven other leaders of various armed groups. Thirty-six were identified as responsible for crimes under international law but not recommended for prosecution because they spoke truthfully and expressed remorse. President Johnson-Sirleaf was included in the list of supporters of armed groups, and the TRC recommended that she be banned from running for public office for 30 years. In July, President Johnson-Sirleaf committed to work with all key stakeholders to implement the TRC's recommendations, but no progress had been made by the end of the year.

Independent National Human Rights Commission

After substantial delays, progress was made towards constituting the Independent National Human Rights Commission. In August, President Johnson-Sirleaf nominated seven members, including the Chairman. The Senate had not confirmed the nominations by the end of the year.

Violence against women and girls

Rape and other forms of sexual violence against women and girls remained widespread. The vast majority of reported cases of rape involved girls under the age of 16. Of the 807 reported cases of rape in Montserrado County in the first six months of 2009, 77 involved girls under the age of five; 232 involved girls aged between five and 12; and 284 involved girls and young women aged between 13 and 18. It remained difficult to estimate the total number of rapes, especially of women, because of stigmatization and rejection by the families and communities of the survivors. According to international organizations working in Liberia on sexual and gender-based violence issues, the large majority of rapes were committed by a man known to the victim/survivor – either a close relative or neighbour.

■ A 12-year-old girl from Bong County was reportedly raped by four men, including her stepfather. The girl was thrown out of her home after the rape and labelled as "mad" and "possessed by the devil".

■ In February, after waiting eight months for a case of multiple rape of a 14-year-old girl to go to circuit court in Margibi County, a closed-door session between the judge, the defence, the girl and the prosecutor effectively resulted in the case being dropped. It was alleged that the girl was coerced into dropping the case. The accused was released.

The government created a special court to deal with gender-based violent crimes. By November it had conducted four trials, three of which resulted in convictions.

Traditional harmful practices continued, including female genital mutilation (FGM) and trial by ordeal, whereby the guilt or innocence of the accused is determined in an arbitrary manner and in some cases in Liberia has resulted in the death of the accused.

Justice system

Serious challenges remained regarding the police, judiciary and prison sector. The judiciary lacked the capacity to hear cases in a timely manner, contributing to a backlog in the criminal justice system. Local experts estimated that the chronic delays meant that 92 per cent of prisoners were pre-trial detainees.

Prisons also remained ill-equipped, resulting in prisoner escapes throughout the year. In April, 50 inmates escaped from a maximum security prison in south-eastern Liberia. In November, an attempted escape of around 50 inmates in Monrovia was aborted by UNMIL troops.

Amnesty International visit/reports

🚌 Amnesty International delegates visited Liberia in March.

📓 Liberia: After the Truth – Liberians need justice (AFR 34/001/2009)

📓 Lessons from Liberia – Reintegrating women in post-conflict Liberia (AFR 34/002/2009)

LIBYA

SOCIALIST PEOPLE'S LIBYAN ARAB JAMAHIRIYA

Head of state:	Mu'ammar al-Gaddafi
Head of government:	al-Baghdadi Ali al-Mahmoudi
Death penalty:	retentionist
Population:	6.4 million
Life expectancy:	73.8 years
Under-5 mortality (m/f):	20/19 per 1,000
Adult literacy:	86.8 per cent

Freedom of expression, association and assembly continued to be severely curtailed and the authorities showed little tolerance of dissent. Critics of the government's human rights record were punished. Former detainees at Guantánamo Bay returned to Libya by US authorities continued to be detained; one died in custody, apparently as a result of suicide. Foreign nationals suspected of being in the country irregularly, including refugees and asylum-seekers, were detained and ill-treated. An official investigation began into the killing of prisoners at Abu Salim Prison in 1996 but no details were disclosed and some of the victims' relatives who had campaigned for the truth were arrested. Hundreds of cases of enforced disappearance and other serious human rights violations committed in the 1970s, 1980s and 1990s remained unresolved, and the Internal Security Agency (ISA), implicated in those violations, continued to operate with impunity.

Background

In February, Mu'ammar al-Gaddafi became Chairperson of the African Union and in September addressed the UN General Assembly (of which Libya held the presidency) for the first time. Also in September Libya marked 40 years under Mu'ammar al-Gaddafi's rule. Negotiations between the EU and Libya on a framework agreement continued.

On 20 August, Abdelbaset Ali Mohmed al-Megrahi, the Libyan convicted of the 1988 bombing of Pan Am Flight 103 over Scotland in the UK, was released by the Scottish authorities and returned to Libya after he was confirmed to have terminal cancer.

In October, the authorities agreed to a visit by the UN Working Group on Arbitrary Detention, but they neither specified a date nor did they invite the UN Special Rapporteur on torture, despite a pending request.

L

In November, Switzerland suspended the normalization of relations with Libya, following the Libyan authorities' incommunicado detention of two Swiss businessmen, Rachid Hamdani and Max Goeldi, from 18 September to 9 November. In November, the men were convicted of immigration offences and sentenced to 16-month prison terms and fines of LYD2,000 (approximately 1,000 euros). The men, who remained in the Swiss embassy at the end of the year, also faced commercial and tax charges.

Repression of dissent

The authorities released at least two prisoners of conscience but rearrested one of them and continued to detain others. Activities that amount to the peaceful exercise of freedom of expression and association remained criminalized in the Penal Code and Law 71 of 1972.

■ Jamal el-Haji and Faraj Saleh Hmeed, detained since February 2007 for attempting to organize a peaceful demonstration, were released on 10 March. Jamal el-Haji was arrested on 9 December and charged with insulting the judiciary after he complained about his treatment in detention.

■ Fathi el-Jahmi, a renowned critic of the political system detained as a prisoner of conscience almost continuously since March 2002, during which he had access to only sporadic and inadequate medical care, was flown from Libya to Jordan for urgent medical treatment on 5 May. He died on 21 May. No independent investigation was known to have been opened by the Libyan authorities into the circumstances leading to the deterioration of his health and the cause and circumstances of his death.

■ Abdelnasser al-Rabbasi, arrested in January 2003 and serving a 15-year prison sentence for "undermining the prestige of the Leader of the revolution" for writing an email critical of Mu'ammar al-Gaddafi to the *Arab Times* newspaper, remained in Abu Salim Prison.

■ 'Adnan el-'Urfi, a lawyer, was arrested on 9 June following his call to the radio programme *Good Evening Benghazi* in May, in which he recounted human rights violations endured by one of his clients and criticized Libya's judicial system. He was cleared of all charges by a court in Benghazi in September. The prosecution appealed; he remained at liberty pending the outcome of the appeal.

Counter-terror and security

The imprisoned leadership of the Libyan Islamic Fighting Group (LIFG) was reported to have renounced violence following continued negotiations with the Gaddafi International Charity and Development Foundation (GDF), headed by Saif al-Islam al-Gaddafi. In March, the GDF announced that 136 members had been released over the previous two years. Forty-five more members were released in October, along with 43 others alleged to be members of "jihadist" groups. The GDF published a list of those released in October, calling on the Secretary of the General People's Committee to assist their social reintegration.

■ In June, Muhammad Hassan Abou Sadra, a victim of arbitrary detention according to the UN Working Group on Arbitrary Detention, was released after more than 20 years.

■ Abu Sufian Ibrahim Ahmed Hamuda and Abdesalam Safrani, who were returned from detention at Guantánamo Bay by the US authorities in September 2007 and December 2006 respectively, continued to be detained at Abu Salim Prison. The Libyan authorities refused to disclose their legal status. Three other Libyan nationals held at Guantánamo Bay were cleared for release by US authorities in September but had not been returned to Libya by the end of the year.

■ Abdelaziz Al-Fakheri, also known as Ibn Al Sheikh Al Libi, was reported to have committed suicide in Abu Salim Prison on 9 May. He had been returned to Libya in late 2005 or early 2006 after detention by US forces as a terror suspect and had been continuously detained since his return. The authorities said they had opened an investigation and said later that he had committed suicide but provided no details.

■ Mahmoud Mohamed Aboushima, suspected of belonging to the LIFG, who was arrested in July 2005 shortly after returning from the UK, remained in Abu Salim Prison at the end of 2009 despite a High Court ruling of July 2007 confirming a lower court order that he be released.

Migrants, refugees and asylum-seekers

The authorities continued to detain suspected irregular migrants, some of whom were reported to have been ill-treated, and thousands of whom were subsequently deported. The authorities also failed to afford the protection required by international law to refugees and asylum-seekers. In May, the Italian authorities began to send irregular migrants intercepted at sea to Libya, where they were detained. UNHCR, the UN refugee agency, said that by September it had granted refugee status to 206 of the 890 people sent back from Italy to Libya whose cases it had examined. In November, UNHCR's Libyan partner organization announced plans to open health clinics in four detention centres.

■ On 10 August, security forces reportedly used excessive force, including live ammunition, knives and sticks, against up to 200 foreign nationals seeking to escape from the Ganfouda Detention Centre near Benghazi, reportedly causing deaths and serious injuries. Most of the escapees were recaptured and returned to Ganfouda. Some inmates were reported to have been assaulted by security officials following the escape attempt.

Impunity

Throughout 2009, relatives of the hundreds of prisoners believed to have been killed at Abu Salim Prison in 1996 held peaceful protests in Benghazi, Ajdebia and other cities to demand the truth, justice and reparation. The authorities informed some families that prisoners had been killed, and in some cases issued death certificates, but many families rejected the offer of financial compensation as it was conditional on their not seeking judicial redress. In September, the authorities appointed a judge to head an investigation into the incident, but neither his mandate nor other details of the investigation were disclosed. In October, the authorities announced plans to demolish Abu Salim Prison, prompting an outcry by some families of victims who feared the destruction of evidence.

The security forces, particularly the ISA, continued to operate with impunity, and detained and interrogated individuals suspected of dissent or terrorism-related activities, while holding them incommunicado and denying them access to lawyers.

■ On 26 March, three members of the Organizing Committee of Families of Victims of Abu Salim in Benghazi were arrested. Fouad Ben Oumran, Hassan El-Madani and Fathi Tourbil were at the forefront of the demonstrations by families of victims. They and two others arrested on 28 March were released days later without being formally charged.

On 28 October, the General People's Committee for Justice invited people to contact it if they had been

detained by "security bodies" without trial or after acquittal or completion of sentences to the Committee in the framework of "national reconciliation". The Secretary of the Committee reportedly said that victims would receive financial compensation for every month spent in prison, and that the "door remained open" for judicial redress. However, the authorities did not publicly apologize for the human rights violations committed, nor were perpetrators brought to justice.

Discrimination against women

Women continued to face discrimination in both law and practice. Some were prosecuted and convicted for *zina* (having sexual relations outside of wedlock); at least one woman was sentenced to flogging.

■ On 21 October, a group of women from a state-run care centre in Benghazi demonstrated against alleged sexual harassment by officials at the centre. Following the demonstration, officials reportedly put pressure on the women to retract their allegations. On 26 October, defamation charges were initiated against Mohamed Al-Sarit, the journalist who reported on the protest, apparently on the basis of complaints made by some of the women. Investigations were reported to have been initiated into the women's allegations of sexual harassment but no suspected perpetrators were tried.

Death penalty

The death penalty was retained for a large number of offences, including for the peaceful exercise of the right to freedom of expression and association. At least four men were reported to have been executed – one Nigerian and three Egyptian nationals – but the real number may have been higher as the authorities did not disclose details of executions. An amnesty marking the 40th anniversary of the Fateh Revolution in September commuted to life imprisonment all death sentences of those convicted in criminal cases before 1 September. Eight other people under sentence of death were pardoned and 11 had their sentences commuted to various prison terms.

Amnesty International visit/report

🚗 Amnesty International delegates were permitted to visit Libya for the first time in over five years in May.

📄 Libya: Amnesty International completes first fact-finding visit in over five years (MDE 19/003/2009)

L

LITHUANIA

REPUBLIC OF LITHUANIA

Head of state:	Dalia Grybauskaitė (replaced Valdas Adamkus in July)
Head of government:	Andrius Kubilius
Death penalty:	abolitionist for all crimes
Population:	3.3 million
Life expectancy:	71.8 years
Under-5 mortality (m/f):	14/9 per 1,000
Adult literacy:	99.7 per cent

A parliamentary investigation concluded that Lithuanian officials co-operated in the construction of a Central Intelligence Agency (CIA) secret prison in Lithuania during the US-led "war on terror". A new law banned materials from schools that might promote same-sex and other relationships. The UN Committee against Torture criticized the government for not incorporating the crime of torture into domestic law.

Counter-terror and security

The authorities came under international scrutiny in August and November following allegations that up to eight terrorist suspects were held and questioned in secret by the CIA in 2004 and 2005 in a detention facility in Antaviliai, near Vilnius. A subsequent investigation by the parliamentary Committee on National Security and Defence reported in December that state security officials had assisted in constructing a secret prison for terrorist suspects on Lithuanian territory. However, the Committee did not establish that suspects were actually imprisoned and interrogated there. It concluded that CIA aircraft had landed without border checks and that security officials had failed to notify the President or the Prime Minister, in violation of domestic law. Human rights groups called for the investigation to continue and to determine whether human rights violations were committed in relation to the secret prison.

Rights of lesbian, gay, bisexual and transgender people

In July parliament adopted the Law on the Protection of Minors against the Detrimental Effect of Public Information, despite a presidential veto in June. The law, to come into effect in March 2010, banned from schools, public places and the media any materials that "agitate for homosexual, bisexual and polygamous relations" and could be viewed by children. The law was widely criticized as institutionalizing homophobia and violating the rights to freedom of expression and freedom from discrimination. The EU suggested it might infringe the Treaty on European Union, which provides sanctions against member states that violate "EU common values". No final parliamentary vote on a proposal to remove its discriminatory provisions had taken place by the end of the year.

Prison conditions

The UN Committee against Torture expressed concern in January at reports of the prolonged pre-trial and administrative detention of minors and adults and the resulting high risk of ill-treatment. The Committee noted that detention conditions remained poor, with several cases of overcrowding, lack of hygiene and unsuitable infrastructures. It called for torture as defined by the UN Convention against Torture to be made a crime under domestic law.

Amnesty International reports

- Amnesty International condemns adoption of homophobic law in Lithuania (EUR 53/005/2009)
- Lithuania: Investigation of allegations of CIA secret prison must be effective and impartial (EUR 53/007/2009)
- Lithuania: Parliament moves to criminalize homosexuality – act now! (EUR 53/008/2009)

MACEDONIA

THE FORMER YUGOSLAV REPUBLIC OF MACEDONIA

Head of state:	Gjorge Ivanov (succeeded Branko Crvenovski in May)
Head of government:	Nikola Gruevski
Death penalty:	abolitionist for all crimes
Population:	2 million
Life expectancy:	74.1 years
Under-5 mortality (m/f):	17/16 per 1,000
Adult literacy:	97 per cent

Little progress was made in prosecuting war crimes arising from the 2001 internal conflict. Measures were taken to address impunity for ill-treatment by the police and prison conditions. Roma continued to suffer discrimination.

Background

Greece continued to dispute the name of the country. In January a hearing opened at the International Court of Justice in proceedings initiated by Macedonia in November 2008; both countries claimed that the other had violated a 1995 interim agreement, in which Macedonia had temporarily agreed to use the name the Former Yugoslav Republic of Macedonia. Greece had agreed not to block Macedonia's membership of international organizations but had blocked membership of NATO in 2008.

In October the European Commission (EC) recommended opening negotiations on accession, but in December EU Foreign Ministers postponed their decision at Greece's request.

NGOs expressed concerns at measures taken by the government to reinforce Macedonia's claims to a historic identity (including the building of monuments at public expense), and the increasing influence of the Macedonian Orthodox Church on the secular state. The Constitutional Court in April abolished Article 26 of the Law on Primary Education which had provided for the introduction of religious education.

Justice system – war crimes

Proceedings in the case of the "Mavrovo" road workers, returned to Macedonia for prosecution from the International Criminal Tribunal for the former Yugoslavia (Tribunal), were adjourned in May pending extradition from Germany of one of the accused. The Macedonian workers were allegedly abducted in August 2001 by the ethnic Albanian National Liberation Army, ill-treated, sexually violated and threatened with death before being released.

No progress was reported in three other cases returned by the Tribunal.

Impunity continued for the enforced disappearance in 2001 of three ethnic Albanians and the abduction of 13 ethnic Macedonians and one Bulgarian.

Torture and other ill-treatment

In February Macedonia ratified the Optional Protocol to the Convention against Torture; the Ombudsman's Office was appointed as the national preventive mechanism to give effect to the Protocol, and was empowered to co-operate with NGOs.

Both police and NGOs reported a decline in torture and other ill-treatment. This followed the disbanding of the special "Alfi" police units outside Skopje; improvements in investigations by the Ministry of Interior Sector for Internal Control and Professional Standards (SICPS); and the introduction of custody records at police stations. However, judges and prosecutors failed to initiate investigations into allegations of ill-treatment, even when detainees brought before the court showed signs of ill-treatment.

In March, following an investigation into the alleged beating of Jovica Janevski at Tetovo Police Station in 2008, the SICPS referred the case to the Tetovo Public Prosecutor, who had previously failed to open an investigation into the allegations.

The Ministry of Justice initiated a Strategic Plan to address "deplorable" prison conditions reported by the European Committee for the Prevention of Torture in 2008, including the urgent refurbishment of several prisons, facilities for prisoners, and the strengthening and training of prison staff.

In June, the European Court of Human Rights made a preliminary consideration of an application made by Jasmina Sulja, the partner of Sabri Asani, an ethnic Albanian who died after allegedly being beaten while in police custody in January 2000. No effective investigation had been carried out, denying Jasmina Sulja an effective remedy.

Counter-terror and security

The Prosecutor failed to respond to a claim filed by Khaled el-Masri in January against Macedonia for its

M

role in his unlawful abduction, detention and ill-treatment for 23 days in 2003, before being transferred to the custody of US authorities and flown to Afghanistan, where he was allegedly subjected to torture and other ill-treatment. The European Court of Human Rights held preliminary hearings following his application against Macedonia.

Freedom of expression

In March, the police failed to protect around 150 students – demonstrating against a government proposal to build a church in Skopje's central square – from attack by a large counter-demonstration, reportedly organized by the Macedonian Orthodox Church. Public order charges were brought against nine demonstrators and seven counter-demonstrators. Three student organizers were charged with failing to protect public safety. In April a parliamentary committee called for an investigation; the SICPS found that police had acted correctly. A November march in Skopje on the UN Day of Tolerance passed without incident.

Discrimination

Anti-discrimination legislation, required as part of the EU accession process, did not reach the statutes. The draft failed to meet international and EU standards and many NGOs complained that they had not been consulted in the drafting process.

In April the Constitutional Court ruled unconstitutional provisions of the 2008 Law on Health Insurance on the payment of child benefit only to mothers living in municipalities with an annual birth rate below 2.1 children per 1,000 people. These provisions would have discriminated against ethnic Albanian and other mothers from minority communities.

Roma

Progress on addressing discrimination against Roma remained uneven. A registration programme, coordinated by UNHCR, the UN refugee agency, and implemented by Romani NGOs, significantly reduced the numbers of undocumented Roma.

Romani children's access to education was improved by government measures to provide free text books and transport, and scholarships for secondary students. Building work began on a secondary school in Šuto Orizari, a predominantly Roma municipality. However, an increasing number of children attended effectively segregated schools.

The EC in November reported negatively on Macedonia's progress regarding the Roma. Revised National Action Plans (NAP) for the Decade of Roma Inclusion were not adopted until May.

The government failed to allocate any funds to implement the NAP for Improving the Status of Romani Women. UNIFEM, the UN Development Fund for Women, supported research into Romani women's experience of state services.

Some 140 homeless Roma who had protested about their living conditions in Čičino Selo were evicted at night in September to a holiday centre, where they had no access to education, health care or work. Another 20 families were threatened with eviction from the Aerodrom municipality of Skopje. The government failed to provide health care and housing to homeless Romani children as young as nine years of age, reported to be intravenously injecting heroin.

Refugees

A Law on Asylum and Temporary Protection established an administrative court to hear appeals against rejection of refugee status. However, few of the 1,700 Roma and Ashkalia from Kosovo, who had been granted subsidiary protection, received access to a full and fair procedure for determining their need for international protection.

According to UNHCR, some 350 people applied to return to Kosovo. Those who remained were eligible for local integration, but the strategy remained to be approved by the government.

Women's rights

In May, Macedonia ratified the Council of Europe Convention on Action against Trafficking in Human Beings, which entered into force in September. However, legislation giving effect to the Convention was not implemented in practice. The 2006 Law on Equality between Men and Women remained to be fully implemented.

Amnesty international visit/report

Amnesty International delegates visited Macedonia in October.

Amnesty International's Concerns in Macedonia: January-June 2009 (EUR 65/002/2009)

MADAGASCAR

REPUBLIC OF MADAGASCAR

Head of state:	Andry Nirina Rajoelina (replaced Marc Ravalomanana in March)
Head of government:	Camille Albert Vital (replaced Cécile Manorohanta in December, who replaced Eugène Mangalaza in December, who replaced Monja Roindofo in October who replaced Charles Rabemananjara in March)
Death penalty:	abolitionist in practice
Population:	19.6 million
Life expectancy:	59.9 years
Under-5 mortality (m/f):	105/95 per 1,000
Adult literacy:	70.7 per cent

A political crisis sparked widespread human rights violations. Security forces used excessive force against demonstrators, killing dozens of people and injuring hundreds. Members of the opposition were arbitrarily arrested and detained. Freedom of peaceful assembly and expression was denied. The right to a fair trial was not respected. Impunity for human rights violations reigned.

Background

On 17 March, Andry Nirina Rajoelina, former mayor of Antananarivo, proclaimed himself President of the High Transitional Authority (Haute Autorité de la Transition, HAT) following months of tension with the government of President Marc Ravalomanana. Andry Rajoelina publicly accused Marc Ravalomanana of misusing the country's wealth and called for his resignation. He also organized mass demonstrations against the government. Under pressure, President Ravalomanana transferred his authority to a military directorate which in turn transferred it to Andry Rajoelina. The Malagasy High Constitutional Court validated both transfers of authority. The new President later suspended the National Assembly and Senate, and declared an unlimited "state of exception", suspending many constitutional rights. The HAT was not recognized by regional and international bodies, and Madagascar was suspended by the African Union.

An International Contact Group convened to find a solution to the political crisis. An agreement was signed in August in Maputo, Mozambique by all political parties involved in the crisis, including Andry Rajoelina and former Presidents Didier Ratsiraka, Albert Zafy and Marc Ravalomanana, but it was not implemented. On 6 October, Eugène Mangalaza was appointed Prime Minister. An additional agreement was signed in November in Addis Ababa, Ethiopia. In December, President Rajoelina appointed Colonel Camille Albert Vital as Prime Minister.

In March, the HAT established the Commission nationale mixte d'enquête (CNME) as an "operative instrument enabling the HAT to exercise its judicial and security activities relating to unlawful acts committed before, during and after the crisis". The CNME replaced in practice the prosecutor's office and the regular judicial system. The CNME was later replaced by the Forces d'intervention spéciale (FIS) with a similar mandate. The two institutions were perceived by many as HAT political bodies used to repress political opponents.

Excessive use of force and unlawful killings

Security forces under both governments used excessive force against demonstrators, resulting in deaths and injuries. No independent and impartial investigations were conducted into such incidents.

■ Photojournalist Ando Ratovonirina was among at least 31 people killed by Marc Ravalomanana's Presidential Guard during a demonstration on 7 February at Ambohitsorohitra presidential palace in Antananarivo. Members of the Presidential Guard fired live ammunition at unarmed demonstrators approaching the palace. Scores of people were also injured.

■ In April, at least four supporters of former President Ravalomanana were killed and 70 wounded by HAT security forces during demonstrations in Antananarivo.

Arbitrary arrests and detentions

Political opponents of President Ravalomanana's government were arbitrarily arrested before the HAT came to power, and after March supporters of former President Ravalomanana were arbitrarily arrested and detained by HAT security forces, especially by members of the CNME and FIS. Some people arrested during demonstrations were held for months without trial.

■ On 20 February, Jean Théodore Rajivenson, lecturer at the University of Antananarivo and supporter of Andry Rajoelina, was arrested and charged with

M

endangering state security, participating in unauthorized demonstrations and arson. He was acquitted by an Antananarivo court and released on 19 March.

■ On 29 April, Manandafy Rakotonirina, who had been designated Prime Minister by Marc Ravalomanana on 10 April, was arrested by the CNME at Hotel Carlton in Antananarivo along with at least six other people. All were charged with illegal gathering, damage to public property and illegal possession of firearms. Manandafy Rakotonirina was also charged with impersonating the prime minister. On 23 September, he was sentenced to a suspended prison sentence of two years; the other six received suspended sentences of between six and 12 months. They were all released.

■ Senator Naike Eliane was arrested on 12 September and accused, among other things, of participating in an unauthorized demonstration. She was released on 22 September. Her trial was continuing.

Freedom of expression – journalists

Media outlets and journalists were targeted by officials before and after the HAT come to power. Journalists received threats via their mobile phones and some went into hiding. In January, the Ravalomanana government closed down Radio Viva; it had already closed Tele Viva on 13 December 2008. Both are owned by Andry Rajoelina. The HAT closed down private television station Tele Mada and Radio Mada, both owned by former President Ravalomanana in March, followed by other pro-Ravalomanana media outlets.

■ Evariste Anselme Ramanantsoavi, a journalist with Radio Mada, was arrested by HAT security officers on 5 May and charged with endangering state security and spreading false information. He was released on 20 May after a court sentenced him to a fine of 1 million ariary (around 385 euros). After he appealed, he started to receive anonymous threats by telephone.

Unfair trials

On 3 June, an Antananarivo criminal court sentenced in their absence former President Ravalomanana and his Minister of Finance, Haja Nirina Razafinjatovo, to four years in prison and a fine of US$70 million for compensation for alleged abuse of office. The trial was not made public and the defendants could not challenge the accusations.

Amnesty International visit/reports

🚐 Amnesty International delegates visited Madagascar in June.

📄 Madagascar: Investigate killings by security forces (AFR 35/001/2009)

📄 Madagascar: Human rights overlooked in resolving the current political crisis, 6 July 2009

MALAWI

REPUBLIC OF MALAWI

Head of state and government:	Bingu wa Mutharika
Death penalty:	abolitionist in practice
Population:	15.3 million
Life expectancy:	52.4 years
Under-5 mortality (m/f):	125/117 per 1,000
Adult literacy:	71.8 per cent

Prisons remained overcrowded and without adequate facilities. Two gay men were ill-treated by police and detained after publicly celebrating their engagement.

Background

The Democratic Progressive Party led by President wa Mutharika won presidential and parliamentary elections on 19 May amid allegations that police had disrupted opposition party meetings and that state media coverage was biased.

Prison conditions

Prisons were overcrowded, most holding more than twice their capacity. In December, for example, Maula Prison (Central region), built for 700 prisoners, housed about 2,200; Zomba Prison (South region), built for 900 inmates, housed 2,176; Chichiri Prison in Blantyre, built for 700 prisoners, housed 1,800; and Mzuzu Prison (Northern region), built for 200 inmates, housed 412. The overcrowding resulted in the spread of contagious diseases, including tuberculosis and scabies.

Female juvenile offenders were held with adult inmates; there are no separate facilities for such prisoners.

Trials of opposition politicians

■ The trial continued of former President Bakili Muluzi,

accused of involvement in a 2008 coup plot. He faced charges of treason and corruption. On 7 December, the High Court dropped 50 of the 60 charges against him. The trial was delayed to allow him to travel abroad for medical treatment. Several other politicians opposed to President wa Mutharika arrested at the same time and released on bail alleged they were being politically persecuted.

■ There was no progress in the trial of former Vice-President Dr Cassim Chilumpha, arrested in April 2006 on suspicion of treason. He remained free on bail.

Police

On 2 December, the National Assembly passed the Police Bill amid protests from human rights groups and opposition parties that it would give police excessive powers, including the power to search without a warrant. The police have a long record of carrying out unlawful searches as well as arbitrary arrests and detentions of government critics, including opposition politicians and journalists. The President had not signed the Police Bill into law by the end of the year.

Discrimination – abuse and detention of gay men

■ Steven Monjeza and Tiwonge Chimbalanga were arrested on 28 December, two days after they had a traditional engagement ceremony (*chinkhoswe*) in Blantyre's Chirimba township. They were charged with "unnatural offences" and "indecent practices between males" under sections 153 and 156 of the Penal Code. If convicted, they face up to 14 years in prison with hard labour. The two men were assaulted in police custody. Both were subject to forcible psychological assessment. Tiwonge Chimbalanga was also forced to undergo an anal examination in hospital to establish whether or not he had had sexual relations with men. Forced anal examination constitutes cruel, inhuman and degrading treatment.

MALAYSIA

MALAYSIA
Head of state:	Yang di-Pertuan Agong Tuanku Mizan Zainal Abidin
Head of government:	Najib Tun Razak (replaced Abdullah Ahmad Badawi in April)
Death penalty:	retentionist
Population:	27.5 million
Life expectancy:	74.1 years
Under-5 mortality (m/f):	12/10 per 1,000
Adult literacy:	91.9 per cent

Freedom of expression was restricted, with bloggers prosecuted and peaceful demonstrators frequently arrested. At least two people died in police custody. Migrant workers, refugees and asylum-seekers faced arrest, detention, and ill-treatment in detention camps. Malaysia rejected recommendations made under the UN Universal Periodic Review (UPR) to guarantee the right to peaceful assembly, and to ratify the UN Refugee Convention and the UN Migrant Workers Convention.

Background

Najib Tun Razak became Prime Minister in April. Political tensions increased in Perak state, located north of the capital Kuala Lumpur and formerly controlled by the opposition People's Alliance (PA), following three defections from the party. After a meeting with the Prime Minister, the Sultan of Perak ordered the PA Chief Minister to resign in February. During a state assembly session in May, when the National Front government representative Zambry Abdul Kadir was expected to be appointed as the new Chief Minister, the opposition Speaker V. Sivakumar was forcibly removed by police officers. Dozens of short-term arrests were made before and after the assembly session.

Freedom of expression

Freedom of expression was severely curtailed, with the authorities using various laws, including the Communication and Multimedia Act 1998 (CMA 1998), to crush critical opinion.

■ Independent news portal Malaysiakini reported on and posted two videos of a protest held in August by Muslims against the relocation of a Hindu temple to

M

their neighbourhood. The government's internet regulatory agency ordered Malaysiakini to remove the videos, threatening to prosecute them under the CMA 1998, alleging offensive content. Charges against them remained pending.

■ Following a nationwide crackdown on bloggers in March, eight bloggers faced imprisonment and fines after being charged under the CMA 1998 for posting critical comments against the Sultan of Perak over the Perak political crisis. An opposition parliamentarian, Karpal Singh, was charged under the Sedition Act for threatening to sue the Sultan, claiming that the Sultan breached the State's constitution. One blogger pleaded guilty with the remaining cases still pending. All were freed on bail.

■ Mohamad Asri Zainul Abidin, a religious leader, was charged in November under the Selangor Islamic Administration Enactment for conducting a religious discourse without government authorization. His trial remained pending while he was freed on bail. If convicted, he faces two years' imprisonment and/or fines of up to 3,000 Malaysia Ringgit (US$873).

■ In October, several police reports were lodged against Sisters in Islam, a women's rights organization, after they criticized caning as a punishment for Muslims. At least two of their leaders were questioned by police under the Sedition Act.

Arbitrary arrests and detentions

The authorities arrested hundreds of peaceful demonstrators, detaining them for up to 24 hours, in an attempt to stifle dissent. Five prisoners of conscience – leaders of the Hindu Rights Action Force (HINDRAF) detained under the Internal Security Act (ISA) – were released. Ten other ISA detainees were also released. Nine people reportedly remained in detention under the ISA.

■ Wong Chin Huat was arrested in May under the Sedition Act after calling for a protest against the government over the Perak crisis. That same month, Mohamad Sabu, the Vice-President of the opposition Pan-Malaysian Islamic Party (PAS), and at least 14 others, were arrested for participating in or planning protests over the Perak crisis. Five lawyers representing the latter 14 were also arrested. They were all released after being held overnight.

■ In August, almost 600 people were briefly arrested following an anti-ISA rally. Sixty-three were held overnight, including PA Vice-President Sivarasa Rasiah.

■ In September, 16 members of HINDRAF, including former ISA detainee P. Uthayakumar, were briefly detained while attempting to hold a candlelight vigil in Kuala Lumpur.

Deaths in custody

■ Extensive signs of torture were discovered on the body of Kugan Ananthan, who died in police custody in January. In October, one police officer was charged with causing him grievous bodily harm.

■ In July, Teoh Beng Hock, political secretary to an opposition leader, died after falling from an upper floor of the Malaysian Anti-Corruption Commission Selangor headquarters. The previous evening, the police had taken him for questioning as a witness in an investigation into the abuse of state funds by the opposition state government. An inquest into the death was ongoing.

Violence against women and girls

Reports of sexual abuse, including rape, by timber company workers against Penan women and girls in Baram village, Sarawak state, formed the basis of a report published in September by a government task force investigating the issue. The report confirmed that women and girls as young as 10 had been raped by timber company employees. However, state officials denied the involvement of company employees in the rapes and police dropped further investigations.

Cruel, inhuman and degrading punishment

People continued to be caned for various offences.

■ In June, the government announced that since 2002 they had sentenced 47,914 migrants to be caned for immigration offences, with 34,923 canings already carried out by 2008.

■ In July, the Shariah High Court in Pahang state sentenced Kartika Dewi to six strokes of the cane and a fine for consuming alcohol. In September, Nazarudin Kamaruddin was sentenced to six strokes of the cane and one year's imprisonment for drinking alcohol. Mohamad Shahrin and Nadiah Hussin were sentenced by the Selangor state Islamic court to six strokes of the cane for trying to have premarital sex. All were Muslim.

Refugees and migrants

Migrants, including asylum-seekers and refugees,

were often arrested and detained for long periods. The government made no distinction between migrant workers, asylum-seekers and refugees. UNCHR, the UN refugee agency, had registered 49,000 people of concern as of May. Eighty-nine per cent were from Myanmar. An estimated 45,000 asylum-seekers remained unregistered.

Conditions in detention centres remained far below international standards. Reports of insufficient food, poor nutrition, poor sanitation and physical abuse persisted.

■ In May, two inmates from Myanmar died from leptospirosis, a bacterial infection caused by contact with water contaminated by animal urine, at the Juru Immigration Depot. In August, a detainee at the KLIA Immigration Depot died after contracting the H1N1 flu virus. Other inmates were hospitalized in both instances.

Death penalty

At least 68 people were sentenced to death by the High Courts while the number of executions was unknown. Malaysia did not support UN UPR recommendations to introduce a moratorium on the death penalty or abolish it. It also did not disclose the number of executions carried out.

Amnesty International visits/report

🚌 Amnesty International delegates visited Malaysia in July and August.

📄 Malaysia: End caning as a punishment for all offences (ASA 28/006/2009)

MALDIVES

REPUBLIC OF MALDIVES

Head of state and government:	Mohamed Nasheed
Death penalty:	abolitionist in practice
Population:	300,000
Life expectancy:	71.1 years
Under-5 mortality (m/f):	31/26 per 1,000
Adult literacy:	97 per cent

In the country's first multi-party elections, the opposition won the majority of parliamentary seats. Parliament's failure to enact the draft penal code

hampered progress towards ensuring justice. At least 180 people, mostly women, were at risk of being flogged. Rising global sea levels continued to threaten the country.

Background

The former president Maumoon Abdul Gayoom's Dhivehi Rayyithunge (Maldivian People's Party) won the majority of seats in the May parliamentary elections. The ensuing political impasse between President Mohamed Nasheed and the opposition-dominated parliament impeded government-proposed reforms. The government continued to call for urgent measures to address global warming in the face of rising sea levels and temperatures. In a meeting with Amnesty International in April, the President reiterated his commitment to protecting human rights and the rule of law.

Torture and other ill-treatment

At least 180 people, mostly women, were at risk of being flogged. The courts had imposed this punishment in recent years for having extramarital sex. The government did not publicly endorse national and international calls for a moratorium on flogging after the last known instance in July, but there were no further floggings by year's end.

■ An 18-year-old woman received 100 lashes on 5 July after being accused of having sex with two men outside marriage. Local journalists reported the woman fainted after being flogged and was taken to hospital for treatment. The woman, who was pregnant at the time of sentencing, had her punishment deferred until after the birth of her child. The court ruled the woman's pregnancy was proof of her guilt. The men involved in the case were acquitted.

Justice system

Parliament failed to enact at least three new bills designed to strengthen human rights protections in the country. These were a bill to make defamation a civil rather than criminal offence, a press freedom bill, and a right to freedom of expression bill.

As in previous years, parliament failed to enact the penal code bill, which aims to remove some of the fundamental flaws in the current criminal justice system, such as the lack of a unified definition of a criminal offence.

There was no move to bring perpetrators of past

M

human rights violations to justice. However, attempts from opposition members of parliament to enact a law providing immunity from prosecution to the former president failed when the Speaker of Parliament declared the move unconstitutional.

Right to adequate housing

After a visit to the Maldives in February, the UN Special Rapporteur on adequate housing said that climate change "jeopardizes the survival of the nation, but more immediately, it jeopardizes the right to housing due to the scarcity of land". The country remained at risk of rising sea levels and coastal erosion.

Amnesty International report

Maldives: Over one hundred people at risk of being flogged, 21 Jul 2009

MALI

REPUBLIC OF MALI

Head of state:	Amadou Toumani Touré
Head of government:	Modibo Sidibé
Death penalty:	abolitionist in practice
Population:	13 million
Life expectancy:	48.1 years
Under-5 mortality (m/f):	193/188 per 1,000
Adult literacy:	26.2 per cent

A draft law equalizing rights for men and women sparked controversy and protests. At least 10 people were sentenced to death; no executions were carried out.

Background

The government and Tuareg armed groups from Niger and Mali concluded another peace agreement in October. The Malian authorities pledged to develop the region of Kidal and the Tuareg armed groups agreed to co-operate with the government in its fight against al-Qa'ida in the Islamic Maghreb (AQIM). In January, a Tuareg armed group released three Malian soldiers held since 2008. The army released members of a Tuareg armed group in June.

In January, four European tourists were abducted by AQIM in northern Mali. Two were released in April and one in July. UK national Edwin Dyer was reportedly executed in June after the UK authorities refused to release Abu Qatada (see United Kingdom entry). Robert Fowler, Canadian UN envoy, and his aide Louis Guay, captured by AQIM in Niger in December 2008, were released in April in Mali. AQIM also said it was holding Pierre Camatte, a French national abducted in northern Mali in November. Other European hostages abducted in Mauritania were reportedly held in Mali (see Mauritania entry).

Women's rights

The Bill for Persons and Family Code, which grants equal rights to women, sparked widespread debate. It makes 18 the minimum age for marriage, and stipulates that both parties must consent to marriage and divorce, and both father and mother have parental authority. It also gives men and women equal inheritance rights.

After Parliament adopted the Code in August, tens of thousands of people – led by religious groups – demonstrated across the country against its adoption. Women's organizations had mixed reactions, most calling for more discussions. President Touré sent the Bill back to Parliament, where it awaited a second reading.

Death penalty

At least 10 people were sentenced to death.
■ In March, Bamako Assize Court sentenced Makan Diarra to death on 12 March for the murder of a six-year-old child. His lawyer pleaded that his client was mentally ill.

MALTA

REPUBLIC OF MALTA

Head of state:	George Abela (replaced Edward Fenech-Adami in April)
Head of government:	Lawrence Gonzi
Death penalty:	abolitionist for all crimes
Population:	0.4 million
Life expectancy:	79.6 years
Under-5 mortality (m/f):	7/7 per 1,000
Adult literacy:	92.4 per cent

Migrants and asylum-seekers' lives were put at risk by delays in sea rescue operations. They continued to be routinely detained on arrival, in contravention of international standards. Conditions in detention remained poor, despite efforts by the authorities to improve some facilities.

Migrants, refugees and asylum-seekers' rights

Rescue at sea

The authorities failed to adequately protect the lives of migrants and asylum-seekers rescued at sea. The Maltese and Italian governments disagreed over which country was responsible for search and rescue operations, which led to delays in responding to distress calls.

■ On 16 April, a Turkish cargo ship, *Pinar*, rescued an estimated 140 people whose boat was at risk of sinking in waters south of Sicily. The ship was prevented from reaching either a Maltese or Italian port because neither country would accept responsibility for the people rescued. The individuals were left stranded for four days with insufficient food and water and forced to sleep on the deck of the ship. They were eventually allowed to disembark at Porto Empedocle, Italy, on 20 April.

■ On 30 April, a Maltese coastguard vessel was prevented by the Italian authorities from disembarking 66 migrants and possible asylum-seekers on the Italian island of Lampedusa. The individuals were rescued by a Tunisian fishing boat and transferred to the Maltese vessel while in Malta's search and rescue zone as designated by international conventions. Despite this, the Maltese authorities initially refused to assist or disembark the migrants and asylum-seekers on Maltese territory. The migrants and asylum-seekers were eventually admitted to Malta.

Detention

In January, the UN Working Group on Arbitrary Detention expressed concerns about the legal basis for detention of migrants and asylum-seekers. The Working Group noted that detention is automatic and mandatory for all irregular migrants, including asylum-seekers; the maximum length of detention is not defined in law and its duration is often not related to individual case assessments.

In practice, the government has applied a maximum one-year detention period for asylum-seekers whose applications are pending. Rejected asylum-seekers and all irregular migrants who have not been forcibly returned to their home countries or to third countries after 18 months' detention are generally released.

Decisions regarding asylum applications and detention can only be challenged before the Immigration Appeals Board, which is not part of the judiciary. This contravenes Article 5(4) of the European Convention on Human Rights, which provides for automatic judicial review of detention.

Conditions in detention remained poor. In Hal Far Centre, more than 500 people were living in tents. The authorities opened a new detention facility in Ta'Kandja and renovated part of the Lyster Centre.

M

MAURITANIA

ISLAMIC REPUBLIC OF MAURITANIA

Head of state:	General Mohamed Ould Abdel Aziz
Head of government:	Moulaye Ould Mohamed Laghdaf
Death penalty:	abolitionist in practice
Population:	3.3 million
Life expectancy:	56.6 years
Under-5 mortality (m/f):	128/112 per 1,000
Adult literacy:	55.8 per cent

Security forces used excessive force against peaceful demonstrators, human rights defenders and members of parliament. Torture and other ill-treatment were frequently reported. Prison conditions remained harsh. Dozens of people suspected of belonging to armed groups were detained without trial. Hundreds of migrants were

held and expelled with no opportunity to challenge the legality of their detention or collective expulsion. No executions were reported, but at least one person was under sentence of death.

Background

General Mohamed Ould Abdel Aziz, who became President in August 2008 after a coup against the democratically elected President Sidi Ould Cheikh Abdallahi, resigned in April from the army to stand in the July presidential elections. His victory was confirmed by the Constitutional Court, although the president of the Independent National Electoral Commission threw doubts on the reliability of the results and resigned.

Mauritania, suspended from the AU after the 2008 coup, was readmitted in June before the presidential elections.

Torture, other ill-treatment and prison conditions

Torture and other ill-treatment were widespread. In September, in a telephone conversation with a journalist, a detainee complained about the systematic use of torture on most inmates.

Despite the release of 68 detainees in September from Dar Naïm, prisons remained overcrowded. Harsh and arbitrary punishments continued to be reported. In Nouadhibou and Dar Naïm prisons, detainees were crammed together in stifling heat. Only old and sick detainees were occasionally allowed to leave their cells. Detainees went on hunger strike to protest against food shortages. Families of detainees staged a sit-in to protest against torture of prisoners suspected of terrorism.

■ Cheikhani Ould Sidina, arrested in 2008 and sentenced to one year in prison for helping his brother to escape from a court, died in Nouakchott prison in April. The Justice Department subsequently announced that it would investigate conditions of detention there.

Excessive use of force

In the first six months of 2009, the security forces regularly used excessive force to prevent demonstrators from protesting against the electoral timetable.

■ In April, two demonstrations were violently repressed. The protests were attended by political parties and civil society organizations, including the Coordination of Democratic Forces – a coalition formed by the National Front for the Defence of Democracy and comprising trade union federations, human rights activists and civil society.

■ On 2 April, police beat human rights defender Boubacar Messaoud, president of SOS Esclaves, an NGO that campaigns against slavery, and several members of parliament, including Kobade Ould Cheick and Mohamed Moustapha Ould Bedredine, and fired tear gas at them as they staged a peaceful protest against the August 2008 coup.

■ On 19 April, many women, including former ministers, members of parliament and human rights defenders, were kicked or beaten with batons and belts by security forces. The women were staging a sit-in in front of the UN headquarters in Nouakchott. Nebghouha Mint Mohamed Vall, former Education Minister, and her daughter were beaten by the police. Another woman lost consciousness and had to be hospitalized after she too was beaten by the police.

Prisoners of conscience – releases

Isselmou Ould Abdelkhader Isselmou, a former Minister of Health detained since September 2008 for criticizing the coup against President Sidi, was provisionally released in February. In June, four other detainees, including the former Prime Minister and the Minister of Public Administration, were released on bail.

Counter-terror and security

At least 12 people, among them Malian nationals suspected of belonging to al-Qa'ida in the Islamic Maghreb (AQIM), were arrested in different parts of the country, including the capital Nouakchott and in the border area with Mali. Among them was a man suspected of involvement in a bombing outside the French Embassy in Nouakchott in August. At the end of the year, more than 60 people suspected or convicted of terrorism offences were in prison.

Abuses by armed groups

Three Spanish aid workers were abducted by AQIM in November, and two Italian tourists were taken hostage in December. All were reportedly transferred to Mali.

Refugees

UNHCR, the UN refugee agency, announced in October that more than 14,000 Mauritanian refugees, comprising over 3,500 families, had returned from Senegal since the start of the year. Since the beginning of the return of refugees in January 2008, nearly 20,000 Mauritanians had come back to Mauritania from neighbouring countries. Out of 12,000 refugees still living in Mali, around 8,000 had expressed a wish to return to Mauritania. Between 1989 and 1991, thousands of Mauritanians fled to neighbouring countries in the aftermath of repression against the black Mauritanian population.

Migrants' rights

More than 1,750 people suspected of trying to migrate to Europe were arbitrarily arrested and held at a detention centre in Nouadhibou for a few days before being expelled. This policy of arrests and collective expulsions by the Mauritanian authorities was the result of intense pressure by the EU, and Spain in particular, in an attempt to combat migration to Europe.

Discrimination and slavery

The report of the Special Rapporteur on contemporary forms of racism was released in March. He noted that the government had taken positive steps to combat discrimination, but expressed concern about the ongoing marginalization of black Mauritanian people in the political, economic and social spheres. He stressed that despite the adoption of laws, notably against slavery, there was still a gap between the legal framework and its application, and that no complaints were being brought before the domestic courts. The Special Rapporteur recommended amending the Constitution to reflect the cultural diversity of the country, and establishing a Commission to examine the root causes of discrimination.

The Special Rapporteur on contemporary forms of slavery, including its causes and consequences, visited Mauritania in October and November. She acknowledged the efforts made by the government and civil society to fight slavery, but considered that "a more holistic, collaborative and sustained approach addressing all forms of discrimination together with poverty at all levels of society is required".

■ The case of a couple arrested for slave practices on a 10-year-old girl was dismissed in April after the prosecutor concluded it was a family matter. SOS Esclaves, which filed the case, complained that the 2007 law criminalizing slavery had not been enforced.

Death penalty

Courts continued to impose the death penalty, although no executions were reported. At the end of the year, at least one person was under sentence of death.

Amnesty International report

Mauritanie: Nouvelle répression par la force de manifestations pacifiques (AFR 38/001/2009)

MEXICO

UNITED MEXICAN STATES

Head of state and government:	Felipe Calderón Hinojosa
Death penalty:	abolitionist for all crimes
Population:	109.6 million
Life expectancy:	76 years
Under-5 mortality (m/f):	22/18 per 1,000
Adult literacy:	92.8 per cent

M

Reports increased of serious human rights violations committed by members of the military carrying out law enforcement activities. Federal, state and municipal police forces also continued to commit serious human rights violations in several states. Women experienced high levels of gender-based violence with little access to justice. Thousands of irregular migrants were abducted, and some murdered, by criminal gangs. Women migrants were often raped. Several journalists and human rights defenders were killed, harassed or faced fabricated criminal charges. Marginalized communities whose lands were sought for economic development were at risk of harassment, forced eviction or denial of their right to adequate information and consultation. The Inter-American Court of Human Rights issued ground-breaking rulings against Mexico in two cases involving grave human rights violations.

Background

Following congressional mid-term elections, the Institutional Revolutionary Party became the largest party in the House of Deputies. In November, a new President of the National Human Rights Commission (Comisión Nacional de los Derechos Humanos, CNDH) was chosen by the Senate. Mexico agreed to implement 83 of the 91 recommendations made by the UN Human Rights Council.

Some 50,000 troops were engaged in law enforcement activities to improve public security and combat organized crime and the drug cartels. According to media reports, more than 6,500 people were killed in violence related to organized crime. The security forces were also frequently the target of attacks.

The US Congress authorized a further US$486 million as part of the Merida Initiative, a three-year regional co-operation and security agreement. Human rights conditions were imposed on 15 per cent of the Initiative's funding. Despite failure to meet human rights conditions, funds continued to be released to Mexico.

Police and security forces

Military abuses and the military justice system

Reports of human rights violations – including extrajudicial executions and other unlawful killings, enforced disappearances, torture and other ill-treatment and arbitrary detention – committed by members of the military increased. The CNDH made 30 recommendations to the Ministry of Defence regarding confirmed cases of abuses during the year, compared with 14 in 2008. Some victims and relatives who tried to file complaints received threats. Human rights violations involving military personnel continued to be investigated and tried within the military justice system. Government officials refused to recognize the scale of abuses or impunity.

■ In August, the National Supreme Court ruled that relatives of four unarmed civilians shot and killed by the army in Santiago de los Caballeros, Sinaloa state, in March 2008, did not have the legal right to challenge the military justice system handling of the case.
■ In March, Miguel Alejandro Gama Habif, Israel Ayala Martínez and Aarón Rojas de la Fuente were forcibly disappeared by members of the army in Nuevo Laredo, Tamaulipas state. Their burned bodies were found in April. Relatives were not allowed to see the bodies or the autopsy report. In May, the Ministry of Defence announced that 12 military personnel had been detained, but no official information was available regarding charges or their trial.
■ In March, 25 municipal police officers were detained by the army and tortured during pre-charge detention (*arraigo*) on a military base in Tijuana, Baja California state. The police were later charged with offences linked to organized crime and transferred to a civilian prison in Tepic, Nayarit state. At the end of the year it was not known if any investigation had been initiated into the allegations of torture.

Police forces

In January, the National Public Security law came into force. This requires increased professionalization and co-ordination of the police and includes some improved human rights protection. In June, the Federal Police law established a single federal police force with new powers to receive criminal complaints and conduct investigations, including electronic surveillance and undercover operations, without adequate judicial controls.

There were several reports of human rights violations, including enforced disappearance; excessive use of force; torture and other ill-treatment; and arbitrary detention committed by municipal, state and federal police. Government commitments to investigate all allegations of torture were not implemented.

■ In February, municipal police agents forcibly disappeared Gustavo Castañeda Puentes in Monterrey, Nuevo León state. Although witness evidence identified the perpetrators, the investigation did not result in the arrest of suspects.
■ In March, federal police illegally detained Jesús Arturo Torres at his home in Chihuahua City, Chihuahua state. Police beat him and threatened him with death during three hours of questioning. He was released without charge. He filed a complaint, but at the end of the year it was not known whether the investigation had made any progress.

Migrants' rights

More than 60,000 irregular migrants, the vast majority Central Americans trying to reach the USA, were detained and deported. Migrants, particularly women and children, were at risk of abuses such as beatings, threats, abduction, rape and murder, mainly by criminal gangs, but also by some public officials.

M

Measures to prevent and punish abuses were inadequate and migrants had virtually no access to justice. The government promoted regional guidelines on the care of child migrants and trained some officials in efforts to improve the protection of child migrants in detention.

In July, the CNDH published a report highlighting the extremely high levels of kidnapping for ransom and other abuses against migrants by criminal gangs. It estimated that as many as 10,000 migrants may have been kidnapped during the previous six months and that in many cases women migrants were sexually assaulted. Official efforts to curb attacks on migrants were completely inadequate.

■ In January, Chiapas state police shot and killed three irregular migrants and wounded others while pursuing the vehicle they were travelling in near San Cristóbal, Chiapas state. The trial of several police officers was pending at the end of the year.

Human rights defenders

In October, a report by the Office of the UN High Commissioner for Human Rights in Mexico documented threats and attacks against human rights defenders by both state officials and private individuals. It also highlighted the lack of effective action to investigate and prevent attacks. Human rights defenders, particularly those working on economic, cultural and social rights, faced fabricated criminal charges and unfair trial proceedings.

■ In February, Indigenous human rights defenders Raúl Lucas Lucía and Manuel Ponce Rosas were abducted, tortured and murdered in Ayutla, Guerrero state, by unidentified gunmen who claimed to be police officers. The two men had been threatened in the past for their work. Raúl Hernández, a prisoner of conscience and activist with another local Indigenous rights organization, remained in prison on a fabricated murder charge at the end of the year. Four others accused in the case, prisoners of conscience Manuel Cruz, Orlando Manzanarez, Natalio Ortega and Romualdo Santiago, were released in March after a federal court concluded there was insufficient evidence against them. Human rights defenders campaigning for justice in both cases received death threats.

■ In August, an unidentified gunman repeatedly shot and almost killed Salomón Monárrez of the Sinaloan Civic Front, a human rights organization in Culiacán,

Sinaloa state. An investigation into the shooting was continuing at the end of the year.

Freedom of expression – attacks on journalists

Journalists, particularly those working on issues related to public security and corruption, continued to face threats, attacks and abduction. There were reports that at least 12 journalists were murdered during 2009. Investigations into killings, abductions and threats rarely led to the prosecution of those responsible, contributing to a climate of impunity.

Indigenous Peoples and marginalized communities

Indigenous Peoples and members of marginalized communities were frequently subjected to unfair judicial proceedings. The rights of communities to their land and homes were overlooked or challenged in several cases in order to exploit local resources.

■ In September, prisoner of conscience Jacinta Francisco Marcial from Santiago Mexquititlán, Querétaro state, was released during a retrial after the federal prosecutor dropped the case against her. She had been targeted because she was an Indigenous woman living in poverty and had spent three years in prison for a crime she had not committed. Two other Indigenous women were awaiting sentence in retrials on the same charges and remained in prison at the end of the year.

■ Members of the community of Lomas del Poleo, outside Ciudad Juárez, Chihuahua state, were repeatedly threatened and intimidated by private security guards as part of a six-year campaign to drive the families from their homes so that commercial development of the site could start. An agrarian court was still considering the families' claim to the land at the end of 2009. Despite repeated complaints, the authorities did not prevent or investigate the threats.

Violence against women and girls

Violence against women in the community and home remained widespread in most states. Scores of cases of murder in which women had been abducted and raped were reported in Chihuahua and Mexico states. Legal measures to improve the prevention and punishment of gender-based violence were adopted by all states, but implementation of the new laws remained very limited. Impunity for murder and other violent crimes against women remained the norm.

M

■ The murder and abduction of women and girls in Ciudad Juárez continued. At least 35 women were reportedly abducted in 2009 and their whereabouts remained unknown at the end of the year. The state government published a report on advances in the prevention and punishment of the murder of women, but failed to provide a full account of all alleged cases. In November, the Inter-American Court of Human Rights ruled on the "cotton field" (*Campo Algodonero*) case that Mexico was guilty of discrimination and of failing to protect three young women murdered in 2001 in Ciudad Juárez or to ensure an effective investigation into their abduction and murder. The Court ordered a new investigation, reparations for the relatives, investigations of officials and improved measures to prevent and investigate cases of abduction and murder of women and girls.

Sexual and reproductive rights

In an apparent reaction to the Federal District's decriminalization of abortion in 2007, 17 of Mexico's 31 state legislatures passed amendments to state constitutions guaranteeing the legal right to life from the moment of conception. A constitutional challenge to the amendment in Baja California state filed with the National Supreme Court was pending at the end of the year.

The government finally published an updated directive for medical professionals caring for women who have experienced violence. Under the directive, survivors of rape are entitled to receive information on and access to legal abortion. Some state governments informed the media that the directive would not be applied in their states.

Impunity

Impunity for past human rights violations remained entrenched. Little or no action was taken to bring to justice those responsible.
■ Investigations into hundreds of cases of serious human rights violations committed during Mexico's "dirty war" in the 1960s, 1970s and 1980s made no progress and some documents from previous investigations remained unaccounted for.
■ In February, a Supreme Court special investigation concluded that serious human rights violations were committed by police in San Salvador Atenco in May 2006, including sexual assault of detainees. However, it stated that only those directly implicated in abuses

could be held to account, not senior officials who had ordered the operation or failed to prevent or investigate abuses. In September, a special federal criminal investigation into torture, including sexual assault, of 26 women detainees in San Salvador Atenco concluded that 34 state police officers were responsible, but did not press charges and returned the case to the Mexico State Attorney General's Office, which had previously failed to prosecute those responsible. No further information was available on new investigations.
■ In March, a federal court confirmed the closure of the case of genocide against former President Luis Echeverría for the 1968 Tlatelolco student massacre.
■ In October, the Supreme Court finalized its special investigation into serious human rights violations during the political crisis in Oaxaca in 2006. It concluded that the governor and other senior state officials should be held accountable. However, by the end of the year, no further information was available about new investigations to comply with the Court's recommendation. Juan Manuel Martínez remained in prison accused of the murder of US journalist Brad Will in October 2006 in Oaxaca, despite the lack of evidence against him and the failure of federal authorities to conduct a full and thorough investigation to identify those responsible.
■ In December, the Inter-American Court of Human Rights found Mexico responsible for the enforced disappearance of Rosendo Radilla by the army in Guerrero state in 1974. It ordered a new civilian investigation, reparations for the relatives and reform of the military penal code to end military jurisdiction over the investigation and trial of human rights cases.

Amnesty International visits/report

🚌 Amnesty International delegates visited Mexico in February and June.
📄 Mexico: New reports of human rights violations committed by the military (Index: AMR 41/058/2009)

MOLDOVA

REPUBLIC OF MOLDOVA

Head of state:	Mihai Ghimpu (replaced Vladimir Voronin in September)
Head of government:	Vladimir Filat (replaced Zinaida Greceanîi in September)
Death penalty:	abolitionist for all crimes
Population:	3.6 million
Life expectancy:	68.3 years
Under-5 mortality (m/f):	26/21 per 1,000
Adult literacy:	99.2 per cent

Allegations of torture and ill-treatment remained widespread and the perpetrators continued to enjoy impunity. Police failed to uphold and protect the right to freedom of assembly. Human rights defenders faced harassment as a result of their activities.

Background

Moldova's ruling Communist Party won the parliamentary elections on 5 April for the third time running, amidst widespread claims of electoral fraud. Peaceful protests in the capital, Chişinău, began on 6 April. They became violent on 7 April and resulted in the storming of the presidential and parliamentary buildings. A re-run of the elections was held on 29 July which resulted in a majority for the opposition parties.

Torture and other ill-treatment

Following the demonstrations in Chişinău, hundreds of people, including minors, were rounded up and detained by police. International and local NGOs collected testimonies from over 100 detainees, their families and lawyers, claiming that they had been subjected to torture or other ill-treatment. The Council of Europe's Commissioner for Human Rights reported that during his visit to detention centres following the events in April, the majority of people interviewed by his delegation alleged ill-treatment by police officers.

■ Oxana Radu was among a group of 36 young people who had come from Cahul in the south of the country in two minibuses to witness the events. They were stopped as they were leaving Chişinău after midnight on 8 April, and then escorted to the General Police Commissariat. Oxana Radu, her sister and one other woman were taken directly into the police station. She told Amnesty International that she was led into a room where there was a female and a male police officer. She was forced to strip naked. The male police officer said: "You're cold, we will warm you up." She stated that she was forced to perform squats while naked and was threatened and sworn at as she did so. She was then taken to a cell with four other women and her younger sister. They were reportedly left for two days without food or water, access to a lawyer or the possibility of contacting their families. Oxana Radu was accused of having shouted at a policeman and sentenced to five days' administrative detention by a judge in the police station. She and two other women were taken to the police station in Drochia in the north of the country to serve their sentences. She was released at 2 am on 14 April.

Impunity

A culture of impunity among police officers continued, encouraged by the low rate of prosecutions for acts of torture and other ill-treatment, the failure to conduct prompt, thorough and impartial investigations and the lack of adequate punishment for violations.

■ The government delegation reported to the UN Human Rights Committee that as of September, 101 complaints of torture or other ill-treatment by police officers had been received, and 25 criminal investigations had been started in connection with the events in April. However, the number of complaints lodged against the police for ill-treatment did not reflect the scale of the problem. Intimidation and harassment of victims and witnesses resulted in under-reporting of torture and other ill-treatment and contributed to impunity.

■ On 16 June the European Court of Human Rights ruled unanimously that Sergei Gurgurov had been a victim of torture in 2005, and in July the Prosecutor General's office opened a criminal case, almost four years after Sergei Gurgurov first alleged that he had been tortured by police officers. The Prosecutor General's office had previously responded to all requests for criminal investigations by saying that the injuries Sergei Gurgurov claimed were the result of torture by police officers had been self-inflicted.

M

Freedom of assembly

Despite the progressive Law on Assemblies which was passed in 2008, police and local authorities continued to unduly restrict the right to freedom of peaceful assembly by banning demonstrations, imposing limitations and detaining peaceful protesters.

■ On 29 January, Anatol Matasaru was detained outside the offices of the Prosecutor General in Chişinău, as he held a one-man protest dressed in a pig suit and using audio equipment to play the sound of a pig squealing. He was protesting the failure of the Prosecutor General to open an investigation following his complaint about police ill-treatment in 2006. As part of the protest, he displayed images showing pigs in different contexts, with text criticizing inaction by prosecutors. Police arrived within minutes of the beginning of the protest and detained Anatol Matasaru for approximately five hours. He was charged with failing to inform the mayor's office about the protest (although this was not a requirement of the Law on Assemblies), failing to abide by the orders of the police, resisting arrest, and insulting public officials. Anatol Matasaru alleged that he was punched by a police officer while in detention. The charges were dropped by Rîşcani district court in Chişinău in February.

■ On 3 February, police reportedly failed to protect peaceful demonstrators who were attacked by a group of masked men. The demonstration was organized by Amnesty International Moldova and local human rights organizations Hyde Park, Promo Lex, the Resource Centre for Human Rights and the Institute for Human Rights. They were protesting against previous failures by the police to uphold the rights to freedom of assembly, association and expression, and to call on the Prosecutor General's office to investigate these failures. Shortly after gathering in front of the Prosecutor General's office in central Chişinău, the demonstrators were attacked by approximately 10 men, some wearing masks, who sprayed paint at them, punched and hit them. Igor Grosu, the Chair of Amnesty International Moldova, was hit from behind and had to be treated in hospital for a head injury requiring several stitches. A member of the Helsinki Committee for Human Rights was punched in the face. The demonstrators called the police immediately, but reported that no officers came to their aid. After the participants had successfully chased off the attackers the police again refused to come and collect the

evidence which remained of the attack, such as masks and spray-paint cans.

Human rights defenders

In April, at least seven NGOs involved in monitoring human rights violations following the events in Chişinău received letters from the Ministry of Justice. The letters asked each organization to explain its position towards the riots, as well as any measures taken by the organization to prevent and stop the violence and to enforce the Law on Assemblies. These seven and another four organizations also received subpoenas from their local tax inspectorates, dated 24 April, asking them to present financial documents for 2008 and 2009, and identify their sources of income and expenditure by 28 April. On 28 April, the office of Amnesty International in Chişinău was visited by representatives from the local tax inspectorate, who requested that the organization provide a list of paying members and other documents. In a letter to Amnesty International the Prosecutor General's office replied that the checks had been routine and that there was "no causal relationship to the events of 7 April."

International justice

By the end of 2009, Moldova had still not ratified the Rome Statute of the International Criminal Court, despite a decision by the Constitutional Court in 2007 that Moldova could ratify the Rome Statute without requiring a change in the Constitution.

Amnesty International visits/reports

🚍 Amnesty International delegates visited in April and July.

📓 Moldova: Memorandum – Amnesty International's concerns relating to policing during and after the events of 7 April 2009 in Chişinău (EUR 59/003/2009)

📓 Police torture and other ill-treatment: it's still "just normal" in Moldova (EUR 59/009/2009)

MONGOLIA

MONGOLIA
Head of state: **Tsakhia Elbegdorj (replaced Nambaryn Enkhbayar in June)**
Head of government: **Batbold Sukhbaatar (replaced Sanjaagiin Bayar in October)**
Death penalty: **Retentionist**
Population: **2.7 million**
Life expectancy: **66.2 years**
Under 5-mortality (m/f): **49/40 per 1,000**
Adult literacy: **97.3 per cent**

Law enforcement officials continued to commit human rights abuses with impunity. Authorities failed to prevent, investigate and punish attacks against lesbian, gay, bisexual and transgender people including attacks by law enforcement officials. Information on the use of the death penalty remained a state secret.

Background

In July 2008, a riot broke out in the capital, Ulaanbaatar, amid allegations of widespread electoral fraud – five people were killed and hundreds injured.

On 1 July 2009, the Parliamentary Sub-committee on Human Rights set up a four-member Working Group to investigate allegations that law enforcement officials subjected people to torture and other ill-treatment and illegal detention during the July 2008 riot. The Working Group also investigated violations of the right to a fair trial. A public hearing was held on 2 December to hear testimony from the public, NGOs, lawyers and public officials.

Impunity

Allegations of law enforcement officials committing torture and other ill-treatment were frequently dismissed by the State General Prosecutor's Office with no or inadequate investigation.

In July, the Parliament passed an Amnesty Law which led to over 2,192 people being released for minor crimes and misdemeanours committed before 24 June 2009. Those released included people being detained for alleged crimes committed during the July 2008 riot.

An investigation by the Special Investigation Unit into the case of four senior police officials suspected of authorizing and distributing live ammunition and 10 police officers suspected of using live ammunition in July 2008 was completed on 15 February. Further procedures to initiate prosecution were stalled until November because the defendants and their lawyers did not return the case files to the Special Investigation Unit. It was unclear how the Amnesty Law would impact on the prosecutions.

Death penalty

All aspects of the death penalty are considered a state secret. The families and lawyers of those on death row received no prior notification of execution and the bodies of those executed were never returned to their families.

■ The President commuted the sentences of all those on death row who appealed for clemency to 30 years. One was Buuveibaatar, a 33-year-old man found guilty of murdering his former girlfriend's boyfriend in January 2008.

Freedom of expression – journalists

The National Police Agency issued contracts to broadcasting stations which, if signed, required them to co-operate with the police when reporting on public disorder situations. Broadcasting stations would have to rely on police information and assist the police in dispersing rallies, demonstrations and marches. Fear of reprisals continued to result in self-censorship. The authorities continued to restrict access to information.

Legal developments

Mongolia acceded to the UN Convention on the Rights of Persons with Disabilities.

Rights of lesbian, gay, bisexual and transgender people

The State Registration General Agency officially recognized the LGBT Centre in December. The Agency had previously rejected the application for recognition stating that it conflicted with "Mongolia's traditions and customs" and had the potential "to set the wrong example for youth and adolescents".

Torture and other ill-treatment

Torture and other ill-treatment were common in police stations and pre-trial detention centres. Detention conditions were poor and overcrowding was routine.

The Special Investigation Unit of the State General

M

Prosecutor's Office charged with investigating allegations of torture by officials has a staff of 24 to cover the entire country.

Amnesty International visit/report

🚍 Amnesty International delegates visited Mongolia in July.

📃 Where should I go from here? The legacy of the 1 July 2008 riot in Mongolia (ASA 30/003/2009).

MONTENEGRO

REPUBLIC OF MONTENEGRO

Head of state:	Filip Vujanović
Head of government:	Milo Đukanović (re-elected in March)
Death penalty:	abolitionist for all crimes
Population:	0.6 million
Life expectancy:	74 years
Under-5 mortality (m/f):	11/9 per 1,000
Adult literacy:	96.4 per cent

Some progress was made in prosecuting war crimes; freedom of expression was compromised by threats, fines and unresolved political killings; Roma suffered discrimination. The European Commission prepared an opinion on Montenegro's accession to the European Union.

Justice system – war crimes

In July parliament approved a Law on Co-operation with the International Criminal Court; a 2007 bilateral agreement providing US citizens with immunity remained in force.

In March, the Bijelo Polje Special Court for War Crimes and Organized Crime (SCWC) opened proceedings against eight former Yugoslav People's Army (JNA) soldiers, accused of murdering 23 Kosovo Albanian civilians, at Kaluđerski Laz in April 1999.

In May, at Podgorica SCWC, the trial began of five former JNA Montenegrin reservists for the torture and inhumane treatment at Morinj camp of 169 Croatian civilians and prisoners of war between October 1991 and August 1992. Proceedings had been transferred from Bijelo Polje in March, after witnesses had received threats; measures for their protection were subsequently agreed.

Proceedings opened in November against nine former government officials and high-ranking police officers, with five of them being tried in their absence. They had been indicted in January for the enforced disappearance in 1992 of at least 79 refugees from Bosnia and Herzegovina (BiH) who were subsequently handed over to the then Bosnian Serb authorities. S.P., a former police inspector who refused to participate in the disappearances and was forced to retire from the police, had since 1992 continued to receive threats to his life, assaults, and damage to his property. In December, he was granted protection as a witness in proceedings.

Torture and other ill-treatment

In January, the UN Committee against Torture (CAT) urged the authorities to guarantee fundamental legal safeguards to detainees and to promptly investigate allegations of ill-treatment.

In March, Montenegro ratified the Optional Protocol to the Convention against Torture, and in May proposed the Protector of Human Rights and Freedoms as the national prevention mechanism.

The NGO Youth Initiative for Human Rights (YIHR) confirmed a decrease in reported allegations of ill-treatment, following the CAT's recommendations.

Freedom of expression

In April, following a retrial, Damir Mandić was convicted as an accomplice to the murder of Duško Jovanović, former editor of the newspaper *Dan*, and sentenced to 30 years' imprisonment. No other suspects were identified. The newspaper subsequently received threats, including a bomb scare.

In August, the mayor of Podgorica and his son were charged with assaulting two journalists from the newspaper *Vijesti*. No progress was made in investigating the murder of Srdjan Vojičić, bodyguard to author Jevrem Brković, or the serious assault in May 2008 on journalist Mladen Stojović, after he requested police protection following his reports on organized crime in football.

In May, the Prime Minister publicly criticized NGOs and independent journalists, who were subject to punitive fines. In August, Andrej Nikolaidis and the journal *Monitor* were ordered by the Supreme Court to pay 12,000 euros in damages to film director Emir Kusturica.

M

Discrimination

A draft anti-discrimination law was prepared. In November the Minister for Human Rights and Minorities made discriminatory statements about homosexuals.

The UN Committee on the Elimination of Racial Discrimination (CERD) noted in March "continued allegations of police brutality and ill-treatment and lack of prompt and impartial investigations of cases with respect to disadvantaged ethnic groups, particularly Roma." According to the YIHR, 75 per cent of Roma reportedly stated they would not make a complaint if ill-treated.

The CERD further concluded that socio-economic conditions for Roma were "precarious and discriminatory". UNHCR, the UN refugee agency, assisted Roma without birth certificates to obtain identity documents – required for eligibility to social security, health, education and employment.

Refugees and asylum-seekers

According to UNHCR, approximately 4,476 Roma, Askhali and Egyptians from Kosovo remained in Montenegro. A proposed amendment to the Law on Foreigners would allow them, and others displaced from Croatia and BiH, to apply for residency.

Violence against women and girls

In June the US State Department placed Montenegro on its 2009 Watch List of trafficking in persons, as it continued to be a transit country for women and girls trafficked for sexual exploitation, but failed to convict traffickers or identify victims. A draft domestic violence law did not include adequate provisions on the implementation of protection orders.

Amnesty International visit/report

🚗 Amnesty International delegates visited Montenegro in October.

📄 Amnesty International's concerns in Montenegro: January-June 2009 (EUR 66/004/2009)

MOROCCO/ WESTERN SAHARA

KINGDOM OF MOROCCO

Head of state:	King Mohamed VI
Head of government:	Abbas El Fassi
Death penalty:	abolitionist in practice
Population:	32 million
Life expectancy:	71 years
Under-5 mortality (m/f):	43/29 per 1,000
Adult literacy:	55.6 per cent

Attacks increased on freedom of expression, association and assembly in relation to issues viewed as integral to the state's internal or external security. Human rights defenders, journalists seen as transcending red lines in reporting on the monarchy, proponents of self-determination in Western Sahara, and members of the unauthorized political organization Al-Adl wal-Ihsan faced harassment, arrests and prosecutions. Terrorism suspects were arrested and detained, at times incommunicado. Arrests and collective expulsions of migrants continued. Perpetrators of ongoing and past human rights violations enjoyed almost total impunity.

Background

In June, the Party of Modernity and Authenticity, founded by Fouad Ali el Himma, won most seats in local elections, followed by the Istiqlal Party led by Prime Minister Abbas El Fassi. In July, one opposition political figure was given a two-year prison term, and four opposition political figures and a journalist were sentenced to between 20 and 25 years in prison, in a highly politicized case known as the "Belliraj Affair", which was marred by allegations of torture and procedural irregularities.

The stalemate continued in negotiations on the status of Western Sahara between Morocco and the Polisario Front, which calls for an independent state in Western Sahara and runs a self-proclaimed government-in-exile in refugee camps in south-western Algeria. The UN Security Council extended the mandate of the UN Mission for the Referendum in Western Sahara until 30 April 2010 with no provision for human rights monitoring.

M

Freedom of expression

The authorities remained intolerant of views expressed or information published deemed offensive to the monarchy. They seized or suppressed editions of national and international publications containing opinion polls, articles or cartoons about the royal family, and closed down publications. They also prosecuted journalists under various provisions of the Penal Code and Press Code, both of which can be used to punish peaceful expression with imprisonment.

■ Khaled Gheddar and Tawfik Bouashrin, respectively a cartoonist and the director of the daily *Akhbar Al-Youm*, received suspended four-year prison sentences on 30 October for publishing a cartoon depicting the King's cousin, Prince Moulay Ismail, against a backdrop of the Moroccan flag. They were also heavily fined and required to pay damages for showing disrespect to the national flag and offending a member of the royal family. The sentences were confirmed on appeal in December. The Prince exempted both men from paying damages following their apology. Their newspaper was shut down by order of the authorities but reopened under another name.

Judicial proceedings were initiated against a number of publications that commented on the King's health.

■ On 15 October, Idriss Chahtane, publisher of the weekly *Almichaal*, was sentenced to one year in prison by the Court of First Instance of Rabat for publishing false information with "malicious intent". *Almichaal* was shut down in November after his sentence was confirmed on appeal.

Human rights defenders, journalists and others were prosecuted for denouncing corruption and criticizing the authorities.

■ Human rights defender Chekib El-Khiari was sentenced to three years' imprisonment and a heavy fine on 24 June for undermining or insulting public institutions and for violating financial regulations. The ruling was upheld by the Court of Appeal of Casablanca on 24 November. Chekib El-Khiari had publicly alleged that high-ranking officials were involved in drug-trafficking. He remained imprisoned at the end of the year.

Repression of dissent
Sahrawi activists

The authorities tightened restrictions on expression in favour of self-determination for the people of Western Sahara. Sahrawi human rights defenders, activists and others faced continuing harassment, including close surveillance, threats and assault at the hands of security officials, and prosecution on politically motivated charges, apparently to deter or punish them for expressing their views and documenting human rights.

■ Seven Sahrawi activists who visited the Tindouf camps in Algeria run by the Polisario Front were arrested on their return to Morocco on 8 October and referred for trial before the military court in Rabat. They included human rights defenders Brahim Dahane and Ali Salem Tamek, and Dakja Lashgar, a former victim of enforced disappearance. They were charged with threatening state security, including Morocco's "territorial integrity". They were still detained awaiting trial at the end of the year.

■ On 27 August, Ennaâma Asfari, co-president of the Committee for the Respect of Freedoms and Human Rights in Western Sahara, who lives in France, was sentenced to four months in prison and a fine for "contempt" of public officials on duty. His co-defendant, Ali El-Rubia, received a suspended prison term and a fine. Both alleged that they were assaulted by police during arrest on 14 August.

■ On 14 November, on her return to Laayoune from abroad, human rights defender Aminatou Haidar was expelled from the airport to the Canary Islands for allegedly renouncing her citizenship. She was allowed to return on 17 December, having spent over a month on hunger strike in Lanzarote airport to protest against her expulsion.

The authorities restricted the movement of Sahrawi activists and human rights defenders, preventing them from observing trials, documenting violations and meeting foreigners. Some were banned from travelling abroad and had their identification and travel documents confiscated.

■ In October, the authorities prevented five Sahrawi activists from travelling to Mauritania and confiscated their travel and identification documents without providing any reason for the travel ban.

Dozens of Sahrawis were prosecuted on violent conduct charges in connection with demonstrations held in 2009 or previous years; the court proceedings reportedly failed to satisfy international standards of fair trial. Some Sahrawis who advocated independence for Western Sahara were harassed and beaten by Moroccan security forces.

M

Al-Adl wal-Ihsan members

Members of Al-Adl wal-Ihsan continued to face harassment. The group's spokesperson, Nadia Yassine, had been awaiting trial since 2005 for allegedly defaming the monarchy. Her trial was again postponed, to January 2010.

■ In February, security forces assaulted Hakima Moaadab Aloui, a member of Al-Adl wal-Ihsan, when they raided the office in Témara of the Tanwir Association, whose membership includes Al-Adl wal-Ihsan activists. In December, the general prosecution decided that there was not enough evidence to press charges against a government official she had accused of beating her.

Counter-terror and security

In September, the official state news agency reported that a "terrorist" network had been broken up and 24 suspects arrested. Some suspects were reported to have been detained by officials of the Directorate for Surveillance of the Territory, a security force implicated in torturing and otherwise ill-treating detainees in previous years. Some of the detainees were held incommunicado for several weeks and in some cases their families were not officially informed of their arrest and whereabouts.

■ On 4 February, an appeal court in Rabat confirmed the 10-year prison sentence imposed on Said Boujaadia, a Guantánamo Bay detainee returned to Morocco by US authorities in May 2008. His lawyers withdrew from the case in protest at what they considered to be irregularities in the trial. One of them, Tawfik Moussaef, faced disciplinary proceedings for denouncing human rights violations committed against detained terrorism suspects. In April, the Supreme Court upheld lower court rulings that he had breached standards of the legal profession.

■ No steps were known to have been taken by the Moroccan authorities to investigate the allegations of Binyam Mohamed, released from Guantánamo Bay in February, that he had been tortured in Morocco, where he was secretly detained between July 2002 and January 2004.

Hundreds of Islamist prisoners sentenced after the 2003 Casablanca bombings demanded their release or judicial review of their trials, some staging hunger strikes to protest against their detention and prison conditions. Many were convicted on the basis of "confessions" reported to have been obtained under torture.

Migrants' rights

The authorities continued to arrest and expel foreign nationals suspected of being irregular migrants, often without considering their individual protection needs or allowing them to contest their expulsion. Some were reported to have been assaulted and ill-treated at the time of or following their arrest or when being expelled; some were reported to have been dumped at the border with Algeria or Mauritania without adequate food and water.

■ A 29-year-old migrant from Cameroon died on 1 January after being shot by Moroccan security officials when a group of about 50 migrants attempted to reach the fence between Morocco and the Spanish enclave of Melilla. Fourteen others in the group were arrested, beaten and eventually dumped on the border with Algeria near the city of Oujda. No investigation into these incidents was known to have taken place.

Refugees and asylum-seekers

Although Morocco is party to the 1951 Refugee Convention and its 1967 Protocol, the authorities did not issue residency cards or other necessary documents to refugees recognized by UNHCR, the UN refugee agency. On 15 June, a group of refugees staged a sit-in outside the UNHCR office in Rabat to protest against their conditions and call for their resettlement in other countries. Two weeks later, there were clashes between police and refugees when the latter refused to disperse. Five refugees were arrested, convicted of violent conduct, sentenced to one month in prison and fined. They were cleared of the charge of irregular stay. They were reported to have been beaten at the time of arrest.

Freedom of religion

The authorities prevented members of the Alternative Movement for Individual Freedom from publicly breaking the Ramadan fast on 13 September in Mohammadia. At least six members of the group were reportedly arrested or called in for questioning, although none was formally charged. The general prosecution in Rabat banned from travelling abroad two of the group's organizers, Ibtissame Lashgar and Zineb El-Razoui, both of them women.

In March, after the authorities accused Iranian diplomats in Rabat of carrying out activities inimical to the "religious fundamentals" of Morocco, there were reports that a number of suspected Shi'a Muslims

M

were questioned, Shi'a documents were seized, and a school for Iraqi children was closed.

Transitional justice

A list of cases of enforced disappearances investigated by the Equity and Reconciliation Commission was still not published. The Commission, established to investigate gross human rights violations committed between 1956 and 1999, completed its work in November 2005 and the list was due to be published by the Advisory Council on Human Rights, tasked to follow up its work. In September, the Advisory Council said that 17,012 survivors and victims' families had received financial compensation as a result of the Commission's decisions and 2,886 people had been issued with health care cards. However, victims and survivors continued to be denied effective access to justice and the perpetrators had still not been held to account. In June, the UN Working Group on Enforced or Involuntary Disappearances visited Morocco. On 20 August, the King called for judicial reform, as recommended by the Commission, but no reform measures were implemented.

Polisario camps

No steps were known to have been taken by the Polisario Front to address the impunity of those accused of committing human rights abuses in the camps in the 1970s and 1980s.

Amnesty International visit/reports

🚌 Amnesty International's Secretary General and other delegates visited Morocco in March and discussed human rights with the Ministers of Justice and Interior.

📄 No more half measures – addressing enforced disappearances in Morocco and Western Sahara
(MDE 29/005/2009)

📄 Morocco/Western Sahara: Expulsion of human rights defender reflects growing intolerance (MDE 29/012/2009)

MOZAMBIQUE

REPUBLIC OF MOZAMBIQUE

Head of state:	Armando Guebuza
Head of government:	Luisa Diogo
Death penalty:	abolitionist for all crimes
Population:	22.9 million
Life expectancy:	47.8 years
Under-5 mortality (m/f):	162/144 per 1,000
Adult literacy:	44.4 per cent

Police used excessive force during demonstrations and to apprehend suspects. Thirteen detainees died of asphyxiation in an overcrowded police cell; two police officers were held responsible for the deaths. A senior police officer was convicted of murder for an extrajudicial execution committed in 2007.

Background

At least 120 people died as a result of cholera between January and March. In March, the Red Cross suspended its activities in Mongicual district in the northern province of Nampula after three Red Cross workers and two police officers were killed by residents in a violent protest over cholera treatment. Residents accused the Red Cross workers, who were putting chlorine in wells, of contaminating their water supplies with cholera.

A new political party, the Democratic Movement of Mozambique (Movimento Democrático de Moçambique, MDM), was formed in March when the Mayor of Beira city, Daviz Simango, split from the main opposition party, the Mozambique National Resistance (Resistência Nacional Moçambicana, RENAMO). Daviz Simango was one of three presidential candidates in elections held in October, which were won by the incumbent, President Armando Guebuza, and the ruling party, the Front for the Liberation of Mozambique (Frente da Libertação de Moçambique, FRELIMO). There were sporadic acts of violence during the election campaign, most involving the destruction by party activists of their opponents' campaign material. Two police officers were fined by the Murrupula District Court for destroying election posters belonging to RENAMO, and police were criticized for failing to respond to acts of violence by members of FRELIMO. International and national election observers noted irregularities

M

during the elections, including incidents of ballot box stuffing and invalidation of votes cast for opposition candidates. The European Union observer mission, however, believed this did not significantly affect the results.

One of the country's biggest corruption trials started in November. The former Minister of Transport and four former officials of the Mozambique Airports Company, ADM, were accused of stealing nearly US$2 million from the company between 2005 and October 2008.

Police

■ In June, the Maputo Provincial Court in Matola city convicted a senior police officer of the murder of Abranches Penicelo in August 2007. The police officer was sentenced to 22 years' imprisonment and ordered to pay compensation of 500,000Mtn (about US$19,000) to Abranches Penicelo's five children. However, five other officers accused of involvement in the killing were neither charged nor tried. Two other police officers allegedly involved had since died. Following years of police harassment, Abranches Penicelo had been beaten, injected with a toxic substance, shot in the neck, set on fire and left for dead by eight police officers.

There were reports of police officers co-operating with criminals, including by providing them with firearms and police uniforms.

■ Two convicted murderers who escaped from Maputo city police cells in December 2008 were rearrested. Samuel Januário "Samito" Nhare was rearrested in January and Aníbal "Anibalzinho" dos Santos Júnior in August. A third, Luís "Todinho" de Jesus Tomás, who had escaped with the others, was found shot dead in Matola city, Maputo, in January. "Anibalzinho" alleged that their escape had been facilitated by the police.

■ In February, three police officers were arrested on suspicion of collaborating with criminals.

Excessive use of force

Police continued to use excessive force, especially when apprehending suspects and when controlling demonstrations.

■ In January, plain-clothed police shot at four unnamed men who were reportedly attempting to rob a shop selling electrical appliances in the Baixa area of Maputo. The police officers opened fire on two of the suspects as they emerged from the shop, killing one

instantly and injuring the other in the leg. The two other suspects reportedly escaped. Police authorities told Amnesty International that the police officers acted in self-defence when the alleged robbers shot at them. However, they also stated that it was agents of the private security company guarding the shop who had opened fire. No investigation was carried out.

■ In April, a police officer shot and wounded two striking workers at the construction site of the Mozambique national stadium. About 700 workers were striking over low wages, lack of overtime pay and mistreatment by the project's managers. The Maputo city police stated that an investigation would be carried out, but no further information had been released by the end of the year.

■ In September, police fired live ammunition while trying to disperse demonstrations at a sugar plantation in the Marromeu district of Sofala province, injuring two workers. The demonstrations reportedly turned violent when strikers destroyed an ambulance and motorbike, put up barricades and burned part of the sugar plantation. Workers at the sugar plantation were striking over wages. No investigation was known to have been carried out by the end of the year.

Deaths in custody

In March, 13 people died of asphyxiation in an overcrowded police cell in Mongicual. The detainees had been arrested along with others following riots over cholera treatment in the district. In August, the Angoche District Court convicted the officer on duty at the time and the district police commander of manslaughter and sentenced them both to one year's imprisonment. The court acquitted the district head of the criminal investigation police due to lack of evidence.

Amnesty International visit/reports

▨ Amnesty International delegates visited Mozambique in May.

▨ Briefing to the Parliament (assembly) of Mozambique (AFR 41/002/2009)

▨ "I can't believe in justice any more": Obstacles to justice for unlawful killings by police in Mozambique (AFR 41/004/2009)

M

MYANMAR

UNION OF MYANMAR

Head of state:	Senior General Than Shwe
Head of government:	General Thein Sein
Death penalty:	abolitionist in practice
Population:	50 million
Life expectancy:	61.2 years
Under 5-mortality (m/f):	120/102 per 1,000
Adult literacy:	89.9 per cent

Almost 2,200 political prisoners remained behind bars. Most were held in abysmal conditions and many suffered from poor physical and psychological health. The authorities arrested Daw Aung San Suu Kyi, General Secretary of the National League for Democracy (NLD), the main opposition party, and sentenced her to 18 months' further house arrest. Fighting intensified between the army and an aligned ethnic minority Karen armed group, and armed opposition group the Karen National Liberation Army (KNLA). This was accompanied by serious human rights violations and led to thousands seeking refuge in neighbouring Thailand. The authorities continued to target ethnic minority activists involved in various forms of resistance to government policies, practices, and projects.

Background

In August, Daw Aung San Suu Kyi was permitted to meet a US Senator, and in October met with her government liaison officer for the first time since January 2008. In November, she met a high-level mission from the US.

In April, the State Peace and Development Council (SPDC, the military government) proposed that the ethnic minority armed groups that had agreed ceasefires with the government become border guard forces under SPDC command. This was in preparation for national elections in 2010 – the first since 1990 – but negotiations and fighting with such armed groups followed throughout the year. By the end of the year only nine groups agreed to the proposal, most citing a feared loss of territory or control as reasons for their refusal.

Relief, rehabilitation, and reconstruction in the wake of the 2008 Cyclone Nargis continued, while serious food shortages struck Chin and Rakhine

States. Myanmar began building a fence on the border with Bangladesh, which increased tensions between the two countries. The international community raised concerns that the Myanmar government may be seeking nuclear capability.

Political prisoners

Although in February and September the government released more than 13,000 prisoners, there were only 158 known political prisoners among them, including five prisoners of conscience, Ma Khin Khin Leh, U Saw Naing Naing, U Soe Han, Ko Aung Tun, and Khaing Kaung San. These individuals had all been imprisoned for approximately 10 years. At least 50 people were arrested between the September releases and the end of the year and almost 2,200 political prisoners remained.

■ In January, a court sentenced Bo Min Yu Ko (Phyo Gyi), a member of the All Burma Federation of Students Union, to 104 years in prison under various charges including six counts under the Immigration Act.

■ In May, after an unidentified American man entered the property of Daw Aung San Suu Kyi, the authorities arrested her for violating the conditions of the house arrest she had been under since 2003. After a partly closed trial in Yangon's Insein prison, she was sentenced to three years of hard labour, immediately reduced to an additional 18 months of house arrest.

■ In September, the authorities detained Kyaw Zaw Lwin (Nyi Nyi Aung), a man from Myanmar with US citizenship, when he arrived in Myanmar to visit his family – four members of which are prisoners of conscience. While in custody, security officers tortured Kyaw Zaw Lwin and denied him medical treatment. In October, he was tried on charges of fraud and forgery. The authorities publicly stated that Kyaw Zaw Lwin could be sentenced to death if convicted.

Prison conditions

The authorities continued to send and hold political prisoners in prisons far away from their families and friends, despite telling the UN Human Rights Council in March that prisoners receive visits and necessary health treatments. At least 220 political prisoners had been moved to remote prisons since November 2008, making it extremely difficult for families to provide essential assistance. Conditions in prisons continued to be extremely poor, including inadequate food, water and medical care. Authorities frequently kept

M

political prisoners in solitary confinement.

■ In March, Hla Myo Naung, an activist imprisoned nearly 1,500km from his home, was in danger of completely losing his eyesight. He had already gone blind in one eye after being denied specialist medical treatment.

■ Beginning in March, Ko Htay Kywe, a student leader held more than 1,100km from his family, was held incommunicado and in solitary confinement. Prison authorities threatened other prisoners with severe punishment if they spoke to him.

■ In March, Su Su Nway, an NLD campaigner, was hospitalized in a prison over 1,000km from her home. Prison authorities gave her mental health medication which caused her condition to worsen. She was kept in solitary confinement on an intermittent basis as punishment for various offences and denied family visits.

■ In May, Zarganar, a comedian and activist held over 1,400km from his home, was in urgent need of medical attention for various health problems, including an enlarged heart. He lost consciousness in April and was only taken to the hospital 10 days later. Following a visit to Myitkyina prison on 7 December, Zarganar's sister-in-law confirmed that he was suffering from the skin disease pruritus.

Targeting ethnic minorities

The government continued to target ethnic minority activists for their work on political, environmental, and/or religious issues, and for their real or imputed support of ethnic political and armed groups.

■ In January, the authorities arrested, beat, and imprisoned at least 19 Rakhine men and women for possessing documents on human rights and democracy and for forming a political organization. They were sentenced to prison terms of between five and seven years.

■ In January, soldiers beat a Shan woman several times after accusing her of giving rice to Shan insurgents and acting as a guide for them.

■ In February, police arrested two local Kachin youths for surfing banned websites on Myanmar.

■ In March and early April, authorities increased their surveillance of the ceasefire group the New Mon State Party (NMSP), throughout Mon State, questioning them regularly about contacting the media.

■ In June, authorities in Rakhine State arrested Soe Soe on charges of contacting opposition groups in exile,

and sentenced her to six years' imprisonment.

In Rakhine State, systematic persecution of ethnic minority Rohingyas continued unabated, causing thousands to flee to Bangladesh, Thailand or Malaysia, often on boats. In January, the Myanmar navy intercepted one such boat that had recently left Myanmar, and held the 78 Rohingyas on board for six days and beat them severely, before sending them back out to sea. In April, at the regional meetings of the Bali Process, the government publicly refused to recognize Rohingyas either as an existing ethnic minority or as citizens of Myanmar.

Cyclone Nargis-related arrests and imprisonment

At least 29 people who had assisted in private relief work after Cyclone Nargis struck Myanmar in May 2008 remained in prison for activity deemed political by the authorities. At least 18 of them were sentenced to between 10 and 35 years in prison.

■ In October, the authorities arrested at least 10 people for accepting relief donations from abroad. At least seven were members of the local Lin Let Kye ("Shining Star") organization, devoted to relief and social activism.

Armed conflict and displacement

The Myanmar army continued to attack various ethnic minority armed groups, often targeting civilians and causing large-scale displacement. In June, attacks by the army and the government-supported Democratic Karen Buddhist Army (DKBA) internally displaced thousands of ethnic minority Karen civilians and caused 4,800 refugees to flee to Thailand. The DKBA forcibly recruited people during the offensive for both portering and military service, destroyed abandoned villages, and planted land mines in the wake of the exodus.

In August, the most intensive attacks in 10 years against the armed opposition Shan State Army-South and Shan civilians forced more than 10,000 people to relocate; most were internally displaced. The attacks were characterized by extrajudicial executions and sexual abuse. Also in August, the army attacked the Myanmar National Democratic Alliance Army, causing more than 30,000 mostly ethnic minority Kokang to flee into China, almost all of whom subsequently returned to Myanmar. Internal displacement increased to over 500,000 people.

M

Development-related violations

The army committed human rights violations in connection with official development projects, including forced labour, killings, beatings, land confiscation, forced farming, restrictions on movement, and confiscation of property. Battalions providing security for the Yadana, Yetagun and Kanbauk-Myiang Kalay natural gas pipelines in Tanintharyi Division and Kayin State forced civilians to work on barracks, roads and sentry huts. Authorities also confiscated land without compensation in relation to the Shwe gas project in Rakhine State, and targeted villagers suspected of opposing or questioning the project. Authorities arrested, detained and interrogated local villagers, forcing some to flee the area.

Child soldiers

The Burmese army and government-backed militias continued to systematically recruit, use and imprison child soldiers, both directly and through recruiting agents. Several ethnic minority armed groups also continued recruiting children. The government failed to align its action plan against the recruitment and use of child soldiers with international standards, despite a verbal commitment in September 2007 to do so in the "near future". The government took no steps towards developing a formal disarmament, demobilization and reintegration programme that would ensure that all child soldiers are released and returned to their families.

The ILO continued to receive and address reports of child soldier recruitment by officials. By the end of the year, the ILO had received 131 complaints concerning under-age recruitment since February 2007. Fifty-nine children had been discharged from the military. The authorities continued to maintain that children only join the military voluntarily, and typically punished perpetrators of under-age recruitment with only a reprimand. The authorities also released from prison and discharged three of four known child soldiers who had been sentenced and imprisoned for desertion.

International scrutiny

In January and February, the UN Secretary-General's Special Adviser visited Myanmar and briefed the UN Security Council the following month. In February, the UN Special Rapporteur on the situation of human rights in Myanmar visited the country, and presented a report in March to the UN Human Rights Council. Also in February, the Thai Foreign Minister conducted informal talks with the Karen National Union (KNU) with the permission of the Myanmar government. The UN High Commissioner for Refugees visited Myanmar in March. In both April and June, meetings of the Bali process, aimed at deterring human trafficking and smuggling and preventing illegal migration in Asia and the Pacific, were held and the situation of the Rohingya in Myanmar was discussed.

Following the arrest of Daw Aung San Suu Kyi in May, the UN Security Council issued a press statement expressing concern and calling for the release of all political prisoners. ASEAN, the UN High Commissioner for Human Rights, and the UN Special Rapporteur on the situation of human rights in Myanmar also issued statements on her arrest. The EU tightened its economic sanctions against Myanmar.

In June, the UN Secretary-General visited Myanmar. The UN Representative for Children and Armed Conflict visited Myanmar in July. In August, the UN discussed with the government the development of a joint action plan to address children in armed conflict under Security Council Resolutions 1612 and 1882. In October, the UN Security Council Working Group issued its conclusions on Children and Armed Conflict in Myanmar in accordance with the resolutions. In December, the UN General Assembly adopted a resolution on the human rights situation in Myanmar.

After extending its list of individuals and business networks subjected to targeted financial sanctions in January, and announcing in February that it would conduct a review of its policy on Myanmar, in September the USA concluded that it would maintain its economic sanctions but begin dialogue with the Myanmar government. In August, a US Senator visited Myanmar. In November the US government sent a high-level mission.

Death penalty

In October, a court in Laogai, Shan State, sentenced at least one child soldier to death for killing a person who may also have been a child soldier.

M

Amnesty International reports

▤ Open letter to the governments of Bangladesh, India, Indonesia, Malaysia, Myanmar and Thailand on the plight of the Rohingyas (ASA 01/001/2009)

▤ Myanmar: Daw Aung San Suu Kyi's new sentence "shameful", 11 August 2009

NAMIBIA

REPUBLIC OF NAMIBIA

Head of state and government:	**Hifikepunye Pohamba**
Death penalty:	**abolitionist for all crimes**
Population:	**2.2 million**
Life expectancy:	**60.4 years**
Under-5 mortality (m/f):	**58/45 per 1,000**
Adult literacy:	**88 per cent**

Presidential and National Council elections were held in November amid reports of inter-party violence. A long-running treason trial continued with no sign of concluding.

Background

In the run-up to the presidential and National Council elections held on 27 and 28 November, members of the ruling South West Africa People's Organization (SWAPO) and opposition parties clashed. SWAPO members were accused of disrupting campaign meetings of other political parties.

■ On 27 October, about 300 SWAPO supporters blocked supporters of the Rally for Democracy and Progress (RDP) from campaigning in Outapi, Omusati region. SWAPO activists claimed that RDP members had used provocative language when seeking to recruit supporters.

■ On 8 November, RDP and SWAPO supporters threw stones at each other after SWAPO supporters confronted RDP activists who had arrived in Outapi to attend a rally. Three people were arrested during the clashes.

Caprivi treason trial

The treason trial of detainees arrested following the 1999 attacks by a secessionist group, the Caprivi Liberation Army, continued with no indication that it

was near conclusion. Most of the 117 detainees spent their 10th year in custody. The trial started in 2004.

Discovery of mass graves

Mass graves were discovered in northern Namibia. Some of the bodies were suspected to be those of about 30 San-speaking men who allegedly disappeared from military custody in western Caprivi after they were detained on suspicion of being part of the 1999 secessionist attacks. The National Society for Human Rights published the names of some of the victims.

NEPAL

FEDERAL DEMOCRATIC REPUBLIC OF NEPAL

Head of state:	**Ram Baran Yadav**
Head of government:	**Madhav Kumar Nepal (replaced Pushpa Kamal Dahal in May)**
Death penalty:	**abolitionist for all crimes**
Population:	**29.3 million**
Life expectancy:	**66.3 years**
Under-5 mortality (m/f):	**52/55 per 1,000**
Adult literacy:	**56.5 per cent**

Nepali human rights defenders reported hundreds of killings and abductions by state forces and armed groups. Public insecurity escalated as a growing number of armed groups took violent action against civilians. The police used unnecessary and excessive force to dispel political and rights-based demonstrations. Torture of detainees was widely reported.

Background

Commitments made in Nepal's 2006 Comprehensive Peace Accord to uphold civil, political, economic, social and cultural rights remained unfulfilled. Political division and proliferation of armed groups threatened the peace process. The ruling Communist Party of Nepal-Maoist (CPN-M) government, headed by Prime Minister Pushpa Kamal Dahal, fell in May and was replaced by a coalition government led by Madhav Kumar Nepal. Maoist party supporters staged protests and general strikes, including a blockade of parliament. Efforts to draft a new constitution made little progress. Despite the state's declared support for the UN Draft Principles on eliminating discrimination based on work or descent (which addresses caste inequalities), discrimination against Dalits and women persisted with impunity.

Transitional justice

Efforts to establish a Truth and Reconciliation Commission (TRC) stalled. Nepali critics of a draft TRC bill, pending since 2007, noted shortcomings, among them the proposed commission's lack of independence from political influence, inadequate witness protection, and a proposal to grant it the power to recommend amnesty for perpetrators of serious human rights violations.

Enforced disappearances

Both sides of the conflict that ended in 2006 subjected people to enforced disappearances. According to the ICRC, more than 1,300 people remained unaccounted for by year's end. A draft bill criminalizing enforced disappearance lapsed in June, and a Commission of Inquiry into disappearances was not set up. The proposed bill failed both to employ a definition of enforced disappearance consistent with international law, and to recognize enforced disappearance as a possible crime against humanity. On 30 August, Amnesty International issued a joint memorandum with eight prominent Nepali and international organizations calling for improvements to bring the draft in line with international standards.

Impunity

Impunity continued for perpetrators of human rights abuses during the conflict – no cases were tried before a civilian court. Survivors of violations reported that police refused to file complaints or investigate cases. The authorities failed to implement court-ordered arrests of military personnel accused of human rights violations.
■ In December, the government promoted a high ranking army officer implicated in human rights violations, including torture, arbitrary detention and enforced disappearances, during the conflict. The UN High Commissioner for Human Rights expressed particular concern about this, and opposed his promotion pending investigation.

Police abuse

Police continued to employ unnecessary and excessive force to quell demonstrations, including beating protesters with *lathis* (long wooden sticks) and gun butts. Torture and other ill-treatment of detainees, and killings of people suspected of being affiliated with armed groups in faked "encounters", were reported.

Abuses by armed groups

Over 100 armed groups operated in Nepal's Terai region and committed human rights abuses, including abductions of members of the Pahadi (hill) community and bomb attacks on public places.
■ On 9 April, police shot and killed Parasuram Kori, after members of the leftist Terai-based armed group Janatantrik Terai Mukti Morcha (JTMM-J) fired at a police patrol team. The victim's mother said that her son and two others had been abducted by the JTMM-J three days earlier.

The Young Communist League, the youth wing of the CPN-M, were also responsible for killings, assaults and abductions.

Child soldiers

Over 2,500 former child soldiers remained in cantonments (military areas where, under the Comprehensive Peace Accord, the CPN-M had agreed to be quartered). In July, the government announced plans to discharge them and more than 1,000 "illegal recruits" inducted after 2006, a process that was to finish by November. But the two sides failed to reach an agreement on a discharge and rehabilitation plan, which remained stalled as of mid-October. Releases had not commenced by the end of the year, but were announced for early January 2010.

Torture and other ill-treatment

National laws providing safeguards against torture fell short of international standards, and remained inadequately implemented.
■ In July, police tortured Bhakta Rai and Sushan Limbu after the latter was arrested on a minor charge in Urlabari, south-eastern Nepal. Police beat them in a jail cell, then stripped them to their underwear in the street, assaulted them with iron rods and forced them to crawl on their knees and elbows over stony ground. Both sustained serious injuries. Following a successful court petition, the men were granted access to lawyers and

provided with medical care, but officers involved in their torture were not suspended, and no investigation was launched.

Violence against women and girls

Women human rights defenders were threatened, assaulted and killed. Dowry deaths and sexual violence continued. Legislative weakness and inadequate policing obstructed prosecution of domestic and sexual violence cases. Police refused to record cases of violence against women, or to provide information to women human rights defenders on the status of investigations.

■ Uma Singh, a journalist for Radio Today FM and member of the Women's Human Rights Defender Network, was attacked on 11 January by a group of armed men. She was severely mutilated and died on her way to hospital in Kathmandu.

In August, Amnesty International launched an action demanding that the Prime Minister ensure accountability in the case of Maina Sunuwar, a 15-year-old girl who was tortured to death by members of the Nepal Army in February 2004. In December, one of the accused, Major Niranjan Basnet, was expelled from a UN peacekeeping mission and repatriated to Nepal. Amnesty International called on the Nepal army to hand him over to civilian authorities.

Legal and institutional developments

The government stalled ratification of the Rome Statute of the International Criminal Court despite a commitment from Nepal's then Minister of Foreign Affairs. In July, Amnesty International submitted more than 13,000 appeal letters to the new Minister of Foreign Affairs Sujata Koirala, calling for the government to proceed with ratification. The Minister agreed to begin the process, but by year's end no progress had been made.

NETHERLANDS

KINGDOM OF THE NETHERLANDS

Head of state:	Queen Beatrix
Head of government:	Jan Peter Balkenende
Death penalty:	abolitionist for all crimes
Population:	16.6 million
Life expectancy:	79.8 years
Under-5 mortality (m/f):	6/5 per 1,000

Asylum-seekers were transferred to Greece, despite continuing concern about their lack of access to a fair asylum-determination procedure there. Accelerated asylum-determination procedures, detentions of asylum-seekers and migrants, the extension of pre-trial detention and the denial of legal assistance during police questioning of criminal suspects gave rise to concern.

Refugees, asylum-seekers and migrants

Following a court ruling in May, the government resumed transfers of asylum-seekers to Greece for determination of their asylum claims under the "Dublin II" Regulation, despite serious concerns about asylum-determination procedures and detention conditions in Greece.

In June, the government proposed amendments to the Aliens Act. If implemented, all asylum claims would be processed within eight days, including in complex cases. In July, the UN Human Rights Committee (HRC) expressed concern that existing "accelerated procedures", allowing determination of asylum applications within 48 working hours, and the proposed eight-day procedure, might not allow asylum-seekers to substantiate their claims adequately, putting them at risk of forcible return.

According to government figures, thousands of irregular migrants and asylum-seekers were taken into immigration detention centres during the year and held on a remand regime. Those detained included vulnerable individuals, such as trafficking and torture survivors, with little consideration given to alternatives to detention. Even unaccompanied minors, whom the government asserted had no legitimate claim to remain or reside in the Netherlands, continued to be detained.

Some people whose immigration detention began

in 2008 were held for more than 12 months, as Dutch law provides no maximum time limit on immigration detention.

Counter-terror and security

In March, the Council of Europe Commissioner for Human Rights expressed concern at measures adopted by the authorities with the stated aim of combating terrorism, including: vague and broad definitions of crimes that may lead to unjustifiable restrictions on human rights and freedoms; provisions under the Investigation and Prosecution of Terrorist Offences Act permitting detention on mere suspicion of a "terrorist crime"; and an extension of maximum pre-trial detention from 90 days to two years for people charged with "terrorism offences".

The HRC expressed concern about the denial of legal counsel for criminal suspects during police questioning and possible pre-trial detention periods of up to two years. It criticized certain provisions of the Witness Identity Protection Act, which allow the defence to be excluded during the questioning of witnesses whose identity has been withheld from the defence for "national security reasons". It also expressed concern about the power of local mayors to issue administrative "disturbance orders", allegedly to combat terrorism, without judicial authorization or oversight of the measures imposed under such orders.

Guantánamo Bay detainees

In July, the government stated that it would consider accepting the transfer of some individuals detained at the US naval base at Guantánamo Bay.

Discrimination

The Council of Europe Commissioner for Human Rights expressed concern about racist, anti-Semitic and other intolerant tendencies in the Netherlands, notably intolerance against Muslims.

In June, legislation was passed obliging municipalities from 1 January 2010 to collect data on discriminatory incidents, and provide access to a support service for those who wished to report discrimination.

NEW ZEALAND

NEW ZEALAND
Head of state:	Queen Elizabeth II represented by Anand Satyanand
Head of government:	John Key
Death penalty:	abolitionist for all crimes
Population:	4.3 million
Life expectancy:	80.1 years
Under-5 mortality (m/f):	6/5 per 1,000

The government indicated a willingness to support the UN Declaration on the Rights of Indigenous Peoples. Asylum-seekers were put at risk of persecution by the passenger screening process of the new Immigration Act. Maori were disproportionally represented both among those arrested and processed by the criminal justice system and among prisoners.

Indigenous Peoples' rights

In its Universal Periodic Review (UPR) in July, the government stated that it "would like to move to support" the UN Declaration on the Rights of Indigenous Peoples as long as it did not interfere with the current domestic framework for resolving Indigenous Peoples' rights claims.

Concerns were raised that Maori were being discriminated against by the Foreshore and Seabed Act 2004, which was passed to settle Maori's claim to foreshore and seabed title. These concerns prompted the establishment of an independent Ministerial Review Panel which recommended that the Act be repealed and new legislation drafted. Maori rights under the Treaty of Waitangi required new legislation to be enforced.

Refugees and asylum-seekers

In November, the Immigration Act came into force, incorporating the passenger processing system. The Act empowered the chief executive of the Immigration Department to refuse a person permission to board an aircraft to travel to New Zealand without giving a reason. This could expose asylum-seekers to harm if they were at risk of persecution in their own countries. The Act also denied failed applicants access to judicial review.

Prison conditions

In September, the Department of Corrections announced that it would be introducing bunk beds in 2010 on a permanent basis even though they already had 21 per cent of beds in shared cells, in contravention of international standards on the treatment of prisoners. In July the Department of Corrections announced that prison cells built from modified shipping containers would be incorporated into the prison system from March 2010 to cope with rising prisoner numbers.

The Corrections (Contract Management of Prisons) Amendment Act 2009 allowed for the privatization of prisons. Concerns were raised about the possible reduction of accountability that could occur within privately managed prisons.

There were disproportionately high numbers of Maori arrested, processed by the criminal justice system and imprisoned.

Legal, constitutional or institutional developments

During its UPR, the Government indicated that it would ratify the Optional Protocol to the UN Convention on the Rights of the Child and become a party to the International Convention for the Protection of All Persons from Enforced Disappearance.

The New Zealand Bill of Rights Act 1990 (BORA) did not have protected legal status, which allowed for the possible enactment of legislation contrary to its provisions. The BORA did not incorporate all the rights provided in the International Covenant on Civil and Political Rights or the International Covenant on Economic, Social and Cultural Rights.

NICARAGUA

REPUBLIC OF NICARAGUA

Head of state and government:	Daniel Ortega Saavedra
Death penalty:	abolitionist for all crimes
Population:	5.7 million
Life expectancy:	72.7 years
Under-5 mortality (m/f):	29/22 per 1,000
Adult literacy:	78 per cent

The total ban on all forms of abortion remained in force. Two thirds of rape victims whose cases were recorded between January and August 2009 were under 18. Intimidation and attacks on government critics increased, raising fears of curbs on the rights to freedom of expression and association.

Background

There were clashes between supporters of the ruling Sandinista National Liberation Front (Frente Sandinista de Liberación Nacional, FSLN) and government critics throughout the year.

Nicaragua remained one of a handful of states in the Americas not to have signed the Rome Statute of the International Criminal Court.

In November a new post of Special Ombudsman for Sexual Diversity was created within the Office of the Human Rights Ombudsman.

Sexual and reproductive rights

The total ban on all forms of abortion remained in force. Nicaraguan Ministry of Health figures showed an increase in maternal deaths during the first 19 weeks of 2009 as compared with the same period in 2008, rising from 20 to 33. Some 16 per cent of the 33 deaths in 2009 were due to complications following unsafe abortions; no such deaths had been recorded in the comparable period in 2008, before the law prohibiting all forms of abortion came into effect.

In May the UN Committee against Torture stated that it was "deeply concerned" that the Nicaraguan government had taken no steps to repeal the law, despite concerns having previously been expressed by three other UN committees.

The Supreme Court of Justice failed to rule on an appeal lodged in July 2008 challenging the constitutionality of the law prohibiting all forms of abortion, despite having committed itself to doing so by 6 May 2009.

Violence against women and girls

Official efforts to combat violence against women and girls were ineffective. Statistics from the Women and Children's Police Unit stated that 1,259 rapes were reported between January and August. Of these, two thirds involved girls aged 17 or under.

■ In August, a 13-year-old girl was stabbed to death with a bayonet by her stepfather, who had been released from prison three days earlier. He had been sentenced to 13 years' imprisonment for the aggravated rape which resulted in the girl's pregnancy, but was released on grounds of ill health after serving only eight months. No notice of his release was given to the girl or her family. There was reportedly no investigation into the court's decision to release him.

Human rights defenders

Women human rights defenders working to promote women's rights and sexual and reproductive rights were harassed by officials.

■ In October, journalist and women's rights activist Patricia Orozco and two colleagues were stopped by police as they were returning from leading a training course for local women's rights promoters. The officers claimed that the women had fled from a previous checkpoint without permission. A debate ensued during which Patricia Orozco was arrested. She was taken to the police station in León and detained for four hours before being released without charge.

The next day an article about the incident was published in the government online magazine *El 19*. The article described the Autonomous Women's Movement, to which Patricia Orozco and one of her two colleagues belong, as "evil" and stated that Patricia Orozco and her colleagues "of uncertain gender" had been returning from a party "where men are not allowed".

Freedom of expression and association

There was a series of incidents involving attacks on journalists, government critics and civil society activists.

■ In November, pro-government supporters in Managua attacked a group of protesters demonstrating against corruption and curbs on freedom of expression.

FSLN supporters threw stones at them, breaking the glass entrance door of a police station where protesters had taken refuge. None of those involved in the attack had been arrested by the end of the year.

The Civil Co-ordinating Committee (Coordinadora Civil, CC), a national network of civil society groups, reported attacks and intimidation of its members by FSLN supporters.

■ In August, CC members were attacked on their way to a cultural event after discussing a proposal for alternatives to the government's existing social and economic policies. More than 30 CC members were reportedly injured.

■ Leonor Martínez, a 24-year-old member of the CC, was attacked by three armed men in October as she returned home from a press conference in Managua on human rights violations. They beat her, breaking her arm in several places, and threatened that if she carried on working with the CC they would kill her and her family. The men had allegedly been involved in previous attacks on CC members. An investigation into the attack was opened. In November, Leonor Martínez received telephone threats which referred to her work with the CC. By the end of the year, no one had been brought to justice for any of the attacks on CC members.

Amnesty International visit/reports

🚍 Amnesty International delegates visited Nicaragua in July.

📄 The total abortion ban in Nicaragua: Women's lives and health endangered, medical professionals criminalized (AMR 43/001/2009)

📄 The impact of the complete ban of abortion in Nicaragua: Briefing to the United Nations Committee against Torture (AMR 43/005/2009)

📄 Nicaragua: Submission to the UN Universal Periodic Review (AMR 43/010/2009)

NIGER

REPUBLIC OF NIGER

Head of state:	Mamadou Tandja
Head of government:	Ali Badjo Gamatié (replaced Seyni Oumarou in October)
Death penalty:	abolitionist in practice
Population:	15.3 million
Life expectancy:	50.8 years
Under-5 mortality (m/f):	171/173 per 1,000
Adult literacy:	28.7 per cent

Numerous protests took place against a constitutional amendment allowing a third term for the President. In response, the President dissolved key institutions and granted himself emergency powers. The security forces harassed and detained political leaders, journalists and human rights activists. The government and Tuareg-led armed opposition signed a peace agreement.

Background

In May, President Tandja dissolved Parliament after the Constitutional Court rejected attempts to amend the Constitution by referendum to allow him a third term. In June, he dissolved the Constitutional Court and granted himself emergency powers. In August, the President overwhelmingly won the referendum (boycotted by opposition parties) to change the Constitution. This resulted in protests led by opposition parties, civil society activists and trade unions who denounced a "constitutional coup". In October, the ruling party won parliamentary elections (also boycotted by the opposition), despite calls by the Economic Community of West African States (ECOWAS) to postpone the vote. As a result, Niger was suspended from ECOWAS.

In April, two Canadian diplomats abducted in Niger in December 2008 by al-Qa'ida in the Islamic Maghreb (AQIM) were released in Mali.

In October, several Tuareg armed groups signed a comprehensive peace agreement with the government, with all Tuareg factions agreeing to disarm. As a result, the state of emergency, in place in the Agadez region since 2007, was lifted in November.

Repression of dissent

The authorities repressed demonstrations against the referendum and President Tandja's rule, and arrested several political opponents.

■ In June, Mamadou Issoufou, former member of parliament and leader of the main opposition party, the Nigerien Party for Democracy and Socialism (Parti nigérien pour la démocratie et le socialisme, PNDS), was briefly detained, allegedly after calling on security forces to stop obeying President Tandja's orders.

■ In July, opposition activist Alassane Karfi was arrested and sent to Koutoukalé high-security prison after criticizing the referendum process on television. He was charged with "provoking the creation of a crowd" and was released on bail in October.

Human rights defenders

Human rights activists, notably members of the United Front for the Protection of Democracy (Front uni pour la sauvegarde des acquis démocratiques, FUSAD), were repeatedly harassed by the police when protesting against the constitutional amendment. Demonstrations that were mostly peaceful were dispersed with tear gas.

■ In August, Marou Amadou, a human rights activist and President of FUSAD, was arrested for calling for protests against the government. Following a judicial decision, he was released the next day but immediately rearrested. He was charged with "running an unauthorized association". He was released on bail in September.

Freedom of expression – the media

President Tandja issued a decree in July which could be used to censor information deemed to "endanger state security or public order" and which swept aside the authority of the national media regulatory agency.

■ In April, Seyni Amadou, director of Dounia TV, and another journalist, Elhadj Idi Abdou, were briefly arrested and charged with "broadcasting false information" after criticizing French President Nicolas Sarkozy's visit to Niger. In June, the Dounia media group was closed down for several days for airing a statement from the opposition accusing President Tandja of staging a coup.

■ In August, Abdoulaye Tiémogo, the publishing manager of the independent newspaper *Le Canard Déchaîné*, was sentenced to three months' imprisonment for having "discredited a court decision"

N

by commenting on the arrest warrant against former Prime Minister Hama Amadou. He was released after two months.

Impunity

President Tàndja granted a blanket amnesty to all members of the Tuareg armed opposition following the October peace agreement. The amnesty, also covering the Nigerien security forces, entrenched the climate of impunity and closed any avenues for justice and redress for human rights abuses committed by both sides during the conflict. About 100 Tuareg remained held without trial for their alleged involvement in the armed opposition, even though they should have been released under the amnesty.

Amnesty International reports

📄 Niger-Mali: Amnesty International calls for the release of hostages reportedly held by Al-Qa'ida in the Islamic Maghreb (AFR 43/001/2009)
📄 Niger: Appel à la libération inconditionnelle et immédiate de M. Amadou Arou (AFR 43/002/2009)

NIGERIA

FEDERAL REPUBLIC OF NIGERIA

Head of state and government:	Umaru Musa Yar'Adua
Death penalty:	retentionist
Population:	154.7 million
Life expectancy:	47.7 years
Under-5 mortality (m/f):	190/184 per 1,000
Adult literacy:	72 per cent

The police continued to commit with impunity a wide range of human rights violations, including unlawful killings, torture and other ill-treatment, and enforced disappearances. Some people were targeted for failing to pay bribes. Several people were tortured to death in police detention. Prisoners were held in appalling conditions, many of whom had been awaiting trial for years. The government intimidated and harassed human rights defenders and journalists. Violence against women remained endemic, and abuses against people suspected of same-sex relationships continued. Forced evictions affected thousands of people across the country.

At least 58 people were sentenced to death, bringing to more than 870 the number of prisoners on death row. Many were sentenced after unfair trials. However, the government announced a "self-imposed moratorium" on executions. In the Niger Delta, clashes continued in the first half of the year between armed groups and the security forces, resulting in many deaths, including of bystanders. The security situation improved after the President offered an amnesty to members of armed groups in August.

Background

In February, Nigeria's human rights situation was examined by the UN Universal Periodic Review (UPR) Working Group. In June, Nigeria announced it accepted 30 of the 32 recommendations made by the UPR Working Group.

In July, Nigeria acceded to the International Convention for the Protection of All Persons from Enforced Disappearance, the Convention on the Prevention and Punishment of the Crime of Genocide, and the Optional Protocol to the Convention against Torture.

In March, the Executive Secretary of the National Human Rights Commission (NHRC), Kehinde Ajoni, was dismissed and subsequently replaced by Roland Ewubare. Her removal may have been arbitrary. By the end of 2009, a bill aimed at strengthening the effectiveness of the NHRC had still not been passed. Since November 2007, the NHRC had not had a governing council.

In July, more than 800 people, including 24 police officers, died during a week of clashes between members of the religious group Boko Haram and security forces in Borno, Kano, Katsina and Yobe states. On 26 July, members of Boko Haram attacked a police station in Bauchi state. Boko Haram's leader, Muhammad Yusuf, was arrested on 30 July in Maiduguri, Borno state. Later that day the police announced that he had been killed while attempting to escape. On 13 August, Michael Kaase Aondoakaa, the Attorney General of the Federation and Minister of Justice, stated that Muhammad Yusuf had been killed in police custody. The government announced it would investigate all the killings, but no further developments were made public.

In November, the ECOWAS Community Court of Justice ruled that Nigerians have a legal and human right to education, following a case brought by the Nigerian NGO Socio-Economic Rights and Accountability Project.

President Umaru Musa Yar'Adua, who went to Saudi Arabia for medical treatment in November, had not returned to Nigeria by the end of the year nor handed over his powers to the Vice-President.

In December, a clash between a religious group and the police in Bauchi state resulted in the death of at least 65 people, including children.

Unlawful killings and enforced disappearances

Hundreds of people died at the hands of the police. Many were unlawfully killed before or during arrest in the street or at roadblocks, or subsequently in police detention. Others were tortured to death in police detention. A large proportion of these unlawful killings may have constituted extrajudicial executions. Many other people disappeared after arrest. The families of such victims rarely receive redress and are often left with no answers. Most perpetrators remain unpunished. Although the police have mechanisms to receive complaints from the public, these complaints are often unprocessed.

■ Police shot and injured Christian Onuigbo on 19 March while he was parking his car in Jiwa, Federal Capital Territory. He spent the night at Jiwa police station and was taken to hospital the next morning. Staff at the hospital refused to treat him without a police report, which was finally submitted at 4pm. Christian Onuigbo died the following day.

■ Aneke Okorie, an *Okada* (motorcycle taxi) rider, was shot after he failed to pay a bribe to the police at a checkpoint in Emene, Enugu state, on 15 May. He died on the way to hospital. An eyewitness told Amnesty International that the police officer shot Aneke Okorie in the stomach and then hung his gun around Aneke Okorie's neck to suggest that the police officer had been attacked by an armed robber. In September, the police officer was dismissed and prosecuted; he was awaiting trial at the end of the year.

■ Stanley Adiele Uwakwe and Faka Tamunotonye Kalio were arrested on 10 May and brought to Old GRA detention centre in Port Harcourt. After several days, they were transferred to another police station, but officers there told relatives that the men were not in detention. Unofficially, relatives were informed that the men had been killed by the police.

Torture and other ill-treatment

The police frequently used torture and other ill-treatment when interrogating suspects and there was no standardized mechanism to prevent such practices. Confessions extracted under torture continued to be used as evidence in court.

■ On 19 November, three *Okada* riders were accused by community members of theft and handed over to the police. The men said their motorbikes had been stolen by the community. They were held for seven days by the Special Anti-Robbery Squad (SARS) in Borokiri, Port Harcourt, and beaten every night with the butt of a gun and an iron belt. They also said they were given water mixed with chemicals to drink, which caused internal wounds. The same water was poured over their bodies, causing pain and a rash. After an NGO lodged a complaint, the men were released on bail.

Justice system

Despite repeated government pledges to address the problems in the criminal justice system, little progress was made. A review of the Police Act (1990) started in 2004 had still not resulted in new law. The vast majority of recommendations made in previous years by two presidential commissions, the UN Special Rapporteur on extrajudicial, summary or arbitrary executions, and the UN Special Rapporteur on torture were not implemented.

Seven out of 10 inmates in prison were pre-trial detainees. Many had been held for years awaiting trial in appalling conditions. Few could afford a lawyer and the government-funded Legal Aid Council had fewer than 100 lawyers for the whole country.

The Federal Ministry of Justice said it arranged lawyers to take up the cases of prisoners without legal representation. However, by the end of 2009 the impact of the scheme was not evident and prison overcrowding had not improved. The scheme did not address the causes of delays in the criminal justice system.

In July, the Lagos State Governor signed the Magistrates' Court Bill into law; suspects must be brought to court within 24 hours and only qualified legal practitioners can prosecute them.

In August, the new Interior Minister, Dr Shetima Mustapha, reiterated the commitment to reform prisons. At the end of 2009, most justice sector reform bills were still pending before the National Assembly.

Death penalty

At least 58 people were sentenced to death. At the end of the year, around 860 men and 11 women were on death row. Hundreds of them had not received a fair trial.

No steps were taken to implement the recommendations made in 2004 by the National Study Group on the Death Penalty and in 2007 by the Presidential Commission on Reform of the Administration of Justice to adopt a moratorium on executions. In February, however, at the fourth session of the UPR, the Minister of Foreign Affairs stated that Nigeria continued to exercise "a self-imposed moratorium" on executions.

In June, the Governor of Lagos state pardoned and released three death row prisoners. A further 29 prisoners in Lagos state had death sentences commuted to life imprisonment and eight others to various prison terms.

Kidnapping was made a capital offence in six states – Abia, Akwa Ibom, Anambra, Ebonyi, Enugu and Imo – and a bill to this end remained pending in Delta state.

Violence against women

Violence against women remained pervasive, including domestic violence, rape and other forms of sexual violence by state officials and private individuals. The authorities consistently failed to exercise due diligence in preventing and addressing sexual violence by both state and non-state actors, leading to an entrenched culture of impunity.

While some states in Nigeria have adopted state legislation to protect women from discrimination and violence, the UN Women's Convention had yet to be implemented at federal and state level almost 25 years after its ratification.

Rights of lesbian, gay, bisexual and transgender people

Human rights abuses against individuals suspected of same-sex sexual relations continued. Nigeria's Criminal Code penalizes consensual same-sex sexual conduct between adults. Islamic law in Nigeria criminalizes "sodomy" and in some states makes it punishable by death.

The Same Gender Marriage (Prohibition) Bill 2008, which would introduce criminal penalties for marriage ceremonies between people of the same sex and for people witnessing or helping to formalize such marriages, was debated by government but not passed into law.

Freedom of expression

Human rights defenders and journalists critical of the government faced increased intimidation and harassment. At least 26 journalists were arrested by the State Security Service or police. Some were released after a few hours while others were detained incommunicado for up to 12 days. In addition, media offices were raided, TV stations shut down and journalists threatened and beaten by police and security forces.

■ In September, Bayo Ohu, Assistant News Editor of *The Guardian* newspaper, was killed in his home in Lagos in suspicious circumstances. Apart from his mobile phone and laptop, nothing was stolen.

■ In November, three journalists were arrested in Port Harcourt after they published a story about a shooting incident in Bundu, Port Harcourt. One was released after two days, the other two after five days. They were charged with publishing false news.

In November, the African Commission on Human and Peoples' Rights urged the federal government to withdraw the Nigerian Press Council and the Practice of Journalism in Nigeria Bill 2009, which would restrict freedom of expression if passed into law.

By the end of 2009, the Freedom of Information Bill, first presented in 1999, remained pending before the National Assembly.

Niger Delta

In the first six months of 2009, armed groups and gangs kidnapped dozens of oil workers and their relatives, including children, and attacked many oil installations. The security forces, including the military, continued to commit human rights violations in the Niger Delta, including extrajudicial executions, torture and other ill-treatment, and destruction of homes. According to reports, the Joint Task Force (JTF), which combines troops of the army, navy, air force and the mobile police, frequently raided communities. Such raids often happened following clashes between the JTF and militants, often resulting in the death of bystanders.

■ In May, a clash between the JTF and armed groups in Delta state led to two weeks of fighting between the two sides as well as land and air strikes by the JTF on communities and militants' camps across the Warri South and South West local government areas in Delta state. The area was occupied by the JTF for several months, with residents only able to return in August. Most houses were destroyed. Amnesty International was told that at least 30 bystanders, including children, were killed and many more wounded as a result of the JTF intervention.

In October, most leaders and members of armed groups in the Niger Delta accepted an amnesty offered by the federal government in August. The amnesty covered "offences associated with militant activities in the Niger Delta". While the security situation subsequently improved, there appeared to be no plan to address the causes of the conflict.

Pollution and environmental damage caused by the oil industry continued to have a serious impact on people living in the Niger Delta. More than 60 per cent of residents depend on the natural environment for their livelihood. Communities in the Niger Delta frequently had no access to basic information about the impact of the oil industry on their lives.

The laws and regulations to protect the environment continued to be poorly enforced. Government agencies responsible for enforcement were ineffective and, in some cases, compromised by conflicts of interest.

The Petroleum Industry Bill, which would reform Nigeria's oil industry legislation, remained pending. However, it fails to address the social and human rights impacts of the oil industry.

Right to adequate housing – forced evictions

Forced evictions continued throughout Nigeria. The authorities failed to provide compensation or alternative housing to people forcibly evicted from their homes. Some communities faced their third forced eviction.

In Port Harcourt, capital of Rivers state, forced evictions were carried out throughout the year along the waterfront, affecting thousands of people.
■ On 28 August, thousands of people were forcibly evicted from Njemanze Community, Port Harcourt.
■ On 12 October in Bundu Community, Port Harcourt, at least three people died and 11 were seriously injured after combined troops of the JTF and police used firearms to disperse a crowd demonstrating against intended demolitions and blocking their entry into the community.

Amnesty International visits/reports

🚌 Amnesty International delegates visited Nigeria in June/July and November/December.

📄 Nigeria: A new chance to commit to human rights – Implementation of the outcome of the Universal Periodic Review (AFR 44/014/2009)

📄 Nigeria: Petroleum, pollution and poverty in the Niger Delta (AFR 44/017/2009)

📄 Nigeria: Killings by security forces in Northern Nigeria (AFR 44/028/2009)

📄 Nigeria: Thousands facing forcible eviction (AFR 44/032/2009)

📄 Nigeria: Promoting and protecting human rights – A ten point national agenda (AFR 44/035/2009)

📄 Killing at will – Extrajudicial executions and other unlawful killings by the police in Nigeria (AFR 44/038/2009)

OMAN

SULTANATE OF OMAN

Head of state and government:	**Sultan Qaboos bin Said**
Death penalty:	retentionist
Population:	2.8 million
Life expectancy:	75.5 years
Under-5 mortality (m/f):	14/13 per 1,000
Adult literacy:	84.4 per cent

Women and girls, and members of two tribes, continued to face discrimination. A journalist was prosecuted for exposing state censorship.

Discrimination
Women and girls

Women and girls continued to face discrimination in law, particularly family law, and in practice.

Aal Tawayya and Aal Khalifayn tribes

Around 15 people belonging to Aal Tawayya and Aal Khalifayn tribes continued to suffer economic and social problems due to a 2006 Interior Ministry decision to rename their tribes "Awlad Tawayya" and "Awlad Khalifayn", affiliating them to the main al-Harithi tribe. This reduced their status to that of "*akhdam*", effectively servants of al-Harithi tribe. A 2008 court action against the Ministry's decision failed. The government said it had addressed the tribes' grievance but some members of the tribes were reported to still face difficulties in renewing their

O

identity cards, which are needed to register businesses, obtain travel documents, and arrange matters such as divorce and inheritance.

Children's rights

In June, the UN Committee on the Rights of the Child, when examining Oman's compliance with the UN Children's Convention, expressed concern about continuing discrimination against children born out of wedlock; abuses and ill-treatment within the family and in institutions; and disparities in access to health and education faced by children in rural areas and children of foreign nationals. Among other things, the Committee urged the government to establish a minimum age of criminal responsibility, create an independent national human rights institution, and re-examine reservations Oman entered when ratifying the Convention.

Freedom of expression

■ 'Ali al-Zuwaydi, a journalist and moderator of a section of the Sablat Oman Forum website, was sentenced to 10 days in prison and fined in April for publicizing a government directive instructing a radio programme not to broadcast live calls or accept calls from people who wished to comment on military, security and judicial issues or anything concerning the head of state. He was released as he had already spent more than 10 days in jail.

Ill-treatment

■ Wosim Tahan, a Syrian computer engineer and resident of Oman for around two years, was reportedly ill-treated in police custody following his arrest in July for unknown reasons. He was held incommunicado at Mahda Prison for four days and was reported to have not been given food for around 36 hours. He was denied prompt access to his family, was not allowed to see a lawyer, and had no opportunity to challenge his detention. In October, the government told Amnesty International that Wosim Tahan had entered Oman illegally and had been deported, but did not say when or give any further details.

PAKISTAN

ISLAMIC REPUBLIC OF PAKISTAN

Head of state:	Asif Ali Zardari
Head of government:	Yousuf Raza Gilani
Death penalty:	retentionist
Population:	180.8 million
Life expectancy:	66.2 years
Under-5 mortality (m/f):	85/94 per 1,000
Adult literacy:	54.2 per cent

Millions of Pakistanis suffered abuses as a result of a sharp escalation in armed conflict between the government and armed groups. Pakistani Taleban and other anti-government groups targeted civilians throughout the country, while security forces used indiscriminate and disproportionate force and carried out suspected extrajudicial executions. In areas controlled by the Pakistani Taleban and allied armed groups, civilians faced severe abuses, including arbitrary arrest and detention; torture and other ill-treatment; a near total absence of due judicial process; stringent restrictions on freedom of expression and assembly; religious and ethnic discrimination; and violence and discrimination against women and girls. Violence against minorities increased, with the government failing to prevent attacks or punish perpetrators. There were no executions, although 276 people were sentenced to death.

Background

Following nationwide protests led by Pakistani lawyers, Iftikhar Chaudhry was reinstated on 16 March as Chief Justice. He had been dismissed from his post in November 2007 by then President Pervez Musharraf. On 31 July, the Supreme Court ruled that President Musharraf had violated the Constitution when he declared emergency rule on 3 November 2007. In August, a criminal case was filed against him for illegally detaining judges of the higher judiciary in 2007. On 16 November, the Supreme Court resumed hearing cases of enforced disappearances that had been interrupted by the 2007 emergency.

Violence in Balochistan escalated in January after Baloch armed groups called off a ceasefire begun in mid-2008. Hostage-taking and unlawful killings by armed groups were countered by violations, including arbitrary arrests and enforced disappearances, by state agents.

Pakistani Taleban and related insurgent groups consolidated their hold in the Federally Administered Tribal Areas (FATA) and expanded their reach into parts of the North West Frontier Province (NWFP), most notably the densely populated Swat valley. The army continued its operations against insurgents, focusing particularly on Swat in April, on Khyber Agency in FATA from September, and on South Waziristan from October. Insurgents killed hundreds of civilians and injured thousands more in attacks across the country, including attacks targeting mosques and schools.

On 13 April, the Pakistani Taleban in Swat forced President Zardari to sign the Nizam-e-Adl (Order of Justice) Regulation. The Regulation formally established courts implementing the Taleban's harsh interpretation of Islamic law in Malakand Division. The peace pact broke down when the Pakistani Taleban continued armed incursions into neighbouring Buner in mid-April. The Taleban's actions, and the resulting army operations that began on 26 April, displaced more than 2 million people, joining some half a million Pakistanis who had already fled their homes as a result of the conflict between the Pakistani Taleban and government security forces. The South Waziristan operation prompted over two thirds of the region's 450,000 population to flee.

Legal, constitutional or institutional developments

The pre-charge detention period for suspects held for interrogation under the Anti-Terrorism Act was extended from 30 to 90 days on 2 October.

On 19 August, the Ministry of Human Rights informed Parliament that of the 11,000 human rights cases registered by it countrywide over the past three years – most of them in Sindh Province – more than 8,000 had not been investigated by the police or had been dismissed.

On 4 August, the National Assembly passed the Domestic Violence (Prevention and Protection) Bill. It lapsed after the Senate failed to pass it and the government did not set up a mediation committee to resolve differences.

President Zardari announced a reform package for FATA in August. It included lifting the ban on political party activities and limited reform of the colonial-era Frontier Crimes Regulation, which deprives FATA residents of most rights afforded under international law and the Pakistani Constitution. Implementation of these reforms remained pending.

On 24 November, Prime Minister Gilani presented comprehensive proposals to reduce the military presence in Balochistan, release Baloch political detainees except those involved in "terrorism", release "disappeared" people and initiate economic uplift programmes. Twenty disappeared people were reportedly released in late November and in December; 89 criminal cases registered against political activists were withdrawn. On 10 December, the Prime Minister reportedly stated that of 992 Baloch victims of enforced disappearance, 262 had already been released and the rest would be released soon.

Insurgency in FATA, NWFP and Balochistan

Insurgents abducted and unlawfully killed thousands of people, including tribal elders, teachers, journalists, other professionals, and internally displaced people returning to their homes. In 87 suicide attacks, 1,299 people were killed and 3,633 injured, many of them civilians. In the past two years, the Taleban destroyed over 200 schools in Swat, including more than 100 girls' schools. According to local officials, these attacks disrupted the education of more than 50,000 pupils from primary to college level.

Taleban groups set up informal Islamic "courts" in areas under their control and "tried" and punished scores of people, particularly women, accused of breaching their harsh interpretation of Islamic law. Punishments included public floggings and executions.

The Pakistani military at times used indiscriminate or excessive force in attacks on suspected Taleban hideouts, leading to high numbers of civilian casualties. Security forces detained family members of suspected insurgents, including children, to force them to surrender.

State-supported but unregulated tribal lashkars (militias), formed by elders in NWFP and designated tribal areas to counter the Taleban and protect tribal villages, detained and in some cases killed Taleban suspects.

Journalists reporting the insurgency in the

P

Northwest and Balochistan were targeted by the government as well as by armed groups, resulting in under-reporting of abuses. At least 10 journalists lost their lives in the course of their work.

■ Afghan journalist Janullah Hashimzada was killed on 24 August in Jamrud, Khyber Agency; his colleagues believed that the Taleban were responsible. That same month, the Quetta-based newspaper *Asaap* closed after security and intelligence personnel were sent to their office to censor their work.

■ On 7 July, insurgents in Buner set fire to the house of Behroz Khan, a journalist with Geo TV.

Internally displaced people

In addition to some 500,000 people displaced earlier from FATA as a result of the conflict, more than 2 million people fled the fighting in Swat which began in April (see Afghanistan entry). The government failed to ensure the rights of the displaced – over half of them children – to security, health, food, shelter and education. In October, the security forces harassed Mehsud tribespeople fleeing the fighting in South Waziristan and detained scores of Mehsuds under the collective responsibility clause of the Frontier Crimes Regulation.

Torture and other ill-treatment

Dozens of detainees were tortured to death or killed, and other extrajudicial executions were reported amid widespread impunity for such violations.

■ Christian minority member Fanish Masih, aged 19, was found dead on 15 September in Sialkot prison where he had been held in solitary confinement. Prison authorities claimed that he had committed suicide but his relatives reportedly noted bruises consistent with torture on his forehead, arms and legs. Three prison officials were suspended for negligence, but no criminal charges were brought against them.

■ More than 250 bodies of suspected militants were reportedly found in Swat after mid-July, some hanging from poles, warning the Taleban of the same fate.

Enforced disappearances

New instances of enforced disappearances were reported. Despite the resumption of Supreme Court hearings of disappearance cases in November, the fate and whereabouts of hundreds of disappeared people remained unknown.

■ In October, a district court in Abbottabad declared former President Musharraf a suspect in the case of the alleged abduction of Atiq-ur Rehman, a scientist at the Pakistan Atomic Energy Commission, who disappeared on 25 June 2004.

■ On 18 August, the army stated it was holding 900 prisoners arrested in Swat who would be handed over to relevant agencies. Their identity, whereabouts and fate remained unknown.

■ On 3 April, three Baloch activists, Ghulam Mohammad Baloch, Lala Muni, and Sher Mohammad Baloch, were abducted by men in civilian clothing from their lawyer's office on the very day that the anti-terrorism court cleared them of charges of causing unrest. They were reportedly taken away in Frontier Corps vehicles. They were found dead on 8 April. Ghulam Mohammad Baloch was a member of a committee to ascertain the identity of some 800 victims of enforced disappearance. The Balochistan High Court set up a judicial inquiry in April, and in September called on the intelligence agencies to assist the investigation of the murders after police had complained about their lack of co-operation.

Zakir Majeed Baloch, a social worker and vice-chairman of the Baloch Students Organization, was according to family members picked up on 8 June by intelligence agency personnel near Mastung, Balochistan. Police refused to register the family's complaint. His fate and whereabouts remain unknown.

Discrimination – religious minorities

Members of religious minorities suffered increasing abuses, including abduction, murder, intimidation, and harassment, as state officials failed to protect them and adequately prosecute perpetrators. The Taleban imposed *jizia*, a tax payable by non-Muslims living under Muslim rule, on Sikhs, Hindus and Christians, or in some cases expelled them outright. Sectarian violence between the Sunni and Shi'a communities increased in Kurram Agency as Sunni Taleban exerted their control.

■ At least 14 members of the Ahmadiyya community, including children, were arrested on charges of blasphemy which carries the mandatory death penalty. At least 11 Ahmadis and nine Christians were killed for their faith in separate incidents.

■ On 29 January, five Ahmadis, including one minor, were detained on spurious charges of blasphemy in Layyah district, Punjab Province, with no evidence or

P

witnesses to support the charges against them. They were released on bail.

■ In Gojra, Punjab, over 1,000 people attacked the Christian quarter on 1 August, burning six people alive, including a seven-year-old child. Seventeen others were injured, one of whom died later. The attack was a response to rumours that Christians had torn pages of the Qur'an in neighbouring Korian. A judicial inquiry, ordered by the Punjab Chief Minister, submitted its findings to Punjab authorities in early September; they were not made public. Of 42 people arrested on charges stemming from the attack in Gojra, 35 were released on bail.

Violence against women and girls

Women continued to be victims of "honour killings", with 960 incidents reported. In September, the Punjab law minister announced that crimes against women would be tried under the Anti-Terrorism Act.

■ In NWFP and the tribal areas, Taleban groups closed or burned down girls' schools, forced women to wear a veil and prohibited them from leaving their homes unless accompanied by male relatives. Several women were punished, shot dead or mutilated for alleged "immoral" activities.

Legal redress sought for abuses of women's rights remained difficult to obtain.

■ On 27 April, Ayman Udas, a Pashtun singer from Peshawar, was shot dead, reportedly by her two brothers who viewed her divorce, remarriage and artistic career as damaging to family honour. No one was arrested.

Children's rights

Child labour, domestic violence, sexual abuse, and forcing girls into marriage to settle disputes continued. The government rarely took action to prevent such abuses or to ensure punishment of the perpetrators. In October, the Sindh Assembly heard that 4,367 child labour victims had been recovered between May 2008 and April 2009 in that province alone and handed over to an NGO for their rehabilitation.

The army on several occasions presented children to the media, stating that they had been found in Taleban camps where they were allegedly trained for suicide missions.

■ In August, 11 boys, including three apparently under 10 years old, appeared before journalists in Mingora

"visibly traumatized". They said that they had been held in Taleban camps along with hundreds of other boys.

The Juvenile Justice System Ordinance of 2000 remained inadequately implemented. Its provision to detain children separately from adults remained unimplemented.

Death penalty

The Human Rights Commission of Pakistan recorded 276 new death sentences, with 7,700 people remaining under sentence of death. No executions were carried out.

Promises made in 2008 to commute all death sentences to life imprisonment remained unfulfilled. In September, President Zardari called on provincial governments to submit recommendations on commuting the death penalty to prison terms of 24 to 30 years. On 31 August, the Supreme Court suspended an order passed by the Lahore High Court in April under which death sentences would not be imposed on women and juveniles in narcotics cases.

Amnesty International visit/reports

🚌 An Amnesty International delegate visited Pakistan in May.

📄 Pakistan: Resolve hundreds of Baluch "disappearances" (ASA 33/001/2009)

📄 Pakistan: Lahore attack shows government must do more to protect civilians (ASA 33/002/2009)

📄 Pakistan: Government should take concrete action to amend or abolish the blasphemy laws within a year (ASA 33/008/2009)

📄 Pakistan: Amnesty International welcomes Supreme Court move to hear disappearances cases (ASA 33/011/2009)

📄 Pakistan: Government must prepare for South Waziristan displacement crisis, 16 October 2009

P

PALESTINIAN AUTHORITY

PALESTINIAN AUTHORITY

Head of Palestinian Authority:	Mahmoud Abbas
Head of government:	Salam Fayyad
Death penalty:	retentionist
Population:	4.3 million
Life expectancy:	73.3 years
Under-5 mortality (m/f):	23/18 per 1,000
Adult literacy:	93.8 per cent

During Operation "Cast Lead", the 22-day military offensive launched by Israel that ended on 18 January, Hamas forces and militias in the Gaza Strip continued to fire indiscriminate rockets and mortars into Israel, and within Gaza they abducted political opponents and former detainees alleged to have "collaborated" with the Israeli intelligence services; some were summarily killed, others were beaten or shot in the legs. Throughout the year, Palestinian Authority (PA) security forces in the West Bank and Hamas security forces and militias in Gaza arbitrarily detained hundreds of members or sympathizers of rival factions without charge or trial and often tortured and otherwise ill-treated them. Security agencies under the PA in the West Bank and the de facto administration in Gaza used excessive force when confronting armed rivals, causing a number of civilian deaths. The PA in the West Bank and Hamas in Gaza continued to clamp down on freedom of expression. Military courts in the West Bank and Gaza sentenced 17 people to death; no executions were carried out.

Background

Israel's occupation of the West Bank, including East Jerusalem, and the Gaza Strip continued. In this context, two separate non-state Palestinian authorities operated with limited powers: in the West Bank, the caretaker government of the PA under Prime Minister Salam Fayyad appointed by President Mahmoud Abbas of the Fatah party; and in the Gaza Strip, the Hamas de facto administration under former PA Prime Minister Isma'il Haniyeh. Inter-factional tension continued between Fatah and Hamas despite attempts at reconciliation sponsored by the Egyptian government.

Armed groups affiliated to Hamas largely complied with the ceasefire with Israel declared in late January, but other Palestinian armed groups linked to the Popular Front for the Liberation of Palestine (PFLP), Fatah and Islamic Jihad continued to fire rockets and mortars into southern Israel periodically throughout the year; although indiscriminate, these did not cause Israeli civilian fatalities.

The Israeli military blockade of Gaza, in force since June 2007, continued to have a devastating impact on food security, health and civilian infrastructure. The humanitarian crisis caused by the blockade was exacerbated by Operation "Cast Lead" (see Israel and the Occupied Palestinian Territories entry), which destroyed more than 3,000 homes and damaged a further 20,000. Scores of civilian buildings, including hospitals, clinics and schools, were also damaged. The Israeli authorities restricted the entry of basic commodities such as fuel and imposed a total ban on the import of cement, so tunnels running under the Gaza-Egypt border were increasingly used to smuggle in goods. The inherently unsafe tunnels were made more dangerous by attacks by Israeli forces; dozens of people, including children, were killed and injured in the tunnels.

In September, the UN Human Rights Council's Goldstone report accused both Israel and Hamas of war crimes in Gaza and southern Israel during Operation "Cast Lead", and recommended that those responsible be brought to justice. The Hamas de facto administration did not establish any independent or impartial investigation into the conduct of Palestinian armed groups; Hamas officials said only that they were prepared to conduct internal investigations.

Unlawful killings

During and immediately following Israel's military operation in the Gaza Strip, Hamas forces and militias there engaged in a campaign of abductions, deliberate and unlawful killings, torture and death threats against people they accused of "collaborating" with Israel and other opponents and critics. More than 30 individuals were summarily killed. Scores of others were shot in the legs, kneecapped or otherwise injured in ways intended to cause permanent disability, or they were severely beaten or otherwise tortured or ill-treated. These abuses were committed with impunity, with the apparent approval of the Hamas leadership.

■ Saleh Jahjouh from Beit Hanoun was shot dead in al-Shifa' Hospital on 21 January. He had been held at Gaza Central Prison accused of "collaboration" with Israel but was moved to the hospital after being injured in an Israeli air attack on the prison.

In addition to the targeted killings, at least five civilian bystanders were killed and injured in the West Bank and Gaza Strip during violent clashes between Palestinian security forces and armed groups.

■ On 31 May, one civilian was killed in the West Bank town of Qalqiliya during a gunfight between PA police and armed supporters of Hamas who were resisting arrest. Three policemen and two armed members of Hamas were also killed.

■ On 14 and 15 August, at least four civilians were killed and others injured in Rafah in the Gaza Strip during a clash between Hamas security forces and members of Jund Ansar Allah, an armed group that claims allegiance to al-Qa'ida. In all, some 24 people were killed and more than 100 injured in the gunfight.

Abuses by armed groups

The armed wing of Hamas and other Palestinian armed groups based in Gaza fired hundreds of rockets and mortars into southern Israel before Hamas declared a ceasefire on 18 January. The attacks killed three civilians and severely injured at least four others. Several homes were also damaged.

■ Seven-year-old Uriel Elazarov was seriously injured by shrapnel when a rocket exploded in Bersheva, southern Israel, on 15 January. Five other civilians were injured in the same attack.

After 18 January, the PFLP, Fatah and Islamic Jihad continued sporadically to fire rockets and mortars from Gaza into southern Israel.

Hamas continued to deny the captured Israeli soldier Gilad Shalit access to the ICRC or visits from his family. In October, Hamas issued a video of Gilad Shalit that showed he was still alive and in captivity.

Justice system

The judicial systems in the West Bank and Gaza remained extremely problematic. The PA continued to prohibit former members of the judiciary and security forces from working for the Hamas de facto administration in Gaza, and to pay them for not working. Hamas continued to use alternative prosecutors and judges who often lacked the necessary training and qualifications. In the West

Bank, PA security forces frequently failed to comply with court decisions calling for them to release specific detainees.

Arbitrary arrests and detentions

In the West Bank and Gaza hundreds of people were arbitrarily arrested and held without charge or trial. Those detained were often suspected of involvement with a rival political party.

Torture and other ill-treatment

Detainees held in the West Bank and Gaza were frequently beaten, subjected to sleep deprivation, and forced to spend long periods handcuffed in painful stress positions (*shabeh*) during the interrogation period. Complaints of torture were rarely investigated.

Deaths in custody

In the West Bank, three detainees died while being detained by PA security forces; all three were reportedly arrested because of suspected involvement with Hamas and were alleged to have been tortured or otherwise ill-treated in custody.

■ Haitham Amr, a nurse, was arrested at his home near Hebron on 11 June by members of the PA's General Intelligence Service; his death was announced four days later. His body had extensive and severe bruising and the Minister of the Interior later acknowledged that he had been tortured in detention. In an unusual move, the PA opened a military trial against the officers accused of involvement in his death.

In Gaza, at least four men died in the custody of Hamas security forces; three of them were alleged to have been tortured.

■ Zayad Ayash Jaradat, a resident of Rafah, died in March while in the custody of Hamas police in the Gaza Strip after being detained under criminal charges. He was alleged to have died as a result of beatings by the police. The Ministry of the Interior dismissed 11 police officers, who were detained and expected to be brought to trial before a military court.

Freedom of expression

The Palestinian authorities in both the West Bank and Gaza curtailed media freedom and took action against media and journalists who criticized them.

In January in the West Bank, PA security forces detained and threatened journalists who reported the violent suppression of demonstrators protesting against the Israeli attack on Gaza. Throughout the year the security forces arrested and harassed media

P

workers of al-Aqsa and al-Quds satellite channels, media outlets seen as aligned with Hamas. In July, the PA government ordered al-Jazeera to suspend its operations, but was quickly forced to retract this by a public outcry.

■ Khaled Amayreh was arrested and detained without charge for three days in January by the PA's Preventative Security Agency in Hebron. He was interrogated about an interview with al-Quds TV in which he had criticized the PA's response to the Israeli attack on Gaza.

In Gaza on 14 August, the Hamas Ministry of the Interior banned journalists from accessing Rafah during fighting between the Hamas security forces and Jund Ansar Allah. In November, Hamas prevented a meeting of journalists organized by the International Federation of Journalists from taking place.

■ Sari al-Qudweh, editor of *al-Sabah* newspaper, was detained by the Hamas de facto administration in Gaza in June. Hamas security officers also searched his home and closed the newspaper's offices. Sari al-Qudweh was released on 19 August.

Violence against women and girls

Five women and a 16-year-old girl were reported to have been victims of so-called honour killings, most carried out by male relatives. Perpetrators of such killings, when tried and convicted, generally receive inappropriately lenient sentences, often being imprisoned for less than three years.

■ On 23 July, Fadia Jawdat al-Najjar, a divorced mother of five, was killed in Gaza. Her father, Jawdat al-Najjar, handed himself in to the police on 24 July and confessed to beating his daughter to death. He was charged with her murder and at the end of 2009 was awaiting trial.

Death penalty

Courts in the West Bank and Gaza continued to sentence people to death, particularly for murder and "collaboration", although no executions were carried out. In the West Bank, PA military courts handed down three death sentences for alleged "collaboration" and treason; in Gaza, Hamas military courts sentenced 14 people to death on charges of "collaboration", treason and murder.

Amnesty International visits/reports

🚍 Amnesty International delegates visited the West Bank and Gaza Strip in January, February, June, July, October and November.

▤ Palestinian Authority: Hamas' deadly campaign in the shadow of the war in Gaza (MDE 21/001/2009)

▤ Israel/Gaza: Operation "Cast Lead" – 22 Days of Death and Destruction (MDE 15/015/2009)

▤ Troubled waters – Palestinians denied fair access to water (MDE 15/027/2009)

PAPUA NEW GUINEA

PAPUA NEW GUINEA

Head of state:	Queen Elizabeth II represented by Paulias Matane
Head of government:	Michael Somare
Death penalty:	Abolitionist in practice
Population:	6.7 million
Life expectancy:	60.7 years
Under-5 mortality (m/f):	70/68 per 1,000
Adult literacy:	57.8 per cent

Sorcery-related killings increased. The government did little to effectively address the situation or to bring the perpetrators to justice. Women and girls suffered physical and sexual violence, and those responsible were seldom brought to justice. Police continued to forcibly evict communities from mining areas. HIV infection rates were the highest in the region, but access to testing, treatment, care and prevention were not adequately met.

Unlawful killings

■ In January, a group of men stripped a woman naked, gagged and burned her alive at Kerebug rubbish dump in Mount Hagen, after she was suspected of practising witchcraft. Provincial police commanders in Eastern Highlands and Chimbu admitted that there were more than 50 sorcery-related killings in their provinces in 2008.

■ In February, villagers shot dead a 60-year-old man, threw his body into a fire and burned his son alive after accusing them of causing the death of a prominent member of the community by sorcery.

Violence against women and girls

Physical, psychological and sexual abuse continued to be a major problem.

■ In April, a police officer was charged with the rape and abduction of a 13-year-old girl in Port Moresby.

■ In May, police officers in Lae reportedly killed a female sex worker and beat and badly injured another.

Right to health – HIV

HIV infection rates were the highest in the Pacific Region. According to WHO statistics published in October, an estimated 1.4 per cent of the population lived with HIV. Information gathering and monitoring of HIV rates was very patchy.

Despite attempts to improve health care for people living with HIV, they still faced problems with palliative care, stigmatization and discrimination. Health care and social workers lacked training and many trained medical staff emigrated.

■ In a historic court case, a man was fined Kina 2,000 (US$705) by the court in Western Province for "unlawfully stigmatizing" a girl for taking an HIV test. He had publicly accused her of having AIDS outside the hospital where she had gone for testing.

Forced evictions

Between April and July, police officers raided villages in the highlands, forcibly evicting people from their homes, burning down at least 97 houses and destroying their belongings, gardens and livestock. These incidents took place in the "special mining lease" area within which the Porgera Joint Venture operates one of the largest mines in the country. The police acted without prior notice or discussion and without alternative accommodation or other assistance being made available. Police acted violently in carrying out the forced evictions, including threatening residents with guns and firing weapons. Police beat some residents and reportedly raped three women during the forced evictions.

Amnesty International visits

🚌 Amnesty International delegates visited Papua New Guinea in July, August and September.

PARAGUAY

REPUBLIC OF PARAGUAY

Head of state and government:	Fernando Lugo
Death penalty:	abolitionist for all crimes
Population:	6.3 million
Life expectancy:	71.7 years
Under-5 mortality (m/f):	44/32 per 1,000
Adult literacy:	94.6 per cent

The government took some steps to fulfil promises on human rights and strengthen institutions, but failed to deliver on key promises regarding land reform and Indigenous Peoples' rights. There were reports of police ill-treatment in some rural areas. There were some developments in bringing to justice those responsible for past human rights abuses.

Background

Steps were taken to strengthen the institutional framework for human rights protection within the executive, but clear indications of how these would be reflected in the operation of the legislature or judiciary were lacking. Concerns remained about the effectiveness of key bodies such as the Human Rights Ombudsman's Office and the Paraguayan Indigenous Institute.

Violence attributed to the Army of the Paraguayan People armed group, including the kidnapping of landowner Fidel Zavala in October, resulted in security concerns in some areas.

In May the government announced a state of emergency across western departments of Paraguay following a serious drought that led to food security problems among Indigenous and campesino (peasant farmer) communities.

Indigenous Peoples' rights

While the authorities took some steps to ensure the provision of basic services to Indigenous communities, they failed to address Indigenous Peoples' land claims, tackle discrimination or monitor effectively the use of members of Indigenous communities as forced labour in remote areas.

In October, the Senate rejected a bill to expropriate the traditional lands of the Yakye Axa community from their current owners and return them to the community, despite an overdue deadline for the

P

implementation of an Inter-American Court of Human Rights ruling ordering the return of the lands. No substantive progress was made in returning land to the Sawhoyamaxa community, in line with a 2006 Inter-American Court ruling. A third case, relating to the Xákmok Kásek community, was pending before the Inter-American Court at the end of 2009.

In November, the Senate Human Rights Commission apparently supported the eviction of around 150 Ava Guaraní families from their traditional lands in the Itakyry district. The eviction order was cancelled later that month after a public outcry. Community members reported being sprayed subsequently with apparently toxic pesticides from a small airplane. This was confirmed by a Health Ministry report. More than 200 people were reportedly affected and several required hospital treatment.

There were reports that pesticides were used near Indigenous communities, in violation of national regulations. The Paraguayan Indigenous Institute linked the death of 12 Mbyá Guaraní Indigenous people between June and August 2009 in the Aba'í District of the Caazapá department to possible contamination from pesticides used on neighbouring wheat and soya crops.

The deteriorating living conditions endured by some landless communities, coupled with inadequate access to essential services, led to serious health problems and preventable deaths. In early 2009, six members of the Sawhoyamaxa Indigenous community died after suffering from diarrhoea and vomiting.

Despite government promises, deforestation in the northern Chaco continued, further endangering the Ayoreo-Totobiegosode Indigenous Peoples living in the area.

A UN study published in March highlighted the widespread violation of labour rights suffered by Indigenous Peoples in the Chaco region, and the continued use of forced and child labour on ranches.

Land disputes

Campesino groups continued to demand a land reform process that would address their needs. Some groups carried out demonstrations, road blocks and occupations in support of their demands. A number of people were killed or injured in the context of land disputes and during law enforcement activities.

■ In May, the body of 30-year-old campesino leader Enrique Brítez Irala was found hanging from a tree in the La Fortuna Agroganadera in the Jejuí colony, Choré district, San Pedro department. He had been involved in a dispute with a local landowner. Campesino groups reported that Enriquez Brítez Irala, who went missing three days before his body was found, had been tortured and claimed suggestions he had committed suicide were false. Investigations were under way at the end of the year.

Police and security forces

Police officers were accused of injuring dozens of people during a raid on a campesino encampment in the Toro Blanco neighbourhood of Caaguazú. The officers were looking for those suspected of involvement in an assault on nearby commercial premises in July. Around 50 people were subsequently detained and charged with resisting arrest and public order offences. They were awaiting trial at the end of the year.

Impunity

Some significant progress was made in bringing to justice some high-profile perpetrators of human rights abuses during the military government of General Alfredo Stroessner (1954-1989). By the end of 2009, some 13,700 applications for reparations had been made to the Ombudsman after modifications to legislation on compensation were made in 2008. In October, the Defence Minister authorized the unsealing of files dating from the military regime, giving human rights activists investigating human rights violations during this period access to this information for the first time.

■ In May, Sabino Augusto Montanaro, Interior Minister between 1968 and 1989, was arrested after voluntarily returning to Paraguay from exile in Honduras. He faced trial for a series of human rights violations including crimes allegedly committed as part of Operation Condor, a joint plan by Southern Cone military governments in the 1970s and 1980s to eliminate opponents.

■ In August, a judge ordered the extradition of Norberto Bianco, an army doctor at the Campo de Mayo military hospital, to Argentina to face trial for his alleged role in the illegal detention of more than 30 women and the subsequent appropriation of their children in 1977 and 1978. He was awaiting extradition at the end of the year.

■ In June, former diplomat Francisco Ortiz Téllez was arrested in connection with the enforced disappearance of Agustín Goiburú, a leading opponent of the Stroessner government, in 1977. Francisco Ortiz Téllez was under house arrest at the end of the year awaiting the outcome of his appeal.

Amnesty International visit/report

🚗 Amnesty International delegates visited Paraguay in March and met with President Lugo and other officials.

📃 "We're only asking for what is ours" – Indigenous Peoples in Paraguay (AMR 45/005/2009)

PERU

REPUBLIC OF PERU
Head of state and government:	Alan García Pérez
Death penalty:	abolitionist for ordinary crimes
Population:	29.2 million
Life expectancy:	73 years
Under-5 mortality (m/f):	38/27 per 1,000
Adult literacy:	89.6 per cent

Thirty-three people were killed, including 23 police officers, and at least 200 protesters were injured when police dispersed a road blockade led by members of Indigenous communities. Indigenous leaders were intimidated and harassed. Human rights defenders continued to be threatened. Violations of women's sexual and reproductive rights remained a concern.

Background

Throughout the year, there was increasing social unrest and discontent over government policies, in particular in relation to extractive projects and legislation on the use of resources and land. This led to nationwide mobilizations and strikes that paralysed the country for weeks.

The armed opposition group Shining Path (Sendero Luminoso) remained active in some parts of the Andean region and there were reports of armed confrontations with the military and police.

Indigenous Peoples' rights

Thousands of Indigenous demonstrators staged a road blockade for more than 50 days in the Amazon region in protest against a series of decree laws, which, they argued, affected their fundamental right to land and resources and thus their livelihoods.

Excessive use of force and ill-treatment

On 5 June, 33 people, including 23 police officers, were killed and at least 200 protesters were injured as the police intervened to disperse the road blockade. Police used excessive force to disperse the crowd, injuring and killing bystanders. Protesters killed 11 police officers whom they were holding hostage, and another 12 during the police operation. The whereabouts of a police official who participated in the operation remained unknown at the end of the year. In the aftermath, scores of detainees reported ill-treatment by police.

Justice system

At least 18 people faced charges for disturbances during the protests and the killing and injuring of police officers, but little progress was made in bringing to justice members of the security forces responsible for human rights violations against protesters. In addition, six Indigenous leaders were charged with rebellion, sedition and conspiracy against the state, charges which appeared not to be based on reliable evidence.

Legal and institutional developments

Four working groups, which included representatives of Indigenous Peoples, were set up to investigate the violence that occurred on 5 June, review the decree laws which sparked the protests, issue recommendations for a mechanism for consultation with Indigenous Peoples, and propose a National Plan of Development in the Amazon. In December, the Commission set up by the working group investigating the 5 June clashes presented its report to the Ministry of Agriculture. However, two members of the Commission, including its president, refused to endorse the report on the grounds that the Commission lacked the necessary time and resources to conduct full investigations and that the report lacked impartiality.

Corporate accountability

In January, photographs were published relating to the ill-treatment of 29 people, and the killing of one man while in detention in 2005 following protests

P

against a British mining project in the north-west of the country. The protesters alleged that they were tortured by police and the mine's security guards. In March 2009, the Public Prosecutor charged police officers with torture, but decided not to pursue either the mining company or its security guards. However, the victims brought an action against the company in the UK and in October a High Court injunction was issued against Monterrico Metals in the UK. The High Court ruling was pending at the end of the year.

In December, police shot dead two men and injured eight other villagers in Cajas-Canchaque, Carmen de la Frontera district, Huancabamba province. Police reportedly opened fire during an operation to arrest one of those suspected of involvement in an arson attack on a Rio Blanco Copper encampment on 1 November in which three mine employees were killed.

Maternal mortality

Some measures were taken to reduce maternal mortality, which remained high in rural areas and among Indigenous Peoples. In March a National Plan for the Reduction of Maternal Mortality was introduced which included measures to increase access to health facilities, including emergency obstetric care, and improve community participation. However, there were concerns about how this plan would link up with existing policies.

Sexual and reproductive rights

Steps were taken towards decriminalizing abortion in certain circumstances, including when the pregnancy is the result of rape.

In November, however, the Constitutional Tribunal ruled that the state could not distribute or sell oral emergency contraception. This ruling disadvantaged women on low incomes unable to afford this contraception, which remained available in chemists.

The rights of lesbian, gay, bisexual and transgender people

Lesbian, gay and transgender people continued to face discrimination and ill-treatment.
■ In January, Techi, a transgender woman, was kidnapped and tortured by members of a local neighbourhood watch patrol in the town of Tarapoto, San Martín province. The trial of three people accused of carrying out the attack on Techi was continuing at the end of the year.

Human rights defenders

Human rights defenders were threatened and intimidated. The authorities failed to send a clear message that such acts would not be tolerated or to ensure effective investigations into these threats. In September, an anonymous caller threatened to poison human rights defender and former president of the 2001 Truth and Reconciliation Commission Salomón Lerner Febres; his two guard dogs had been poisoned earlier that month.
■ In September, human rights defender Gisela Ortiz Perea was accused in a national newspaper of being a leading member of Shining Path in what appeared to be an attempt to intimidate her for her continued support to victims of human rights violations during the government of Alberto Fujimori (1990-2000).

Impunity

In April, former President Alberto Fujimori was sentenced to 25 years' imprisonment for grave human rights violations. However, impunity remained a concern. Scores of cases of reported killings by police officers were not investigated amid serious concerns that a 2007 decree law was being used to prevent investigations into alleged extrajudicial executions. The decree law reformed the Penal Code and exempts from prosecution police officers who injure or kill suspects while on duty.

There was no progress in implementing the recommendations of the 2001 Truth and Reconciliation Commission set up to investigate human rights violations committed during the internal armed conflict (1980-2000).

Little progress was made regarding the 1,000 cases of past human rights violations filed with the Public Prosecutor's Office since 2003. The Ministry of Defence continued to withhold information on cases involving military personnel.

The Reparations Council, a body set up in 2006 to create a record of victims of human rights violations during the two decades of internal armed conflict so that they could claim reparation, had to suspend its work in November owing to lack of resources.

Amnesty International visits/reports

🚍 Amnesty International delegates attended the trial of Alberto Fujimori in April and visited Peru in July and August for research purposes.

📋 Fatal flaws: Barriers to maternal health in Peru (AMR 46/008/2009)

📋 Peru: Bagua, six months on (AMR 46/017/2009)

PHILIPPINES

REPUBLIC OF THE PHILIPPINES

Head of state and government:	Gloria Macapagal-Arroyo
Death penalty:	abolitionist for all crimes
Population:	92 million
Life expectancy:	71.6 years
Under-5 mortality (m/f):	32/21 per 1,000
Adult literacy:	93.4 per cent

With 2010 as the self-imposed deadline by the government to "crush" the communist insurgency, the military failed to differentiate between New People's Army (NPA) fighters and civilian activists and human rights defenders in rural areas, resulting in displacement and unlawful killings. The military subjected civilians to secret detention, torture and other cruel, inhuman and degrading treatment. Both sides carried out politically motivated killings and enforced disappearances. A culture of impunity continued as almost no perpetrators were brought to justice. In July, the government began actively pursuing the resumption of formal peace negotiations with the National Democratic Front (NDF) and the Moro Islamic Liberation Front (MILF).

Hundreds of thousands remained displaced. Indigenous Peoples living in remote areas throughout the country, and the *Moros* (Philippine Muslims) in Mindanao were particularly affected. Privately armed militias and death squads carried out unlawful killings. Indigenous Peoples suffered both as a result of the conflict and from forced evictions from their lands in the interest of extraction industries.

Internal armed conflict

In December, the President signed into law "An Act Defining and Penalizing Crimes Against International Humanitarian Law, Genocide and Other Crimes Against Humanity".

Moro Islamic Liberation Front

In July, the army and the MILF agreed to stop military operations after a year of fighting in Mindanao Island, southern Philippines. In September, they signed a framework agreement for an International Contact Group to serve as guarantors to the peace negotiations. In October, they signed an agreement on civilian protection that reconfirmed their obligations under humanitarian law and human rights law and designated an International Monitoring Team and NGOs to carry out monitoring and civilian protection functions. Formal peace talks resumed in December.

In December, the government estimated that there were some 125,000 internally displaced people in Maguindanao province. Only 20 per cent of displaced families lived in centres for the displaced. Many lived in tents unsuitable for long-term shelter, especially given frequent typhoons and floods. Living conditions were poor, with unclean water, inadequate sanitation and high levels of malnutrition.

National Democratic Front

In June, the government and the NDF agreed to work towards the resumption of formal peace talks to end the 40-year sporadic armed conflict. The NDF are linked to the Communist Party of the Philippines (CPP) and the NPA.

In July, the government lifted its four-year suspension of the Joint Agreement on Safety and Immunity Guarantee to allow the NDF to prepare for talks that had been stalled since 2005. However, military efforts to flush out the NPA resulted in the displacement of thousands, including Indigenous Peoples, from forested lands throughout the country.

■ In July and August, some 1,800 people from 15 Indigenous communities in Surigao del Sur province, 400 people from seven communities in North Cotabato province, and 500 people from seven communities in Davao del Sur fled after government troops entered their communities. Their economic activities were affected and their movement was restricted. Some community members were intimidated into joining Task Force Gantangan – Bagani Force, a government-backed paramilitary unit composed of Indigenous Peoples tasked to fight the NPA. Some had returned home by the end of the year.

P

Unlawful killings

In a follow-up report on the Philippines in April the UN Special Rapporteur on extrajudicial, summary or arbitrary executions stated that the government had not implemented reforms to ensure command responsibility for human rights violations; that impunity for unlawful killings remained widespread; and witness protection remained inadequate. In addition, the CPP and the NPA had failed to reduce unlawful killings.

■ In March, unidentified assailants shot dead anti-mining activist Eliezer Billanes in South Cotabato province in broad daylight. He had just returned from a meeting with soldiers to discuss his safety concerns.

■ In June, five soldiers beat and shot dead Katog Sapalon, a charcoal maker, in front of his family in Maguindanao province. A family member said that the soldiers repeatedly asked if he was a member of the MILF.

■ In September, armed men killed Catholic priest and human rights defender Father Cecilio Lucero in Northern Samar province. He had been travelling with an armed police bodyguard for security.

■ In November, more than 100 members of paramilitary groups, together with the private army of a powerful political clan, massacred more than 60 people, including 33 journalists and media personnel in Maguindanao province. Those killed were filling out a certificate of nomination for a provincial governor candidate.

Torture and other ill-treatment, enforced disappearances

Torture continued to be practised in military facilities and secret detention centres. In May, the UN Committee Against Torture expressed concern about the "numerous, ongoing, credible and constant allegations... of routine and widespread use of torture and ill-treatment of suspects in police custody, especially to extract confessions" and that those "committed by law enforcement and military services personnel were seldom investigated or prosecuted".

■ In January, the military abducted Mansur Salih, a tricycle driver from Maguindanao province, during a raid on his village. The military held him incommunicado in a secret detention centre where he was beaten and repeatedly given electric shocks. He was fed only once every three days. Mansur Salih was made to sign a document he had not read, before he

surfaced in April and was charged with arson.

■ In May, the military reportedly abducted Melissa Roxas, an American citizen of Philippine descent, in Tarlac province. The military beat her and subjected her to near-suffocation with plastic bags. Melissa Roxas said that she was mistakenly identified by her abductors as the former secretary-general of leftist labour group Migrante.

In November, the Anti-torture Bill became law.

Indigenous Peoples' rights

Free, prior and informed consent, enshrined in Philippine law, continued to be circumvented or denied in practice. In August, the UN Committee on the Elimination of Racial Discrimination expressed concern that Indigenous Peoples were not adequately consulted with regard to infrastructure and natural resource exploitation projects. The Committee also highlighted the effect internal displacement had on the livelihoods, health and education of Indigenous Peoples.

■ In October, about 100 armed police and a demolition crew violently dispersed residents from a protest site in Didipio, Nueva Vizcaya province. The residents were protesting against the forced eviction of hundreds of Indigenous Peoples and rural dwellers from their homes in Didipio to make way for mining exploration. The police reportedly used unnecessary and excessive force and threw tear gas at the residents.

Freedom of expression

The government accused activists and left-leaning NGOs of being communist supporters. Activists were targeted in criminal lawsuits, known as SLAPP suits (Strategic Lawsuits Against Public Participation).

Amnesty International visits/report

🚗 Amnesty International delegates visited the Philippines in March, April, May and December.

📘 Shattered Lives: Beyond the 2008-2009 Mindanao Armed Conflict (ASA 35/003/2009)

POLAND

REPUBLIC OF POLAND

Head of state:	Lech Kaczyński
Head of government:	Donald Tusk
Death penalty:	abolitionist for all crimes
Population:	38.1 million
Life expectancy:	75.5 years
Under-5 mortality (m/f):	9/7 per 1,000
Adult literacy:	99.3 per cent

The results of an investigation into Poland's alleged involvement in the US-led renditions (unlawful transfers of terrorist suspects between countries) and secret detention programme remained classified. Poland was referred to the European Court of Justice for failing to incorporate into national law the EU legislation prohibiting gender discrimination. International bodies criticized the impediments faced by women in accessing certain reproductive health services, including abortion, even when their lives were at risk. Poland was criticized for the use of criminal defamation legislation.

Counter-terror and security

The National Public Prosecutor continued to investigate allegations that Poland hosted a secret detention facility where "high value detainees" were interrogated by the US Central Intelligence Agency (CIA) in 2002 and 2003. In April, Roman Giertych, former head of a parliamentary commission, said that he had presented documentary evidence of potentially criminal acts to the government in 2006. Findings of the Commission remained classified. Former officials, including former President Aleksander Kwasniewski, denied the allegations, but acknowledged ongoing co-operation between the CIA and the Polish intelligence agency.

Also in April the TVP television station and the *Rzeczpospolita* newspaper published new evidence of Poland's involvement, including a flight book from Szymany airport where US jets were reported to have landed regularly in 2002 and 2003.

In July the National Public Prosecutor informed Amnesty International that his office had initiated an investigation in March 2008 into possible infringements of authority by public servants in connection with secret CIA operations in Europe.

However, the scope and methodology of the investigation would not be made public, as it was classified information.

Discrimination

In May Poland was referred to the European Court of Justice by the European Commission for failing to incorporate into national law EU legislation prohibiting gender discrimination in access to, and supply of, goods and services. The anti-discrimination legislation had not been adopted by the end of December. However, the government did prepare a draft law to strengthen the powers of the Commissioner for the Protection of Civil Rights to act as an equality body.

Sexual and reproductive rights

Women had difficulty accessing abortion services within the health system even when permitted by law, including in cases when their lives were at risk. Medical service providers and health institutions were not held accountable for denying access to lawful health services or for the consequences of that denial on women's health and lives. The UN Committee on Economic, Social and Cultural Rights criticized Poland for not guaranteeing basic sexual and reproductive health services such as contraception and family planning services.

Parliament adopted the Patients' Rights and the Ombudsperson for Patients' Rights Act in June, which allows any patient to file an objection against a physician's opinion or ruling. Its enactment followed a 2007 ruling by the European Court of Human Rights in *Tysiąc v Poland* that Poland violated the right to respect for private life because it provided no timely or effective means for women to appeal against doctors' decisions to deny them access to abortion services. However, the new law required the Medical Board to rule on a complaint within 30 days, a delay that could be too long for certain medical procedures and thus constitute a violation of the right to health. In addition, the Medical Board was allowed to return a patient's complaint unanswered if they were unable to cite the legal basis of the rights or obligations being claimed. The need to hire a lawyer was a serious disincentive for patients in low or middle income groups.

■ In June the European Court of Human Rights asked the government to clarify the circumstances of the death in September 2004 of a 25-year-old pregnant woman, Z. In the months before her death, she was

P

diagnosed with ulcerative colitis and an abscess that required three operations to remove. Z was admitted to a number of hospitals, but none would perform a full endoscopy and other diagnostic examinations for fear of risking the life of the foetus, despite appeals from her family. Z miscarried on 5 September 2004 in the fifth month of pregnancy and died from septic shock on 29 September 2004.

Justice system

The European Court of Human Rights ruled on pre-trial detentions and prison overcrowding in Poland.
■ In February, in *Kauczor v Poland*, the Court concluded that numerous cases of excessively lengthy detention on remand revealed a "malfunctioning of the Polish criminal justice system" that affected large numbers of individuals.
■ In *Jamrozy v Poland*, the Court ruled in September that the extensive length of pre-trial detention – more than two years – violated the right to trial within a reasonable time or to release pending trial.
■ In October the Court found Poland in violation of the prohibition of torture or degrading treatment. Krzysztof Orchowski had passed most of his prison sentence in a cell with a personal space smaller than 3m² and at times 2m². The government acknowledged that prison overcrowding was systemic.

Freedom of expression

Criminalizing defamation, an offence punishable by up to two years' imprisonment for journalists (Article 212 of the criminal code), had – in at least one case – an adverse effect on freedom of expression.
■ In February the European Court of Human Rights found that Poland had violated the right to freedom of expression. In 2000 journalist Jacek Długołęcki was convicted of insulting a politician under Article 212 and fined. The ruling stated that the penalty amounted to a form of censorship and that the conviction was likely to deter journalists from contributing to public discussion or performing their task as public watchdog.

Refugees and asylum-seekers

Refugees and asylum-seekers continued to experience difficulties in accessing health care services and the labour market. In December some 200 asylum-seekers, mostly people from Georgia and Chechnya, travelled to Strasbourg without tickets or identity documents as a way of protesting at the conditions of refugees and asylum-seekers in Poland.

Amnesty International report

Poland: Briefing to the UN Committee on Economic, Social and Cultural Rights (EUR 37/002/2009)

PORTUGAL

PORTUGUESE REPUBLIC

Head of state:	Aníbal António Cavaco Silva
Head of government:	José Sócrates Carvalho Pinto de Sousa
Death penalty:	abolitionist for all crimes
Population:	10.7 million
Life expectancy:	78.6 years
Under-5 mortality (m/f):	6/5 per 1,000
Adult literacy:	94.9 per cent

The judicial investigation into alleged complicity by Portuguese authorities with the illegal transfer of prisoners to Guantánamo Bay was closed in May on the grounds of lack of evidence. Two former Guantánamo Bay detainees took up residency in Portugal. Domestic violence led to numerous deaths. Investigations into allegations of torture by law enforcement officials proceeded slowly, with evidence of impunity.

Counter-terror and security

At the end of May the judicial investigation into suspected CIA rendition flights and other illegal transfers of prisoners to Guantánamo Bay alleged to have crossed through Portuguese territory was closed by the public prosecutor on the grounds of insufficient evidence. Ana Gomes, a Portuguese member of the European Parliament, submitted an appeal in July calling for the investigation to be continued, arguing that it had been inadequate. She cited numerous shortcomings, including the failure to take testimony from relevant intelligence service officials, the foreign affairs and defence ministers, former prime ministers, US embassy officials, or the directors of the Portuguese Civil Aviation Institute and air traffic control authorities. She also criticized the failure of the prosecutor to request clarification from the Ministry of Foreign Affairs about whether its exceptional authorizations to the USA allowing "the transport of contentious material and people" included the transfer of prisoners to secret detention centres. The appeal was rejected in September by the public prosecutor, who stated that the additional investigatory measures requested were "irrelevant".

On 28 August, two Syrian detainees at Guantánamo Bay were released and transferred to Portugal. They were not able to return to Syria due to the risk of torture and other serious human rights violations. The Portuguese government granted both men residence permits on humanitarian grounds, and confirmed that no charges would be brought against them.

Violence against women and girls

The Portuguese Association for Victim Support registered 15,904 complaints concerning domestic violence in 2009. These included 16 murders.

Torture and other ill-treatment

Criminal investigations into allegations of torture and other ill-treatment by law enforcement officials continued in 2009.

■ On 22 May the Criminal Court of Faro issued its sentence in the case of the torture of Leonor Cipriano. The court recognized that she had been tortured in police custody in 2004, but acquitted all three police officers, claiming that it was impossible to identify exactly who had been responsible. A fourth officer was convicted of giving false testimony and another was convicted of falsifying documents. Leonor Cipriano's appeal was pending at the end of the year.

■ By the end of the year, no trial date had been set for three judicial police officers accused of torturing Virgolino Borges in March 2000. The case was due to go to trial in November 2008 but was delayed pending further medical examinations requested by the defence. Virgolino Borges said that he had been tortured by police officers who punched him and beat him on the soles of his feet with a wooden post while in custody. The investigation had been closed in 2005 by the public prosecutor, who stated that Virgolino Borges' injuries could have been self-inflicted. Virgolino Borges appealed against this decision to the Lisbon region courts: first to the Tribunal de Instrução and then to the Tribunal da Relação, which in November 2005 ordered that the case go to trial.

PUERTO RICO

COMMONWEALTH OF PUERTO RICO
Head of state: Barack H. Obama (replaced
                                  George W. Bush in January)
Head of government: Aníbal Aceveda-Vilá
Death penalty: abolitionist for all crimes
Population: 4 million
Life expectancy: 79 years
Under-5 mortality (m/f):   9/8 per 1,000

There were reports of police ill-treatment during attempts to enter an informal settlement where residents were under a government eviction order.

Excessive use of force

There were reports of excessive use of force by police against the community of Villas de Sol in Toa Baja in August during a police operation to gain access to the area. According to reports, police deployed pepper spray and used batons against a group of residents who were obstructing their access. A number of people were reportedly taken to hospital, including a woman who was eight months pregnant.

Right to adequate housing

The Villas de Sol Community of 211 families in Toa Baja, many of whose members were from the Dominican Republic, was under an eviction order from the government. In August, the water and electricity supplies to the community were turned off and temporary supplies provided by the town authorities. There were concerns about the quality of the water in the tanks and about reported toxicity from the electrical generators. In November, a complaint was made on behalf of the community to the UN Special Rapporteur on adequate housing. Later that month, the 31 December deadline for the eviction of the community was extended by six months.

Police and security forces

In August, a jury in a US federal court convicted four San Juan Municipal Police officers in connection with the death in custody of Jose Antonio Rivera Robles in 2003. The four officers were awaiting sentencing at the end of the year.

P

QATAR

STATE OF QATAR

Head of state:	Shaikh Hamad bin Khalifa al-Thani
Head of government:	Shaikh Hamad bin Jassim bin Jabr al-Thani
Death penalty:	retentionist
Population:	1.4 million
Life expectancy:	75.5 years
Under-5 mortality (m/f):	10/10 per 1,000
Adult literacy:	93.1 per cent

Women faced discrimination and violence. Migrant workers were exploited and abused, and inadequately protected under the law. Hundreds of people continued to be arbitrarily deprived of their nationality. Sentences of flogging were passed. Death sentences continued to be handed down, although no executions were carried out.

Discrimination and violence against women

Women continued to face discrimination in law and practice and were inadequately protected against violence within the family. Family law makes it much easier for men to divorce than women.

Despite a 2008 reform to the law on compensation equalizing provisions for men and women, an appeal court in April overturned a lower court's decision that had adhered to the reform and ruled that compensation for the death of a woman and her daughter was to be valued at half that of her husband and their son, in accordance with Shari'a law.

In April, Qatar acceded to the Convention on the Elimination of All Forms of Discrimination against Women but with reservations relating to equality of women under the law, within marriage and in terms of guardianship of children.

Freedom of expression

At least 11 foreign nationals were convicted of blasphemy, three of whom received maximum seven-year prison sentences for using words considered insulting to Islam. They included a Syrian man convicted of "insulting Islam in a fit of rage" for uttering a blasphemous word when the credit on his mobile phone ran out during a conversation. The court also ordered that he be deported. It was not

clear whether the prison sentence was enforced in his and other cases.

At least 52 other foreign nationals were convicted of charges relating to "illicit sexual relations" and either deported or sentenced to imprisonment followed by deportation.

Debate continued about a possible new press and publications law to replace Law No.8 of 1979, which prescribes imprisonment for criticizing religion, the army and the Emir.

Migrants' rights

Migrant workers, who make up more than 80 per cent of Qatar's population, continued to be exposed to, and inadequately protected against, abuses and exploitation by employers. Women migrant domestic workers were particularly at risk of exploitation and abuses such as beatings, rape and other sexual violence.

A new sponsorship law passed in February to regulate the entry, exit, residence and work of foreign nationals introduced some improvements. Notably, it requires that sponsor employers no longer retain employees' passports after visa formalities have been completed. It also allows women employees in independent employment to sponsor the entry into and residence in Qatar of their husbands and children.

Discrimination – denial of nationality

The government continued to deny Qatari nationality to hundreds of people who were consequently denied employment opportunities, social security and health care in Qatar, or denied entry to the country. They had no means of remedy before the courts. Most were members of al-Murra tribe, which was partly blamed for a coup attempt in 1996.

Cruel, inhuman and degrading punishments

At least 18 people, mostly foreign nationals, were sentenced to flogging of between 40 and 100 lashes for offences related to "illicit sexual relations" or alcohol consumption. Only Muslims considered medically fit were liable to have such sentences carried out. It was not known if any of the sentences were implemented.

Death penalty

At least three people were sentenced to death and up to five death sentences were upheld in 2009. At least 27 people were on death row at the end of the year.

Amnesty International report

Qatar: Submission to the UN Universal Periodic Review (MDE 22/001/2009)

ROMANIA

ROMANIA

Head of state:	Traian Băsescu
Head of government:	Emil Boc
Death penalty:	abolitionist for all crimes
Population:	21.3 million
Life expectancy:	72.5 years
Under-5 mortality (m/f):	20/15 per 1,000
Adult literacy:	97.6 per cent

The results of the Senate's investigation into Romania's alleged involvement in the US-led renditions (unlawful transfers of terrorist suspects between countries) and secret detention programme remained classified. Government surveys demonstrated widespread discrimination against Roma by the majority population. Several cases of forced evictions of Roma were reported.

Background

A political crisis was triggered by an attempt to reform the pension system as one of the conditions of an International Monetary Fund loan, and Emil Boc's government was forced to resign in October. After the presidential elections, the president reappointed Emil Boc as the Prime Minister, and his new government was approved by the parliament in December. The Romanian Academic Society reported in November that the country's health system might be close to collapse in 2010.

A new Civil Code and Criminal Code were adopted in June. The Criminal Code introduced "aggravating circumstances" in cases of crimes perpetrated with discriminatory intent, and punished incitement to hatred or discrimination. However, these codes were not in force at the end of the year, as new procedural codes had not been adopted.

There was strong opposition by local NGOs to the content of the codes. The Association for the Defence of Human Rights in Romania – the Helsinki Committee (APADOR-CH) criticized, among other things, an Article in the procedural codes that seemed to allow the use of information gained through torture as evidence in criminal proceedings.

Counter-terror and security

The New York Times newspaper reported in August that a secret US Central Intelligence Agency (CIA) prison had been constructed in Bucharest. The government denied this and emphasized that it co-operated with all the international commissions set up to investigate the allegations of the existence of CIA detention centres on their territory. The European Commission reacted with a repeated call for full, independent and impartial investigations to establish the truth.

In a response to a request by the APADOR-CH, the government confirmed that some CIA-operated aircraft took off and landed on Romanian territory, as had previously been identified by a Council of Europe report.

The report of the Senate commission of inquiry, which had investigated allegations in 2006 and 2007 regarding the existence of CIA detention centres in Romania and was adopted in 2008, remained classified.

Discrimination – Roma

There was widespread prejudice against Romani people among the majority population. Roma continued to experience discrimination in access to education, health care and housing, including lack of secure tenure. According to the government-sponsored Inter-ethnic Barometer 2009, 55 per cent of the respondents believed that Roma should not be allowed to travel abroad as they damaged the reputation of the country and over 43 per cent agreed that they would not hire Roma because they regarded them as "lazy and thieving". The newspaper *Jurnalul Național* called for a popular legislative initiative to enforce the term "Țigan" instead of Roma. Romani and human rights NGOs expressed concerns about the negative connotations of the term "Țigan". Cases of violence against Romani

R

communities, including the destruction of properties, were reported.

■ On 31 May, in Sanmartin, as a response to an alleged conflict between a group of local Roma and a non-Roma man, 400 non-Romani people reportedly attacked houses inhabited by Roma, damaging dozens of homes and properties. According to the NGO Romani CRISS, as a result of the attacks 170 Roma fled their homes and sought refuge in the woods, in the fields and on the streets, fearing for their safety. An informal local commission for dialogue (comprised mostly of the non-Roma population) was formed, which drafted a community agreement outlining obligations for the Roma. Following the adoption of this agreement, from June until August the Roma in Sanmartin allegedly continued to suffer harassment from local non-Roma people who gathered regularly in groups of 100 to 150 people, going round the Romani houses in the village allegedly to monitor the fulfilment of these obligations. Romanian NGOs expressed concerns over the lack of response of the authorities to ensure the safety of the community and the investigations of the attacks on Romani houses.

■ The European Court of Human Rights took into consideration the government's admission that there was a lack of remedies for the enforcement of the rights guaranteed by the European Convention in the case of *Tănase and others v Romania*, including the prohibition of torture, right to a fair trial, right to respect for private and family life, right to an effective remedy and prohibition of discrimination. In 1991, a crowd of more than 2,000 non-Roma, together with the priest and mayor, had burned or otherwise damaged the houses of 24 Romani people in Bolintin Deal. Following the attacks, the entire Romani community in the village fled their houses and were left homeless for a month. In May, the government committed to paying damages totalling €565,000, and undertook to implement a series of measures to prevent and fight discrimination and to improve living conditions for the Roma community.

Right to adequate housing

Romani people continued to experience segregation in housing. The UN Special Rapporteur on adequate housing raised concerns about the housing conditions of poor and vulnerable groups, including Roma, and urged Romania to consider ratifying Article 31 on the right to adequate housing under the Revised European Social Charter. There were several cases of violations of the right to adequate housing.

■ Five years after they were forcibly evicted from a building in the centre of Miercurea Ciuc, approximately 75 Romani people, including families with young children, continued to live in inadequate housing conditions, hidden behind a sewage treatment plant on the outskirts of the town. Since they were relocated there by the municipal authorities, they lived in metal cabins and shacks which were overcrowded, lacked fresh air and offered little protection from the cold and rain. The sanitation facilities remained inadequate, with only four toilet cubicles for the whole community. The proximity of the location to the sewage treatment plant violated the 300m protection zone established by national law to separate human habitation from potential toxic hazards. The municipality failed in its obligation to ensure the provision of adequate alternative housing. In 2008, members of the community assisted by Romani CRISS had filed a complaint with the European Court of Human Rights alleging violations of human rights enshrined in the European Convention.

Torture and other ill-treatment

■ In April, the European Court of Human Rights found Romania in violation of the prohibition of torture. Nicu Olteanu was arrested in 1997 by the police on suspicion of stealing six bottles of mineral water. He complained that he was shot in the left foot by a policeman at the local police station after he attempted to escape, and that he did not receive appropriate medical assistance despite his injuries. In addition to the bullet wound, his medical report mentioned cuts on his right leg and right forearm. The ruling stated that the authorities had violated his right not to be subjected to inhuman or degrading treatment, and that the degree of force used against Nicu Olteanu was excessive and unjustified. The ruling also stated that the authorities had failed to carry out an effective and impartial investigation into his allegations.

Mental health institutions

■ In December, two NGOs, the Center for Legal Resources and Interights, filed an application with the European Court of Human Rights on behalf of five patients who died at the Poiana Mare Psychiatric Hospital in 2004. The patients allegedly died from a combination of poor care, inadequate treatment and substandard living conditions. In 2004, the hospital was visited by the European Committee for the

Prevention of Torture which raised concerns about the treatment of patients, as well as the living conditions, and asked the authorities to take urgent measures to address these problems.

Amnesty International visits

🚋 Amnesty International delegates visited Romania in January, May and October.

RUSSIAN FEDERATION

RUSSIAN FEDERATION

Head of state:	Dmitry Medvedev
Head of government:	Vladimir Putin
Death penalty:	abolitionist in practice
Population:	140.9 million
Life expectancy:	66.2 years
Under-5 mortality (m/f):	18/14 per 1,000
Adult literacy:	99.5 per cent

Human rights defenders, lawyers and journalists were threatened and physically attacked; some were killed. A climate of impunity for these crimes prevailed, with police failing to investigate effectively. Human rights abuses were increasingly reported in the North Caucasus. In a number of cases, criminal suspects were allegedly subjected to torture and other ill-treatment to extract confessions. The Russian authorities failed to investigate fully human rights violations carried out by the armed forces in the August 2008 conflict with Georgia. Concerns continued about the failure to uphold fair trial standards. Government officials spoke out against racism, but racist attacks still took place on a regular basis. In November the Constitutional Court decided in favour of fully abolishing the death penalty.

Background

The government voiced its intention to fight corruption. In December, President Dmitry Medvedev ordered the reform of the Interior Ministry as a response to the public's anger about police abuses. The Russian Federation's human rights record was assessed under the UN Universal Periodic Review in February. Concerns were raised about the recent murders of journalists, the independence of the judiciary, extremism and hate crimes as well as the situation in the North Caucasus.

Insecurity in the North Caucasus

Unlawful killings, extrajudicial executions, excessive use of force, enforced disappearances, torture and other ill-treatment in custody, and arbitrary detention continued to be reported in Chechnya, Ingushetia and Dagestan. Armed groups killed government officials, and suicide bombers killed law enforcement officials and civilians. Victims of human rights abuses feared reprisals if they sought redress.

Chechnya

In April the Russian government announced an end to the Counter-Terrorism Operation, but reports of serious human rights violations, in particular enforced disappearances, continued. A complete list of those who have disappeared since 1999 had still not been compiled. The investigation of mass graves by the authorities was ineffective, lacking systematic procedures and adequate forensic facilities. Families of internally displaced people faced eviction from temporary accommodation without adequate alternative housing or compensation. There were reports that properties belonging to families of alleged members of armed groups were destroyed.

The Russian authorities failed to conduct effective investigations into violations established by the European Court of Human Rights. Those submitting cases to the Court faced intimidation and harassment.

■ In July Natalia Estemirova, from the Memorial Human Rights Centre in Grozny, was abducted outside her home and murdered. Her body was later found with gunshot wounds in neighbouring Ingushetia.

■ In August the bodies of human rights activists Zarema Sadulayeva and her husband, Alik (Umar) Dzhabrailov, were found in the boot of a car in Grozny. They had both been shot. Zarema Sadulayeva was the head of the local charity, Let's Save the Generation, which helped children injured during the armed conflict in Chechnya. In October the authorities said that Alik Dzhabrailov was the target of the abduction but that his wife had insisted on going with him.

■ In October, aid worker Zarema Gaisanova was taken from her home in Grozny. Prosecutors told her mother that she was alive but that they did not have access to

R

her. Chechen TV reported that Chechen President Ramzan Kadyrov had led an operation targeting fighters in a neighbour's home.

Ingushetia
The assassination attempt in June of Ingushetian President Yunus-Bek Yevkurov, seen as a moderating influence in the most unstable of the Russian Caucasian republics, raised fears about an escalation of violence.

■ In May hearings began at Nazran City Court into the August 2008 killing of Magomed Evloev, a prominent opposition figure to the previous government and owner of an independent website in Ingushetia. In December a police officer was convicted of causing his death by negligence and given a two-year prison sentence.

■ In October Maksharip Aushev, a friend of Magomed Evloev, who also opposed the previous government, and who had run Magomed Evloev's website after his death, was shot dead while travelling in neighbouring Kabardino-Balkaria. In December his mother- and brother-in-law were killed when a car in which they were travelling, with his widow and other relatives, was blown up.

Journalists who attempted to report allegations of torture and unlawful killings were threatened and had to leave Ingushetia. Armed groups indiscriminately killed civilians, including during suicide attacks. There were reports of traders being shot by members of armed groups for selling alcohol.

Dagestan
Amidst a high level of violence and lawlessness, human rights defenders and journalists were threatened or killed, and disappearances and torture continued to be reported.

■ The office of the NGO Mothers of Dagestan for Human Rights was destroyed in a suspected arson attack in August. In the same month leaflets were distributed in Makhachkala, Dagestan's capital, calling for a blood feud against Svetlana Isaeva and Gulnara Rustamova, members of the NGO, and against other Dagestani human rights activists and journalists. They were accused of being members of illegal armed groups. The criminal investigation into the threats, opened in October, was ineffective. No measures were taken by the authorities to protect members of the NGO.

■ In August the body of Malik Akhmedilov, an investigative journalist who had written about unsolved killings of Dagestani officials, was found in a car in Makhachkala. He had been shot dead.

■ In August Artur Butaev, Islam Askerov and Arsen Butaev were abducted and allegedly beaten and ill-treated while being interrogated in an unknown building. Islam Askerov and Arsen Butaev managed to escape and went into hiding. Three days days later the remains of Artur Butaev and two other men, Gadzhi Gudaliev and Amiraslan Islamov, were found in a burned-out car near Makhachkala.

Kabardino-Balkaria
■ In February the Supreme Court ruled that, in accordance with new legislation, the trial of 58 individuals accused of an attack on public buildings in Nalchik in October 2005 should take place without a jury. In March the trial opened at the Supreme Court of Kabardino-Balkaria. The health of several detainees had reportedly deteriorated as a result of harsh conditions in pre-trial detention, including the lack of medical care. According to his lawyer, detainee Rasul Kudaev was denied medical aid for hepatitis C. Appeals by his lawyer for confession statements allegedly made under torture or duress to be excluded from the case material were ignored. Rasul Kudaev had previously been detained at the US naval base in Guantánamo Bay, Cuba.

Armed conflict
A report by the Independent International Fact-Finding Mission on the Conflict in Georgia, commissioned by the EU and published in September, confirmed that violations of international human rights and humanitarian law were committed by Georgian, Russian and South Ossetian forces in 2008 and called on all sides of the conflict to address the consequences of the war. By the end of the year, no full investigations had been conducted by any side into the violations of human rights and international humanitarian law that took place during the 2008 war and in its immediate aftermath. A general lack of accountability persisted and there had been no comprehensive efforts undertaken to bring any of those responsible to justice.

Freedom of expression and human rights defenders
Amendments to the law on NGOs, which came into force in August, eased registration, inspection and reporting procedures. However, legislation regulating

civil society organizations remained open to abuse.

Independent civil society remained under threat, especially but not only in the North Caucasus. Human rights defenders, journalists and opposition activists across the Russian Federation were subjected to attacks and threats. Some were killed. Investigations into such attacks and threats remained inadequate. Officials accused human rights defenders and NGOs of supporting "extremism" or working for foreign secret services. Under the law to combat extremist activities, law enforcement agencies targeted violent opponents and peaceful dissenters alike. The UN Human Rights Committee, during its examination of Russia's compliance with the International Covenant on Civil and Political Rights, raised concerns about the lack of protection for human rights defenders and journalists.

■ In January, lawyer and human rights defender Stanislav Markelov and *Novaya Gazeta* journalist Anastasia Baburova were shot dead in central Moscow. Two suspects were arrested in November.

■ In February a jury acquitted all those charged with involvement in the 2006 killing of journalist Anna Politkovskaya. In September the Supreme Court ordered a new investigation following an appeal from her family. The new investigation combined the case against the three alleged accomplices to the crime with the investigation into those responsible for carrying out the murder and for ordering it.

■ In March, human rights defender Lev Ponomarev was kicked and beaten by three men near his Moscow home.

■ In October, in a civil libel case, Moscow's Tverskoi District Court fined Oleg Orlov, head of Memorial Human Rights Centre, for libelling Chechen President Ramzan Kadyrov when he accused him of responsibility for the July murder of human rights defender Natalia Estemirova. Appeals by both sides – against the judgement and against the amount of compensation awarded – had not been heard by the end of the year. Later in October a criminal defamation charge, based on the same evidence and punishable by up to three years' imprisonment, was brought against Oleg Orlov.

■ In May Aleksei Sokolov, head of an NGO campaigning against torture and ill-treatment in prisons and detention centres, was detained, allegedly on suspicion of taking part in a 2004 robbery. In July Sverdlovsk Regional Court ordered his discharge and release. However, the police immediately detained him again, allegedly on suspicion of a different crime. In a closed hearing in August, Ekaterinburg District Court ordered his remand in custody on the grounds that, as a member of the region's public commission for oversight of places of detention, he could meet and influence men convicted of the 2004 robbery. Amid numerous procedural violations, his detention was extended into 2010.

The right to freedom of assembly was restricted for members of the political opposition and for human rights activists. Several people were sentenced to police detention solely for attempting to exercise their right to freedom of assembly. The Moscow authorities repeatedly denied requests to hold demonstrations in support of the right to freedom of assembly, and arrested and fined dozens of people who attempted to demonstrate publicly.

■ In January, four members of the opposition coalition, the Other Russia, were detained by police in Nizhnii Novgorod and sentenced to five days' administrative detention, apparently with the sole purpose of preventing them from attending a demonstration three days later. Neither police reports nor the court hearings gave specific information about the allegations against them.

■ A gay pride march was banned in May by the Moscow authorities, which provided no alternative date or location as required in law. Police later briefly detained several people who attempted to hold a march, as well as counter-demonstrators.

■ Opposition activist Eduard Limonov was given a 10-day prison sentence for allegedly refusing to obey police orders during an unauthorized demonstration in October.

In this climate of intolerance for independent views, freedom of expression was also curtailed in the arts and sciences.

■ In July the trial began of Yuri Samodurov, former director of Moscow's Sakharov Museum, and Andrei Yerofeev, an art curator, on a charge of inciting hatred that carries a sentence of up to five years' imprisonment. They were charged in connection with a 2007 Moscow exhibition of works that had been rejected by other galleries, intended to promote debate on freedom and art.

Torture and other ill-treatment

Regional commissions for public oversight of places of detention started to function from January onwards. They were appointed in several Russian regions

R

following the adoption of enabling legislation in September 2008. There were widespread reports of torture or other ill-treatment in places of detention, including alleged denial of medical aid. In a few cases, law enforcement officials were convicted of abuse of office in connection with such reports. However, allegations that the authorities failed to investigate effectively such abuses remained frequent.

■ In February and April, Zubair Zubairaev, an ethnic Chechen, was reportedly beaten and otherwise ill-treated by prison officers in a prison colony in Volgograd region. During a visit in April his lawyer saw marks on his shoulders and across his chest. No medical help was provided and the injuries he received were not recorded. Possibly as a result of his complaints about his treatment, Zubair Zubairaev was transferred to a different colony.

■ Sergei Magnitskii, a lawyer, died in pre-trial detention in Moscow in November. A criminal investigation into his death was opened following information that he had been denied medical treatment.

Unfair trials

Trial procedures frequently failed to meet international standards of fair trial. In some cases there were concerns that the treatment of suspects was politically motivated. In September the Parliamentary Assembly of the Council of Europe called on the Russian Federation, among others, to adopt reforms to increase judicial independence and end the harassment of defence lawyers.

■ In February, former YUKOS oil company owner Mikhail Khodorkovskii and his former colleague Platon Lebedev, serving eight-year prison sentences following conviction for tax evasion and fraud in 2005, were transferred from pre-trial detention in Chita to face trial on new charges of money laundering and embezzlement. In March the new trial began in Moscow, amid concerns that it would fail to meet international standards of fair trial and that the further prosecution may have been politically motivated. The rights of the two defendants to adequate time and facilities to prepare their defence for the second trial appeared to have been violated.

Racism

The authorities recognized racially or ethnically motivated violence as a "threat to national security".

However, an effective programme of action to tackle racially motivated violence and racial discrimination by law enforcement officials has still to be implemented.

According to the NGO the SOVA Centre, by the end of the year at least 71 people had died and more than 330 were injured in 36 Russian regions as a result of racially motivated attacks. Anti-racist campaigners were also targeted by right-wing groups.

■ In November, 26-year-old Ivan Khutorskoi was shot and killed near his home. He had participated in a number of anti-fascist public actions and had been threatened and attacked by unidentified people.

According to statistics from the Interior Ministry, in the first four months of the year 105 people were accused of, or under investigation for, "extremist" crimes, which included cases of racially motivated murder.

Death penalty

In November the Constitutional Court decided to extend a 10-year moratorium on executions and recommended abolishing the death penalty completely. The moratorium was due to expire when all regions had introduced jury trials, which was planned to happen in January 2010. The Court said the path towards full abolition was irreversible.

Violence against women and girls

Research by NGOs showed that violence against women in the family was widespread. There were no statistics provided by the government, and government support for crisis centres and telephone helplines remained inadequate. There were only some 20 shelters across the country for women fleeing domestic violence. Many of these were open solely to those with residential registration in the local region, including Moscow's single shelter, which provided space for only 10 women. No legal measures specifically addressed violence against women in the family.

Amnesty International visit/reports

🚌 An Amnesty International delegate visited North Ossetia in July.

📖 Civilians in the aftermath of war – the Georgia-Russia conflict one year on (EUR 04/001/2009)

📖 Russian Federation: Rule without law – human rights violations in the North Caucasus (EUR 46/012/2009)

📖 Russian Federation: Briefing to the UN Human Rights Committee (EUR 46/025/2009)

RWANDA

REPUBLIC OF RWANDA

Head of state:	Paul Kagame
Head of government:	Bernard Makuza
Death penalty:	abolitionist for all crimes
Population:	10 million
Life expectancy:	49.7 years
Under-5 mortality (m/f):	167/143 per 1,000
Adult literacy:	64.9 per cent

The authorities tightly controlled political space in advance of the 2010 presidential elections and freedom of expression was unduly restricted by broad laws on genocide ideology. Human rights defenders continued to exercise self-censorship to avoid confrontations with the authorities. Conventional courts still fell short of fair trial standards despite continued improvements to Rwanda's justice system. Rwanda sought to address some failings within its criminal justice system which were cited by the International Criminal Tribunal for Rwanda (ICTR) when it refused to transfer cases in 2008. No country extradited genocide suspects to Rwanda.

Background

International donors, pleased with economic developments and Rwanda's rapprochement with the Democratic Republic of Congo (DRC), rarely raised human rights violations publicly.

Rwanda's relations with the DRC improved following a peace deal early in the year to end the rebellion by the Rwandan-backed National Congress for the Defence of the People (CNDP). In January, Rwanda joined Congolese government forces in a joint military offensive against the Democratic Liberation Forces of Rwanda (FDLR) in North-Kivu province. Military operations against the FDLR were strongly criticized from a human rights perspective (see DRC entry). The Netherlands and Sweden did not reinstate direct budgetary assistance which they had suspended in December 2008 following the release of a UN report demonstrating Rwandan support for the CNDP.

Rwanda joined the Commonwealth of Nations and restored diplomatic relations with France in November.

Freedom of expression

Freedom of expression remained severely restricted.

Journalists

In August, the government introduced a media law which placed undue restrictions on press freedom, including a requirement that Rwandan journalists possess a degree or certificate in journalism as a precondition to practising. Some journalists who were critical of the government continued to be excluded from government press conferences.

■ On 25 April, the BBC Kinyarwanda service was suspended by the Rwandan government after it aired a trailer for a show discussing forgiveness after the 1994 genocide. The government argued, without basis, that the broadcast constituted genocide denial, which is a criminal offence in Rwanda. The advertisement included Faustin Twagiramungu, a former presidential candidate, opposing attempts to have all Hutus apologize for the genocide as not all had participated in it. The broadcast also contained an excerpt from a man of mixed ethnicity reflecting on why the government had not allowed relatives of those killed by the Rwandan Patriotic Front (RPF) to grieve. The BBC service was reinstated in June following negotiations between the BBC and the government.

Law on genocide ideology

The authorities used broadly defined genocide ideology laws to silence dissent, including criticisms of the ruling RPF party and demands for justice for RPF war crimes. As of August 2009, there were reportedly 912 people in prison (356 awaiting trial; 556 convicted and sentenced) on genocide ideology charges. Some cases resulted in acquittals, often following a period of prolonged pre-trial detention.

Although the law covers some acts that can constitute hate speech, it requires no link to any genocidal act and is extremely vague. For example, it penalizes people with a 10- to 25-year prison term for "dehumanizing" a group of people by "laughing at one's misfortune" or "stirring up ill feelings". It penalizes young children with sentences of up to 12 months at a rehabilitation centre, and those aged 12 to 18 with prison sentences of between five and twelve and a half years.

Human rights defenders

Human rights defenders continued to self-censor their work to avoid confrontations with the authorities. There were reports that some NGOs continued to be infiltrated by members of the ruling RPF party.

R

Freedom of association

The government actively impeded the registration of nascent opposition political parties. The Social Party Imberakuri was registered in August after several delays, but the Green Party still awaited its registration in late 2009 and had difficulty securing police clearance for meetings.

Prisoners of conscience

Charles Ntakirutinka, a former government minister, remained in Kigali Central Prison, serving a 10-year sentence due to end in 2012. He was convicted, in an unfair trial, of inciting civil disobedience and associating with criminal elements. His co-accused, former President Pasteur Bizimungu, was released by presidential pardon in 2007.

Justice system

Rwanda sought to address some of the failings within its criminal justice system, which were impugned by the ICTR when it refused to transfer cases to Rwanda in 2008. In May, Rwanda amended the 2007 transfer law, allowing witnesses residing abroad to testify by video link, deposition or before a judge sitting in a foreign jurisdiction. The amendment also provided for legal aid to indigent defendants transferred or extradited.

A special witness protection service for such cases was housed within the Supreme Court to respond to concerns that some defence witnesses would be averse to approaching the Witness and Victim Support Unit within the Prosecutor's Office.

A draft law clarifying the nature of "special provisions" attached to life sentences was pending approval at year's end. Abolition of the death penalty in 2007 led to the introduction of two types of life sentence: life imprisonment and life imprisonment with special provisions, which would be served in isolation. The draft law requires prisoners to be kept in individual cells for 20 years, raising concerns that some prisoners would be subjected to prolonged solitary confinement. Rwanda does not have the capacity to keep prisoners in individual cells. The draft law would allow prisoners to exercise and receive visits only from members of their immediate family. It violates the right to health in medical emergencies, as a convicted prisoner could not access medical treatment outside prison without the approval of three prison doctors.

As of October, there were 62,821 people in prison.

Prison overcrowding continued to be a problem, despite a significant reduction in the prison population due to community service and annual prisoner releases.

Gacaca proceedings

Gacaca trials, whose procedures fail to meet international fair trial standards, were expedited with the objective of completing all outstanding cases by December. The 31 July deadline for new accusations before gacaca was extended in some areas. Some gacaca trials were reportedly marred by false accusations, corruption, and difficulties in calling defence witnesses. In December, with several appeals and revisions pending, the deadline to end gacaca was extended to the end of February 2010. After the closure of gacaca, new accusations were to be presented before conventional courts.

International justice

International Criminal Tribunal for Rwanda

The ICTR's mandate to finish all first-instance trials was extended to end of June 2010, according to UN Security Council Resolution 1901. The apprehension of two suspects indicted by the ICTR, Grégoire Ndahimana and Idelphonse Nizeyimana, and their transfer to Arusha from the DRC and Uganda respectively, marked growing regional co-operation between countries to support justice for the genocide.

Universal jurisdiction – Genocide suspects living abroad

Judicial proceedings against genocide suspects took place in many countries including Belgium, Canada, Finland and the USA. Extradition hearings against genocide suspects continued in Finland, Sweden and the UK. No country extradited genocide suspects to Rwanda for trial.

Due to concerns over the protection of defence witnesses and fears of executive interference with the judiciary, a UK High Court ruling overturned the UK's initial decision to extradite to Rwanda four Rwandans wanted on genocide charges. Finland ruled against extradition, deciding instead to try François Bazaramba under universal jurisdiction (see Finland entry). The court travelled to Rwanda to hear evidence from prosecution witnesses. Sweden was the first country to rule in favour of extradition, but Sylvère Ahorugeze's extradition was halted pending an appeal at the European Court of Human Rights.

The Rwandan government reported that it had over 500 genocide suspects under investigation around the world. It also stated that some African countries had not co-operated with its investigations.

Impunity

War crimes and crimes against humanity committed by the RPF and the Rwandan Patriotic Army (RPA) before, during and after the genocide were not prosecuted. There were no new criminal investigations or prosecutions initiated against former RPA fighters accused of committing war crimes and crimes against humanity. The ICTR did not issue indictments against any RPF commanders implicated in such abuses. Neither did the ICTR recall the RPF file that was transferred to the government of Rwanda, resulting in the prosecution of two junior commanders. This was despite concerns that the trial, whose verdict was pronounced in October 2008, fell short of international fair trial standards and that those who directed the killings were not prosecuted.

Rights of lesbian, gay, bisexual and transgender people

In late December, the lower house of the Rwandan parliament rejected an amendment to the Penal Code, which would have criminalized same-sex relations and their promotion. Following significant pressure from Rwandan civil society and the diplomatic community, the Minister of Justice issued a public statement stating that homosexuality would not be criminalized, as sexual orientation was a private matter.

Refugees and asylum-seekers

The deadline for voluntary repatriation of Rwandan refugees from Uganda lapsed. This followed concerns raised that repatriation may not have been voluntary given that Uganda's assistance to Rwandan refugees was due to cease after 31 July, according to the voluntary repatriation agreement signed between the Rwandan government, the Ugandan government and the UN High Commissioner for Refugees on 22 April. Some refugees reported that they were stopped from cultivating their land. The ending of such assistance may have forced refugees who continued to have a well-founded fear of persecution in Rwanda to return there.

Amnesty International visits/report

Amnesty International delegates visited Rwanda in September and October.

Finland: Universal jurisdiction put into practice against suspect in Rwandan genocide (EUR/20/001/2009)

SAUDI ARABIA

KINGDOM OF SAUDI ARABIA
Head of state and government: **King Abdullah bin 'Abdul 'Aziz Al-Saud**
Death penalty: retentionist
Population: 25.7 million
Life expectancy: 72.7 years
Under-5 mortality (m/f): 26/17 per 1,000
Adult literacy: 85 per cent

The authorities used a wide range of repressive measures to suppress freedom of expression and other legitimate activities. Hundreds of people were arrested as suspected terrorists. Thousands of others arrested in the name of security in previous years remained in jail; they included prisoners of conscience. Some 330 security suspects received unfair trials before a newly constituted but closed specialized court; one was sentenced to death and 323 were sentenced to terms of imprisonment. Women continued to face severe discrimination in law and practice, despite some signs of reform. The state did little to tackle widespread violence against women, particularly against domestic workers. Shi'a Muslims and others were targeted for practising their faith. The rights of migrants, refugees and asylum-seekers were violated. The administration of justice remained shrouded in secrecy and was summary in nature. Torture and other ill-treatment of detainees were systematic and carried out with impunity. Sentences of flogging were regularly imposed. The death penalty was used extensively. At least 69 people were executed, including two juvenile offenders.

Background

In February, during the UN Human Rights Council's (UNHRC) Universal Periodic Review of human rights

S

in Saudi Arabia, the government undertook to introduce various reforms while asserting that the country's laws were based on religious concepts. In May, Saudi Arabia was re-elected to the UNHRC.

In February, for the first time a woman was appointed to be a deputy minister in the government, and the Supreme Court began to function as the highest court of appeal as provided for under the 2007 Law of the Judiciary. The Courts of Cassation were also replaced by courts of appeal.

In July, the government introduced the country's first law against human trafficking, said to be a significant problem; those convicted of trafficking face up to 15 years' imprisonment and a fine.

Attacks by members or supporters of al-Qa'ida were reported. In August, the Deputy Interior Minister was reported to have been wounded in an assassination attempt by a suicide bomber. In October, the Interior Ministry said two men had been killed in a clash with security forces and militants in Jizan province and that six Yemeni nationals had been arrested.

In the last months of 2009, the conflict in Yemen's Sa'da region spilled over into Saudi Arabia and several Saudi Arabian soldiers were reported to have been killed by Yemeni rebel fighters. Saudi Arabian jets attacked the Yemeni rebels; it was unclear whether the authorities took adequate precautions to protect civilians from such attacks. The government sought to close the border to refugees fleeing from the conflict. Those who crossed from Sa'da were forcibly returned to Yemen.

Counter-terror and security

The authorities used a range of repressive measures in the name of countering terrorism, undermining embryonic legal reforms. Vague and broadly written anti-terrorism laws were used to suppress freedom of expression and other legitimate activities. The security forces failed to respect even these laws, knowing they could act with impunity.

Hundreds of people were detained on security grounds in 2009, adding to the thousands arrested in previous years; all were held in virtual secrecy. Many were suspected supporters of Islamist groups. Typically, such detainees are held without charge or trial for months or years for investigation and interrogation, and without any means of challenging their detention. Most are held without access to

lawyers and some are not permitted to see or communicate with their families for months or years. They are held in prisons where torture and other ill-treatment are rife and used to obtain self-incriminating "confessions". If charged, they face grossly unfair trials, conducted in secret and without defence lawyers and in which defendants are questioned briefly by a three-man panel about their "confessions". Sentences range from death to flogging and terms of imprisonment. Some of those imprisoned are held beyond the expiry of their sentence. Others are held for indefinite periods for "re-education".

■ In July, the government announced that 330 accused had been tried before a newly constituted specialized criminal court. Three were acquitted while 323 were sentenced to prison terms of up to 30 years, one was sentenced to death and three were banned from travelling abroad. Some of the 323 were said to have received additional punishments of fines or forced residence; others would be released only after "repenting". No details of the charges were disclosed or of the evidence on which defendants had been convicted, and no information was given about hundreds of others scheduled to be tried before the same court.

Prisoners of conscience

The authorities continued to detain peaceful government critics and human rights activists, including some arrested in previous years. They were prisoners of conscience.

■ Seven men arrested in February 2007 in connection with a petition calling for detainees to be given fair trials or released and advocating the establishment of a human rights organization, continued to be detained without trial throughout 2009. They were held in solitary confinement at Dhahban prison. The Interior Ministry accused the seven – Al-Sharif Saif al-Ghalib, Dr Saud al-Hashimi, Abdel Rahman Khan, Musa al-Qirni, Fahd al-Qirshi, Sulieman al-Rushudi and Abdel Rahman al-Shumayri – of collecting money to fund terrorism, but they strongly denied this. In October, the Court of Grievances heard an appeal against the detention of Abdel Rahman al-Shumayri. In December, the Interior Ministry said that it was preparing to bring him to trial, but no proceedings had taken place by the end of the year.

Torture and other ill-treatment

Torture and other ill-treatment were common and committed with impunity. Methods used included severe beatings, electric shocks, suspension, sleep deprivation and insults.

■ Dr Saud al-Hashimi, a prisoner of conscience held in solitary confinement since his arrest in February 2007, was reported to have been tortured and otherwise ill-treated several days after he began a hunger strike in June to protest against his continuing detention. He was said to have been stripped to his underwear, shackled and dragged to an extremely cold cell, where he was held for five hours.

Discrimination and violence against women

Women continued to face severe discrimination in law and practice. Women had to have a male guardian to travel outside their home, get married or access many public services. Women remained banned from driving. In June, however, Saudi Arabian officials told the UNHRC that the government would take steps to reduce discrimination against women, although no significant changes had been introduced by the end of the year.

In April, the Special Rapporteur on Violence against Women issued a report on her visit to Saudi Arabia in 2008. It noted modest reforms, but concluded that the high level of discrimination against women compromised their rights and dignity. It found too that various factors, including women's lack of autonomy and economic independence, practices surrounding divorce and child custody, the absence of a law criminalizing violence against women, and inconsistencies in law enforcement and the administration of justice, prevented many women from escaping abusive environments. It further noted that violence against female domestic workers was not sufficiently recognized by the state.

The media highlighted several cases of violence against women.

■ In February, a 23-year-old unmarried woman who was raped by five men after she accepted a lift, was sentenced by the District Court in Jeddah to one year in prison and 100 lashes for fornication outside marriage and trying to abort the resultant foetus. It was not clear what action was taken against her alleged rapists.

■ In July, a man shot dead his two sisters after the religious police arrested the women for associating with men not related to them. The murders were carried out in front of the father; he "pardoned" his son on the grounds that he had been defending the family's honour and there were contradictory reports as to whether he was brought to justice.

After negative publicity about the consequences for women of early marriage, there were moves by official bodies to address the issue.

Freedom of religion

Shi'a Muslims and at least one Christian were targeted for their beliefs. Eighteen Isma'ili Shi'a Muslims, 17 of whom had been serving 10-year prison sentences since 2000, were released. Most were prisoners of conscience.

■ In January, Hamoud Saleh al-Amri was arrested after announcing on his blog that he had converted from Islam to Christianity. He was released in late March on condition that he did not travel abroad or appear in the media.

■ At least 10 Shi'a Muslims, including six boys aged between 14 and 16, were arrested in March in Eastern Province and detained incommunicado in connection with a demonstration on 27 February against arrests of Shi'a visitors to the tomb of the Prophet Muhammad in Madina. Several of the boys were released within a few weeks but it was not clear what happened to the others.

■ In March, security forces were reported to have arrested several Shi'a Muslims in the city of al-'Awamiya for protesting against an order for the arrest of a leading Shi'a cleric and imam for criticizing attacks on Shi'a pilgrims and alleged discrimination against the Shi'a community.

Migrants' rights

Employers and state officials abused the rights of migrant workers with impunity. Domestic workers, particularly women, were made to work up to 18 hours a day and some were subjected to sexual or other abuse.

About 500 migrant workers and others detained in Riyadh's al-Shumaisi deportation centre went on hunger strike in September to protest against their prolonged detention and overcrowded and filthy conditions. Some had valid passports and airline tickets to leave Saudi Arabia, but they were not permitted to challenge their detention and were held for up to seven months before being deported. Several were reported to have died in detention.

S

Mohammed Saquib, an Indian national who had fled from his employer, died in al-Shumaisi deportation centre on 30 August, apparently from tuberculosis and lack of adequate medical treatment.

Refugees and asylum-seekers

The authorities continued to deny entry to some refugees and asylum-seekers. From August, they closed the southern border with Yemen in order to prevent the entry of people fleeing the conflict in Yemen's Sa'da region.

■ Twenty-eight Eritreans continued to be restricted to a camp near Jizan city; they were believed to have been there since 2005.

Cruel, inhuman and degrading punishments

Sentences of flogging continued to be passed and implemented. Some people convicted of theft were sentenced to have their hands amputated.

■ On 25 March, a court in Makkah sentenced a man to 15 years in jail and 40,000 lashes for the attempted rape and manslaughter of a young woman; she was killed by a truck when she ran into a road to escape from him.

■ On 24 July, the right hand of Hasan bin Ayyash Ahmed Sagheer, a Yemeni national convicted of theft, was amputated.

■ On 28 September, around 20 teenagers were flogged in public in Khobar and Dammam, each receiving at least 30 lashes, following a riot in Khobar the previous week.

Death penalty

The death penalty continued to be used extensively. Unlike previous years, no one was known to have been executed solely for drugs offences. Defendants facing capital charges received grossly unfair trials, including denial of legal representation and conviction solely on the basis of "confessions" allegedly extracted using torture.

At least 69 people were executed and 141 remained on death row, although the latter figure was believed to be much higher. Among those executed were two women, two juvenile offenders and 19 foreign nationals.

■ On 10 May, two juvenile offenders – Sultan bin Sulayman bin Muslim al-Muwallad, a Saudi Arabian, and 'Issa bin Muhammad 'Umar Muhammad, a

Chadian – were among five men beheaded in Madina after grossly unfair trials. They were convicted of crimes allegedly committed when they were aged 17, including the abduction and rape of children.

Amnesty International visits/reports

🖘 The authorities continued to deny Amnesty International access to Saudi Arabia to investigate human rights.

▣ Saudi Arabia: Assaulting human rights in the name of counter-terrorism (MDE 23/009/2009)

▣ Saudi Arabia: Countering terrorism with repression (MDE 23/025/2009)

SENEGAL

REPUBLIC OF SENEGAL

Head of state:	Abdoulaye Wade
Head of government:	Souleymane Ndéné Ndiaye (replaced Cheikh Hadjibou Soumaré in April)
Death penalty:	abolitionist for all crimes
Population:	12.5 million
Life expectancy:	55.4 years
Under-5 mortality (m/f):	125/114 per 1,000
Adult literacy:	41.9 per cent

In southern Casamance a resumption of sporadic fighting between people alleged to be members of a separatist movement and the Senegalese army resulted in the displacement of hundreds of people. Torture against detainees was used by the police and condoned by the judiciary. Repression of gay men increased. Independent media and journalists were harassed in an attempt to stifle freedom of expression. The trial of former Chadian President Hissène Habré did not begin.

Background

A resumption of sporadic attacks against military targets by people alleged to belong to the Democratic Forces of Casamance Movement (Mouvement des forces démocratiques de Casamance, MFDC) undermined the fragile status quo in southern Casamance reached after the 2004 peace agreement. In September and October, several soldiers were killed. In response, the Senegalese air force bombed areas thought to include MFDC bases.

In March, an opposition coalition won local elections against a background of protests against rising food prices, shortages of key commodities and power cuts.

Internally displaced people – Casamance
The resumption of intermittent hostilities in Casamance led to the displacement of hundreds of people from their homes in the outskirts of Ziguinchor, the main city in Casamance. Some people fled areas that were bombed by Senegalese military airplanes. Others, notably around Baraf village near Ziguinchor, were forcibly expelled from their homes by alleged members of the MFDC and forbidden from returning to cultivate their fields.

Freedom of expression
Independent media and journalists were targeted in an attempt to stifle freedom of expression and criticism of President Abdoulaye Wade and his government.
■ In March, three community radio stations in Dakar were suspended for two months for commenting on the local elections. The authorities withdrew the suspension after four days on condition that the stations stopped commenting on political issues during election campaigns.
■ In August, three journalists with Le Quotidien newspaper were summoned by police for interrogation for two days after publishing an article criticizing President Wade and government ministers.

Discrimination – lesbian, gay, bisexual and transgender people
Men faced harassment, arbitrary arrest, torture and unfair trial because of their suspected engagement in consensual same-sex sexual relationships.
■ In January, nine men were sentenced to eight years' imprisonment for "indecent conduct and unnatural acts and conspiracy" on the basis of confessions extracted by security forces under torture. The men had been arrested following anonymous accusations about their sexual behaviour. They were all released in April after the Dakar Appeal Court overturned the convictions.
■ In June, three men and a teenage boy were arrested in the city of Darou Mousty, Louga region, after being anonymously denounced for alleged sexual acts "against nature". The teenager was released and the

three adults were sentenced in August to prison terms ranging from two to five years' imprisonment. The men lodged an appeal, which had not been heard by the end of the year.

Torture and other ill-treatment
Several cases of torture and other ill-treatment of detainees in police stations were documented. Confessions extracted under torture were used to convict people after unfair trials.
■ In January, more than 20 students and young people detained after riots in the gold-mining town of Kédougou, about 700km south-east of Dakar, were reportedly tortured in order to extract confessions and incriminate others. Some of the detainees were given electric shocks. Others were beaten, kicked and punched while naked. Although several detainees told the court during their trial that they had been tortured, the judges and the prosecutor did not order an inquiry into the allegations. Nineteen defendants were sentenced to prison terms on the basis of their "confessions". They were pardoned in March by President Wade.

International justice – Hissène Habré
The authorities asserted throughout the year that the trial of Chad's former President Hissène Habré could not begin until they had received a certain amount of financial assistance, which international donors considered excessive. In 2006, the AU had called on Senegal to try Hissène Habré, who was living in exile in Senegal, for torture and other crimes committed during his rule.

In February, President Wade threatened to lift the judicial surveillance under which Hissène Habré had been placed and to remit him to the AU. A few days later, Belgium filed a case against Senegal before the International Court of Justice (ICJ) asking the ICJ to compel Senegal to take measures to prevent Hissène Habré from fleeing the country and to either prosecute him or extradite him to Belgium for trial. In May, the ICJ rejected the Belgian request.

In September, Hissène Habré's complaint against Senegal started to be examined before the ECOWAS Community Court of Justice for violations by Senegal of the African Charter on Human and Peoples' Rights, notably relating to the principle of non-retroactivity of penal legislation. The Court had not taken a decision on the issue by the end of the year.

S

Amnesty International visit/report

🚃 In April, an Amnesty International delegation visited Senegal to research human rights issues.

📑 Senegal: Authorities must protect nine men at risk of homophobic attack, 27 April 2009

SERBIA

REPUBLIC OF SERBIA, INCLUDING KOSOVO

Head of state:	Boris Tadić
Head of government:	Mirko Cvetković
Death penalty:	abolitionist for all crimes
Population:	9.9 million
Life expectancy:	73.9 years
Under-5 mortality (m/f):	15/13 per 1,000
Adult literacy:	96.4 per cent

Serbia made some progress in prosecuting war crimes in domestic courts. Discrimination against minority communities continued in both Serbia and Kosovo, where inter-ethnic violence persisted. A police and justice mission led by the European Union (EU) assumed responsibilities of the UN Interim Administration Mission in Kosovo (UNMIK). More refugees were forcibly returned to Kosovo.

General political developments

In December the Chief Prosecutor to the International Criminal Tribunal for the former Yugoslavia (Tribunal) reported positively on Serbia's progress on co-operation with the Tribunal. The EU subsequently unblocked Serbia's interim trade agreement, and Serbia applied for EU candidacy status pending a decision on unfreezing a Stabilization and Association Agreement. Progress had previously remained dependent on the arrest of former Bosnian Serb General Ratko Mladić and former Croatian-Serb leader Goran Hadžić, indicted by the Tribunal.

In December the International Court of Justice considered submissions on the legality of Kosovo's 2007 unilateral declaration of independence, which 64 countries had recognized by the end of the year.

Serbia

International justice

The Tribunal convicted five Serbian political, police and military leaders in February of war crimes and crimes against humanity. Former Yugoslav Deputy Prime Minister Nikola Šainović, Yugoslav Army (VJ) General Nebojša Pavković and Serbian police General Sreten Lukić were convicted of the deportation, forcible transfer, murder and persecution (including rape) of thousands of ethnic Albanians during the 1999 Kosovo conflict, and each sentenced to 22 years' imprisonment. Former VJ Colonel General Vladimir Lazarević and General Chief of Staff Dragoljub Odjanić were convicted of aiding and abetting deportations, forcible transfer and other inhumane acts, and each sentenced to 15 years' imprisonment. Former President Milan Milutinović was acquitted.

Proceedings opened in January against former Assistant Interior Minister Vlastimir Đorđević, indicted for crimes against humanity and war crimes in Kosovo. He was charged with responsibility for crimes by police under his command leading to the deportation of 800,000 Albanian civilians, the enforced disappearance of more than 800 ethnic Albanians, and leading a conspiracy to conceal their bodies which were transported to Serbia for reburial.

Proceedings were suspended in January against Vojislav Šešelj, Serbian Radical Party leader, indicted for crimes against humanity and war crimes in Croatia and Bosnia and Herzegovina (BiH). He was convicted in July for contempt of court for disclosing the identities of protected witnesses.

In October the Appeals Chamber considered the Prosecution's application for a retrial of Kosovo Albanian Ramush Haradinaj, acquitted of war crimes in 2008.

Justice system: war crimes

Proceedings continued at the Belgrade Special War Crimes Chamber in cases related to BiH, Croatia and Kosovo.

In April, four Serbian police officers were convicted and sentenced to between 13 and 20 years' imprisonment for the murder of 48 members of the Berisha family and Abdullah Elshani, in Suva Reka/Suharekë, Kosovo, in March 1999. Two senior commanders were acquitted.

In June, four members of the Scorpions paramilitary group were convicted of murdering 20

Albanian civilians in Podujevo/ë in March 1999, and sentenced to between 15 and 20 years' imprisonment.

In September, two former police officers were acquitted of the post-war disappearance of the Albanian-American Bytiçi brothers. The prosecution immediately appealed the verdict.

The trial continued of the ethnic Albanian Gnjilane/Gjilan Group accused of the imprisonment, torture and abuse (including rape) of 153 civilians, and the murder of at least 80 of them, in 1999; 34 individuals were still missing. Eight accused were tried in their absence.

In November, five men suspected of killing 23 Roma civilians in Sjeverin in BiH in 1992 were arrested. Allegedly the Roma were imprisoned and tortured, men were forced to sexually abuse each other and women were repeatedly raped.

Investigations continued into the alleged post-war abduction and torture of Serbs by the Kosova Liberation Army at the Yellow House near Burrel in Albania.

Torture and other ill-treatment

In January the European Committee for the Prevention of Torture reported on its November 2007 visit to places of detention in Serbia. There were fewer allegations than on previous visits but ill-treatment, including disproportionate force on arrest, continued.

The UN Committee against Torture (CAT) in July found that Besim Osmani was in June 2000 subjected to cruel, inhuman or degrading treatment or punishment during the forced eviction of a settlement in Belgrade. The CAT noted that the "infliction of physical and mental suffering [was] aggravated by… his Roma ethnic origin… a minority historically subjected to discrimination and prejudice." The authorities had failed to open an investigation, denying Besim Osmani the rights to have his case promptly and impartially investigated and to receive compensation.

Prison conditions

The European Committee for the Prevention of Torture reported severe overcrowding and "dilapidated" detention conditions, especially in Belgrade District Prison. Prisoners were reportedly ill-treated in the Požarevac-Zabela Correctional Institution, abuse that was apparently concealed by alteration of the register of "coercive means". Psychiatric patients were hit with truncheons in Belgrade Special Prison hospital.

The Committee expressed concerns about the quality of prisoners' medical records.

According to a local NGO, in January lawyers for detainee N.N. were refused access to his medical records. N.N. had alleged that his arm was broken in 2008 by prison guards at Niš Correctional Centre. In November, 12 security staff were arrested on suspicion of abusing and torturing detainees at Leskovac District Prison in January.

Amendments to the Law on Execution of Penal Sanctions adopted in August improved the internal complaints system. A by-law on internal oversight was not adopted, nor had a National Protection Mechanism required under the Optional Protocol to the UN Convention against Torture been established by the end of the year.

Rights of lesbian, gay, bisexual and transgender people

In March an Anti-Discrimination Law was adopted. It had earlier been withdrawn under pressure from the Serbian Orthodox Church and other religious institutions. They objected to articles guaranteeing freedom of religion and the right to non-discrimination on the grounds of sexual orientation and gender identity.

In September the Belgrade Pride march did not take place, after the authorities at the last moment refused to provide security on the agreed route, because of threats from right-wing groups.

Discrimination – Roma

In June the Council of Europe Advisory Committee on the Framework Convention for the Protection of National Minorities recommended that the judicial system address discrimination against minorities more efficiently, and that action be taken to issue identification documents and to tackle discrimination against Roma in education, employment, health and housing.

In June G.H., an internally displaced person from Kosovo, was reportedly attacked by 10 unknown individuals in Belgrade. G.H. was taken to hospital with pulmonary damage, but later discharged himself. Without identity documents he was not eligible for medical care, nor would the police investigate his case. Three attacks on the same community were reported in July. No one was brought to justice.

The inhabitants of several unlawful Romani settlements were forcibly evicted.

S

■ Displaced people from Kosovo were evicted in April from a temporary settlement at Blok 67 in New Belgrade to make way for the June 2009 Student Games. Temporary alternative accommodation was provided, but local residents attempted to set containers on fire to prevent Roma from moving in. Some 60 families accepted alternative accommodation without water or electricity. Others remained at Blok 67 without permanent shelter. A fence erected around them in June for the duration of the games restricted their freedom of movement.

Human rights defenders

Women human rights defenders, in particular those addressing war crimes, transitional justice and corruption, were subject to continued threats to their lives and property, media attacks and malicious prosecutions. The authorities failed to protect them. In June anti-fascist activists were twice attacked by the right-wing group Honour (Obraz) because of their support for evicted Roma.

Violence against women

Amendments to the Criminal Code increased penalties for domestic violence and trafficking, and introduced the offence of knowingly exploiting a trafficked person. A draft law on domestic violence was criticized by NGOs for failing to strengthen protection mechanisms and to ensure the prosecution of those who violated protection orders.

Kosovo

In accordance with a 2008 UN plan, UNMIK retained a role in relations between Serbia and Kosovo. Some of its responsibilities were taken over by an EU-led police and justice mission (EULEX).

A Constitutional Court was established to review legislation and receive complaints of human rights violations by the Kosovo authorities. In June the Kosovo Assembly appointed an Ombudsperson.

In September, 22 members of the NGO Self-Determination! (Vetevendosje!) were arrested for damaging EULEX vehicles during a demonstration against a protocol on co-operation between the Serbian Ministry of Interior and EULEX police.

The ruling Democratic Party of Kosovo won local elections in November which were marred by violence. Despite provisions for the decentralization of municipalities, Kosovo Serbs largely boycotted the elections and failed to win municipalities where they formed a majority.

Justice system: war crimes

EULEX and the Ministry of Justice established mixed judicial panels and an Office of Special Prosecutors, which included local prosecutors, to address war crimes and other serious crimes.

In March Gani Gashi was convicted of the murder, attempted murder and grievous bodily harm of ethnic Albanians in 1998 and sentenced to 17 years' imprisonment.

In September, four Kosovo Serbs were arrested in Novo Brdo/Novobërdë on suspicion of war crimes including the inhumane treatment, unlawful arrest and detention of Kosovo Albanians in 1999.

In October, in a retrial of the Llapi Group ordered by the Supreme Court, Latif Gashi, Nazif Mehmeti and Rrustem Mustafa-Remi were convicted of the torture and inhumane treatment of civilian detainees at Llapashtica/Lapaštica in 1998-9. They were sentenced to between three and six years' imprisonment. The Albanian member of the judicial panel made public his disagreement with the verdict.

Enforced disappearances and abductions

More than 1,800 families in Kosovo and Serbia still did not know the fate of family members at the end of the year. EULEX had in December 2008 taken responsibility for the Office of Missing Persons and Forensics (OMPF). By December 101 mortal remains had been exhumed and 83 returned to their families; 400 previously unidentified remains were sent to the International Commission for Missing Persons for identification through DNA analysis. Investigations were opened in a few cases.

Families of the disappeared held repeated demonstrations calling for the return of missing relatives. Amendments to the 2006 Law on Civilian Victims of War providing compensation to relatives of the disappeared had not been introduced by the end of the year.

Torture and other ill-treatment

In January the European Committee for the Prevention of Torture reported on its March 2007 visit to places of detention in Kosovo then under UNMIK's control. It reported the denial of detention rights and ill-treatment by Kosovo Police Service officers, and criticized conditions in most psychiatric and social welfare institutions. The Committee also described ill-treatment in several prisons by the elite Intervention Unit, including the beating of juvenile males at Lipjan/Lipljan Correctional Centre.

S

Impunity

In March the Special Representative of the UN Secretary-General (SRSG), citing security reasons, refused to allow a public hearing before the UNMIK Human Rights Advisory Panel (HRAP) relating to UNMIK's failure to bring to justice members of the Romanian Formed Police Unit. An internal investigation had found them responsible for the death of two men, Mon Balaj and Arbën Xheladini, on 10 February 2007 and for the serious injury of two others through the improper use of rubber bullets. Although the HRAP decided a public hearing would take place in June, the SRSG said in May he would not attend the hearing "under the procedure envisaged by the panel". In October an Administrative Directive was adopted which potentially rendered the case inadmissible.

Inter-ethnic crimes

In September the UN Secretary-General reported on the growing number of security-related incidents affecting minority communities. Inter-ethnic tensions between Kosovo Serbs and ethnic Albanians and attacks continued, especially in Serb-dominated north Mitrovicë/a. In July and August Roma were attacked and threatened in Gjilan/Gnjilane and Ferizaj/Uroševac respectively.

In March the Supreme Court overturned the conviction in June 2008 of Kosovo Albanian Florim Ejupi for the bombing in February 2001 of the Niš-Ekspress bus near Podujevë/o in which 11 Serbs were killed and at least 40 injured. A new investigation opened in May.

In April Kosovo Albanian returnees to Kroi i Vitakut/Brđani in north Mitrovicë/a were prevented from rebuilding their houses by Kosovo Serbs. For 10 days EULEX police and troops of the NATO-led Kosovo Force (KFOR) used tear gas and stun grenades against protesters, one of whom was injured. In mid-May Serbs also were allowed to rebuild their houses, and a barbed wire fence was erected between the construction sites, patrolled by EULEX police. In mid-August and September violence again broke out.

Discrimination – Roma

Discrimination against Roma remained pervasive, including in access to education, health care and employment. Few enjoyed the right to adequate housing. The majority remained without personal documents that would enable them to register their residency and status.

The action plan to implement a Strategy for the Integration of Roma, Ashkali and Egyptians had yet to be implemented. An estimated 75 per cent of Romani women were illiterate and had little access to protection from domestic violence. In October NGOs alleged discrimination against Roma applicants for "multi-ethnic" apartments in the predominantly Serbian village of Llapje Sellë/Laplje Selo.

In June the HRAP declared partially admissible a case brought against UNMIK by 143 displaced Romani, Ashkali and Egyptian residents of UNMIK-administered camps in northern Mitrovicë/a. The residents alleged they had suffered lead poisoning and other health problems from the Trepçë/Trepča smelter and mining complex.

Forcible returns

Several EU member states and Switzerland negotiated bilateral agreements with Kosovo on the forcible return of minorities, including Roma. Kosovo Serbs were forcibly returned from Luxembourg in November. A return and reintegration strategy agreed by the Kosovo authorities and UNMIK in 2007 was not adequately resourced or implemented by government and municipal authorities.

In November UNHCR, the UN refugee agency, in considering needs for international protection, stated that Serbs, Roma and Albanians in a minority situation continued to face persecution or serious harm through cumulative discriminatory acts. During 2009, according to UNHCR, 2,962 individuals were forcibly returned to Kosovo from other European countries, including 2,492 ethnic Albanians and 470 members of minority communities. There were 193 individuals – 47 Serbs, 127 Roma and 19 Albanians (returned to a minority situation) – from communities UNHCR considered to be in need of continued international protection.

Violence against women

The OMPF reported on 400 cases of sexual assaults in Kosovo between 2003 and 2008, in which only 10 per cent of suspects were forensically examined. Over a third of victims were under the age of 16. A 2009 survey found that the majority of sexual assaults were not reported to the authorities.

S

Amnesty International visits/reports

🚗 Amnesty International delegates visited Serbia and Kosovo in February.

▤ Serbia: Burying the past – 10 years of impunity for enforced disappearances in Kosovo (EUR 70/007/2009)

⬛ Serbia: Human rights defenders at risk (EUR 70/014/2009)

⬛ Concerns in the Balkans: Serbia, including Kosovo, January-June 2009 (EUR 70/016/2009)

⬛ Serbia: Briefing to the Human Rights Committee (EUR 70/015/2009)

SIERRA LEONE

REPUBLIC OF SIERRA LEONE

Head of state and government:	Ernest Bai Koroma
Death penalty:	retentionist
Population:	5.7 million
Life expectancy:	47.3 years
Under-5 mortality (m/f):	160/136 per 1,000
Adult literacy:	38.1 per cent

Violence erupted in March between supporters of the ruling All People's Congress (APC) and the opposition Sierra Leone People's Party (SLPP), during which people were seriously injured and there were allegations of rape and other sexual assaults. Sexual and gender-based violence against women continued, including harmful traditional practices such as female genital mutilation (FGM). The government made efforts to reduce the high rate of maternal mortality.

Background

Political violence erupted between APC and SLPP supporters in three areas of the country in March in the run-up to local elections. In Pujehun in the south, violence between 9 and 12 March left several people seriously injured. In Freetown, violence between 13 and 16 March resulted in injuries and the looting of the SLPP headquarters; there were also allegations of rape and other sexual assault of SLPP supporters. In Kenema between 13 and 14 March, violence and arson attacks targeted APC supporters.

In April, a Joint Communiqué Adherence Committee facilitated by the UN and the Political Parties Registration Commission was established and agreed by APC and SLPP representatives, which helped to defuse tensions. In July, the government appointed a Commission of Inquiry to investigate the reasons for the violence and the allegations of rape and other sexual assaults. An independent review

panel was not constituted. The same month, the Independent Media Commission reported that radio stations owned by the APC and SLPP appeared to have contributed to the violence with hate speech, and that their licences would be withdrawn. Members of civil society were concerned that the ruling of the commission threatened freedom of expression.

In September and October, the government deployed soldiers to help police in response to public concerns about the police's response to a sharp rise in armed robberies.

In May, the government launched the Agenda for Change, its second Poverty Reduction Strategy Paper. It was used as the framework to seek donor funding at the Sierra Leone Investment and Donor Conference held in London, the UK, in November.

The Anti-Corruption Commission (ACC) made significant progress. In February, four public officers were indicted on various counts of corruption. In June, two former senior officials of the Sierra Leone Broadcasting Service and the former Ombudsman were convicted of misappropriation of funds and sentenced to jail and/or heavy fines. In May, the ACC reviewed the work of the Ministry of Health and Sanitation and made several recommendations to improve the health care delivery system and reduce the risk of corrupt practices in the Ministry. In October, the Minister of Health was charged with corruption and subsequently dismissed. A fast-track anti-corruption court with dedicated judges and prosecutors, which had been proposed by the ACC in 2008, had not been established by the end of the year.

Some progress was made in implementing the recommendations of the Truth and Reconciliation Commission (TRC) – established after the 1991-2002 civil war – but no follow-up committee was appointed and the constitutional review process stalled. The mandate of the UN Integrated Peacebuilding Office in Sierra Leone (UNIPSIL) was renewed in September for a further year.

Special Court for Sierra Leone

The prosecution case in the trial of former Liberian President Charles Taylor before the Special Court for Sierra Leone (SCSL) in The Hague ended on 27 February, and included 91 witnesses. He faced 11 charges of war crimes and crimes against humanity committed during the civil war in Sierra Leone. The

S

defence case began on 13 July; Charles Taylor was the sole witness during the rest of 2009.

On 26 October, the Appeals Chamber of the SCSL upheld the convictions of the Revolutionary United Front leaders Issa Sesay, Morris Kallon and Augustine Gbao on nearly all counts. The convictions were the first for attacks on UN peacekeepers as a violation of international humanitarian law and for forced marriage as an inhumane act constituting a crime against humanity. In October, all eight of the convicted men were transferred to Rwanda, honouring a March agreement with the SCSL, to serve their prison sentences. The sentences ranged from 15 to 52 years, with credit given for time served in detention at the SCSL. No prison facility within Sierra Leone meets the required international standards. In November, the SCSL handed over its detention facilities to the Sierra Leone prison service to be used to house female prisoners.

Reparations programme
The reparations programme, set up under the TRC, devoted most of 2009 to identifying 28,000 war victims, implementing symbolic reparations in 18 chiefdoms, and making available fistula surgery for victims of sexual violence. The only funds for the reparation programme, drawn from the peace-building fund, ran out in late 2009 and the government took no steps to ensure funding for the future.

Maternal mortality
In July, the National Human Rights Commission released its second annual report, which highlighted among other things the high rate of maternal mortality. In September, Amnesty International released a report and delegates, including the Secretary General, toured Sierra Leone to raise awareness about the issue. On 23 September at the UN General Assembly, President Koroma announced plans for providing free care for pregnant and lactating women, and for children under five. Implementation of the plans was expected to start in April 2010.

Violence and discrimination against women
Using the Child Rights Act (2007), NGOs made some gains in their campaign to stop the practice of FGM among girls below the age of 18. Some traditional leaders imposed by-laws in their communities outlawing the practice of FGM for children.

■ In February, four women journalists were abducted, stripped and forced to parade naked through the streets of Kenema by women initiators of FGM who said that the journalists were disrupting their tradition. After the journalists were released, the police took no action against the alleged attackers.

There were allegations that women were raped and otherwise sexually assaulted during the March political violence. The Commission of Inquiry set up in July concluded that sexual violence did take place but that rape did not. No action was taken against those alleged to have perpetrated sexual violence. Civil society and women's rights groups contested the findings of the inquiry.

■ A woman in the northern district of Kono was barred from chieftaincy elections in November because of her gender.

Freedom of expression
The Sierra Leone Association of Journalists filed a suit in the Supreme Court in February seeking to repeal archaic seditious libel provisions. The case remained pending at the end of the year.

Concern was raised by the UN in July that some of the provisions of the Sierra Leone Broadcasting Corporation Act passed in 2009 could undermine the independence of the broadcasting corporation. President Koroma gave assurances that this would not be the case.

In July, the Independent Media Commission announced that licences of political party radio stations would be withdrawn because of the March political violence, a move opposed by civil society groups. The SLPP filed an action challenging the decision.

Death penalty
No new death sentences were passed by ordinary courts. Nine men and three women – Sia Beke, Mankaprie Kamara and Nallay Foday – remained on death row. Five of the men had been on death row for six years.

■ In October, the conviction against Marie Sampa Kamara, who had been sentenced to death for murder, was overturned and she was released.

In August, a member of the military convicted after a court martial for a killing was sentenced to death by firing squad. Under martial law, the President must sign the death sentence; this had not happened by the end of the year.

In October, President Koroma called for the death penalty to be imposed for armed robbery. However, no further action was taken.

Amnesty International visit/reports

🚌 In September, Amnesty International delegates, including the Secretary General, visited Sierra Leone. They toured the country for 12 days to raise awareness about the high rate of maternal mortality and related issues, and met senior government officials including the Minister of Health, Minister of Gender and Vice-President.

📄 Sierra Leone: Lives cut short – make pregnancy and childbirth safer (AFR 51/001/2009)

📄 Sierra Leone: President Koroma must commute all death row prisoners (AFR 51/003/2009)

📄 Sierra Leone: Out of reach – the cost of maternal health in Sierra Leone (AFR 51/005/2009)

📄 Sierra Leone: End maternal mortality – join our campaign (AFR 51/006/2009)

📄 Sierra Leone: Investment in the health sector needed to implement free care policy (AFR 51/014/2009)

SINGAPORE

REPUBLIC OF SINGAPORE

Head of state:	S.R. Nathan
Head of government:	Lee Hsien Loong
Death penalty:	retentionist
Population:	4.7 million
Life expectancy:	80.2 years
Under-5 mortality (m/f):	4/4 per 1,000
Adult literacy:	94.4 per cent

Laws were tightened to limit freedom of expression and assembly, and used to intimidate and punish increasingly outspoken critics and opposition activists. Information about the application of the death penalty was very limited. Criminal offenders were sentenced to caning.

Freedom of expression and assembly

Numerous lawsuits by the authorities created a climate of fear for people with dissenting views. Government critics and human rights defenders, including former prisoners of conscience, remained undeterred and held public gatherings, wrote articles and challenged the ruling People's Action Party's dominance.

■ Dr Chee Soon Juan, secretary-general of the opposition Singapore Democratic Party (SDP), faced several charges, including two counts of speaking in public without a permit. He was fined S$10,000 (US$7,100) or 10 weeks' imprisonment under the Public Entertainments and Meetings Act (PEMA).

■ SDP member Yap Keng Ho faced charges relating to the sale of the SDP newspaper during the 2006 elections. He opted to serve a 20-day jail sentence after refusing to pay a S$2,000 (US$1,400) fine.

Both men also faced multiple charges of illegal assembly and illegal procession.

In April, the authorities announced the Public Order Act 2009 (POA). The POA imposed further controls on freedom of expression, the right to peaceful assembly and the right to form associations. It was first used against five Falun Gong protesters who were charged with illegal assembly. The POA complements and strengthens provisions of existing legislation, including PEMA and the Miscellaneous Offences Act, which have been used previously to suppress peaceful demonstrations.

The POA also empowers law enforcement officers to stop people filming and exhibiting films of law enforcement activities. Amendments to the Films Act limit the filming of unauthorized protests and of anyone not authorized to seek election.

Detention without trial

Approximately 20 suspected Islamist militants continued to be held under the Internal Security Act (ISA). Two individuals, held since 2002 under the ISA, were released.

The government announced that 366 individuals had been held without trial over the past five years under the Criminal Law (Temporary Provisions) Act, but 272 were released over the same period.

Death penalty

Reporting of death sentences, executions and other related information was limited. At least one person, Tan Chor Jin, was executed in January, and at least six others were known to have been sentenced to death by the courts. The actual number of executions and death sentences is believed to be much higher.

Torture and other ill-treatment

Caning remained a form of punishment for a number of offences under Singapore law, including immigration offences. At least five individuals were sentenced to caning, mostly for sexual offences such as rape. Military service remained compulsory, and under military regulations conscientious objectors and others who failed to comply could be caned and imprisoned for offences such as non-compliance with lawful orders and insubordination.

Migrants' rights

One quarter of Singapore's population were migrants.
■ Work permits for two Myanmar nationals, who had worked in Singapore for 11 years, were not renewed, following their active support for Myanmar's pro-democracy movement.

SLOVAKIA

SLOVAK REPUBLIC

Head of state:	Ivan Gašparovič
Head of government:	Robert Fico
Death penalty:	abolitionist for all crimes
Population:	5.4 million
Life expectancy:	74.6 years
Under-5 mortality (m/f):	9/8 per 1,000

Roma continued to face discrimination and violence at the hands of both state authorities and private individuals, and were still largely denied equal access to education, housing and health.

Background

Despite assuming the Presidency of the Decade for Roma Inclusion 2005–2015 in June, Slovakia failed to acknowledge serious structural deficiencies in the country's educational system which continued to segregate many Roma children into an inferior system.

In April, Slovakia ratified the Revised European Social Charter with the exception of Article 31 on the right to housing. The amendment to the penal law that introduced the concept of crimes of extremism entered into force in September. The amendment was criticized by Slovakian NGOs, who argued that the definition of extremism is vague and that the amendment does not address the structural causes of the problem. The law was adopted in June despite a veto by the President.

Citing grounds of procedural deficiencies, in July the Supreme Court annulled the November 2008 decision of the Ministry of Interior to ban a right-wing group known as the Slovak Brotherhood (Slovenská Pospolitosť). The Ministry had declared the group unconstitutional and illegal in spreading national, racial, religious and political hatred. The Ministry announced it would issue a new ban.

The Slovak Brotherhood organized a series of rallies between August and December conveying anti-Roma messages. One of the group's leaders, Marián Kotleba, was charged on 22 August with defaming nationality, race and belief.

Discrimination – Roma

Education

In September, the UN Human Rights Council raised concerns under the Universal Periodic Review about the situation of the Romani minority in Slovakia, including the disproportionate enrolment of Romani children in special schools.

In May, the European Commission against Racism and Intolerance (ECRI) recommended that data be collected to monitor the impact of public policies on minorities, including Roma. Due to lack of data disaggregated by ethnicity and gender, the government was unable to assess the composition of different types of schools.

Although discrimination and segregation are prohibited by legislation, effective legal and policy measures that would ensure implementation in practice were still not in place. Romani children continued to be segregated in schools and classes providing inferior education.

In May, ECRI urged Slovakia to take measures to remove Roma children who had no disabilities from special elementary schools and integrate them into mainstream education. It also urged that allegations of discriminatory practices against Roma in schools be investigated, and that policies be introduced to prevent placing children from minority groups in separate classes.

In September, the Roma Education Fund reported that the proportion of Romani children attending

S

special schools was almost 60 per cent, and the proportion in special classes with substandard education in mainstream schools was 85.8 per cent. It called on the government to abolish special primary schools for children with mild mental disability.

■ The special school in Pavlovce nad Uhom underwent further inspections in 2009. In 2008, 99.5 per cent of the pupils were Roma, and were often transferred to the school without any assessment. An inspection carried out between April and May demonstrated that there were still many Romani children in the special school who had never been diagnosed with mental disability. The State School Inspectorate recommended that the school's director be dismissed; he resigned in November.

Housing

In May, ECRI urged the government to take urgent measures to protect Roma from being forcibly evicted, and to ensure that measures to improve housing conditions consider the need to integrate Roma with the general population.

The Ministry of Infrastructure and Regional Development and the municipal authority of the town of Sabinov were found to have discriminated against Roma by evicting them from municipally owned apartments in the town centre. Both the ministry and the municipality appealed against the decision.

In October, the Ostrovany municipality began building a wall dividing the Roma settlement from the rest of the village. The initiative was criticized by the government's Plenipotentiary for Roma Communities, who said that construction of the wall raised concerns about segregation and potential violation of the law.

Forced sterilization of Romani women

In a response to the outcome of the Universal Periodic Review, Slovakia announced that it had adopted legislative measures, including requiring health workers to seek informed consent for sterilization and the definition of a new criminal offence of "illegal sterilization". However, according to the Centre for Civil and Human Rights (Poradňa pre občianske a ľudské práva), the Ministry of Health Care failed to issue any implementing guidelines on sterilizations and informed consent for health workers. In addition, the authorities were still failing to carry out thorough, impartial and effective investigations into all cases of alleged forced sterilizations.

In April, in the case of *K.H. and others v. Slovakia,* the European Court of Human Rights found Slovakia

in violation of the right to private and family life and the right to access to court. The case involved eight Romani women who suspected that the reason for their infertility might be that a sterilization procedure was performed on them during their Caesarean delivery in hospitals in eastern Slovakia. The women were refused full access to the official documentation relating to their medical treatment. The Court ruled that the state must give access to files containing personal data, and must permit copies to be made. The government requested that the case be reviewed by the Grand Chamber of the European Court of Human Rights.

Torture and other ill-treatment

There were some positive developments in legal cases regarding police officers accused of torture, and at least one further report of ill-treatment by officers was received.

■ In September, the Supreme Court confirmed the sentences of six former police officers who were convicted of ill-treatment and the unlawful death of Karol Sendrei, a 51-year-old Romani man who died in police custody in 2001. The two officers principally responsible were sentenced to eight and a half years' imprisonment.

■ Seven police officers were accused of ill-treating six Romani boys in Košice police station in April, after a newspaper published graphic video footage of the abuse. In May, the General Prosecutor informed Amnesty International that racial motivation would be considered.

Counter-terror and security

Non-refoulement

In December, Mustafa Labsi, an Algerian national, escaped from the camp for asylum-seekers in the village of Rohovce. He was detained in Austria, where he was still held at the end of the year pending his return to Slovakia. Mustafa Labsi had been convicted in his absence in Algeria of crimes of terrorism and sentenced to life imprisonment. Algeria requested his extradition in 2007. In 2008 the Constitutional Court in Slovakia had ruled that he could not be deported to Algeria where he faced serious human rights violations, including torture and other ill-treatment.

In October the regional court in Bratislava upheld a decision by the Migration Office to reject Mustafa

Labsi's application for asylum. In December, his lawyer appealed against the judgement to the Supreme Court.

Right to health

Reproductive rights

In June, parliament adopted an Amendment to the Law on Health Care and Health Care Services, introducing a 48-hour waiting period for women seeking an abortion on request. This breaches WHO guidelines which state that waiting periods unnecessarily delay care and decrease safety. The Amendment also stipulated that personal data such as identity numbers should be collected to record the women seeking abortions.

Amnesty International visit/reports

🚌 Amnesty International delegates visited Slovakia in September.

📋 Slovakia: Joint open letter regarding case of police abuse of Romani boys (EUR 72/002/009)

📋 Slovakia: Roma children still lose out – segregation persists in Slovak schools despite new law (EUR 72/004/2009)

📋 Human Rights Council adopts Universal Periodic Review outcome on Slovakia: Amnesty International urges enhanced protection of the human rights of Roma (EUR 72/005/2009)

SLOVENIA

REPUBLIC OF SLOVENIA

Head of state:	Danilo Türk
Head of government:	Borut Pahor
Death penalty:	abolitionist for all crimes
Population:	2 million
Life expectancy:	78.2 years
Under-5 mortality (m/f):	5/4 per 1,000
Adult literacy:	99.7 per cent

The authorities failed to restore the rights of people (known as the "erased") whose permanent residency status was unlawfully revoked in 1992. Despite some government measures discrimination against Roma, especially in access to housing and education, continued.

Discrimination

The 'erased'

The authorities still failed to guarantee the rights of former permanent residents of Slovenia originating from other former Yugoslav republics, whose legal status was unlawfully revoked in 1992. It resulted in violations of their economic and social rights. Some of them were also forcibly removed from the country.

In November, the government submitted a draft law to parliament which would retroactively restore the status of the "erased". By the end of the year the law had not been adopted.

The authorities did not present any plans on further steps to ensure that the "erased" were granted reparation for past human rights violations such as restoration of their economic, social and cultural rights, compensation or an official apology.

The parliamentary and public discussion on the "erased" was marred by xenophobic statements by several parliamentarians throughout the year.

Roma

In spite of some steps taken by the government towards improving the situation for the Roma community, discrimination continued.

Enrolment of Romani children in pre-school education was very low, which put them at a disadvantage compared to their peers when they entered primary education. In December, the government announced an initiative to increase attendance of Romani children in pre-school

S

programmes. Some progress was made in addressing the consequences of past segregation of Romani pupils. After several years of campaigning by human rights and Roma organizations, the authorities started an external and independent evaluation of Roma education in September. However, this evaluation did not include the so called "Bršljin model" which had previously resulted in the de facto segregation of Romani pupils.

Many Roma experienced inadequate housing conditions, including lack of security of tenure, access to water, sanitation facilities and electricity. Romani settlements were very often isolated and segregated. In some cases, where planned evictions were supposed to take place the community had not been properly informed and consulted.

In November, a draft National Roma Programme was presented to the general public and for consultation with NGOs. The programme outlined measures to improve the situation of the Roma community for the period 2010-2015. It covered several social aspects where Roma face discrimination, such as housing, education, employment and access to health.

Amnesty International report

Slovenia: Submission to the UN Universal Periodic Review (EUR 68/004/2009)

SOLOMON ISLANDS

Head of state:	Queen Elizabeth II represented by Sir Frank Kabui (replaced Nathaniel Waena in July)
Head of government:	Derek Sikua
Death penalty:	abolitionist for all crimes
Population:	0.5 million
Life expectancy:	65.8 years
Under-5 mortality (m/f):	56/57 per 1,000
Adult literacy:	76.6 per cent

Informal settlements in Honiara, the capital, continued to grow rapidly. The authorities did little to provide adequate access to clean water, sanitation and health services for thousands of people living there. Violence against women and girls remained prevalent across the country.

Right to adequate housing

Thousands of people in Honiara live in informal settlements which have mushroomed since the 1980s and 1990s due to high rural to urban migration and high unemployment. The government remained unwilling or unable to address poor sanitary and living conditions there, and provide adequate alternative housing to settlement dwellers.

The government failed to address the poor water supplies in the settlements around Honiara and thousands of people continued to drink contaminated stream water. Inhabitants of other settlements often had to walk more than a kilometre every day to fetch water due to the lack of a water and road infrastructure.

Many other settlements had no access to electricity. Scores of people were forced to scavenge at the Ranadi rubbish dump in the outskirts of Honiara to feed themselves and to find building materials for their homes. The authorities made no meaningful attempt to prevent scavenging or educate scavengers on the health and safety risks of this practice. Many homes were poorly constructed with scraps of tin, wood and plastic. Lack of space in some settlements forced several families to share toilets with poor hygienic conditions.

Violence against women and girls

At least 64 per cent of women between the ages of 15 and 49 experienced violence in the home, according

S

to a government-sponsored survey completed in January by the Secretariat of the Pacific Community, a regional inter-governmental organization. In August, the government used these findings to draw up a national plan of action to address domestic violence in the country. The survey results were published in November.

Amnesty International visit

🚌 An Amnesty International delegate visited the country in August.

SOMALIA

SOMALI REPUBLIC
Head of state of Transitional Federal Government: **Sheikh Sharif Sheikh Ahmed (replaced Adan Mohamed Nuur Madobe in January)**
Head of government of Transitional Federal Government: **Omar Abdirashid Ali Sharmarke (replaced Nur Hassan Hussein in February)**
Head of Somaliland Republic: **Dahir Riyaale Kahin**
Death penalty: **retentionist**
Population: **9.1 million**
Life expectancy: **49.7 years**
Under-5 mortality (m/f): **186/174 per 1,000**

Armed conflict between armed groups and Transitional Federal Government (TFG) forces continued despite the withdrawal of Ethiopian troops in January. Thousands of civilians were killed and hundreds of thousands displaced by indiscriminate warfare, bringing the number of people internally displaced since 2007 to up to 1.55 million. The humanitarian crisis deepened, compounded by insecurity and threats against aid agencies. Humanitarian workers, journalists and human rights activists faced considerable risks, including killings and abductions, in the course of their work. Serious human rights abuses, including war crimes, remained unpunished. The TFG controlled only part of the capital Mogadishu and there was no effective justice system. Armed groups controlled vast areas of south and central Somalia where they carried out unlawful killings and torture. In semi-autonomous Puntland, a new regional government was elected and a spate of

killings of officials and civilians threatened relative stability.

Background

Following the 2008 Djibouti peace agreement, the Transitional Federal Parliament was enlarged and elected Sheikh Sharif Sheikh Ahmed, former Alliance for the Re-liberation of Somalia-Djibouti leader, as TFG President on 30 January.

Attacks continued against the TFG, particularly by al-Shabab ("youth") militias. In early January, an al-Shabab faction took Baidoa city, where Parliament used to sit. Despite the withdrawal of Ethiopian troops and the adoption by Parliament of Islamic law in April, armed groups launched a new offensive against the TFG in and around Mogadishu on 7 May. Among the groups were the Hizbul Islam coalition led by Sheikh Hassan Dahir Aweys, who returned to Somalia from Eritrea in April, and al-Shabab factions. In June, the TFG reached an agreement with the Ahlu Sunna Wal Jama'a armed group, which had fought against al-Shabab in central Somalia in January. Allies Hizbul Islam and al-Shabab clashed from September onwards in and around Kismayo.

The African Union Mission in Somalia (AMISOM), comprising 5,200 Burundian and Ugandan troops and mandated to protect TFG institutions, was increasingly attacked by armed groups. AMISOM troops allegedly responded with indiscriminate shooting and shelling, resulting in civilian deaths. Al-Shabab claimed responsibility for at least three suicide attacks – an attack on 22 February in Mogadishu killed 11 Burundian soldiers; an attack on 18 June on a hotel in Beletweyne killed the TFG Minister of Security and over 20 others, including an aid worker; and an attack on 17 September on AMISOM's base near the Mogadishu airport killed at least 21 people, including the Deputy Force Commander, in retaliation for a reported US helicopter strike on 14 September against suspected al-Qa'ida member Saleh Ali Saleh Nabhan near Barawe.

On 18 December, Mohamed Suleiman Barre and Ismail Mohamed Arale were released from the US detention centre at Guantánamo Bay and returned to Somaliland.

Despite international support, including transfers of weapons and ammunition by the USA, and the training of TFG troops by states including France, the TFG struggled to integrate and enlarge its security

S

forces. On 23 December, the UN Security Council imposed sanctions, including an arms embargo, on Eritrea, accused of supporting Somali armed groups in violation of the UN arms embargo on Somalia. The UN Security Council continued to request the UN Secretary-General to plan for the relocation of UN operations into Somalia and for an eventual UN force.

Human rights abuses, including recruitment of children into armed forces, were raised in reports by the UN Secretary-General, the UN Independent Expert on Human Rights in Somalia, and the Representative of the UN Secretary-General on internally displaced persons. International and local calls to end impunity for crimes under international law did not translate into concrete steps by the TFG or the international community to establish a commission of inquiry into such crimes.

Hijacking of ships and kidnapping of maritime crews by pirates increased and expanded far beyond the Gulf of Aden, despite international naval patrols and renewed commitment by the Puntland authorities to try pirates. The Puntland authorities faced more insecurity, including killings of officials and civilians. Among those killed were five Pakistani Muslim clerics in Galkayo in August.

Indiscriminate attacks

All parties to the conflict used mortars and heavy weapons in areas populated or frequented by civilians. Mogadishu civilians were particularly affected, as armed groups launched attacks from residential areas, and the TFG and AMISOM allegedly fired indiscriminately in response. As a result, numerous civilians were killed and injured.

■ On 2 February, at least 10 civilians were killed and a dozen injured on Maka al-Mukarama road in Mogadishu when AMISOM soldiers allegedly opened fire after an explosion targeted their vehicle. The results of an AMISOM investigation into the incident were not publicly available by the end of the year.

■ On 17 June, a mosque in the Karan district in northern Mogadishu was hit by a mortar at dusk after a day of fighting between the TFG, AMISOM and armed groups. Thirteen worshippers leaving after prayers were killed.

■ On 11 September, the Martini hospital for disabled war veterans and a prison were hit by mortars during an attack by armed groups on the Mogadishu port. At least 11 people, including three children, were killed in the

hospital. Four guards in the prison were killed and a dozen people were injured. Armed groups denied responsibility for the shelling.

Displacement

Fighting and insecurity were a major cause of displacement. In January, fighting between al-Shabab and Ahlu Sunna Wal Jama'a in Dhusamareb and Guri El in central Somalia displaced 50,000 to 80,000 people.

The UN estimated that after the armed groups' offensive against the TFG in Mogadishu in May, over 255,000 people fled the capital, including 65,000 who had returned since January hoping for improved security. Many joined previously displaced people along the Afgoye corridor outside Mogadishu, which by the end of the year hosted some 366,000 people in squalid settlements.

Civilians also fled to neighbouring countries; more than 50,000 crossed the border with Kenya to reach refugee camps in Dadaab. Others undertook dangerous sea journeys across the Gulf of Aden to reach Yemen. According to the UN, almost 32,000 Somalis arrived in Yemen in 2009; 309 Somali and other nationals died, including by drowning, during the journey.

Restrictions on humanitarian aid

Up to 3.7 million people were in need of humanitarian support during the year because of armed conflict, displacement, droughts and floods, yet humanitarian operations remained under-funded. Humanitarian operations were further impeded by fighting and insecurity, killings and abductions of humanitarian workers, and threatening statements and restrictions against aid agencies, although many roadblocks were dismantled in areas under the control of armed groups. At least 10 humanitarian workers were killed and a further seven kidnapped. Ten aid workers abducted in 2008 remained hostages. Fighting in May and June in Mogadishu forced aid staff to flee compounds and temporarily halt humanitarian operations.

■ Three World Food Programme (WFP) workers were killed by gunmen during the year. On 6 January, Somali national Ibrahim Hussein Duale was shot dead while monitoring school feeding in a WFP-supported school in Yubsan village, six kilometres from Garbahare in the Gedo region. On 8 January, Somali national Mohamud

Omar Moallim was shot dead while monitoring food distribution to displaced people in a camp north-west of Mogadishu. On 22 December, the WFP head of security guards in Beletweyne was shot dead in the town.

■ Two Médecins Sans Frontières foreign medical workers were abducted on 19 April in Bakool region and released on 28 April. The organization suspended its operations in Bakool, which included one health centre serving some 250,000 people and four health posts, because of lack of security.

■ On 17 May, following its capture of the city of Jowhar, al-Shabab raided the compound of UNICEF, the UN Children's Fund. It destroyed or looted humanitarian supplies, including vaccines and nutritional supplies for malnourished children, affecting over 100,000 child beneficiaries. The UNICEF compound was still occupied by al-Shabab at the end of the year.

■ In June, the al-Shabab faction in Kismayo accused humanitarian organizations of being behind the conflict in Somalia. On 25 October, al-Shabab closed the office of a Somali aid agency, ASEP, which operates in Beled Hawo, along the Somali-Kenyan border in Gedo region, allegedly for spying for Western governments.

Threats against journalists and civil society

The space for freedom of expression and independent reporting on the situation in Somalia further narrowed. Intimidation of Somali journalists and civil society organizations by armed groups increased, including through the threat of killings, closure of radio stations and occupation of NGO offices. Nine journalists were killed during the year, including at least three in targeted killings. The dangers forced many Somali activists to flee the country. Insecurity and the risk of kidnappings hindered visits by foreign observers. Cases of harassment of journalists were also reported in Puntland.

■ On 7 June, Mukhtar Mohamed Hirabe, director of Radio Shabelle, was shot dead by unknown gunmen in Bakara market. His colleague Ahmed Omar Hashi was injured in the shooting. Mukhtar Mohamed Hirabe was the third Radio Shabelle journalist to be killed and the second radio director to be murdered in 2009.

■ On 1 October, the al-Shabab faction in Baidoa entered the premises of Radio Warsan, asked the station to stop broadcasting and detained two of its journalists for two days, reportedly accusing them of broadcasting music contrary to Islam. On 21 October, al-Shabab in Baidoa closed Radio Warsan and Radio Jubba.

■ On 2 June, director of Somali Universal Satellite TV Ibrahim Mohamed Hussein was abducted by masked gunmen in the Afgoye district; he was released days later. Two foreign journalists, Canadian reporter Amanda Lindhout and Australian photographer Nigel Brennan, were freed on 25 November. They had been held hostage since their kidnapping in Afgoye on 23 August 2008. Two Somali men abducted with them were freed on 15 January.

■ Between 19 and 21 August, armed groups looted the offices of the Peace and Human Rights Network, an umbrella of civil society organizations, in the KM5 area of Mogadishu.

■ On 2 November, al-Shabab reportedly closed three women's organizations in Beled Hawo in Gedo region, claiming that Islam does not allow women to work.

■ On 3 December, a suicide bomber detonated explosives at a medical graduation ceremony in Mogadishu. The attack killed at least 23 people, including medical students, university staff, three journalists and three TFG ministers, and injured at least 56 others. No one claimed responsibility for the attack.

Justice system

There was no effective functioning and centralized justice system in south and central Somalia. The UN Development Programme continued to provide capacity-building support for detention facilities, courts and police forces. The Office of the High Commissioner for Human Rights agreed with the TFG to provide technical assistance in human rights and support for the fight against impunity.

In Puntland, which had a functioning justice system, there were reports of arbitrary detentions and unfair trials.

Abuses by armed groups

Al-Shabab factions unlawfully killed and punished people they accused of spying or not conforming to their own interpretation of Islamic law. In areas under their control, there was an alarming rise in public killings, including stonings to death, as well as amputations and floggings. Al-Shabab factions also desecrated graves of Sufi religious leaders and put restrictions on women's dress and freedom of movement.

S

■ On 25 June, Ali Mohamudi Geedi, Osmail Kalif Abdule, Jeylani Mohamed Had and Abdulkadir Adow Hirale had their right hands and left feet amputated by al-Shabab in front of a crowd in Suqahola in Mogadishu. They were accused of robbery.

■ On 28 September, an al-Shabab firing squad publicly killed Mohamed Ali Salad and Hassan Moallim Abdullahi, whom they accused of spying for AMISOM and the US Central Intelligence Agency (CIA).

■ On 16 October, al-Shabab forces in northern Mogadishu reportedly flogged women for wearing bras, claiming this was against Islam.

■ On 7 November, Abas Hussein Abdirahman was stoned to death in front of a crowd in Merka. He was reportedly accused of a sexual offence.

■ On 13 December, Mohamed Abukar was stoned to death in Afgoye by Hizbul Islam members. He was accused of sexual intercourse outside marriage with a woman, who was given 100 lashes.

Somaliland

The Republic of Somaliland, which declared independence in 1991, continued to seek international recognition, although Somaliland people focused their political attention on repeated delays in national elections. In late September, President Dahir Riyaale Kahin and two Somaliland opposition party leaders signed an agreement brokered by Ethiopian mediators to create a new election commission, fix a flawed voter registration list, and reschedule elections for 2010.

During the period leading up to the agreement, Somaliland government officials regularly arrested and briefly detained independent journalists. The government also maintained security committees which carried out arbitrary arrests; more than 200 individuals were detained in 2009. Human rights defenders censored their own reporting out of fear that they could be arrested or their organizations shut down.

Three protesters were killed and six injured during a demonstration on 12 September. Police fired tear gas and bullets to disperse a crowd outside a parliament building, which was closed several days earlier after a gun was drawn during a parliamentary session.

Tensions remained high in border areas claimed by the semi-autonomous Puntland Region of Somalia. Somaliland continued to host displaced Somalis without sufficient international support.

Death penalty

The TFG reportedly established a military court in Mogadishu to try soldiers accused of criminal offences in October. The court reportedly sentenced six soldiers to death, including three in their absence, for murder.

In Puntland, at least six people were sentenced to death for murder, including two tried in their absence. No executions were known to have been carried out.

■ On 27 April, Ifraah Ali Aden was sentenced to death after a summary trial by the court of first instance in Bossaso, Puntland, after being found guilty of murdering another woman. She was convicted the day after the murder.

Amnesty International visit/reports

🚗 Amnesty International delegates visited Somaliland in September.

📄 Somalia: Human Rights Challenges – Somaliland Facing Elections (AFR 52/001/2009)

📄 Somalia: End indiscriminate shelling in Mogadishu (AFR 52/005/2009)

📄 Somalia: Amnesty International calls for accountability and safeguards on arms transfers to Somalia's Transitional Federal Government (AFR 52/006/2009)

📄 Somalia: Unlawful killings and torture demonstrate al-Shabab's contempt for the lives of civilians (AFR 52/009/2009)

📄 Somalia: Protection of civilians should be a paramount concern for the UN Security Council, 16 January 2009

📄 Somalia: Allegations of AU force firing on civilians need investigating, 5 February 2009

SOUTH AFRICA

REPUBLIC OF SOUTH AFRICA
Head of state and government: Jacob G. Zuma (replaced
     Kgalema Motlanthe in May)
Death penalty: abolitionist for all crimes
Population: 50.1 million
Life expectancy: 51.5 years
Under-5 mortality (m/f):   79/64 per 1,000
Adult literacy: 88 per cent

Increased incidents of torture and extrajudicial executions by police were reported. Refugees and migrants continued to suffer discrimination and displacement in large-scale incidents of violence. Advocates of housing rights were threatened and attacked with impunity. High levels of violence against women and girls were reported, along with failures by the authorities to provide adequate support to survivors of such abuse. An estimated 5.7 million people were living with HIV, with women continuing to be disproportionately affected.

Background

Elections in April resulted in a new government under the African National Congress (ANC) President, Jacob Zuma. The ANC secured 65.9 per cent of the vote and control over eight of the nine provinces. An Independent Electoral Commission official in KwaZulu-Natal province was prosecuted for forgery and violating the electoral code, the first such case since 1994.

Persistent poverty, rising levels of unemployment and violent crime, together with the crisis in the public health sector, posed significant challenges for the new government. Political tensions emerged within the ANC, the trade union congress and Communist Party alliance over economic policy, with frequent trade union-led workers' strikes. Corruption and nepotism impeded community access to housing and services, and led to the collapse of some municipal governments and to widespread protests among affected communities. The volatile situation contributed to increased incidents of violence against foreign nationals, who were perceived as competing for scarce economic resources.

Political developments continued to affect the independence and integrity of the administration of justice. In April, the Acting National Director of Public Prosecutions (NDPP), Mokotedi Mpshe, withdrew corruption charges against Jacob Zuma on grounds of improper interference in the case.

In August, the Judicial Services Commission (JSC), without a formal hearing, ruled that the Judge President of the Western Cape High Court, John Hlophe, was not guilty of gross misconduct after an apparent attempt to influence two judges preparing a judgement affecting the case against Jacob Zuma. A minority of JSC members disagreed with the ruling.

In November, President Zuma appointed Menzi Simelane as NDPP. He had previously been under disciplinary investigation by the Public Service Commission (PSC) after the Ginwala commission of inquiry found his testimony untruthful and without basis in law. The PSC findings had not been made public by the end of the year.

Torture and other ill-treatment

Incidents of torture and other ill-treatment by police of detained crime suspects were reported. Corroborated cases included the use of suffocation and electric shock torture. Incidents of torture rose, according to the police oversight body, the Independent Complaints Directorate (ICD). From April 2008 to March 2009 they investigated 828 incidents of assault with intent to cause grievous bodily harm, some of which amounted to torture. Suspects in several cases were interrogated and assaulted while held without any record of their arrest. Despite continuing efforts by the South African Human Rights Commission and civil society organizations, South Africa did not ratify the Optional Protocol to the Convention against Torture.

The Judicial Inspectorate of Prisons received over 2,000 complaints of assaults against prisoners by prison warders between April 2008 and March 2009. In October, a provision in the new Correctional Services Amendment Act, which compels prison officials to report any use of force to the Inspecting Judge immediately, became operational. Overcrowding remained a serious problem, with 19 prisons "critically overcrowded".

■ Sidwel Mkwambi died in February while in the custody of the Bellville South Organized Crime Unit (OCU). Police claimed he had jumped out of a moving police vehicle, but his injuries were not consistent with their claims. In May, the provincial minister for police

S

ordered them to co-operate with the ICD-led investigation. The ICD referred the case to the prosecuting authorities for a decision on charges against 14 members of the OCU.

Extrajudicial executions

In September, the Minister of Police and the National Commissioner of Police announced legislative and other measures to respond with maximum force against armed criminals and perpetrators of attacks against police officers.

In June, the ICD reported a 15 per cent increase in deaths in custody and "as a result of police action" over the past two reporting years. KwaZulu-Natal province showed the highest increase, 47 per cent, from 175 to 258 deaths.

■ Bongani Mkhize, chairperson of the Maphumulo Taxi Association, was shot dead by members of the National Intervention Unit on 3 February, allegedly after he opened fire on them. His death, which appeared to be linked to investigations into the murder of a police commissioner, occurred despite a ruling three months earlier by the Durban High Court restraining police from "unlawfully killing" him. The court heard evidence that his name was on a list of suspects, all of whom by October that year had been shot dead, several after being arrested and interrogated by the police.

■ An unidentified man was shot dead on 29 October in Durban while apparently fleeing the police after a suspected vehicle theft. Witnesses heard gunshots and saw his body hanging on a security fence near an apartment building. The police attempted to mislead independent investigators and also told the media that he had electrocuted himself on the fence. However, medical evidence indicated he died from a high velocity gunshot injury to his spine. There was no evidence of electrical injury.

Right to adequate housing – forced evictions

In September, leaders and supporters of the community-based economic and social rights movement, Abahlali baseMjondolo (Abahlali), fled their homes in the Kennedy Road informal settlement near Durban, following an attack by armed men. Their houses were destroyed and they were threatened with further violence. The attackers identified their targets by name and in ethnic terms, as amaMpondo (Xhosa-speakers). Subsequently 13

Abahlali supporters, all Xhosa-speakers, were arrested and charged in connection with the deaths on 27 September of two men during the night of the attack. However, no charges were brought against anyone for the attacks on Abahlali supporters. By the end of the year, one of the 13 arrested Abahlali supporters had charges against him withdrawn, and 12 still faced charges, with seven of them released on bail.

In October, the Constitutional Court declared section 16 of the KwaZulu-Natal Elimination and Prevention of Re-emergence of Slums Act 6 (2007) to be inconsistent with the Constitution and invalid. The case against the Act had been brought in the courts by Abahlali in 2008. The October ruling affected thousands of people living in informal housing and with insecure land tenure.

Despite the impact of their successful litigation, Abahlali's community-based work remained severely disrupted by the violent events of September.

Refugees and migrants

Violations of the rights to life and physical integrity of refugees and migrants, and attacks on their property, occurred throughout the year. Incidents of violence led to large-scale displacements of non-national communities in De Doorns, Siyathemba/Balfour and Polokwane, along with other serious incidents elsewhere. Somali and Zimbabwean nationals were particularly targeted. The police response to incidents varied from complicity or negligence to, in some cases, a visible effort to prevent violence from escalating. Towards the end of the year the work of civil society and humanitarian organizations was beginning to achieve an improved police emergency response.

President Zuma publicly condemned xenophobia and the destruction of property of foreign nationals. Progress was made in drafting a National Action Plan to Combat Racism, Racial Discrimination, Xenophobia and Related Intolerance. Durable solutions remained difficult to achieve for some displaced refugees, particularly from conflict countries. Incidents of forcible returns continued to occur.

The political and economic crisis in Zimbabwe fuelled the flow of migrants and asylum-seekers into South Africa. In April, the government introduced a 90-day visa-free entry for Zimbabweans and announced plans for immigration permits for Zimbabweans already in the country. The permits had

not been implemented by the end of the year. An informal shelter for Zimbabweans in the border town of Musina was abruptly closed in March, with many occupants seeking shelter in Johannesburg, particularly at the Central Methodist Mission (CMC). By the end of the year, several thousand Zimbabweans were still sheltering at the CMC with the authorities failing to meet their humanitarian needs.
■ In July, the police arrested hundreds of mainly Zimbabwean nationals for "loitering" near the CMC. Medical evidence indicated that in some cases the detainees had been beaten, kicked, pepper sprayed and shocked with electric stun guns. Some were verbally abused as *makwerekwere* (foreigners) by police. All 350 detainees were released uncharged three days later. In October, the CMC and Lawyers for Human Rights sought an order in the High Court declaring the arrests unlawful and prohibiting the further use of the anti-loitering municipal by-law. The case was ongoing at the end of the year.

Violence against women and girls

A new ministry for Women, Youth, Children and People with Disability was announced.

High levels of violence against women and girls continued to be reported, although comparisons with previous years were difficult due to the changed legal framework for recording these crimes. Police figures for the year ending March 2009 indicated a 10.1 per cent increase in sexual offences, including rape, against adults and children, with over 30,000 against women 18 years or older.

In June, the South African Medical Research Council published results of a survey showing that more than two fifths of the men interviewed had been physically violent to an intimate partner.

The ICD reported to Parliament in February that its inspection of 430 police stations showed many were failing to comply with their obligations under the Domestic Violence Act (DVA). There were also a number of substantiated complaints brought against the police, including failing to arrest the perpetrator for non-compliance with a Protection Order, to advise complainants of their options under the DVA and for "chasing away" complainants.

NGOs and support organizations reported that the police had not received adequate or in some cases any training on their obligations under the sexual offences and domestic violence laws. By the end of

the year, the authorities had established 17 out of the targeted 50 planned one-stop centres for the provision of treatment, support and access to justice for survivors of gender-based violence. In July, the Minister of Police announced he would review the decision to close the specialized family violence and sexual offences units. Research confirmed that the decision in 2006 to close the units led to a deterioration in services and a reduced rate of arrests and convictions.

In November, the Equality Court reserved judgement in a complaint of hate speech brought by the NGO Sonke Gender Justice. The complaint was brought against the ANC Youth League president, for public comments which appeared to denigrate women who reported being raped.

Right to health – people living with HIV/AIDS

An estimated 5.7 million people were living with HIV, according to UNAIDS. By July the number of AIDS patients receiving antiretroviral treatment (ART) had increased to an estimated 870, 000, about half of those who needed it. Poor government planning and staffing shortages left some hospitals with shortages of ART drugs and unable to start treatment for new patients. In October, the budget allocation for HIV drugs was increased.

Women continued to be disproportionately affected and infected by HIV and AIDS. In June the South African Human Sciences Research Council's national HIV prevalence survey showed that 15- to 19-year-old females had a prevalence rate of over six per cent, more than twice the rate for males of the same age group, and rising to over 32 per cent among 25- to 29-year-old women. African women aged 20 to 34 years were identified as the population group most at risk in the country.

On 1 December, World AIDS Day, the government announced a new drive to scale up voluntary HIV testing, among other new measures to combat the epidemic.

International justice

Following civil society protests, the government confirmed in August that it would act on the International Criminal Court arrest warrant against the President of Sudan if he travelled to South Africa, despite the position taken at the African Union Heads

S

of State and Government Summit in Sirte, Libya in July.

In December, human rights organizations sought an order in the Pretoria High Court declaring unlawful the South African authorities' decision not to initiate an investigation into alleged crimes against humanity committed in Zimbabwe by individuals known to travel to South Africa.

Amnesty International visits/reports

🚌 Amnesty International delegates visited South Africa in March, July/August and November.

📑 Human rights concerns in South Africa: Memorandum sent to the South African government, August 2009 (AFR 53/008/2009)

📑 South Africa: Failure to conduct impartial investigation into Kennedy Road violence is leading to further human rights abuses (AFR 53/011/2009)

SPAIN

KINGDOM OF SPAIN

Head of state:	King Juan Carlos I de Borbón
Head of government:	José Luis Rodríguez Zapatero
Death penalty:	abolitionist for all crimes
Population:	44.9 million
Life expectancy:	80.7 years
Under-5 mortality (m/f):	5/5 per 1,000
Adult literacy:	97.9 per cent

Allegations of torture and other ill-treatment by law enforcement officials continued, but reportedly decreased in police stations which had installed CCTV systems. Reforms to asylum legislation recognized gender and sexual orientation as grounds for persecution, but increased procedural restrictions on applying for asylum. The authorities continued to hold detainees incommunicado, despite repeated calls from international human rights bodies for this practice to be abolished. The armed Basque group Euskadi Ta Askatasuna (ETA) continued its campaign of violence, claiming responsibility for killing two people. Victims of gender-based violence, and human trafficking in particular, continued to lack adequate state protection and assistance. There was little progress in investigating enforced disappearances and mass graves relating to the Spanish Civil War and the Franco regime. Government measures to tackle racism were inadequate. The application of universal jurisdiction for international crimes was restricted following legislative reform.

Torture and other ill-treatment/police and security forces

Allegations of torture and other ill-treatment by law enforcement officials continued. Following the introduction in 2008 of comprehensive CCTV systems in Catalan autonomous police stations, a national NGO network reported that complaints of ill-treatment against Catalan police officers had gone down by almost 40 per cent compared to 2007. None of the complaints they recorded related to ill-treatment occurring inside a police station. However, the national police and Civil Guard had still not implemented these measures, except with detainees held incommunicado, and only then when specifically requested by a judge.

The Public Prosecutor's annual report stated that there had been more than 230 complaints of torture and other ill-treatment by law enforcement officials during the year. No steps had been taken to create an independent police complaints commission, despite repeated recommendations by international human rights bodies, including the UN Human Rights Committee.

■ No date was set for the trial of the two police officers charged with killing Osamuyia Akpitaye while he was being forcibly deported from Spain in June 2007.

■ In June a video was published on the internet showing the degrading treatment of a Senegalese man during an attempt to forcibly deport him from Spain. The footage showed him lying on his stomach on the tarmac at Madrid airport, his arms and legs tied together behind his back and apparently being gagged by plain-clothes police officers. The officers then picked him up off the ground, still tied up, and put him into the back of a police van after the pilot refused to allow him to board in these conditions.

■ In June, three police officers accused of ill-treating a detainee at Les Corts autonomous Catalan police station in Barcelona in March 2007 were convicted of assault and sentenced to a €600 fine. A fourth officer was acquitted. Concealed camera footage showed the officers kicking and beating the detainee.

Migrants' rights, refugees and asylum-seekers

Migrants and asylum-seekers continued to risk their lives attempting to reach Spain along dangerous land and sea routes, although official figures showed a 45 per cent decrease in arrivals by boat compared to the previous year. Spain continued to have one of the lowest asylum recognition rates in the EU.

In February, police trade unions reported that officers at the Vallecas police station in Madrid had received orders to arrest a specified monthly quota of irregular migrants; similar instructions were reported by police in other parts of the country. The Minister of the Interior publicly denied that such a policy existed. NGOs across Spain reported an increase in racially motivated identity checks by police over the course of the year; this was believed to be as a result of migration control measures.

In October, Spain ratified Protocol 4 of the European Convention on Human Rights, which prohibits collective expulsion of foreign nationals.

The reform of the asylum law, adopted in October, broadens the grounds for granting refugee status or subsidiary protection to include individuals persecuted on the grounds of gender or sexual orientation. However, it also excludes EU citizens from seeking asylum, eliminates the possibility of claiming asylum in Spanish embassies abroad, and increases the grounds for excluding an individual from refugee status on the basis of undefined, vague criteria such as "constituting a danger to national security".

The Law on Foreigners was amended in October. The amendments grant NGOs access to migration detention centres, but increase the maximum period of detention of irregular migrants from 40 to 60 days.

Counter-terror and security

The authorities continued to hold in incommunicado detention people suspected of involvement in terrorism-related activities, despite repeated calls from international human rights bodies for this practice to be abolished. Under current legislation, detainees held incommunicado have severely restricted access to legal representation and are at increased risk of torture and other ill-treatment.

In its concluding observations of 19 November, the UN Committee against Torture (CAT) reiterated its concern that Spain's incommunicado detention regime for cases involving terrorism or armed groups weakened necessary legal safeguards against acts of torture or ill-treatment. The CAT called upon Spain to amend the incommunicado regime with a view to abolishing it.

■ Following the refusal of the Public Prosecutor and investigating judge to examine the allegations of torture made before the investigating court by Mohammed Fahsi, in June his lawyer submitted a formal complaint in relation to the treatment received by Mohammed Fahsi while he was detained incommunicado by the Civil Guard in January 2006. No response had been received by the end of the year. In September, Mohammed Fahsi and eight other men were put on trial on terrorism-related charges. In December the four-year limit on pre-trial detention for people accused of serious crimes was reached, and he was released awaiting sentence.

■ In May the Supreme Court acquitted Sabino Ormazabal and seven other men previously convicted of "collaborating with terrorism" in the so-called "Macroproceso 18/98" trial. A woman who had been convicted of membership of a terrorist organization was also acquitted. The UN Special Rapporteur on human rights and counter-terrorism and the UN Human Rights Committee had raised concerns in 2008 about the excessively broad and imprecise nature of some articles of Spanish counter-terrorism legislation, including those applied in this case, which may not be in line with international law.

Abuses by armed groups

ETA claimed responsibility for numerous bomb attacks during the year, including a car bomb which killed two Civil Guard officers in Mallorca and an attack on a Civil Guard barracks in the Basque Country, both in July.

Children's rights

Children living in state-run children's homes were exposed to human rights violations. There were complaints of negligence, forced medication, excessive use of force and mental and physical abuse by staff. A study published by the Spanish Ombudsperson in 2008 highlighted similar issues.

Violence against women and girls

Despite some positive developments in recent years, women continued to be killed by their partners and former partners. Migrant women who were victims of

S

domestic violence continued to face additional difficulties in obtaining justice and specialist services. The institutional response to other forms of gender-based violence, including human trafficking for sexual exploitation, remained inadequate. There was no institutionalized system for identifying victims of sex trafficking or referring them for assistance. Victims of gender-based violence seeking redress faced numerous obstacles, including lack of compensation for the psychological effects of violence.

■ Eight years after being run over and stabbed 15 times by her ex-husband, Ascensión Anguita had still received no compensation for the attack, and her recovery was impeded by inadequate institutional support. She remained unable to work and was diagnosed with post-traumatic stress disorder, living on a monthly disability allowance of €401. In July 2008, her ex-husband became entitled to six days leave a month from prison, during which time Ascensión Anguita had to leave her home and go into hiding. The police told her they did not have sufficient resources to protect her.

Racism

The National Human Rights Plan launched in 2008 contained a provision to establish a comprehensive National Strategy to Combat Racism; however, at the end of the year this had still not begun, contrary to the recommendations of the UN Committee on the Elimination of Racial Discrimination and the EU Monitoring Centre on Racism and Xenophobia. The Council for Advancement and Equal Treatment, established by law in 2003, was still not operational. According to the 2009 annual report of the EU Fundamental Rights Agency, published in June, this leaves Spain as one of only four EU countries that do not have a national equality body producing statistics on complaints about racism. Spain is also one of just six EU member states that do not collect or publish official data on racist crimes.

Enforced disappearances

In September, Spain ratified the International Convention for the Protection of All Persons from Enforced Disappearance, but enforced disappearance is still not criminalized in Spanish law.

In December 2008 the National Criminal Court ruled that it was not competent to investigate cases of enforced disappearances dating from the Spanish

Civil War and early years of the rule of Francisco Franco; it therefore referred the 114,266 suspected cases of enforced disappearance to the 43 local criminal courts in whose jurisdiction the mass graves had been found. Subsequently, 13 courts classified the cases as ordinary crimes and closed the investigations on the grounds that the crimes had passed the statute of limitations (which sets a maximum period of time that legal proceedings may be initiated after a specific crime). Only three of the local courts classified the cases as crimes under international law (which have no expiry date). These investigations were ongoing at the end of the year.

On 11 March the Senate rejected a draft law calling on the government to take on the task of locating, exhuming and identifying the remains of victims of the Civil War and the rule of Francisco Franco. This was in contradiction to the 2007 Law of Historical Memory, which contained provisions to help families locate and recover the remains of their loved ones. The 2007 law itself falls short of international standards relating to the right to reparation for victims and relatives of victims of gross human rights violations.

International Justice

In October, parliament adopted an amendment to the Law on the Judiciary, which would restrict the application of universal jurisdiction. Thirteen cases under investigation in Spain could be closed as a result. The amendment limits universal jurisdiction to cases in which the victims are Spanish or in which Spain has a "relevant connecting link", where the alleged perpetrator is in Spain, and as long as no effective investigation or prosecution has already begun in another country or international court. The criteria for determining what constitutes "effective" in this context were not defined. The legislative amendment was passed without specific debate.

Amnesty International visit/reports

🚃 Amnesty International delegates visited Spain in November.

📄 Spain: Out of the Shadows – time to end incommunicado detention (EUR 41/001/2009)

📄 Spain: Adding insult to injury – police impunity two years on (EUR 41/010/2009)

📄 Spain: Briefing to the Committee against Torture (EUR 41/004/2009)

S

SRI LANKA

DEMOCRATIC SOCIALIST REPUBLIC OF SRI LANKA
Head of state and government: Mahinda Rajapaksa
Death penalty: abolitionist in practice
Population: 20.2 million
Life expectancy: 74 years
Under-5 mortality (m/f):   21/18 per 1,000
Adult literacy: 90.8 per cent

Some 300,000 Tamil civilians were displaced by armed conflict, and subsequently detained in government camps. Those suspected of ties with the Liberation Tigers of Tamil Eelam (LTTE) – more than 12,000 – were detained separately. Many were held incommunicado and sometimes in facilities not designed to hold prisoners or in secret places of detention. Civilians were trapped for months prior to the conflict's end in May without adequate food, shelter, sanitation and medical care, or access to humanitarian aid. The LTTE used civilians as human shields and used threats and violence to prevent them from fleeing the conflict zone. Government artillery killed and wounded civilians, including patients in hospitals and medical workers. The government failed to address impunity for past human rights violations, and continued to carry out enforced disappearances and torture. Hundreds of Tamils continued to be detained in the south for lengthy periods without charge under special security legislation. Human rights defenders and journalists were killed, assaulted, threatened and jailed. Police killings of criminal suspects intensified.

Background

In May, the Sri Lankan government declared victory over the LTTE, ending more than 25 years of armed conflict. But an end to fighting did not end the government's reliance on draconian security legislation or stem human rights violations.

Armed conflict

Both the Sri Lankan government and the LTTE violated international humanitarian law. The government used heavy weaponry indiscriminately in areas densely populated with civilians. The LTTE forcibly recruited adults and children as combatants, used civilians as human shields against the approaching government forces, and attacked civilians who tried to escape. Independent accounts from the conflict areas were limited as access by the media, the UN and humanitarian agencies was restricted. According to UN estimates, thousands of civilians died in the fighting. Displaced people reported enforced disappearances of young men separated from their families by the military as civilians crossed into government territory and underwent military screening to identify LTTE combatants.

The government did not begin to reopen the A9 highway – the only land route to the Jaffna Peninsula – until July, thus severely restricting civilian access to humanitarian supplies during the first half of the year. Private vehicles were banned until late December.

Internally displaced people

By the end of May, civilians displaced by fighting were confined to government camps in the north and east where conditions were crowded and unsanitary. Many thousands of other civilians also remained displaced from earlier stages of the conflict. The Sri Lankan government initially banned humanitarian agencies from the newly established camps, which were run by the military, but gradually eased restrictions to allow delivery of relief material. Humanitarian workers were not permitted to speak to displaced people. Visits by journalists were tightly controlled, and no independent human rights monitoring was permitted. The ICRC lost access to the displaced when the government directed them to downgrade activities after fighting concluded. By year's end, restrictions on freedom of movement had been relaxed, but over 100,000 people remained in the camps.

Abuses by armed groups
LTTE

The LTTE recruited children as fighters and punished people who resisted forced recruitment. They imposed a strict pass system, hindering thousands of families from the Wanni region from moving to safer areas. As conflict intensified and territory controlled by the LTTE diminished, they actively prevented civilians from escaping, including shooting at those who tried to flee.

The LTTE also deliberately targeted civilians. They

S

launched indiscriminate attacks outside the conflict zone, including suicide bombings and an aerial assault on Colombo.

■ On 10 March, a suicide bombing of a Muslim religious procession in southern Sri Lanka killed 14 civilians and injured 50.

Government-allied armed groups

Armed groups allied with the government were used for counter-insurgency, including the Eelam People's Democratic Party, the People's Liberation Organization of Tamil Eelam, and the Tamil People's Liberation Front (TMVP). Members carried out enforced disappearances and hostage-taking for ransom, unlawful killings, and recruitment of child soldiers, including from camps housing internally displaced people. TMVP members and cadres loyal to the former TMVP leader, V. Muralitharan (known as Karuna), were accused by local parents of child recruitment in Batticaloa district. Internecine violence between supporters of the two factions resulted in civilian deaths.

Enforced disappearances

The government continued to carry out enforced disappearances as part of its counter-insurgency strategy. Enforced disappearances were reported in many parts of the country, particularly in northern and eastern Sri Lanka and in Colombo.

Arbitrary arrests and detentions

The security forces used emergency regulations to arrest and detain many thousands of Tamils suspected of LTTE links. People were arrested in various contexts, including in displacement camps, during search operations and at security checkpoints throughout the country.

■ On 26 March, more than 300 people, most of them Tamil, were arrested in a search operation conducted between 6pm and 6am in the town of Gampaha, about 24km north-west of Colombo.

Hundreds of people remained detained without charge in police lock-ups and southern prisons under the Prevention of Terrorism Act and emergency regulations on suspicion of links to the LTTE; in November, 20 were released for lack of evidence.

■ On 18 September, some 36 Tamil prisoners on hunger strike protesting against their prolonged detention without trial at Welikada jail said they were beaten by prison guards. Beatings by prison guards in November injured 22 Tamil prisoners, seven of them seriously.

Extrajudicial executions

Police killings of criminal suspects escalated after President Mahinda Rajapaksa ordered a crackdown on underworld activity in July. At least five alleged gang leaders were abducted and killed in July alone.

■ In mid-August, thousands of Sri Lankans took to the streets to protest against the killing of two young men by police in Angulana, a suburb of Colombo, after a woman with police links accused them of harassment. Witnesses say the victims were beaten and otherwise tortured before being taken out of the station; their bodies were found the next day.

Impunity

Investigations into human rights violations by the military and police stalled. Court cases did not proceed as witnesses refused to come forward for fear of reprisals. In June, a Presidential Commission of Inquiry, established to look into serious violations of human rights committed since 2006, was disbanded without completing its mandated tasks. Of the 16 cases referred, only seven were investigated, with reports on five finalized. No reports were made public and no inquiry resulted in prosecutions.

People suspected of committing human rights violations continued to hold responsible positions in government. Minister of National Integration Vinayagamoorthy Muralitharan (alias Karuna) and Chief Minister of the Eastern Province Sivanesathurai Chandrakanthan (alias Pillayan) were reportedly responsible for abducting teenagers to serve as child soldiers, and holding as hostage, torturing and unlawfully killing civilians and people suspected of links to the LTTE. Both men were formerly LTTE members. There was no official investigation into any allegations of abuse.

■ In September, Joseph Douglas Peiris and four other police officers were released on bail by the Supreme Court after they challenged convictions related to enforced disappearances carried out in July 1989. In August, a Gampaha court had sentenced the men to five years' hard labour for abducting two brothers (one of whom was killed) with intent to murder, and keeping the youths in illegal custody. The crimes were committed in the context of government counter-insurgency operations. The case took 20 years to prosecute.

Human rights defenders

Human rights defenders continued to be subjected to arbitrary arrests, enforced disappearances, attacks and threats.

■ Sinnavan Stephen Sunthararaj of the Centre for Human Rights and Development was abducted by uniformed men in May, just hours after his release from two months in police detention without charge. He remained missing at year's end.

■ Five doctors who provided eyewitness accounts of civilian casualties in the final phase of the armed conflict were detained by the Sri Lankan army in May. In July, they were apparently compelled to publicly recant their earlier reports of Sri Lankan military attacks on civilians. Four of the five were released in August and permitted to resume work. The fifth, Dr Sivapalan, was released in late December.

■ In August, Dr Paikiasothy Saravanamuttu, Director of the Colombo-based Centre for Policy Alternatives, received an anonymous letter posted to his home address, threatening to kill him if the EU withdrew Sri Lanka's Generalized System of Preference Plus tariff concession, which was in jeopardy because of Sri Lanka's failure to live up to its human rights commitments. In September he was detained and questioned by police at Bandaranaike International airport.

Journalists

Journalists were killed, physically assaulted, abducted, intimidated and harassed by both government personnel and members of armed groups. Little effort was made to investigate attacks or bring perpetrators to justice.

■ Lasantha Wickrematunge, outspoken critic of the Sri Lankan government and editor of the *Sunday Leader* newspaper, was shot and killed on his way to work on 8 January.

■ On 1 June, unidentified assailants abducted and assaulted Poddala Jayantha, General Secretary of the Working Journalists Association in Sri Lanka. His attackers called him a traitor, shaved his beard, beat him with iron bars, broke his leg and crushed his fingers, saying it was to prevent him from writing.

■ On 31 August, journalist and prisoner of conscience Jayaprakash Sittampalam Tissainayagam was sentenced to 20 years' hard labour on terrorism charges for articles he wrote in 2006 criticizing the military's treatment of civilians in eastern Sri Lanka. His colleagues V. Jasiharan and V. Vallarmathy were

released in October after 19 months in detention. The charges were dropped when they agreed not to pursue a fundamental rights complaint against the authorities.

Amnesty International visit/reports

🚍 The authorities denied Amnesty International permission to visit the country.

📋 Stop the War on Civilians in Sri Lanka: A briefing on the humanitarian crisis and lack of human rights protection (ASA 37/004/2009)

📋 Twenty years of make-believe. Sri Lanka's Commissions of Inquiry (ASA 37/005/2009)

📋 Letter to the Security Council: The situation in Sri Lanka (ASA 37/009/2009)

📋 Sri Lanka: Government misrepresentations regarding the scale of the crisis (ASA 37/012/2009)

📋 Unlock the Camps in Sri Lanka (ASA 37/016/2009)

SUDAN

REPUBLIC OF SUDAN
Head of state and government: **Omar Hassan Ahmed Al Bashir**
Death penalty: **retentionist**
Population: **42.3 million**
Life expectancy: **57.9 years**
Under-5 mortality (m/f):   **117/104 per 1,000**
Adult literacy: **60.9 per cent**

Widespread human rights abuses by the government and armed groups continued. The conflict in Darfur was less intense than in previous years but nevertheless continued, with attacks on civilians and humanitarian convoys among violations of international humanitarian law committed by all sides to the conflict. Hundreds of civilians were killed. Violence against women, including rape, remained widespread, particularly during attacks on villages and near camps of internally displaced persons (IDPs). In Southern Sudan, armed clashes escalated as did ethnic conflicts, resulting in more than 2,500 deaths and the displacement of more than 350,000 people. In March, the International Criminal Court (ICC) issued an arrest warrant against President Omar Al Bashir for war crimes and crimes against humanity. Following this, the government stepped up repression of human rights defenders, political opponents and ordinary civilians, and expelled and closed down international and national humanitarian organizations. More than 60 people were sentenced to death, 54 by special counter-terrorism courts, and at least nine were executed. Torture and other ill-treatment were widely reported. The use of cruel, inhuman and degrading punishments persisted; at least 12 women were flogged after police arrested them mainly for wearing trousers.

Background

Tensions mounted between the National Congress Party (NCP), the ruling party, and the Sudan People's Liberation Movement (SPLM), the ruling party in Southern Sudan, particularly over legal reforms and the demarcation of Abyei's borders that were defined in July by the Permanent Court of Arbitration, which sits in The Hague. The Court decided that the oil fields of Heglig and Bamboo belonged to the North, which was contested by the SPLM.

Disputes also continued between the NCP and the SPLM over aspects of the 2005 Comprehensive Peace Agreement and the South Sudan Referendum Bill, which was passed in December.

The national elections, which were supposed to be held by April, were delayed until April 2010. The voters' registration process, which lasted from November to December, was impeded by several factors, including lack of access to registration points.

In June, the UN Human Rights Council did not renew the mandate of the Special Rapporteur on the Human Rights Situation in Sudan and decided to replace the Special Rapporteur with an Independent Expert on the situation of human rights in Sudan. Mohamed Chande Othman, a former judge from Tanzania, was appointed on 2 October.

Preliminary consultations were held in Doha under the auspices of the Qatari government and in collaboration with the AU-UN joint chief mediator for Darfur, Djibril Bassole, to discuss the prospects of a new peace agreement for Darfur. In February, the government of Sudan and the Justice and Equality Movement (JEM), one of the main Darfur-based armed opposition groups, signed the "goodwill and confidence building agreement" following a week of negotiations in Doha. The two parties committed to finding a peaceful resolution to the conflict. The agreement contained provisions to exchange those involved in the conflict who had been captured, including people arrested following the JEM attack on Khartoum in May 2008, as well as ceasing arrests of displaced people and allowing access to humanitarian aid for the displaced. The agreement broke down after the ICC issued the arrest warrant against President Al Bashir, and after the government refused to surrender hundreds of detainees arrested after the 2008 JEM attack on Khartoum.

International justice

On 4 March, the ICC issued an arrest warrant against President Al Bashir for two counts of war crimes and five counts of crimes against humanity. The AU and League of Arab States expressed their support for President Al Bashir and requested the Security Council to defer the case under Article 16 of the Rome Statute of the ICC. The request was not granted.

The warrant against President Al Bashir was the third issued by the ICC relating to Darfur. The

Sudanese government refused to co-operate or surrender any of the suspects. Ali Kushayb, one of the former leaders of the Janjaweed, the government-allied militia, against whom an arrest warrant was issued by the ICC in 2007, reportedly remained at liberty. Ahmed Haroun, former State Minister for Humanitarian Affairs, against whom the ICC also issued an arrest warrant in 2007, was appointed governor of South Kordofan in May.

On 7 May, the ICC's pre-trial chamber issued a sealed summons for Bahar Idriss Abu Garda, the alleged co-perpetrator of three war crimes in the Haskanita attack against peacekeepers of the African Union Mission in Sudan (AMIS) in 2007. Bahar Idriss Abu Garda voluntarily appeared before the ICC on 18 May.

In March, the AU formed a panel on Darfur, headed by former South African President Thabo Mbeki, to investigate ways of securing peace, justice and reconciliation in the region. In October, the panel submitted its report to the AU. Among other recommendations, it called for the creation of a hybrid court comprising Sudanese judges as well as AU-appointed judges from other countries to prosecute the most serious crimes committed in Darfur. The report was subsequently endorsed by the AU's Peace and Security Council.

Armed conflict – Darfur

Despite a reduction in attacks and the return of some displaced people to their home villages, conflict persisted in Darfur. Civilians continued to bear the brunt of the fighting, with hundreds of civilians killed. Attacks on villages led to the displacement of thousands of civilians.

Attacks on humanitarian workers and convoys, and on the joint UN-AU Mission in Darfur (UNAMID) also continued. According to the UN Office for the Coordination of Humanitarian Affairs (OCHA) in September, three UNAMID staff and seven national humanitarian staff were killed and 12 humanitarian staff and 10 UNAMID staff were wounded in the first eight months of the year. UNAMID still lacked essential equipment and fell short of the pledged strength of 26,000 uniformed troops required to fulfil its mandate to protect civilians.

■ In January, JEM entered Muhajeria, a town in south Darfur that was previously controlled by the Sudan Liberation Army/Minni Minawi branch (SLA/MM), the only Darfur-based armed opposition group to have signed the 2006 Darfur Peace Agreement with the Sudanese government. Both sides engaged in fighting and the shelling of civilian areas, and government planes bombed the town killing scores of civilians and injuring hundreds, and causing the displacement of most of the town's population. In February, around 6,000 people sought safe haven around the UNAMID base in Muhajeria. The government asked UNAMID to leave Muhajeria, but it refused to do so.

Access to humanitarian aid

On 4 March, immediately after the ICC issued its warrant of arrest against President Al Bashir, the government expelled 13 international humanitarian organizations and closed down three national human rights and humanitarian organizations. The government said some of the organizations' papers were not in order and accused others of providing information to the ICC.

The expulsions removed 40 per cent of all aid workers from Sudan and threatened to have a dramatic impact on the humanitarian situation in Darfur, in the transitional areas (Abyei, Blue Nile and South Kordofan) and eastern Sudan – all home to significant numbers of vulnerable people relying on humanitarian aid.

In June, the government announced that it would allow the entry and registration of new organizations and their staff. However, the three national humanitarian and human rights organizations remained closed – the Khartoum Centre for Human Rights and Environmental Development, the Sudan Social Development Organization (known as SUDO) and the Amal Centre for the Rehabilitation of Victims of Torture in Khartoum – leaving a significant gap in humanitarian services and the monitoring and reporting of human rights violations in Darfur and Sudan in general. The National Intelligence and Security Services (NISS) harassed staff of these organizations, raided their offices and froze their assets.

Violence against women

Rape and other violence against women continued to be widespread during attacks on villages and in the vicinity of IDP camps, especially when women ventured outside. Organizations offering protection services, particularly to survivors of sexual violence in Darfur, were seriously affected by the expulsions and closures of humanitarian organizations.

S

Armed conflict – Southern Sudan

Armed clashes between different ethnic communities continued. More than 2,500 people were reportedly killed and more than 350,000 were displaced. The violence mostly affected remote areas. The worst affected state was Jonglei, where at least 2,000 were killed, according to UN estimates.

Attacks increased on civilians by the Lord's Resistance Army (LRA), an armed group that originated in northern Uganda. According to the UN Office of the High Commissioner for Human Rights (OHCHR), the LRA's attacks in Southern Sudan could amount to war crimes, with 27 confirmed attacks between December 2008 and March 2009.

The increase of violence across southern Sudan was exacerbated by poor rainfall, leading to a dire humanitarian situation. The lack of cultivation and access to fields, as well as the difficulty for humanitarian agencies to travel, increased food insecurity, with the threat of famine affecting an estimated 1.5 million people.

Arbitrary detentions, torture and other ill-treatment

The NISS continued to detain people arbitrarily and hold them incommunicado, particularly in Khartoum and Darfur after the ICC issued the warrant of arrest for President Al Bashir. NISS personnel raided the offices of several Sudanese NGOs, took away files and arrested some of their staff. They also arrested staff of international humanitarian organizations seen by the government as possible suppliers of information to the ICC. Human rights defenders were particularly affected by the wave of arrests and many fled the country.

A new National Security Bill, adopted by parliament in December, retains the power of the NISS to detain people without charge for four and a half months and maintains immunity from prosecution for security officers.

■ On 21 October, Adam Suleiman Sulman, one of the 103 defendants sentenced to death by special counter-terrorism courts (see below), died in a police hospital in Khartoum two days after he was taken there from Kober prison. He was still in shackles. Adam Suleiman Sulman had been tortured during his detention. He also had a mental disorder that was reportedly exacerbated by his detention and torture. He died of tuberculosis and was denied adequate health care,

despite warnings by his lawyer that he needed urgent medical attention.

Unfair trials – special courts

Between July 2008 and June 2009, 103 individuals were sentenced to death by special counter-terrorism courts. The defendants were convicted collectively after unfair trials of crimes relating to their alleged participation in the JEM attack on Khartoum in May 2008. The special courts were set up in the aftermath of the attack in application of the 2001 Counter-Terrorism Act. The "confessions" of most defendants were allegedly extracted under torture and were accepted by the courts as the main evidence to secure their conviction. Many defendants were only given access to a lawyer after their trial had begun. All but one defendant, who died in custody (see above), were awaiting the outcome of appeals at the end of the year.

Death penalty

In addition to those sentenced to death by the special courts, at least six people were sentenced to death by ordinary courts and nine were executed.

■ Nine men accused in relation to the murder of newspaper editor Mohamed Taha, who was found beheaded in September 2006, were executed on 13 April after the Supreme Court upheld their death sentences. Although all nine retracted their confessions in court alleging they had been extracted under torture, the Appeal Court accepted their "confessions" as evidence against them. All nine were from Darfur.

■ Four men were sentenced to death in June by the Court of First Instance in Khartoum for the killing of USAID employee John Granville and his driver Abdel Rahman Abbas on 1 January 2008. After the family of Abdel Rahman Abbas pardoned the four men, as they are entitled to do under Islamic law in Sudan, the Court of Appeal sent the case back to the Court of First Instance which upheld the death sentences on 12 October. Three of the defendants alleged that their confessions had been extracted under torture.

Enforced disappearances and incommunicado detention

Around 200 of the approximately 1,000 people arrested following the attack by the JEM on Khartoum in May 2008 remained unaccounted for, according to a June report by the Special Rapporteur on the situation of human rights in the Sudan. At the end of 2009, the government had still not named the detainees, clarified their status or whereabouts, or allowed them access to their families and lawyers.

Freedom of expression – freedom of the press

The print media was heavily censored in the first nine months of the year. The NISS visited newspapers daily and censored articles they considered harmful to the government or ruling party, or covered sensitive issues such as the ICC or Darfur. This prompted protests by journalists and media owners, including the voluntary suspension of their publications. A new press law, passed in June, maintained restrictions on journalists, such as fines against journalists and publications for alleged press offences, and the powers of the National Press and Publication Council to close down newspapers. On 27 September, President Al Bashir lifted the censorship, imposed 18 months earlier by the NISS, and the government called on editors in return to adhere to a journalistic "ethical code" that could mean they would not address issues that would have been censored in the past.

Journalists continued to be intimidated and arrested by the NISS. Foreign journalists were harassed and expelled reportedly for covering issues seen as sensitive or harmful to Sudan.

■ On 2 March, Zouhir Latif, a Tunisian journalist who was also working for the UN World Food Programme, was expelled after he had been detained by the NISS for three days. Zouhir Latif had covered stories on Darfur, including a battle in Muhajeria in February.

Cruel, inhuman and degrading punishments

Cruel, inhuman and degrading punishments, including flogging, continued to be passed and implemented.

■ In July, 13 women, including journalist Lubna Ahmed Hussein, were arrested in a restaurant in Khartoum for wearing trousers, which was deemed "indecent or immoral dress" by the public order police officers who arrested the women. Ten of the women were sentenced to 10 lashes each under Article 152 of the Criminal Act. The flogging was carried out. Lubna Hussein took her case to an ordinary court, which in

September convicted and fined her. She led a public campaign against Article 152 and announced she would be appealing against her conviction.

Amnesty International reports

▦ Empty promises on Darfur: International community fails to deliver (AFR 54/001/2009)

▦ Sudan: Death penalty – 82 Darfuri men (AFR 54/012/2009)

▦ Sudan: Amnesty International calls for arrest of President Al Bashir, 4 March 2009

▦ Sudan: Execution of nine potentially innocent men shows flaws of death penalty, 14 April 2009

▦ Sudanese authorities must abolish the punishment of flogging and repeal discriminatory laws, 24 August 2009

SURINAME

REPUBLIC OF SURINAME

Head of state and government:	Runaldo Ronald Venetiaan
Death penalty:	abolitionist in practice
Population:	0.5 million
Life expectancy:	68.8 years
Under-5 mortality (m/f):	35/26 per 1,000
Adult literacy:	90.4 per cent

The trial of 25 people accused of carrying out extrajudicial executions in 1982 resumed following unnecessary delays. The lack of protection of Indigenous Peoples' rights remained a concern.

Impunity – trial developments

In January, the military trial of 25 people accused of extrajudicial executions in 1982 resumed after a six-month adjournment. The trial had begun in November 2007 following 25 years of impunity. Among the defendants was former President Lieutenant Colonel Désiré (Dési) Delano Bouterse, who took power in a military coup in 1980 and was replaced in 1987. Dési Bouterse and 24 other men were charged with the killing of 13 civilians and two army officers who were arrested by the military authorities and executed the next day in Fort Zeelandia, a military base in Paramaribo, in December 1982.

The presiding judge rejected a motion filed in 2008 by the defence to ban the media from covering the

S

trial. Witnesses, including former soldiers, testified before the military court stating that Dési Bouterse was at Fort Zeelandia on the morning of the first killings. In August, a civilian witness, brother of one of the victims, told the court that during an interview, a former high-ranking officer, who later died, had implicated Dési Bouterse in the killing of two of the victims. Dési Bouterse denied any involvement in the killings. The trial was continuing at the end of the year.

Indigenous Peoples' rights

In February, the UN Committee on the Elimination of Racial Discrimination considered Suriname's report. In its concluding observations in March, the Committee urged Suriname to ensure legal acknowledgement of the collective rights of Indigenous Peoples. These encompass the rights to own, develop, control and use their lands, resources and communal territories according to customary laws and the traditional land-tenure system, and to participate in the exploitation, management and conservation of the associated natural resources. The Committee invited Suriname to update and approve the draft Mining Act, in line with its previous recommendations to ensure that Indigenous and Tribal Peoples are fully consulted and their informed consent is obtained regarding matters affecting their interests. The Committee also invited the state party to identify practical methods to strengthen judicial procedures in order to give Indigenous Peoples effective protection and remedies against acts of discrimination.

SWAZILAND

KINGDOM OF SWAZILAND

Head of state:	King Mswati III
Head of government:	Barnabas Sibusiso Dlamini
Death penalty:	abolitionist in practice
Population:	1.2 million
Life expectancy:	45.3 years
Under-5 mortality (m/f):	111/92 per 1,000
Adult literacy:	79.6 per cent

The rights to freedom of association, expression and assembly continued to be repressed. Security legislation was used to violate people's rights. Police used excessive force against peaceful demonstrators. Torture and the unjustified use of lethal force by law enforcement officials were reported. Nearly 70 per cent of Swaziland's population lived in poverty and a quarter of the population required food aid. Women and girls continued to be disproportionately affected by violence, poverty and the country's HIV pandemic.

Background

The new government that took office in October 2008 continued to respond to political opposition and dissent by using the 2008 Suppression of Terrorism Act (STA). In July, civil society organizations met in Manzini and called for greater protection of human rights, including rights linked to health, education, housing and security, and for an end to violence against women and the repeal of the STA. The government's National Smart Partnership Dialogue, held in August, was criticized by political organizations and civil society for failing to be inclusive.

In September, the government announced the appointment of the Commission on Human Rights and Public Administration, which had been pending since the new Constitution came into force in 2006. However, the King appointed the Commissioners without enabling legislation and full public consultation or involvement in the nominations.

Delays in judicial appointments began to be addressed, but there were continuing concerns about effective guarantees of judicial independence.

Counter-terror and security

Despite growing domestic and international criticism, the government declared it would not amend the STA. The authorities also used other security legislation to arrest and prosecute government critics.

■ On 3 June, human rights lawyer Thulani Maseko was arrested under the Sedition and Subversive Activities Act, allegedly for uttering words "with a subversive intention" at a public gathering. Following court appearances, he was remanded into custody at Sidwashini Maximum Security Prison. On 10 June, his lawyers obtained a High Court order to allow him confidential legal access and two days later he was released on bail. No trial date had been set by the end of the year.

■ In July, police arrested political activists Mphandlana Shongwe and Norman Xaba at a civil society gathering in Manzini, apparently for shouting slogans and wearing T-shirts associated with organizations proscribed as terrorist in 2008 under the STA. They were released on bail. No trial date had been set by the end of the year.

■ On 21 September, on the first day of the trial, the High Court acquitted Mario Masuku, President of the proscribed People's United Democratic Movement (PUDEMO), of a charge brought against him under the STA. The court found that the state's evidence was either inadmissible or failed to prove the case.

■ The trial of the remanded South African national Amos Mbedzi on subversion and other charges in connection with the attempted bombing of a bridge in 2008 was postponed until March 2010.

■ Sixteen defendants charged in 2006 with treason in connection with bombing incidents were not brought to trial. They remained out of custody under conditional bail. The government had still not made public the report of an inquiry into their allegations of torture in pre-trial detention.

Freedom of association, expression and assembly

The sweeping and imprecise provisions of the STA and associated severe penalties continued to intimidate government critics. Civil society activists and government opponents reported increased incidents of harassment, searches and seizures of materials, and monitoring of electronic communications, telephone calls and meetings, some of which were disrupted by the police.

The media and journalists faced continuous pressure and some overt acts of intimidation. Police increasingly pressed journalists to name their sources and to refrain from publishing certain information which, under the STA, could associate them with the activities of organizations declared to be terrorist. *The Times of Swaziland* was pressured to stop publishing the weekly columns of a government critic, Mfomfo Nkhambule.

■ On 21 May, the Supreme Court ruled, in a case brought by trade unions and political organizations, that there was no conflict between the right of Swazi citizens to form and join political parties under Section 25 of the Constitution, and Section 79, which allows participation in elections only on the basis of "individual merit". A dissenting ruling, by Justice Thomas Masuku, had found that the substantive right to freedom of association protected under Section 25 was nullified by Section 79 and that this derogation could not be reasonably justified.

Torture and excessive use of force

Police and other security officials, including informal policing groups, continued to use excessive force against criminal suspects, political activists and unarmed demonstrators. Incidents of torture and other ill-treatment were also reported. The problem of impunity for such abuses remained unaddressed. Although the new Commissioner of Police, Isaac Magagula, stressed the need to respond to the public's concern about crime without resorting to "police brutality" and limited police use of lethal force to circumstances where the lives of police or others were at risk, victims of police abuses continued to have no access to an independent complaints investigation body.

■ On 16 April church and labour union organizers had to call off a march for free education after violence erupted. A breakaway group damaged property and assaulted a police officer. The security forces used disproportionate force against some demonstrators, including a man whom they beat with batons, kicked, strangled and stamped on apparently because he had insulted the national flag.

■ On 4 September, Wandile Dludlu, president of SWAYOCO, the Swaziland Youth Congress, was unlawfully arrested by four police officers near the border with South Africa. He was taken to a forested area near Bhunya and interrogated about weapons

S

while being subjected to repeated suffocation torture, with his hands and ankles tied tightly behind him. About seven hours later the police dumped him, uncharged, in Mbabane. He needed hospital treatment for injuries and psychological trauma consistent with his allegations. He lodged a criminal complaint against named police officers at Mbabane police station, but by the end of the year the investigation had not resulted in any arrests. He also lodged a civil claim for damages.

■ On 21 September, Correctional Services security officers, without issuing a warning to disperse, assaulted political activists who had gathered peacefully to wait for the release of Mario Masuku (see above) from Matsapha Central Correctional facility. The security officers also demanded that journalists stop filming and photographing their actions. They seized cameras and other reporting equipment and verbally abused, threatened and physically assaulted several journalists. The police investigation into the incident had not resulted in any arrests by the end of the year. In addition, no publicly known steps were taken by the authorities against the Department of Correctional Services, despite public calls for an inquiry into the violence and the intimidation of media workers.

Poverty, HIV and the right to health

Swaziland's HIV prevalence rate remained the highest in the world. Most recent available UNAIDS statistics indicated that 42 per cent of pregnant women attending antenatal clinics in 2008 were HIV positive. Access to antiretroviral treatment for AIDS continued to increase, but lack of access to adequate daily food, particularly in rural areas, continued to impede the ability of people living with AIDS to adhere to the treatment, which must be taken with food at regular intervals daily.

An estimated 256,383 people required food aid. Fifteen per cent of households were headed by orphaned children.

In October on World Poverty Day, the UN Resident Coordinator expressed concern that there were no signs of abatement in poverty levels.

Substantial gender differences in rates of poverty and HIV infection persisted, with women disproportionately affected and infected. Women continued to experience violations of their sexual and reproductive rights through violence or threats of violence from male partners refusing to use condoms.

In November, the Campaign on Accelerated Reduction of Maternal Mortality in Swaziland was launched with official support. The maternal mortality ratio was estimated to be 370 per 100,000 live births in 2006.

Women's and children's rights

In March, the High Court ruled that the government was obliged, under the Constitution, to provide children with free primary school education. However, the Prime Minister stated that the ruling could only be implemented in phases from 2010.

Finalization of draft legislation affecting women's right to equality under the law and on children's rights continued to be delayed, despite the appointment of additional legislative drafters by the Ministry of Justice to speed up the reform of laws in conflict with the Constitution.

In October, parliament passed the People Trafficking and People Smuggling (Prohibition) Bill.

Death penalty

Although the 2006 Constitution permits the use of capital punishment, no executions have been carried out since 1983. No new death sentences were imposed in 2009. Three people remained under sentence of death.

Amnesty International visit/reports

🚌 Amnesty International delegates visited Swaziland in March.

▤ Swaziland: Suppression of Terrorism Act undermines human rights in Swaziland (AFR 55/001/2009) (joint publication with the Human Rights Institute of the International Bar Association)

▤ Swaziland: An atmosphere of intimidation – Counter-terrorism legislation used to silence dissent in Swaziland (AFR 55/004/2009)

▤ Swaziland: Amnesty International condemns use of excessive force against media workers and political activists by prison officials (AFR 55/006/2009)

SWEDEN

KINGDOM OF SWEDEN

Head of state:	King Carl XVI Gustaf
Head of government:	Fredrik Reinfeldt
Death penalty:	abolitionist for all crimes
Population:	9.2 million
Life expectancy:	80.8 years
Under-5 mortality (m/f):	4/4 per 1,000

The government did not exclude resorting to "diplomatic assurances" to send people to countries where they may face torture or other ill-treatment. Two victims of rendition (unlawful transfer of suspects between countries) were denied residence permits. Deportations of asylum-seekers whose claims had not been finally determined gave rise to concern.

Counter-terror and security

In April, the UN Human Rights Committee (HRC) noted that Sweden had not excluded the future use of "diplomatic assurances" to permit the sending of individuals to countries where they may face torture or other ill-treatment. It recommended that the government should ensure that no one, including anyone suspected of terrorism, was exposed to the danger of torture or other ill-treatment.

■ In November, partly based on information never disclosed to Ahmed Agiza and Mohammed El Zari, the government dismissed their appeals against the refusal to grant them residence permits, thus denying them full reparation for the grave violations they suffered as a result of their rendition on a CIA-leased plane from Sweden to Egypt in December 2001. The authorities did not heed calls for an in-depth investigation into the reasons for the expulsion of the two men.

Guantánamo Bay detainees

In February, the Stockholm Migration Court recognized Adel Abdul Hakim, a Chinese national of Uighur ethnicity released from US custody in Guantánamo Bay in 2006, as a refugee. This decision overturned the June 2008 refusal by the Migration Board to grant him a residence permit.

Torture and other ill-treatment

The HRC expressed concern about the failure to guarantee the right of detained criminal suspects to access a doctor; the reported number of self-inflicted deaths in prisons; and the absence of an effective and independent police complaints body.

In December, the European Committee for the Prevention of Torture stated that the authorities had taken insufficient measures to allay its concerns regarding legal safeguards against ill-treatment in police custody; the imposition of restrictions on remand prisoners; and the isolation of certain categories of sentenced prisoners.

■ An investigation into the death of Johan Liljeqvist, a 24-year-old man who had died in April 2008 following his arrest by the police in Gothenburg, was reopened in October amid reports that police investigators had attempted to cover up the extent of the injuries he had sustained.

In December, the Parliamentary Ombudsman criticized the use of pepper spray by the police in certain circumstances. These included in vehicles and on police premises against individuals whom the police already had under control; where there was no threat of violence; or as an inducement to follow police orders.

Sweden failed to introduce torture as a crime in its penal code.

Refugees, asylum-seekers and migrants

The HRC expressed concern about deportations of asylum-seekers whose claims had not been finally determined; the use, in some expulsion cases, of information undisclosed to those facing expulsion; and the lengthy detentions of some asylum-seekers. Both the HRC and the European Committee for the Prevention of Torture expressed concern about the holding of immigration detainees in remand prisons.

Despite recommendations from UNHCR, the UN Refugee Agency, that all states halt forcible returns to central and southern Iraq and Eritrea, 285 Iraqis were forcibly returned to the former and several Eritreans to the latter.

Asylum-seekers who wished to challenge their transfer to another EU member state under the Dublin II Regulation were not entitled to a suspensive in-country appeal (which would suspend their transfer pending the outcome of the appeal). Those detained while awaiting transfer were denied the right to an appointed legal representative, including in respect of challenges to their detention pending transfer.

In June, the UN Committee on the Rights of the

S

Child expressed concern over the authorities' failure to sufficiently consider the best interests of children seeking asylum, and the large number of unaccompanied children disappearing from reception centres. In November, the government announced it would form a commission to review the system for dealing with unaccompanied asylum-seeking children and their housing needs.

Violence against women and girls

The HRC expressed concern about the high prevalence of violence against women, the lack of shelters for women in some municipalities and the continuing occurrence of female genital mutilation (within migrant communities).

Discrimination

The HRC noted the increase of reported racially motivated crimes. The CRC expressed concern at discrimination against and xenophobic and racist attitudes towards children of ethnic minorities, refugee and asylum-seeking children and children belonging to migrant families.

SWITZERLAND

SWISS CONFEDERATION

Head of state and government:	**Hans-Rudolf Merz**
Death penalty:	**abolitionist for all crimes**
Population:	**7.6 million**
Life expectancy:	**81.7 years**
Under-5 mortality (m/f):	**6/5 per 1,000**

There was concern at a rise in racism and xenophobia in public discourse. Ill-treatment by law enforcement officials was alleged, including apparently racially motivated incidents. Violence against women and human trafficking continued despite legislative measures to combat them.

Racism and discrimination

Voters in a referendum held on 29 November supported a constitutional amendment to ban the construction of minarets. During the referendum campaign, the Muslim minority was severely stigmatized by political propaganda expressed by defenders of the ban. Responding to the referendum, the European Commission against Racism and Intolerance (ECRI) expressed concern that "an initiative that infringes human rights can be put to vote".

The ECRI's periodic report on Switzerland, published in September, expressed concern at increasingly racist and xenophobic political discourse, particularly in relation to the Swiss People's Party. It also expressed concern at the limited effectiveness of the criminal law provision against racism and called for improved training of legal professionals in its application.

The report recommended that civil and criminal laws to combat racism be enhanced, in particular by introducing a provision allowing for increased penalties for racially motivated offences.

The Commission welcomed measures to improve integration of foreign nationals. However, the report also noted widespread racial discrimination in access to services. Migrant children were particularly obstructed from accessing education. Travelling communities were not provided with sufficient appropriate transit sites and must therefore stop in places not designated for this purpose, generating tensions with local people.

Police and security forces

In October, the UN Human Rights Committee expressed concern about ongoing reports of police ill-treatment, in particular against asylum-seekers and migrants. The Committee called for the creation of independent mechanisms to investigate complaints against the police.

Migrants' rights, refugees and asylum-seekers

A federal law entered into force on 1 January which provides that all negative decisions on naturalization must state the reasons and be open to judicial appeal.

In October, the UN Human Rights Committee expressed concern that people whose asylum applications had been rejected were subjected to inadequate living conditions and lacked access to health care.

On 12 June, parliament approved an amendment to the Civil Law which prohibits Swiss nationals or legally resident non-nationals from marrying irregular migrants and rejected asylum-seekers.

At the end of the year, no final decision had been taken by the Federal Administrative Court regarding asylum appeals submitted to Switzerland in 2008 by three detainees held at the US detention centre in Guantánamo Bay. Nevertheless, the Court reversed the decision of the Migration Office on one of the detainees and sent his case back for further inquiry, stating that his defence arguments had not been properly evaluated.

In December, the Federal Council confirmed that it would grant humanitarian protection to an Uzbek detainee held at Guantánamo Bay, and that the detainee would be received by the Canton of Geneva once a memorandum of understanding had been agreed by US and Swiss authorities. At the end of the year, the Swiss government left open the possibility of accepting more Guantánamo detainees if other cantonal authorities agreed to receive them.

Violence against women and girls

In August, the UN Committee on the Elimination of Discrimination against Women welcomed legislation introduced to combat violence against women and human trafficking but noted the continued prevalence of these human rights abuses. The Committee also expressed concern that support services for victims of trafficking had been established only in a limited number of cantons and that legislation on protection of victims was applied inconsistently.

The Committee called for the establishment of more support services for victims of gender-based violence and action to eliminate discrimination against women of ethnic minority communities and migrant women. The UN Human Rights Committee expressed concern that the Foreign Nationals Act impedes migrant women who have been subjected to domestic violence from acquiring or renewing their residency permit after a divorce.

Institutional developments

Switzerland ratified the Optional Protocol to the Convention against Torture in September. In October, the Federal Council appointed a commission of 12 people as a national torture prevention mechanism.

In July, the Federal Council stated that the creation of an independent national human rights institution was "premature" and instead authorized the creation of a university-based human rights centre as a pilot project. This centre would provide advice and analysis on human rights issues on demand to clients, including governmental and private bodies. Human rights organizations criticized the proposal, however, for failing to comply with internationally recognized criteria on such institutions ("The Paris Principles").

Amnesty International reports

- Switzerland: Banning the construction of minarets would violate international human rights law (EUR 43/001/2009)
- Switzerland votes against religious freedom, 30 November 2009

SYRIA

SYRIAN ARAB REPUBLIC

Head of state:	Bashar al-Assad
Head of government:	Muhammad Naji al-'Otri
Death penalty:	retentionist
Population:	21.9 million
Life expectancy:	74.1 years
Under-5 mortality (m/f):	21/16 per 1,000
Adult literacy:	83.1 per cent

The government remained intolerant of dissent. Critics, human rights defenders, alleged opponents of the government and others were detained, often for prolonged periods; some were sentenced to prison terms after unfair trials. Torture and other ill-treatment remained common, and were committed with impunity; there were several suspicious deaths in custody. The government failed to clarify the circumstances in which prisoners were killed at Sednaya Military Prison in 2008 and, again, took no steps to account for thousands of victims of enforced disappearances in previous years. Women faced legal and other discrimination and violence. The Kurdish minority remained subject to discrimination, and thousands of Syrian Kurds were effectively stateless. At least eight prisoners were executed.

Background

Relations between Syria and Lebanon continued to improve, but there was a marked deterioration in relations with Iraq. There were renewed discussions

S

towards an Association Agreement with the European Union.

In November, the International Atomic Energy Agency said that it had not been able to investigate whether a facility destroyed by the Israeli air force in 2007 had been used for nuclear development purposes as the government had been unwilling to co-operate.

Repression of dissent

Syria remained under a national state of emergency in force continuously since 1963 and which, over many years, has been used to suppress and punish even peaceful dissent. This pattern continued throughout 2009. Political activists, human rights defenders, bloggers, Kurdish minority activists and others who criticized the government or exposed human rights violations were subject to arbitrary arrest and often prolonged detention or were sentenced to prison terms after unfair trials before the grossly deficient Supreme State Security Court (SSSC) or Military and Criminal Courts. They included prisoners of conscience. Others, including former detainees, were subject to travel bans.

■ Muhannad al-Hassani, a prominent human rights lawyer detained in July, remained in prison awaiting trial at the end of the year accused of "weakening nationalist sentiment" and disseminating "false news" – the stock charges used to prosecute critics – and other offences. The charges arose from his publication on the internet of reports of trials before the SSSC. Held at 'Adra Prison near Damascus, he could be imprisoned for 15 years if convicted. On 10 November, the Bar Association decided to ban him from practising law for publicly exposing the failure of the SSSC to uphold defendants' rights to defence and to fair trial.

■ Haytham al-Maleh, aged 78, a veteran human rights lawyer and government critic arrested in October, also faced trial for allegedly "weakening nationalist sentiment", spreading "false news" and "slandering a governmental body" because of comments he made in a telephone interview with a Europe-based satellite TV channel in September. He too faced up to 15 years' imprisonment if convicted.

■ Mesh'al al-Tammo, spokesperson of the Kurdish Future Current in Syria, an unauthorized political party, was sentenced to three and a half years in prison in May by the Damascus Criminal Court for "weakening nationalist sentiment" and disseminating "false news".

In November, the same court sentenced Sa'dun Sheikhu and two other members of the unauthorized Kurdish Azadi Party in Syria to three-year prison terms for "weakening nationalist sentiment" and "inciting sectarian or racial strife or provoking conflict between sects and various members of the nation." The charges apparently arose from articles in their party newspaper criticizing discrimination against Syria's Kurdish minority.

■ Kareem 'Arabji, a blogger, was sentenced to three years in prison by the SSSC in September for disseminating "false news" and "weakening nationalist sentiment". He had moderated the internet youth forum www.akhawia.net prior to his arrest in June 2007. He was reported to have been tortured and otherwise ill-treated during his prolonged incommunicado detention.

■ Habib Saleh, a pro-reform activist, was sentenced to three years in prison by the Damascus Criminal Court in March for "weakening nationalist sentiment" and spreading "false news". The charges related to several articles criticizing the government that he had written and published on the internet prior to his arrest on 7 May 2008.

■ Khaled Kenjo, a member of the Kurdish minority, was arrested in September, 12 days after he was forcibly returned to Syria from Germany, where he had unsuccessfully sought asylum. He was charged with "broadcasting abroad false news that could harm the reputation of the state". The charge apparently related to his participation, while in Germany, in activities to promote Kurdish minority rights in Syria. On 30 December, Qamishli Military Court ordered his release without dropping the charge. According to Khaled Kenjo, he was tortured in custody.

■ Aktham Naisse, a human rights lawyer, was one of at least 11 human rights defenders and political activists who were prevented from travelling abroad in 2009.

Counter-terror and security

Suspected Islamists and supporters of the Muslim Brotherhood, which remained outlawed in Syria, faced arrest, prolonged detention and unfair trials, mostly before the SSSC. Defendants convicted of belonging to the Muslim Brotherhood are routinely sentenced to death and then have their sentences immediately commuted to 12-year prison terms. Hundreds of suspected Islamists and others accused of security offences were believed to be held at

S

Sednaya Military Prison and other prisons, and to be subject to harsh treatment regimes.

■ Nabil Khilioui and eight other alleged Islamists, mostly from Deir al-Zour, continued to be detained incommunicado at an unknown location following their arrest in August 2008.

■ Two women – Bayan Saleh 'Ali and Usra al-Hussein – were released in April and July respectively after being held incommunicado for months apparently for contacting an international organization about the detention since 2002 of Usra al-Hussein's husband by the US authorities at Guantánamo Bay.

■ Ziad Ramadan, a former work colleague of a suspect in the 2005 assassination of former Lebanese Prime Minister Rafiq al-Hariri, continued to be detained without trial although the Special Tribunal for Lebanon informed the Syrian authorities that it saw no grounds for his detention. He has been held since July 2005.

Torture and other ill-treatment

Torture and other ill-treatment were reported to be common in police stations, security agencies' detention centres, and prisons. These abuses were committed with impunity. The SSSC and other courts continued to convict defendants on the basis of "confessions" that the defendants alleged were extracted under torture while they were held incommunicado in pre-trial detention.

Seven suspicious deaths in custody were reported but the authorities apparently took no action to investigate them or the allegations of torture made by detainees.

■ Jakarkhon 'Ali, a member of the Kurdish minority, was reported to have been tortured by beatings, electric shocks and being forced to stand for up to 20 hours each day while he was held incommunicado by Military Security officials following his arrest on 20 June. He was released without charge on 3 October.

■ Yusuf Jabouli and Mohammed Amin al-Shawa died in Military Security custody in January, the former after several days' detention and the latter after he had been detained for more than four months. Their families were not permitted to examine the bodies and Military Security officials attended the funerals. Unofficial sources alleged that both men had died as a result of torture. The authorities disclosed no information and were not known to have investigated the deaths.

Impunity

The authorities failed to clarify the circumstances in which at least 17 prisoners and five other people were, according to reports, killed at Sednaya Military Prison in July 2008. No investigation was known to have been carried out. In July, the authorities allowed some family visits to the prison for the first time since the July 2008 events, but at least 43 families were not permitted to visit or have any contact with imprisoned relatives, increasing concern that they may have been among those killed in July 2008.

■ In February, the Defence Minister closed an investigation into the killings of Sami Ma'touq and Joni Suleiman on 14 October 2008, apparently by Military Security officials, but it was unclear whether any action was taken against the officials alleged to be responsible for the deaths. Two witnesses to the killings, Hussam Mussa Elias and Qaher Deeb, and a lawyer, Khalil Ma'touq, were reported to have been harassed and intimidated when they persisted in demanding accountability.

Women's rights

Women continued to be denied equality with men under the law, notably the Personal Status Law covering rights to marriage and inheritance rights, and the Penal Code, which prescribes lower penalties for murder and other violent crimes committed against women in which defence of family "honour" is considered a mitigating factor. On 1 July, President Bashar al-Assad issued Legislative Decree 37. This replaced Article 548 of the Penal Code, which had exempted perpetrators of "honour crimes" from any penalty, and instituted a penalty of at least two years' imprisonment for men convicted of killing or injuring women relatives on grounds of "honour". However, no amendment was made to other Penal Code articles prescribing reduced sentences for crimes deemed to have been committed in the name of "honour".

At least 13 women and one man were reported to have been victims of "honour killings".

■ In October, a court in Zablatani near Damascus convicted Fayez al-'Ezzo, arrested in 2007, of stabbing his 16-year-old sister Zahra al-'Ezzo to death in January 2007 because she had been kidnapped and raped by a family friend. The court ruled that the killing was "motivated by honour" and therefore sentenced him to only two and a half years in prison. He was released

S

immediately as he had spent that period in prison awaiting the verdict. In November, Zahra al-'Ezzo's husband appealed before the highest court of appeal against the ruling, demanding a harsher sentence. The court had not reached a decision by the end of the year.

Discrimination – Kurdish minority

Kurds, who comprise up to 10 per cent of the population and reside mostly in the north-east, continued to face identity-based discrimination, including restrictions on use of their language and culture. Thousands were effectively stateless and so denied equitable access to social and economic rights.

■ Suleiman 'Abdelmajid Osso of the Yekiti Kurdish Party in Syria and 15 other men were detained incommunicado for almost two months after peacefully celebrating the Kurdish festival of Newruz in March. They were all charged with "inciting sectarian strife" and participating in a public gathering. They were all released on bail in May and June and were awaiting trial at the end of 2009.

■ Jamal Sa'doun and three other members of a band were awaiting trial on the charge of "inciting sectarian strife" for performing Kurdish songs at a wedding celebration in Derek near the town of al-Hassaka.

Refugees and asylum-seekers

Hundreds of thousands of Iraqi refugees remained in Syria, many of whom faced economic and other problems because they did not have the right to work or did not possess valid visas, so opening them to the possibility of deportation to Iraq. Palestinian refugees who were long-term residents of Iraq were not permitted entry and some remained at a desolate camp at al-Tanf, in the border area between Iraq and Syria.

Iranian Ahwazi Arab asylum-seekers remained at risk of forcible return to Iran.

Death penalty

At least seven men were sentenced to death after being convicted of murder and at least eight prisoners were executed, including four who were executed at Aleppo Central Prison in August. The true number of executions may have been higher as the authorities rarely disclose information about executions.

Amnesty International reports

◻ Syria: Elderly Prisoner of Conscience charged (MDE 24/030/2009)

◻ Syria: Lifetime law practice ban against Muhannad al-Hassani sends chilling message (MDE 24/032/2009)

◻ Syria: Kurdish minority rights activists jailed (MDE 24/033/2009)

◻ Trial of Kurds in Syria likely to be a "parody of justice", 15 December 2009

TAIWAN

TAIWAN	
Head of state:	Ma Ying-jeou
Head of government:	Wu Den-yih (replaced Liu Chao-shiuan in September)
Death penalty:	retentionist

In March, Taiwan ratified the International Covenant on Civil and Political Rights and the International Covenant on Economic, Social and Cultural Rights. In December, an implementation act provided for a review of all laws, regulations, ordinances and administrative measures to ensure they are aligned to the Covenants within two years. A national human rights reporting system will be established to monitor implementation.

Death penalty

The 2006 moratorium on the death penalty remained de facto only, despite the Minister of Justice announcing her intention to move towards abolition in 2008. The court of final appeal upheld the death sentence of 13 people, bringing the total number of inmates awaiting execution to 44. There are a total of 79 individuals on death row.

With ratification of the International Covenants, the number of crimes punishable by death is expected to fall from 52 (under 11 acts) to 20.

■ On 6 August 2009, the Supreme Court overturned portions of the original rulings against Chiou Ho-shun. Chiou Ho-shun was sentenced to death for robbery, kidnapping, blackmail and murder in 1989. He has been detained for over 21 years while the cases have bounced between the High Court and the Supreme Court.

T

Freedom of expression and assembly

Despite public demand, there was no progress on the government's proposal to amend the Assembly and Parade Law.

■ In May and June, two leaders of human rights organizations, Lee Min Tsong and Lin Chia Fan, were prosecuted for leading assemblies without permits during the visit of a semi-official Chinese delegation in November 2008. The two cases were still pending at the end of the year.

Violence against women and girls

In January, the legislature passed a law against human trafficking. In November, Article 80 of the Social Order Maintenance Act, which imposes penalties on prostitutes but not their clients, was declared unconstitutional by the Council of Grand Justices. The Ministry of the Interior announced that it plans to decriminalize the sex industry.

Refugees and asylum-seekers

In November, two versions of a new draft Law on Refugees were submitted to the Cabinet. The draft excluding refugees from China, who are dealt with in the Act Governing Relations Between People on the Two Sides of the Strait, was submitted to the Legislative Yuan in December.

TAJIKISTAN

REPUBLIC OF TAJIKISTAN

Head of state:	Emomali Rakhmon
Head of government:	Okil Okilov
Death penalty:	abolitionist in practice
Population:	7 million
Life expectancy:	66.4 years
Under-5 mortality (m/f):	83/74 per 1,000
Adult literacy:	99.6 per cent

The authorities failed to adequately address violence against women. Freedom of expression remained restricted. The government continued to exert tight control over the exercise of religion. Reports of torture and other ill-treatment by law enforcement officers continued.

Violence against women

Between a third and a half of women in Tajikistan have experienced physical, psychological or sexual abuse by husbands or other family members. Despite some initial steps by the government to combat domestic violence, women's access to the criminal justice system was restricted, and services to protect victims of domestic violence such as shelters and adequate alternative housing were virtually non-existent. Women massively under-reported violence against them, fearing reprisals or because of inadequate response by the police and judiciary, resulting in virtual impunity for the perpetrators. Domestic violence was widely justified as a "family matter" by the authorities wishing to promote traditional gender roles. Women and girls were even more vulnerable to domestic violence because of early and unregistered marriages and an increased early drop-out rate from school. The draft law on protection from domestic violence, in preparation for several years, was still not presented to parliament.

Freedom of religion

The Jehovah's Witnesses remained banned across the country and members of the Sunni missionary group Jamaat-ut Tabligh came under increased pressure. In March, President Rakhmon signed a new law, making it mandatory for religious groups to register with the authorities before 1 January 2010. To obtain the registration the applicant must prove that

T

the group has existed in Tajikistan for at least five years. The law also states that all published or imported religious literature must be approved by the government. The Muslim community is singled out for special restrictions, with limits imposed on the number of mosques and state approval required for the appointment of imams. Cathedral mosques are only permitted in towns with more than 10,000 inhabitants. Religious organizations now require the permission of the Ministry of Culture's Religious Affairs Committee before attending religious conferences abroad or inviting foreign visitors.

■ In February, the Supreme Court rejected an appeal by the Jehovah's Witnesses against their ban, declared by the government in October 2007.

■ The authorities continued to close, confiscate and destroy Muslim and Christian places of worship, without explanation. In April, the Higher Economic Court rejected an appeal by the Grace Sunmin Church against the confiscation of their place of worship in the capital, Dushanbe. Compensation offered was insufficient to build another church.

■ In August, the Supreme Court sentenced five members of Jamaat-ut Tabligh to between three and six years' imprisonment for "public appeals to overthrow the constitutional order". The Court claimed that the sentences were based on a 2006 alleged ban of the group as an "extremist and terrorist organization", but provided no evidence of such a ban, whose existence was disputed. The accused rejected the charges, insisting that they had no political agenda and that the movement's activities were based on the values of Sunni Islam's Hanafi school, the majority religion in Tajikistan.

Torture and ill-treatment

Reports of torture and ill-treatment by law enforcement officials continued, in particular to extract confessions in police detention during the first 72 hours, the maximum period suspects could be held without charge.

■ On 27 June, Khurshed Bobokalonov, a specialist at the Tajikistani Oncology Centre, died after being arrested by the police. He had been walking along the street when police stopped him and accused him of being drunk. He protested, and some 15 policemen bundled him into a police car. The Ministry of the Interior claimed that he died of a heart attack on the way to the police station. His mother reported injuries

on her son's face and body, and on 22 July the Minister of the Interior announced an investigation into possible "death through negligence". There was no public information about the progress of the investigation by the end of the year.

Freedom of expression – journalists

Independent newspapers and journalists continued to face criminal and civil law suits for criticizing the government, resulting in self-censorship of the media. In October, the government introduced a new decree obliging journalists to request, in writing, information such as laws, policies and government statements, and pay a fee of 25 Somoni (around US$4.50) per page. The Tajikistani National Alliance of Independent Media said the decree violated the Constitution's guarantee of free access to information.

Amnesty International visit/reports

🚌 Amnesty International representatives visited Tajikistan in July.

📄 Violence is not just a family matter: Women face abuse in Tajikistan (EUR 60/001/2009)

📄 Women and girls in Tajikistan: Facing violence, discrimination and poverty (EUR 60/002/2009)

📄 Remove barriers to girls' education in Tajikistan (EUR 60/005/2009)

TANZANIA

UNITED REPUBLIC OF TANZANIA

Head of state:	Jakaya Kikwete
Head of government:	Mizengo Peter Pinda
Head of Zanzibar government:	Amani Abeid Karume
Death penalty:	abolitionist in practice
Population:	43.7 million
Life expectancy:	55 years
Under 5-mortality (m/f):	112/100 per 1,000
Adult literacy:	72.3 per cent

The killing of albino people in some parts of the country continued and the government's overall response remained inadequate. Thousands of Burundian refugees complained of government efforts to force them to return to their country despite fears of persecution upon return. There was a high prevalence of violence against women and girls, and most perpetrators were not held accountable.

Background

Talks between the ruling Chama Cha Mapinduzi party and the opposition Civic United Front regarding power-sharing and legal and electoral reform in semi-autonomous Zanzibar, which broke down in 2008, were not restarted. This raised fears of political violence in Zanzibar during the forthcoming political campaigns for the general elections scheduled for 2010.

Discrimination – attacks on albino people

Killings and mutilation of albino people continued, driven by cultural beliefs that albino body parts will make people rich. Reports indicated that over 20 albino people were killed in 2009, bringing the total to over 50 in two years. Although dozens of people suspected of involvement in the murder and mutilation of albino people were arrested, cases concerning only two killings were concluded in court. The first, in September, found three men guilty of murder; the second, in November, convicted four men. Police investigations of such cases remained slow and the overall government effort to prevent attacks on albino people was inadequate.

International scrutiny

In July the UN Human Rights Committee issued its concluding observations after considering Tanzania's fourth periodic report submitted under the International Covenant on Civil and Political Rights. The Committee expressed concerns about the continued high prevalence of gender-based violence, in particular domestic violence and the lack of effective and concrete measures to combat female genital mutilation; the under-resourcing of the human rights institution – the Commission for Human Rights and Good Governance; the ill-treatment of detainees by law enforcement officials; and the failure to recognize and protect the rights of minorities and Indigenous peoples, including in relation to the negative impact of projects such as game parks on the traditional way of life of these communities. The Committee also noted the government's failure to implement its previous recommendations.

Refugees and asylum-seekers

More than 36,000 Burundian refugees in Mtabila refugee camp in western Tanzania were at risk of forcible return. Many of the refugees had their homes set on fire or were threatened with arson by individuals acting under instructions of Tanzanian authorities. Despite evidence of several attempts to forcibly return refugees, the authorities denied the use of coercion and said that the return process was voluntary as part of a tripartite agreement between the governments of Tanzania and Burundi and the UNHCR, the UN refugee agency. The government announced that it was committed to the closure of the camp and the return home of the refugees by the end of the year. However, very few refugees registered for the voluntary repatriation exercise. No procedures were in place to assess any individual claims by refugees and asylum-seekers of genuine and well-founded fears of persecution upon return to their home country.

Freedom of expression

The government lifted the ban it had imposed in October 2008 on the weekly *MwanaHALISI* newspaper. However, a number of journalists, in both mainland Tanzania and Zanzibar, reported threats and complained of harassment in relation to media stories about high-ranking individual politicians.

The redrafted Media Services Bill, which regulates the media and includes input from civil society on a 2007 draft bill, had not been published or submitted to parliament by the end of the year.

T

Violence against women and girls

Reports on violence against women and girls, including domestic violence, marital rape and marriage of young girls, remained widespread. Female genital mutilation continued to be practised, including in some urban areas.

Local civil society organizations recorded a very low rate of prosecutions for perpetrators of gender-based violence.

Right to health

The maternal mortality ratio continued to be high, with between 8,000 and 13,000 women dying every year, according to reports. This was attributed mainly to an acute dearth of health facilities and qualified medical professionals, particularly in rural areas.

Prison conditions

Prison conditions – both on the mainland and in Zanzibar – continued to be harsh and there were reports of torture and other ill-treatment. Local human rights groups recorded a marginal decrease in prison overcrowding and noted that the problem was mainly due to delays in adjudicating court cases and an inadequate use by courts of non-custodial sentences. According to the Legal and Human Rights Centre and Zanzibar Legal Services Centre, almost half of the prison population comprised pre-trial detainees.

Death penalty

Courts continued to hand down death sentences. As of May, the government stated that 292 prisoners were being held under sentence of death.

A petition filed by three civil society organizations in 2008 challenging the constitutionality of the death penalty remained pending in the High Court.

Amnesty International visit/reports

🚌 An Amnesty International delegate visited mainland Tanzania in October.

📄 Four Tanzanians sentenced to death for killing an albino man, 3 November 2009

📄 Tanzania: Burundian refugees must not be intimidated to return home, 29 June 2009

THAILAND

KINGDOM OF THAILAND

Head of state:	King Bhumibol Adulyadej
Head of government:	Abhisit Vejjajiva
Death penalty:	retentionist
Population:	67.8 million
Life expectancy:	68.7 years
Under-5 mortality (m/f):	13/8 per 1,000
Adult literacy:	94.1 per cent

Freedom of expression suffered a significant setback in 2009 with tens of thousands of Thai websites blocked for allegedly defaming the royal family, and a number of people arrested. The government made little progress in resolving the conflict in the deep south, which was rocked by violence throughout the year. Muslim insurgents raised the level of their brutality, targeting civilians as well as the security forces. Impunity for human rights violations by the authorities continued with no successful prosecutions for a sixth consecutive year. Refugees and asylum-seekers from Myanmar and Laos were forcibly returned to their countries of origin where they risked serious human rights abuses.

Background

For the first time in eight years, the Democrat Party headed the new coalition government, remaining in power throughout 2009. The political conflict that polarized the nation in 2008 continued between the conservative and royalist People's Alliance for Democracy (PAD) and the United Front of Democracy against Dictatorship (UDD) which is loosely affiliated with deposed Prime Minister Thaksin Shinawatra. The authorities invoked Part II of the Act on Internal Security for the first time in April when demonstrations by the UDD resulted in violence as Thailand hosted an ASEAN summit. They did so five more times throughout the year, including in parts of the deep south, replacing Martial Law there. During the ASEAN summit the police fired live rounds, seriously injuring several people. The authorities then terminated the summit. Later that month, unknown assailants tried to assassinate PAD leader Sondi Limthongkul, firing more than 100 bullets in broad daylight.

An internal armed conflict in the deep south continued throughout the year, with the number of dead in the last six years totalling almost 4,000. The government's various attempts to decrease the role of the military in policy and funding decisions did not reduce the violence. In June, six unknown assailants opened fire on the Al-Furquan mosque in Narathiwat province, killing 10 Muslim worshippers and seriously injuring 12 others.

Freedom of expression

In January, the Senate established a subcommittee to oversee legal action taken against those deemed to have violated the *lèse-majesté* law. This law prohibits any word or act which defames, insults or threatens the royal family. Also in January, the government created a website to enable citizens to report someone for purported violation of the law. Throughout the year, the Ministry of Information and Communication Technology, in co-operation with the Royal Thai Army, blocked tens of thousands of websites for allegedly breaching the 2007 Computer-related Crimes Act by commenting on the monarchy. In March, police raided the office of online newspaper *Prachatai*, and briefly detained its director. Three people received prison terms of three to 18 years for violating the *lèse-majesté* law, bringing to four the total number of convictions in the past two years.

■ On 3 April, a court sentenced Suwicha Thakhor to 10 years in prison for material he posted on his blog which was deemed to have defamed the monarchy.

■ On 28 August, a court sentenced Darunee Chanchoengsilapakul to 18 years in prison for remarks she made at a rally in 2008.

Impunity

In January, the Prime Minister called for an investigation into three incidents of ethnic minority Rohingyas being pushed back onto the high seas by Thai security forces (see below). However, no one was prosecuted. That same month, the Prime Minister publicly pledged to resolve the enforced disappearance case of Muslim lawyer Somchai Neelapaijit, but no progress was made or new prosecution initiated. In April, despite previous findings that Thai security forces used disproportionate force which killed 32 people in the Krue-Se mosque in 2004, and a post-mortem inquest identifying three ranking officers as responsible for the killings, the government announced that there would be no prosecutions. In May, a post-mortem

inquest into the 2004 Tak Bai incident in which 78 people died in custody, failed to acknowledge the circumstances that caused their deaths and so discouraged any future prosecution. By the end of the year – one year after a post-mortem inquest determined that Yapha Kaseng died of blunt force trauma while in custody – the government had not begun a prosecution against security officials responsible for his torture and killing in the deep south.

Internal armed conflict

2009 saw a spike in the number and brutality of attacks in the deep south by Muslim insurgents targeting Thai security forces and civilians they deemed to be co-operating or collaborating with the authorities. Other attacks were indiscriminate, killing or injuring many. Insurgents beheaded at least eight people. Violence intensified during the holy month of Ramadan, with at least 32 attacks reported in which at least 35 people were killed and over 80 people injured.

■ On 12 March, Laila Paaitae Daoh, a human rights defender, was shot and killed in broad daylight in Yala province. She was the fourth member of her family to be killed in the south and is survived only by her three young children.

■ On 27 April, nine people were killed and two others injured in five separate attacks on the eve of the fifth anniversary of the Krue-Se mosque incident.

■ On 15 June, a rubber tapper in Yala province was stabbed to death before being beheaded. His body was later burned and left on the plantation, while his head was found impaled on a shovel close by.

■ On 25 August, 20 people were injured when a car bomb exploded in Narathiwat province.

Refugees and migrants

In January, Thai authorities placed 200 ethnic minority Rohingyas from Myanmar and Bangladesh on a boat that had been stripped of its motor, and returned them to sea without a clear destination and with limited provisions. They had been detained on an island for several weeks previously and denied access to UNHCR, the UN refugee agency. At least two people subsequently died. This brought the total number of refugees and migrants pushed back to sea in two months to approximately 1,200. Also in January, authorities intercepted another boat of 78

T

Rohingyas and detained them throughout the year. UNHCR was permitted to speak with them, but two people died, reportedly from lack of medical care.

Throughout the year, Thai authorities continued to return groups of Lao Hmong individuals, including asylum-seekers, from a camp in Phetchabun province amidst questions that returns were not voluntary. In late December, Thai authorities forcibly repatriated all of the Lao Hmong – around 4,500 – from Phetchabun, as well as 158 recognized refugees detained in Nong Khai province since November 2006. UNHCR had not been permitted access to the larger group, while all 158 had been recognized as refugees and accepted for resettlement by several countries, but denied departure from Thailand. Among them were 87 children, some born in detention.

A national verification process for migrant workers began in July. However, the Thai government did not publicize or explain the process to migrants, and officials and unofficial agents exploited migrants' consequent lack of awareness for financial gain.

Death penalty

In August, the authorities executed via lethal injection two drug traffickers, Bundit Charoenwanich and Jirawat Phumpruek, in the first executions carried out in Thailand since 2003.

Amnesty International report

Thailand: Torture in the southern counter-insurgency (ASA 39/001/2009)

TIMOR-LESTE

DEMOCRATIC REPUBLIC OF TIMOR-LESTE

Head of state:	José Manuel Ramos-Horta
Head of government:	Kay Rala Xanana Gusmão
Death penalty:	abolitionist for all crimes
Population:	1.1 million
Life expectancy:	60.7 years
Under-5 mortality (m/f):	92/91 per 1,000
Adult literacy:	50.1 per cent

Impunity persisted for grave human rights violations committed during Timor-Leste's 1999 independence referendum and the previous 24 years of Indonesian occupation. The judicial system remained weak and access to justice was limited. The police and security forces continued to use unnecessary and excessive force. Levels of domestic violence remained high.

Background

In February, the UN Security Council voted unanimously to extend its mission for another year. In September, a National Commission for the Rights of the Child was established and the government signed the Optional Protocol to the International Covenant on Economic, Social and Cultural Rights. All 65 camps for internally displaced people were officially closed during the year. However, around 100 families remained in transitional shelters.

Justice system

In June, a new Penal Code came into force which incorporated the Rome Statute provisions but was insufficient to challenge impunity for past crimes. The Penal Code made abortion a punishable offence in most cases. A Witness Protection Law which came into force in July contained some serious shortcomings, such as the failure to include victims of crime under the definition of "witness". In spite of an increased number of judges and lawyers in the districts, access to justice remained limited.

Police and security forces

There were at least 45 allegations of human rights violations committed by the police and eight by the military, in particular ill-treatment and unnecessary or excessive use of force. Accountability mechanisms for the police and military were weak. Holding

T

accountable those responsible for the 2006 violence, which erupted after the dismissal of one third of the country's military, remained slow and incomplete but a number of cases were investigated, awaited trial or completed. No members of the security forces were held accountable for the violence during the 2008 state of emergency.

Violence against women and girls

High levels of sexual and gender-based violence remained. Women reporting violence were often encouraged to resolve the cases through traditional mechanisms, rather than seeking remedy through the criminal justice system.

Impunity

Reports by both the Commission for Reception, Truth and Reconciliation (CAVR) and the Indonesia-Timor-Leste Truth and Friendship Commission (CTF) documenting human rights violations had not been debated in parliament by year's end. However, in a positive move, a parliamentary resolution on the establishment of a follow-up institution on the CAVR/CTF recommendations was passed in mid-December. The Prosecutor General did not file any new indictments based on findings of the UN Serious Crimes Investigation Team into crimes committed in 1999. Only one person remained in jail for these crimes.

■ On 30 August, the government released Martenus Bere, a militia leader indicted by the UN for crimes against humanity committed in 1999. He returned – a free man – to Indonesia in October.

In August, the President rejected calls to set up an international tribunal for past crimes. In September, a National Victims' Congress called for an international tribunal.

Amnesty International visits/report

🚗 Amnesty International delegates visited Timor-Leste in June and July.

📓 'We cry for justice': Impunity persists 10 years on in Timor-Leste (ASA 57/001/2009)

TOGO

REPUBLIC OF TOGO

Head of state:	Faure Gnassingbé
Head of government:	Gilbert Fossoun Houngbo
Death penalty:	abolitionist for all crimes
Population:	6.6 million
Life expectancy:	62.2 years
Under-5 mortality (m/f):	105/91 per 1,000
Adult literacy:	53.2 per cent

The death penalty was abolished. Several detainees died in detention reportedly as a result of torture or other ill-treatment. More than 30 people were arrested on political grounds, including military personnel; some were held incommunicado. The authorities curtailed freedom of expression.

Death penalty

In June, parliament abolished the death penalty for all crimes. Death sentences were commuted to life imprisonment.

Deaths in custody

Several people died in detention probably as a result of torture or other ill-treatment.

■ Kossi Koffi died in March on the day he was transferred to Lomé civil prison after eight days in custody. He was reportedly tortured or otherwise ill-treated at the National Intelligence Agency (NIA).

Political prisoners

■ In April, at least 32 men, including Kpatcha Gnassingbé, brother of President Faure Gnassingbé, were arrested for an alleged coup attempt. Most were charged with offences against the security of the state, conspiracy, rebellion and "voluntary violence", and were held at the NIA. Others were charged with inciting violence and held at Kara civil prison in the north. Some of the detainees were held incommunicado and several were denied family visits. Lawyers were sometimes denied access to their clients.

■ Vincent Sodji, member of the opposition Union of Forces for Change, was arrested in October in Badou, apparently for possessing military uniforms and guns. He was still held without charge at Atakpamé civil prison in central Togo at the end of the year.

T

Freedom of expression

Freedom of expression was curtailed to stifle criticism of the authorities. In April, after the alleged coup attempt, the High Council for Broadcasting and Communication (Haute autorité de l'audiovisuel et de la communication) called on the media to show restraint on how information is used and suspended all interactive shows on radio and television until further notice.

■ In July, a peaceful demonstration by Journalists for Human Rights was dispersed by security forces.

Impunity

The government established the Truth, Justice and Reconciliation Commission in February to shed light on human rights violations committed between 1958 and 2005. The Decree creating the Commission did not clarify its powers and no provisions were made to bring to justice perpetrators of abuses.

Amnesty International reports

📖 Togo: À quand la justice? (AFR 57/001/2009)

📖 Togo: Quinzième pays d'Afrique à abolir la peine de mort (AFR 57/002/2009)

TRINIDAD AND TOBAGO

REPUBLIC OF TRINIDAD AND TOBAGO

Head of state:	George Maxwell Richards
Head of government:	Patrick Manning
Death penalty:	retentionist
Population:	1.3 million
Life expectancy:	69.2 years
Under-5 mortality (m/f):	37/28 per 1,000
Adult literacy:	98.7 per cent

At least 39 people were killed by police, some in circumstances suggesting that the killings may have been unlawful. At least 11 people were sentenced to death; there were no executions.

Background

In January the government tabled a working document on constitutional reform before Parliament. Proposed changes included replacing the UK-based Judicial Committee of the Privy Council with the Caribbean Court of Justice as the country's highest court, and the creation of a Ministry of Justice.

Police and security forces

At least 39 people were killed by police. Eyewitness testimonies and other evidence indicated that some of these killings may have been unlawful.

■ In January, 52-year-old George Ashby was fatally shot three times in the chest by police as he was returning from work to his home near Rio Claro. Police claimed that when they stopped his car they were shot at and returned fire. His family believed it was a case of mistaken identity. His killing led to a three-day protest by local residents. A police investigation was continuing at the end of the year.

■ In August, 19-year-old Tyrone Peters was found dead in his cell at the police station in La Horquetta, Arima. The first autopsy substantiated police claims that he had hanged himself; officers claimed he had used his jeans to commit suicide. However, his family claimed he was fully clothed when they saw his body in the cell. A second autopsy, requested by the family, reportedly found that he had died as a result of being throttled. Investigations were continuing at the end of the year.

Violence against women and children

In October the Leader of Government Business in the Senate announced that there had been a four-fold increase in deaths as a result of domestic violence between 2004 and 2008 and a 60 per cent increase in complaints of domestic violence over the same period. Women's organizations acknowledged that the rise in the number of complaints may have been linked to improved police responses to reports, but noted that the government needed to do more to support survivors of domestic violence, including increasing the number of shelters.

Death penalty

At least 11 people were sentenced to death; no executions took place.

In July the authorities moved to execute Ronald Tiwarie, despite the fact that his appeal was pending before the Inter-American Commission on Human Rights. His case was deferred after his lawyers filed a constitutional motion to the High Court; the motion was pending at the end of 2009. Ronald Tiwarie remained on death row at the end of the year, despite the fact that in August his death sentence became eligible for commutation under a 1993 ruling of the Judicial Committee of the Privy Council which deemed that more than five years under sentence of death would constitute inhuman and degrading treatment.

Amnesty International report

Trinidad and Tobago: First execution in 10 years threatened (AMR 49/001/2009)

TUNISIA

REPUBLIC OF TUNISIA

Head of state:	Zine El 'Abidine Ben 'Ali
Head of government:	Mohamed Ghannouchi
Death penalty:	abolitionist in practice
Population:	10.3 million
Life expectancy:	73.8 years
Under 5-mortality (m/f):	24/21 per 1,000
Adult literacy:	77.7 per cent

Freedom of expression, association and assembly remained severely restricted. Government critics, including journalists, human rights defenders and student activists, were harassed, threatened and prosecuted. Hundreds of people were convicted following unfair trials on terrorism-related charges. Torture and other ill-treatment continued to be reported, and prisoners were subjected to harsh prison conditions. At least two death sentences were imposed, but the government maintained a moratorium on executions.

Background

President Zine El 'Abidine Ben 'Ali was re-elected for a fifth consecutive term in October amid reports of restrictions on political opponents and repression of dissent.

Political prisoners – releases

In November, 68 prisoners were released to mark the 22nd anniversary of the accession of President Ben 'Ali. They included prisoners of conscience. In all cases, their release was conditional. Former political prisoners are usually placed under administrative control orders governing their place of residence. They are also required to report regularly to the police and denied passports and other official documents.

■ Among those released were Adnan Hajji and 17 others who had been sentenced on appeal to up to eight years in prison for protesting in 2008 against growing unemployment, poverty and rising living costs in the Gafsa region. Their trials were unfair. The courts disregarded and failed to investigate their allegations of torture and other ill-treatment.

The presidential pardon did not apply to prisoners sentenced in their absence who had yet to be apprehended.

T

■ Fahem Boukadous, a TV journalist sentenced in his absence to six years in prison for his reporting of the Gafsa protests, appealed against his conviction in November and remained at liberty.

Freedom of expression and association

People who criticized the government or exposed official corruption or human rights violations faced harassment, intimidation and physical assault by state security officers. They were also prosecuted and imprisoned on trumped-up charges and targeted in smear campaigns in the pro-government media. The abuses were committed with impunity, with complaints rarely investigated. Critics were subjected to overt and oppressive surveillance, and their phone and internet connections were disrupted or cut. The authorities blocked websites and maintained close control over the media.

■ The authorities shut down Radio Kalima, an independent radio station, on 30 January, four days after it began broadcasting from abroad by satellite. Police blockaded its office, harassed its staff and placed Sihem Bensedrine, the editor-in-chief, under investigation for allegedly using a broadcasting frequency without a licence.

■ On 4 April, the Tunis Court of Appeal confirmed the one-year prison sentence imposed on prisoner of conscience Sadok Chourou for "maintaining a banned organization". In interviews with the media he had commented on the political situation in Tunisia and called for Ennahda, a banned Islamist organization, to be authorized to resume its political activities. He had been conditionally released in November 2008 after serving 18 years in prison. Following his re-imprisonment his previous conditional release was revoked so that he must complete the remaining year of the original sentence as well as the new prison term.

■ In August, the executive board of the National Syndicate of Tunisian Journalists (Syndicat national des journalistes tunisiens) was ousted after publishing a report in May which criticized the lack of press freedom in Tunisia. Government supporters within the syndicate held a special congress and elected a new executive board. The new board then obtained a court order requiring the ousted board members to vacate the syndicate's premises.

■ Hamma Hammami, spokesperson of the unauthorized Tunisian Workers' Communist Party (Parti communiste des ouvriers tunisiens), was beaten by men believed to be plain-clothes police at Tunis airport on 29 September. He had just returned from France, where he had publicly criticized the elections, President Ben 'Ali and corruption.

■ In November, dissenting journalist Taoufik Ben Brik was sentenced to six months' imprisonment on politically motivated charges after an unfair trial.

Human rights defenders

Human rights defenders were harassed with oppressive surveillance, threats and assaults. Often, they were physically prevented by state security officials from attending meetings or gatherings where human rights were to be discussed. The authorities continued to block the registration of several human rights NGOs, impeding and restricting their activities, and prevented some registered organizations from holding public and other meetings.

■ Human rights lawyer Samir Ben Amor was not permitted to visit any of his clients in custody from August onwards. The authorities gave no reason. He acts for many suspects in terrorism-related cases.

■ In October, the car of lawyer and human rights defender Abderraouf Ayadi was damaged with a dangerous substance by unidentified people, believed to be security officials, when he was due to drive Hamma Hammami and Radhia Nasraoui, a lawyer and human rights defender, and the couple's daughter. The couple's home was placed under heavy police surveillance in October and they were summoned to appear before the criminal police to answer unspecified charges. They lodged formal complaints, but no investigations were known to have been opened.

■ In December, human rights activist Zouheir Makhlouf was sentenced after an unfair trial to three months' imprisonment and a heavy fine after he posted on a social networking site a video denouncing pollution as well as lack of infrastructure and basic services in the industrial zone of the city of Nabeul.

Counter-terror and security

In August, the government amended the anti-terrorism law of 2003 to strengthen its anti-money laundering provision and to remove other provisions requiring that the identity of judges, prosecutors and police officers investigating cases in counter-terrorism trials be kept secret.

The authorities continued to arrest and prosecute people suspected of involvement in terrorism-related

T

activities. In most cases, uncharged detainees were held incommunicado for longer than the six days permitted by law, without their families and lawyers being informed, and their arrest dates were falsified to conceal their period of enforced disappearance.

Trials under the anti-terrorism law were unfair. Suspects were denied prompt access to a lawyer, and denied adequate time to consult their lawyers and prepare their defence. Confessions allegedly obtained under torture were accepted as evidence by the courts without question or investigation. Some defendants were reported to have been tried and sentenced for the same offence more than once.

At least four Tunisian terrorism suspects were forcibly returned to Tunisia by other states despite fears that they would face torture or other ill-treatment and unfair trial.

■ In April, the Italian authorities forcibly returned Mehdi Ben Mohamed Khalaifia, who had previously been sentenced in his absence to 10 years in prison on terrorism-related charges in Tunisia. On arrival, he was immediately detained incommunicado and held for 12 days, twice the legal maximum, during which he alleges that he was beaten, kicked and slapped by interrogators, suspended in contorted positions and threatened with rape. He appealed against his sentence, which in September was reduced to two years.

■ Sami Ben Khemais Essid, who was retried by civil and military courts and sentenced to 12 years' imprisonment following his forcible return from Italy in 2008, was taken from prison to the Interior Ministry in January and June, interrogated and, he alleges, tortured. New charges were brought against him and he was denied access to his lawyer.

■ The authorities failed to investigate the enforced disappearance of Abbes Mlouhi, who was arrested in 2005. Before his arrest he had been interrogated several times at the Interior Ministry in relation to his membership of al-Tabligh wa Daaoua, an Islamic religious group.

Torture and other ill-treatment

Torture and other ill-treatment in police stations and detention centres, including the Interior Ministry's Department of State Security, continued to be reported. Some detainees were held incommunicado beyond the limit allowed by law, with their arrest dates falsified by police to cover this up. Detainees were at particular risk of torture or other ill-treatment when they were being held incommunicado. The courts, however, routinely disregarded torture allegations made by defendants and convicted them on the basis of confessions allegedly obtained under torture. No official investigations into torture allegations were known to have been carried out after complaints were filed, and security forces continued to operate with impunity.

■ Ramzi Romdhani, serving a prison sentence totalling 29 years imposed in 2008 after he was convicted under the 2003 anti-terrorism law in nine separate cases, alleged that he had been tortured and otherwise ill-treated by guards at Mornaguia Prison in April. In August, he was taken to the State Security Department where, he alleged, security officials tortured him with electric shocks, suspended him by the limbs, hanged him by the neck for a few seconds and threatened him with death. He said that in December he was again tortured for two days by State Security Department officers. He sustained serious eye injuries.

Death penalty

At least two people were sentenced to death, but there were no executions. The government has maintained a de facto moratorium on executions since 1991, but prisoners remain on death row, where they are not permitted contact with their families or lawyers.

Amnesty International visit/reports

🚗 Amnesty International delegates visited Tunisia in September/October and met human rights defenders, journalists and victims and their relatives.

📄 Tunisia: Routine muzzling of dissent mars upcoming presidential elections (MDE 30/013/2009)

📄 Tunisia: Continuing abuses in the name of security (MDE 30/010/2009)

📄 Behind Tunisia's "economic miracle": inequality and criminalization of protest (MDE 30/003/2009)

T

TURKEY

REPUBLIC OF TURKEY

Head of state:	Abdullah Gül
Head of government:	Recep Tayyip Erdoğan
Death penalty:	abolitionist for all crimes
Population:	74.8 million
Life expectancy:	71.7 years
Under-5 mortality (m/f):	36/27 per 1,000
Adult literacy:	88.7 per cent

Little progress was made on enhancing human rights protections. Reports of torture and other ill-treatment persisted, as did criminal prosecutions limiting the right to freedom of expression. The legitimate work of human rights defenders was hampered by excessive administrative scrutiny and judicial harassment. In many cases alleged human rights violations by state officials were not investigated effectively, and the chances of bringing law enforcement officials to justice remained remote. Unfair trials continued, especially under anti-terrorism legislation which was used to prosecute children under the same procedures as adults. Prison regimes showed little improvement, and access to appropriate medical treatment was commonly denied. No progress was made in recognizing the right to conscientious objection to military service, and the rights of refugees and asylum-seekers continued to be violated. Lesbian, gay, bisexual and transgender people faced discrimination in law and practice, and protections for women and girls subjected to violence remained inadequate.

Background

In January a new state-owned radio and television channel was launched to provide Kurdish-language broadcasting. However, restrictions on the use of languages other than Turkish in political affairs and public and private education for children remained in force.

The Kurdistan Workers' Party (PKK) declared a ceasefire in March that remained in force at the end of the year. Despite the ceasefire, further armed clashes with the Turkish armed forces resulted in loss of life.

In May, 44 people died after a shooting in the village of Bilge/Zangirt in the south-eastern province of Mardin. According to an official announcement, most of the alleged perpetrators were village guards, a paramilitary force employed by the state to fight the PKK. Guards were also among those killed. The trial of those accused of involvement in the killings began in September.

Parliament legislated in June to enable the clearing of an estimated 600,000 mines along the Syrian border. The law did not resolve the issue of landmines in other areas of Turkey's territory nor of the stockpile of landmines that Turkey maintains.

In July, construction of the Ilısu dam on the Tigris River in eastern Turkey was put on hold after the three EU states that had provided export credit guarantees withdrew them. Their decision reflected concerns that the project would not meet agreed standards, including human rights guarantees. The dam was expected to displace at least 55,000 people.

Turkey and Armenia signed an agreement in October aimed at normalizing relations. At the end of the year the agreement awaited ratification by their respective parliaments.

In November parliament began discussing an initiative aimed at addressing the human rights concerns of citizens of Kurdish origin and ending the conflict with the PKK. The government indicated steps to enhance human rights protections but no timeline for implementation.

In December the Constitutional Court ruled to close the pro-Kurdish Democratic Society Party on the grounds that it was a "focus of activities against the independence of the state, its indivisible integrity within its territory and nation". The party was closed under laws that failed to uphold international standards on freedom of association.

Freedom of expression

People who expressed non-violent but dissenting opinions – particularly criticisms of the armed forces or of the position of Kurds and Armenians in Turkey – faced criminal investigation and prosecution. Among those frequently prosecuted were writers, journalists, Kurdish political activists and human rights defenders.

Numerous laws allowed the state to limit freedom of expression. Investigations and prosecutions for insulting the Turkish nation (Article 301 of the Penal Code), punishable by up to two years' imprisonment, continued to be initiated, although most were denied permission to proceed by the Minister of Justice.

T

In August prosecutors acting on behalf of the head of the armed forces brought a criminal complaint under Article 301 against journalist Mehmet Baransu. It was based on an article in the national newspaper *Taraf* about an alleged armed forces plot to destabilize the government. Permission for the investigation to proceed was pending at the end of the year.

Conscientious objectors and their supporters continued to be prosecuted under Article 318 of the Penal Code for publicly asserting the right to refuse compulsory military service.

■ In May the trial began in Istanbul of Oğuz Sönmez, Mehmet Atak, Gürşat Özdamar and Serkan Bayrak on a charge of "alienating the public from the institution of military service" (Article 318). They had publicly supported conscientious objector Mehmet Bal in 2008. All four were acquitted.

■ The trial of Sami Görendağ, Lezgin Botan and Cüneyt Caniş, on charges brought under Article 318 following similar protests, continued at the end of the year.

A large number of prosecutions under anti-terrorism legislation targeted free expression about the Kurdish issue in Turkey, and frequently resulted in the imposition of custodial sentences.

■ Osman Baydemir, Democratic Society Party Mayor of the south-eastern city of Diyarbakır, was convicted of "making propaganda for an illegal organization" (Article 7/2 of the Anti-Terrorism Law) in April. He was charged in connection with a speech he made during a protest against a Turkish military operation into northern Iraq in 2008. An appeal was pending at the end of the year.

Threats of violence from unidentified individuals continued against people who expressed dissenting opinions. Police protection was available to some of those at risk.

■ In September anti-racist group DurDe received emailed threats of violence after it brought a criminal complaint against the head of the armed forces.

The authorities closed websites by means of arbitrary administrative orders and court rulings, often without reasons being provided.

Human rights defenders

Human rights defenders were prosecuted for their legitimate work monitoring and reporting human rights violations. Certain prominent individuals were subjected to regular criminal investigations. There was excessive administrative scrutiny by officials, and in some cases judicial proceedings were used to bring closure cases against human rights organizations.

■ Ethem Açıkalın, head of the Adana branch of the Human Rights Association (İHD), faced seven ongoing prosecutions as a result of his work as a human rights defender. In October he was convicted of "inciting enmity or hatred among the population" and sentenced to three years' imprisonment for criticizing the state government's imprisonment in 2008 of children involved in protests, including against withdrawal of family health care benefits. An appeal was pending at the end of the year.

■ In December Muharrem Erbey, Vice-President of İHD and head of its Diyarbakır branch, was arrested on suspicion of membership of the Kurdish Communities Union (KCK) which is alleged to be part of the PKK. The police interrogated him about his work for İHD, and reportedly seized data on human rights abuses from İHD's Diyarbakır office. He remained in pre-trial detention at the end of the year.

Torture and other ill-treatment

Torture and other ill-treatment continued to be reported, with many abuses taking place away from official places of detention. Those accused of ordinary crimes, as well as people accused of politically motivated offences, were vulnerable to ill-treatment.

■ In January the trial began in Istanbul of 60 state officials, including police officers and prison guards, on charges connected with the death in custody of Engin Çeber in October 2008. Some of the accused faced charges of torture. The trial continued at the end of the year.

■ In October Resul İlçin died from head injuries after being detained in the south-eastern province of Şırnak. A statement from the governor's office pre-empting the official investigation indicated that the death did not result from ill-treatment.

Impunity

Investigations into alleged human rights abuses by state officials remained largely ineffective and the chances of bringing officials to justice were remote. During the year no independent human rights mechanism or independent monitoring of places of detention was adopted.

In January the parliamentary Human Rights Inquiry Committee reported on prosecutions of law enforcement officials in Istanbul in 2003-8. It found

T

that, in 35 criminal cases against 431 officers, not one conviction had followed. In June the Criminal Procedure Code was amended to allow the prosecution of military officials in civilian courts.

■ In October the Supreme Court of Appeals ruled that a gendarmerie officer charged following a fatal shooting in the south-eastern province of Siirt should not face punishment. The shooting occurred when unarmed civilians threw stones at the officers' vehicle and chanted slogans. Although the court recorded that the shooting was disproportionate, it acquitted the officer because of "the gravity of the physical attack…, the fact that it continued increasingly despite the warnings and the totality of the conditions of the region".

■ In September, Ceylan Önkol, a young teenager, was killed in an explosion near her home in the Lice district of south-eastern Turkey. Witnesses said she had been grazing cattle close to Tapantepe gendarmerie station and reported hearing the sound of a mortar immediately before the explosion. Neither a full autopsy nor a prompt crime scene investigation was carried out. The authorities said that "security reasons" prevented them from visiting the scene until three days after the death.

■ The prosecution of Ergenekon, an alleged ultra-nationalist network with links to state institutions, continued. Those accused included both serving and retired senior members of the armed forces. The court accepted a second indictment in March and a third in September. However, the prosecution was not broadened to include an investigation of alleged human rights violations.

Prison conditions

Allegations of ill-treatment on transfer to prison persisted and, in a number of cases, prisoners' access to appropriate medical treatment was denied.

■ Emrah Alişan, who was serving a three-year prison sentence, made an application for release on medical grounds in April. The application was supported by medical reports stating that his health condition could not be treated while in prison. The reports indicated that his health had deteriorated significantly while he was in prison and that he was paralyzed and dependent on nursing care. He remained in prison at the end of the year.

Prisoners' rights to associate with other prisoners were frequently not enforced.

■ In November five prisoners were sent to the high security prison on the island of İmralı where PKK leader Abdullah Öcalan had been imprisoned in isolation for 10 years. It was announced that the six prisoners would be able to associate with each other for up to 10 hours a week, in keeping with regulations applicable to all prisoners in Turkey's high security prisons.

On occasion, children were held in prison alongside adults, and generally prison regimes for children did not differ from those of adult prisoners. Notably, there was no provision for child prisoners to continue their education.

Unfair trials

Protracted and unfair trials persisted, especially of suspects prosecuted under anti-terrorism legislation. Children were prosecuted under the same procedures as adults and convicted under unfair laws on the basis of unsubstantiated and unreliable evidence for their alleged participation in sometimes violent demonstrations.

■ In March, 14-year-old A.Y. was convicted on charges of making propaganda for a terrorist organization and of membership of a terrorist organization. He allegedly participated in a demonstration in October 2008. He was sentenced to three years, one month and 15 days in prison. An appeal was pending at the end of the year.

Prisoners of conscience – conscientious objectors

Conscientious objection to military service was not allowed and no civilian alternative was available. Laws allowing the repeated prosecution and conviction of conscientious objectors remained in force.

■ In December, Enver Aydemir was rearrested in Istanbul for refusing to perform military service. He told his lawyer that he was repeatedly beaten at Maltepe Military Prison. At the end of the year he remained in pre-trial detention on charges of persistent insubordination and desertion.

■ In November, three soldiers were convicted of beating conscientious objector Mehmet Bal in June 2008 and sentenced to three months and 10 days' imprisonment. All four men had been prisoners in Hasdal Military Prison. Neither the senior officer who allegedly ordered the attack on Mehmet Bal nor any other official at the prison faced prosecution.

Rights of lesbian, gay, bisexual and transgender people

Discrimination in law and practice continued against people based on their sexual orientation and gender identity. Five transgender women were murdered, and in only one case was a conviction secured.

■ The trial began in January of the father of a gay man, Ahmet Yıldız, who was shot dead in 2008 in a suspected "honour" crime. Ahmet Yıldız had previously complained of threats from relatives. His father was not arrested and the trial started in his absence.

■ The NGO Lambda Istanbul, which supports the rights of lesbian, gay, bisexual and transgender (LGBT) people, won its appeal against closure in the Supreme Court of Appeals in January. However, the ruling left open the possibility that LGBT organizations could be closed for "encouraging others to become lesbian, gay, bisexual or transgender".

■ In October prosecutors sought to close LGBT solidarity organization Black Pink Triangle after the Izmir Governor's office said that its statute breached "Turkish moral values and family structure".

Refugees and asylum-seekers

Recognized refugees, registered asylum-seekers and others in need of protection were arbitrarily denied access to the asylum procedure and sometimes detained. Some were returned to countries where they risked persecution.

■ In September the European Court of Human Rights found in the case of *Abdolkhani and Karimnia v Turkey* that the refugees had been unlawfully detained for more than a year. The applicants were eventually released in October, but many others detained in similar circumstances remained in detention and the provision declared unlawful in the judgement remained in force.

Violence against women and girls

The number of shelters available for women survivors of domestic violence remained woefully inadequate and far below the one for every settlement of 50,000 people required by domestic law. In September a government protocol was signed to facilitate greater cooperation between state institutions in protecting survivors of domestic violence.

■ In June the European Court of Human Rights ruled in the case of *Opuz v Turkey* that the authorities had failed in their obligation to protect the applicant and her

mother from violence. The court found violations of the rights to life and the prohibitions on torture and of discrimination. It ruled that the state's failure – even if unintentional – to protect women against domestic violence breached women's right to equal protection of the law, and that general and discriminatory judicial passivity in Turkey created a climate conducive to domestic violence.

Amnesty International visits/reports

� Amnesty International delegates visited Turkey in January, February, March, April, May, July, August and October, including to observe trials.

📓 Stranded – Refugees in Turkey denied protection (EUR 44/001/2009)

📓 Turkey: German, Swiss and Austrian governments withdraw financial support for Turkey's Ilısu dam project where human rights violations were a risk (EUR 44/004/2009)

📓 Turkey: Submission to the UN Universal Periodic Review – Eighth session of the UPR Working Group of the Human Rights Council, May 2010 (EUR 44/005/2009)

📓 Turkey: Amnesty International welcomes improvement in detention conditions of Abdullah Öcalan after 10 years in isolation (EUR 44/006/2009)

📓 Turkey: Constitutional Court rules in favour of closure of pro-Kurdish Democratic Society Party (EUR 44/007/2009)

TURKMENISTAN

TURKMENISTAN	
Head of state and government:	Gurbanguly Berdymukhamedov
Death penalty:	abolitionist for all crimes
Population:	5.1 million
Life expectancy:	64.6 years
Under-5 mortality (m/f):	72/56 per 1,000
Adult literacy:	99.5 per cent

The whereabouts of dozens of victims of forced disappearance in 2002 remained unknown. Prisoners of conscience continued to be imprisoned for peacefully expressing their beliefs. Freedom of expression, association and religion continued to be restricted.

Enforced disappearances

The authorities continued to withhold information to relatives and the public about the whereabouts of dozens of people arrested and convicted following the alleged armed attack on former President Saparmurad Niyazov in November 2002. Letters from their relatives to various governmental officials remained unanswered.

■ The whereabouts of Boris Shikhmuradov, Minister of Foreign Affairs under former President Saparmurad Niyazov, remained unknown. He was sentenced to 25 years' imprisonment in a closed trial in December 2002, increased the following day to life imprisonment by the People's Council which was abolished in 2008. Since then, Boris Shikhmuradov's family have had no news of him. His wife wrote repeatedly to government officials, but received no response. In September 2007, during a visit to Columbia University in the USA, President Berdymukhamedov was quoted as saying he was "positive" that Boris Shikhmuradov was alive. This continues to be the only information about his fate since his life sentence was imposed.

Repression of dissent

All printed and electronic media remained under state control. The authorities continued to block websites run by exiled members of the opposition and dissidents. Journalists working with foreign independent media outlets were harassed by law enforcement and national security service officials. The authorities continued to put pressure on family members of exiled members of the opposition by putting them on a "black list" of people barred from leaving the country.

■ Osmankuly Khallyev, correspondent of Radio Free Europe/Radio Liberty News Service (RFE/RL) in Lebap province, continued to suffer harassment by local governmental officials because of his work for RFE/RL's Turkmen service. In January he was put under house arrest after covering the parliamentary elections in December 2008. He told RFE/RL that his son, his daughter-in-law and son-in-law were sacked as a punishment for his co-operation with RFE/RL. He complained to the local Prosecutor's Office but received no response.

■ On 15 November, Ovez Annaev died aged 46 after being denied permission to travel to Moscow for treatment for heart disease which was not available in Turkmenistan. He and other members of his family were barred from leaving the country after his brother-in-law, Kudayberdy Orazov, exiled leader of the opposition movement Vatan (Motherland), was

sentenced to life imprisonment in his absence after the November 2002 attack on former President Saparmurad Niyazov.

Prisoners of conscience

■ On 6 November Andrei Zatoka, an environmental activist, was released after Dashoguz Regional Court reconsidered his case and commuted his initial sentence to a fine of 1,000 Manat (about US$350). He had been sentenced on 29 October, after an unfair trial, to five years' imprisonment for "hooliganism" and injuring a man who had attacked him at a market on 20 October. He told Amnesty International that he was released on the condition that he would renounce his Turkmenistani citizenship and leave the country. After paying the fine, he and his wife had to leave Turkmenistan for Russia on 7 November with only a few belongings, and fearing that the government would confiscate his freehold apartment. Amnesty International believes that he was targeted because of his peaceful work as an environmental activist.

The authorities continued to use false criminal charges to suppress peaceful dissent.

■ Human rights activists Annakurban Amanklychev and Sapardurdy Khadzhiev remained in detention after being sentenced in August 2006, after an unfair trial, to seven years' imprisonment for illegal possession or sale of ammunition or firearms. Both had been associated with the exiled NGO the Turkmenistan Helsinki Foundation.

Freedom of religion – Jehovah's Witnesses

■ In July, according to the international human rights organization Forum 18, two young Jehovah's Witnesses, Shadurdi Ushotov and Akmurat Egendurdiev, were sentenced to two years and 18 months respectively in a labour camp for refusing to perform compulsory military service.

■ In May, Serdar Town Court lifted the suspension of the two-year prison sentences imposed on brothers Sakhetmurad and Mukhammedmurad Annamamedov, both Jehovah's Witnesses, and they were arrested to serve the remaining 18 months of their sentences. On 3 June, the two brothers lodged appeals at the Regional Court in Balkanabad against the lifting of the suspension of their prison sentences. On 30 June the court rejected their appeal.

T

UGANDA

REPUBLIC OF UGANDA

Head of state and government:	Yoweri Kaguta Museveni
Death penalty:	retentionist
Population:	32.7 million
Life expectancy:	51.9 years
Under 5-mortality (m/f):	129/116 per 1,000
Adult literacy:	73.6 per cent

Law enforcement officials were not held to account for human rights violations including unlawful killings, torture and other ill-treatment. The government attacked freedom of expression and press freedom. Despite a high prevalence of gender-based violence, there was little progress in bringing perpetrators to justice and implementing long-promised legislative reforms. Lesbian, gay, bisexual and transgender (LGBT) people continued to face discrimination and other human rights violations, and a draft law threatened to further entrench discrimination against them. Death sentences were passed; there were no executions.

Background

A major corruption case in which a former health minister, two deputies and a government official faced criminal charges of embezzlement and abuse of office remained in court. The charges relate to the management of the Global Fund against HIV/AIDS, Tuberculosis and Malaria.

Armed conflict

Despite the reported conclusion of peace talks in 2008, no final peace agreement was signed by the government and the Lords Resistance Army (LRA) in relation to the conflict in northern Uganda. However, there was relative calm in the region.

There was little progress in implementing agreements reached under the peace process in 2008 – including agreements on accountability and reconciliation, and on disarmament, demobilization and reintegration (DDR Agreement). In particular, no justice mechanisms were set up to investigate human rights abuses committed during the conflict and no comprehensive government reparations programmes were established to assist victims and survivors to rebuild their lives.

In spite of a joint military operation by the armed forces of Uganda, Sudan and the Democratic Republic of the Congo (DRC) between late 2008 and early 2009, the LRA continued to commit human rights abuses, including unlawful killings and abductions of hundreds of civilians, in the DRC, Central African Republic and Southern Sudan.

International Criminal Court – arrest warrants

Arrest warrants issued in 2005 by the International Criminal Court (ICC) for Joseph Kony, the LRA leader, and three LRA commanders remained in force, but were not implemented by the Ugandan or regional governments.

Even though Uganda is a state party to the Rome Statute of the ICC and therefore obliged to arrest and surrender to the ICC anyone named in an arrest warrant, President Museveni announced in July and October that Sudanese President Omar Hassan Ahmed Al Bashir, against whom the ICC issued an arrest warrant in March 2009, could visit Uganda (see Sudan entry).

Internally displaced people

The majority of internally displaced people in the conflict-affected northern region left the camps and returned to their homes. It was estimated that up to 65 per cent of the original displaced population returned to their villages of origin and 15 per cent went to transit sites outside camps. Most of those who returned to their villages faced lack of access to clean water, health care, schools and other essential public services. Over 400,000 displaced people remained in camps and in dire need of humanitarian assistance.

U

Torture and other ill-treatment

The government failed to ensure that suspected perpetrators of torture and other ill-treatment by the police and other state security services were brought to justice. Victims and survivors were rarely granted access to justice and legal remedies. Up to 71 per cent of the Uganda Human Rights Commission's compensation awards since 2001 remained unpaid by the government. Most complaints submitted to the Commission by victims of human rights violations related to torture and other cruel, inhuman and degrading treatment or punishment.

Violence against women and girls

Reports indicated a continued high prevalence of gender-based violence, particularly domestic violence. Perpetrators were rarely brought to justice and women faced considerable constraints in their attempts to access justice.

In December, parliament passed a Bill specifically outlawing and providing for the punishment of the practice of female genital mutilation and measures for protecting victims. The Bill was awaiting presidential assent to become law at the end of the year. A number of bills were pending, including one that would provide a new legal framework for legal rights within and the dissolution of marriage, and another that would criminalize domestic violence.

Trial of Kizza Besigye

The trial of opposition leader Kizza Besigye and others accused of treason remained pending in the High Court in Kampala. A legal application filed by the accused in the Constitutional Court, challenging the continuation of the trial, had not been determined by the end of the year.

Two cases of murder filed in 2007 in two other courts against people co-accused with Kizza Besigye also remained pending.

September riots – unlawful killings and other violations

Demonstrations and riots took place on 10-13 September in Kampala and elsewhere over the government's decision to stop a delegation from Uganda's Buganda Kingdom from visiting the eastern district of Kayunga to join celebrations of National Youth Day on 12 September. The police said the visit was stopped to prevent possible violence between supporters of the Kabaka, king of the Baganda people, and a local ethnic group in Kayunga – the Banyala, which opposes the Kabaka's authority.

Up to 27 people were reportedly killed during the riots. At least half of them died after being shot by police and security personnel. The government did

not conduct an independent and impartial investigation into the killings by security forces, some of which may have been unlawful, in order to bring those responsible for human rights violations to justice.

Hundreds of individuals were arrested in connection with the riots. Dozens were charged with serious offences, including terrorism, and faced the death penalty. They were detained for days and weeks without being charged or brought before a judge – well beyond the limit prescribed by the Constitution. Many of them testified that they had been tortured or otherwise ill-treated in detention.

Freedom of expression

Following the September riots, the Broadcasting Council – a government body mandated to control broadcast content – arbitrarily ordered the closure of four radio stations. This was reportedly over failures before and during the riots to comply with the minimum broadcasting standards provided for under the Electronic Media Act, 2000. The stations were not given adequate notice of the closures or explanations for them, nor were they given an opportunity to appeal. The Council also ordered the discontinuation of some radio programmes during this period. By the end of the year, two of the stations remained closed.

Large sections of the media faced government intimidation and official threats over their reporting during the riots.

■ Kampala-based journalist Robert Kalundi Sserumaga was arbitrarily arrested, detained and tortured because of comments he made during a radio talk show about the tension between the government and the Buganda Kingdom, and the riots. He sustained serious injuries as a result of the torture. He was subsequently charged with sedition. The case remained pending in court.

General attacks by the authorities on freedom of expression and press freedom continued. Several criminal cases involving journalists charged with criminal libel, sedition and "the publication of false news" remained pending in court.

The government did not withdraw the Regulation of Interception of Communications Bill, 2007 or respond to human rights concerns raised about it. If passed into law, the Bill would significantly restrict the right to freedom of expression.

Refugees and asylum-seekers

In April, a joint communiqué signed by the UNHCR, the UN refugee agency, and the governments of Uganda and Rwanda indicated the governments' intention to repatriate about 20,000 Rwandan refugees living in Uganda. The communiqué stated that assistance to Rwandan refugees would end on 31 July 2009. The deadline for repatriation was later extended to the end of September. Affected refugees complained that the withdrawal of humanitarian and other assistance, the lack of procedures to determine any well-founded fears of persecution upon return, and the failure to provide alternative durable solutions under the UN Refugee Convention process created conditions that would lead to forced return. Few refugees voluntarily registered for the exercise and returned home.

Dozens of refugees in refugee settlement camps and urban areas reported instances of arbitrary arrests, unlawful detention and torture or other ill-treatment by government authorities. Perpetrators were rarely brought to justice.

Discrimination – lesbian, gay, bisexual and transgender people

In September, the Anti-Homosexuality Bill sponsored by a member of the ruling party was published and listed for consideration by Parliament. In light of existing laws that prohibit "carnal knowledge of any person against the order of nature" and the constitutional ban on same-sex marriage, the Bill, if enacted into law, would further criminalize LGBT people and perpetuate discrimination against and stigmatization of them.

The Bill provides for extremely punitive measures, including the death penalty for the offence of "aggravated homosexuality" and life imprisonment for the offence of "homosexuality", and seeks to introduce other new offences such as "the failure to report the offence of homosexuality". In addition, the Bill aims to criminalize "promotion of homosexuality", which would significantly hamper the work of human rights defenders and curtail the right to freedom of expression, association and assembly in relation to advocacy on LGBT rights. The Bill remained pending before Parliament at the end of the year.

LGBT people and rights activists continued to face arbitrary arrests, unlawful detention, torture and other ill-treatment by police and other security personnel.

Death penalty

In January, Uganda's highest court – the Supreme Court – upheld a 2005 judgement of the Constitutional Court that the mandatory application of the death penalty is unconstitutional. The Court also decided that death sentences that courts had been obliged to impose, which applied to the vast majority of more than 400 appellants in the case, should be commuted to life imprisonment. However, the Supreme Court also ruled that the death penalty remains constitutional.

Civilian and military courts continued to impose the death penalty. There were no executions.

Amnesty International visits/reports

🚍 Amnesty International delegates conducted research in Uganda in January, August, September and October.

📄 Uganda: Amnesty International calls on the Ugandan government to abolish the death penalty (AFR 59/001/2009)

📄 Uganda: Incommunicado detention/torture and other ill-treatment (AFR 59/002/2009)

📄 Ugandan "Anti-Homosexuality Bill" threatens liberties and human rights defenders, 15 October 2009

📄 Uganda: Amnesty International says government obliged to arrest Sudanese President, 16 October 2009

U

UKRAINE

UKRAINE

Head of state:	Viktor Yushchenko
Head of government:	Yuliya Timoshenko
Death penalty:	abolitionist for all crimes
Population:	45.7 million
Life expectancy:	68.2 years
Under-5 mortality (m/f):	18/13 per 1,000
Adult literacy:	99.7 per cent

Refugees and asylum-seekers were at risk of forcible return. People detained pending extradition had no possibility to challenge the legality of extradition and detention. The authorities failed to respond adequately to racist attacks. Reports of torture and ill-treatment in police detention continued, and perpetrators of human rights violations enjoyed impunity. Freedom of assembly continued to be under threat.

Rights of refugees and asylum-seekers

Ukraine continued to violate the right to asylum by failing to provide adequate and fair asylum procedures and by *refoulement*, or forcibly returning asylum-seekers and refugees to countries where they faced the risk of serious human rights violations. During the year Amnesty International raised four cases of *refoulement* with the Ukrainian government. On 25 August, changes to a Council of Ministers Regulation governing the entry of foreigners and stateless persons to Ukraine came into force. This required nationals of listed countries and stateless people to carry at least 12,620 Ukrainian hryvna (about €1,000). The application of this new regulation to asylum-seekers was contrary to international refugee law, and it amounted to *refoulement*.

■ On 31 August, six nationals of the Democratic Republic of the Congo (DRC) arrived at Boryspil airport, but were not allowed to leave the airport and were deported to the DRC via Dubai on 2 September. Reportedly, one of them was beaten when he tried to claim asylum; his claim was ignored and he was then drugged to make him sleep. According to the State Border Guard Service, the DRC nationals were not allowed to enter Ukraine because they had less than €1,000 each.

■ The Prosecutor General exercised his right to oversee the legality of all court decisions and overturned the decisions which had granted refugee status to 15 asylum-seekers from Afghanistan, Belarus and Uzbekistan. He based his decision on minor omissions, such as the absence of a medical check or the failure to document employment in the country of origin. According to UNHCR, the UN refugee agency, these do not constitute legitimate grounds to refuse refugee status. The asylum-seekers had no avenue of appeal against decisions of the Prosecutor General.

Torture and other Ill-treatment/impunity

There were continued reports of torture and other ill-treatment by law enforcement officials and of the authorities' failure to carry out effective and independent investigations into such allegations. Between January and October, 13 human rights NGOs belonging to the Ukrainian Helsinki Human Rights Union received 165 complaints about torture and other ill-treatment, of which 100 related to police actions. Ukraine ratified the Optional Protocol to the UN Convention against Torture in 2006, but had still not set up a national mechanism for monitoring places of detention in accordance with its obligations under the Protocol.

■ On 24 March, Vadim Glavatyi was sentenced at Podil regional court to nine years' imprisonment for rape and robbery. He appealed against the sentence and the appeal was pending at the end of the year. Since September 2006, Vadim Glavatyi had reportedly been subjected to torture and other-ill-treatment on three occasions by police officers from Podil district police station to make him confess, first to robbery, and then to rape, resulting in injuries which required hospital treatment. In October, the Kyiv Prosecutor replied to a letter from Amnesty International stating that there were no grounds to start criminal proceedings against officers of Podil police station. The letter stated that other police officers from Podil police station were investigating the alleged ill-treatment by their colleagues.

Racism

Limited steps were taken to counter racially motivated crimes and to make statistics available. Despite a joint instruction on 6 February by the Prosecutor General's office and the Ministry of Internal Affairs to collect data on racist crimes and results of investigations, no statistics were available by the end of the year. Racially motivated crimes continued to be prosecuted as "hooliganism" with no recognition of the racist element of the crime. According to the Diversity Initiative, a coalition of local NGOs and international organizations, 23 racist incidents were recorded up to October. During this period seven criminal cases were opened into racist incidents, all under charges of "hooliganism".

■ In interviews recorded by the Vinnytsya Human Rights Group three asylum-seekers from Somalia stated that they were detained and taken to a police station on 28 February, where two of them were beaten by police officers, reportedly in revenge for the kidnapping of Ukrainian sailors by Somali pirates. The allegations were denied by the Vinnytsya District Prosecutor's office. UNHCR received an assurance from the Prosecutor General's office that another investigation would be conducted but no results were communicated. Later the Vinnytsya Human Rights Group was informally notified that the two alleged perpetrators were no longer employed by the police.

Prisoner of conscience

Ukrainian legislation failed to provide any procedure for those detained awaiting extradition to challenge the legality of their extradition and of their detention.

■ On 7 July, the Balaklava district court refused to consider an appeal by Igor Koktysh against his detention pending extradition to Belarus, confirming the absence of any remedy within the extradition procedure. Igor Koktysh had been detained since 25 June 2007 following an application by Belarus for his extradition to face a charge of murder, a crime which carries the death penalty in Belarus. He had already been acquitted of this charge and released in 2001, and the Supreme Court had confirmed the verdict on 1 February 2002. On 11 April 2002, the Prosecutor General of Belarus appealed against the acquittal and the case was returned to court for a retrial. Igor Koktysh was an opposition activist and worked to rehabilitate young drug users. He moved to Ukraine in October 2003 where he continued to support the Belarusian opposition during the presidential elections in 2006. In October 2007, he applied to the European Court of Human Rights against his extradition and detention. The court urged Ukraine not to extradite him to Belarus until it had considered his case, and the possibility that the charge against Igor Koktysh had been fabricated by the Belarusian authorities to punish him for the peaceful exercise of his right to freedom of expression.

Freedom of assembly

On 3 June, the parliament approved the draft Law on Assembly at its first reading. The draft law had been criticized by NGOs for its failure to comply with international human rights standards. It required five days' notice before any action, and made no allowance for spontaneous gatherings; it allowed the use of force by law enforcement officers with no requirement for restraint, and it failed to incorporate the duty of the state to ensure that the right to peaceful assembly was respected.

Enforced disappearance

On 27 January, the Parliamentary Assembly of the Council of Europe passed a resolution welcoming the conviction of three former police officers for the murder of the investigative journalist Georgiy Gongadze, but called for the instigators and organizers to be held to account "without regard to the rank and position of the suspects". Georgiy Gongadze disappeared on 22 July 2000, and his headless body was found in November the same year. On 23 July, nine years after the disappearance, Oleksiy Pukach, a former lieutenant general in the Ministry of Internal Affairs, was arrested and charged with the killing.

U

UNITED ARAB EMIRATES

UNITED ARAB EMIRATES

Head of state:	Shaikh Khalifa bin Zayed Al Nahyan
Head of government:	Shaikh Mohammed bin Rashid Al Maktoum
Death penalty:	retentionist
Population:	4.6 million
Life expectancy:	77.3 years
Under-5 mortality (m/f):	10/12 per 1,000
Adult literacy:	90 per cent

Women and foreign migrant workers faced legal and other discrimination. Hundreds of Palestinians and Lebanese long-term residents were ordered to leave the country on the grounds of national security. A defendant in a terrorism trial alleged that he was tortured in pre-trial detention. At least 13 people were sentenced to death; no executions were reported.

Background

A proposed draft media law was adopted by the Federal National Council (parliament) in January. It was criticized by journalists, lawyers and others because of its adverse implications for media freedom. It had not been ratified by the end of the year.

In March, the government pledged to implement 36 of 74 recommendations made by the UN Human Rights Council in December 2008 during its Universal Periodic Review of human rights in the United Arab Emirates (UAE). These included recommendations relating to women's rights, the rights of migrant workers and the ratification of international human rights treaties. However, the government said it would not abolish the death penalty or allow workers substantive rights, such as the right to form a trade union.

In August, the UN Committee on the Elimination of Racial Discrimination urged the UAE authorities to improve protection of the rights of foreign workers. In October, the UN Special Rapporteur on racism urged the authorities to regularize the situation of Bidun, who remain stateless and so barred from accessing certain categories of employment as well as state health care and other services.

In October, the UAE President issued a decree concerning mobilization in response to internal or external threats to national security. Among other things, the decree provides for the imposition of the death penalty against people convicted of disclosing information that harms the state.

Counter-terror and security

In September, seven UAE nationals and one Afghan national were tried in Abu Dhabi before the Federal Supreme Court on terrorism-related charges. The eight were believed to have been among 21 people arrested in October 2008; charges against 13 others were dropped and they were released. In October, six of the eight defendants were released on bail, apparently to await trial in 2010. Some of those arrested were alleged to have been tortured in detention.

■ In October, Naji Hamdan, a US national, was convicted on terrorism-related charges after a closed trial before the Federal Supreme Court in Abu Dhabi. He denied the charges. He was sentenced to 18 months' imprisonment, but was released in November and deported.

The authorities ordered hundreds of long-term foreign residents to leave the country on national security grounds. Those affected were Palestinians, notably from Gaza, and Lebanese Shi'a Muslims. Some were said to have been resident in the UAE for up to 30 years.

Torture and other ill-treatment

■ Naji Hamdan (see above) said in court that he had been tortured in pre-trial detention by being strapped into "an electric chair" and beaten about the head until he lost consciousness. Neither the court nor the responsible authorities appeared to take any steps to investigate his allegations.

■ In May, the authorities arrested Shaikh Issa bin Zayed Al Nahyan, a member of Abu Dhabi's ruling family, after the broadcasting abroad of footage taken in 2004 in which he appeared to be torturing a man with an electric cattle prod. The authorities said they had previously investigated the incident and had taken no action because the matter had been settled privately between the perpetrator and the victim. The Shaikh was charged together with six others, including some in their absence; their trial was continuing at the end of 2009.

Discrimination – women and migrant workers

Women continued to suffer discrimination in law and practice. Foreign migrant workers, who make up a large proportion of the UAE's workforce and many of whom are employed in construction, faced exploitation, abuse and poor living conditions. Media reports suggested that some women survivors of rape did not report the crime to the police for fear that they would be charged with engaging in illicit sex.

■ Marnie Pearce, a UK national, was released in April after she had served 68 days of a three-month sentence imposed for adultery, which is prohibited in the UAE even when carried out in private between consenting adults. Adultery is punishable by death although lesser punishments can be imposed. The law covering adultery and its application have had a discriminatory impact on women.

Death penalty

Thirteen men were sentenced to death by courts in Dubai and Sharjah; no executions were known to have been carried out.

■ In June, the Supreme Court set aside the death sentence imposed on Shahid Bolsen because he had not had access to a lawyer at his trial.

UNITED KINGDOM

UNITED KINGDOM OF GREAT BRITAIN AND
NORTHERN IRELAND

Head of state:	Queen Elizabeth II
Head of government:	Gordon Brown
Death penalty:	abolitionist for all crimes
Population:	61.6 million
Life expectancy:	79.3 years
Under-5 mortality (m/f):	6/6 per 1,000

Reports implicating the UK in grave violations of human rights of people held overseas continued to emerge. Calls for independent investigations into the UK's role in these violations went unheeded. The government's attempts to return people to countries known to practise torture on the basis of "diplomatic assurances" (unenforceable promises from the countries where these individuals were to be returned) continued. The European Court of Human Rights found that, by detaining a number of foreign nationals without charge or trial (internment), the UK had violated their human rights. The implementation of measures adopted with the stated aim of countering terrorism led to human rights violations, including unfair judicial proceedings. The executive gained powers to circumvent and undermine the independence of coroners' inquests. Twenty years after Patrick Finucane's death, an inquiry into state collusion in his killing had yet to be established.

Counter-terror and security
Torture and other ill-treatment

Further reports emerged that grave human rights violations had been committed with the knowledge, complicity and, in some cases, in the presence of UK intelligence officers, including in Bangladesh, Egypt, Pakistan and the United Arab Emirates, and that UK officials had attempted to cover up the UK's involvement. In August, two Parliamentary Committees expressed concern about the UK's involvement in the torture of "terror suspects" held abroad. However, calls for independent investigations into the UK's role in these and other gross violations of human rights perpetrated in the context of the so-called war on terror, including into the UK's involvement in the US-led rendition programme (the unlawful

U

transfers of terrorist suspects between countries), went unheeded.

■ In February, Binyam Mohamed, an Ethiopian national formerly residing in the UK, was released from US custody at Guantánamo Bay, Cuba, where he had been held since 2004, and returned to the UK. He had been detained in Pakistan in April 2002 and then transported under the US-led rendition programme to Morocco, then to Afghanistan, and then on to Guantánamo Bay. The US government did not dispute that his treatment amounted to torture or other ill-treatment. UK judges ruled repeatedly during the year that the UK government should disclose what the US Central Intelligence Agency told the UK's Security Service (MI5) and what the UK's Secret Intelligence Service (MI6) knew of the unlawful treatment of Binyam Mohamed. They also made clear that "the relationship of the United Kingdom Government to the United States authorities in connection with [Binyam Mohamed] was far beyond that of a bystander or witness to the alleged wrongdoing." The UK government's appeal against the disclosure rulings was pending at the end of the year. In March it was announced that the police would begin an investigation into the allegations of possible criminal wrongdoing.

■ By the end of the year, Shaker Aamer, a Saudi Arabian national, was the only known remaining former UK resident still held in Guantánamo Bay. Following his capture in Afghanistan he had been detained by US military authorities in various locations and ultimately in Guantánamo Bay. In December, the High Court of England and Wales ordered the UK authorities to disclose certain documents to support his case that any confessions he might have made during his detention had been induced by ill-treatment by US and UK officials, thereby discrediting such confessions and improving his prospects of release.

■ In February, the government admitted that, contrary to earlier statements, two individuals captured by UK forces in Iraq in 2004 and transferred to US detention had subsequently been moved to a US detention facility in Afghanistan. The US government categorized them as "unlawful enemy combatants". There was concern that efforts to identify them were being hampered by the UK government.

In December, the UK All Party Parliamentary Group on Extraordinary Rendition began legal proceedings in the USA, requesting disclosure from various US security agencies about the UK's role in the US-led rendition programme. This included the unlawful transfer of two people through the UK territory of Diego Garcia, and the handover in Iraq by UK special forces to US forces of other individuals who were then flown to Afghanistan.

Deportations

Attempts continued to deport individuals alleged to pose a threat to "national security" to countries where they would be at risk of grave human rights violations, including torture. The government continued to argue that "diplomatic assurances" were sufficient to reduce the risk they would face.

■ In February, two Algerian nationals, referred to in legal proceedings in the UK as "RB" and "U", and Omar Othman (also known as Abu Qatada), a Jordanian national, lost their appeals before the Appellate Committee of the House of Lords (the Law Lords) against deportation to their respective countries on "national security" grounds. In all three cases the government was relying on "diplomatic assurances", given by the Algerian and Jordanian governments respectively, claiming that they would sufficiently reduce the risk that the men would be subjected to grave human rights violations, including torture, on their return.

The following day, the European Court of Human Rights issued interim measures indicating to the government that Omar Othman should not be deported to Jordan. At the end of the year, his case was pending.

■ In April, 10 Pakistani students in the UK were arrested and detained under suspicion of involvement in terrorism. They were later released without charge but immediately rearrested and detained again, pending deportation on "national security" grounds. They were held in high security prisons. By December, eight of them had abandoned their appeals against deportation and had returned to Pakistan.

In December, the High Court of England and Wales ruled against the government and the Special Immigration Appeals Commission (SIAC). It held that, even in the context of bail proceedings before the SIAC, a fair hearing required sufficient disclosure, and that exclusive reliance on secret material would breach fair trial standards.

Internment

In February, the Grand Chamber of the European Court of Human Rights unanimously ruled that, by

U

interning nine foreign nationals on suspicion of terrorism, the UK had violated their right to liberty. Detaining them without charge or trial had discriminated unjustifiably between them and UK nationals. The Court also found that four of the nine had not been able to effectively challenge the allegations against them because the open material on which the government had relied consisted purely of general assertions and the national court's decision to maintain their detention was based solely or to a decisive degree on secret material to which neither they nor their lawyers of choice had had access. The Court also held that each of the nine had been denied the right to compensation for the above violations.

"Control orders"

As of 10 December there were 12 "control orders" in force under the Prevention of Terrorism Act 2005. The Act gives a government minister unprecedented powers to issue "control orders" to restrict the liberty, movement and activities of people purportedly suspected of involvement in terrorism, on the basis of secret intelligence.

■ In June, the Law Lords applied the judgement of the European Court of Human Rights (see above) and allowed the appeals of three individuals, referred to as "AF", "AN" and "AE", against the imposition of "control orders", finding that it had breached their right to a fair hearing. The Law Lords ruled unanimously that sufficient disclosure must be given to "AF", "AN" and "AE". The judgement ruled that people subjected to "control orders" had to be given sufficient information about the allegations against them to enable them to mount an effective defence, and that, where the case against the "controlee" was based solely or to a decisive degree on closed materials, fair trial standards would not be met.

■ In August, Mahmoud Abu Rideh, a stateless Palestinian who was originally interned in December 2001 under powers enacted in the aftermath of the September 2001 attacks in the USA and then made subject to a "control order" since March 2005, said that he could no longer stay in the UK and wished to leave. Following the threat of legal proceedings, the government agreed to provide him with a certificate of travel that permitted him to leave and re-enter the UK for up to five years. Nonetheless, almost as soon as Mahmoud Abu Rideh had left the country, the government cancelled his certificate of travel, and ordered his permanent exclusion from the UK.

Armed forces in Iraq

In June, the European Court of Human Rights declared partly admissible the application lodged against the UK on behalf of Faisal Attiyah Nassar Al-Saadoon and Khalaf Hussain Mufdhi, two Iraqi nationals. They were arrested and detained in 2003 in Iraq in UK-run detention facilities. In December 2008, they were transferred to Iraqi custody despite substantial grounds for believing that they were at risk of being subjected to an unfair trial before the Iraq High Tribunal followed by execution, and in spite of the European Court of Human Rights' interim measures indicating that the UK government should not transfer them to the Iraqi authorities until further notice.

In May, ruling against the government, the Court of Appeal of England and Wales confirmed that UK soldiers on military service in Iraq were entitled to benefit from the rights guaranteed by the Human Rights Act 1998.

■ At the end of the year, a public inquiry under the Inquiries Act 2005 into the circumstances surrounding the death of Baha Mousa was ongoing. He died at a UK-run detention facility in Iraq in September 2003, having been tortured by UK troops over a period of 36 hours.

In November, the government announced a public inquiry under the Inquiries Act 2005 into the case of Khuder al-Sweady and five other Iraqi men. Among other things, the case concerns complaints that Khuder al-Sweady was murdered and five other Iraqis were tortured or otherwise ill-treated by UK soldiers while being detained in Iraq in 2004.

Legal developments

In November, parliament passed the Coroners and Justice Act 2009. It gave the executive powers to order the suspension of a coroner's inquest and institute instead an inquiry under the Inquiries Act 2005, maintaining that the latter would be adequate to investigate the cause of death.

Police and security forces

In April, the policing of demonstrations at the G-20 Summit in London gave rise to concern. There were reports of disproportionate use of force; the use of weapons such as batons and shields during charges against demonstrators; and the intentional removal of police identification numbers.

U

Publicly available video footage appeared to show that on 1 April a police officer wearing a helmet and balaclava struck Ian Tomlinson, a 47-year-old newspaper seller, with a baton on the back of his leg, and pushed him over. At the time of contact, Ian Tomlinson had his back to a line of riot police, his hands in his pockets, and was walking away from them. Ian Tomlinson collapsed and died shortly afterwards. The police only admitted that contact had occurred following publication of the footage. By the end of the year, one police officer was being investigated on suspicion of manslaughter.

■ In February, the Crown Prosecution Service of England and Wales announced that there was insufficient evidence that any offence had been committed by any individual police officers in relation to the killing of Jean Charles de Menezes, a Brazilian national shot dead by police officers in London in 2005. The decision appeared to sanction impunity for the killing. In November, the Metropolitan police agreed to pay compensation to Jean Charles de Menezes' family.

■ In March, the Chief Commissioner of London police agreed to pay Babar Ahmad compensation and exemplary damages after admitting that in December 2003 police officers had subjected him to a violent, sustained and unprovoked assault, including by twice placing him in a life-threatening neck-hold.

Northern Ireland

Dissident republican groups claimed responsibility for the killings in March of two soldiers, Mark Quinsey and Patrick Azimkar, and of police constable Stephen Paul Carroll.

In June, journalist Suzanne Breen won her fight against the application by the Police Service of Northern Ireland for her to hand over materials relating to the killings of the two soldiers. The Recorder of Belfast ruled that to give the material to the police would endanger her life and acknowledged that the protection of the confidentiality of sources for journalists was part of the right to freedom of expression.

Collusion and political killings

In January, the Consultative Group on the Past set up by the government in 2007 recommended establishing an independent commission to deal with the legacy of the past by combining processes of reconciliation, justice and information recovery.

■ Twenty years after the killing of prominent human

rights lawyer Patrick Finucane, the government continued to renege on its commitment to establish an independent inquiry into state collusion in his death.

Three public inquiries into allegations of state collusion in the killings of Robert Hamill, Rosemary Nelson, a human rights lawyer, and Billy Wright finished taking evidence. Final reports were expected in 2010. The exclusion from a number of sessions of each inquiry of family members and their lawyers gave rise to concern.

Discrimination – Roma

Following an increase in the preceding months in verbal and physical attacks, in June over 100 Roma fled their homes in Belfast.

Refugees, asylum-seekers and migrants

In October, contrary to the advice of UNHCR, the UN refugee agency, the government attempted to forcibly return 44 Iraqis to Baghdad. On arrival the Iraqi authorities accepted only 10 and the other 34 Iraqis were flown back to the UK and detained on arrival.

In November, the government conceded that all non-Arab Darfuris, regardless of their political or other affiliations, were at risk of persecution in Darfur and that internal relocation elsewhere in Sudan was not currently available.

In December, the Royal Colleges of Paediatrics and Child Health, General Practitioners and Psychiatrists issued a joint statement calling for an immediate end to the administrative detention of children under Immigration Act powers on the basis that it was "shameful", "damaging", and "permanently harmful to children's health".

In July, the Chief Inspector of Prisons of England and Wales found that conditions at a privately run immigration detention centre, Tinsley House, near London, were "wholly unacceptable" for women and children and that conditions had worsened since the last inspection to an "encroaching 'prison culture'". Concern was expressed about the detention of families for over 72 hours, and some for many weeks.

Violence against women and girls

In November, the government launched a strategy to address violence against women in line with commitments made under the 1995 United Nations Beijing Platform for Action.

In November, the government announced a three-month pilot project to address the human rights crisis facing women at risk of violence and who have insecure immigration status.

Amnesty International visits/reports

🚐 Amnesty International delegates observed court proceedings in England throughout the year, including challenges to "control orders", appeals against deportations with assurances, and legal actions brought against the government by former Guantánamo detainees.

📄 United Kingdom: The case of Binyam Mohamed - "championing the rule of law"? (EUR 45/001/2009)

📄 UK/Northern Ireland: Patrick Finucane - twenty years on, still no inquiry (EUR 45/002/2009)

📄 Independent investigation into alleged UK involvement in torture long overdue (EUR 45/009/2009)

UNITED STATES OF AMERICA

UNITED STATES OF AMERICA
Head of state and government: Barack H. Obama (replaced George W. Bush in January)
Death penalty: retentionist
Population: 314.7 million
Life expectancy: 79.1 years
Under-5 mortality (m/f):   7/8 per 1,000

One hundred and ninety-eight detainees remained held in the Guantánamo detention centre at the end of 2009, despite a commitment by the new administration to close the facility by 22 January 2010. Executive reviews to determine which detainees could be released, prosecuted or transferred to other countries were initiated. By the end of the year, most Guantánamo detainees who were the subjects of habeas corpus petitions were still waiting for their cases to be heard. At least five detainees were referred for trial before revised military commissions and one other was transferred to federal court jurisdiction. Further details emerged of torture and other ill-treatment of detainees held in the Central Intelligence Agency (CIA) secret detention programme, terminated by President Obama.

Concerns persisted about conditions in prisons,

jails and immigration detention centres. The long-term isolation of thousands of prisoners in super-maximum security facilities continued to fall short of international standards. Dozens of people died after being stunned by police Tasers (electro-shock weapons). At least 105 people were sentenced to death and 52 executions were carried out during the year.

Women belonging to racial, ethnic and national minorities were more likely to die in pregnancy or childbirth than women from other sectors of the population, reflecting disparities based on poverty and race in health care provision.

Counter-terror and justice

Detentions at Guantánamo

In January, the indefinite detention without charge in the US naval base at Guantánamo Bay, Cuba, of foreign nationals designated as "enemy combatants" entered its eighth year. On 22 January, President Obama signed an executive order for the closure of the detention facility within a year. He ordered an executive review to determine which detainees could be released or prosecuted and what other "lawful means" existed for the disposition of individuals who the review determined could neither be tried by US authorities nor transferred to other countries.

The US authorities continued to refuse to allow the release into the US mainland of any Guantánamo detainee who could not be returned to his home country. In February, the Court of Appeal overturned a 2008 order by a federal judge for the release into the USA of 17 Uighur men held without charge at Guantánamo since 2002 and who could not be returned to China. In June, four of the Uighur detainees were transferred to Bermuda, and in October another six were released in Palau.

On 18 November, President Obama acknowledged that his deadline for closure of the detention facility would not be met. By the end of the year, 198 detainees remained in Guantánamo. Forty-nine detainees were transferred out of the base during 2009. A Yemeni man, Mohammad al Hanashi, died in Guantánamo in June, bringing to five the number of detainees reported to have committed suicide in the base.

Military commissions

In October, following a review of the prosecution options for Guantánamo detainees, President Obama

U

signed into law the 2010 National Defense Authorization Act, which included the Military Commissions Act (MCA) of 2009, amending provisions of the MCA passed three years earlier.

In November, the Attorney General announced that the Justice Department was referring five Guantánamo detainees for trial by military commission.

■ Canadian national Omar Khadr remained in US custody at the end of the year, facing a military commission trial for an alleged war crime committed when he was 15 years old (see Canada entry).

Transfers to federal court

■ In June, Ahmed Khalfan Ghailani, held in secret US custody for two years before being transferred to Guantánamo in 2006, was transferred to New York to face trial in a federal court on charges relating to the 1998 bombings of the US embassies in Tanzania and Kenya.

■ In November, Attorney General Eric Holder announced that five Guantánamo detainees previously facing military commission trials – Khalid Sheikh Mohammed, Walid bin Attash, Ramzi bin al-Shibh, 'Ali 'Abd al-'Aziz and Mustafa al Hawsawi – would be transferred for trial in federal courts on charges relating to the attacks in the USA of 11 September 2001. The five men were still held in Guantánamo at the end of the year.

■ In March, Ali Saleh Kahlah al-Marri, a Qatari national held since June 2003 in indefinite military custody in the USA, was transferred to civilian custody to face charges in a federal court. He entered a guilty plea on a charge of "conspiracy to provide material support and resources to a foreign terrorist organization" and was sentenced to 100 months' imprisonment. The judge reduced the sentence by nine months "to reflect the very severe conditions" in which Ali al-Marri had been held between 23 June 2003 and late 2004.

Habeas corpus proceedings for Guantánamo detainees

By the end of the year, 18 months after the Supreme Court ruled in *Boumediene v. Bush* that detainees held in Guantánamo were "entitled to a prompt habeas corpus hearing" to challenge the lawfulness of their detention, most of those who had lodged petitions had still not received a hearing. In a majority of the cases in which a decision was made, the detainee was found to be unlawfully held. A number of detainees who received such decisions continued

to face indefinite detention at Guantánamo while the administration decided how to respond.

In November the Attorney General told a Senate hearing that there remained a possibility that, once the review of Guantánamo cases was completed, there would be a number of detainees whom the administration would seek to continue to detain without charge under "the laws of war".

Detentions in Bagram, Afghanistan

The US military continued to hold hundreds of detainees, including a number of children, without access to lawyers or the courts in Bagram air base in Afghanistan (see also Afghanistan entry). Litigation continued in US federal courts about whether Bagram detainees could have access to the US courts to challenge the lawfulness of their detention.

On 2 April, a federal judge ruled that three of the four Bagram detainees whose habeas corpus petitions were before him could challenge their detention. The three were non-Afghan nationals, while the fourth was an Afghan. In September, the government appealed against this ruling. The appeal was pending at the end of the year.

CIA secret detention programme

In April, the Director of the Central Intelligence Agency (CIA) confirmed that, pursuant to an executive order on interrogations signed by President Obama on 22 January, the CIA was no longer using any "enhanced interrogation techniques" or operating "detention facilities or black sites". He also confirmed that the CIA retained the authority to detain individuals on a "short-term transitory basis".

In April, the administration released four Justice Department memorandums from 2002 and 2005 providing legal approval for various "enhanced interrogation techniques" against detainees held in secret CIA custody. The techniques included forced nudity, prolonged sleep deprivation, and "waterboarding" (simulated drowning). Among other things, the memorandums revealed that Abu Zubaydah, the subject of the 2002 memorandum, had been "waterboarded" more than 80 times in August 2002, and Khaled Sheikh Mohammed some 183 times in March 2003. President Obama and Attorney General Holder stressed that anyone who had relied "in good faith" on the advice in the memorandums would not be prosecuted.

In August further details of the torture and other ill-treatment of detainees held in the CIA programme were released into the public domain. Attorney General Holder announced a "preliminary review" into whether "federal laws were violated in connection with the interrogation of specific detainees at overseas locations".

The administration resisted further release of details of the actual treatment of detainees in the now-terminated secret CIA programme on the grounds of national security.

Detainee interrogation and transfer policy
In August, the Special Task Force on Interrogations and Transfer Policies, set up under the 22 January executive order on interrogations, issued its recommendations to the President. These included the formation of a High-Value Detainee Interrogation Group and guidance for interrogators from the military and other agencies.

Impunity and lack of remedy
Impunity and lack of remedy persisted for human rights violations committed during what the Bush administration termed the "war on terror".

In January, the Convening Authority for the military commissions, Susan J. Crawford, revealed that she had dismissed charges against Guantánamo detainee Mohamed al-Qahtani in 2008 because he had been tortured in US custody. By the end of the year no criminal investigation had been opened into the case.

In a policy U-turn, the new administration moved to block publication of a number of photographs depicting abuse of detainees in US custody in Afghanistan and Iraq. In October new legislation granted the Pentagon the authority to suppress photographs deemed harmful to national security.

On 4 November in Milan, Italy, 22 US agents or officials of the CIA and one military officer were convicted of crimes for their involvement in the abduction of Usama Mostafa Nasr (Abu Omar), who was abducted in Milan and transferred to Egypt where he was allegedly tortured. The US officials were tried in their absence.

Torture and other ill-treatment – electro-shock weapons
At least 47 people died after being struck by police Tasers, bringing to more than 390 the number of such deaths since 2001. Among them were three unarmed teenagers involved in minor incidents and an apparently healthy man who was shocked for 49 continuous seconds by police in Fort Worth, Texas, in

May. These and other cases raised further concern about the safety and appropriate use of such weapons.

■ Fifteen-year-old Brett Elder died in Bay City, Michigan, in March, after being shocked by officers responding to reports of unruly behaviour at a party. The coroner ruled that the boy, who was of small stature, died from alcohol-induced excited delirium, with the Taser shocks a contributory factor.

Prison conditions
Thousands of prisoners were held in long-term isolation in US super-maximum security prisons, where conditions in many cases fell short of international standards for humane treatment.

■ Scores of prisoners at Tamms CMAX facility in Illinois – many of them mentally ill – had spent 10 or more years confined to solitary cells for 23 hours a day, with inadequate treatment or review of their status. Prisoners had no work, educational or recreational programmes and little contact with the outside world. In September, following appeals from community and human rights groups, the new Director of Corrections introduced a 10-point reform plan, which included Transfer Review Hearings for each inmate, more mental health monitoring and an opportunity for prisoners to undergo General Educational Development (basic education) testing.

In October, a US federal appeals court ruled that constitutional protection against shackling pregnant women during labour had been clearly established by decisions of the US Supreme Court and lower courts.

Migrants and asylum-seekers
Tens of thousands of migrants, including asylum-seekers, were routinely detained, in violation of international standards. Many were held in harsh conditions and had inadequate access to health care, exercise and legal assistance. In August, the government announced a number of proposed changes, including strengthening federal oversight of immigration detention facilities and consultation on alternatives to detention. However, it declined to make nationwide standards governing conditions in detention enforceable by law.

In May, the UN Special Rapporteur on extrajudicial, summary or arbitrary executions expressed concern about deaths of migrants in Immigration and Customs Enforcement (ICE) custody

U

resulting from inadequate medical care. He found that more deaths had occurred than the 74 officially recorded since 2003 and urged that ICE be required to promptly and publicly report all deaths in custody, with each death fully investigated.

Health and reproductive rights

In May, Dr George Tiller was shot dead in Wichita, Kansas, by an anti-abortion activist. Dr Tiller had been subjected to a series of threats and attacks for providing lawful late-term abortions to women whose pregnancies presented a grave risk to their health or who were carrying non-viable foetuses. After Dr Tiller's murder, the federal government increased security protection for some other abortion providers. However, threats and harassment of doctors and clinics continued.

Right to health – maternal mortality

The number of preventable deaths from pregnancy-related complications remained high, costing the lives of hundreds of women during the year. There were inequalities in access to maternal health care based on income, race, ethnicity or national origin, with African American women nearly four times more likely to die of pregnancy-related causes than white women. An estimated 52 million people under 65 had no health insurance in early 2009, a rise over the previous year.

Trade embargo against Cuba

President Obama lifted some travel restrictions to Cuba, allowing Cuban-Americans to visit relatives in Cuba and send money home. However, he extended the USA's 47-year trade embargo against Cuba, which limited Cubans' access to medicines, endangering the health of millions (see Cuba entry).

Conscientious objectors

In August, Travis Bishop, a sergeant in the US army, was sentenced to one year in prison for refusing to serve in Afghanistan because of his religious beliefs. His application for conscientious objector status was still pending when he was court-martialled. He is one of several US soldiers imprisoned in recent years for refusing to deploy to Iraq or Afghanistan.

Unfair trials

In August, the US Parole Commission denied release on parole to Leonard Peltier, despite concerns about the fairness of his 1977 conviction for murder. The former American Indian Movement activist had spent more than 32 years in prison for the murders of two Federal Bureau of Investigation (FBI) agents in June 1975.

In June, the US Supreme Court declined to hear an appeal against the 2001 convictions of five men imprisoned on charges of acting as unregistered agents for the Cuban government and related offences. In May 2005, the UN Working Group on Arbitrary Detention had stated that their detention was arbitrary because of the failure to guarantee them a fair trial.

Death penalty

Fifty-two people were executed during the year, bringing to 1,188 the total number of prisoners executed since the US Supreme Court lifted a moratorium on the death penalty in 1976 and allowed executions to resume in January 1977.

In September, Ohio attempted and failed to execute Romell Broom, a 53-year-old African American man. The lethal injection team spent some two hours attempting to find a useable vein, before giving up. In November, the state authorities announced that they had decided to switch from using three drugs in lethal injections to one. On 8 December, Ohio executed Kenneth Biros using this method.

Texas executed 24 people during the year and in June carried out its 200th execution under the current governor, Rick Perry. During the year, Governor Perry faced intense criticism over the case of Cameron Willingham, who was executed in Texas in 2004. Details continued to emerge that the arson murders of which he was convicted may have been the result of an accidental fire.

Nine people were released from death rows during the year on grounds of innocence, bringing to more than 130 the number of such cases since 1976.

In March, New Mexico became the USA's 15th abolitionist state when the state governor signed into law a bill abolishing the death penalty.

Amnesty International reports

📄 USA: The promise of real change – President Obama's executive orders on detentions and interrogations (AMR 51/015/2009)

📄 USA: Out of sight, out of mind, out of court? The right of Bagram detainees to judicial review (AMR 51/021/2009)

📄 USA: Right to an effective remedy – Administration should release Guantánamo Uighurs into the USA now (AMR 51/023/2009)

📄 USA: Different label, same policy? Administration drops 'enemy combatant' label in Guantánamo litigation, but retains law of war framework for detentions (AMR 51/038/2009)

📄 USA: Detainees continue to bear costs of delay and lack of remedy: Minimal judicial review for Guantánamo detainees 10 months after Boumediene (AMR 51/050/2009)

📄 USA: Too much cruelty, too little clemency: Texas nears 200th execution under current governor (AMR 51/057/2009)

📄 USA: Federal court rejects government's invocation of 'state secrets privilege' in CIA 'rendition' cases (AMR 51/058/2009)

📄 USA: 'Unconscionable and unconstitutional': Troy Davis facing fourth execution date in two years (AMR 51/069/2009)

📄 USA: Trials in error: Third go at misconceived military commission experiment (AMR 51/083/2009)

📄 USA: Blocked at every turn. The absence of effective remedy for counter-terrorism abuses (AMR 51/120/2009)

URUGUAY

EASTERN REPUBLIC OF URUGUAY

Head of state and government:	**Tabaré Vázquez Rosas**
Death penalty:	**abolitionist for all crimes**
Population:	**3.4 million**
Life expectancy:	**76.1 years**
Under-5 mortality (m/f):	**18/15 per 1,000**
Adult literacy:	**97.9 per cent**

The law continued to grant impunity to those responsible for human rights violations under the military government (1973-1985).

Background

José Mujica won the November presidential elections.

Uruguay's human rights record was assessed under the UN Universal Periodic Review in May and the government accepted all the recommendations made.

Impunity for past violations

In October, a referendum was held on the proposed annulment of the 1986 Law on the Expiration of the Punitive Claims of the State (Expiry Law), which prevents cases of alleged violations committed during the military-backed governments from being reopened. However, the proposal failed to gain the majority needed to overturn the law.

In the run-up to the referendum, the Uruguayan Supreme Court delivered a landmark ruling that the Expiry Law was unconstitutional. The ruling was given in the case of Nibia Sabalsagaray, a young activist who was tortured and killed in 1974. This ruling and decisions made by the Executive to limit the application of the law were important steps towards bringing perpetrators of past human rights violations to justice.

In August, a law on reparations for victims of state repression under Uruguay's military government (1973-1985) and the previous civilian regime (1968-1973) was passed by the Senate.

■ In March, eight former military and police officials were sentenced to between 20 and 25 years' imprisonment for their role in the deaths of 28 people in Operation Condor, a joint plan by Southern Cone military governments in the 1970s and 1980s to eliminate opponents.

■ In October, Gregorio Álvarez, former general and de facto president between 1980 and 1985, was sentenced to 25 years in prison for killing 37 activists in Argentina in 1978. A former marine was sentenced to 20 years' imprisonment in the same case for killing 29 people.

■ In November, the former police photographer Nelson Bardecio was extradited from Argentina to Uruguay to face charges in connection with the enforced disappearance of the student Héctor Castagnetto in 1971. He was detained awaiting trial at the end of the year.

Prison conditions

U

The Special Rapporteur on torture visited Uruguay in March and concluded that conditions of detention were critical. He denounced the situation in Libertad Penitentiary in which convicted prisoners and pre-trial detainees were "held together like animals in metal boxes for almost 24 hours a day". After the visit, he recommended a fundamental reform of the criminal justice and penitentiary systems.

There were reports of overcrowding, ill-treatment, inadequate health care, insufficient food supplies as well as of poor conditions for juveniles in detention and excessive use of force by security agents. According to the Parliamentary Commissioner for the Penitentiary System, more than 60 per cent of the prison population were in pre-trial detention or awaiting final sentence.

Violence against women and girls

Women who experienced gender-based violence continued to face obstacles in obtaining protection, justice and reparation. Lack of resources and inadequate training of the judiciary hindered the implementation of legislation on domestic violence. According to official figures, 23 women were killed between November 2008 and October 2009.

UZBEKISTAN

REPUBLIC OF UZBEKISTAN

Head of state:	Islam Karimov
Head of government:	Shavkat Mirzioiev
Death penalty:	abolitionist for all crimes
Population:	27.5 million
Life expectancy:	67.6 years
Under-5 mortality (m/f):	63/53 per 1,000
Adult literacy:	96.9 per cent

The authorities persisted in their refusal to allow an independent, international investigation into the mass killing of protesters in Andizhan in 2005. Human rights defenders and journalists continued to be targeted, and some were sentenced to prison terms after unfair trials. Dozens of members of minority religious Islamic groups were given long prison terms after unfair trials. The space for freedom of religion and belief contracted further. In waves of arbitrary detentions, the security forces swept up a range of individuals and their relatives suspected of involvement with banned Islamist parties and armed groups accused of attacks throughout the country. Thousands of people convicted of involvement with Islamic movements and Islamist parties remained imprisoned in harsh

and life-threatening conditions. Reports of torture or other ill-treatment continued.

International scrutiny

Four years after the killing of hundreds of mainly peaceful demonstrators by the security forces in Andizhan on 13 May 2005, the authorities still refused to initiate or allow an independent, international investigation into the events. The government failed to release all imprisoned human rights defenders or meet other human rights benchmarks set by the EU in 2005 when it imposed a visa ban on 12 officials and an arms embargo following the killings. The government considered the matter closed, as it had informed a UN Universal Periodic Review of human rights in December 2008 when its representatives once more denied the use of excessive or disproportionate force.

In October the EU unconditionally lifted the arms embargo on Uzbekistan despite the government's failures to meet the EU's human rights benchmarks.

Counter-terror and security

New waves of arbitrary detentions followed reported attacks in the Ferghana Valley and the capital, Tashkent, in May and August and the killings of a pro-government imam and a high-ranking police officer in Tashkent in July. The authorities blamed the Islamic Movement of Uzbekistan (IMU), the Islamic Jihad Union (IJU) and the unregistered Islamist Hizb-ut-Tahrir party, banned in Uzbekistan, for the attacks and killings. The IJU claimed responsibility for attacks on a police station, a border checkpoint and a government office in Khanabad on 26 May, as well as a suicide bombing at a police station in Andizhan the same day. At least three people died in a shoot-out between unidentified armed men and security forces in Tashkent on 29 August. In September at least 90 men were detained during a counter-terrorism operation in Dzhizzakh.

Among the dozens detained as suspected members or sympathizers of the IMU, the IJU and Hizb-ut-Tahrir were men and women who attended unregistered mosques, studied under independent imams, had travelled or studied abroad, or had relatives who lived abroad or were suspected of affiliation to banned Islamist groups. Many were believed to have been detained without charge or

U

trial for lengthy periods. There were reports of torture and unfair trials.

■ In September, at the start of the first trial of suspects in the 26 May attacks in Khanabad, human rights activists reported that the trial was closed, despite earlier assurances by the Prosecutor General that it would be open and fair.

■ At least 30 men were arrested in October in Sirdaria on suspicion of involvement in the July killings in Tashkent and of being members of Hizb-ut-Tahrir. Relatives of some of the accused said the men had no connections with Hizb-ut-Tahrir or armed groups but merely practised their faith in unregistered mosques. In October relatives alleged that some of the accused had been tortured in pre-trial detention in an attempt to force them to confess to participating in the July killings. One mother said her son's face was swollen and his body covered in bruises, that needles had been inserted in the soles of his feet and electric shocks applied to his anus, and that he had difficulty eating, standing and walking.

Torture and other ill-treatment

There were continued reports of widespread torture or other ill-treatment of detainees and prisoners, and the authorities failed in most cases to conduct prompt and impartial investigations into torture allegations. Several thousand people convicted of involvement with Islamic movements and Islamist parties banned in Uzbekistan continued to serve long prison terms under conditions that amounted to cruel, inhuman and degrading treatment.

■ In January an appeals court in Tashkent upheld the prison sentences of up to 17 years of four police officers convicted in December 2008 of torture. The officers had been convicted of killing 30-year-old Muzaffar Tuichev in the town of Angren in March 2008. Relatives said he had been detained to extort money from him, and that up to 15 police officers had beaten and tortured him for several hours.

■ Poet and government critic Yusuf Dzhuma, sentenced to five years' imprisonment in April 2008 for allegedly resisting arrest and causing bodily harm, was said in November to be emaciated, ill and barely able to walk. He was reportedly held in punishment cells for periods of up to 11 days, and on one occasion handcuffed, hung by his hands from the ceiling and repeatedly beaten. He told his family that, during a visit to Yaslik prison camp by delegates of the ICRC, he had

been transferred to a prison in Nukus, denied food and drink, refused access to a toilet and held naked in very cold conditions.

■ In November the independent human rights organization Ezgulik reported that two sisters arrested in Tashkent in May on charges of hooliganism and robbery were repeatedly raped in custody by police officers. Their family said the charges were fabricated. They were subsequently sentenced to six and seven years in prison. One of the sisters reportedly became pregnant as a result of the rapes and tried to kill herself. In December the General Prosecutor's office said it would investigate.

Human rights defenders

Human rights defenders and independent journalists continued to be harassed, beaten and detained, although the authorities repeatedly denied this.

Although some human rights defenders were conditionally released in 2008 and 2009, others remained in prison following conviction in previous years.

■ At least 10 human rights defenders were still held in cruel, inhuman and degrading conditions, serving long prison terms imposed after unfair trials. They had limited access to relatives and legal representatives, and were reportedly tortured or otherwise ill-treated.

At least three human rights defenders were sentenced to long prison terms during the year on allegedly fictitious charges brought to punish them for their work, in particular for defending farmers' rights.

■ The health of 60-year-old Norboi Kholzhigitov, a member of the Human Rights Society of Uzbekistan serving a 10-year prison sentence imposed in 2005 for libel and fraud, deteriorated so seriously that his family feared for his life. The charges against him were reportedly fabricated to punish him for his human rights activities on behalf of farmers. He was denied appropriate medical care for diabetes and high blood pressure, but was transferred to a prison hospital in December.

■ In July Dilmurod Saidov, a journalist and human rights defender, was sentenced to 12 years and six months in prison for fraud and bribery after an unfair trial. He was believed to have been imprisoned for defending the rights of farmers in the Samarkand region and exposing corruption by local authorities. He was said to be gravely ill in prison with tuberculosis. During his trial, all the prosecution witnesses withdrew

U

their accusations, saying that the prosecuting authorities had forced them to make false statements. An appeals court upheld the sentence in October.

■ In October Farkhad Mukhtarov, a long-standing member of the Human Rights Alliance of Uzbekistan, was sentenced after a reportedly unfair trial to five years in prison for bribery and fraud relating to property deals. The charges were believed to have been politically motivated to punish him for his human rights activities. An appeal court upheld the sentence.

Human rights activists and journalists were summoned for police questioning, placed under house arrest or routinely monitored by uniformed or plain-clothes officers. Others reported being beaten by the police or by people suspected of working for the security forces. Relatives also alleged that they were threatened and harassed.

■ In April Elena Urlaeva, a leading member of the Human Rights Alliance, was assaulted by two unidentified men as she was leaving her home with her five-year-old son early in the morning. She said they threatened her with a knife, beat her and asked why she was still in the country. The same week her son sustained concussion and bruising after being beaten by an unidentified young man at a playground. She was among a group of human rights defenders who were prevented by police from publicly commemorating the fourth anniversary of the Andizhan killings and detained as they left their homes on the morning of 13 May. Seven were detained at police stations for over seven hours; others were held under house arrest.

■ Bakhtior Khamroev and Mamir Azimov, members of the Human Rights Society of Uzbekistan, were briefly detained in Dzhizzakh in November to prevent them meeting Bakhodir Choriev, a recently returned exile and leader of the unregistered political opposition movement Birdamlik. Bakhtior Khamroev was reportedly punched in the face by a plain-clothes police officer and dragged from the car in which he was sitting with Bakhodir Choriev, who was also assaulted when he got out of the car. The same day Mamir Azimov was taken to a district police station for questioning about the intended meeting. He said officers punched him in the kidneys and slapped his head, made him stand with his legs apart holding a chair above his head for over an hour, and threatened that his legs and arms would be broken if he sought medical help on release or reported the ill-treatment. Bakhodir Choriev was forced to leave the country in December.

■ In December a researcher with the international NGO Human Rights Watch was assaulted in the town of Karshi by an unidentified attacker, then detained by police and deported from Uzbekistan. At least three human rights activists she had intended to meet in Karshi and Margilan were briefly detained.

Freedom of religion

Religious communities continued to be under strict control by the government, which restricted their right to freedom of religion. Those most affected were members of unregistered groups such as Christian Evangelical congregations and Muslims worshipping in unregistered mosques.

■ Suspected followers of the Turkish Muslim theologian, Said Nursi, were convicted in a series of trials. The charges against them included membership or creation of an illegal religious extremist organization and publishing or distributing materials threatening the social order. According to independent religious experts, Said Nursi represented a moderate and non-violent interpretation of Islam. By October at least 68 men had been sentenced to prison terms of between six and 12 years following seven unfair trials. Appeals against the sentences were rejected.

More trials were reportedly pending at the end of the year but it was not clear how many more individuals had been detained. Reportedly, some of the verdicts were based on confessions obtained under torture in pre-trial detention; defence and expert witnesses were not called; access to the trials was in some cases obstructed; and other trials were closed. Before the start of the trials national television denounced the accused as "extremists" and "a threat to the country's stability", compromising their right to be presumed innocent before trial.

Amnesty International reports

▥ Uzbekistan: Submission to the Human Rights Committee, 96th session, (EUR 62/002/2009)

▥ Uzbekistan: Health condition of POC deteriorating, Norboi Kholzhigitov (EUR 62/003/2009)

U

VANUATU

REPUBLIC OF VANUATU

Head of state:	Iolu Johnson Abil (replaced Kalkot Mataskelekele in September)
Head of government:	Edward Natapei
Death penalty:	Abolitionist for all crimes
Population:	0.2 million
Life expectancy:	69.9 years
Under-5 mortality (m/f):	39/29 per 1,000
Adult literacy:	78.1 per cent

Rural to urban migration led to a growth in informal settlements in Port Vila. Many of the settlements were overcrowded and had inadequate access to clean water, sanitation and housing. Violence against women continued to increase, with perpetrators seldom brought to justice.

Right to adequate housing

Increased rural to urban migration and a lack of employment opportunities forced many people to live in informal settlements in Port Vila. Many of the settlements were overcrowded, had little or no access to clean water, no sanitation and poor housing conditions. More than 500 people who lived in Seaside Togoa, a settlement in the middle of Port Vila, shared four toilets and two showers. A number of other settlements in Port Vila, including Black Sands, Fresh Wota and Olen were badly overcrowded and had poor public security, with many children not attending school. Many people from settlements had to scavenge in a rubbish dump outside Port Vila for food, water and building materials.

Violence against women

Violence against women continued to increase. Perpetrators were seldom brought to justice due to a lack of police training on domestic violence and on the provisions of the new Family Protection Act (FPA). The FPA, enacted by Parliament in June 2008, was the first legislation on gender-based violence in the Pacific Islands. During a Universal Periodic Review in May, the government committed itself to fully implementing the provisions of the FPA.

The government pledged to review its commitments under the UN Women's Convention (CEDAW).

Amnesty International visit

Amnesty International delegates visited Vanuatu in August.

VENEZUELA

BOLIVARIAN REPUBLIC OF VENEZUELA

Head of state and government:	Hugo Chávez Frías
Death penalty:	abolitionist for all crimes
Population:	28.6 million
Life expectancy:	73.6 years
Under-5 mortality (m/f):	24/19 per 1,000
Adult literacy:	95.2 per cent

Attacks, harassment and intimidation of those critical of government policies, including journalists and human rights defenders, were widespread. Unfounded charges were brought against those who opposed government policies. More special courts and prosecutor's offices specializing in gender-based violence were established. However, the implementation of the 2007 law to eradicate violence against women remained slow.

Background

In February, the limit on presidential terms was removed, following a referendum.

Social unrest increased; there were nearly twice as many protests between January and August as in the whole of 2008. The protests were sparked by issues such as discontent over labour rights and basic services, including a new education law opposed by the private education sector and the political opposition.

The National Assembly debated the possibility of legal reforms to regulate the use and possession of small arms, including harsher sentences for possession of weapons. According to the National Assembly's Security and Defence Commission, there were between nine and 15 million illegal firearms in circulation.

Reforms to the armed forces in October included provisions allowing the creation of militias.

Ten police officers charged with criminal offences in the context of the 2002 attempted coup against President Chávez were sentenced to up to 30 years'

V

imprisonment in April. They were convicted of homicide and grievous bodily harm against anti-coup protesters amid concerns that not all of those who committed acts of violence in the context of the attempted coup had been brought to justice.

Human rights defenders

Human rights defenders and victims of human rights violations and their relatives seeking justice and redress continued to be attacked, threatened and harassed by the security forces.

■ In August, two men shot at José Luis Urbano, President of the Foundation for the Defence of the Right to Education, an NGO working to promote and defend the constitutional right to free education for all. He and other members of the Foundation had been the targets of a series of attacks and threats. By the end of the year, nobody had been brought to justice for this attack or for the shooting in 2007 which left José Luis Urbano seriously injured. No protection measures had been put in place for him, his family or other members of the Foundation by the end of 2009.

■ In October, Oscar Barrios was shot dead in the town of Guanayén, Aragua State, by two armed men dressed in similar clothing to that worn by police officers. The shooting followed a six-year campaign of harassment and intimidation against the Barrios family which began after they reported the killing of Narciso Barrios by police officers in 2003. Further killings of family members took place: Luis Barrios was killed in 2004 and Rigoberto Barrios in 2005. The Inter-American Commission on Human Rights called on Venezuela to take the necessary measures to guarantee the right to life and security of the Barrios family and to bring those responsible for the killings to justice.

■ In November, human rights defender Mijail Martínez was shot dead in Lara state. He had been working with the Committee of Victims Against Impunity in Lara on a documentary film featuring the stories of people who had suffered human rights violations at the hands of police officers. By the end of the year nobody had been brought to justice for the killing and no protection had been provided for the family.

Freedom of expression

Journalists were harassed, intimidated and threatened. At least 34 radio stations had their licences revoked for non-compliance with statutory telecommunications regulations. However, as noted in August by the Special Rapporteur for Freedom of Expression of the Inter-American Commission on Human Rights, the authorities' public statement that these stations "play[ed] at destabilizing Venezuela" indicated that their editorial stance could have been the actual reason behind the closure.

There was concern that a draft law which would criminalize the dissemination of information in media outlets which was "false" and could "harm the interest of the state" could undermine freedom of information and expression. The law remained before the National Assembly at the end of the year.

In August, staff at the Caracas offices of the television channel Globovisión were attacked by armed men. Teargas grenades were thrown and one of the security guards was beaten. Globovisión was widely regarded as opposing government policies. In January, the Inter-American Court of Human Rights issued a ruling ordering the authorities to investigate reports of intimidation and physical and verbal attacks against Globovisión staff. No investigation had been initiated by the end of the year.

Repression of dissent

Members of opposition political parties were harassed, threatened and intimidated, including by the use of spurious criminal charges. On several occasions the security forces failed to intervene when government supporters physically attacked suspected opponents.

■ In January, pro-government activists carrying iron bars, machetes and firearms forced their way into the Fundación Ateneo cultural centre in Caracas. They were protesting at the centre's decision to organize a seminar commemorating the anniversary of the creation of Bandera Roja, a left-wing political party opposed to the government. The police failed to intervene.

■ In September, Julio César Rivas, a student and leader of the United Active Youth of Venezuela, was detained and charged with "organizing armed groups". He remained in a high-security prison for more than two weeks before being released on bail. He had been protesting in Valencia against the new law on education. His trial had not started by the end of the year.

■ In August, Richard Blanco, Prefect of Caracas and President of the opposition Brave People's Alliance was detained together with 11 civil servants. They had been protesting against the new education law which came into effect in August. In October, the 11 civil servants were released pending trial. Despite a reported lack of credible evidence against him, Richard Blanco remained in prison at the end of the year awaiting trial on charges of inciting violence resulting in injury to a police officer.

Violence against women and girls

Progress in the investigation and prosecution of cases of domestic violence remained slow. More courts and prosecutors' offices specializing in dealing with gender-based violence were established. However, the numbers remained insufficient to deal with the high volume of cases. The Public Prosecutor's Office in Caracas stated that it had received more than 12,000 complaints between January and August and that only half of those received could be dealt with.

VIET NAM

SOCIALIST REPUBLIC OF VIET NAM

Head of state:	**Nguyen Minh Triet**
Head of government:	**Nguyen Tan Dung**
Death penalty:	**retentionist**
Population:	**88.1 million**
Life expectancy:	**74.3 years**
Under-5 mortality (m/f):	**27/20 per 1,000**
Adult literacy:	**90.3 per cent**

Severe restrictions on freedom of expression and assembly continued. Repression of dissidents intensified with new arrests of political and human rights activists, most of whom had criticized widespread corruption and government policies relating to China. Bloggers were briefly detained. In most cases, national security concerns were cited as a pretext for arrests and criminal investigations. Peaceful protests by Catholics over land ownership were met with excessive force and arrests by police. Members of ethnic and religious minority groups were threatened and harassed. The National Assembly approved the removal of the death penalty for eight crimes, but 21 capital offences remained. At least 59 death sentences were handed down, and

nine executions were reported in the media. No official statistics on the death penalty were made public.

Background

Corruption remained a key public issue. On 30 June, Viet Nam ratified the UN Convention against Corruption. The government rejected key recommendations arising from its Universal Periodic Review. It refused to: amend or repeal national security provisions of the 1999 Penal Code inconsistent with international law; remove other restrictions on dissent, debate, political opposition and the rights to freedom of expression and assembly; and release prisoners of conscience. An increasing demand for land led to the adoption of legislation in October on the provision of compensation, resettlement and work opportunities to residents displaced by development projects.

Freedom of expression – dissidents

Tight controls on freedom of expression continued, including in the print and broadcast media and on the internet. A new wave of arrests began in May, targeting independent lawyers, bloggers and pro-democracy activists critical of government policies. The authorities claimed to have uncovered a plot "infringing upon national security" involving 27 people. One of those arrested was sentenced to five and a half years' imprisonment in December, and at least four others were in pre-trial detention at year's end. They were charged under Article 79 of the national security section of the Penal Code for attempting to overthrow the state, which carries the death penalty. They are affiliated to the Democratic Party of Viet Nam, an exile political group calling for multi-party democracy. All had publicly criticized controversial business deals and border policies relating to China.

■ Le Cong Dinh, a prominent lawyer, was arrested on 13 June. The government immediately launched a propaganda campaign in the state-controlled media against him. In August, state television interrupted regular broadcasts to air video clips with his "confessions". He was held incommunicado, with no visits from family members or lawyers allowed. The Ministry of Justice revoked his licence, forbidding him to practise law.

V

Political prisoners/prisoners of conscience

At least 31 political prisoners, including prisoners of conscience Father Nguyen Van Ly, Nguyen Van Dai and Le Thi Cong Nhan, remained in prison after being sentenced in unfair trials. Others included lawyers, trade unionists and members of independent political and human rights groups. Most of them were convicted of "conducting propaganda" against the state under Article 88 of the Penal Code.

In October, nine dissidents arrested in September 2008 for unfurling banners, distributing leaflets, posting on the internet information criticizing government policies and calling for democracy, were tried. They were all charged under Article 88. The first trial took place at Ha Noi People's court, where poets Tran Duc Thach and Pham Van Troi were sentenced to three and four years' imprisonment respectively.

■ Vu Hung, a physics teacher, received a three-year sentence at the trial. He went on hunger strike in late 2008 after security officers repeatedly beat him during interrogation. He went on hunger strike again following his trial in protest at his sentence and conditions of detention. Police officials had arrested him earlier during a peaceful demonstration in April 2008, when he was beaten before being released.

In the second trial, six men, including writers Nguyen Xuan Ngia, aged 60, and Nguyen Van Tinh, aged 67, were sentenced to between three and six years' imprisonment.

All nine defendants also received up to four years' probation or house arrest on release.

Discrimination – ethnic and religious groups

Security officials continued to arrest, harass and closely monitor members of religious groups perceived to be opponents of the government. The Supreme Patriarch of the banned Unified Buddhist Church of Viet Nam (UBCV), Thich Quang Do, remained under de facto house arrest, and other leaders faced restrictions on movement and close surveillance.

Security forces confronted Catholics and members of the minority Khmer Krom in disputes over land ownership, using unnecessary force against and arresting peaceful protesters.

In September and December, the authorities orchestrated mobs, including plain-clothes police, to intimidate, harass and physically attack almost 380 followers of Buddhist monk Thich Nhan Hanh to force them to leave their monastery in Lam Dong province.

At least six minority Montagnards in the Central Highlands were sentenced in April and September to between eight and 12 years' imprisonment on charges of "undermining national solidarity". An unknown number remained imprisoned since large-scale protests about land confiscation and freedom of religious practice in 2001 and 2004.

Death penalty

After discussions in the National Assembly, members voted to remove the death penalty for eight crimes, including four economic offences, reducing the number of capital offences to 21; the Ministry of Justice had proposed a reduction of 12 crimes. The death penalty for drug trafficking, for which most death sentences are handed down, was retained. The government maintained its policy of secrecy on all aspects of the death penalty, including statistics. According to media reports 59 people were sentenced to death during the year, and nine executions were reported by the media.

Amnesty International reports

- Viet Nam should release peaceful critics (ASA 41/005/2009)
- Viet Nam: Prisoner of conscience sentenced (ASA 41/008/2009)
- Viet Nam: Prisoner of conscience, Le Cong Dinh (ASA 41/002/2009)

YEMEN

REPUBLIC OF YEMEN

Head of state:	Ali Abdullah Saleh
Head of government:	Ali Mohammed Mujawar
Death penalty:	retentionist
Population:	23.6 million
Life expectancy:	62.5 years
Under-5 mortality (m/f):	84/73 per 1,000
Adult literacy:	58.9 per cent

The authorities detained thousands of people in connection with protests in the south and elsewhere, and amid renewed fighting in Sa'da in the north. Most of those detained were released or tried. Others, mostly arrested in previous years, were sentenced to death or prison terms after unfair trials before the Specialized Criminal Court (SCC). Torture and other ill-treatment were reported, and there was at least one suspicious death in custody. The authorities failed to investigate these and other violations, including alleged unlawful killings by government forces. The government tightened controls on the media. Women remained subject to discrimination and violence. The authorities afforded protection to refugees and asylum-seekers from Somalia, but forcibly returned terrorism suspects to Saudi Arabia despite the risks they faced there. At least 30 people were executed.

Background

Parliamentary elections scheduled for 2009 were postponed for two years in the face of mounting unrest, protests in the south against alleged discrimination and advocating independence, and an upsurge in fighting in Sa'da Governorate in the north between government forces and members of the Shi'a minority Zaidi community.

There were continuing attacks by armed groups, including al-Qa'ida in the Arabian Peninsula. In March, four South Koreans and a Yemeni man were killed by a bomb explosion in Shibam in Hadhramawt. Three health workers and three children kidnapped by unknown people in June from al-Jumhuriya Hospital in Sa'da were still missing at the end of the year; the government said that the six were still alive, but no further details were available. Three other health workers kidnapped with them, all women, were

killed. In December, the government intensified attacks on what they said were al-Qa'ida strongholds, killing scores of people, including children and other relatives of suspects. On 25 December, a failed attempt to blow up a plane over Detroit in the USA drew international attention to al-Qa'ida in Yemen as the Nigerian national involved was reported to have received training in Yemen.

In May, Yemen's human rights record was considered by the UN Human Rights Council under its process of Universal Periodic Review. It urged Yemen to fulfil its human rights obligations, including ending the execution of juvenile offenders.

Sa'da conflict

The long-running conflict in the northern Sa'da Governorate between government forces and armed supporters of the late Zaidi Shi'a cleric Hussain Badr al-Din al-Huthi resumed with new intensity from August, when the government launched a military offensive codenamed Scorched Earth that included aerial bombing and deployment of ground troops. Over 190,000 people had been displaced by the fighting since 2004, according to UNHCR, the UN refugee agency, in December, and an unknown number of civilians were killed in 2009.

Both sides were believed to have committed serious human rights abuses. The government accused the rebel forces of killing civilians and captured soldiers, while the rebels alleged that government forces had carried out indiscriminate attacks, and tortured and killed al-Huthi supporters. In November, the fighting spread across the border with Saudi Arabia, despite the Saudi Arabian government's attempts to seal the frontier and deny access to people fleeing the conflict. There was also fighting between Saudi Arabian forces and armed al-Huthi supporters.

The government closed off the area of fighting to the media and independent observers, making it difficult to obtain independent information about the conflict. The authorities were reported to have detained many suspected supporters of the rebels, but they did not disclose their number or other information, such as their legal status, where they were being held and under what conditions. Nor, it appeared, did they carry out independent and impartial investigations into alleged killings of civilians by their forces.

Y

■ At least 80 civilians were reported to have been killed when the Yemeni air force bombed Adi village in the Harf Sufyan district of 'Amran, a governorate bordering Sa'da, in September. A government-appointed commission was said to have investigated the killings, but no findings were announced.

■ Muhammad al-Maqálih, a journalist and member of the Socialist Party who had criticized government policies, particularly in Sa'da, became a victim of enforced disappearance. He was abducted from a Sana'a street in September, apparently by security officials. The authorities refused to disclose his whereabouts and legal status or allow him access to his family or a lawyer, but acknowledged in December that he was being held by the security forces.

Over 100 alleged al-Huthi supporters were brought to trial before the SCC, whose procedures in practice fail to satisfy international standards of fair trial. At least 34 of them were sentenced to death and at least a further 54 were given prison terms of up to 15 years for forming an armed gang and committing violent crimes, including killing soldiers, in 2008, in the Bani Hushaysh district north of Sana'a. They were arrested in 2008 together with at least 50 others who were released uncharged. They were tried before the SCC in separate groups.

Unrest in the south

Throughout most of 2009, there were protests in the south, particularly in Aden, against alleged discrimination by the government against southerners and in support of calls for the south to regain the status of an independent state, so breaking the union of 1990. Many of the protests were peaceful, but others became violent. Government forces were reported to have used excessive, including lethal, force against protesters, tens of whom were killed.

■ On 3 July, security forces were reported to have shot dead 'Ali Ahmed La'jam in his home in front of his family, even though he posed no threat. No independent investigation was known to have been carried out.

The authorities also carried out waves of arrests. Most of the detainees were quickly released, but some remained in prolonged detention. Among them were prisoners of conscience, including Salim 'Ali Bashawayh (see below). Others were charged and brought to trial before the SCC.

■ Qassim 'Askar Jubran, a former diplomat, and Fadi Ba'oom, a political activist, who were charged with endangering national unity by organizing protests and calling for the independence of the south, appeared before the SCC in Sana'a in June. Their trial was still in progress at the end of 2009.

Torture and other ill-treatment

There were new reports of torture and other ill-treatment of detainees by police and prison guards. The most commonly cited methods were beatings on the body with sticks and rifle butts, kicking and punching, and suspension by the wrists and ankles. The purpose appeared to be to punish and to extract "confessions" from detainees that could be used against them in court.

■ Tens of detainees held in connection with protests in the south were reported to have been beaten and subjected to tear gas at al-Mukalla Central Prison in August after chanting demands in support of the independence of the south and for demanding their release. Seven who were seen as ringleaders, including Salim 'Ali Bashawayh, were suspended by their wrists and ankles for several hours, causing them severe pain. They had been arrested in May after a peaceful protest calling for the release of political prisoners.

■ Tawfiq Bassam Abu Thabit died in October while detained at the Political Security Prison in Sana'a. He had been wounded by shrapnel during armed clashes in Sa'da in 2008 and detained at a military checkpoint when his family were trying to take him for medical treatment. The authorities gave no reason for his death, which was possibly the result of medical neglect or ill-treatment. No investigation was known to have been conducted.

In November, Yemen's application of the UN Convention against Torture was considered by the Committee Against Torture; the Committee urged the government to take immediate measures to eradicate torture.

Cruel, inhuman and degrading punishments

Flogging continued to be used as punishment for alcohol and sexual offences.

Counter-terror and security

In addition to trials connected to the conflict in Sa'da and protests in the south, at least 24 people were

Y

tried by the SCC for alleged links to al-Qa'ida, including eight who were sentenced to prison terms of up to seven years after being convicted of planning terrorist acts. Sixteen others, referred to as the Tarim Cell or the Brigades of the Soldiers of Yemen, were convicted by the SCC in July of carrying out acts of terrorism in 2007 and 2008; six were sentenced to death and the other 10 were sentenced to prison terms of up to 15 years.

Over 90 Yemenis continued to be held by the US authorities at Guantánamo Bay, Cuba. The body of one, Muhammad Ahmad Abdullah Saleh, was returned to Yemen for burial following his death at the prison in June. Salim Hamdan, who was detained following his return to Yemen in November 2008, was released in January. Six Yemenis returned to Yemen in December were detained for several days before being released without charge. Media reports suggested that the US authorities planned to send all or most of the remaining Yemeni detainees for "rehabilitation" in Saudi Arabia, apparently against the wishes of the Yemeni government.

Freedom of expression – the media

The government increased controls over the media. In May it established a court to try cases related to the media. The authorities also confiscated newspapers, denied some access to state-owned printing facilities and, in the case of *al-Ayyam*, one of the largest-circulation daily newspapers, sent in troops to prevent it publishing in May and besieged its offices in Aden.

Discrimination and violence against women and girls

In March, the government amended the nationality law to enable Yemeni women married to foreign men to pass on their nationality to their children. However, women continued to face discrimination under the law and in practice. They were also subjected to early and forced marriage and, it was believed, suffered high levels of violence within the family. Maternal mortality rates remained significantly higher than in most other countries in the region. In February, parliament approved a draft law to raise the marriage age for girls to 17, but it had not been enacted by the end of the year.

■ Twelve-year-old Fauzia al-'Amudi died in September while giving birth. She had been married when aged 11

to a 24-year-old man, and was in labour for almost two days before she could reach the nearest hospital, almost 100km away.

Refugees and asylum-seekers

The authorities continued to afford protection to thousands of Somalis. At least 77,000 people were reported by UNHCR in December to have entered Yemen since January, mostly after making the perilous journey across the Red Sea. Others were believed to have drowned while attempting the crossing. The authorities detained and forcibly returned nationals of other countries, however, without allowing them access to asylum procedures.

■ 'Ali 'Abdullah al-Harbi and four other Saudi Arabian nationals were forcibly returned to Saudi Arabia in April without being given access to asylum procedures or any means to contest their deportations. The five were reportedly suspected supporters of al-Qa'ida and were at risk of serious human rights violations in Saudi Arabia.

Death penalty

At least 53 people were sentenced to death and at least 30 prisoners were executed. Hundreds of people were believed to be on death row. More than 70 were under sentence of death in Ta'iz Central Prison alone.

■ 'Ali Mousa was executed in January after spending over 30 years in prison. Convicted of murdering a relative, he was believed to be mentally ill. According to reports, he did not die when first shot so the executioner then shot him in the head at close range.

■ In March, the SCC sentenced three men to death after unfair trials – Abdul Karim Laliji and Hani Muhammad for spying for Iran; and Bassam al-Haydari for spying for Israel.

Amnesty International visit/reports

🚍 Amnesty International delegates visited Yemen in February to conduct research.

📄 Yemen's dark side: Discrimination and violence against women and girls (MDE 31/014/2009)

📄 Suggested recommendations to states included in the fifth round of Universal Periodic Review – May 2009 (IOR 41/012/2009)

Y

ZIMBABWE

REPUBLIC OF ZIMBABWE

Head of state and government:	Robert Mugabe
Death penalty:	retentionist
Population:	12.5 million
Life expectancy:	43.4 years
Under-5 mortality (m/f):	100/88 per 1,000
Adult literacy:	91.2 per cent

The human rights situation improved slightly with the setting up of a unity government in February. However, harassment and intimidation persisted of human rights defenders, political activists and supporters of the Movement for Democratic Change (MDC-T) led by Prime Minister Morgan Tsvangirai. Scores of people perceived to be critics of the former ruling Zimbabwe African National Union (ZANU-PF) were targeted for arrest. State institutions controlled by ZANU-PF continued to target perceived political opponents, putting strain on the fragile unity government. Tensions within state institutions fuelled attacks on MDC-T activists in rural areas as well as on some commercial farms.

The economy showed the first signs of improvement since the crisis began in 2000. The Zimbabwe dollar was scrapped and hard currencies such as the US dollar and South African rand were used instead. This brought inflation under control and improved availability of food in shops. However, many poor households had no access to foreign currencies and could not afford fees for education and health care. Intervention by humanitarian agencies led to health facilities and schools reopening; most had closed in 2007.

Background

On 27 January, Southern African Development Community (SADC) leaders held an extraordinary summit in South Africa to try to break the political impasse in Zimbabwe that followed the signing of the Global Political Agreement (GPA) on 15 September 2008. The three parties to the GPA – ZANU-PF, MDC-T and the MDC led by Arthur Mutambara – had reached a deadlock over the allocation of key ministries.

Following the SADC intervention, Morgan Tsvangirai was sworn in as Prime Minister on 11 February with two deputies – Arthur Mutambara of the MDC and Thokhozani Khupe of the MDC-T. Other members of the unity government were sworn in on 14 February. However, the unity government remained fragile mainly due to President Mugabe's refusal to implement parts of the GPA. ZANU-PF argued that the MDC-T had not done enough to lobby for the end of targeted sanctions imposed by the EU and the USA. In October, the MDC-T boycotted three cabinet meetings in protest over delays in implementing the GPA. The MDC-T only resumed attending cabinet meetings after a SADC-convened summit on 5 November. The summit gave the parties 30 days to resume dialogue to resolve the impasse. By the end of the year, none of the major issues had been resolved.

Victims of the 2005 mass forced evictions continued to live in deplorable conditions.

Freedom of expression, association and assembly

Suppression of human rights defenders and perceived political opponents of ZANU-PF persisted. Scores of human rights and political activists were arrested and charged after exercising their rights.

The Attorney General's office continued to invoke Section 121 of the Criminal Procedures and Evidence Act (CPEA) to prolong the detention of human rights defenders and political activists who would normally have been granted bail. Section 121 allows a further seven days in detention to allow the state to lodge an appeal with a higher court.

■ At least 18 political prisoners were held on what were believed to be trumped-up charges brought by the former ZANU-PF government. On 2 March, Jestina Mukoko and Broderick Takawira were bailed and released after spending three months in custody. Thirteen others were subsequently released on bail. Three – Gandhi Mudzingwa and Kisimusi Dhlamini, both MDC-T officials; and Andrison Manyere, a journalist – were granted bail on 9 April. The authorities opposed the bail but failed to file an appeal within the seven-day period stipulated by Section 121 of the CPEA. The three were released on 17 April only to be redetained within days by police. Gandhi Mudzingwa and Kisimusi Dhlamini remained in hospital receiving treatment for injuries sustained by torture in custody. They were finally granted bail on 13 May and released. All the detainees needed treatment as a result of torture and other ill-treatment in custody.

■ The trial of Jestina Mukoko and 17 other victims of abduction in 2008 started at the beginning of the year. However, on 28 September the Supreme Court ordered a permanent stay to the criminal prosecution against Jestina Mukoko on the grounds that state security agents had violated her constitutional rights.

■ Seven members of Women of Zimbabwe Arise (WOZA), all of them women, were arrested in Bulawayo on 17 June and denied access to their lawyers after participating in a peaceful demonstration. The next day, while Amnesty International's Secretary General was holding a press conference at the Meikles Hotel in Harare, four WOZA activists, a cameraman from the state-owned *Herald* newspaper and an independent journalist were arrested and beaten by police about 50 metres from the hotel. The WOZA activists were denied access to medical treatment as a punishment for their activism and detained overnight. The independent journalist and cameraman were released the same day.

■ On 5 August, four student leaders from the Zimbabwe National Students Association – Clever Bere, Kudakwashe Chakabva, Archieford Mudzengi and Brian Rugodo – were arrested at the University of Zimbabwe for distributing T-shirts. They were charged with contravening the Criminal Law (Codification and Reform Act) by participating in a gathering with intent to promote public violence, breach of the peace and "bigotry". They were released on bail on 7 August.

■ On 25 October, Cephas Zinhumwe, the Executive Director of the National Association for NGOs (NANGO), and Dadirai Chikwengo, NANGO board chairperson, were arrested in the town of Victoria Falls after NANGO convened a workshop for NGO directors. The two were released on bail on 27 October charged with contravening the Public Order and Security Act (POSA) for allegedly failing to notify the regulating authority of an intention to hold a "public political gathering". They were acquitted on 25 November.

■ On 28 October, Thulani Ndhlovu and Ndodana Ndhlovu from the Zimbabwe Election Support Network were arrested in Dete, Hwange District. They were charged under the POSA for holding meetings allegedly without police clearance. Ndodana Ndhlovu was released on the day of arrest, while Thulani Ndhlovu was released on bail on 30 October.

■ On 8 November, Lovemore Matombo, President of the Zimbabwe Congress of Trade Unions (ZCTU), together with four other ZCTU activists – Michael Kandukutu, Percy Mcijo, Dumisani Ncube and Nawu Ndlovu – were arrested in the town of Victoria Falls after holding a trade union meeting. They were charged under the POSA for organizing what the state alleged was an illegal meeting. They were released on 12 November when the case was dismissed by a magistrates' court.

■ On 20 November, 32 activists from Gweru appeared before a magistrates' court. They had been arrested in December 2008 after participating in a peaceful demonstration and charged under the POSA. However, when they were summoned to court, the charges were changed to destruction of property and chanting insults against President Mugabe.

Harassment of lawyers and judicial officers

Harassment and intimidation continued of lawyers representing human rights and political activists, and of court officials.

■ On 14 May, Alec Muchadehama, a lawyer who was representing journalist Andrison Manyere and two MDC-T officials, was arrested at the magistrates' court in Harare by police officers from the Law and Order Section. He was charged with defeating or obstructing the course of justice for "unlawfully causing the release" of Kisimusi Dhlamini, Gandhi Mudzingwa and Andrison Manyere by misinforming and misdirecting High Court officials. He was detained overnight. He was acquitted on 10 December. In a related case, Constance Gambara, the High Court clerk who facilitated the temporary release of the three detainees, was arrested on 6 May on charges of criminal abuse of public duty. She was granted bail on 8 May, but the state invoked Section 121 of the CPEA and she remained in custody with her nine-month-old baby. She was released on 14 May after the state withdrew its appeal against bail. She was also acquitted on 10 December.

Impunity

No meaningful measures were taken to bring to justice perpetrators of serious human rights violations during the state-sponsored violence and torture of political opponents of ZANU-PF in the run-up to the second round of the presidential elections in June 2008. At least 200 people were killed and over 9,000 injured in the violence. A few isolated prosecutions were recorded. The Organ on National Healing created by the government did not prioritize bringing the perpetrators to account, nor did the Ministries of

Z

Defence and Home Affairs see the need for urgent institutional reform to combat impunity. Throughout 2009, elements within the army, police and intelligence services felt able to continue targeting human rights activists and members of the MDC-T for human rights violations.

The Attorney General's office was either unwilling to investigate alleged human rights violations or was complicit in them.

Torture and other ill-treatment

Torture and other ill-treatment of detainees persisted. No perpetrators were brought to justice.

■ In September the Supreme Court of Zimbabwe ruled among other things that Jestina Mukoko (see above) had been tortured by state security agents who abducted and held her incommunicado in December 2008. Despite this, no investigation was carried out.

■ At least 95 soldiers were arrested in October in Harare on suspicion of breaking into an armoury at Pomona barracks and stealing 21 guns. They were reportedly tortured while being interrogated by members of the Central Intelligence Organization, Military Intelligence Corps and Military Police. At least two of them died as a result of the injuries sustained. One was reported to have committed suicide while in solitary confinement. Pascal Gwezere, a transport manager for the MDC-T who was charged with the same offence, was detained by state security agents from his home in Harare on 27 October and tortured. He was denied access to medical treatment. He was released on 24 December on bail after the Supreme Court upheld an earlier bail ruling by the High Court.

Manfred Novak, the UN Special Rapporteur, was barred from entering Zimbabwe on 28 October. The government withdrew the invitation two days earlier on the grounds that an SADC delegation was in the country assessing the performance of the unity government.

Justice system – independence of the judiciary

Magistrates' courts found themselves under pressure after passing decisions not favourable to the Attorney General's office. The lower courts came under increased pressure in cases against MDC-T officials and human rights defenders, often seeing judicial officers themselves facing trumped-up charges at the instigation of the Attorney General's office. The

charges were intended to instil fear among judicial officers, undermining their independence and impartiality.

■ Livingstone Chipadza, Manicaland acting regional magistrate, was arrested in March after he granted bail to Roy Bennett, MDC-T treasurer-general. He was accused of "criminal abuse of office" after sanctioning the release of Roy Bennett from remand, and detained for several days in deplorable prison conditions before being released on bail. On 4 August the charges against him were dismissed.

■ Chioniso Mutongi, a magistrate who was presiding over the trial of human rights lawyer Alec Muchadehama, resigned on 3 November. She alleged that she had been harassed by prosecution authorities after she convicted judicial officer Andrew Kumire of contempt of court and sentenced him to five days in prison. Andrew Kumire walked out of court and was later granted bail by another magistrate in unexplained circumstances. The conviction of Andrew Kumire was later confirmed by the High Court on review. Chioniso Mutongi received several anonymous threatening telephone calls and said that she had not received protection from the Chief Magistrate's Office.

Death penalty

At least seven people were sentenced to death in 2009, bringing the number of people on death row at the end of the year to at least 52.

Amnesty International visits/reports

🚗 Amnesty International delegates visited Zimbabwe in March, May, June and October. In June, Amnesty International's Secretary General visited Zimbabwe and met senior government officials, including Vice President Joice Mujuru, and Minister of Defence Emmerson Mnangagwa, AU and EU diplomats as well as human rights defenders and survivors of human rights violations. In July, the Secretary General met Prime Minister Morgan Tsvangirai in the UK.

📰 Zimbabwe: A five point human rights agenda for the inclusive government (AFR 46/009/2009)

📰 Zimbabwe: Moving from words to action (AFR 46/025/2009)

Z

A Bosnian Muslim woman in a temporary centre for internally displaced people north of Sarajevo, Bosnia and Herzegovina in October 2009. Many people remained unable to go back to their pre-war places of residence.

A Uighur woman in Urumqi, Xinjiang Uighur Autonomous Region, north-west China, July 2009. Police cracked down on initially peaceful Uighur protesters, triggering violent riots and heightened ethnic tension between Uighurs and Han.

AMNESTY INTERNATIONAL REPORT 2010
PART THREE: SELECTED HUMAN RIGHTS TREATIES

A Palestinian woman covers her face as smoke rises following an explosion during an Israeli strike in Gaza city, 14 January 2009. The strike was part of a 22-day military offensive code-named Operation "Cast Lead".

SELECTED INTERNATIONAL AND REGIONAL HUMAN RIGHTS TREATIES

(AT 31 DECEMBER 2009)

SELECTED INTERNATIONAL HUMAN RIGHTS TREATIES

SELECTED REGIONAL HUMAN RIGHTS TREATIES

States which have ratified or acceded to a convention are party to the treaty and are bound to observe its provisions. States which have signed but not yet ratified have expressed their intention to become a party at some future date; meanwhile they are obliged to refrain from acts which would defeat the object and purpose of the treaty.

	International Covenant on Civil and Political Rights (ICCPR)	(first) Optional Protocol to the ICCPR	Second Optional Protocol to the ICCPR, aiming at the abolition of the death penalty	International Covenant on Economic, Social and Cultural Rights (ICESCR)	Optional Protocol to the ICESCR	Convention on the Elimination of All Forms of Discrimination against Women (CEDAW)	Optional Protocol to CEDAW	Convention on the Rights of the Child (CRC)	Optional Protocol to the CRC on the involvement of children in armed conflict	International Convention on the Elimination of All Forms of Racial Discrimination	Convention against Torture and Other Cruel, Inhuman or Degrading Treatment or Punishment
Afghanistan	●			●		●		●	●	●	●28
Albania	●	●	●	●		●		●	●	●	●
Algeria	●	●		●		●		●	●	●	●22
Andorra	●	●	●			●		●	●	●	●22
Angola	●	●		●		●	●	●	●		
Antigua and Barbuda						●		●	●	●	●
Argentina	●	●	●	●	○	●	●	●	●	●	●22
Armenia	●	●		●	○	●	●	●	●	●	●
Australia	●	●	●	●		●	●	●	●	●	●22
Austria	●	●	●	●		●	●	●	●	●	●22
Azerbaijan	●	●	●	●	○	●	●	●	●	●	●22
Bahamas	●			●		●		●		●	○
Bahrain	●			●		●		●		●	●
Bangladesh	●			●		●	●10	●	●	●	●
Barbados	●	●		●		●		●		●	
Belarus	●	●		●		●		●	●	●	●
Belgium	●	●	●	●	○	●		●	●	●	●22
Belize	●			○		●	●10	●	●	●	●
Benin	●	●		●		●	○	●	●	●	●
Bhutan						●		●	●	○	
Bolivia	●	●		●		●	●	●	●	●	●22
Bosnia and Herzegovina	●	●	●	●		●	●	●	●	●	●22
Botswana	●					●		●	●	●	●
Brazil	●	●	●	●		●	●	●	●	●	●22
Brunei Darussalam						●		●			
Bulgaria	●	●	●	●		●	●	●	●	●	●22
Burkina Faso	●	●		●		●	●	●	●	●	●
Burundi	●			●		●	○	●	●	●	●22

Optional Protocol to the Convention against Torture	International Convention for the Protection of All Persons from Enforced Disappearance (not yet into force)	Convention relating to the Status of Refugees (1951)	Protocol relating to the Status of Refugees (1967)	Convention relating to the Status of Stateless Persons (1954)	Convention on the Reduction of Statelessness (1961)	International Convention on the Protection of the Rights of All Migrant Workers and Members of Their Families	Rome Statute of the International Criminal Court	
		●	●				●	Afghanistan
●	●	●	●	●	●	●	●	Albania
	○	●	●	●		●	○	Algeria
							●	Andorra
		●	●				○	Angola
		●	●	●			●	Antigua and Barbuda
●	●	●	●	●		●	●	Argentina
●	○	●	●	●	●		○	Armenia
○		●	●	●	●		●	Australia
○	○	●	●	●	●		●	Austria
●	○	●	●	●	●	●		Azerbaijan
		●	●				○	Bahamas
							○	Bahrain
						○	○	Bangladesh
				●			●	Barbados
		●	●					Belarus
○	○	●	●	●			●	Belgium
		●	●	●		●	●	Belize
●		●	●			○	●	Benin
								Bhutan
●	●	●	●	●	●	●	●	Bolivia
●	○	●	●	●	●	●	●	Bosnia and Herzegovina
		●	●	●			●	Botswana
●	○	●	●	●	●		●	Brazil
								Brunei Darussalam
	○	●	●				●	Bulgaria
○	●	●	●			●	●	Burkina Faso
	○	●	●				●	Burundi

● state is a party

● state became party in 2009

○ signed but not yet ratified

○ signed in 2009, but not yet ratified

10 Declaration under Article 10 not recognizing the competence of the CEDAW Committee to undertake confidential inquiries into allegations of grave or systematic violations.

22 Declaration under Article 22 recognizing the competence of the Committee against Torture (CAT) to consider individual complaints.

28 Reservation under Article 28 not recognizing the competence of the CAT to undertake confidential inquiries into allegations of systematic torture if warranted.

12 Declaration under Article 12(3) accepting the jurisdiction of the International Criminal Court (ICC) for crimes in its territory.

124 Declaration under Article 124 not accepting the jurisdiction of the ICC over war crimes for seven years after ratification.

* Signed the Rome Statute but have since formally declared their intention not to ratify.

** Ratified or acceded but subsequently denounced the treaty.

	International Covenant on Civil and Political Rights (ICCPR)	(first) Optional Protocol to the ICCPR	Second Optional Protocol to the ICCPR, aiming at the abolition of the death penalty	International Covenant on Economic, Social and Cultural Rights (ICESCR)	Optional Protocol to the ICESCR	Convention on the Elimination of All Forms of Discrimination against Women (CEDAW)	Optional Protocol to CEDAW	Convention on the Rights of the Child (CRC)	Optional Protocol to the CRC on the involvement of children in armed conflict	International Convention on the Elimination of All Forms of Racial Discrimination	Convention against Torture and Other Cruel, Inhuman or Degrading Treatment or Punishment
Cambodia	●	○		●		●	○	●	●	●	●
Cameroon	●	●		●		●		●	○	●	●22
Canada	●	●	●	●		●	●	●	●	●	●22
Cape Verde	●	●	●	●		●		●	●	●	●
Central African Republic	●	●		●		●		●		●	
Chad	●	●		●		●		●	●	●	●
Chile	●	●	●	●	○	●	○	●	●	●	●22
China	○			●		●		●	●	●	●28
Colombia	●	●	●	●		●	●10	●	●	●	●
Comoros	○			○		●		●		●	○
Congo (Republic of)	●	●		●	○	●	○	●		●	●
Cook Islands						●		●	●		
Costa Rica	●	●	●	●		●	●	●	●	●	●22
Côte d'Ivoire	●	●		●		●		●		●	●
Croatia	●	●	●	●		●	●	●	●	●	●22
Cuba	○			○		●	○	●	●	●	●28
Cyprus	●	●	●	●		●	●	●	○	●	●22
Czech Republic	●	●		●		●	●	●	●	●	●22
Democratic Republic of the Congo	●	●		●		●		●	●	●	●
Denmark	●	●	●	●		●	●	●	●	●	●22
Djibouti	●	●	●	●		●		●	○	○	●
Dominica	●			●		●		●	●		
Dominican Republic	●	●		●		●	●	●	○	●	○
Ecuador	●	●	●	●	○	●	●	●	●	●	●22
Egypt	●			●		●		●	●	●	●
El Salvador	●	●		●	○	●	○	●	●	●	●
Equatorial Guinea	●	●		●		●	●	●		●	●28
Eritrea	●			●		●		●	●	●	

Optional Protocol to the Convention against Torture	International Convention for the Protection of All Persons from Enforced Disappearance (not yet into force)	Convention relating to the Status of Refugees (1951)	Protocol relating to the Status of Refugees (1967)	Convention relating to the Status of Stateless Persons (1954)	Convention on the Reduction of Statelessness (1961)	International Convention on the Protection of the Rights of All Migrant Workers and Members of Their Families	Rome Statute of the International Criminal Court	
●		●	●			○	●	Cambodia
○		●	●			○	○	Cameroon
		●	●		●		●	Canada
	○	●	●			●	○	Cape Verde
		●	●				●	Central African Republic
	○	●	●	●	●		●	Chad
●	●	●	●			●	●	Chile
		●	●					China
	○	●	●	○		●	●124	Colombia
	○					○	●	Comoros
○	○	●	●			○	●	Congo (Republic of)
							●	Cook Islands
●	○	●	●	●	●		●	Costa Rica
		●	●				○12	Côte d'Ivoire
●	○	●	●	●			●	Croatia
	●							Cuba
●	○	●	●				●	Cyprus
●		●	●	●	●		●	Czech Republic
		●	●				●	Democratic Republic of the Congo
●	○	●	●	●	●		●	Denmark
		●	●				●	Djibouti
		●	●				●	Dominica
		●	●		○		●	Dominican Republic
○	●	●	●	●		●	●	Ecuador
		●	●			●	○	Egypt
		●	●		○	●		El Salvador
		●	●					Equatorial Guinea
							○	Eritrea

● state is a party
● state became party in 2009
○ signed but not yet ratified
○ signed in 2009, but not yet ratified

10 Declaration under Article 10 not recognizing the competence of the CEDAW Committee to undertake confidential inquiries into allegations of grave or systematic violations.

22 Declaration under Article 22 recognizing the competence of the Committee against Torture (CAT) to consider individual complaints.

28 Reservation under Article 28 not recognizing the competence of the CAT to undertake confidential inquiries into allegations of systematic torture if warranted.

12 Declaration under Article 12(3) accepting the jurisdiction of the International Criminal Court (ICC) for crimes in its territory.

124 Declaration under Article 124 not accepting the jurisdiction of the ICC over war crimes for seven years after ratification.

* Signed the Rome Statute but have since formally declared their intention not to ratify.

** Ratified or acceded but subsequently denounced the treaty.

	International Covenant on Civil and Political Rights (ICCPR)	(first) Optional Protocol to the ICCPR	Second Optional Protocol to the ICCPR, aiming at the abolition of the death penalty	International Covenant on Economic, Social and Cultural Rights (ICESCR)	Optional Protocol to the ICESCR	Convention on the Elimination of All Forms of Discrimination against Women (CEDAW)	Optional Protocol to CEDAW	Convention on the Rights of the Child (CRC)	Optional Protocol to the CRC on the involvement of children in armed conflict	International Convention on the Elimination of All Forms of Racial Discrimination	Convention against Torture and Other Cruel, Inhuman or Degrading Treatment or Punishment
Estonia	●	●	●	●		●		●	○	●	●
Ethiopia	●			●		●		●		●	●
Fiji						●		●	○	●	
Finland	●	●	●	●	○	●	●	●	●	●	●22
France	●	●	●	●		●	●	●	●	●	●22
Gabon	●			●	○	●		●	○	●	●
Gambia	●	●		●		●		●	○	●	○
Georgia	●	●	●	●		●	●	●		●	●22
Germany	●	●	●	●		●	●	●	●	●	●22
Ghana	●	●		●	○	●	○	●	○	●	●22
Greece	●	●	●	●		●	●	●	●	●	●22
Grenada	●			●		●		●		○	
Guatemala	●	●		●	○	●	●	●	●	●	●22
Guinea	●	●		●		●		●		●	●
Guinea-Bissau	○	○	○	●	○	●	●	●	○	○	○
Guyana	●	●		●		●		●		●	●
Haiti	●					●		●	○	●	
Holy See								●	●	●	●
Honduras	●	●	●	●		●		●	●	●	●
Hungary	●	●	●	●		●	●	●	○	●	●22
Iceland	●	●	●	●		●	●	●	●	●	●22
India	●			●		●		●	●	●	○
Indonesia	●			●		●	○	●	○	●	●
Iran	●			●				●		●	
Iraq	●			●		●		●	●	●	
Ireland	●	●	●	●		●	●	●	●	●	●22
Israel	●			●		●		●	●	●	●28
Italy	●	●	●	●	○	●	●	●	●	●	●22

Optional Protocol to the Convention against Torture	International Convention for the Protection of All Persons from Enforced Disappearance (not yet into force)	Convention relating to the Status of Refugees (1951)	Protocol relating to the Status of Refugees (1967)	Convention relating to the Status of Stateless Persons (1954)	Convention on the Reduction of Statelessness (1961)	International Convention on the Protection of the Rights of All Migrant Workers and Members of Their Families	Rome Statute of the International Criminal Court	
●		●	●				●	Estonia
		●	●				●	Ethiopia
		●	●	●			●	Fiji
○	○	●	●	●	●		●	Finland
●	●	●	●	●	○		●124	France
○	○	●	●			○	●	Gabon
		●	●				●	Gambia
●		●	●				●	Georgia
●	◐	●	●	●	●		●	Germany
○	○	●	●			●	●	Ghana
	○	●	●	●			●	Greece
	○							Grenada
●	○	●	●	●	●		●	Guatemala
○		●	●	●		●	●	Guinea
		●	●			○	○	Guinea-Bissau
						○	●	Guyana
	○	●	●				○	Haiti
		●	●	○				Holy See
●	●	●	●	○		●	●	Honduras
		●	●	●	◐		●	Hungary
○	○	●	●				●	Iceland
	○							India
							○	Indonesia
		●	●				○	Iran
								Iraq
○	○	●	●	●	●		●	Ireland
		●	●	●	○		○*	Israel
○	○	●	●	●			●	Italy

● state is a party
◐ state became party in 2009
○ signed but not yet ratified
○ signed in 2009, but not yet ratified

10 Declaration under Article 10 not recognizing the competence of the CEDAW Committee to undertake confidential inquiries into allegations of grave or systematic violations.

22 Declaration under Article 22 recognizing the competence of the Committee against Torture (CAT) to consider individual complaints.

28 Reservation under Article 28 not recognizing the competence of the CAT to undertake confidential inquiries into allegations of systematic torture if warranted.

12 Declaration under Article 12(3) accepting the jurisdiction of the International Criminal Court (ICC) for crimes in its territory.

124 Declaration under Article 124 not accepting the jurisdiction of the ICC over war crimes for seven years after ratification.

* Signed the Rome Statute but have since formally declared their intention not to ratify.

** Ratified or acceded but subsequently denounced the treaty.

	International Covenant on Civil and Political Rights (ICCPR)	(first) Optional Protocol to the ICCPR	Second Optional Protocol to the ICCPR, aiming at the abolition of the death penalty	International Covenant on Economic, Social and Cultural Rights (ICESCR)	Optional Protocol to the ICESCR	Convention on the Elimination of All Forms of Discrimination against Women (CEDAW)	Optional Protocol to CEDAW	Convention on the Rights of the Child (CRC)	Optional Protocol to the CRC on the involvement of children in armed conflict	International Convention on the Elimination of All Forms of Racial Discrimination	Convention against Torture and Other Cruel, Inhuman or Degrading Treatment or Punishment
Jamaica	●	**		●		●		●	●	●	
Japan	●			●		●		●	●	●	●
Jordan	●			●		●		●	●	●	●
Kazakhstan	●	●		●		●	●	●	●	●	●22
Kenya	●			●		●		●	●	●	●22
Kiribati						●		●			
Korea (Democratic People's Republic of)	●			●		●		●			
Korea (Republic of)	●	●		●		●	●	●	●	●	●22
Kuwait	●			●		●		●	●	●	●28
Kyrgyzstan	●	●		●		●	●	●	●	●	●
Laos	●			●		●		●	●	●	
Latvia	●	●		●		●		●	●	●	●
Lebanon	●			●		●		●	○	●	●
Lesotho	●	●		●		●	●	●	●	●	●
Liberia	●	○	●	●		●	○	●	○	●	●
Libya	●	●		●		●		●	●	●	●
Liechtenstein	●	●	●	●		●	●	●	●	●	●22
Lithuania	●	●	●	●		●	●	●	●	●	●
Luxembourg	●	●	●	●	○	●	●	●	●	●	●22
Macedonia	●	●	●	●		●	●	●	●	●	●
Madagascar	●	●		●	○	●	○	●	●	●	●
Malawi	●	●		●		●	○	●	○	●	●
Malaysia						●		●			
Maldives	●	●		●		●	●	●	●	●	●
Mali	●	●		●	○	●	●	●	●	●	●
Malta	●	●	●	●		●		●	●	●	●22
Marshall Islands						●		●			
Mauritania	●			●		●		●		●	●28

Optional Protocol to the Convention against Torture	International Convention for the Protection of All Persons from Enforced Disappearance (not yet into force)	Convention relating to the Status of Refugees (1951)	Protocol relating to the Status of Refugees (1967)	Convention relating to the Status of Stateless Persons (1954)	Convention on the Reduction of Statelessness (1961)	International Convention on the Protection of the Rights of All Migrant Workers and Members of Their Families	Rome Statute of the International Criminal Court	
		●	●			●	○	Jamaica
	●	●	●				●	Japan
							●	Jordan
●	●	●	●					Kazakhstan
	○	●	●				●	Kenya
				●	●			Kiribati
								Korea (Democratic People's Republic of)
		●	●	●			●	Korea (Republic of)
							○	Kuwait
		●	●			●	○	Kyrgyzstan
	○							Laos
		●	●	●	●		●	Latvia
●	○							Lebanon
		●	●	●	●		●	Lesotho
●		●	●	●	●	○	●	Liberia
			●	●	●			Libya
●	○	●	●	●	●			Liechtenstein
	○	●	●	●			●	Lithuania
○	○	●	●	●			●	Luxembourg
●	○	●	●	●			●	Macedonia
○	○	●		**			●	Madagascar
		●	●	●			●	Malawi
								Malaysia
●	○							Maldives
●	●	●	●			●	●	Mali
●	○	●	●				●	Malta
							●	Marshall Islands
		●	●			●		Mauritania

● state is a party

● state became party in 2009

○ signed but not yet ratified

○ signed in 2009, but not yet ratified

10 Declaration under Article 10 not recognizing the competence of the CEDAW Committee to undertake confidential inquiries into allegations of grave or systematic violations.

22 Declaration under Article 22 recognizing the competence of the Committee against Torture (CAT) to consider individual complaints.

28 Reservation under Article 28 not recognizing the competence of the CAT to undertake confidential inquiries into allegations of systematic torture if warranted.

12 Declaration under Article 12(3) accepting the jurisdiction of the International Criminal Court (ICC) for crimes in its territory.

124 Declaration under Article 124 not accepting the jurisdiction of the ICC over war crimes for seven years after ratification.

* Signed the Rome Statute but have since formally declared their intention not to ratify.

** Ratified or acceded but subsequently denounced the treaty.

	International Covenant on Civil and Political Rights (ICCPR)	(first) Optional Protocol to the ICCPR	Second Optional Protocol to the ICCPR, aiming at the abolition of the death penalty	International Covenant on Economic, Social and Cultural Rights (ICESCR)	Optional Protocol to the ICESCR	Convention on the Elimination of All Forms of Discrimination against Women (CEDAW)	Optional Protocol to CEDAW	Convention on the Rights of the Child (CRC)	Optional Protocol to the CRC on the involvement of children in armed conflict	International Convention on the Elimination of All Forms of Racial Discrimination	Convention against Torture and Other Cruel, Inhuman or Degrading Treatment or Punishment
Mauritius	●	●		●		●	●	●	●	●	●
Mexico	●	●	●	●		●	●	●	●	●	●[22]
Micronesia						●		●	○		
Moldova	●	●	●	●		●	●	●	●	●	●
Monaco	●		●	●		●		●	●	●	●[22]
Mongolia	●	●		●	○	●	●	●	●	●	●
Montenegro	●	●	●	●	○	●	●	●	●	●	●[22]
Morocco	●			●		●		●	●	●	●[22]
Mozambique	●		●			●		●	●	●	●
Myanmar						●		●			
Namibia	●	●	●	●		●	●	●	●	●	●
Nauru	○	○						●	○	○	○
Nepal	●	●	●	●		●	●	●	●	●	●
Netherlands	●	●	●	●	○	●	●	●	●	●	●[22]
New Zealand	●	●	●	●		●	●	●	●	●	●[22]
Nicaragua	●	●	●	●		●		●	●	●	●
Niger	●	●		●		●	●	●		●	●
Nigeria	●			●		●	●	●	○	●	●
Niue								●			
Norway	●	●	●	●		●	●	●	●	●	●[22]
Oman						●		●	●	●	
Pakistan	○			●		●		●	○	●	○
Palau								●			
Panama	●	●	●	●		●	●	●	●	●	●
Papua New Guinea	●			●		●		●		●	
Paraguay	●	●	●	●	○	●	●	●	●	●	●[22]
Peru	●	●		●		●	●	●	●	●	●[22]
Philippines	●	●	●	●		●	●	●	●	●	●

Optional Protocol to the Convention against Torture	International Convention for the Protection of All Persons from Enforced Disappearance (not yet into force)	Convention relating to the Status of Refugees (1951)	Protocol relating to the Status of Refugees (1967)	Convention relating to the Status of Stateless Persons (1954)	Convention on the Reduction of Statelessness (1961)	International Convention on the Protection of the Rights of All Migrant Workers and Members of Their Families	Rome Statute of the International Criminal Court	
●							●	Mauritius
●	●	●	●	●		●	●	Mexico
								Micronesia
●	○	●	●				○	Moldova
	○	●					○	Monaco
	○						●	Mongolia
●	○	●	●	●		○	●	Montenegro
	○	●	●			●	○	Morocco
	○	●	●				○	Mozambique
								Myanmar
		●	●				●	Namibia
							●	Nauru
								Nepal
○	○	●	●	●	●		●	Netherlands
●		●	●		●		●	New Zealand
●		●	●			●		Nicaragua
	○	●	●		●	●	●	Niger
●	●	●	●			●	●	Nigeria
								Niue
○	○	●	●	●	●		●	Norway
							○	Oman
								Pakistan
								Palau
	○	●	●				●	Panama
		●	●					Papua New Guinea
●	○	●	●			●	●	Paraguay
●		●	●			●	●	Peru
		●	●	○		●	○	Philippines

	International Covenant on Civil and Political Rights (ICCPR)	(first) Optional Protocol to the ICCPR	Second Optional Protocol to the ICCPR, aiming at the abolition of the death penalty	International Covenant on Economic, Social and Cultural Rights (ICESCR)	Optional Protocol to the ICESCR	Convention on the Elimination of All Forms of Discrimination against Women (CEDAW)	Optional Protocol to CEDAW	Convention on the Rights of the Child (CRC)	Optional Protocol to the CRC on the involvement of children in armed conflict	International Convention on the Elimination of All Forms of Racial Discrimination	Convention against Torture and Other Cruel, Inhuman or Degrading Treatment or Punishment
Poland	●	●	○	●		●	●	●	●	●	[28]●[22]
Portugal	●	●	●	●	○	●	●	●	●	●	●[22]
Qatar						●		●	●	●	●
Romania	●	●	●	●		●	●	●	●	●	●
Russian Federation	●	●		●		●	●	●	●	●	●[22]
Rwanda	●		●	●		●	●	●	●	●	●
Saint Kitts and Nevis						●	●	●		●	
Saint Lucia						●		●		●	
Saint Vincent and the Grenadines	●	●		●		●		●			●
Samoa	●					●		●			
San Marino	●	●	●	●		●	●	●	○	●	●
Sao Tome and Principe	○	○	○	○		●	○	●		○	○
Saudi Arabia						●		●		●	●[28]
Senegal	●	●		●	○	●	●	●	●	●	●[22]
Serbia	●	●	●	●		●	●	●	●	●	●[22]
Seychelles	●	●	●	●		●	○	●	○	●	●[22]
Sierra Leone	●	●		●		●	○	●	●	●	●
Singapore						●		●	●		
Slovakia	●	●	●	●	○	●	●	●	●	●	●[22]
Slovenia	●	●	●	●	○	●	●	●	●	●	●[22]
Solomon Islands				●	○	●		●	○	●	
Somalia	●	●		●				○	○	●	●
South Africa	●	●	●	○		●	●	●	●	●	●[22]
Spain	●	●	●	●	○	●	●	●	●	●	●[22]
Sri Lanka	●	●		●		●		●	●	●	●
Sudan	●			●				●	●	●	○
Suriname	●	●		●		●		●	○	●	
Swaziland	●			●		●		●		●	●

Optional Protocol to the Convention against Torture	International Convention for the Protection of All Persons from Enforced Disappearance (not yet into force)	Convention relating to the Status of Refugees (1951)	Protocol relating to the Status of Refugees (1967)	Convention relating to the Status of Stateless Persons (1954)	Convention on the Reduction of Statelessness (1961)	International Convention on the Protection of the Rights of All Migrant Workers and Members of Their Families	Rome Statute of the International Criminal Court	
●		●	●				●	Poland
○	○	●	●				●	Portugal
								Qatar
●	○	●	●	●	●		●	Romania
		●	●				○	Russian Federation
		●	●	●	●	●		Rwanda
		●					●	Saint Kitts and Nevis
							○	Saint Lucia
		●	●	●			●	Saint Vincent and the Grenadines
	○	●	●				●	Samoa
							●	San Marino
		●	●			○	○	Sao Tome and Principe
								Saudi Arabia
●	●	●	●	●	●	●	●	Senegal
●	○	●	●	●		○	●	Serbia
		●	●			●	○	Seychelles
○	○	●	●			○	●	Sierra Leone
								Singapore
	○	●	●	●	●		●	Slovakia
●	○	●	●	●			●	Slovenia
		●	●				○	Solomon Islands
		●	●					Somalia
○		●	●				●	South Africa
●	●	●	●	●			●	Spain
						●		Sri Lanka
		●	●				○*	Sudan
		●	●				●	Suriname
	○	●	●	●	●			Swaziland

● state is a party

● state became party in 2009

○ signed but not yet ratified

○ signed in 2009, but not yet ratified

10 Declaration under Article 10 not recognizing the competence of the CEDAW Committee to undertake confidential inquiries into allegations of grave or systematic violations.

22 Declaration under Article 22 recognizing the competence of the Committee against Torture (CAT) to consider individual complaints.

28 Reservation under Article 28 not recognizing the competence of the CAT to undertake confidential inquiries into allegations of systematic torture if warranted.

12 Declaration under Article 12(3) accepting the jurisdiction of the International Criminal Court (ICC) for crimes in its territory.

124 Declaration under Article 124 not accepting the jurisdiction of the ICC over war crimes for seven years after ratification.

* Signed the Rome Statute but have since formally declared their intention not to ratify.

** Ratified or acceded but subsequently denounced the treaty.

	International Covenant on Civil and Political Rights (ICCPR)	(first) Optional Protocol to the ICCPR	Second Optional Protocol to the ICCPR, aiming at the abolition of the death penalty	International Covenant on Economic, Social and Cultural Rights (ICESCR)	Optional Protocol to the ICESCR	Convention on the Elimination of All Forms of Discrimination against Women (CEDAW)	Optional Protocol to CEDAW	Convention on the Rights of the Child (CRC)	Optional Protocol to the CRC on the involvement of children in armed conflict	International Convention on the Elimination of All Forms of Racial Discrimination	Convention against Torture and Other Cruel, Inhuman or Degrading Treatment or Punishment
Sweden	●	●	●	●		●	●	●	●	●	●22
Switzerland	●		●	●		●	●	●	●	●	●22
Syria	●			●		●		●	●	●	●28
Tajikistan	●	●		●		●	○	●	●	●	●
Tanzania	●			●		●	●	●	●	●	
Thailand	●			●		●	●	●	●	●	●
Timor-Leste	●		●	●	○	●	●	●	●	●	●
Togo	●	●		●	○	●		●	●	●	●22
Tonga								●		●	
Trinidad and Tobago	●	**		●		●		●		●	
Tunisia	●			●		●	●	●	●	●	●22
Turkey	●	●	●	●		●	●	●	●	●	●22
Turkmenistan	●	●	●	●		●	●	●	●	●	●
Tuvalu						●		●			
Uganda	●	●		●		●		●	●	●	●
Ukraine	●	●	●	●	○	●	●	●	●	●	●
United Arab Emirates						●		●		●	
United Kingdom	●		●	●		●	●	●	●	●	●
United States of America	●			○		○		○	●	●	●
Uruguay	●	●	●	●	○	●	●	●	●	●	●22
Uzbekistan	●	●		●		●		●		●	●
Vanuatu	●					●	●	●		●	
Venezuela	●	●	●	●		●	●	●	●	●	●22
Viet Nam	●			●		●		●	●	●	
Yemen	●			●		●		●	●	●	●
Zambia	●	●		●		●	○	●	○	●	●
Zimbabwe	●			●		●		●		●	

Optional Protocol to the Convention against Torture	International Convention for the Protection of All Persons from Enforced Disappearance (not yet into force)	Convention relating to the Status of Refugees (1951)	Protocol relating to the Status of Refugees (1967)	Convention relating to the Status of Stateless Persons (1954)	Convention on the Reduction of Statelessness (1961)	International Convention on the Protection of the Rights of All Migrant Workers and Members of Their Families	Rome Statute of the International Criminal Court	Country
●	○	●	●	●	●		●	Sweden
●		●	●	●			●	Switzerland
						●	○	Syria
		●	●			●	●	Tajikistan
	○	●	●				●	Tanzania
							○	Thailand
○		●	●			●	●	Timor-Leste
○		●	●			○		Togo
								Tonga
		●	●	●			●	Trinidad and Tobago
	○	●	●	●	●			Tunisia
○		●	●			●		Turkey
		●	●					Turkmenistan
		●	●					Tuvalu
	○	●	●	●		●	●	Uganda
●		●	●				○	Ukraine
							○	United Arab Emirates
●		●	●	●	●		●	United Kingdom
			●				○*	United States of America
●	●	●	●	●	●	●	●	Uruguay
							○	Uzbekistan
	○							Vanuatu
	○		●				●	Venezuela
								Viet Nam
		●	●				○	Yemen
		●	●	●			●	Zambia
		●	●	●			○	Zimbabwe

● state is a party

● state became party in 2009

○ signed but not yet ratified

○ signed in 2009, but not yet ratified

10 Declaration under Article 10 not recognizing the competence of the CEDAW Committee to undertake confidential inquiries into allegations of grave or systematic violations.

22 Declaration under Article 22 recognizing the competence of the Committee against Torture (CAT) to consider individual complaints.

28 Reservation under Article 28 not recognizing the competence of the CAT to undertake confidential inquiries into allegations of systematic torture if warranted.

12 Declaration under Article 12(3) accepting the jurisdiction of the International Criminal Court (ICC) for crimes in its territory.

124 Declaration under Article 124 not accepting the jurisdiction of the ICC over war crimes for seven years after ratification.

* Signed the Rome Statute but have since formally declared their intention not to ratify.

** Ratified or acceded but subsequently denounced the treaty.

	African Charter on Human and Peoples' Rights (1981)	Protocol to the African Charter on the Establishment of an African Court on Human and Peoples' Rights (1998)	African Charter on the Rights and Welfare of the Child (1990)	Convention Governing the Specific Aspects of Refugee Problems in Africa (1969)	Protocol to the African Charter on Human and Peoples' Rights on the Rights of Women in Africa (2003)
Algeria	●	●	●	●	○
Angola	●	○	●	●	●
Benin	●	○	●	●	●
Botswana	●	○	●	●	
Burkina Faso	●	●	●	●	●
Burundi	●	●	●	●	○
Cameroon	●	○	●	●	○
Cape Verde	●		●	●	●
Central African Republic	●	○	○	●	○
Chad	●	○	●	●	○
Comoros	●	●	●	●	●
Congo (Republic of)	●	○	●	●	○
Côte d'Ivoire	●	●	●	●	○
Democratic Republic of the Congo	●	○		●	●
Djibouti	●	○	○	○	●
Egypt	●	○	●	●	
Equatorial Guinea	●	○	●	●	○
Eritrea	●		●		
Ethiopia	●	○	●	●	○
Gabon	●	●	●	●	○
Gambia	●	●	●	●	●
Ghana	●	●	●	●	●
Guinea	●	○	●	●	○
Guinea-Bissau	●	○	●	●	●
Kenya	●	●	●	●	○
Lesotho	●	●	●	●	●
Liberia	●	○	●	●	●
Libya	●	●	●	●	●
Madagascar	●	○	●	○	○

	African Charter on Human and Peoples' Rights (1981)	Protocol to the African Charter on the Establishment of an African Court on Human and Peoples' Rights (1998)	African Charter on the Rights and Welfare of the Child (1990)	Convention Governing the Specific Aspects of Refugee Problems in Africa (1969)	Protocol to the African Charter on Human and Peoples' Rights on the Rights of Women in Africa (2003)
Malawi	●	●	●	●	●
Mali	●	●	●	●	●
Mauritania	●	●	●	●	●
Mauritius	●	●	●	○	○
Mozambique	●	●	●	●	●
Namibia	●	○	●	○	●
Niger	●	●	●	●	○
Nigeria	●	●	●	●	●
Rwanda	●	●	●	●	●
Sahrawi Arab Democratic Republic	●		○		○
Sao Tome and Principe	●				
Senegal	●	●	●	●	●
Seychelles	●	○	●	●	●
Sierra Leone	●	○	●	●	○
Somalia	●	○	○	○	○
South Africa	●	●	●	●	●
Sudan	●	○	●	●	○
Swaziland	●	○	○	●	○
Tanzania	●	●	●	●	●
Togo	●	●	●	●	●
Tunisia	●	●	○	●	
Uganda	●	●	●	●	○
Zambia	●	○	●	●	●
Zimbabwe	●	○	●	●	●

SELECTED TREATIES
REGIONAL
AFRICAN UNION

● state is a party
● state became party in 2009
○ signed but not yet ratified
○ signed in 2009, but not yet ratified

This chart lists countries that were members of the African Union at the end of 2009.

	American Convention on Human Rights (1969)	Protocol to the American Convention on Human Rights to Abolish the Death Penalty (1990)	Additional Protocol to the American Convention on Human Rights in the Area of Economic, Social and Cultural Rights	Inter-American Convention to Prevent and Punish Torture (1985)	Inter-American Convention on Forced Disappearance of Persons (1994)	Inter-American Convention on the Prevention, Punishment and Eradication of Violence Against Women (1994)	Inter-American Convention on the Elimination of All Forms of Discrimination against Persons with Disabilities (1999)
Antigua and Barbuda						●	
Argentina	●[62]	●	●	●	●	●	●
Bahamas						●	
Barbados	●[62]					●	
Belize						●	
Bolivia	●[62]		●	●	●	●	●
Brazil	●[62]	●	●	●	○	●	●
Canada							
Chile	●[62]	●	○	●	○	●	●
Colombia	●[62]		●	●	●	●	●
Costa Rica	●[62]	●	●	●	●	●	●
Cuba*							
Dominica	●					●	○
Dominican Republic	●[62]		○	●		●	●
Ecuador	●[62]	●	●	●	●	●	●
El Salvador	●[62]		●	●		●	●
Grenada	●					●	
Guatemala	●[62]		●	●	●	●	●
Guyana						●	
Haiti	●[62]		○	○		●	●
Honduras	●[62]			○	●	●	
Jamaica	●					●	○
Mexico	●[62]	●	●	●	●	●	●
Nicaragua	●[62]	●	○	●	○	●	●
Panama	●[62]	●	●	●	●	●	●

	American Convention on Human Rights (1969)	Protocol to the American Convention on Human Rights to Abolish the Death Penalty (1990)	Additional Protocol to the American Convention on Human Rights in the Area of Economic, Social and Cultural Rights	Inter-American Convention to Prevent and Punish Torture (1985)	Inter-American Convention on Forced Disappearance of Persons (1994)	Inter-American Convention on the Prevention, Punishment and Eradication of Violence Against Women (1994)	Inter-American Convention on the Elimination of All Forms of Discrimination against Persons with Disabilities (1999)
Paraguay	●62	●	●	●	●	●	●
Peru	●62		●	●	●	●	●
Saint Kitts and Nevis						●	
Saint Lucia						●	
Saint Vincent and the Grenadines						●	
Suriname	●62		●	●		●	
Trinidad and Tobago						●	
United States of America	○						
Uruguay	●62	●	●	●	●	●	●
Venezuela	●62	●	○	●	●	●	●

● state is a party
● state became party in 2009
○ signed but not yet ratified
○ signed in 2009, but not yet ratified

This chart lists countries that were members of the Organization of American States at the end of 2009.

62 Countries making a Declaration under Article 62 recognize as binding the jurisdiction of the Inter-American Court of Human Rights (on all matters relating to the interpretation or application of the American Convention).

*   In 2009 the General Assembly of the Organization of American States (OAS) adopted resolution AG/RES.2438 (XXXIX-O/09), which resolves that the 1962 resolution that excluded the Cuban government from its participation in the OAS, ceases its effects. The 2009 resolution states that the participation of Cuba in the OAS will be the result of a process of dialogue initiated at the request of the government of Cuba.

	European Convention for the Protection of Human Rights and Fundamental Freedoms (ECHR) (1950)	Protocol No. 6 to the ECHR concerning the abolition of the death penalty in times of peace (1983)	Protocol No. 12 to the ECHR concerning the general prohibition of discrimination (2000)	Protocol No. 13 to the ECHR concerning the abolition of the death penalty in all circumstances (2002)	Framework Convention on the Protection of National Minorities (1995)	Council of Europe Convention on Action against Trafficking in Human Beings	European Social Charter (revised) (1996)	Additional Protocol to the European Social Charter Providing for a System of Collective Complaints (1995)
Albania	●	●	●	●	●	●	●	
Andorra	●	●	●	●		○	●	
Armenia	●	●	●	○	●	●	●	
Austria	●	●	○	●	●	●	○*	○
Azerbaijan	●	●	○		●		●	
Belgium	●	●	○	●	○	●	●	●
Bosnia and Herzegovina	●	●	●	●	●	●	●	
Bulgaria	●	●		●	●	●	●	**
Croatia	●	●	●	●	●	●	○*	●
Cyprus	●	●	●	●	●	●	●	●
Czech Republic	●	●	○	●	●		○*	○
Denmark	●	●		●	●	●	○*	○
Estonia	●	●	○	●	●		●	
Finland	●	●	●	●	●	○	●	●
France	●	●		●		●	●	●
Georgia	●	●	●	●	●		●	
Germany	●	●	○	●	●	○	○*	
Greece	●	●	○	●	○	○	○*	●
Hungary	●	●	○	●	●	○	●	○
Iceland	●	●	○	●	○	○	○*	
Ireland	●	●	○	●	●	●	●	●
Italy	●	●	○	●	●	○	●	●
Latvia	●	●	○	○	●	●	○*	
Liechtenstein	●	●	○	●	●			
Lithuania	●	●		●	●	○	●	

SELECTED TREATIES

REGIONAL COUNCIL OF EUROPE

	European Convention for the Protection of Human Rights and Fundamental Freedoms (ECHR) (1950)	Protocol No. 6 to the ECHR concerning the abolition of the death penalty in times of peace (1983)	Protocol No. 12 to the ECHR concerning the general prohibition of discrimination (2000)	Protocol No. 13 to the ECHR concerning the abolition of the death penalty in all circumstances (2002)	Framework Convention on the Protection of National Minorities (1995)	Council of Europe Convention on Action against Trafficking in Human Beings	European Social Charter (revised) (1996)	Additional Protocol to the European Social Charter Providing for a System of Collective Complaints (1995)
Luxembourg	●	●	●	●	○	●	○*	
Macedonia	●	●	●	●	●	●	○*	
Malta	●	●		●	●	●	●	
Moldova	●	●	○	●	●	●	●	
Monaco	●	●		●			○	
Montenegro	●	●	●	●	●	●	○	
Netherlands	●	●	●	●	●	○	●	●
Norway	●	●	○	●	●	●	●	●
Poland	●	●		○	●	●	○*	
Portugal	●	●	○	●	●	●	●	●
Romania	●	●	●	●	●	●	●	
Russian Federation	●	○	○		●		●	
San Marino	●	●	●	●	●	○	○	
Serbia	●	●	●	●	●	●	●	
Slovakia	●	●	○	●	●	●	●	○
Slovenia	●	●	○	●	●	●	●	○**
Spain	●	●	●	●	●	●	○*	
Sweden	●	●		●	●	○	●	●
Switzerland	●	●		●	●	○		
Turkey	●	●	○	●		○	●	
Ukraine	●	●	●	●	●	○	●	
United Kingdom	●	●		●	●	●	○*	

● state is a party

● state became party in 2009

○ signed but not yet ratified

○ signed in 2009, but not yet ratified

This chart lists countries that were members of the Council of Europe at the end of 2009.

* State is a party to the European Social Charter of 1961, which is gradually being replaced by the European Social Charter (revised). The revised Charter embodies in one instrument all rights guaranteed by the Charter of 1961, its Additional Protocol of 1988 and adds new rights and amendments.

** Declaration under Article D of the European Social Charter (revised) recognizing the competence of the European Committee of Social Rights to consider collective complaints.

Armed al-Shabab fighters patrol Bakara Market in Mogadishu, Somalia, on 29 June 2009. Thousands of civilians were killed and hundreds of thousands displaced as the conflict between armed groups and the Transitional Federal Government continued.

AMNESTY INTERNATIONAL REPORT 2010

PART FOUR

10

An Awá child looks at the coffins of 12 Awá, including seven children, killed in August 2009. All parties to Colombia's internal armed conflict targeted civilians, with Indigenous Peoples particularly hard hit in 2009.

AMNESTY INTERNATIONAL
SECTIONS

Algeria ❖ Amnesty International,
10, rue Mouloud ZADI
(face au 113 rue Didouche Mourad),
Alger Centre, 16004 Alger
email: amnestyalgeria@hotmail.com
www.amnestyalgeria.org

Argentina ❖ Amnistía Internacional,
Uruguay 775, 4ºB,
C1015ABO Ciudad de Buenos Aires
email: contacto@amnesty.org.ar
www.amnesty.org.ar

Australia ❖ Amnesty International,
Locked Bag 23, Broadway NSW 2007
email: supporter@amnesty.org.au
www.amnesty.org.au

Austria ❖ Amnesty International,
Moeringgasse 10, A-1150 Vienna
email: info@amnesty.at
www.amnesty.at

Belgium ❖
Amnesty International **(Flemish-speaking)**,
Kerkstraat 156,
2060 Antwerpen
email: amnesty@aivl.be
www.aivl.be
Amnesty International **(francophone)**,
Rue Berckmans 9,
1060 Bruxelles
email: aibf@aibf.be
www.aibf.be

Benin ❖ Amnesty International,
Carré 865, Immeuble François Gomez,
Quartier Aidjedo (une rue après le Centre
d'Accueil en venant de la BIBE),
Cotonou
email: amnestybenin@yahoo.fr

Bermuda ❖ Amnesty International,
PO Box HM 2136, Hamilton HM JX
email: aibda@ibl.bm

Canada ❖
Amnesty International **(English-speaking)**,
312 Laurier Avenue East, Ottawa,
Ontario, K1N 1H9
email: info@amnesty.ca
www.amnesty.ca
Amnistie internationale **(francophone)**,
6250 boulevard Monk, Montréal,
Québec, H4E 3H7
www.amnistie.ca

Chile ❖ Amnistía Internacional,
Oficina Nacional, Huelén 164 - Planta Baja,
750-0617 Providencia, Santiago
email: info@amnistia.cl
www.amnistia.cl

Côte d'Ivoire ❖ Amnesty International,
04 BP 895, Abidjan 04
email: amnesty.ci@aviso.ci

Denmark ❖ Amnesty International,
Gammeltorv 8, 5 - 1457 Copenhagen K.
email: amnesty@amnesty.dk
www.amnesty.dk

Faroe Islands ❖ Amnesty International,
Hoydalsvegur 6, FO-100 Tórshavn
email: amnesty@amnesty.fo
www.amnesty.fo

Finland ❖ Amnesty International,
Ruoholahdenkatu 24, D 00180 Helsinki
email: amnesty@amnesty.fi
www.amnesty.fi

France ❖ Amnesty International,
76 boulevard de la Villette,
75940 Paris, Cédex 19
email: info@amnesty.fr
www.amnesty.fr

Germany ❖ Amnesty International,
Heerstrasse 178, 53111 Bonn
email: info@amnesty.de
www.amnesty.de

Greece ❖ Amnesty International,
Sina 30, 106 72 Athens
email: athens@amnesty.org.gr
www.amnesty.org.gr

Hong Kong ❖ Amnesty International,
Unit D, 3/F, Best-O-Best Commercial Centre,
32-36 Ferry Street, Kowloon
email: admin-hk@amnesty.org.hk
www.amnesty.org.hk

Iceland ❖ Amnesty International,
Þingholtsstræti 27, 101 Reykjavík
email: amnesty@amnesty.is
www.amnesty.is

Ireland ❖ Amnesty International,
1st Floor, Ballast House,
18-21 Westmoreland St, Dublin 2
email: info@amnesty.ie
www.amnesty.ie

Israel ❖ Amnesty International,
PO Box 14179, Tel Aviv 61141
email: info@amnesty.org.il
www.amnesty.org.il

Italy ❖ Amnesty International,
Via Giovanni Battista De Rossi 10,
00161 Roma
email: info@amnesty.it
www.amnesty.it

Japan ❖ Amnesty International,
4F Kyodo Bldg, 2-2 Kandanishiki-cho,
Chiyoda-ku, Tokyo 101-0054
email: info@amnesty.or.jp
www.amnesty.or.jp

Korea (Republic of) ❖ Amnesty International,
Gwanghwamun PO Box 2045, Jongno-gu,
110-620 Seoul,
email: info@amnesty.or.kr
www.amnesty.or.kr

Luxembourg ❖ Amnesty International,
Boîte Postale 1914, 1019 Luxembourg
email: info@amnesty.lu
www.amnesty.lu

Mauritius ❖ Amnesty International,
BP 69, Rose-Hill
email: amnestymtius@erm.mu
www.amnestymauritius.org

Mexico ❖ Amnistía Internacional,
Tajín No. 389, Col. Narvarte,
Del. Benito Juárez,
CP 03020 Mexico DF
email: contacto@amnistia.org.mx
www.amnistia.org.mx

Morocco ❖ Amnesty International,
281 avenue Mohamed V,
Apt. 23, Escalier A,
Rabat
email: amorocco@sections.amnesty.org

Nepal ❖ Amnesty International,
PO Box 135, Amnesty Marga, Basantanagar,
Balaju, Kathmandu
email: info@amnestynepal.org
www.amnestynepal.org

Netherlands ❖ Amnesty International,
Keizersgracht 177, 1016 DR Amsterdam
email: amnesty@amnesty.nl
www.amnesty.nl

New Zealand ❖ Amnesty International,
PO Box 5300, Wellesley Street, Auckland
email: info@amnesty.org.nz
www.amnesty.org.nz

Norway ❖ Amnesty International,
Tordenskioldsgate 6B, 0106 Oslo
email: info@amnesty.no
www.amnesty.no

Paraguay ❖ Amnistía Internacional,
Tte. Zotti No. 352 casi Emilio Hassler,
Barrio Villa Morra, Asunción
email: ai-info@py.amnesty.org
www.py.amnesty.org

Peru ❖ Amnistía Internacional,
Enrique Palacios 735-A, Miraflores, Lima 18
email: amnistia@amnistia.org.pe
www.amnistia.org.pe

Philippines ❖ Amnesty International,
18 A Marunong Street, Barangay Central,
Quezon City 1101
email: section@amnesty.org.ph
www.amnesty.org.ph

Poland ❖ Amnesty International,
ul. Piękna 66a, lokal 2, I piętro, 00-672, Warszawa
email: amnesty@amnesty.org.pl
www.amnesty.org.pl

Portugal ❖ Amnistia Internacional,
Av. Infante Santo, 42, 2°, 1350 - 179 Lisboa
email: aiportugal@amnistia-internacional.pt
www.amnistia-internacional.pt

Puerto Rico ❖ Amnistía Internacional,
Calle Robles 54, Suite 6, Río Piedras, 00925
email: amnistiapr@amnestypr.org
www.amnistiapr.org

Senegal ❖ Amnesty International,
303/GRD Sacré-coeur II, Résidence Arame SIGA,
BP 35269, Dakar Colobane
email: asenegal@sections.amnesty.org
www.amnesty.sn

Sierra Leone ❖ Amnesty International,
PMB 1021, 16 Pademba Road, Freetown
email: amnestysl@gmail.com

Slovenia ❖ Amnesty International,
Beethovnova 7, 1000 Ljubljana
email: amnesty@amnesty.si
www.amnesty.si

Spain ❖ Amnistía Internacional,
Fernando VI, 8, 1° izda, 28004 Madrid
email: info@es.amnesty.org
www.es.amnesty.org

Sweden ❖ Amnesty International,
PO Box 4719, 11692 Stockholm
email: info@amnesty.se
www.amnesty.se

Switzerland ❖ Amnesty International,
PO Box, CH-3001 Berne
email: info@amnesty.ch
www.amnesty.ch

Taiwan ❖ Amnesty International,
3F., No. 14, Lane 165, Sec. 1,
Sinsheng S. Rd, Da-an District,
Taipei City 106
email: amnesty.taiwan@gmail.com
www.amnesty.tw

Togo ❖ Amnesty International,
2322 avenue du RPT,
Quartier Casablanca,
BP 20013, Lomé
email: aitogo@cafe.tg
www.amnesty.tg

Tunisia ❖ Amnesty International,
67 rue Oum Kalthoum,
3ème étage, escalier B,
1000 Tunis
email: admin-tn@amnesty.org

United Kingdom ❖ Amnesty International,
The Human Rights Action Centre,
17-25 New Inn Yard,
London EC2A 3EA
email: sct@amnesty.org.uk
www.amnesty.org.uk

United States of America ❖ Amnesty International,
5 Penn Plaza, 16th floor, New York, NY 10001
email: admin-us@aiusa.org
www.amnestyusa.org

Uruguay ❖ Amnistía Internacional,
Wilson Ferreira Aldunate 1220,
CP 11.100, Montevideo
email: oficina@amnistia.org.uy
www.amnistia.org.uy

Venezuela ❖ Amnistía Internacional,
CCS182576,
Av. Venezuela con Calle Sorocaima,
Res. Esedra P.B. Local #1, Casillero 936,
El Rosal, Caracas 1060
email: info@aiven.org
www.aiven.org

Hungary ❖ Amnesty International,
Rózsa u. 44, II/4, 1064 Budapest
email: info@amnesty.hu
www.amnesty.hu

Malaysia ❖ Amnesty International,
A-3-3A, 8 Avenue, Jalan Sungai Jernih,
8/1, Section 8, 46050, Petaling Jaya,
Selangor
email: amnesty@tm.net.my
www.aimalaysia.org

Mali ❖ Amnesty International,
Immeuble Soya Bathily, Route de l'aéroport,
24 rue Kalabancoura,
BP E 3885, Bamako
email: amnesty.mali@ikatelnet.net

Moldova ❖ Amnesty International,
PO Box 209, MD-2012 Chişinău
email: info@amnesty.md
www.amnesty.md

Mongolia ❖ Amnesty International,
PO Box 180, Ulaanbaatar 210648
email: aimncc@magicnet.mn
www.amnesty.mn

Slovakia ❖ Amnesty International,
Karpatska 11, 811 05 Bratislava
email: amnesty@amnesty.sk
www.amnesty.sk

Turkey ❖ Amnesty International,
Abdülhakhamid Cd. No. 30/5, Talimhane,
Beyoğlu, Istanbul
email: posta@amnesty.org.tr
www.amnesty.org.tr

Ukraine ❖ Amnesty International,
vul. Kravchenko, 17, kv.108, Kiev
email: info@amnesty.org.ua
www.amnesty.org.ua

AMNESTY INTERNATIONAL
STRUCTURES

Burkina Faso ❖ Amnesty International,
Rue 17.548, 08 BP 11344, Ouagadougou 08
email: aiburkina@fasonet.bf

Czech Republic ❖ Amnesty International,
Provaznická 3, 110 00, Prague 1
email: amnesty@amnesty.cz
www.amnesty.cz

AMNESTY INTERNATIONAL
PRE-STRUCTURES

Croatia ❖ Amnesty International,
Praška 2/III, 10000 Zagreb
email: admin@amnesty.hr
www.amnesty.hr

Thailand ❖ Amnesty International,
90/24 Lat Phrao Soi 1, Lat Yao,
Chatuchak, Bangkok 10900
email: info@amnesty.or.th
www.amnesty.or.th

AMNESTY INTERNATIONAL
SPECIAL PROJECTS

There are Amnesty International Special Projects in the following countries:

Ghana, Kenya, South Africa, Zimbabwe.

AMNESTY INTERNATIONAL
GROUPS

There are also Amnesty International groups in some 30 countries and territories around the world.

More information on Amnesty International groups and Amnesty International Special Projects can be found online at www.amnesty.org.

AMNESTY INTERNATIONAL
OFFICES

International Secretariat (IS)
Amnesty International,
Peter Benenson House,
1 Easton Street,
London WC1X 0DW,
United Kingdom
email: amnestyis@amnesty.org
www.amnesty.org

ARABAI (Arabic translation unit)
c/o International Secretariat,
Peter Benenson House, 1 Easton Street,
London WC1X 0DW,
United Kingdom
email: arabai@amnesty.org
www.amnesty.org/ar

Éditions Francophones d'Amnesty International (EFAI)
47 rue de Paradis,
75010 Paris,
France
email: ai-efai@amnesty.org
www.amnesty.org/fr

Editorial Amnistía Internacional (EDAI)
Calle Valderribas, 13,
28007 Madrid, Spain
email: edai@edai.org
www.amnesty.org/es

European Association Office
Amnesty International European Association
Rue de Trèves 35, B-1040 Brussels,
Belgium
email: amnesty-eu@aieu.be
www.amnesty-eu.org

IS Beirut – Middle East and North Africa Regional Office
Amnesty International,
PO Box 13-5696, Chouran Beirut 1102 - 2060,
Lebanon
email: mena@amnesty.org

IS Dakar – Africa Human Rights Education Office
Amnesty International,
SICAP Sacré Coeur Pyrotechnie Extension,
Villa No. 25, BP 47582, Dakar,
Senegal
email: KGaglo@amnesty.org

IS Geneva – UN Representative Office
Amnesty International,
22 rue du Cendrier, 4ème étage,
CH-1201 Geneva,
Switzerland
email: uaigv@amnesty.org

IS Hong Kong – Asia Pacific Regional Office
Amnesty International,
16/F Siu On Centre, 188 Lockhart Rd, Wanchai,
Hong Kong
email: admin-ap@amnesty.org

IS Kampala – Africa Regional Office
Amnesty International,
Plot 20A Kawalya Kaggwa Close,
PO Box 23966,
Kampala,
Uganda
email: ai-aro@amnesty.org

IS Moscow – Russia Resource Centre
Amnesty International,
PO Box 212, Moscow 119019,
Russian Federation
email: msk@amnesty.org
www.amnesty.org.ru

IS New York – UN Representative Office
Amnesty International,
777 UN Plaza, 6th Floor,
New York, NY 10017,
USA
email: aiunny@amnesty.org

IS Paris – Research Office
Amnesty International,
76 boulevard de la Villette,
75940 Paris, Cédex 19,
France
email: pro@amnesty.org

I WANT TO HELP

WHETHER IN A HIGH-PROFILE CONFLICT OR A FORGOTTEN CORNER OF THE GLOBE, **AMNESTY INTERNATIONAL** CAMPAIGNS FOR JUSTICE AND FREEDOM FOR ALL AND SEEKS TO GALVANIZE PUBLIC SUPPORT TO BUILD A BETTER WORLD

WHAT CAN YOU DO?

Activists around the world have shown that it is possible to resist the dangerous forces that are undermining human rights. Be part of this movement. Combat those who peddle fear and hate.

- Join Amnesty International and become part of a worldwide movement campaigning for an end to human rights violations. Help us make a difference.

- Make a donation to support Amnesty International's work.

Together we can make our voices heard.

I am interested in receiving further information on becoming a member of Amnesty International

name

address

country

email

I wish to make a donation to Amnesty International (donations will be taken in UK£, US$ or euros)

amount

please debit my: Visa ☐   Mastercard ☐

number ☐☐☐☐☐ ☐☐☐☐☐ ☐☐☐☐☐ ☐☐☐☐

expiry date

signature

Please return this form to the Amnesty International office in your country.
(See pages 394-397 for further details of Amnesty International offices worldwide.)
If there is not an Amnesty International office in your country, please return this form to the International Secretariat in London:
Peter Benenson House, 1 Easton Street, London WC1X 0DW, United Kingdom

www.amnesty.org

INDEX OF SELECTED TOPICS*

A

arbitrary arrests
Afghanistan 57; Angola 63; Belgium 77; Chad 101; Equatorial Guinea 135-6; Gambia 146-7; Guinea 158; Guinea-Bissau 159; India 168; Iran 173; Korea (Republic of) 201; Madagascar 214-15; Malaysia 218; Palestinian Authority 255; Sri Lanka 302

arbitrary detention
Afghanistan 57; Belgium 77; Chad 101; Egypt 131; Equatorial Guinea 135-6; Europe and Central Asia 33; Gambia 146-7; Guinea 158; Guinea-Bissau 159; Honduras 163; India 168; Iran 173; Iraq 177, 179; Jordan 191; Korea (Democratic People's Republic of) 199; Korea (Republic of) 201; Lebanon 206; Madagascar 214-15; Malaysia 218; Malta 221; Palestinian Authority 255; Sri Lanka 302; Sudan 306; United States of America 344-5

armed conflict
Afghanistan 55-6; Africa 2, 3; Americas 15; Asia-Pacific 22-3; Colombia 108; Congo, Democratic Republic of the 122; Georgia 148; India 167; Myanmar 237; Philippines 261; Russian Federation 270; Sri Lanka 301; Sudan 305, 306; Thailand 321; Uganda 333; Yemen 355-6

armed groups
Afghanistan 55-6; Brazil 85; Central African Republic 99; Chad 100-01; Colombia 109-10; Côte d'Ivoire 114; India 167; Iraq 177; Mauritania 222; Middle East and North Africa 42; Myanmar 237; Nepal 240; Nigeria 249; Pakistan 251-2; Palestinian Authority 255; Somalia 291-2, 293-4; Spain 299; Sri Lanka 301-2

asylum-seekers
Asia-Pacific 28-9; Australia 68; Austria 69; Bahamas 71; Belgium 77; Bulgaria 89; Burundi 92; Canada 97; China 107; Congo, Republic of 113; Denmark 126; Egypt 133; Eritrea 138; Europe and Central Asia 33; Finland 143-4; France 145; Germany 150; Greece 152-3; Ireland 181; Italy 186-7; Japan 190; Kenya 197; Korea (Republic of) 201; Laos 204; Libya 210-11; Malta 221; Montenegro 231; Morocco/Western Sahara 233; Netherlands 241; New Zealand 242; Poland 264; Rwanda 275; Saudi Arabia 278; Spain 299; Sweden 311-12; Switzerland 312-13; Syria 316; Taiwan 317; Tanzania 319; Turkey 331; Uganda 335; Ukraine 336; United Kingdom 342; United States of America 345-6; Yemen 357

C

child soldiers
Chad 101; Congo, Democratic Republic of the 123; Myanmar 238; Nepal 240

children's rights
Congo, Democratic Republic of the 123; Equatorial Guinea 136; Haiti 161-2; Ireland 181; Oman 250; Pakistan 253; Spain 299; Swaziland 310

conscientious objectors
Finland 144; Greece 154; Israel and the Occupied Palestinian Territories 185; Korea (Republic of) 201; Turkey 329, 330; United States of America 346

conscription for military service
Eritrea 138; Finland 144

corporate accountability
Africa 7; Canada 97; Côte d'Ivoire 114; Ecuador 129; India 168; Peru 259-60

counter-terror and security
Albania 60-1; Americas 18; Australia 68; Austria 69; Belgium 78; Bosnia and Herzegovina 83; Canada 97; Denmark 125; Egypt 131; Europe and Central Asia 32-3; France 145-6; Germany 149-50; Hungary 165; India 167; Ireland 180; Italy 187; Jordan 191; Kazakhstan 194; Kuwait 202; Kyrgyzstan 202-3; Libya 210; Lithuania 212; Macedonia 213-14; Mauritania 222; Morocco/Western Sahara 233; Netherlands 242; Poland 263; Portugal 264-5; Romania 267; Saudi Arabia 276; Slovakia 288-9; Spain 299; Swaziland 309; Sweden 311; Syria 314-15; Tunisia 326-7; United Arab Emirates 338; United Kingdom 339; United States of America 343; Uzbekistan 348-9; Yemen 356-7

cruel, inhuman and degrading punishments
(see also torture and other ill-treatment)
Iran 175; Malawi 217; Malaysia 218; Qatar 266; Saudi Arabia 278; Sudan 307; Yemen 356

D

death penalty
Afghanistan 58; Albania 62; Americas 19; Bahamas 71; Bahrain 73; Bangladesh 74; Belarus 75; Benin 78; Burkina Faso 89; Cameroon 96; Canada 97; China 105; Congo, Democratic Republic of the 124; Cuba 118; Egypt 133; Ethiopia 141; Europe and Central Asia 38-9; Gambia 147; Ghana 151; Guatemala 156; Guyana 161; India 170; Indonesia 172; Iran 176; Iraq 177; Jamaica 189; Japan 190; Jordan 193; Kenya 197-8; Korea (Democratic People's Republic of) 199; Korea (Republic of) 201; Kuwait 202; Laos 204; Lebanon 207; Libya 211; Malaysia 219; Mali 220; Mauritania 223; Middle East and North Africa 45; Mongolia 229; Myanmar 238; Nigeria 248; Pakistan 253; Palestinian Authority 256; Qatar 267; Russian Federation 272; Saudi Arabia 278; Sierra Leone 285-6; Singapore 286; Somalia 294; Sudan 306; Swaziland 310; Syria 316; Taiwan 316; Tanzania 320; Thailand 322; Togo 323; Trinidad and Tobago 325; Tunisia 327; Uganda 335; United Arab Emirates 339; United States of America 346; Viet Nam 354; Yemen 357

deaths in custody
Australia 68; Benin 78; China 105; Egypt 132; Eritrea 138; France 144-5; Italy 187; Malaysia 218; Mozambique 235; Palestinian Authority 255; South Africa 295-6; Togo 323; United States of America 345-6; Yemen 357

detention without trial
Bulgaria 88; China 105; Israel and the Occupied Palestinian Territories 184-5; Singapore 286

discrimination
Bosnia and Herzegovina 82; Burundi 92; Finland 144; Slovakia 287-8; Switzerland 312; Tanzania 319; United Arab Emirates 339

discrimination – minorities
Asia-Pacific 24; Bosnia and Herzegovina 82; Croatia 116-17; Dominican Republic 128; Egypt 133; Estonia 139; Greece 154; India 169; Iran 175; Macedonia 214; Malaysia 218; Mexico 225; Middle East and North Africa 48; Morocco/Western Sahara 233; Myanmar 237; Netherlands 242; Oman 249-50; Pakistan 252-3; Qatar 266; Serbia 283; Slovenia 289; Syria 316; Viet Nam 354

discrimination – Roma

Bulgaria 88; Croatia 116; Czech Republic 120-1; Europe and Central Asia 35; Finland 144; Greece 154; Hungary 165-6; Italy 186; Macedonia 214; Montenegro 231; Romania 267-8; Serbia 281-2, 283; Slovakia 287-8; Slovenia 289-90

discrimination – women

(see also violence against women and girls)

Africa 8; Albania 62; Iran 174; Lebanon 206; Libya 211; Oman 249; Poland 263; Qatar 266; Saudi Arabia 277; Sierra Leone 285; United Arab Emirates 339; Yemen 357

E

enforced disappearances

Albania 59, 61; Americas 11, 12; Bosnia and Herzegovina 82; Chad 101; Gambia 147; Korea (Democratic People's Republic of) 199; Lebanon 206-7; Morocco/Western Sahara 234; Nepal 240; Nigeria 247; Pakistan 252; Philippines 262; Serbia 282; Spain 300; Sri Lanka 302; Sudan 306-7; Turkmenistan 331-2; Ukraine 337; Yemen 356

excessive use of force

Belgium 78; Georgia 149; Guinea 156-7; Honduras 163; India 168; Israel and the Occupied Palestinian Territories 184; Jordan 192; Madagascar 215; Mauritania 222; Mozambique 235; Peru 259; Puerto Rico 265; Swaziland 309-10

extrajudicial executions

Africa 4; Americas 12; Asia-Pacific 23; Bangladesh 74; Colombia 109; Guinea 156-7; South Africa 296; Sri Lanka 302

F

forced evictions

Africa 7; Angola 62-3; Cambodia 26, 93; Chad 102; Equatorial Guinea 135; Ghana 151; India 168; Israel and the Occupied Palestinian Territories 184; Italy 186, 188; Nigeria 249; Papua New Guinea 257; South Africa 296; Zimbabwe 358

freedom of assembly

Belarus 75-6; Benin 78; Congo, Republic of 112-13; Egypt 132; Estonia 139; Europe and Central Asia 36; Georgia 148-9; Jordan 191-2; Moldova 228; Russian Federation 270-1; Singapore 286; Swaziland 309; Taiwan 317; Ukraine 337; Zimbabwe 358-9

freedom of association

Burundi 90; Cameroon 95; Cuba 117-18; Djibouti 127; Egypt 132; Honduras 164; Iran 174-5; Jordan 191-2; Korea (Democratic People's Republic of) 199; Rwanda 274; Swaziland 309; Tunisia 326; Zimbabwe 358-9

freedom of expression

Albania 61; Azerbaijan 70; Burundi 90-1; Congo, Democratic Republic of the 124; Congo, Republic of 112-13; Estonia 139; Ethiopia 140-1; Guinea-Bissau 159-60; Honduras 164; Indonesia 170-1; Iran 174-5; Italy 188; Kenya 197; Korea (Democratic People's Republic of) 199; Laos 204; Macedonia 214; Malaysia 217-18; Nicaragua 244; Philippines 262; Qatar 266; Russian Federation 270-1; Rwanda 273; Senegal 279; Sierra Leone 285; Singapore 286; Taiwan 317; Togo 324; Turkey 328-9; Zimbabwe 358-9

freedom of expression - internet

Bahrain 72; China 104; Cuba 117-18; Egypt 132; Iran 174; Korea (Republic of) 200; Malaysia 218

freedom of expression – journalists

Afghanistan 56; Albania 61; Angola 63-4; Armenia 67; Bahrain 72; Cambodia 93-4; Cameroon 95; Chad 101-2; China 104; Côte d'Ivoire 114; Croatia 116; Djibouti 127; Egypt 132; Eritrea 138; Ethiopia 141; Europe and Central Asia 36; Fiji 142-3; Gambia 147; Georgia 149; Guinea 158; Honduras 164; Iraq 179; Kenya 197; Korea (Republic of) 201; Kuwait 201-2; Kyrgyzstan 203; Madagascar 216; Mexico 225; Middle East and North Africa 44; Mongolia 229; Montenegro 230; Morocco/Western Sahara 232; Nicaragua 244; Niger 245-6; Nigeria 248; Oman 250; Pakistan 251-2; Palestinian Authority 255-6; Poland 264; Rwanda 273; Somalia 293; Sri Lanka 303; Sudan 307; Swaziland 309; Tajikistan 318; Tanzania 319; Tunisia 326; Uganda 334; Venezuela 352; Viet Nam 353; Yemen 357

freedom of expression – lèse majesté

Bahrain 72; Jordan 191-2; Morocco/Western Sahara 232; Thailand 321

freedom of expression – minorities

Indonesia 171; Malaysia 217-18

freedom of movement

Congo, Republic of 112-13; Cuba 117-18

freedom of religion

Armenia 67; China 105-6; Egypt 133; Eritrea 137; Europe and Central Asia 36; Fiji 143; Indonesia 171; Iran 175; Kazakhstan 195; Laos 204; Malaysia 218; Morocco/Western Sahara 233-4; Pakistan 252-3; Saudi Arabia 277; Tajikistan 317-18; Turkmenistan 332; Uzbekistan 350; Viet Nam 354;

H

health [right to]

Afghanistan 57; Bulgaria 88-9; Burkina Faso 89; Croatia 117; Guyana 161; Haiti 161; Hungary 166; Indonesia 172; Ireland 181; Papua New Guinea 257; South Africa 297; Swaziland 310; Tanzania 320; United States of America 346

health, women's

Czech Republic 121; Dominican Republic 128; El Salvador 134; Peru 260; Poland 263-4; Sierra Leone 285; Slovakia 288, 289

housing [right to]

Albania 59; Angola 62-3; Brazil 86; Bulgaria 88; Czech Republic 121; Egypt 133; Equatorial Guinea 135; Ghana 151; Kenya 197; Maldives 220; Nigeria 249; Puerto Rico 265; Romania 268; Slovakia 288; Solomon Islands 290; South Africa 296; Vanuatu 351

human rights defenders

Africa 5-6; Albania 61; Americas 19; Angola 63; Asia-Pacific 23; Azerbaijan 70-1; Belarus 76; Brazil 87; Burkina Faso 89; Burundi 91; Cambodia 93; Cameroon 95; Chad 102; China 104-5; Colombia 111; Congo, Democratic Republic of the 124; Djibouti 127; Ecuador 129; Estonia 139; Ethiopia 140-1; Europe and Central Asia 31; Gambia 147; Guatemala 156; Guinea 157-8; Honduras 163, 164; Indonesia 171; Iran 174; Kenya 196; Kyrgyzstan 203; Mexico 225; Middle East and North Africa 41; Moldova 228; Nicaragua 244; Niger 245; Nigeria 248; Peru 260; Russian Federation 270-1; Rwanda 273; Serbia 282; Sri Lanka 303; Syria 314; Tunisia 326; Turkey 329; Uzbekistan 349-50; Venezuela 352; Zimbabwe 358-9

I

impunity

Afghanistan 55; Africa 4-5; Americas 11; Argentina 65; Armenia 66-7; Asia-Pacific 23; Bolivia 79-80; Brazil 84; Cameroon 96; Central African Republic 99; Chile 103; Colombia 111; Congo, Democratic Republic of the 124; Croatia 116; Ecuador 129-30; El Salvador 134; Europe and Central Asia 33-4, 37; Guatemala 155; Guinea 157; Haiti 162; India 168-9; Indonesia 171-2; Israel and the Occupied Palestinian Territories 185; Kenya 195-6; Liberia 208; Libya 211; Mexico 226; Moldova 227; Mongolia 229; Nepal 240; Niger 246; Paraguay 258-9; Peru 260; Rwanda 275; Serbia 283; Sri Lanka 302; Suriname 307-8; Syria 315; Thailand 321; Timor-Leste 323; Togo 324; Turkey 329-30; Ukraine 336; United States of America 345; Uruguay 347; Zimbabwe 359-60

Indigenous Peoples' rights

Americas 17-18; Argentina 65; Asia-Pacific 26; Australia 67; Bangladesh 74; Bolivia 80; Brazil 87; Canada 96; Chile 102-3; Colombia 108-9; El Salvador 134; Mexico 225; New Zealand 242; Paraguay 257-8; Peru 259; Philippines 261, 262; Suriname 308

internally displaced people

Afghanistan 57; Africa 6; Asia-Pacific 21; Bosnia and Herzegovina 82-3; Chad 101; Congo, Democratic Republic of the 123; Georgia 148; Iraq 179; Kenya 196; Middle East and North Africa 42; Myanmar 237; Pakistan 252; Senegal 279; Somalia 292; Sri Lanka 301; Uganda 333

international justice

Africa 3-4; Americas 13-14; Bosnia and Herzegovina 81; Cambodia 93; Canada 97; Central African Republic 98-9; Congo, Democratic Republic of the 124-5; Croatia 115; Finland 143; Moldova 228; Rwanda 274-5; Serbia 280; South Africa 297-8; Spain 300; Sudan 304-5; Uganda 333;

international scrutiny

Colombia 111; Korea (Democratic People's Republic of) 199; Myanmar 238; Tanzania 319; Uzbekistan 348

J

justice system

Afghanistan 57; Argentina 65; Bolivia 79; Bosnia and Herzegovina 81-2; Burundi 91; China 105; Colombia 110; Croatia 115-16; Ghana 152; Haiti 162; Iran 174; Israel and the Occupied Palestinian Territories 184-5; Jamaica 189; Japan 190; Liberia 209; Macedonia 213; Maldives 219-20; Mexico 224; Montenegro 230; Nepal 240; Nigeria 247; Palestinian Authority 255; Peru 259; Poland 264; Rwanda 274; Serbia 280-1, 282; Somalia 293; Timor-Leste 322; Zimbabwe 360

L

land rights

Brazil 86; Burundi 92; Germany 150-1; Paraguay 258

legal developments

Afghanistan 56; Australia 68; Bangladesh 74; Burundi 91; Cambodia 94; Colombia 109; Fiji 142; Finland 144; France 146; Germany 151; Ireland 180; Italy 186; Korea (Democratic People's Republic of) 199; Korea (Republic of) 201; Mongolia 229; Nepal 241; New Zealand 243; Pakistan 251; Peru 259; Saudi Arabia 275-6; Switzerland 313; United Kingdom 341

lesbian, gay, bisexual and transgender people

Africa 7-8; Americas 17; Bulgaria 89; Cameroon 95; China 107; Egypt 132-3; Europe and Central Asia 35; Greece 154; Guyana

160-1; Honduras 164; Hungary 166; India 170; Jamaica 189; Latvia 204-5; Lithuania 212; Malawi 217; Middle East and North Africa 48; Mongolia 229; Nigeria 248; Peru 260; Rwanda 275; Senegal 279; Serbia 281; Turkey 331; Uganda 335

M

migrants' rights

Albania 61-2; Americas 14; Angola 64; Asia-Pacific 25-6; Austria 69; Bahamas 71; Bahrain 72-3; Belgium 77-8; Cyprus 119; Dominican Republic 128; Egypt 133; Europe and Central Asia 33; France 145; Germany 150; Greece 152-3; Haiti 162; Italy 186-7, 221; Jordan 192; Korea (Republic of) 200; Kuwait 202; Libya 210-11; Malaysia 218-19; Malta 221; Mauritania 223; Mexico 224-5; Middle East and North Africa 47-8; Morocco/Western Sahara 233; Netherlands 241-2; Qatar 266; Saudi Arabia 277-8; Singapore 287; South Africa 296-7; Spain 299; Sweden 311-12; Switzerland 312-13; Thailand 321-2; United Kingdom 342; United States of America 345-6

P

police and security forces

Angola 63; Australia 68; Austria 69; Bahamas 71; Belgium 78; Brazil 84-5; Canada 97; Cyprus 119; Denmark 126; Djibouti 127; Dominican Republic 127-8; France 144-5; Germany 150; Guatemala 155; Haiti 162; Indonesia 171; Ireland 180; Kenya 196; Korea (Republic of) 200; Malawi 217; Mexico 224; Middle East and North Africa 44; Mozambique 235; Nepal 240; Paraguay 258; Puerto Rico 265; Somalia 291-2; Spain 298; Switzerland 312; Timor-Leste 322-3; Trinidad and Tobago 324; United Kingdom 341-2

political prisoners

Cameroon 95; Eritrea 137-8; Ethiopia 140; Myanmar 236; Togo 323; Tunisia 325-6; Viet Nam 354; Zimbabwe 358

prison conditions

Albania 59; Argentina 66; Benin 78; Brazil 85-6; Cameroon 95-6; Equatorial Guinea 136; Ghana 151; Greece 153-4; Ireland 180; Israel and the Occupied Palestinian Territories 185; Kazakhstan 194; Laos 204; Lithuania 212; Malawi 216; Mauritania 222; Myanmar 236-7; New Zealand 243; Serbia 281; Tanzania 320; Turkey 330; United States of America 345; Uruguay 347-8

prisoners of conscience

Belarus 76; Cuba 117; Equatorial Guinea 135-6; Eritrea 137-8; Ethiopia 140; Finland 144; Israel and the Occupied Palestinian Territories 185; Mauritania 222; Rwanda 274; Saudi Arabia 276; Tunisia 326; Turkey 330; Turkmenistan 332; Ukraine 337; Viet Nam 354

R

racism

Austria 68; China 107; Europe and Central Asia 34; Hungary 165; Korea (Republic of) 200; Mauritania 223; Russian Federation 272; Spain 300; Sweden 312; Switzerland 312; Ukraine 336-7

refoulement

Europe and Central Asia 32; Slovakia 288-9

refugees

Asia-Pacific 24-5, 28-9; Australia 68; Belgium 77; Bosnia and Herzegovina 82-3; Bulgaria 89; Burundi 92; Canada 97; Chad 101; China 107; Congo, Democratic Republic of the 123; Cyprus

119; Denmark 126; Egypt 133; Eritrea 138; Finland 143-4; France 145; Germany 150; Greece 152-3; Iraq 179; Ireland 181; Italy 186-7; Japan 190; Jordan 192; Kenya 197; Korea (Republic of) 201; Laos 204; Lebanon 205-6; Libya 210-11; Macedonia 214; Malaysia 218-19; Malta 221; Mauritania 223; Middle East and North Africa 48; Montenegro 231; Morocco/Western Sahara 233; Netherlands 241; New Zealand 242; Poland 264; Rwanda 275; Saudi Arabia 278; South Africa 296-7; Spain 299; Sweden 311-12; Switzerland 312-13; Syria 316; Taiwan 317; Tanzania 319; Thailand 321-2; Turkey 331; Uganda 335; Ukraine 336; United Kingdom 342; Yemen 357

repression of dissent
Africa 5-6; Asia-Pacific 24-5; Bangladesh 73; Congo, Republic of 113; Ethiopia 141; Europe and Central Asia 35-6; Libya 210; Middle East and North Africa 43; Morocco/Western Sahara 232-3; Niger 245; Syria 314; Turkmenistan 332; Venezuela 352-3; Viet Nam 353

T

torture and other ill-treatment
Albania 59; Angola 63; Austria 68-9; Azerbaijan 70; Bangladesh 73-4; Benin 78; Bosnia and Herzegovina 83; Brazil 85-6; Bulgaria 88; China 105; Congo, Democratic Republic of the 124; Czech Republic 121; Denmark 126; Egypt 131, 132; Equatorial Guinea 136; Eritrea 138; Europe and Central Asia 37-8; Greece 153; Guinea 157; Guinea-Bissau 159-60; Guyana 160; Iran 173-4, 175; Israel and the Occupied Palestinian Territories 185; Italy 187; Jordan 191; Kazakhstan 193-4; Korea (Democratic People's Republic of) 199; Kyrgyzstan 203; Latvia 205; Macedonia 213; Maldives 219; Mauritania 222; Middle East and North Africa 45; Moldova 227; Mongolia 229-30; Montenegro 230; Nepal 240-1; Nigeria 247; Oman 250; Pakistan 252; Palestinian Authority 255; Philippines 262; Portugal 265; Romania 268-9; Russian Federation 271-2; Saudi Arabia 277; Senegal 279; Serbia 281, 282; Singapore 287; Slovakia 288; South Africa 295-6; Spain 298; Sudan 306; Swaziland 309-10; Sweden 311; Switzerland 313; Syria 315; Tajikistan 318; Tunisia 327; Turkey 329; Uganda 333-4; Ukraine 336; United Arab Emirates 338; United Kingdom 339-40; United States of America 345; Uzbekistan 349; Yemen 356; Zimbabwe 360

trafficking in human beings
Albania 58; Americas 14; Greece 154; Ireland 181

transitional justice
Burundi 91; Morocco/Western Sahara 234; Nepal 240

truth and reconciliation commissions
Africa 3; Burundi 91; Colombia 15; Kenya 196-7; Morocco/Western Sahara 48-9; Nepal 240; Sierra Leone 284-5

U

unfair trials
Argentina 65; Bangladesh 73-4; Egypt 131-2; Iran 174; Iraq 178; Israel and the Occupied Palestinian Territories 185; Kazakhstan 194; Lebanon 207; Madagascar 216; Malawi 216-17; Middle East and North Africa 45; Namibia 239; Russian Federation 272; Sudan 306; Turkey 330; United Kingdom 341; United States of America 346

unlawful killings
Africa 4-5; Americas 14-15; Congo, Democratic Republic of the 122-3; Côte d'Ivoire 113-14; Dominican Republic 128; Equatorial Guinea 136; Gambia 147; Guinea-Bissau 159; Honduras 163; India 167-8; Iran 173; Israel and the Occupied Palestinian Territories 183; Jamaica 188-9; Madagascar 215; Nigeria 247; Palestinian Authority 254-5; Papua New Guinea 256; Philippines 262; Somalia 293-4; South Africa 296; Uganda 334

V

violence against women and girls
Afghanistan 56; Albania 58; Americas 16-17; Argentina 66; Armenia 66; Asia-Pacific 23; Australia 68; Bahamas 71; Bangladesh 74; Belarus 76; Burundi 91; Cambodia 94; Canada 96-7; Chad 101; Congo, Democratic Republic of the 123; Cyprus 119; Denmark 126; Dominican Republic 128; El Salvador 134; Europe and Central Asia 38; Fiji 143; Finland 143; Georgia 148; Ghana 151; Guatemala 155-6; Guinea 157; Guyana 160; Haiti 162; Honduras 164; Hungary 166; Iraq 178, 179; Jamaica 189; Japan 190; Jordan 192-3; Kenya 196; Lebanon 206; Liberia 208-9; Malaysia 218; Mexico 225-6; Montenegro 231; Nepal 241; Nicaragua 244; Nigeria 248; Pakistan 253; Palestinian Authority 256; Papua New Guinea 257; Portugal 265; Qatar 266; Russian Federation 272; Saudi Arabia 277; Serbia 282, 283; Sierra Leone 285; Solomon Islands 290-1; South Africa 297; Spain 299-300; Sudan 305; Sweden 312; Switzerland 313; Taiwan 317; Tajikistan 317; Tanzania 320; Timor-Leste 323; Trinidad and Tobago 325; Turkey 331; Uganda 334; United Kingdom 342-3; Uruguay 348; Vanuatu 351; Venezuela 353; Yemen 357

W

war crimes
Croatia 115-16; Macedonia 213; Montenegro 230; Serbia 280-1, 282

women's rights
(see also violence against women and girls)
Americas 17; Bolivia 80; Chile 103; Ireland 181; Kuwait 202; Macedonia 214; Mali 220; Mexico 226; Middle East and North Africa 46-7; Nicaragua 243-4; Swaziland 310; Syria 315-16

workers' rights
Brazil 86; Greece 153; India 169-70

*This is an index of topics based around the subheadings that appear in the A-Z of country entries. It should be used by the reader only as a navigational tool, not as a statement of Amnesty International's human rights concerns in a particular country or territory.

Police disperse a demonstration in Tegucigalpa, Honduras, 23 September. People protesting against the army-backed coup that forced President José Manuel Zelaya Rosales from power in June often faced excessive force.